Student Quick Tips

Use this Student Quick Tips guide for a quick and easy start with McGraw-Hill Connect. You'll get valuable tips on registering, doing assignments, and accessing resources, as well as information about the support center hours.

Getting Started

TIP: To get started in Connect, you will need the following:

- Your instructor's Connect Web Address

    Sample of Connect Web Address:

    http://www.mcgrawhillconnect.com/class/instructorname_section_name

- Connect Access Code

TIP: If you do not have an access code or have not yet secured your tuition funds, you can click "Free Trial" during registration. This trial will provide temporary Connect access (typically three weeks) and will remind you to purchase online access before the end of your trial.

Registration and Sign In

1. Go to the Connect Web Address provided by your instructor
2. Click on **Register Now**
3. Enter your email address

TIP: If you already have a McGraw-Hill account, you will be asked for your password and will not be required to create a new account.

4. Enter a registration code or choose **Buy Online** to purchase access online

5. Follow the on-screen directions

TIP: Please choose your Security Question and Answer carefully. We will ask you for this information if you forget your password.

6. When registration is complete, click on **Go to Connect Now**

7. You are now ready to use **Connect**

Trouble Logging In?

- Ensure you are using the same email address you used during registration

- If you have forgotten your password, click on the "Forgot Password?" link at your Instructor's Connect Course Web Address

- When logged into Connect, you can update your account information (e.g. email address, password, and security question/answer) by clicking on the *"My Account"* link located at the top-right corner

Home (Assignments)

TIP: If you are unable to begin an assignment, verify the following:

- The assignment is available (start and due dates)

- That you have not exceeded the maximum number of attempts

- That you have not achieved a score of 100%

- If your assignment contains questions that require manual grading, you will not be able to begin your next attempt until your instructor has graded those questions

TIP: Based on the assignment policy settings established by your Instructor, you may encounter the following limitations when working on your assignment(s):

- Ability to Print Assignment

- Timed assignments – once you begin a "*timed assignment,*" the timer will not stop by design

TIP: "*Save & Exit*" vs. "*Submit*" button

- If you are unable to complete your assignment in one sitting, utilize the "*Save & Exit*" button to save your work and complete it at a later time

- Once you have completed your assignment, utilize the "*Submit*" button in order for your assignment to be graded

Library

TIP: The *Library* section of your Connect account provides shortcuts to various resources.

- If you purchased ConnectPlus, you will see an *eBook* link, which can also be accessed from the section information widget of the *Home* tab

- *Recorded Lectures* can be accessed if your instructor is using *Tegrity Campus* to capture lectures. You may also access recorded lectures when taking an assignment by clicking on the projector icon in the navigation bar

- Many McGraw-Hill textbooks offer additional resources such as narrated slides and additional problems, which are accessible through the *Student Resources* link

Reports

TIP: Once you submit your assignment, you can view your available results in the *Reports* tab.

- If you see a dash (-) as your score, your instructor has either delayed or restricted your ability to see the assignment feedback

- Your instructor has the ability to limit the amount of information (e.g. questions, answers, scores) you can view for each submitted assignment

Need More Help?

CONTACT US ONLINE

Visit us at:

www.mcgrawhillconnect.com/support

Browse our support materials including tutorial videos and our searchable Connect knowledge base. If you cannot find an answer to your question, click on "Contact Us" button to send us an email.

GIVE US A CALL

Call us at:

1-800-331-5094

Our live support is available:

Mon-Thurs: 8 am – 11 pm CT
Friday: 8 am – 6 pm CT
Sunday: 6 pm – 11 pm CT

COMMUNICATION MATTERS

Second Edition

KORY FLOYD

Arizona State University

COM 113 Fundamentals of Speech Communication

University of Nevada-Reno

4 5 6 7 8 9 0   DCM DCM   15 14 13

ISBN-13: 978-1-25-911250-8
ISBN-10: 1-25-911250-0

Learning Solutions Consultant: Elizabeth Wildes
Project Manager: Vanessa Estrada
Cover Photo Credits: © BananaStock/PictureQues

Dear Readers:

I can still recall how my family reacted when I said I wanted to study communication. *You already know how to communicate,* I remember one relative saying. Communication seemed like common sense to my family members, so they weren't entirely sure why I needed a PhD just to understand it.

As it turns out, my relatives are like a lot of other people in this regard. Because each of us communicates in some form nearly every day of our lives, it's hard not to think of communication as completely intuitive. What can we possibly learn from research and formal study that we don't already know from our lived experience? Aren't we all experts in communication already?

For the sake of argument, let's say we were. Why, then, do we so often misunderstand each other? Why is our divorce rate so high? How come it seems like women and men speak different languages? What accounts for the popularity of self-help books, relationship counselors, and talk shows? If we're all experts at communicating, why do we often find it so challenging? Maybe communication isn't as intuitive as we might think.

When I wrote the first edition of *Communication Matters,* my goal was to help readers see how communication not only affects their social relationships but also influences their happiness, career objectives, and quality of life. I wanted to guide students through their personal experience of communication, illuminate the value of engaging in a critical investigation of processes and behaviors, and help readers actively apply the course material to their own life experiences.

Our world is changing quickly these days—and so, too, are the ways we communicate. In the last few years, we've seen people use computer-mediated communication in unprecedented ways. Deployed servicemen watch the birth of their children live via Skype. Political protestors organize rallies with less than a day's notice on Twitter. Adults given up for adoption as infants use Facebook to find their biological parents. And despite the growth of these newer platforms, e-mail is far from dead: Most adults in a recent survey said their e-mail load either stayed the same or increased over the past year. Each new technology shrinks our world just a little more, requiring effective communicators to adapt their behaviors accordingly. This new edition of *Communication Matters* focuses on teaching the adaptability skills students need in an ever-changing communication world.

An ideal textbook not only engages and excites students; it also provides relevant, contemporary, and high-quality support for instructors. *Communication Matters,* Second Edition, offers Connect, a flexible, groundbreaking online learning platform that features LearnSmart, an adaptive diagnostic; hands-on learning activities; quizzes; and a fully integrated e-book. Connect enables instructors to better tailor class time to student needs and gives students more opportunities than ever for communication skills practice and assessment. I hope you will find this new edition of *Communication Matters* and its extensive instructional support to comprise a well-integrated package of engaging and contemporary materials for the introductory course.

Name: Kory Floyd

Education: I got my undergraduate degree from Western Washington University, my Masters degree from the University of Washington, and my PhD from the University of Arizona

Current jobs: Professor, book writer

Favorite job growing up: Singing busboy

Worst childhood memory: Getting sent to the principal's office in third grade. (It's possible I haven't told my parents about that.)

Best childhood memory: The birth of my sister and brother

Hobbies: Playing piano, singing, reading, traveling, playing Wii tennis

Pets: I have a puppy named Buster. There's also a kitty who lives in our neighborhood and visits me every now and then.

Favorite recent book: The Social Animal, by David Brooks

Favorite TV show: NCIS (the original one)

Places I love: Iceland, Starbucks, my brother's house

BRIEF CONTENTS

CONTENTS

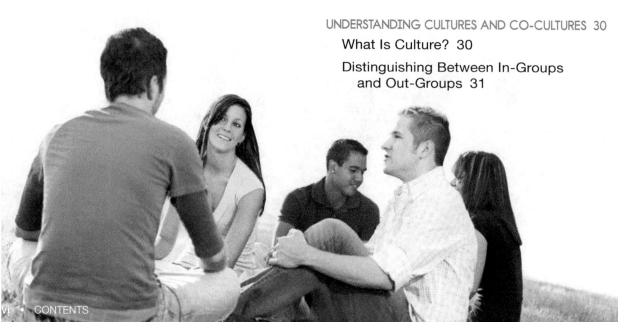

PART THREE
Communication in the Public Sphere 259

BOXES

THE COMPETENT COMMUNICATOR

PUTTING COMMUNICATION TO WORK

Communication Matters

Because great communicators are made, not born.

We all communicate, all the time. We interact with loved ones, friends, colleagues, peers, bosses, and clients, and we do so in numerous ways every day—in person as well as remotely, using a dizzying number of devices to stay connected. Consequently, many of us believe we're experts, that good communication is based on personal instincts. *Communication Matters* became one of the most successful new offerings in introductory communication because it debunks that myth, revealing why the study of communication is more complex and more essential than it seems. Throughout *Communication Matters'* highly interactive program, well-known communication scholar Kory Floyd uses fresh examples and thorough coverage to illustrate to students that our instincts aren't as good as we think they are. And Floyd's integrated and proven solutions show students how great communication can be learned.

Communication Matters reflects our increasingly diverse, interactive, and digital world, which requires us to make numerous communication choices every day and adapt how we behave within different audiences, situations, and media. Its hands-on features urge students to consider which choices are likely to be effective and which less so. *Communication Matters* guides students toward better choices by moving them from the personal to the critical to the active and adaptive. It prompts students to question their assumptions, helps them to move beyond their personal daily communication experiences, and challenges them to think critically about why and how they communicate in the ways they do. The result: Students are able to internalize core communication principles, adapt their communication behavior more effectively, and actively apply those strategies to all aspects of their lives.

Program components that invite students to go beyond superficial ideas about communication:

Connect Communication, McGraw-Hill's groundbreaking, interactive learning platform, offers a range of flexible digital learning solutions that improve student readiness and performance. Connect Communication integrates a media-rich eBook with groundbreaking activities and assignments that help students to study more effectively and efficiently. This flexible platform, which has full integration with the Blackboard CMS and features single-sign-on capability with a host of other Learning Management Systems, also makes the management and grading of assignments easier for instructors. Connect Communication includes the adaptive study tool LearnSmart, a full suite of speech preparation tools, video-based activities, self-assessments, chapter quizzes, and more.

NEW Content enhancements driven directly by student activity.

LearnSmart, McGraw-Hill's adaptive learning system, assesses student knowledge of course content and maps out a personalized study plan for success. Accessible within Connect Communication, *LearnSmart* uses a series of adaptive questions to pinpoint the concepts students do understand—and those they don't. This online tool is popular with students and instructors alike because it helps students to learn faster and study more efficiently, and it enables instructors to customize classroom lectures and activities to meet their students' needs.

For the second edition, the Floyd program has capitalized on and leveraged the data generated by the more than 10,000 introductory communication students using *LearnSmart* for Floyd's *Communication Matters,* analyzing the questions that students struggled to answer and identifying common trouble spots in the course coverage. As a result, the program's new digital activities and questions focus more heavily and deeply on these concepts, so that more help, more guidance, and more practice and being offered in the areas where students need them the most.

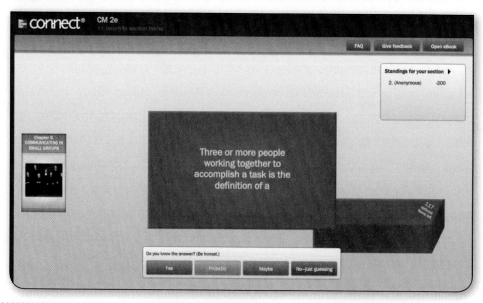

NEW Current communication theory, research, and scholarship and new, effective examples of communication concepts and principles.

Based on the most current research and scholarship, Floyd's text presents and investigates communication theories, processes, and application systematically, using story-telling to connect concepts to students' own experiences. Research and examples have been revised and updated throughout the text, and a new vignette has been added to the beginning of every chapter—a real-life introductory example of that chapter's topic.

THE DARK SIDE OF COMMUNICATION

Cultural Intolerance: Discrimination against Muslim Students on U.S. College Campuses

Nineteen-year-old college senior Nohayia Javed was walking to her residence hall on a Saturday night when she was grabbed from behind, thrown to the ground, and kicked in the ribs by a young man yelling anti-Islamic slurs. An emergency room exam later revealed that Javed had sustained multiple bruises and a dislocated shoulder. It's fortunate that few Muslim students at U.S. colleges and universities have endured similar physical attacks—yet during the years of the U.S. wars in Iraq and Afghanistan, many have felt like outsiders. Some receive hostile looks or threatening e-mail messages. Others feel excluded from social events where they once would have felt welcome. Some have been the target of verbal abuse blaming all Muslims for the terrorist actions of a few.

Distinguishing between in-groups and out-groups may be a natural tendency among human beings and other species, but it can lead us to make erroneous judgments about others. After 19 Islamic extremists carried out deadly attacks on the United States on September 11, 2001, many Muslims—even those born in the United States, such as Javed—felt as though they were being treated as terrorists simply because they shared a cultural and religious background with the hijackers. Although the attacks were genuine atrocities, in truth the vast majority of Muslims had nothing to do with them. In fact, many major Islamic organizations explicitly condemned the terrorist strikes.

Such discrimination against Muslims provides evidence of how, during times of stress or uncertainty, it may be especially easy to make broad generalizations about groups of people. For competent communicators, however, it is vitally important to remember not to condemn an entire group based on the actions of a few individuals.

SOURCES: Kerr, M. (2009, May 17). Muslims face discrimination and intolerance. *The Statesman*. Retrieved February 17, 2010, from www.sbstatesman.com/2.892/muslims-face-discrimination-and-intolerance-1.38633; Woods, T. (2006, April 5). Muslim student believes attacker came from off campus. *Waco Tribune-Herald*, accessed November 13, 2011, www.wacotrib.com/news/content/news/stories/2006/04/05/04052006wacmuslim.html.

A "Dark Side of Communication" feature in each chapter takes a close-up look at a specific dark side topic and promotes discussion of mature, effective ways of dealing with its challenges in people's lives (and communicative experiences).

"Fact or Fiction?" boxes in every text chapter and online "Misconceptions" quizzes in Connect Communication prompt students to question their assumptions about seemingly self-evident communication questions.

Fact or fiction?

More Is More: When It Comes to Forming Perceptions, More Information Is Always Better

People sometimes criticize others for making snap judgments or arriving at their impressions on the basis of limited information. After listening to only one speech, for example, you decide to vote for a political candidate without learning anything else about him or her. It's easy to see how such on-the-spot judgments can be misleading and how our perceptions might be more accurate if we had additional information.

In many cases, it's true: when we form perceptions of others, our first impressions can be misleading. Research shows, however, that in certain cases our snap judgments are surprisingly accurate. Perhaps even more surprising is that, although gathering additional information about someone can make our perceptions *more* accurate, it can also make them *less* accurate.

You may think, for instance, that your long-time friends would describe you more accurately than strangers would. An interesting experiment proved

otherwise, however. Participants described themselves on personality inventories and then asked their close friends to describe them on the same inventories. As you might expect, the friends' reports matched the participants' self-reports fairly well. The researchers next asked complete strangers to walk through the participants' residence hall rooms and then describe the participants' personalities. That is, they filled out descriptions of the participants without even meeting them, based only on the limited information they got from browsing around their rooms.

The strangers were more accurate than the close friends in describing participants' personalities. That result suggests that having more information about a person—as you would if you had known that person for years—does not necessarily make your perceptions of him or her more accurate. More information is sometimes better, but not always.

ASK YOURSELF

- Why are snap judgments sometimes accurate? What clues might we be subconsciously noticing that help us interpret a situation quickly yet accurately?
- When have you made snap judgments that turned out to be inaccurate? What led you to form those perceptions?

SOURCE: Gosling, S. D., Ko, S. J., Mannarelli, T., & Morris, M. E. (2002). A room with a cue: Personality judgments based on offices and bedrooms. *Journal of Personality and Social Psychology, 82*, 379–398.

Online "Know Yourself" activities in Connect Communication deepen students' understanding of the various views of different communication concepts by applying those various views to their own thoughts. Based on each student's responses, a customized summary shows how the student's views correlate with the various views of a communication concept.

What Is Your Primary Listening Style?

1. Which of the following statements most likely describes why you might enjoy taking a class from a specific instructor?

- a. The instructor explains everything in a clear concise way.
- b. The instructor provides examples that relate the course to the interests of her students.
- c. The instructor does not waste class time and lets the students leave when they are finished with their work.
- d. The instructor provides a lot of class time for students to think about the course content.

Question 1 of 6   next

Results

More ways to develop, practice, and apply communication skills, competencies, and adaptive strategies

NEW **The second edition of *Communication Matters* places a stronger emphasis on the need for students to develop adaptability—to audience, situation, and medium—as a core communication skill.** Coverage of this theme has been integrated throughout the text. Additionally, **"Adaptability" boxes in each chapter present students with short communication scenarios, asking students to contemplate the choices and adaptations they might make at a given decision point** and requiring students to incorporate multiple skills taught in the chapter.

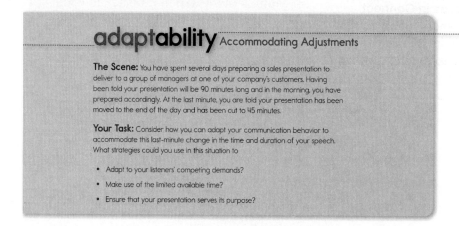

adaptability Accommodating Adjustments

The Scene: You have spent several days preparing a sales presentation to deliver to a group of managers at one of your company's customers. Having been told your presentation will be 90 minutes long and in the morning, you have prepared accordingly. At the last minute, you are told your presentation has been moved to the end of the day and has been cut to 45 minutes.

Your Task: Consider how you can adapt your communication behavior to accommodate this last-minute change in the time and duration of your speech. What strategies could you use in this situation to

- Adapt to your listeners' competing demands?
- Make use of the limited available time?
- Ensure that your presentation serves its purpose?

"The Competent Communicator" boxes in each chapter present students with a self-assessment of a particular communication skill or tendency. These boxes were designed with the underlying idea that for students to improve their communication skills and ability, they need to reflect on how they communicate now.

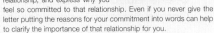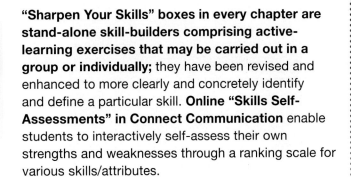

SHARPEN Your Skills:
Relational commitment

Write a letter to your romantic partner, one of your parents, or another person with whom you have a close relationship, and express why you feel so committed to that relationship. Even if you never give the letter putting the reasons for your commitment into words can help to clarify the importance of that relationship for you.

"Sharpen Your Skills" boxes in every chapter are stand-alone skill-builders comprising active-learning exercises that may be carried out in a group or individually; they have been revised and enhanced to more clearly and concretely identify and define a particular skill. **Online "Skills Self-Assessments" in Connect Communication** enable students to interactively self-assess their own strengths and weaknesses through a ranking scale for various skills/attributes.

A text and online program that reflects today's diverse, complex, and ever-changing world and that bridges communication theory with real-life applications:

NEW **"Get Connected" sections in every chapter focus on communication issues that arise within CMC-based platforms**—in people's personal lives, in their workplaces, and in online classrooms. Topics include netiquette, online co-cultures, avatars, and predicting relational dissolution on Facebook.

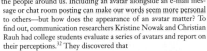

getCONNECTED

Personal Appearance of Avatars

We often feel powerless and frustrated when forced to wait for others. Many waiting areas even lack clocks to reduce complaints about the passage of time.

As a nonverbal channel, personal appearance is influential not only in face-to-face interaction but also online. When interacting in cyberspace, many people use avatars as representations of themselves. Although avatars are not "real" people, they signify real people, and so we become accustomed to perceiving them in many of the same ways we perceive the people around us. Including an avatar alongside an e-mail message or chat room posting can make our words seem more personal to others—but how does the appearance of an avatar matter? To find out, communication researchers Kristine Nowak and Christian Rauh had college students evaluate a series of avatars and report on their perceptions.[32] They discovered that

- Avatars should look as human as possible, rather than looking like animals or inanimate objects.
- Avatars should have a defined gender, rather than appearing androgynous.
- Communicators prefer avatars that look like themselves.

THE USE OF TIME

Chronemics is the way we use time. You might not immediately think of time usage as nonverbal behavior, but the way we give (or

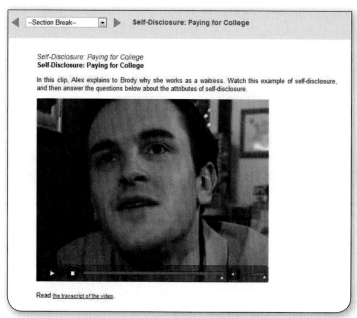

Technology and Computer-Mediated Communication (CMC). With integrated examples in every chapter, as well as coverage of social networking, e-mail, texting, IMing, and more, *Communication Matters* explores the opportunities and challenges students encounter as they rely more and more on new technologies for communication in all areas of their lives.

Online Video Activities in Connect Communication. Engaging video clips from current pop-culture sources are used to illustrate and test student understanding of communication concepts.

NEW **"Putting Communication to Work," a popular feature from the first edition that highlights the link between communication skills and success in the workplace,** has been revised and streamlined to profile the diverse career options for communication students through a job description and corresponding work responsibilities.

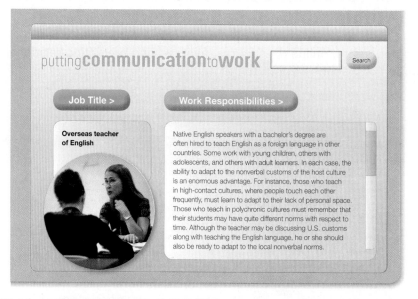

With its emphasis on diversity, *Communication Matters* probes the ways that students' personal roots and contexts, and those of their communication partners, affect their communication. To set the foundation for this central theme, Chapter 2, "Communication and Culture," surveys the crucial role of culture in communication and illuminates how differences in individuals' mental and physical abilities can be the basis of a co-culture—examining, for example, the values and customs of the deaf community and the impact of those factors on their communication. Other chapters consider the communicative diversity of socially marginalized groups such as the elderly, the homeless, and sexual minorities.

Tools that help beginning students get more practice time and become more effective at public speaking:

Speech Capture in Connect gives instructors the ability to evaluate speeches live, using a fully customizable rubric. Instructors can also upload speech videos on behalf of students, as well as create and manage peer review assignments. In addition, students can upload their own videos for self-review and/or peer review.

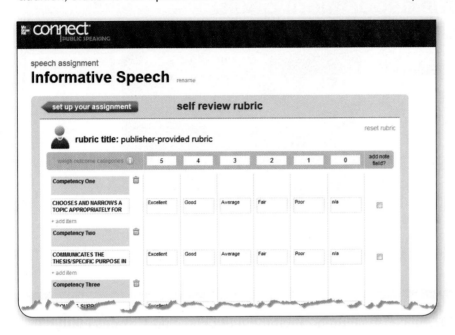

Outline Tool, with enhanced user interface. The Outline Tool guides students systematically through the process of organizing and outlining their speeches. Instructors can customize parts of the outliner or turn it off if they don't want their students to use it.

Topic Finder, as well as access to EasyBib and Survey Monkey online tools. The Topic Finder helps students to select a topic for speech assignments. EasyBib is a web-based tool that simplifies and automates the formatting of citations and bibliographies. Survey Monkey, also a web-based tool, helps students to create and manage audience-analysis questionnaires.

NEW McGraw-Hill SpeechPrep app.

On-the-go students can practice their speeches on their Apple- or Android-based smartphones or tablets using the McGraw-Hill SpeechPrep app. This mobile tool is designed to help students create and organize note cards, as well as practice, record, time, and review speeches. To learn more or download the app, search "Speech Prep" in iTunes, the App Store, or the Android Market.

create

A program that can be customized and tailored to your students, your introductory communication courses, and your department goals.

CREATE, because customization for your course needs does matter.
Design your ideal course materials with McGraw-Hill's Create! Rearrange or omit chapters, combine material from other sources, upload your syllabus or any other content you have written to make the perfect resource for your students. Search thousands of leading McGraw-Hill textbooks to find the best content for your students, then arrange it to fit your teaching style. You can even personalize your book's appearance by selecting the cover and adding your name, school, and course information. When you order a Create book, you receive a complimentary review copy. Get a printed copy in 3 to 5 business days or an electronic copy (eComp) via e-mail in about an hour. Register today at **www.mcgrawhillcreate.com**, and craft your course resources to match the way you teach.

Three additional full chapters, written by Kory Floyd for *Communication Matters*, are available exclusively through McGraw-Hill's Create customization site:

- **Chapter 16, Communicating in Organizations**
- **Chapter 17, Communication and Media**
- **Chapter 18, Communication and Health**

ADDITIONAL RESOURCES FOR INSTRUCTORS

Instructor's Manual. Written and updated by the author, the Instructor's Manual provides a range of tools for each chapter to help to structure the course and use the *Communication Matters* text effectively for particular course needs— discussion questions, assignment ideas, lecture ideas, and other resources.

Test Bank. The Test Bank offers multiple-choice questions, true/false questions, fill-in-the-blank questions, and essay questions for each chapter.

PowerPoints for each chapter created and updated by the author.

McGraw-Hill **Campus** A one-stop teaching and learning experience.

McGraw-Hill Campus is the first of its kind institutional service providing faculty with **true single sign-on access to all of McGraw-Hill's course content, digital tools, and other high-quality learning resources from any learning management system (LMS).** This innovative offering allows for secure and deep integration and seamless access to any of our course solutions such as McGraw-Hill Connect®, McGraw-Hill Create™, McGraw-Hill LearnSmart™, or Tegrity®. McGraw-Hill Campus includes access to our entire content library, including e-books, assessment tools, presentation slides, and multi-media content, among other resources, providing faculty open and unlimited access to prepare for class, create tests/quizzes, develop lecture material, integrate interactive content, and much more.

Visit coursesmart.com to purchase registration codes for this exciting new product.

CourseSmart offers thousands of the most commonly adopted textbooks across hundreds of courses from a wide variety of higher education publishers. It is the only place where faculty can review and compare the full text of a textbook online, and it provides immediate access, obviating the environmental impact of requesting a printed exam copy. At CourseSmart, students can save up to 50% off the cost of a printed book, reduce their impact on the environment, and gain access to powerful web tools for learning, including full text search, notes and highlighting, and e-mail tools for sharing notes among classmates. Learn more at **www.coursesmart.com.**

Chapter-by-Chapter Changes

CHAPTER 1: New chapter-opening vignette • Updated opening example • New table on computer-mediated communication • "Sharpen Your Skills" element revised and made more concrete, and skills clearly identified • Historical information on action model added • New example for perceptual filters • New "Get Connected" section added on netiquette • New "Adaptability" feature added on cultivating communication competence • Updated list of qualities sought by employers • "Putting Communication to Work" streamlined and example changed to be more directly relevant to chapter topic • First edition "By the Numbers" deleted or incorporated into chapter • Research findings updated

CHAPTER 2: New chapter-opening vignette • New tables on "The Average World Citizen" and on Facebook culture • New "Adaptability" feature added on showing cultural sensitivity • New list of culturally universal characteristics • "Sharpen Your Skills" element revised and made more concrete, and skills clearly identified • "Dark Side of Communication" rewritten with more contemporary example • New "Get Connected" section added on online co-cultures • "Putting Communication to Work" streamlined and example changed to be more directly relevant to chapter topic • First edition "By the Numbers" deleted or incorporated into chapter • Research findings updated

CHAPTER 3: New chapter-opening vignette • Updated examples for image management and collaborative image management • "Dark Side of Communication" rewritten to focus on mental illness • "Sharpen Your Skills" element revised and made more concrete, and skills clearly identified • "Get Connected" section repurposed on online image management • New "Adaptability" feature added on identifying stereotypes • First edition "By the Numbers" deleted or incorporated into chapter • Research findings updated

CHAPTER 4: New chapter-opening vignette • "Putting Communication to Work" streamlined • Expanded section and new figure for dialects • New "Adaptability" feature added on practicing persuasion • Updated examples for defamation and for hate speech • "Sharpen Your Skills" element revised and made more concrete, and skills clearly identified • "Get Connected" section repurposed on online hate speech • First edition "By the Numbers" deleted or incorporated into chapter • Research findings updated

CHAPTER 5: New chapter-opening vignette • Updated figures for American Sign Language • New "Get Connected" section added on avatars • "Sharpen Your Skills" element revised and made more concrete, and skills clearly identified • "Putting Communication to Work" streamlined and example changed to be more directly relevant to chapter topic • New "Adaptability" feature added on enacting expressiveness • New "Adaptability" feature added on considering candidates • First edition "By the Numbers" deleted or incorporated into chapter • Research findings updated

CHAPTER 6: New chapter-opening vignette • "Sharpen Your Skills" element revised and made more concrete, and skills clearly identified • "Sharpen Your Skills" on open-mindedness added • "Get Connected" section repurposed on avoiding information overload online • First edition "By the Numbers" deleted or incorporated into chapter • Research findings updated

CHAPTER 7: New chapter-opening vignette • "Get Connected" section repurposed on meeting social needs online • "Dark Side of Communication" on cyberbullying updated • "Sharpen Your Skills" on avoiding cyberbullying added • "Sharpen Your Skills" element revised and made more concrete, and skills clearly identified • Table 7.2 on Friendship Rules updated with new research • "Putting Communication to Work" streamlined and example changed to be more directly relevant to chapter topic • New "Adaptability" feature added on deliberating disclosures • First edition "By the Numbers" deleted or incorporated into chapter • Research findings updated

CHAPTER 8: New chapter-opening vignette • Discussion of same-sex marriage laws updated • New "Get Connected" section added on predicting relational dissolution with Facebook • Table of confirming messages updated with example messages • Table of disconfirming messages updated with example messages • Popular culture examples updated throughout • "Sharpen Your Skills" element revised and made more concrete, and skills clearly identified • New "Adaptability" feature added on civilizing conflict • First edition "By the Numbers" deleted or incorporated into chapter • Research findings updated

CHAPTER 9: New chapter-opening vignette • "Get Connected" section repurposed on success in online group communication • "Sharpen Your Skills" element revised and made more concrete, and skills clearly identified • "Putting Communication to Work" streamlined and example changed to be more directly relevant to chapter topic • Popular culture examples updated throughout • New "Adaptability" feature added on promoting positivity • First edition "By the Numbers" deleted or incorporated into chapter • Research findings updated

CHAPTER 10: New chapter-opening vignette • New "Get Connected" section added on leadership in online small groups • "Dark Side of Communication" discussion of coercion updated • "Sharpen Your Skills" element revised and made more concrete, and skills clearly identified • New "Adaptability" feature added on selecting strategies • First edition "By the Numbers" deleted or incorporated into chapter • Research findings updated

CHAPTER 11: "Get Connected" section repurposed on computer-mediated communication in audience analysis • "Fact or Fiction?" expanded to include details for evaluating information found online • Audience analysis section expanded • "Sharpen Your Skills" element revised and made more concrete, and skills clearly identified • Examples updated throughout • "Putting Communication to Work" streamlined and example changed to be more directly relevant to chapter topic • Speech topic examples expanded • New "Adaptability" feature added on accommodating adjustments • First edition "By the Numbers" deleted or incorporated into chapter • Research findings updated

CHAPTER 12: New opening vignette • More examples of purpose statements added • "Sharpen Your Skills" added on evaluating the credibility of information found online • Section on speech introductions expanded to include two additional techniques • "Sharpen Your Skills" element revised and made more concrete throughout, and skills clearly identified • APA and MLA citation examples updated • Examples updated throughout • New "Adaptability" feature added on finding facts • First edition "By the Numbers" deleted or incorporated into chapter

CHAPTER 13: Stage fright section repurposed to focus more on public speaking anxiety • "Putting Communication to Work" streamlined and example changed to be more directly relevant to chapter topic • "Sharpen Your Skills" element revised and made more concrete throughout, and skills clearly identified • Section added on cultural norms and their effects on speech delivery styles • Examples updated throughout • "Adaptability" feature added on presenting proficiently • First edition "By the Numbers" deleted or incorporated into chapter

CHAPTER 14: New "Get Connected" section on using online resources in an informative speech • Examples updated throughout • "Sharpen Your Skills" element revised and made more concrete throughout, and skills clearly identified • New "Adaptability" feature added on adapting to audience boredom • First edition "By the Numbers" deleted or incorporated into chapter

CHAPTER 15: New "Get Connected" section on persuasion via text messaging • Examples updated throughout • "Sharpen Your Skills" element revised and made more concrete throughout, and skills clearly identified • "Putting Communication to Work" streamlined and example changed to be more directly relevant to chapter topic • New "Adaptability" feature added on adapting to audience hostility • First edition "By the Numbers" deleted or incorporated into chapter

APPENDIX: "Get Connected" section repurposed on persuasion via text messaging • Research citations updated throughout • "Sharpen Your Skills" element revised and made more concrete throughout, and skills clearly identified • "Putting Communication to Work" streamlined and example changed to be more directly relevant to chapter topic • New "Adaptability" feature added on adapting to anxiety during a job interview • First edition "By the Numbers" deleted or incorporated into chapter

CONTRIBUTORS

I am very grateful to the thoughtful, astute instructors across the country who offered insights and suggestions that improved and enhanced Communication Matters, *Second Edition:*

Manuscript Reviewers

Lisa Heller Boragine, *Cape Cod Community College*
Christy Burns, *Jacksonville State University*
Mattea Garcia, *Indiana State University, Terre Haute*
Brent Goken, *Illinois Central College*
Chris Harper, *Arkansas State University*
Brent Kice, *Frostburg State University*
Kimberly Kline, *University of Texas at San Antonio*
Kurt Lindemann, *San Diego State University*
Thomas Morra, *Northern Virginia Community College—Annandale*
Carol Paulnock, *Saint Paul College*
Elesha Ruminski, *Frostburg State University*
Shari Santoriello, *Suffolk Community College—Riverhead*
Richard Underwood, *Kirkwood Community College*
Charlene Widener, *Hutchinson Community College*
Karen Wolf, *Suffolk Community College—Riverhead*

Connect Reviewers

Wade Cornelius, *Doña Ana Community College*
Brent Kice, *Frostburg State University*
Kimberly Kline, *University of Texas at San Antonio*
Kurt Lindemann, *San Diego State University*
Danna Prather, *Suffolk Community College—Selden*
Rhonda Richardson, *Phoenix College*

Elesha Ruminski, *Frostburg State University*
Kirsten Stantz, *Bowling Green State University*
Adam Vellone, *Miami Dade College*
Karen Wolf, *Suffolk Community College—Riverhead*

Design Reviewers

Sandra Brisiel, *Delaware Technical Community College*
Pamela Brooks, *Arizona State University Polytechnic*
Anna Carmon, *Indiana University—Purdue University Columbus*
Margaret Chojnacki, *Barry University*
Jenny Erickson, *Normandale Community College*
Jodi Gaete, *Suffolk County Community College*
Charles Goehring, *San Diego State University*
Kurt Lindemann, *San Diego State University*
Laura Marqua, *Joliet Junior College*
Thomas Morra, *Northern Virginia Community College—Annandale*
Liz O'Brien, *Phoenix College*
Susan Olson, *Mesa Community College*
Marcie Pachter, *Palm Beach State College*
Whitney Pisani, *Collin College*
Elesha Ruminski, *Frostburg State University*
Kelly Stockstad, *Austin Community College—Cypress Creek*
Adam Vellone, *Miami Dade College*
Jenny Warren, *Collin College*

ACKNOWLEDGMENTS

Few endeavors of any significance are achieved in isolation. There are always others who help us rise to—and exceed—our potential in nearly everything we do. I am delighted to acknowledge and thank those whose contributions and support are responsible for the book you are now reading.

This was my second book with McGraw-Hill, and I could not ask for a better team of editors, managers, and publishers to work with. I am indebted to Mika De Roo, Susan Gouijnstook, Rhona Robbin, Mike Ryan, David Patterson, Elisa Adams, Clare Cashen, Suzie Flores, Jamie Daron, Mel Valentin, Debra Kubiak, Keith McPherson, Mary Reeg, Shawntel Schmitt, and Ayelet Arbel for the consistent, professional support I received from each of them. I'm also grateful for the excellent contributions of Janet Byrne Smith, Marianne Musni, Katie Klochan, Meghan Campbell, and Shawn Coenen to the digital components available for the book in Connect.

My students, colleagues, and administrators at Arizona State University have, as always, been a joy to work with and a tremendous source of encouragement. Undertaking a project of this size can be daunting, and it is so valuable to have a strong network of professional support on which to draw.

I am eternally grateful for the love and support of my family and my lifelong friends. One needn't be an expert on communication to understand how important close personal relationships are—but the more I learn about communication, the more appreciative I become of the people who play those roles in my life. You know who you are, and I thank you from the bottom of my heart.

COMMUNICATION:
A FIRST LOOK

What We Have Here Is a Failure to Adapt

Comedian Kathy Griffin is known for pushing boundaries. She frequently uses coarse language and off-color jokes in her stand-up routines, and she often seems unafraid—if not genuinely eager—to make her listeners uncomfortable. Griffin's irreverent style of humor has made her famous . . . but when she takes it too far, it also gets her into trouble. Such was the case in July 2009 when she performed at the famed Apollo Theater in Harlem as a guest of Rev. Al Sharpton. Although her audience comprised both adults and children of various ethnicities, Griffin began her performance with adult language and sexually explicit humor. Within minutes, the audience booed her off the stage, and she has since been banned from the Apollo for life. Griffin's supporters said she was simply performing the type of comedy for which she is known. Critics noted, however, that she should have been more aware of who her audience was. Had she thought more about her listeners—and adapted her communication style to them—she may well have avoided such an embarrassing incident.

As You READ

- What needs does communication help us meet?
- How does communication work, and what misconceptions do we have about it?
- What particular skills characterize competent communicators?

Why We Communicate

Just as Kathy Griffin seeks to entertain people by communicating humor, we communicate with others to affect several dimensions of our lives. For example, we communicate to form personal relationships, to maintain them, and to end them. We communicate to order dinner at a restaurant, negotiate a car loan, and buy music online. Through communication behaviors, teachers instruct us, advertisers persuade us, and actors entertain us. Very little about our lives isn't influenced by the way we communicate.

Because communication affects so many aspects of our existence, learning how to communicate effectively helps improve our lives in multiple ways. As you'll see, effective communication depends not only on having the right message but also on shaping that message to meet the needs of your audience. Griffin's example illustrates the negative outcomes of failing to adapt a message for listeners. This course will help you develop the tools you need to understand the communication process and the skills you need to adapt your communication behavior to others.

In a series of demonstrations called "Occupy Wall Street," thousands marched in New York and other cities starting in the fall of 2011 to protest wealth inequity and corporate influence over government. Similar demonstrations in recent years have used Facebook and Twitter to exchange information efficiently among protesters. Many involved in Occupy Wall Street found an even more effective means of communication in a smartphone app called "Vibe," which allows users to post short Twitter-like messages. Unlike Tweeters, however, Vibe users can make their messages anonymous and choose how long they will be viewable before disappearing. They can also decide how far their messages will travel, even restricting them to devices within 150 feet of the user's phone. Protesters in New York used Vibe to send each other instant information about where to meet and how to avoid run-ins with police. Even though the app was created only in May 2011, it already supports over a thousand messages a day.[1]

Digital technologies such as Vibe give us unprecedented communication abilities. **Communication** is the process by which we use signs, symbols, and behaviors to exchange information and create meaning.[2] Never before has it been so easy to communicate with others—but what draws us to do so? *Why* do we communicate? As you'll see in this section, communication is vital to many different aspects of life, from filling physical and everyday needs to experiencing relationships, spirituality, and identity.

• **communication** The process by which people use signs, symbols, and behaviors to exchange information and create meaning.

COMMUNICATION ADDRESSES PHYSICAL NEEDS

We humans are such social beings that when we are denied the opportunity for interaction, our mental and physical health can suffer. That is a major reason why solitary confinement is considered such a harsh punishment. Several studies have shown that when people are prevented from having contact with others for an extended period, their health can quickly deteriorate.[3] Similarly, individuals who feel socially isolated because of poverty, homelessness, mental illness, or other stigmatizing situations can suffer even physical pain owing to their lack of interaction with others.[4]

We literally cannot survive without human communication, as a bizarre experiment in the thirteenth century helped to show. Frederick II, emperor of Germany, wanted to know what language humans would speak naturally if they weren't taught any particular one. To find out, he placed 50 newborns in the care of nurses who were instructed only to feed and bathe the babies but not to speak to or hold them. The emperor never discovered the answer to his question because all the infants died.[5] Clearly, Frederick's experiment was unethical by modern standards—that is, it did not follow established principles that guide people in judging whether something is morally right or wrong. Such an experiment wouldn't be repeated today. However, more recent studies in orphanages and adoption centers, conducted according to ethical guidelines, have convincingly shown that human interaction—especially touch—is critical for infants' survival and healthy development.[6]

		TABLE 1.1

TABLE 1.1

COMMUNICATING
IN CYBERSPACE

1.6	Average number of e-mail accounts per U.S. e-mail user
87	Percentage of U.S. teenagers who sleep with, or next to, their cell phone
120	Number of friends the average Facebook user has
10,000	Tweets posted per second immediately following news of Steve Jobs's death in October 2011
6,403,120	Number of fans on Barack Obama's Facebook fan page
20,000,000	Number of Skype users in the United States
88,000,000	Number of .com domain names
294,000,000,000	Average number of e-mail messages sent worldwide per day

Take note of how you compare to these averages. Do you have more e-mail accounts or Facebook friends than average, or fewer? Do you sleep next to your cell phone? Are you an average communicator in these ways, or do you differ from the average?

◀ **HOW DO YOU COMPARE?**

SOURCES: Radicati Group; Pew Research Center; Facebook; Time, Inc.; Skype; Pingdom. Statistics are from November 2011.

Positive social interaction keeps adults healthy, too. Research shows that people without strong social ties such as close friendships and family relationships are more likely to suffer major ailments (such as heart disease and high blood pressure) and to die prematurely than are people who have close, satisfying relationships.[7] They are also more likely to suffer basic ailments, such as colds, and they often take longer to recover from illnesses and injuries.[8] Certainly, not everyone needs the same amount of interaction to stay healthy. Nevertheless, communication plays an important role in maintaining human health and well-being.

• **relational needs** The essential elements people seek in their relationships with others.

COMMUNICATION MEETS RELATIONAL NEEDS

Besides our physical needs, each of us also has **relational needs**—the essential elements we look for in our relationships with other people. As communication scholar Rebecca Rubin and her colleagues have found, relational needs include companionship, affection, and the ability to relax and escape our problems.[9] We don't necessarily have the same needs in all our relationships—you probably value your friends for somewhat different reasons than you value your relatives, for instance. The bottom line, though, is that we need relationships in our lives, and communication is a large part of how we establish and maintain them.[10]

Many features of our day-to-day lives are designed to promote the development of human relationships. Neighborhoods, schools, workplaces, malls, theaters, and restaurants are all social settings in which we regularly interact with others in some way. Technology is also an avenue for promoting our relationships. Cell phones let us call or exchange text messages with virtually anyone at the touch of a button; the Internet offers multiple ways of connecting with others, and many people have met new friends or romantic partners online.[11] Table 1.1 provides an idea of how much of our lives are spent communicating in cyberspace alone. Just imagine how challenging it would be to form and maintain

Communication technology connects us in unprecedented ways. Friend-tracking software, such as Google Latitude, lets people map one another's movements on their cell phones and iPads.

strong social relationships if you did not have the ability to communicate with others. The lack of communication channels is a common experience for many immigrants, who often struggle to adapt to their new culture and to learn its language—and who may feel lonely or ignored in the process.[12]

Some scholars believe our need for relationships is so fundamental that we can hardly get by without them.[13] For example, research has shown that having a rich social life is one of the most powerful predictors of a person's overall happiness.[14] The single most important predictor of happiness in life—by far—is the degree to which an individual has a happy marriage.[15] Marital happiness is more important than income, job status, education, leisure time, or anything else in accounting for how happy people are with their lives. On the negative side, people in distressed marriages are much more likely to suffer from major depression, and they even report being in worse physical health than their happily married counterparts.[16]

The cause-and-effect relationship between marriage and happiness isn't a simple one. It may be that strong marriages promote happiness and well-being, or it may be that happy, healthy people are more likely than others to be married. Whatever the reason, personal relationships clearly play an important role in our lives, and communication helps us form and maintain them.

COMMUNICATION FILLS IDENTITY NEEDS

Are you curious? Laid-back? Caring? Impatient? Each of us can probably come up with a long list of adjectives to describe ourselves, but here's the critical question: How do you *know* you are those things? In other words, how do you form an identity?

The ways we communicate with others—and the ways others communicate with us—play a major role in shaping the way we see ourselves.[17] As we'll consider in Chapter 3, people form their identities partly by comparing themselves to others. If you consider yourself intelligent, for instance, what that really means is that you see yourself as more intelligent than most other people. If you think you're shy, you see most other people as more outgoing than you are.

One way we learn how we compare to others is by communicating with those around us. If people treat you as intelligent or shy, you may begin to believe that you have those characteristics. In other words, those qualities will become part of your self-image. As Chapter 3 explains, identity develops over the course of life, and communication plays a critical role in driving that process. Good communicators also have the ability to emphasize different aspects of their identities in different situations. For example, at work it might be important for you to portray your organized, efficient side, whereas at a pool party you might choose to project your fun-loving nature and sense of humor.

COMMUNICATION MEETS SPIRITUAL NEEDS

An important aspect of identity for many people is their spirituality. Spirituality includes the principles someone values in life ("I value loyalty" or "I value equal treatment for all people"). It also encompasses a person's *morals*, or notions about right and wrong ("It's never okay to steal, no matter what the circumstances" or "I would lie to save a life, because life is more important than honesty"). Finally, spirituality includes beliefs about the meaning of life, such as personal philosophies, awe of nature, belief in a higher purpose, and religious faith and practices ("I trust in God" or "I believe I will reap what I sow in life").

A 2010 survey of more than 112,000 U.S. college students found that many consider some form of spirituality to be an important part of their identity.[18] Almost half said they consider integrating spirituality into their lives to be essential or very important. For those in the study, spirituality didn't necessarily include formal religion; over 68 percent of those surveyed believed people can grow spiritually without being religious. For people who include spirituality as a part of their identity, communication provides a means of expressing and sharing spiritual ideas and practices with one another.

Communication lets people express their faith and spirituality.

COMMUNICATION SERVES INSTRUMENTAL NEEDS

Finally, people communicate to meet their practical, everyday needs, which researchers call **instrumental needs.** Some instrumental needs have short-term objectives, such as ordering a drink in a bar, scheduling a haircut on the telephone, filling out a rebate card, and raising your hand when you want to speak in class. Others encompass longer-term goals, such as getting a job and earning a promotion. The communicative behaviors entailed in serving instrumental needs may not always contribute directly to our health, relationships, identity, or spirituality. Each behavior is valuable, however, because it serves a need that helps us get through daily life.

• **instrumental needs**
Practical, everyday needs.

Meeting instrumental needs may not seem as interesting as forging new relationships or as meaningful as expressing spiritual beliefs. But it is important for two reasons. The first reason is simply that we have many instrumental needs. In fact, most of the communication in which we engage on a day-to-day basis is probably mundane and routine—not heavy, emotionally charged conversations but instrumental interactions such as talking to professors about assignments and taking customers' orders at work. The second reason instrumental needs are important is that many of them—such as buying food at the store and ordering clothes online—have to be met before other needs—for example, maintaining high-quality relationships and finding career fulfillment—can be satisfied.[19]

SHARPEN Your Skills: *Communication needs*

Using the Internet to help you, locate a speech or written statement made by an Occupy Wall Street protester. In a short paragraph, identify how, if at all, the speech or statement reflected the communicator's physical, relational, identity, spiritual, or instrumental needs.

The Nature and Types of Communication

When 14-year-old Santiago Ventura left his home in the Mexican state of Oaxaca for farm work in Oregon, he had no way of foreseeing the tragedy that would befall him. After the fatal stabbing of a fellow farm worker at a party, Ventura was questioned by a Spanish-speaking police officer. Ventura spoke neither Spanish nor English, however, but only the native language of Mixtec Indians. During questioning, he never made eye contact with the officer, because Mixtec Indians believe that it is rude to look people directly in the eye. Owing to his poor grasp of Spanish, Ventura simply answered "yes" to all the officer's questions, leading the officer to presume his guilt. After a trial in which his lawyer forbade him to testify because of his English-language limitations, Ventura was convicted of murder and sentenced to 10 years to life in prison. Only after 5 years of protests by immigration advocates and jurors who were unconvinced of Ventura's guilt did another judge set aside the verdict, freeing Ventura from his wrongful imprisonment.

Had we been involved in Ventura's case, many of us would have interpreted his words and behaviors the same way the arresting officer did. If they asked Ventura whether he had committed a crime and he replied "yes" while also avoiding eye contact, most reasonable people would conclude that he was guilty. As his story illustrates, however, it is easy to misunderstand others when we don't adapt to their communication styles. Even seemingly straightforward communication behaviors can easily be misinterpreted, sometimes with tragic consequences. Ventura's problems began when the officer attributed the wrong meaning to his words and behaviors. How do people express and interpret meaning accurately? What accounts for our ability to communicate in the first place?

We begin this section by examining different ways to understand the communication process. Next, we look at some important characteristics of communication and consider various approaches to thinking about communication in social interaction. Finally, we explore five types of communication in which humans engage. Even though you communicate all the time, you'll find there is still much to learn about communication's central role in life.

VARIOUS MODELS EXPLAIN THE COMMUNICATION PROCESS

• **model** A formal description of a process.

How would you describe the process of communicating? Even researchers have answered that question in different ways over the years. A formal description of a process such as communication is called a **model.** In this section we look at three different models that communication scholars have developed over the years: the action, interaction, and transaction models. The action model was developed first, then the interaction model, and finally the transaction model. In that sense, those models demonstrate how communication researchers have defined and described communication over time.

Communication as Action In the **action model,** which is based on ideas generated in the 1940s by mathematicians Claude Shannon and Warren Weaver, we think of communication as a one-way process.[20] To illustrate, let's say that you need to leave work early next Tuesday to attend parent–teacher conferences at your children's school, and you're getting ready to ask your supervisor for permission. The action model starts with the **source**—the individual who has a thought that he or she wishes to communicate. In our example, the source is *you.* To convey the idea that you'd like to leave early, you must **encode** it, which means to put your idea in the form of language or a gesture that your supervisor can understand. Through that process, you create a **message,** which consists of the verbal and/or nonverbal elements of communication to which people give meaning.[21] In this example, your message might be the question, "Would it be all right if I left work a couple of hours early next Tuesday?"

According to the action model, you would then send your message through a communication **channel,** which is a type of pathway for conveying messages. For example, you can pose your question to your supervisor face-to-face, or you can send it by e-mail, through a text message, or by means of a phone call. Selecting the most

• **action model** A model describing communication as a one-way process.

• **source** The originator of a thought or an idea.

• **encode** To put an idea into language or gesture.

• **message** Verbal and nonverbal elements of communication to which people give meaning.

• **channel** A pathway through which messages are conveyed.

appropriate channel is a matter of adapting to the communication context. You adapt to a context when you remember that the same communication behaviors don't work best in every situation. To be successful, rather, you must identify the goals you wish to accomplish, consider the options available to you at the time, and make a strategic decision about how to communicate. If your message is brief and unambiguous—such as the time a meeting begins—you might choose to send that message by e-mail or text message in order to be efficient and save time. When asking if you can leave work early, however, consider that your supervisor may want more detail about your request and may also need assurances that you won't get behind in your work. A face-to-face or telephone conversation might allow you to accomplish those goals better than a text message or e-mail would, since they allow you to communicate more rapidly and to assess facial expressions and tone of voice as sources of meaning.

In the action model, your supervisor acts as the **receiver** of the message, the person who will **decode** or interpret it. The communication process also includes **noise,** which is anything that interferes with a receiver's ability to attend to your message. The major types of noise are *physical noise* (such as background conversation in the office or static on the telephone line), *psychological noise* (such as other concerns your supervisor is dealing with that day), and *physiological noise* (such as fatigue or hunger). Any of these could prevent your supervisor from paying full attention to your question.

You can see that the action model is linear: A source sends a message through some channel to a receiver, and noise interferes with the message somehow (Figure 1.1). Many of us talk and think about the communication process in that linear manner. For example, when you ask someone "Did you get my message?" you are implying that communication is a one-way process. However, human communication is usually more of a back-and-forth exchange than a one-way process—more similar to tennis than to bowling. Over time, researchers responded to that observation by creating an updated model of communication known as the interaction model.

Communication as Interaction The **interaction model** takes up where the action model leaves off. It includes all the same elements: source, message, channel, receiver, noise, encoding, and decoding, but it differs from the action model in two basic ways. First, the interaction model recognizes that communication is a two-way process. Second, it adds two elements to the mix: feedback and context.[22]

If you've taken physics, you know that every action has a reaction. A similar rule applies to communication. Let's say you're telling your officemate, Simone, about a long-lost friend with whom you recently made contact on Facebook. As you relate your story, Simone nods along and says "Uh-huh" to show she's listening—or maybe

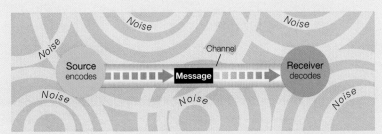

FIGURE 1.1

ACTION MODEL OF COMMUNICATION

In the action model of communication, a sender encodes a message and conveys it through a communication channel for a receiver to decode.

• **receiver** The party who interprets a message.

• **decode** To interpret or give meaning to a message.

• **noise** Anything that interferes with the encoding or decoding of a message.

• **interaction model** A model describing communication as a process shaped by feedback and context.

FIGURE 1.2
INTERACTION MODEL OF COMMUNICATION

The interaction model of communication explains that our messages are shaped by the feedback we receive from others and by the context in which we interact.

- **feedback** Verbal and nonverbal responses to a message.

- **context** The physical or psychological environment in which communication occurs.

- **transaction model** A model describing communication as a process in which everyone is simultaneously a sender and a receiver.

she yawns because she was out late the night before. She might also ask you questions about when you originally met this person or how you got back in touch. In other words, Simone *reacts* to your story by giving you **feedback,** or various verbal and nonverbal responses to your message. Thus, Simone is not just a passive receiver of your message—instead, she is an active shaper of your conversation.

Now let's imagine that you're sharing your story with Simone while you're having coffee in a crowded employee café. Would you tell your story any differently than if the two of you were alone? What if you were in a classroom on campus? What if your parents were in the same room? All those situations are part of the **context,** or the environment you're in. Your environment includes both the physical and the psychological context. The *physical context* reflects where you are physically interacting with each other. In contrast, the *psychological context* includes factors that influence people's states of mind, such as the formality of the situation, the level of privacy, and the degree to which the situation is emotionally charged. According to the interaction model, we take context into account when we engage in conversation. That is, we realize that what is appropriate in certain contexts may be inappropriate in others, and we adapt our behaviors accordingly.

By taking account of feedback and context, the interaction model presents the communication process more realistically than the action model does. In the case of your telling Simone about your long-lost friend, for instance, your story and Simone's feedback would probably be affected by where you were speaking, how many other people could overhear you (if any), and whether those people were coworkers, classmates, family members, or strangers. The interaction model is illustrated in Figure 1.2.

Although the interaction model is more realistic than the action model, it still has limitations. One drawback is that it doesn't represent how complex communication can be. During conversations, it often seems as though both people are sending and receiving information simultaneously rather than simply communicating back and forth, one message at a time. To understand that aspect of communication, we turn to the transaction model, currently the most complete and widely used of the three models.

Communication as Transaction Unlike the action and interaction models, the **transaction model** of communication doesn't distinguish between the roles of source and receiver. Nor does it represent communication as a series of messages going back and forth. Rather, it maintains that both people in a conversation are simultaneously sources *and* receivers. In addition, it illustrates that the conversation flows in both directions at the same time.[23] As a consequence, each person must continuously adapt his or her communication behaviors to those of the other person, in order to keep the conversation flowing smoothly.

To understand the transaction model, imagine that you've taken your car in for service and you're describing to the mechanic the noise your engine has been making. As you speak, a confused look falls across the mechanic's face. According to the interaction model, that facial expression would constitute feedback to your message. The transaction model recognizes that you will interpret that expression not only as feedback to your message but also as a message in and of itself, making the mechanic a source and you a receiver. Note that this process occurs while you're describing your car problems to the mechanic. In other words, you are both sending messages to and receiving messages from the other at the same time. Figure 1.3 depicts the transaction model.

Not only does the transaction model reflect the complex nature of communication, but it also leads us to think about context more broadly. It suggests that our communication is affected not just by the physical or psychological environment but also by our experience, gender, social class, and even the history of our relationship with the person or persons to whom we're talking. As we'll see throughout this book, communication is also influenced by our culture—the collection of shared values, beliefs, and behaviors of a group of people.

If you have a history with the car

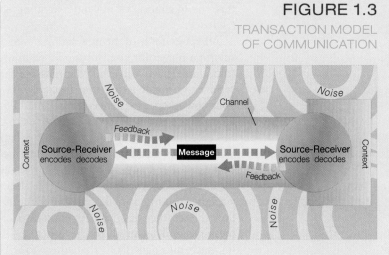

FIGURE 1.3

TRANSACTION MODEL OF COMMUNICATION

The transaction model recognizes that both people in a conversation are simultaneously senders and receivers.

mechanic, you might help him understand your problem by referring to car trouble you've had in the past. If he isn't a native speaker of your language, you might have to speak more slowly and clearly than you otherwise would. Sometimes it's a challenge to consider how cultural aspects of context might affect the way you communicate. According to the transaction model, however, they are always with you.

Adapting to the Communication Context Clearly, then, researchers have different ways of understanding the communication process. Instead of debating which model is right, it's more helpful to look at the useful ideas each model offers. When we do so, we find that each model fits certain situations better than others. You can use that information to adapt to the communication constraints of each model.

For instance, sending a text message to your professor is a good example of the action model. You're the source, and you convey your message through a written channel to a receiver (your professor). Noise includes any difficulty your professor experiences in opening the message or understanding the intent of your message because of the language you have used. When the linear model is in play, you can remember that the likelihood of misunderstanding is high because there is no opportunity for feedback.

An apt example of the interaction model is the communication that occurs when you submit a report for your job, and a team of coworkers comments on it in writing. You (the source) have conveyed your message through your report, and your coworkers (the receivers) provide written feedback. Noise includes any difficulties that either you or your coworkers experience in understanding what everyone has said. In that situation, your coworkers and you send messages to one another, but not at the same time. You therefore have time to interpret, and perhaps misinterpret, one another's meanings.

Most conversations are good examples of the transaction model, because both parties are sending and receiving messages simultaneously. That process occurs, for instance, when you strike up a conversation with someone sitting next to you on an airplane. You might make small talk about where each of you is traveling that day or how the weather has been. As you do so, each of you is sending verbal and nonverbal messages and feedback to the other and is simultaneously receiving and interpreting such messages from the other. Your conversation is affected by the context, in that you may communicate only to pass the time until you land. It is also affected by noise, including turbulence during the flight and the sound of the flight attendants' announcements. A face-to-face conversation requires you to adapt your communication behaviors to the other person's on an ongoing basis, as each of you helps to construct the conversation you're having.

Each model, then, is more useful in some situations than in others. The action model and interaction model are too simplistic to describe most face-to-face conversations, but when you're just leaving a note for someone or submitting a report for feedback, those models can describe the situation quite well. The transaction model, which many experts consider the most comprehensive of the three models, better describes complex face-to-face communications. As you come across examples of different communication situations in this book, you might ask yourself how well each model fits them.

Now that we've looked at different models of communication, let's consider some of communication's most important characteristics.

COMMUNICATION HAS MANY CHARACTERISTICS

Describing the communication process requires more than just mapping out how it takes place. We also need to catalog its important features. In this section, we'll discover that

- Communication relies on multiple channels.
- Communication passes through perceptual filters.
- People give communication its meaning.
- Communication has literal meanings and relational implications.
- Communication sends messages, whether intentional or unintentional.
- Communication is governed by rules.

Communication Relies on Multiple Channels How many different ways do people communicate with one another? Facial expressions telegraph how a person is feeling. Gestures and tone of voice help others to interpret his or her messages. Touch can signal feelings such as affection and aggression. Even a person's clothing and physical appearance communicate messages about that individual to others.

• channel-rich contexts
Communication environments involving many channels at once.

• channel-lean contexts
Communication environments involving few channels at once.

Some situations are **channel-rich contexts**—environments that incorporate multiple communication channels at once. In face-to-face conversations, for instance, you can pay attention to people's words, see their expressions and gestures, hear their tone of voice, and feel their touch at the same time. You can evaluate the information from all those channels simultaneously. Other situations are **channel-lean contexts**—environments that use relatively fewer channels.[24] Tweeting, for instance, relies on text alone; you don't experience a person's voice or gestures on Twitter. As a consequence, you pay more attention to the words, because that's all you have to go on.

Communication Passes through Perceptual Filters Anything you put through a filter—such as air, water, or light—comes out a little bit differently than it went in. The same happens when we communicate: what one person says is not always exactly what the other person hears. The reason is that we all "filter" incoming communication through our perceptions, experiences, biases, and beliefs.

Let's say you're listening to a senator speak on television. The way you process and make sense of the speech probably depends on how much you agree with the senator's ideas or whether you belong to the same political party. Two people with different political viewpoints may listen to the same speech yet hear something very different. One may hear a set of logical, well thought-out ideas, while the other may hear nothing but lies and empty promises.

Perceptual filters can also influence how different people understand the same words. For instance, some trains in New Jersey's subway system are designated "quiet cars." Since the quiet car program started, passengers have disagreed about the proper meaning of "quiet." Some believe it calls for complete silence, whereas others believe they have a right to talk quietly, or whisper. Everyone agrees on which cars are the quiet cars, but their perceptual filters give them different interpretations of what that designation means.

Many aspects of our lives can influence our perception of communication. Whether we're aware of it or not, our ethnic and cultural background, gender, religious beliefs, socioeconomic status, intelligence, education, level of physical attractiveness, and experiences with illness, disease, and death can all act as filters, coloring the way we see the world and the way we make sense of communication. The officer who questioned Santiago Ventura filtered Ventura's behaviors through his own cultural expectations by assuming, incorrectly, that everyone from Mexico speaks Spanish and that lack of eye contact is a sign of dishonesty.

Because of people's different perceptual filters, the definition of "quiet" in the quiet cars of public transportation systems has been a point of debate and contention.

People Give Communication Its Meaning When we write or speak, we choose our words deliberately so that we can say what we *mean*. What is the source of that meaning? Words have no meaning by themselves; they're just sounds or marks on a piece of paper or a monitor. A word is a **symbol,** or a representation of an idea, but the word itself isn't the idea or the meaning. The meaning of words— and of many other forms of communication—comes from the people and groups who use them.

• **symbol** A representation of an idea.

Almost all language is arbitrary in the sense that words mean whatever groups of people decide they mean. As a result, we can't assume that other people understand the meanings we intend to communicate just because we understand what we mean. For instance, what is a mouse? If you asked that question 40 years ago, the answer would have been "a small rodent that likes cheese and gets chased by cats." Today, however, many people know a mouse as a pointing device for navigating within a computer screen. As another example, what is a robot? In the United States, it's a humanlike machine that performs mechanical tasks, but in South Africa, it's a traffic light.

COMMUNICATION HAS LITERAL MEANINGS AND RELATIONAL IMPLICATIONS

Nearly every verbal statement has a **content dimension,** or the literal information the communicator is communicating.[25] When you say to your friend, "I'm kind of unhappy today," the content dimension of your message is that you're feeling sad, depressed, or angry. When your housemate says, "We're out of cereal again," the content dimension of the message is that you have no cereal left.

• **content dimension** Literal information that is communicated by a message.

There's often more to messages than their literal content, though. Many messages also carry signals about the nature of the relationship in which they're shared. Those signals make up the **relational dimension** of the message. For example, by telling your friend that you're feeling unhappy, you may also be sending the message, "I feel comfortable enough with you to share my feelings" or, "I want you to help me feel better." Likewise, you might interpret your housemate's statement that you're out of cereal as also saying, "I'm sure you're aware of this, but I'm just reminding you," or you might take it as meaning, "I'm irritated that you never replace the food you use up." Even though messages like those are unspoken, we often infer meanings about our relationships from the tone and manner in which the statements are made.

One way we distinguish between content and relational dimensions is through **metacommunication,** which is communication about communication. Let's say that Jude asks her husband, Han, to read over the speech she is preparing to give at a conference for small-business owners. Han reads the speech and marks it up with critical comments such as, "This argument isn't convincing," "Awkward wording," and "I can't tell what you're trying to say." After reading Han's comments, Jude is disheartened, and Han is confused by her reaction.

Han: *I thought you wanted my feedback. I was just trying to help you make your speech better; that's what you asked for. Why are you taking my comments so personally?*

Jude: *It's not what you said; it's how you said it.*

Dozing off during a meeting sends messages to others, even if those messages are unintentional.

• **relational dimension**
Signals about the relationship in which a message is being communicated.

• **metacommunication**
Communication about communication.

By focusing his attention on Jude's request for feedback, Han is attending to the content dimension of their conversation. He can't understand why Jude is upset, because Jude had asked him for his feedback. To Jude, however, Han's comments are overly harsh and insensitive, and they imply that he doesn't care about her feelings. Jude is focusing on the relational dimension of their conversation. To highlight that distinction, she metacommunicates with Han by explaining that her hurt feelings were caused not by what Han said but by *the way he said it.* That phrase conveys Jude's thoughts about her communication with Han; thus, it is metacommunicative.

Communication Sends Messages, Intentional and Unintentional

Much of what we communicate to others is deliberate. When you set up a job interview, for instance, you do so intentionally, having thought about why you want the job and how you will respond to the interviewer's questions. Very rarely do you schedule an interview by accident.

You may communicate a number of other messages, however, without intending to. For example, have you ever tried hard to stay awake in an important meeting? Despite your efforts to look engaged and interested, you might not have been aware that your slouching posture and droopy eyelids were signaling your fatigue, perhaps after a long day of working at a part-time job and attending classes. In that instance, your behavior was sending unintentional messages.

Whether unintentional messages should qualify as communication has been a focal point of debate among communication scholars for many years. Some researchers believe that only deliberate, intentional messages are a part of communication and that if you don't intend to communicate, you aren't communicating.[26] Others subscribe to the belief that "you cannot *not* communicate," meaning that absolutely everything you do has communicative value.[27] The validity of that idea is addressed in the "Fact or Fiction?" box.

Communication Is Governed by Rules

Rules tell us what behaviors are required, preferred, or prohibited in various social contexts.[28] Some rules for communication are **explicit rules,** meaning someone has clearly articulated them. Perhaps

• **explicit rules** Rules that have been clearly articulated.

Fact or *fiction*?

You Cannot *Not* Communicate

Some of the research findings you'll encounter in this course will make intuitive sense to you, and others will be more challenging. Although our intuition is right much of the time, it can also fail us, and that is just one reason why the systematic study of communication is so useful. In the "Fact or Fiction?" boxes throughout this book, we'll examine some of the more intuitively appealing ideas we hold about communication to see how valid they are.

For instance, Paul Watzlawick, an Austrian-born communication theorist, proposed that "one cannot *not* communicate." He believed that every behavior sends some message, whether intentional or not, so all behavior has communicative value. Because people are engaged in some type of behavior—watching television, crying, sleeping, dancing—at every moment, they cannot help but continuously communicate, according to Watzlawick. Other researchers have pointed out, however, that Watzlawick's idea treats all

behavior as communication, and they have argued instead that unintentional behaviors are not necessarily communicative. If you don't *intend* for your behavior to convey a message, they believe, you aren't engaging in communication.

My own position lies somewhere in between. Although I don't believe every possible behavior is a form of communication, neither do I think behaviors must be intentional to have communicative value. I would suggest that even unintended messages—such as the ones you might have expressed while trying to stay awake during a meeting—are forms of communication because they still convey meaning. Many aspects of appearance illustrate that idea. For instance, seeing someone in a wheelchair probably leads you to different conclusions than seeing someone in a white lab coat or an orange prison jumpsuit, yet those messages might be unintentional on the other person's part.

ASK YOURSELF

- What do you think about Watzlawick's idea? Did it seem reasonable or unreasonable to you at first? Why?
- When and how do you communicate messages unintentionally?

SOURCES. Motley, M. T. (1990). On whether one can(not) not communicate: An examination via traditional communication postulates. *Western Journal of Communication, 54,* 1–20; Watzlawick, T., Beavin, J., & Jackson, D. (1967). *The pragmatics of human communication.* New York: Norton.

your parents used to say, "Don't talk with your mouth full." Many universities have explicit rules banning hate speech, such as statements that degrade ethnic or sexual minorities, at campus events and in school publications. Facebook enforces specific guidelines regarding the content of text and photos. Those examples are all explicit communication rules because they directly express expectations for communicative behavior.

In contrast, many communication rules are **implicit rules**—rules that almost everyone in a certain social group knows and follows, even though no one has formally articulated them. People in North American cultures, for instance, follow implicit rules when riding in an elevator, such as "Don't get on if it's already full"

• **implicit rules** Rules that have not been clearly articulated but are nonetheless understood.

SHARPEN Your Skills: *Communication rules*

Choose a specific communication situation, such as listening to a distraught friend, talking to a professor about a grade, or watching a political speech. Write down at least five implicit communication rules that apply to that situation. For each, note what would likely happen if someone violated the rule in that situation.

and "Don't make eye contact with others while you're riding." Implicit rules also govern taking turns when you are waiting for some type of service, such as at a bank or grocery store; those rules include "Get into an orderly line" and "Don't cut ahead of someone else."

Most people seem to know and accept implicit rules, even though they usually aren't posted anywhere. They're just a part of everyone's cultural knowledge. Because those rules are implicit, however, their interpretations are likely to vary more from person to person than do understandings of explicit rules. For example, some people believe it is an implicit rule that you shouldn't talk on a cell phone in a crowded environment such as a subway train during rush hour, whereas other people don't see it as inappropriate.

FIVE TYPES OF COMMUNICATION

Communication occurs as five basic types: intrapersonal, interpersonal, small group, public, and mass. They differ primarily with respect to the size of the audience, but they also call for different communication skills.

Intrapersonal Communication

Interpersonal communication occurs between people in the context of their relationships.

• **intrapersonal communication**
Communication with oneself.

The form of communication that addresses the smallest audience is **intrapersonal communication,** the communication you have with yourself. When you mentally remind yourself to do something or rehearse an upcoming conversation in your mind, you are engaging in intrapersonal communication.

Although it may be tempting to equate intrapersonal communication with *cognition*—the act of thinking—your thoughts and memories become communicative only when you put them into words in your mind. Perhaps you have the thought "Don't forget to e-mail Mom about my holiday travel plans." In this instance, you have expressed your thought in words directed at yourself; that is, you have communicated intrapersonally. The same would not be true if you were simply to think of an image, such as a ski slope or a sandy beach, without translating that image into words in your mind.

Interpersonal Communication

• **interpersonal communication**
Communication that occurs between two people in the context of their relationship.

When you exchange instant messages with a friend, talk on the phone with a relative, or visit face-to-face with your supervisor, you are engaging in interpersonal communication. **Interpersonal communication** occurs between two people in the context of their ongoing relationship, and it is the most common form of communication we enact.[29] Even in larger social groups, such as families and organizations, much of our communication is typically interpersonal in nature. We delve more deeply into interpersonal communication in Chapters 7 and 8.

Small Group Communication

• **small group communication**
Communication occurring within small groups of three or more people.

Almost all of us interact in small groups of people, such as sports teams, Bible study groups, organizational departments, and teams of students working on a class project. When we communicate with groups of about 3 to 20 people, we are engaging in **small group communication.** As we'll discover in Chapters 9 and 10, groups have specific ways of making decisions, negotiating power, and working together in the service of their common goals.

Public Communication

• **public communication**
Communication directed at an audience that is larger than a small group.

Public communication occurs when we speak or write to an audience larger than a small group. If you give the welcome speech at a convention for your fraternity or sorority or write a column for the convention's newsletter, you are engaging in public communication. Because your communication targets a larger audience, you might spend more time preparing and practicing your remarks than if you were talking only to a friend or a small group. In Chapters 11 through 15, we examine skills that are helpful for successful public communication.

Mass Communication Communication delivered to a large audience is considered public communication unless it is being transmitted via electronic or print media, such as magazines, television, newspapers, blogs, radio, and websites. Communication transmitted by such media is considered **mass communication.** Newspaper journalists, television personalities, bloggers, and radio announcers are among those whose words are disseminated to vast audiences of people with whom they have little or no personal connection. Because its audience is so large, mass communication works well for distributing news, commentary, and entertainment. It also is effective for marketing products and services through advertisements, but its breadth makes mass communication unsuited for developing relationships or making collective decisions.

• mass communication
Communication to a large audience that is transmitted by media.

Now that we've surveyed the nature and basic types of communication, we'll shift gears and look at some common beliefs about communication that are not as valid as they might seem.

Dispelling Some Communication Myths

In one way or another, you've communicated practically every day of your life. You might therefore feel that you already know what there is to know about communication. As you'll see, however, people have many different ideas about communication. Some of those ideas are not very accurate, which can lead people to make mistakes when communicating with others. In this section we'll examine five common communication myths so that you'll be better able to separate fact from fiction:

1. Everyone is a communication expert.
2. Communication will solve any problem.
3. Communication can break down.
4. Communication is inherently good.
5. More communication is always better.

MYTH: EVERYONE IS A COMMUNICATION EXPERT

Because people communicate constantly, it's easy to believe that just about everyone is an expert in communication. Indeed, in a nationwide survey of American adults conducted by the National Communication Association, fully 91 percent of participants rated their communication skills as above average.[30] Keep in mind, though, that having *experience* with something is not the same as having *expertise.* Many people drive, but that doesn't make them expert drivers. Many people have children, but that doesn't make them parenting experts. Experience can be invaluable, but expertise requires knowledge and ability that go beyond personal experience. Thus, experts in driving, parenting, or communication have training in their fields and a level of understanding that most people who drive, raise children, or communicate don't have.

SHARPEN Your Skills: *Communication experts*

Identify three communication experts outside your college or university. Read about each person's background, and list the training, education, and/or work experiences that make that person an expert in communication. In a brief report, share your findings with your instructor to ensure that you have identified appropriate markers of expertise for each person.

MYTH: COMMUNICATION WILL SOLVE ANY PROBLEM

The classic Paul Newman movie *Cool Hand Luke* (1967) featured a prison warden who had his own special way of dealing with inmates. Whenever things went wrong, he would say, "What we've got here is a failure to communicate," after which he would beat the inmate unconscious and send him to solitary confinement. Sometimes it seems as though

we could solve almost any problem—especially in our relationships—if only we could communicate better. It's easy to blame a lack of communication when things go wrong. Yet the fact is that poor communication isn't the cause of every problem.[31]

On his television talk show *Dr. Phil*, psychologist Phil McGraw often counsels couples encountering difficulties in their relationships. Suppose Connie and Andy appear on *Dr. Phil* complaining that they have been drifting apart for some time. When they discuss their problems on the show, Connie says she feels they need to communicate better to save their relationship. In the course of their conversation, however, Andy states very clearly that his feelings have changed and he is no longer attracted to Connie.

Will communication ultimately solve this couple's marital problems? No—in fact, it will probably cause Connie to realize that their relationship is already over. Going their separate ways might be better for both of them in the long run, so we could say that communication will help them to come to that realization. Nevertheless, it won't solve the problem of their drifting apart in the first place. Therefore, we must be careful not to assume that better communication can resolve any problem we might face in our relationships.

MYTH: COMMUNICATION CAN BREAK DOWN

Just as we sometimes blame our problems on a lack of communication, many of us also point to a "breakdown" in communication as the root of problems. When marriages fail, the spouses may say it was a breakdown in communication that led to their relational difficulties. When government agencies are slow to respond to a natural disaster, people frequently blame their sluggish response on communication breakdowns within those agencies.

The metaphor of the communication breakdown makes intuitive sense to many of us. After all, our progress on a journey is halted if our car breaks down, so it's easy to think that our progress in other endeavors is halted because our communication has broken down. But communication isn't a mechanical object like a car, a computer, or an iPad. Instead, it's a process that unfolds between and among people over time. It may be easy to blame a breakdown in communication for problems we face in personal relationships or during crisis situations. What is actually happening in those contexts is that we are no longer communicating *effectively*. In other words, the problem lies not with communication itself but with the way we're using it. That is one reason why learning about communication—as you are doing in this class—can be so beneficial.

In many instances, people feel they are talking *but not really* communicating.

MYTH: COMMUNICATION IS INHERENTLY GOOD

Listen to people who are having relationship problems, and you'll hear them say they no longer communicate with their romantic partners, parents, or friends. "Sure, we talk all the time," someone might say, "but we don't really *communicate* anymore." Reflected in that statement is the idea that *talking* means just producing words, but *communicating* means sharing meaning with another person in an open, supportive, and inherently positive manner.[32]

THE DARK SIDE OF COMMUNICATION

Tell Me Lies: Misrepresentations in Online Dating Profiles

Online dating services such as Match.com and Zoosk.com have become enormously popular venues for meeting people and starting new relationships. The profiles participants create on these sites commonly include one or more photographs as well as information about the person's age, height and weight, profession, and interests.

Browsing the profiles of others can help us determine whom we might want to contact and communicate with, but how do we know whether the information is true? Research has shown—perhaps not surprisingly—that a large proportion of online daters put false information in their profiles, usually to make themselves appear more attractive to potential partners. Interestingly, women and men tend to lie about different things. In a study of more than 5,000 online dating participants, communication researcher Jeff Hall and his colleagues found that women are more likely than men to lie about their weight. The researchers also found that men are more likely to lie about their income, interests, personality, and age. The results from such studies encourage us to exercise caution when evaluating the profile of a potential dating partner.

SOURCE: Hall, J. A., Park, N., Song, H., & Cody, M. J. (2010). Strategic misrepresentation in online dating: The effects of gender, self-monitoring, and personality traits. *Journal of Social and Personal Relationships, 27,* 117–135.

Thinking that communication is inherently good is similar to thinking that money is inherently good. Sometimes money is put to positive uses, such as providing a home for your family and donating to a worthy charity. At other times it is put to negative uses, such as providing funding for a terrorist group and gambling away hard-earned income. In either case, it isn't the money itself that is good or bad—rather, it's the way it is used.

We can make the same observation about communication. We can use communication for positive purposes, such as expressing love for our parents and comforting a grieving friend. We can also use it for negative purposes, such as intimidating and deceiving people. In fact, deception has become common in certain communication venues, such as in online personal ads, as "The Dark Side of Communication" explains (see box).

Regarding the "dark side" terminology: In recent years, several scholars in the area of interpersonal communication have been studying what they call the "dark side" of communication, or the ways in which people sometimes use communication to hurt or manipulate others. As you encounter "The Dark Side of Communication" box in each chapter of this book, remember that communication itself is not positive or negative—it's what individuals do with it that makes it good or bad.

MYTH: MORE COMMUNICATION IS ALWAYS BETTER

Antonio thinks that if others don't agree with him, the reason is that they just don't understand him. In those situations, he talks on and on, figuring that others will eventually see things his way if he gives them enough information. Perhaps you know someone like Antonio. Does more communication always produce a better outcome?

When people have genuine disagreements, more talk doesn't always help. In some cases, it can just lead to frustration and anger. A study of consultations between doctors and patients found that the more doctors talked, the more likely they were to get off-track and forget about the patients' problems, a pattern that can translate into worse care for the patient.[33] Another study found that the more people communicated with one another on cell phones, the less happy they were, the less satisfied they were with their families, and the more likely they were to say that their work lives "spilled over" into their family lives.[34]

We've already considered that communication cannot solve every problem, so it shouldn't surprise you to learn that more of it isn't always preferable. Indeed, sometimes it seems as though the less said, the better. As you'll learn in this book, the *effectiveness* of our communication—rather than the *amount*—is often what matters. That fact explains why learning to be a competent communicator is so advantageous.

Building Your Communication Competence

Recently, the National Association of Colleges and Employers asked over a thousand employers around the United States what skills and personal qualities they most look for in new college graduates whom they are considering hiring. As you can see in Table 1.2, communication skill was high on the list.[35] That survey—along with several others like it over the past decade—indicates that being an effective communicator gives job applicants a sizable advantage.[36]

None of us is born a competent communicator. Rather, like driving a car, playing a sport, or designing a web page, communicating competently requires skills we must learn and practice. That doesn't mean that nature doesn't give some people a head start. Indeed, research by communication scientist Michael Beatty shows that genes partly determine some of our communication traits—for example, how sociable, aggressive, or shy we are.[37] No matter which traits we are born with, though, we can still learn how to communicate competently. In this section, we probe what it means to be a competent communicator, which skills are necessary for competent communication, and how we learn them.

COMPETENT COMMUNICATION IS EFFECTIVE AND APPROPRIATE

Think about five people whom you consider to be really good communicators. Who's on your list? Any of your friends or relatives? Classmates or teachers? Politicians? Celebrities? You? You probably recognize that identifying good communicators means first asking yourself what a good communicator is. Even communication scholars find that a tricky question. Nevertheless, most researchers seem to agree that **communication competence** means communicating in ways that are *effective* and *appropriate* in a given situation.[38] Communication scholars Brian Spitzberg and Bill Cupach have spent much of their careers studying effective, appropriate communication. Let's take a closer look at what it means to communicate effectively and appropriately, and also at how we can engage in effective and appropriate communication online.

• communication competence
Using communication that is effective and appropriate for a given situation.

Communicating Effectively Effectiveness describes how well your communication achieves its goals.[39] Suppose you want to persuade your neighbor to donate money to a shelter for abused animals. There are many ways to achieve that goal. You could explain how much the shelter needs the money and identify all the

TABLE 1.2		
PERSONAL QUALITIES MOST SOUGHT BY EMPLOYERS AMONG NEW COLLEGE GRADUATES	**1** Ability to work in a team structure	
	2 Ability to communicate verbally	
	3 Ability to make decisions and solve problems	
	4 Ability to obtain and process information	
	5 Ability to plan, organize, and prioritize work	

SOURCE: National Association of Colleges and Employers (2012). *Job Outlook 2012*. Bethlehem, PA: Author.

putting**communication**to**work**

Job Title >	Work Responsibilities >
Public information officer for nonprofit organization	A public information officer, or PIO, is the public face and voice of an organization. This person speaks to the media and to representatives from government and business about the organization's activities and priorities. On any given day, the PIO might be writing a press release, taking part in a live televised interview, making an announcement to an organization's employees, or giving a presentation about the organization to a group of schoolchildren. The job requires excellent public speaking skills, an ability to consider how messages should be framed, and a high level of skill at adapting to the communication needs of different audiences.

services it provides to animals in need. You could offer to do yard work in exchange for your neighbor's donation. You could even recite the times when you have donated to causes that were important to your neighbor.

Your choice of strategy may partly depend on what other goals you are trying to achieve at the same time. If maintaining a good relationship with your neighbor is also important to you, then asking politely may be the most effective course of action. If all you want is the money, however, and your neighbor's feelings are less important to you, then making your neighbor feel obligated to donate may help you achieve your goal, even though it might not be as acceptable morally.

The point is that no single communication strategy is effective in all situations. Because we often pursue more than one goal at a time, being an effective communicator means using behaviors that meet all the goals we have, in the specific context in which we have them.

Communicating Appropriately for the Social and Cultural Context

Besides being effective, competent communication should also be appropriate. That means it adheres to the rules and expectations that apply in a social situation, as we considered earlier in this chapter. For instance, when a coworker asks, "How are you?" you know that it's appropriate to say, "Fine, how are you?" in return. The coworker probably isn't expecting a long, detailed description of how your day is going, so if you launch into one, he or she may find that response inappropriate. Similarly, it's appropriate in most classrooms to raise your hand and wait to be called on before speaking, so it would be inappropriate in those cases to blurt out your comments.

Communicating appropriately can be especially challenging when you're interacting with people from other cultures. The reason is that many communication rules are culture-specific, so what might be perfectly appropriate in one culture may be inappropriate or even offensive in another.[40] If you're visiting a Canadian household and your hosts offer you food, it's appropriate to accept if you're hungry. In many Japanese households, however, it is inappropriate to accept until you have declined the food twice and your hosts offer it a third time.

Even within a specific culture, expectations can vary according to the social situation. Communication that's appropriate at home might be inappropriate at work and vice versa. Moreover, communication that's appropriate for a socially powerful individual is not necessarily appropriate for everyone. It might not be out of line for your manager to demand better cooperation among the staff during a meeting, although expressing the same demand yourself would be inappropriate.

People who know how to communicate effectively can use their skills to succeed in a wide range of fields. Throughout this book, you'll find descriptions of careers that can make excellent use of a communication degree. In the "Putting Communication to Work" box, you'll also discover the diversity of options available to communication majors.

@getCONNECTED

Competence in Computer-Mediated Communication

Since we do so much of our communicating online these days, we especially need to know how to communicate effectively and appropriately in computer-mediated contexts, by observing the rules of competent online communication known as *netiquette*.[41] Communication researchers offer the following specific suggestions:

- *Clarify anything that might be misunderstood.* Even if you think you understand the other person's message, ask yourself how else you might have interpreted it before you respond. Remember that it is easier to misinterpret someone's words when you cannot see facial expressions or hear tone of voice.

- *Don't respond to another's message in anger.* Instead, give yourself time to calm down and collect your thoughts, and then reply.

- *Use emoticons to express your tone.* If appropriate, add emoticons to your message to let your reader know when you're upset, when you're surprised, and when you're kidding.

- *Remember that your reader may misinterpret your words as well.* Although the meaning of your message may be perfectly clear to you, it may not be to your reader. Before you send the message, consider any ways in which your reader might misunderstand your meaning, and work to make it clearer.

Companies seek to hire employees with excellent communication skills.

Whether face to face or online, communication competence implies both effectiveness and appropriateness. Note that those are characteristics of *communication*, not of people. Thus, the logical follow-up question is whether competent *communicators* share any traits. They do, as we'll see next.

COMPETENT COMMUNICATORS SHARE MANY CHARACTERISTICS AND SKILLS

Look again at your list of five people who are good communicators. What do they have in common? Of course, competence is situation-specific, so what works in one context may not work in another. Good communicators, however, tend to have certain characteristics that help them to behave competently in most situations: They are self-aware, adaptable, empathic, cognitively complex, and ethical.

Competent Communicators Are Self-Aware

Good communicators are aware of their own behavior and its effects on others.[42] Researchers call that awareness **self-monitoring.** People who are "high self-monitors" pay close attention to the way they look, sound, and act in social situations. In contrast, people who are "low self-monitors" often seem oblivious to both their own behaviors and other people's reactions to them. For instance, you may know someone who never seems to notice that he dominates the conversation or who seems unaware that she speaks louder than anyone around her.

Self-monitoring usually makes people more competent communicators because it enables them to see how their behavior fits or doesn't fit in a given social setting. In addition, high self-monitors often have the ability to understand people's emotions and social behaviors accurately.[43]

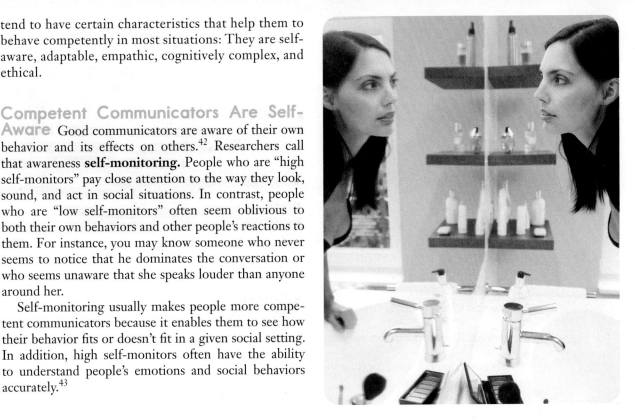

High self-monitors pay close attention to the way they look, sound, and act.

• **self-monitoring**
Awareness of one's behavior and how it affects others.

Competent Communicators Are Adaptable

It's one thing to be aware of your own behavior; it's quite another to able to adapt it to different situations. We've seen that what works in one situation might not be effective in another. Competent communicators are able to assess what will be appropriate and effective in a given context and then modify their behaviors accordingly.[44] As we'll discover in Chapter 11, part of delivering a good speech is being aware of the audience and adapting our behavior accordingly. A competent communicator would speak differently to a group of senior executives than to a group of new hires, for example.

Competent Communicators Are Empathic

Good communicators practice **empathy,** or the ability to be "other-oriented" and to understand other people's thoughts and feelings.[45] When people say "Put yourself in my shoes," they are asking you to consider a situation empathically, from *their* perspective rather than your own. Because people often think and feel differently than you do about the same situation, empathy helps you understand and adapt to their communication behaviors.

• **empathy** The ability to think and feel as others do.

Suppose you want to ask your instructor for a one-week extension on an assignment. You might think, "What's the big deal? It's only a week." To your instructor, however, the extension might mean that she will be unable to complete her grading in time for her planned vacation. If the situation were reversed, how would you feel? An empathic approach would help you consider the situation from the instructor's perspective and tailor your behavior accordingly.

People who don't practice empathy tend to assume that everyone thinks and feels the same way they do, and they risk creating problems when that assumption isn't accurate. How empathic are you? Take the quiz in "The Competent Communicator" box to find out.

Empathy is a particular challenge for individuals with conditions such as autism and Asperger's disorder, both of which impair the ability to interpret other people's nonverbal behaviors. You may have little difficulty judging when a friend is being sarcastic, for instance, because you infer that from his facial expressions and tone of voice. For people with autism or Asperger's disorder, however, those nonverbal signals may not be as evident, making it more challenging to understand and adopt another person's perspective.

Stepping into Others' Shoes: How Empathic Are You?

One of the ways to improve your communication ability is to think about how you communicate now. Each "The Competent Communicator" box will help you to do so by presenting a self-assessment quiz covering a specific communication skill or tendency. For instance, how empathic are you? Indicate how well each of the following statements describes you by assigning it a number between 1 ("not at all") and 7 ("very well").

_____ It makes me sad to see a lonely stranger in a group.

_____ I become nervous if others around me seem nervous.

_____ I tend to get emotionally involved with a friend's problems.

_____ Sometimes the words of a love song can move me deeply.

_____ The people around me have a great influence on my moods.

_____ Seeing people cry upsets me.

_____ I get very angry when I see someone being ill-treated.

_____ I cannot continue to feel okay if people around me are depressed.

_____ I am very upset when I see an animal in pain.

_____ It upsets me to see helpless elderly people.

When you're finished, add up your scores. Your total score should fall between 10 and 70. A score of 10–25 suggests that empathy is a skill you can work on. Learning more about empathy, as you are doing in this class, might help you become more empathic. If you scored between 25 and 55, you are already moderately empathic, and you have a good ability to understand other people's emotions. Continued practice can improve this skill even more. If you scored above 55, you are a highly empathic person. Chances are that this ability helps you to communicate effectively in interpersonal situations.

Remember that your score on this quiz—and on every "The Competent Communicator" quiz in this book—reflects only how you see yourself at this time. If your score surprised you, take the quiz again later in the course to see how studying communication might have changed the way you assess your communication abilities.

SOURCE: Items adapted from Mehrabian, A., & Epstein, N. (1972). A measure of emotional empathy. *Journal of Personality, 40,* 525–543.

Competent Communicators Are Cognitively Complex Let's say you see your friend Annika coming toward you in the hallway at school. You smile and get ready to say hi, but she walks right by as if you're not there. How would you interpret her behavior? Maybe she's mad at you. Maybe she was concentrating on something when she passed and didn't notice anyone around her. Maybe she actually did smile at you and you just didn't see it.

Children with autism often have difficulty interpreting other people's nonverbal behaviors.

The ability to consider a variety of explanations and to understand a given situation in multiple ways is called **cognitive complexity.** As communication scholar Brant Burleson explained, cognitive complexity is a valuable skill because it keeps you from jumping to the wrong conclusion and responding inappropriately.[46] Someone with little cognitive complexity might feel slighted by Annika's behavior and might therefore ignore her the next time they meet. In contrast, someone with more cognitive complexity would remember that behaviors do not always mean what we think they mean. That person would be more open-minded, considering several possible interpretations of Annika's behavior.

SHARPEN Your Skills: *Evaluating competence*

Choose a reality TV show, and consider the characters and their communication behaviors. Based on what you've learned in this section, how would you rate each character in terms of communication competence? What makes some characters more communicatively competent than others? Try to identify specific skills, such as empathy and cognitive complexity, that differentiate the characters from one another. Consider how each person might improve his or her communication competencies. Share your thoughts in a brief report.

Competent Communicators Are Ethical Finally, competent communicators are ethical communicators. **Ethics** are principles that guide us in judging whether something is morally right or wrong. Ethical communication generally dictates that we treat people fairly, communicate honestly, and avoid immoral or unethical behavior. Communicating ethically can be easier said than done, however, because people often have very different ideas about right and wrong. What may be morally justified to one person or one culture may be considered completely unethical to another.

Ethical considerations are often particularly important when we're engaged in compliance-gaining strategies, trying to change the way another person thinks or behaves. Referring back to a previous example: is it ethical to make your neighbor feel obligated to contribute money to your cause? To some people, that strategy would seem unfair, because it may lead your neighbor to donate even if he or she doesn't want to. Depending on why you need the money, however, or what you have done for your neighbor in the past, you might not consider it unethical even if others do.

• **cognitive complexity** The ability to understand a given situation in multiple ways.

• **ethics** Principles that guide judgments about whether something is morally right or wrong.

adaptability Cultivating Competence

The Scene: You're hanging out with several students, some of whom you don't know. One student makes a joke that, although funny, is racially insensitive. You and others laugh, but you then notice that one of the students who didn't laugh is turning red in the face. You wonder if that student is offended by the joke.

Your Task: Consider how you could adapt your communication behavior to defuse this awkward situation. What strategies would you use to

- Practice cognitive complexity?
- Be empathic?
- Communicate ethically?

Competent communicators are aware that people's ideas about ethics vary. They are also aware of their own ethical beliefs, and they communicate in ways that are consistent with those beliefs.

Take one last look at your list of five good communicators. Are they generally aware of their own behaviors and able to adapt them to different contexts? Can they adopt other people's perspectives and consider various ways of explaining situations? Do they behave ethically? These aren't the only characteristics that make someone a competent communicator, but they are among the most important. To the extent that we can develop and practice those skills, we can all become better at the process of communication.

For REVIEW

- **What needs does communication help us meet?** We use communication to help us stay physically healthy, form and maintain important relationships, understand and express our identities, convey our spiritual beliefs, and accomplish mundane, instrumental tasks.

- **How does communication work, and what misconceptions do we have about it?** Communication can be described as action, interaction, or transaction, depending on the situation. Many people mistakenly believe that everyone is a communication expert, communication will solve any problem, communication can break down, communication is inherently good, and more communication is always better.

- **What particular skills characterize competent communicators?** Competent communicators express themselves effectively and appropriately in whatever situation they're in. They are self-aware, adaptable, empathic, cognitively complex, and ethical.

POP QUIZ

Multiple Choice

1. Garry is having difficulty paying attention to what his sister is saying because he is feeling tired and ill. The type of noise that is interfering with his ability to understand his sister is

   a. physical noise.
   b. psychological noise.
   c. cultural noise.
   d. physiological noise.

2. A sign that reads "Please turn off all cell phones" exemplifies an

   a. explicit communication rule.
   b. implicit communication rule.
   c. empathic communication rule.
   d. ethical communication rule.

3. Empathy is best defined as

   a. feeling sorry for someone else.
   b. identifying, feeling, and relating to what others are feeling.
   c. keeping other people's feeling separate from your own.
   d. paying attention to how others are evaluating your social skills.

4. All the following are examples of a psychological context *except*

   a. the formality of the situation.
   b. the level of privacy.

   c. the degree to which the situation is emotionally charged.
   d. the temperature of the room.

5. Research has found that having a strong, positive social network can

   a. increase a person's susceptibility to depression.
   b. decrease a person's susceptibility to colds.
   c. decrease a person's life expectancy.
   d. increase a person's cognitive complexity.

Fill in the Blanks

6. The tendency to behave in morally correct ways is a characteristic of someone who is _____.

7. Most American adults believe a lack of _____ is the number-one cause of divorce.

8. The _____ model is the most contemporary model of human communication.

9. The ability to modify your behavior according to the demands of the situation is known as _____.

10. Communication is _____ if it attends to the rules and expectations that apply in a given social situation.

ANSWERS: 1. d; 2. a; 3. b; 4. d; 5. b; 6. ethical; 7. effective communication; 8. transaction; 9. adaptability; 10. appropriate

KEY TERMS

communication 4
relational needs 5
instrumental needs 7
model 8
action model 8
source 8
encode 8
message 8
channel 8
receiver 9
decode 9
noise 9

interaction model 9
feedback 10
context 10
transaction model 10
channel-rich contexts 12
channel-lean contexts 12
symbol 13
content dimension 13
relational dimension 14
metacommunication 14
explicit rules 14
implicit rules 15

intrapersonal communication 16
interpersonal communication 16
small group communication 16
public communication 16
mass communication 17
communication competence 20
self-monitoring 23
empathy 23
cognitive complexity 25
ethics 25

COMMUNICATION AND CULTURE

A Triumph of Cultural Unity

Cultural barriers needn't stop people from helping one another.
After a catastrophic earthquake killed thousands in Haiti in 2010, people from communities around the world coordinated immediate relief efforts for the Caribbean nation. The governments of the United States, Canada, Israel, Italy, Cuba, Brazil, and the Dominican Republic each sent more than 1,000 disaster relief workers. Humanitarian and religious organizations from Armenia to Zambia sent money, food, medicine, and other supplies to help the struggling survivors. Although efforts to rebuild Haiti's infrastructure continue today, the world's response to the earthquake—and to similar natural disasters elsewhere around the globe—demonstrates that people can work toward a common goal despite their cultural boundaries.

▸ As You READ

- What is culture?
- How does culture influence communication behavior?
- In what ways can we improve our cultural communication skills?

Although few of us may ever take part in an international relief effort, nearly all of us will communicate with people from different cultures at some point. Today's global marketplace makes that increasingly likely. Culture is a powerful influence on communication behavior. It can affect not only how we express ourselves but also how we interpret and react to others. In this chapter, we examine many ways that culture influences us as communicators. We begin by defining culture and considering the sources of our cultural ideas. We then look at some key ways in which cultures differ, focusing in particular on how communication behavior varies from society to society. Finally, we explore strategies for improving our communications with people of other cultures.

Understanding Cultures and Co-Cultures

Even if we don't realize it, our cultural traditions and beliefs influence how we make sense of communication behavior. Each of us is affected by the culture in which we grew up, and we tend to notice other cultures only when they differ from ours. To many people, culture—like an accent—is something that only *other* people have. Let's begin by understanding in what sense we *all* have cultural traits and biases.

• **culture** The totality of learned, shared symbols, language, values, and norms that distinguish one group of people from another.

WHAT IS CULTURE?

We use the term *culture* to mean all sorts of things. Sometimes we connect it to a place, as in "Norwegian culture" and "New England culture." Other times we use it to refer to an ethnic or a religious group, as in "Asian American culture" and "Jewish culture." We also speak of "deaf culture" and "the culture of the rich." What makes a culture?

Although the word *culture* can have different meanings, we define **culture** as the totality of learned, shared symbols,

SHARPEN Your Skills:
Communication challenges

Role-play an interaction you have had with someone whose language, values, or traditions differed markedly from your own. Consider what communication challenges each of you faced. How did you manage those challenges? Ask your instructor and classmates for feedback on how you might have managed them more effectively.

Naturalized citizens bring many different cultural beliefs and practices to the United States.

language, values, and norms that distinguish one group of people from another. That definition tells us that culture isn't a property of countries or ethnicities or economic classes. Rather, it's a property of *people*. We'll refer to the groups of people who share common symbols, language, values, and norms as **societies.**

Each of us identifies with one or more societies, and we are usually keenly aware which ones. It is fundamental to our human nature, in fact, to notice people's similarities and differences with respect to ourselves, so that we know which groups of people we belong to and which ones we are separate from. That distinction comprises the difference between in-groups and out-groups. Who belongs in your in-groups? Take a look at Table 2.1 to see how you compare to the average citizen of the world.

• **societies** Groups of people who share common symbols, language, values, and norms.

DISTINGUISHING BETWEEN IN-GROUPS AND OUT-GROUPS

Researchers use the term **in-groups** to refer to groups we identify with and **out-groups** to describe groups we see as different from us.[1] If you grew up in the American South, for example, you probably see other Southerners as part of your in-group, whereas if you were raised in the Northwest, you do not. Similarly, when you are traveling in foreign countries, the residents may perceive you as an out-group member if you look or sound different from them or if you behave differently.

• **in-groups** Groups of people with which a person identifies.

• **out-groups** Groups of people with which a person does not identify.

In-Groups and Out-Groups, Facebook Style If you're an active social networker on Facebook, you already have an understanding of the difference between in-groups and out-groups. On Facebook, your in-group consists of the people on your friend list. In contrast, your out-group includes people who are not your Facebook friends—among them, those you have "unfriended" or deleted from your friend list. Should Facebook qualify as its own culture? Check out Table 2.2 and see what you think.

The Challenges of Out-Group Status For some people, being perceived as different can be an exciting or intriguing experience, particularly if they do not typically stand out in their regular environments. For others, however, their differences can be stressful. Research shows that many immigrants experience abnormally high levels of stress during their first year in their new homeland.[2] That stress can contribute to disorders such as depression, high blood pressure, and heart disease.[3]

Nearly 7 billion people live on planet Earth. How well do you represent the average person? If we were to identify the single most representative citizen of the planet, that person would:

- **Live in China,** as 19 percent of the world's population does.
- **Be Christian,** as 33 percent of the world's population is.
- **Be male,** as 50.4 percent of the world's population is.
- **Live in a town or city,** as 50.5 percent of the world's population does.
- **Be 29 years old,** which is the median age of the world's population.
- **Make $10,290 per year,** which is the per capita gross world income.
- **Not use the Internet,** as 73 percent of the world's population does not.

TABLE 2.1

THE ULTIMATE IN-GROUP: THE AVERAGE WORLD CITIZEN

In what ways do you fit into this in-group? In what ways do you differ?

◀ •••••••••••••••••••••••••••

HOW DO YOU COMPARE?

SOURCES: U.N.; Population Reference Bureau; CIA *World Factbook,* accessed May 15, 2012, www.cia.gov/library/publications/the-world-factbook/geos/xx.html; accessed May 15, 2012, www.prb.org/Publications/Datasheets/2011/world-population-data-sheet/data-sheet.aspx.

Some researchers point out that our ability to distinguish between people who are similar to and different from ourselves probably helped our ancestors survive by encouraging them to associate with people whose goals and priorities were similar to their own.[4] That tendency to seek out familiar others endures today, as research shows that many people strongly prefer individuals and groups whom they perceive to be similar to themselves. By the same token, many people are more suspicious and less trusting of individuals whose ethnic, national, or cultural background is different from their own.[5] These feelings can make it uncomfortable for an individual to live or work where he or she is considered a minority, especially if the person experiences discrimination on the basis of cultural or ethnic background. For example, read about the experiences of some Muslim students attending U.S. colleges in "The Dark Side of Communication."

The in-group/out-group distinction is a major reason why so many countries struggle with the issue of immigration. How open should a country be to letting people from other societies—whom its own citizens consider to be out-groups—become part of its culture and in-group? Some countries, including Sweden and the United States, have relatively lenient policies that allow many applicants for immigration to enter their borders and eventually become citizens. Other countries have much stricter policies. Denmark, for instance, has drawn criticism in the last decade for significantly toughening its immigration policies and making it harder for foreign-born people to become citizens.[6]

How best to manage immigration—and the population of immigrants living in the country illegally—is currently a highly controversial issue in the United States. In April 2012, for instance, the U.S. Supreme Court heard oral arguments challenging an Arizona law requiring police officers to check the immigration status of anyone they detain. Although supporters claim the law will reduce illegal immigration, opponents say it will result in unfair discrimination against Hispanics, Arizona's largest ethnic minority group. The experiences of Sweden, the United States, and Denmark all illustrate the complex and sometimes contentious relationship between national in-groups and out-groups.

ACQUIRING A CULTURE

How does each of us acquire a culture? Because cultures and societies vary so broadly around the world, it might seem as though we simply inherit our culture genetically, the same way we inherit our eye color and other physical characteristics, but that isn't the case. Culture is not necessarily related to or based on our **ethnicity,** which is our

• **ethnicity** People's perceptions of ancestry or heritage.

THE DARK SIDE OF COMMUNICATION

Cultural Intolerance: Discrimination against Muslim Students on U.S. College Campuses

Nineteen-year-old college senior Nohayia Javed was walking to her residence hall on a Saturday night when she was grabbed from behind, thrown to the ground, and kicked in the ribs by a young man yelling anti-Islamic slurs. An emergency room exam later revealed that Javed had sustained multiple bruises and a dislocated shoulder. It's fortunate that few Muslim students at U.S. colleges and universities have endured similar physical attacks—yet during the years of the U.S. wars in Iraq and Afghanistan, many have felt like outsiders. Some receive hostile looks or threatening e-mail messages. Others feel excluded from social events where they once would have felt welcome. Some have been the target of verbal abuse blaming all Muslims for the terrorist actions of a few.

Distinguishing between in-groups and out-groups may be a natural tendency among human beings and other species, but it can lead us to make erroneous judgments about others. After 19 Islamic extremists carried out deadly attacks on the United States on September 11, 2001, many Muslims—even those born in the United States, such as Javed—felt as though they were being treated as terrorists simply because they shared a cultural and religious background with the hijackers. Although the attacks were genuine atrocities, in truth the vast majority of Muslims had nothing to do with them. In fact, many major Islamic organizations explicitly condemned the terrorist strikes.

Such discrimination against Muslims provides evidence of how, during times of stress or uncertainty, it may be especially easy to make broad generalizations about groups of people. For competent communicators, however, it is vitally important to remember not to condemn an entire group based on the actions of a few individuals.

SOURCES: Kerr, M. (2009, May 17). Muslims face discrimination and intolerance. *The Statesman.* Retrieved February 17, 2010, from www.sbstatesman.com/2.892/muslims-face-discrimination-and-intolerance-1.38633; Woods, T. (2006, April 5). Muslim student believes attacker came from off campus. *Waco Tribune-Herald,* accessed November 13, 2011, www.wacotrib.com/news/content/news/stories/2006/04/05/04052006wacmuslim.html.

---

perception of our ancestry or heritage. Neither is culture necessarily related to our **nationality,** which is our status as a citizen of a particular country. Rather, culture is learned. We acquire our culture by learning the traditions, values, and language of the people who raised us. Researchers use the term **enculturation** to describe the process of acquiring a culture.

For instance, a Cambodian-born citizen raised in the United States will likely adopt the language and practices common to the place where she is brought up. Her ethnicity and citizenship are Cambodian, but her culture is the U.S. culture. Likewise, someone born in New Zealand but raised in Nigeria may adopt the Nigerian culture as his own, even if he is Caucasian.

We learn some of our cultural messages through direct instruction. When a parent tells us to say "thank you" after receiving a gift, or a teacher helps us learn the pledge of allegiance, those experiences impart cultural knowledge in a direct and conscious manner. We learn other cultural lessons through imitation. Perhaps no one had to teach you to face forward and stay quiet while riding in a crowded elevator, for instance; instead you learned that cultural norm by observing others. We can even pick up cultural practices subconsciously, such as when we begin speaking with the accent of those around us without realizing we are doing so.

Although culture is learned, our biology gives us the capacity to learn it. Our genes give us the brains capable of learning and remembering cultural practices and the hands capable of writing cultural stories. They give us the eyes capable of seeing

• **nationality** One's status as a citizen of a particular country.

• **enculturation** The process of acquiring a culture.

Culture is learned. Regardless of our citizenship, most of us learn the language and cultural practices common to the place where we grow up.

cultural symbols and the mouths capable of using language. Our genes don't *determine* our communication behavior, however. Rather, they interact with our cultural environment to shape who we are and how we communicate.

WHAT IS A CO-CULTURE?

When you think about culture as shared language, beliefs, and customs, it may seem as though you belong to many different cultures at once. If you grew up in the United States, you likely feel a part of the U.S. culture. At the same time, if you enjoy comic books, vintage cars, or skateboarding, you may notice that the people who share your interests appear to have their own customs and vocabularies. Or perhaps you observe that people in your generation have different values and customs than people who are older than you—or that different ethnic or religious groups at your school seem to have their own traditions and beliefs. Does each of those groups have a culture of its own? In a manner of speaking, the answer is yes.

• **co-cultures** Groups of people who share values, customs, and norms related to mutual interests or characteristics besides their national citizenship.

Defining Co-Cultures Within many national cultures—such as the Italian, Thai, and U.S. cultures—is a host of other cultural groups that researchers call co-cultures. **Co-cultures** are groups of people who share values, customs, and norms related to mutual interests or characteristics besides their national citizenship. Your co-culture isn't based on the country in which you were born or the national society in which you were raised. Instead, it is composed of smaller groups of people with whom you identify. In many cases, you may identify with your co-cultures as strongly as— or more strongly than—you identify with your national culture.

The Bases of Co-Cultures Some co-cultures form around shared activities or beliefs. If you're into fly fishing, organic gardening, or political activism, there are co-cultures for those interests. Similarly, Buddhists have beliefs and traditions that distinguish them from Baptists, regardless of where they grew up.

Some co-cultures develop around differences in mental or physical abilities. Many deaf populations have values and customs that differ from those of hearing populations, including social customs.[7] Whereas many people are uncomfortable having constant eye contact with another person while talking, deaf people frequently maintain a steady mutual gaze while communicating through sign language. They may also make a point of notifying others in the group if they are leaving the room, even if just for a few moments. Because deaf individuals cannot hear one another call out from another room, this practice makes frantic searches for the absent person unnecessary. Among hearing people, it would be considered annoying to announce every departure from a room. But this and other customs help deaf people interact with one another as members of a shared co-culture.[8] The deaf co-culture also places a strong emphasis on the distinctions between in-group and out-group members. Many individuals who are deaf point out that a person cannot genuinely understand the physical or social experience of deafness unless he

or she is deaf. Consequently, people who are deaf often express a strong preference for interacting with other deaf individuals. They may treat sign language interpreters and the hearing parents of deaf children as "honorary deaf people," but they are frequently hesitant to accept hearing people as part of the deaf co-culture.[9]

Such reluctance was evident when, in 1988, students at Gallaudet University in Washington, D.C., whose undergraduate student body consists entirely of deaf people, staged an eight-day protest demanding the appointment of a deaf president for the university. The board of trustees responded by appointing the first deaf president in the school's 130-year history.

Identifying with Multiple Co-Cultures Many people identify with several co-cultures at once. You might relate to a co-culture for your age group, ethnicity, religion, sexual orientation, musical tastes, and athletic interests, and even your college major. Each may have its own values, beliefs, traditions, customs, and ways of using language that distinguish it from other groups. Some co-cultures even contain smaller co-cultures within them. For example, the deaf co-culture includes people who advocate using only sign language and others who advocate the use of cochlear implants, devices surgically inserted in the ear to help a person hear.

getCONNECTED
Co-Cultures Online

The Internet offers multiple opportunities for people to develop and participate in co-cultures that are specific to the online world. You are probably aware that those who are interested in online games or science fiction, or in the development of free software, can find extensive communities of people with similar interests on the web. Each such community may develop its own terminology, values, and communication practices and interact as a co-culture even though its members may be geographically disbursed.

The Internet also provides opportunities for people to find others who share co-cultural interests that are not unique to the cyberworld. Search engines such as Google and Yahoo host thousands of Usenet groups where people can communicate with others who share their passion for bird watching, silent movies, Eastern philosophy, or African art. The largest such group on Google, for fans of the software Google Earth, currently has over 1.5 billion registered members.[10] Although not all co-cultures are specific to the Internet environment—in the way that, say, online gaming is—they often thrive on the web, where people separated by thousands of miles can communicate whenever they wish.

Components of Cultures and Co-Cultures

Cultures and societies vary enormously. Imagine a group composed of people raised in Saudi Arabia, Vietnam, Iceland, Botswana, Paraguay, Israel, and the U.S. Southwest. The members of each group would differ not only in their native languages but also, most likely, in their religious beliefs, political viewpoints, sports interests, food preferences, clothing, and beliefs about education, marriage, money, and sexuality. Indeed, we might have a harder time identifying the members' similarities than their differences. That's how powerful an influence culture can be.

As we'll see later, values, beliefs, and preferences often vary even among different groups of people within the same country. For example, native Hawaiians, native Texans, and native New Yorkers might vary considerably in their customs and values, even though they were all raised in the United States. Similarly, opera buffs, country music lovers, and jazz fans might seem to have more differences than similarities, even if they grew up in the same community. In short, culture can distinguish not only people with different nationalities but also those with different interests and social characteristics.

The United States has often been called a melting pot to acknowledge that it includes multiple cultural groups. In fact, students are frequently encouraged to learn more about intercultural communication precisely because of the notion that the country's cultural diversity continues to increase. Is that assumption true, though? Check out the "Fact or Fiction?" box to find out.

No matter what their differences, cultures have some common components, as our definition of culture made clear. Those components are symbols, language, values, and norms. Let's take a close look at each one.

CULTURES VARY IN THEIR SYMBOLS

As we saw in Chapter 1, a symbol is something that represents an idea. Words are symbols, for example. In addition, every culture has its own symbols that stand for ideas that are vital to that culture. When we hear that something is "as American as baseball and apple pie," the speaker is using baseball and apple pie as symbols of U.S. life. The U.S. flag, the bald eagle, and "The Star-Spangled Banner" are also common symbols of the United States.

Each society uses symbols that carry particular meanings for its members. For instance, the Chinese national anthem, "Yiyongjun Jinxingqu" ("March of the Volunteers"), serves as a symbol of Chinese culture. Similarly, "Die Stem van Suid-Afrika" ("The Call of South Africa"), the national anthem of South Africa, symbolizes that country's culture. The tartan—a criss-crossed pattern of dyed threads woven together in a textile—serves as an important symbol of Scottish culture, whereas the burqa—an all-covering women's outer garment—is a symbol of Islamic culture.

CULTURES VARY IN THEIR LANGUAGES

Researchers believe there are approximately 6,800 languages used in the world today.[11] Furthermore, according to the New York State Comptroller's Office, more languages are spoken in Queens, New York, than in any other city on earth: 138 at last count.[12] Language allows for written and spoken communication, and it also ensures that cultures and cultural ideas are passed from one generation to the next.

Today, Chinese, Spanish, and English—in that order—are the three most commonly spoken languages in the world. Nearly 2.2 billion people speak one or more of those languages. Moreover, 2010 saw a 2,000% increase in tweets written in Arabic, making Arabic the fastest-growing language on Twitter. Unfortunately, many other languages are in danger of extinction. In fact, researchers believe that at least 10 percent of the world's languages are currently spoken by fewer than 100 people each.[13] We examine language use further in Chapter 4.

In 2010, the French parliament began enforcing a ban on wearing face-covering veils—such as those included in the burqa—in public. Opponents of the ban argue that it violates women's religious freedom. Supporters claim that the veils signify the oppression of women and are inconsistent with the secular culture of France.

CULTURES VARY IN THEIR VALUES

A culture's *values* are the standards it uses to judge how good, desirable, or beautiful something is. In other words, values are cultural ideas about *what ought to be.* Psychological research indicates that U.S. culture values ideas such as equal opportunity, material comfort, practicality, efficiency, achievement, democracy, free enterprise, and individual choice.[14]

Whereas values can vary considerably across cultures, 10 in particular are widely shared and similarly interpreted:[15]

1. *Power:* having prestige, social status, control over resources
2. *Achievement:* acquiring personal success through your own competence
3. *Hedonism:* experiencing fun and pleasure
4. *Stimulation:* having novelty, excitement, challenge in life
5. *Self-direction:* being able to engage in independent thought and action
6. *Universalism:* appreciating and caring about all people and about nature
7. *Benevolence:* enhancing the welfare of people with whom you have contact
8. *Tradition:* respecting the customs and ideas of your culture and religion
9. *Conformity:* observing social norms and inhibiting actions that are likely to harm others
10. *Security:* having safe and stable relationships

Although these 10 values exist across cultures, not every culture emphasizes them to the same degree. As you'll discover in

Whether a kiss is an intimate act between lovers or a routine social greeting may depend on the culture in which it occurs.

Change Is Inevitable: The United States Is Becoming More Culturally Diverse

Communication professors often encourage students to learn more about intercultural communication on the argument that the United States is becoming more diverse over time. Is that notion fact or fiction?

Projections from the U.S. Census suggest that it's a fact. Using data compiled from previous census counts, the U.S. Census Bureau predicts that, over the next half century, the United States will have greater diversity with respect to both ethnicity and age. The table below presents the percentages of the U.S. population that fit each ethnic and age category in 2000 and are projected to fit each category in 2025 and 2050.

As the table illustrates, the U.S. Census Bureau forecasts greater ethnic and age diversity over the next 40 years. For instance, whereas Asian Americans made up 3.8 percent of the population in 2000, they are expected to rise to 8 percent of the population in 2050. Similarly, senior citizens 65 years of age and older were only 12.4 percent of the U.S. population in 2000 but are expected to make up 20.6 percent—more than one-fifth—in just four more decades. Given this growth, the ability to communicate effectively with people from other demographic groups will be increasingly advantageous in the years to come.

Year	Ethnic Category				Age Category		
	African American	White/Caucasian	Asian American	Other Ethnicities	0–19	20–64	65+
2000	12.7	81.0	3.8	2.5	28.5	59.0	12.4
2025	13.7	76.7	5.8	3.8	26.3	55.5	18.2
2050	14.6	72.1	8.0	5.3	26.0	53.4	20.6

2025 percentages for ethnicity represent aggregates of 2020 and 2030 projections. Owing to rounding, some percentages do not sum to 100.

ASK YOURSELF

- What communication challenges will people in the United States face as ethnic and age diversity increases?
- What particular communication skills do you think might help people meet those challenges?

SOURCE: Shrestha, L. B. (2006). *The changing demographic profile of the United States.* Congressional Research Service report for Congress, accessed February 5, 2010, www.fas.org/sgp/crs/misc/RL32701.pdf.

this chapter, tradition, power, and conformity are strongly emphasized in some cultures, whereas achievement and self-direction are more privileged in others.

CULTURES VARY IN THEIR NORMS

Finally, *norms* are rules or expectations that guide people's behavior in a culture. As an example, consider the norms for greeting people when you first meet them. In North American countries, people typically shake hands and make a courteous statement such as "Nice to meet you." In another culture it may be normal to hug, bow, kiss on both cheeks or, in some cases, even to kiss on the lips.

Cultures also vary in their norms for politeness. A behavior that is considered very polite in one culture may be frowned on in another. When receiving a compliment, for instance, people in the United States consider it polite to say "Thank you." By comparison, a Chinese person would consider that reply boastful and would instead respond by suggesting that he or she was not worthy of the compliment.[16]

Even the Internet has its own norms. Netiquette—or network etiquette—consists of the expectations that guide people's online behaviors. Those norms include not forwarding junk mail (also known as *spam*), respecting others' privacy by not forwarding personal messages without permission, using appropriate language and acronyms (such as LOL for "laughing out loud"), and not "flaming," or making hostile and insulting remarks about other Internet users.

DISTINCTIVE FEATURES OF CO-CULTURES

Like cultures, co-cultures often adopt distinctive symbols, language, values, and norms that distinguish their members from outsiders. A co-cultural symbol might be a logo, such as the rainbow flag used by the LGBT (lesbian, gay, bisexual, and transgender) community, or an action, such as genuflecting (bending at least one knee to the ground), a common symbol in certain religious communities. Although co-cultures may not adopt entirely distinctive languages, they frequently use terminology—called *jargon*—that is understood only by others in the same co-culture. Surfers, for instance, might say "getting tubed" to describe being completely covered by the top of a wave, and firefighters call someone who always has trouble gearing up for a fire a "door dancer." We will delve further into the topic of jargon later in this chapter.

Co-cultural groups often arise precisely because their members share specific values. The co-culture of veganism—which promotes diets free of animal products—largely shares values related to the preservation of animal life, whereas the co-culture of Civil War re-enactors—who stage dramatizations of famous Civil War battles to preserve the accurate history of the period—shares values related to the recognition of that major event in U.S. history. Finally, co-cultures adopt their own norms, such as silent worship among Quakers and dressing alike among the community of twins.

> ### SHARPEN Your Skills: *Cultural norms*
>
> Select a culture that seems substantially different from your national culture. Using the Internet, research the values and norms common in that other culture. Create a PowerPoint or video presentation describing them and identifying how others can use that knowledge to communicate effectively with people of that cultural background.

How Culture Affects Communication

If you've ever had difficulty communicating with someone from a different cultural background, then you know how challenging it can be. Dutch social psychologist Geert Hofstede and American anthropologist Edward T. Hall have pioneered the study of cultures and cultural differences in behavior. Their work and that of others points to six cultural differences that influence how people communicate with one another. Those differences—our focus in this section—are related to (1) the emphasis placed on individuals versus groups, (2) the communicative context, (3) power distance, (4) views about masculinity and femininity and about men's and women's roles, (5) orientation toward time, and (6) uncertainty avoidance. We discuss these variations as comparisons—individualistic versus collectivistic, for example—for simplicity's sake. They are more appropriately thought of as sliding scales, however, such that a culture belongs somewhere on a continuum between any two options—it is more or less individualistic, say.

1. INDIVIDUALISTIC VERSUS COLLECTIVISTIC CULTURES

• individualistic culture
A culture in which people believe that their primary responsibility is to themselves.

Cultures differ in how much they emphasize individuals rather than groups. In an **individualistic culture,** people believe their primary responsibility is to themselves. Children in individualistic cultures are raised hearing messages such as "Be yourself," "You're special," and "There's no one else in the world who's just like you." Those messages emphasize the importance of knowing yourself, being self-sufficient, and being true to what you want in life.[17] Indeed, the motto in an individualistic culture might be "I gotta be me!" People in individualistic societies also value self-reliance and the idea that people should "pull themselves up by their own bootstraps"—that is, help themselves when they need help instead of waiting for others to come to their aid. Research shows that the United States, Canada, Great Britain, and Australia are among the most individualistic societies in the world.[18] The United States is so individualistic that *American Idol*—the talent show in which undiscovered singers compete to land lucrative recording contracts and achieve superstar status—is one of television's top-rated programs.

• collectivistic culture
A culture in which people believe that their primary responsibility is to their families, their communities, and their employers.

In contrast, people in **collectivistic cultures** are taught that their primary responsibility is to their families, their communities, and their employers. These cultures focus on the importance of taking care of the needs of the group rather than the individual. People place a high value on duty and loyalty and see themselves not as unique or special but as a part of the group or groups to which they belong. Among the Kabre of Togo, for instance, individuals try to give away many of their material possessions in order to build relationships and benefit their social groups.[19] The motto in a collectivistic culture might be "I am my family and my family is me." Collectivistic cultures include Korea, Japan, and many countries in Africa and Latin America.[20]

How individualistic or collectivistic a culture is can affect communication behavior in several ways. When people in an individualistic culture experience conflict with one another, for instance, they are expected to express it and work toward resolving it. In comparison, people in a collectivistic culture are taught to be much more indirect in the way they handle disagreements, to preserve social harmony. For instance, they may avoid the conflict and hope it will resolve itself or hint at their problems with other people instead of describing them explicitly.[21]

The phenomenal popularity of *American Idol* and the quick rise to fame of each year's winner—2012 winner Phillip Phillips is shown here—reflect the highly individualistic nature of U.S. culture.

Another difference between the two types of culture centers on people's comfort level with public speaking. Many people feel anxious when they have to give a speech, but especially those in collectivistic societies, where people are taught to blend in rather than to stand out. Asserting yourself and standing up for yourself are valued in individualistic cultures, but pressure to adopt these norms can cause embarrassment and shame for people in a collectivistic culture.

Some researchers suggest that the individualistic–collectivistic distinction is the most fundamental way in which cultures differ from one another. Other researchers disagree, maintaining that this distinction by itself cannot adequately characterize cultures.[22] Read on and see what you think.

2. LOW-CONTEXT VERSUS HIGH-CONTEXT CULTURES

If you have traveled much, perhaps you have noticed that people in various parts of the world differ in how direct and explicit their language is. You may have spent time in both low- and high-context cultures in your travels, with *context* here referring to the broad range of factors surrounding every act of communication.

In a **low-context culture,** people are expected to be direct, to say what they mean, and not to "beat around the bush." Individuals in low-context cultures value expressing themselves, sharing opinions, and trying to persuade others to see things their way.[23] The United States is an example of a low-context society, as are Canada, Israel, and most northern European countries.

In contrast, people in a **high-context culture**—such as Korea and the cultures of Native Americans and the Maori of New Zealand—are taught to speak in a much less direct way. Maintaining harmony and avoiding offense are more important than expressing your true feelings.[24] Speech is more ambiguous and people convey much more of their meaning through subtle behaviors and contextual cues, such as facial expressions and tone of voice.

The impact of the communicative context is evident in the ways in which people handle criticism and disagreement in different societies. In a low-context culture, a supervisor might reprimand an irresponsible employee openly, to make an example of the individual. The supervisor would probably be direct and explicit about the employee's shortcomings, the company's expectations for improvement, and the consequences of the employee's failing to meet those expectations.

In a high-context culture, however, the supervisor probably wouldn't reprimand the employee publicly for fear that it would put the employee to shame and cause the worker to "lose face." Criticism in high-context cultures is more likely to take place in private. The supervisor would also likely use more ambiguous language to convey what the employee was doing wrong, "talking around" the issue instead of confronting it directly. To reprimand an employee for repeated absences, for example, a supervisor might point out that responsibility to coworkers is important and that letting down the team would be cause for shame. The supervisor may never actually say that the employee needs to improve his or her attendance record. Instead, the employee would be expected to understand that message by listening to what the supervisor says and paying attention to the supervisor's body language, tone of voice, and facial expressions.

When people from low- and high-context cultures communicate with one another, the potential for misunderstanding is great. To appreciate that point, imagine that you've asked two of your friends to meet you tomorrow evening for a coffee tasting at a popular bookstore café. Tina, who's from a low-context culture, says, "No, I've got a lot of studying to do, but thanks anyway." Lee, who grew up in a high-context culture, nods his head and says, "That sounds like fun." Thus, perhaps you're surprised later when Lee doesn't show up.

How can you account for those different behaviors? The answer is that people raised in a high-context culture are often reluctant to say no—even when they mean no—for fear of causing offense. Another person from Lee's culture might have understood from Lee's facial expression or tone of voice that he didn't intend to go to the coffee tasting. Because you grew up in a low-context society, however, you interpreted his answer and his nods to mean he was accepting your invitation.

3. LOW-POWER-DISTANCE VERSUS HIGH-POWER-DISTANCE CULTURES

Cultures also differ from one another in the degree to which power is distributed within society. Several types of assets can give someone power, including money or other valuable resources, education or expertise, age, popularity, talent, intelligence, and experience. In democratic societies such as the United States and western European nations, people believe in the value of equality across the sexes and groups.

• **low-context culture**
A culture in which people are expected to be direct and to say what they mean.

• **high-context culture**
A culture in which people are taught to speak in an indirect, inexplicit way.

- **low-power-distance culture** A culture in which people believe that no one person or group should have excessive power.

- **high-power-distance culture** A culture in which certain groups, such as the royal family or the members of the ruling political party, have much greater power than the average citizen.

- **masculine culture** A culture in which people cherish traditionally masculine values and prefer sex-specific roles for women and men.

- **feminine culture** A culture in which people cherish traditionally feminine qualities and prefer little differentiation in the roles of women and men.

Saudi Arabia has a high-power-distance culture. Members of the royal family have considerably more power than the average citizen.

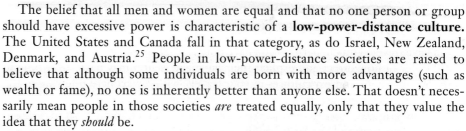

The belief that all men and women are equal and that no one person or group should have excessive power is characteristic of a **low-power-distance culture.** The United States and Canada fall in that category, as do Israel, New Zealand, Denmark, and Austria.[25] People in low-power-distance societies are raised to believe that although some individuals are born with more advantages (such as wealth or fame), no one is inherently better than anyone else. That doesn't necessarily mean people in those societies *are* treated equally, only that they value the idea that they *should* be.

In a **high-power-distance culture,** power is distributed less evenly. Certain groups, such as members of the royal family or the ruling political party, have great power, and the average citizen has much less. People in high-power-distance societies are taught that certain people or groups deserve more power than others and that respecting power is more important than respecting equality. Mexico, Brazil, India, Singapore, and the Philippines are all examples of high-power-distance societies.[26]

Power distance affects many aspects of communication. For example, people in low-power-distance cultures usually expect friendships and romantic relationships to be based on love rather than social status. In contrast, people in high-power-distance cultures often feel pressure to choose friends and mates from within their social class.[27]

Another difference appears in the way people think about authority. Individuals in a low-power-distance society are often taught that it is their right—even their responsibility—to question authority. In such a society it's not unexpected for people to ask "Why?" when a parent or teacher tells them to do something. In comparison, individuals in a high-power-distance society learn to obey and respect those in power, such as parents and teachers, without question.[28]

That difference is also evident in individuals' relationships and communication patterns with their employers. Workers in a low-power-distance culture value *autonomy*—freedom of choice about the way they do their jobs—as well as opportunities to influence decisions that affect them. They might provide their input, for example, through union representatives or employee satisfaction surveys. In contrast, employees in a high-power-distance culture are used to having little or no say about how to do their jobs. Instead, they expect their employers to make the decisions and are more likely to follow those decisions without question.

4. MASCULINE VERSUS FEMININE CULTURES

We usually use the terms *masculine* and *feminine* when we're referring to people. Hofstede has suggested that we can also apply those terms to cultures.[29] In a highly **masculine culture,** people tend to cherish stereotypically masculine values, such as ambition, achievement, and the acquisition of material goods. They also value sex-specific roles for women and men, preferring that men hold the wage-earning and decision-making positions (such as corporate executive) while women occupy the nurturing positions (such as homemaker). Examples of masculine cultures are Austria, Japan, and Mexico.

In a highly **feminine culture,** people tend to value nurturing behavior, quality of life, and service to others, all of which are stereotypically feminine qualities. They also tend *not* to believe that men and women's roles should be strongly differentiated. Therefore, in a feminine culture, it is not unusual for a man to care for children or for a woman to be her family's primary wage earner. Most feminine cultures also provide new mothers with more paid maternity leave than do masculine cultures, so that those mothers can focus their attention on their new infants. Examples of feminine cultures are Sweden, Chile, and the Netherlands.

According to Hofstede's research, the United States has a moderately masculine culture. U.S. adults tend to value sex-differentiated roles—although not as strongly as Austrians, Japanese, and Mexicans do—and they place a fairly high value on stereotypically masculine qualities such as achievement and the acquisition of resources.[30]

5. MONOCHRONIC VERSUS POLYCHRONIC CULTURES

Cultures also vary with respect to their norms and expectations concerning the use of time. Societies that have a **monochronic** concept of time—such as Swiss, Germans, and most Americans—view time as a commodity. People in these cultures save time, spend time, fill time, invest time, and waste time as though time were tangible. They treat time as valuable, believe that "time is money," and talk about making time and losing time.[31]

A monochronic orientation toward time influences several social behaviors. People who think of time as valuable hate to waste it. Therefore, they expect meetings and classes to start on time, and if that doesn't happen, they are willing to wait only so long before leaving. They also expect others to show up when they say they will.

In comparison, societies with a **polychronic** orientation—which include Latin America, the Arab part of the Middle East, and much of sub-Saharan Africa—conceive of time as more holistic and fluid and less structured. Instead of treating time as a finite commodity that must be managed properly to avoid wasting it, people in a polychronic culture perceive it more like a never-ending river, flowing infinitely into the future.[32]

In societies with a polychronic time orientation, schedules are more fluid and flexible than in monochronic societies. In Pakistan, for instance, if you're invited to a wedding that begins at 4:30 in the afternoon and you arrive at 4:25, you will most likely be the first one there. A bank or restaurant may not open at a specified time—as it would be expected to do in a monochronic society—but whenever the owner or manager decides to open. Students in a polychronic society would not expect a professor to begin class at an appointed hour; instead, students would arrive over a period of time, and the class would begin whenever the professor was ready. Further, people in a polychronic culture don't prioritize efficiency and punctuality but instead attach greater value to the quality of life and to their relationships with others.

Check out "Putting Communication to Work" for an example of a career in which communication training can help you interact effectively with people from a wide variety of cultures.

- **monochronic culture**
  A culture that views time as a finite and tangible commodity.

- **polychronic culture**
  A culture that views time as holistic, fluid, and infinite.

- **uncertainty avoidance**
  The extent to which people try to avoid situations that are unstructured, unclear, or unpredictable.

6. UNCERTAINTY AVOIDANCE

Humans have a natural tendency to avoid unfamiliar and uncomfortable situations. In other words, we dislike uncertainty—in fact, uncertainty causes many of us a good deal of stress.[33] Not all cultures find uncertainty to be equally problematic, however. Rather, cultures vary in what Hofstede called **uncertainty avoidance,** or the extent to which people try to avoid situations that are unstructured, unclear, or unpredictable.[34]

Individuals from cultures that are highly uncertainty-avoidant are drawn to people and situations that are familiar, and they are relatively unlikely to

SHARPEN Your Skills: *Adapting to time management*

Interview someone whose career depends heavily on maintaining a tightly managed schedule (such as a person in the travel or broadcast industries). Ask how he or she would manage a customer or coworker who took a polychronic approach to time management.

Job Title >

Work Responsibilities >

International student life coordinator, college or university

Most U.S. colleges and universities have programs to help international students adapt to life in the United States. A student life coordinator may communicate with student applicants from a wide variety of cultures, assisting them with immigration and customs documents, meeting them on arrival, and helping them acclimate to the routines and cultural customs they will experience as students in the United States. This job requires excellent written and oral communication skills, a friendly and patient personality, and a working knowledge of the communication patterns of people from other cultures.

take risks, for fear of failure. They are also uncomfortable with differences of opinion, and they tend to favor rules and laws that maximize security and reduce ambiguity. Argentina, Portugal, and Uruguay are among the countries whose cultures are the most uncertainty-avoidant.

In contrast, people in uncertainty-accepting cultures are more open to new situations and more accepting of people and ideas that are different from their own. They take a "live and let live" approach, preferring as few rules as possible that would restrict their behaviors. Societies with cultures that are highly accepting of uncertainty include Hong Kong, Jamaica, and New Zealand. Hofstede determined that the U.S. culture is more accepting than avoidant of uncertainty, but it is closer to the midpoint of the scale than many countries are. Co-cultures within the United States, however, vary in how tolerant they are of uncertainty. For instance, Amish communities—which adhere to strict guidelines regarding dress, behavior, and the use of modern technology—are often highly uncertainty-avoidant. In comparison, actors, sculptors, and other artists may have a high tolerance for uncertainty if it facilitates their creativity.

Communicating with Cultural Awareness

The opportunity to know and communicate with people from other cultures is greater now than at any time in history. Many U.S. colleges and universities enroll large populations of international students, and social networking online makes it as easy to connect with someone in New Guinea as with someone in New Jersey. Consequently, the ability to communicate effectively with people from different cultural backgrounds has never been a greater advantage. In this section, we explore some essential qualities for communicating with cultural awareness: being open-minded about cultural differences, knowledgeable about cultural communication codes, and flexible and respectful when interacting with others.

Although the United States is relatively accepting of uncertainty, particular groups—such as the Amish—are highly uncertainty-avoidant.

BE OPEN-MINDED ABOUT CULTURAL DIFFERENCES

People with different cultural backgrounds don't just communicate differently—in many cases, they also truly *think* differently. Those differences in communicating and thinking can present real challenges when people from different cultures interact. As we'll see in this section, one way to combat those challenges is to be open-minded about similarities and differences. Open-mindedness requires first being mindful of potential differences and then avoiding the tendency to judge all differences negatively.

Be Mindful People from different cultures are often unaware of *how* they differ. An American college professor might think a Japanese student is being dishonest because the student doesn't look him in the eye when she speaks to him. In the United States, that behavior can suggest dishonesty. In Japan, however, it signals respect. If neither the professor nor the student is aware of how the other is likely to interpret the behavior, it's easy to see how a misunderstanding might arise.

Communicating effectively with people from other cultures requires us to be **mindful,** or aware of how their behaviors and ways of thinking are likely to differ from our own. Unfortunately, being mindful is easier said than done. Many of us operate on what researchers call a *similarity assumption*—that is, we presume that most people think the same way we do, without asking ourselves whether that's true.

Mindfulness of different assumptions is often important when communicating across religious cultures as well. In today's global economy, you are likely to interact with students, customers, or friends whose religious assumptions and practices differ from your own. Being mindful means being sensitive to those differences. When communicating with people who practice Hinduism, for instance, you may want to remember that Hindus believe in a social system, called a *caste system,* in which some people are held in higher esteem than others. Marrying—or even eating with—someone of

• **mindful** Aware—as in being aware of how other cultures' behaviors and ways of thinking are likely to differ from one's own.

a different caste is avoided. Many Hindus also believe that after they die, their soul will return to live on Earth in a new body, human or otherwise. The quality of their next life depends on their actions in this one. Those cultural assumptions differ markedly from those of, say, Muslims. Muslims believe in the fundamental equality of all humans, meaning that no group is held in higher esteem than any other. They also believe they will be sent to Heaven or Hell after death, depending on their deeds in this life.

Questioning our cultural assumptions can be a real challenge because we're often unaware that we hold them in the first place. At the same time, however, it is one of the basic ways in which studying communication and learning about the influences of culture can make us more mindful and competent communicators.

Avoid Ethnocentrism

It's one thing to be *aware* of how patterns of thought and behavior differ among cultures. It's another thing to avoid judging all other cultural practices as inferior to our own.

The first time she traveled through the south of Africa, for instance, Gretchen was put off by some of the cultural practices she encountered. People would kiss her on the lips when they met her for the first time. Strangers sat uncomfortably near her on public buses, and their closeness bothered her even more because few of them used deodorant. Most of the men had multiple wives and took their children to witch doctors when they got sick.

Instead of accepting those characteristics as normal parts of the societies she visited, Gretchen found them backward and wrong. "What messed-up cultures!" she said on returning to the United States. In making that assessment, Gretchen was displaying **ethnocentrism,** the tendency to judge other cultures' practices as inferior to your own. Had she been more open-minded, Gretchen might have learned why people behaved differently than she expected. She may even have come to appreciate that her own cultural practices aren't the only valid ways of interacting with others.

Particularly if you haven't had exposure to a broad range of cultures, it can be easy to believe that your values and traditions are the *right* values and traditions for everyone. If you think that way, consider how much your concept of culture reflects nothing more than where you were raised. Had you been raised in the south of Africa, for instance, you would likely find it normal and right for a man to have several wives and for people to kiss on the lips when they meet, and you would think cultural values and traditions such as Gretchen's were abnormal and wrong. In other words, every cultural group—not just your own—considers its ways of living to be right. When

• **ethnocentrism** The tendency to judge other cultures' practices as inferior to one's own.

Do you react ethnocentrically when you encounter cultural practices that are different from your own?

THE COMPETENT COMMUNICATOR

Who, Me? Being Aware of Ethnocentrism

What do you think about other cultures' values and traditions as compared to your own? On a scale of 1 to 7, indicate your level of agreement with each statement shown below. A score of 7 means you strongly agree; a score of 1 means you strongly disagree.

1 _____ Most other cultures are backward compared with my culture.

2 _____ I see people who are similar to me as virtuous.

3 _____ The values and customs of other cultures have nothing to do with me.

4 _____ People in other cultures just don't know what's good for them.

5 _____ Most people would be happier if they lived like the people in my culture.

6 _____ Lifestyles in other cultures are not as valid as those in my culture.

7 _____ I do not trust people who are different.

8 _____ It is hard for me to respect the customs and traditions of other cultures.

9 _____ Other cultures should try to be more like my culture.

10 _____ People from other cultures act in strange and unusual ways when they come into my culture.

When you're finished, add up your score, which should range from 10 to 70. That is your general ethnocentrism score. If your score is 40 or below, you are relatively low on ethnocentrism. A score above 40 indicates relatively high ethnocentrism.

Ask Yourself

- Were you surprised by your score? Why or why not? What factors do you think your score reflects?
- How can learning about cultural influences on communication affect a tendency toward ethnocentrism?

SOURCE: Items adapted from Neuliep, J. W. (2002). Assessing the reliability and validity of the generalized ethnocentrism scale. *Journal of Intercultural Communication Research, 31,* 201–215.

you communicate with people from other cultures, it is therefore valuable to resist ethnocentrism by remembering that being *different* does not necessarily mean being *wrong*. Perhaps you put a lot of stock in the use of deodorant and view consultations with witch doctors as primitive, but bear in mind that those are simply your cultural values. Although they may seem right to you, they aren't right to everyone.

Overcoming ethnocentrism takes practice. A first step is to recognize any tendencies you might have to judge other cultures' practices as inferior to your own. Check out "The Competent Communicator" to assess where you stand.

BE KNOWLEDGEABLE ABOUT DIFFERENT COMMUNICATION CODES

• **communication codes**
Verbal and nonverbal behaviors whose meanings are often understood only by people from the same culture.

Another requirement for communicating with cultural awareness is to remember that cultures differ from one another in their use of **communication codes,** verbal and nonverbal behaviors whose meanings are often understood only by people from the same culture. Three kinds of communication codes—idioms, jargon, and gestures—differ significantly from society to society, and the variations can make communicating across cultures and co-cultures challenging. Being knowledgeable about those differences can boost the effectiveness of your intercultural communication.

Cultures Use Different Idioms
An *idiom* is a phrase whose meaning is purely figurative; that is, we can't understand its meaning by interpreting the words literally. For example, most Americans know that the idiom "kicking the bucket" has nothing to do with kicking a bucket; it means to die. If you grew up in the United States, you can probably think of several other common idioms, including "a dime a dozen" to mean something that's very common or nothing special, "having two left feet" to mean being a poor dancer, "shaking a leg" to mean hurrying, and "pulling your leg" to mean joking with you.

Every society has its own idioms whose meanings are not necessarily obvious to people from other cultures. In Portugal, for instance, a person who "doesn't give one for the box" is someone who can't say or do anything right. In Finland, if something "becomes gingerbread," that means it goes completely wrong. If someone in Brazil says "Fish don't pull wagons," she is encouraging you to eat red meat. Likewise, if someone in Australia is "as flash as a rat with a gold tooth," he's very pleased with himself. When you interact with people from other cultures, it's very helpful to be aware that they may use phrases that are not familiar to you, and you may be using idioms that are unfamiliar to them.[35]

Cultural differences in language use can also make it difficult to translate phrases and slogans from one culture to the next. As Table 2.3 illustrates, some humorous mistranslations can result.

Cultures Use Different Jargon
A specific form of idiomatic communication—and one that often separates co-cultures in particular—is jargon. As we've seen, *jargon* is language whose technical meaning is understood by people within a given co-culture but not necessarily by those outside it. Your doctor might inform her nurse, for instance, that you have "ecchymosis on a distal phalange," but she would probably tell you that you have

a bruise on your fingertip. Similarly, if your dentist orders a "periapical radiograph," he wants an X ray of the roots of one of your teeth.

Not understanding jargon can make you feel like an outsider. You might even get the impression that doctors and dentists talk that way just to reinforce their in-group status. Jargon can serve an important function, however, by allowing people who use it to communicate with one another in ways that are very specific, efficient, and accurate. Just bear in mind that when you use jargon with people who don't belong to your in-group, they might have difficulty understanding your meaning. Culturally aware communicators know when they need to *code-switch*, or shift between jargon and plain language, in order to be understood by others.

Cultures Use Different Gestures
Cultures also differ a great deal in their use of *gestures*, which are movements, usually of the hand or the arm, that express ideas. The same

TABLE • 2.3

LOST IN TRANSLATION: SOME MISTRANSLATED SLOGANS

Sign in a Bangkok dry cleaner: *Drop your trousers here for best results!*

Sign in a Copenhagen airline ticket office: *We take your bags and send them in all directions.*

Sign in a Hong Kong tailor shop: *Ladies may have a fit upstairs.*

Sign in an Acapulco restaurant: *The manager has personally passed all the water served here.*

Sign in a Moscow hotel room: *If this is your first visit to the USSR, you are welcome to it.*

gesture can have different meanings from society to society. For instance, American parents sometimes play the game "I've got your nose" with infants by putting a thumb between the index and middle finger. That gesture means good luck in Brazil, but it is an obscene expression in Russia and Indonesia. Similarly, holding up an index and pinky finger while holding down the middle and ring finger is a common gesture for University of Texas Longhorns fans. In Italy, however, people use that gesture to suggest that a man's wife has been unfaithful.[36] In some cultures, nodding the head—which Americans take to mean "yes"—actually means "no." Being aware of cultural differences in the meaning of such gestures can steer you away from unintentionally embarrassing yourself or insulting others.

SHARPEN Your Skills: *Gestures*

Select a gesture commonly used in the United States, such as the "OK" gesture or the "thumbs-up" gesture for good luck. Investigate which other cultures use that gesture and what meanings it has there. Write up your results in the form of advice for students planning to travel internationally.

BE FLEXIBLE AND RESPECTFUL WHEN INTERACTING WITH OTHERS

Finally, remember that cultures sometimes vary a good deal in how they communicate. When you interact with people from other cultures, expect some level of ambiguity, be aware of potential differences in access to communication technology, and adapt to the behavior patterns you observe.

Expect Ambiguity Communication experts have long recognized that many people value certainty in their interactions with others.[37] Most of us can recall being in social situations in which we were unsure of what to do or how to act. Such occasions present us with *ambiguity, or a lack of certainty.* Because cultures can differ so substantially in their communication patterns, such ambiguity is common when we interact cross-culturally. It's easy to feel uncomfortable and discouraged when we experience ambiguity and to long for the certainty of our own cultural practices. Good communicators remember, however, that ambiguity is normal when they interact with people from another culture. Instead of fearing the ambiguity, they use it as an opportunity to learn more about the other culture.

Paul and Ethan discovered the value of expecting ambiguity when they traveled to Indonesia one summer. On the bus from the airport on the day they arrived, they were constantly pushed and shoved by other passengers. At their hotel, the guest checking in before them appeared to be haggling with the manager over the cost of the room, and the bargaining delayed Paul and Ethan's check-in. Once they finally reached the check-in desk, the manager refused to take Ethan's credit card when he offered it in his left hand. After completing their transaction, Paul and Ethan were told their luggage would be delivered to their room shortly, yet they waited nearly two hours before it arrived.

As experienced travelers, Paul and Ethan knew they should take the ambiguity of those interactions in stride, however. They soon discovered that Indonesians often push and shove while in crowds but consider jostling to be normal, not an expression of anger or malice. They learned that bargaining over prices is expected in many business transactions and that it is polite to give and receive items only with the right hand, never the left. And because Indonesia is a highly polychronic society, people are far less concerned with punctuality than Paul and Ethan are used to—hence the delayed delivery of the luggage. Ambiguity comes with the territory in intercultural communication and offers a chance to learn about the values and traditions of culturally different people.

Appreciate Differences in Access to Communication Technology

An erroneous assumption many people make when interacting cross-culturally is that everyone has the same access to communication technology, such as the Internet. In fact, such access varies greatly around the world, particularly between countries that are economically *developed* (such as the United States, Germany, France, and Japan) and those that are economically *developing* (such as Bolivia, Angola, Pakistan, and Laos). Internet access even varies within U.S. households, depending on their economic resources.

Social scientists use the term *digital divide* to acknowledge the cultural gap between societies that do and do not have regular Internet access.[38] For instance, whereas electronically scanning a proposal and sending it as an e-mail attachment may be a simple task for you, a potential business client in a developing country may not have easy access to the equipment or the Internet service needed to retrieve it. If you know that ahead of time, you can make alternative arrangements to send your proposal, saving your client frustration—and possibly saving the business transaction.

Figure 2.1 charts the number of people, per 100 inhabitants, with reliable Internet access in the developed and developing world. Notice how the gap has widened—not shrunk—over the years.

Adapt to Others

As you interact with people of other cultures and learn about their customs—particularly those related to communication behavior—it's advantageous to adapt to those customs. To **adapt** means to change your behavior to accommodate what others are doing. If you find that people in a particular social setting are all speaking very quietly, for instance, then lowering your own speaking volume demonstrates adaptation. If others are bowing when they greet a leader or a learned person, you can adapt by doing the same. Good intercultural communicators adapt to the communicative behaviors of their conversational partners to emphasize similarity, convey respect, and promote unity.[39]

During a trip to Toyko in November 2009, for instance, President Barack Obama made headlines when he greeted Japanese emperor Akihito with a nearly 90-degree bow. Although bowing before a foreign head of state drew criticism for the president, it represented his attempt to adapt to the communication culture of Japan, where bowing signifies respect. Four years earlier, President George W. Bush was similarly criticized for holding hands with Saudi Crown Prince Abdullah as the two leaders took a stroll at Bush's ranch. Out of respect for his guest, however, the president was adapting to the communication culture of the Middle East, where holding hands signifies friendship.

• **adapt** To change one's behavior to accommodate what others are doing.

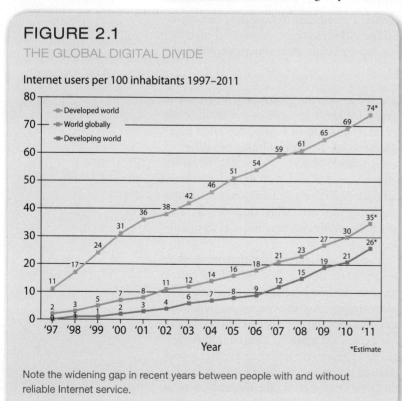

FIGURE 2.1

THE GLOBAL DIGITAL DIVIDE

Internet users per 100 inhabitants 1997–2011

- Developed world
- World globally
- Developing world

Year

*Estimate

Note the widening gap in recent years between people with and without reliable Internet service.

SOURCE: "Internet users per 100 inhabitants 2001–2011," International Telecommunications Union, Geneva, accessed May 2012.

Adaptation can help your intercultural communication flow smoothly, but only if others perceive the adaptation as respectful. If they perceive that you are copying their behavior to mock them, you can cause offense. Whenever Margene speaks to someone with an accent, she inadvertently adopts the same accent in her own speech. If the other speaker doesn't consciously notice, then Margene's adaptation likely helps to make the interaction positive. Researchers know that we like people who adapt to our vocal behavior, because we subconsciously think of them as similar to ourselves.[40] If the other speaker does notice that Margene has adopted his accent, however, he may feel she is making fun of his speech, even if Margene is unaware that she has adapted to his accent in the first place. When you do adapt to another person's behaviors, try not to exaggerate or draw attention to them. Adaptation is likely to be most effective when it appears natural, not forced.

When you adapt your behavior to others, do so in a way that conveys your interest in following their example and accommodating their traditions rather than in a way that mocks or disrespects them. The distinction can be a fine line, but being aware of the potential for conveying disrespect is a crucial first step.

adaptability Showing Sensitivity

The Scene: A family from Libya moves in next door to you. While introducing yourself, you discover that the family consists of a husband with three wives and multiple children. All the parents say they are eager to spend time with you and get to know you.

Your Task: Consider how you would communicate with this family in light of your own beliefs about polygamy. What strategies would you use to

- Be mindful of cultural differences?
- Avoid communicating ethnocentrically?
- Respect your own cultural values as well as those of your neighbors?

- **What is culture?** Culture is the totality of learned, shared symbols, language, values, and norms that distinguish one group of people from another.

- **How does culture influence communication behavior?** Culture influences communication behavior through variations in (1) the emphasis placed on individuals versus groups, (2) the communicative context, (3) power distance, (4) views about masculinity and femininity and about men's and women's roles, (5) orientation toward time, and (6) uncertainty avoidance.

- **In what ways can we improve our cultural communication skills?** We can be open-minded about cultural differences, knowledgeable about cultural communication codes, and flexible and respectful when communicating with people from other cultures.

POP QUIZ

Multiple Choice

1. Garrett's culture has specific rules and expectations that guide people's behavior. We would call those rules and expectations his culture's
   a. symbols.
   b. language.
   c. values.
   d. norms.

2. When Trudy communicates with others, she generally expects them to be direct and to say what they mean. Trudy is probably from a culture that is
   a. high-context.
   b. low-context.
   c. high-power-distance.
   d. low-power-distance.

3. Pieta thinks of time as holistic, fluid, and loosely structured. She does not expect her classes to start on time but to begin whenever the instructor is ready. She is likely from a culture that is
   a. monochronic.
   b. feminine.
   c. masculine.
   d. polychronic.

4. The type of culture in which children are taught to put the needs of their families, villages, and employers ahead of their personal desires or ambitions is called
   a. individualistic.
   b. uncertainty-avoidant.
   c. collectivistic.
   d. low-context.

5. The phrase "kick the bucket" is, for speakers of English, an example of a cultural
   a. idiom.
   b. custom.
   c. symbol.
   d. gesture.

Fill in the Blanks

6. Groups of people who share a common culture are called a _____.

7. The process by which we acquire a culture is called _____.

8. A _____ is a group of people who share values, customs, and norms related to mutual interests or characteristics besides their national citizenship.

(continued)

9. People who are _____ judge other cultural practices as inferior to their own.

10. Good intercultural communicators _____, meaning that they change their behavior to accommodate what others are doing.

KEY TERMS

3

PERCEIVING OURSELVES AND OTHERS

A Romantic Nightmare, Live on the Jumbo-Tron

Proposing to a romantic partner can be one of life's most memorable moments. It certainly was for the young man who proposed to his girlfriend midway through the UCLA-Richmond basketball game at the Los Angeles Sports Arena on December 23, 2011. As the couple appeared on the arena's "jumbo vision" for all in attendance to see, the man pulled a ring from his pocket and said, "I knew that I was going to do this since the first day that I met you, and I figured now was as good a time as any." Once he got on one knee and popped the question, his girlfriend stared at him for several seconds, speechless. Then she stood up, turned, and ran in the other direction—leaving him, ring in hand, rejected in front of a stadium full of people. Within a week, video of the failed proposal had gone viral on YouTube. Suppose you had been in the stands that night. What would you think of this young man? How about the young woman?

▸ As You READ

- How do we form perceptions of others?
- What influences our perceptions?
- How do we manage our image?

Getting along in our social world depends on our ability to understand others and ourselves. Our minds, senses, and experiences help us to form perceptions about people that influence the way we communicate with them. We often hold well-informed perceptions of ourselves and others. Sometimes, however—like the couple at the UCLA basketball game—we may form perceptions on the basis of very limited information, which may or may not be accurate. The more we learn about the perception-making process, the better we will be at understanding and communicating appropriately with the people around us.

How We Perceive Others

Many people would call the selection of a romantic partner one of the most consequential social decisions a person can make, since we could be selecting the person with whom we'll spend the rest of our lives. Because it's such an important decision, you may think most of us would require lots of information to decide whether someone would be a suitable match.

Speed daters might disagree, however. In speed dating, groups of people get together so individuals can visit one another one-on-one for 3- to 8-minute "mini-dates" before moving on to the next person. Whenever two people both want to know more about each other, they each receive the other's contact information and take it from there. Although these mini-dates may seem too short for participants to make serious mate choices, much research has shown that people are surprisingly accurate at evaluating others after very brief periods of time.[1] In fact, our impressions and evaluations of others can be more accurate if we have less—rather than more—information to go on, as the "Fact or Fiction?" box explains.

• **perception** The process of making meaning from environmental experiences.

We form our impressions and evaluations of others by engaging in **perception,** the process of making meaning from what we experience in the world around us. We notice physical experiences—such as fatigue, body aches, and congestion—and perceive that we are ill. We notice environmental experiences—such as cold air, wind, and rain—and we perceive that a storm is underway. When we apply the same process to people and relationships, we engage in *interpersonal perception*, which helps us to make meaning about people from our own and others' behaviors.[2]

As social beings, we are constantly engaged in interpersonal perception. We form impressions and evaluations of others—accurate or not—on the basis of the information available to us. Although our perceptions may seem to take shape instantaneously, we'll find in this section that they actually form in stages, though quickly. We'll also see that several factors can influence the accuracy of our perceptions, including culture, stereotypes, primacy and recency effects, and perceptual sets.

Speed dating relies on short conversations with multiple partners. Research shows that people are sometimes surprisingly accurate at evaluating others after very brief periods of time.

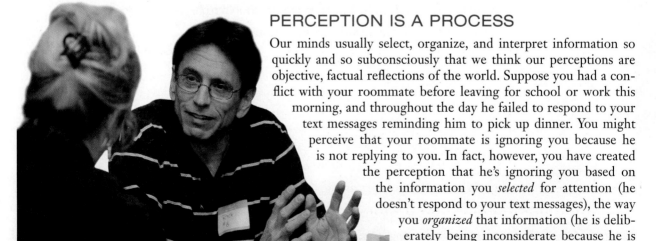

PERCEPTION IS A PROCESS

Our minds usually select, organize, and interpret information so quickly and so subconsciously that we think our perceptions are objective, factual reflections of the world. Suppose you had a conflict with your roommate before leaving for school or work this morning, and throughout the day he failed to respond to your text messages reminding him to pick up dinner. You might perceive that your roommate is ignoring you because he is not replying to you. In fact, however, you have created the perception that he's ignoring you based on the information you *selected* for attention (he doesn't respond to your text messages), the way you *organized* that information (he is deliberately being inconsiderate because he is angry about your conflict), and the way you *interpreted* it (he's ignoring you).[3] That isn't the only perception you could create, however. You might also perceive that he

Fact or *fiction*?

More Is More: When It Comes to Forming Perceptions, More Information Is Always Better

People sometimes criticize others for making snap judgments or arriving at their impressions on the basis of limited information. After listening to only one speech, for example, you decide to vote for a political candidate without learning anything else about him or her. It's easy to see how such on-the-spot judgments can be misleading and how our perceptions might be more accurate if we had additional information.

In many cases, it's true: when we form perceptions of others, our first impressions can be misleading. Research shows, however, that in certain cases our snap judgments are surprisingly accurate. Perhaps even more surprising is that, although gathering additional information about someone can make our perceptions *more* accurate, it can also make them *less* accurate.

You may think, for instance, that your long-time friends would describe you more accurately than strangers would. An interesting experiment proved otherwise, however. Participants described themselves on personality inventories and then asked their close friends to describe them on the same inventories. As you might expect, the friends' reports matched the participants' self-reports fairly well. The researchers next asked complete strangers to walk through the participants' residence hall rooms and then describe the participants' personalities. That is, they filled out descriptions of the participants without even meeting them, based only on the limited information they got from browsing around their rooms.

The strangers were more accurate than the close friends in describing participants' personalities. That result suggests that having more information about a person—as you would if you had known that person for years—does not necessarily make your perceptions of him or her more accurate. More information is sometimes better, but not always.

ASK YOURSELF

- Why are snap judgments sometimes accurate? What clues might we be subconsciously noticing that help us interpret a situation quickly yet accurately?

- When have you made snap judgments that turned out to be inaccurate? What led you to form those perceptions?

SOURCE: Gosling, S. D., Ko, S. J., Mannarelli, T., & Morris, M. E. (2002). A room with a cue: Personality judgments based on offices and bedrooms. *Journal of Personality and Social Psychology, 82,* 379–398.

is having an extremely busy day or that he left his cell phone in his car. The perception you form depends on which pieces of information you attend to and which ones you ignore.

Selection, organization, and interpretation are the three basic stages of perception. Let's examine each in turn.

Selection   Perception begins when one or more of your senses are stimulated. You enter a bagel store and hear a customer placing her order. You see a puppy chewing on an old tennis ball. You smell a coworker's cologne as he walks past. Those sensory experiences of hearing, seeing, and smelling can initiate your formation of perceptions.

In truth, your senses are constantly stimulated by events in your environment. It's impossible, though, to pay attention to everything you're seeing, hearing, smelling, tasting, and feeling at any given moment.[4] When you're watching the puppy play with his tennis ball, you're probably not listening carefully to the news report on the radio. Rather than paying attention to *all* the stimuli in your environment, you engage in **selection,** the process by which your mind and body help you isolate certain stimuli to pay attention to. For example, you notice that your partner didn't take out the garbage, but you overlook that he made dinner three nights in a row. Clearly, the information we attend to influences the perceptions we form. A key point is that we don't necessarily make conscious decisions about which stimuli to notice and which to ignore. How, then, does selection occur? Research indicates that three characteristics in particular make a given stimulus more likely to be selected for attention.

First, being unusual or unexpected makes a stimulus stand out.[5] You might not pay attention to people talking loudly in a restaurant, but if the same loud conversation were to take place in the library, it would grab your attention because it is unusual in that environment. Second, repetition, or how frequently you're exposed to a stimulus, makes it stand out.[6] For example, you're more likely to remember commercials you've seen repeatedly than ones you've seen only once. Similarly, you tend to notice more characteristics about the people you see frequently than about individuals you don't see often, such as their physical appearance and behavior patterns. Third, the intensity of a stimulus affects how much you take notice of it. You are more aware of strong odors than weak scents, and of bright and flashy colors than dull and muted hues.[7]

With so much sensory information available to you, how do you avoid becoming overwhelmed? A part of your brain called the *reticular formation* serves the important function of helping you focus on certain stimuli while ignoring others.[8] It is the primary reason why, when you're having a conversation with a friend in a crowded, noisy coffee shop, you can focus on what your friend is saying and tune out the many other sights and sounds that are bombarding your senses at the time.

Organization Once you've noticed a particular stimulus, the next step in the perception process is **organization,** the classification of information in some way. Organization helps you make sense of the information by allowing you to see its similarities to and differences from other things you know about. To classify a stimulus, your mind applies a **perceptual schema** to it, which is a mental framework for organizing information into categories we call *constructs*.

According to communication researcher Peter Andersen, we use four types of schema to classify information we notice about other people:[9]

1. *Physical constructs* emphasize people's appearance, causing us to notice objective characteristics such as height, age, ethnicity, and body shape, as well as subjective characteristics such as physical attractiveness.

2. *Role constructs* emphasize people's social or professional position, so we notice that a person is a teacher, an accountant, a father, and so on.[10]

3. *Interaction constructs* emphasize people's behavior, so we notice that a person is outgoing, aggressive, shy, or considerate.

4. *Psychological constructs* emphasize people's thoughts and feelings, causing us to notice that a person is angry, self-assured, insecure, or carefree.

Whichever constructs we notice about people—and we may notice more than one at a time—the process of organization helps us determine the ways in which various pieces of information we select for attention are related to one another.[11] If you notice that your neighbor is a Little League softball coach and the father of three children, for example, then those two pieces of information go together because they both relate to the roles he plays. Likewise, if you notice that he seems irritated or angry, those pieces of information go together as examples of his psychological state.

Interpretation After noticing and classifying a stimulus, you have to assign it an **interpretation** to figure out its meaning for you. Let's say one of your coworkers has been especially friendly toward you since last week. She finds numerous occasions to run into you, brings you treats, and offers to run errands for you over her lunch break. Her behavior is definitely noticeable, and you've probably classified it as a psychological construct because it relates to her thoughts and feelings about you.

What is her behavior communicating, though? How should you interpret it? Is she being nice because she's getting ready to ask you for a big favor? Does she want to look good in front of her manager? Or does she like you? If she likes you, does she like you as a friend, or is she making a romantic gesture?

To address those questions, you likely will pay attention to three factors: your *personal experience*, your *knowledge* of this coworker, and the *closeness of your relationship* with her. First, your personal experience helps you to assign meaning to behavior. If some coworkers have been nice to you in the past just to get favors from you later, then you might be suspicious of this person's behavior.[12] Second, your knowledge of the person helps you interpret her actions. If you know she's friendly and nice to everyone, you might interpret her behavior differently than if you notice she's being nice only to you.[13] Finally, the closeness of your relationship influences how you interpret a person's behavior. When your best friend does you an unexpected favor, you probably interpret it as a sincere sign of friendship. In contrast, when a coworker does you a favor, you may be more likely to wonder whether the person has an ulterior motive.[14]

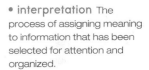

Which constructs would you use to describe these people?

• **interpretation** The process of assigning meaning to information that has been selected for attention and organized.

Our interpretations of another person's behaviors rely on personal experience, knowledge, and the closeness of our relationship with that individual.

The Circular Nature of Perception Although perception occurs in stages, the process is far from linear. Instead, the three stages of perception—selecting, organizing, and interpreting information—all overlap.[15] How we interpret a communication behavior depends on what we notice about it, for example, but what we notice can also depend on the way we interpret it.

Let's assume, for example, that you're listening to a speech by a political candidate. If you find her ideas and proposals favorable, you might interpret her demeanor and speaking style as examples of her intelligence and confidence. If you oppose her ideas, however, you might believe her demeanor and speaking style reflect arrogance or incompetence. Either interpretation, in turn, might lead you to select for attention only those behaviors or characteristics that support your interpretation and to ignore those that don't. So, even though perception happens in stages, the stages don't always take place in the same order. We're constantly noticing, organizing, and interpreting things around us, including other people's behaviors.

As we consider next, perception, like other skills, takes practice. In addition, our perceptions are more accurate on some occasions than others.

WE COMMONLY MISPERCEIVE OTHERS' COMMUNICATION BEHAVIORS

Although we constantly form perceptions of others and of their communication behaviors, we are hardly experts at it. In fact, perceptual mistakes are easy to make. Let's say, for example, that on your overseas trip, you perceive that two adults you see in a restaurant are having a heated argument. As it turns out, you discover that they are not arguing but engaging in behaviors that, in their culture, communicate interest and involvement.

Why do we commit such a perceptual error despite our accumulated experience? The reason is that each of us has multiple lenses through which we perceive the world. Those lenses include our cultural and co-cultural backgrounds, stereotypes, primacy and recency effects, and our perceptual sets. In each case, those lenses have the potential to influence not only our own communication behaviors but also our perceptions of the communication of others.

Cultures and Co-Cultures Influence Perceptions One powerful influence on the accuracy of our perceptions is the culture and co-cultures with which we identify. Recall from Chapter 2 that culture is the learned, shared symbols,

Our feelings about a politician's ideas often influence our interpretation of his or her behaviors.

language, values, and norms that distinguish one group of people—such as Russians, South Africans, or Thais—from another. Co-cultures are smaller groups of people—such as single parents, bloggers, and history enthusiasts—who share values, customs, and norms related to mutual interests or characteristics besides their national citizenship.

Many characteristics of cultures can influence our perceptions and interpretations of other people's behaviors.[16] For instance, we saw in Chapter 2 that people from individualistic cultures frequently engage in more direct, overt forms of conflict communication than do people from collectivistic cultures. In a conflict, then, an individualist might perceive a collectivist's communication behaviors as conveying weakness, passivity, or a lack of interest. Likewise, the collectivist may perceive the individualist's communication patterns as overly aggressive or self-centered. Those perceptions can arise even though each person is communicating in a way that is normal in his or her culture.

The culture and co-cultures with which we identify often influence the accuracy of our perceptions.

Co-cultural differences can also influence perceptions of communication. Teenagers might perceive their parents' advice as outdated or irrelevant, whereas parents may perceive their teenagers' indifference to their advice as naive.[17] Liberals and conservatives may each see the others' communication messages as rooted in ignorance.[18]

Stereotypes Influence Perceptions A **stereotype** is a generalization about a group or category of people that can have a powerful influence on how we perceive others and their communication behavior.[19] Stereotyping is a three-part process:

• stereotype
A generalization about a group or category of people that is applied to individual members of that group.

- First, we identify a group to which we believe another person belongs ("you are a gay man").
- Second, we recall a generalization others often make about the people in that group ("gay men are emotionally sensitive").
- Finally, we apply that generalization to the person ("therefore, you must be emotionally sensitive").

You can probably think of stereotypes for many groups.[20] What stereotypes come to mind for elderly people? How about people with physical or mental disabilities? Wealthy people? Homeless people? Science fiction fans? Immigrants? Athletes? What stereotypes come to mind when you think about yourself?

What stereotypes come to mind when you think of people such as these?

CHAPTER 3 Perceiving Ourselves and Others • 61

Many people find stereotyping distasteful or unethical, particularly when stereotypes have to do with characteristics such as sex, race, and sexual orientation.[21] Unquestionably, because it underestimates the differences among individuals in a group, stereotyping can lead to inaccurate, even offensive, perceptions of other people. It may be true, for instance, that gay men are more emotionally sensitive than straight men, but that doesn't mean *every* gay man is emotionally sensitive. Similarly, people of Asian descent may often be more studious than those from other ethnic groups, but not every Asian is a good student, and not all Asians do equally well in school.[22]

There is variation within almost every group, but stereotypes focus our attention only on the generalizations. In fact, we have a tendency to engage in *selective memory bias*—to remember information that supports our stereotypes while forgetting information that doesn't.[23] During conflict communication, for instance, both women and men tend to remember only their partners' stereotypical behaviors.[24] Men may recall that women nagged and criticized them but might forget that they also listened carefully. Likewise, women may recall that men tuned them out but might overlook their apologies and signs of remorse.

Although perceptions about an individual made on the basis of a stereotype are often inaccurate, they aren't necessarily so.[25] For example, consider the stereotype that women love taking care of children. If you met a woman and assumed (on the basis of that stereotype) that she enjoyed taking care of children, you might be wrong—however, you also might be right. Not every woman enjoys taking care of children, but some do. By the same token, not every Asian person is a good student, but some are. The point is that just because your perception of someone is consistent with a stereotype, that perception isn't necessarily inaccurate. Just as we shouldn't assume that a stereotypical judgment is accurate, we should not assume that it's inaccurate.

Before assuming that your perceptions of others are correct, genuinely get to know those people, and let your perceptions be guided by what you learn about them as individuals. By communicating with them, you can begin to discover how well other people fit or don't fit the stereotypical perceptions you formed of them.

Primacy and Recency Effects Influence Perceptions

As the saying goes, you get only one chance to make a good first impression. There's no shortage of advice on how to accomplish that, from picking the right clothes to polishing your conversational skills. Have you ever noticed that no one talks about the importance of making a good *second* impression?

• **primacy effect** The tendency to emphasize the first impression over later impressions when forming a perception.

According to a principle called the **primacy effect,** first impressions are critical because they set the tone for all future interactions.[26] Our first impressions of someone's communication behaviors seem to stick in our mind more than our second, third, or fourth impressions do. In an early study of the primacy effect, psychologist Solomon Asch found that a person described as "intelligent, industrious, impulsive, critical, stubborn, and envious" was evaluated more favorably than one described as "envious, stubborn, critical, impulsive, industrious, and intelligent."[27]

Notice that most of those adjectives are negative, but when the description begins with a positive adjective *(intelligent)*, the effects of the more negative ones that follow it are diminished.

Asch's study illustrates that the first information we learn about someone tends to have a stronger effect on how we perceive that person than information we receive later.[28] That finding explains why we work so hard to communicate competently during a job interview, on a date, or in other important situations. When people evaluate us favorably at first, they're more likely to perceive us in a positive light from then on.[29]

As most entertainers know, it's equally important to make a good *final* impression, because that's what the audience will remember after leaving. Standup comedians will tell you that the two most important jokes in a show are the first and the last. That advice follows a principle known as the **recency effect,** which says that the most recent impression we have of a person's communication is more powerful than our earlier impressions.[30]

Which is most important, the first or the most recent impression? The answer is that *both* appear to be more important than any impressions we form in between.[31] To grasp this key point, consider the last significant conversation you had with someone. You probably have a better recollection of how the conversation started and ended than you do of what was communicated in between. Figure 3.1 illustrates the relationship between the primacy effect and the recency effect by showing how our first and most recent impressions of people overshadow our other perceptions of them.

Perceptual Sets Influence Perceptions "I'll believe it when I see it," people often say. However, our perception of reality is influenced by more than what we see. Our biases, expectations, and desires can create what psychologists call a **perceptual set,** or a predisposition to perceive only what we want or expect to perceive.[32] An equally valid motto might therefore be "I'll see it when I believe it."

• **recency effect** The tendency to emphasize the most recent impression over earlier impressions when forming a perception.

• **perceptual set** A person's predisposition to perceive only what he or she wants or expects to perceive.

Many successful comedians understand that the final impression they make on an audience is just as important as the first impression.

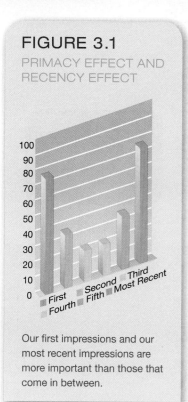

Our first impressions and our most recent impressions are more important than those that come in between.

For example, our perceptual set regarding gender guides the ways we perceive and interact with newborns. Without the help of a contextual cue such as blue or pink baby clothes, we sometimes have a hard time telling whether a dressed infant is male or female. However, research shows that if we're told an infant's name is David, we perceive that child to be stronger and bigger than if the same infant is called, say, Diana.[33] Our perceptual set tells us that male infants are usually bigger and stronger than female ones, so we "see" a bigger, stronger baby when we learn it's a boy. Our perceptions can then affect our communication behavior: We may also hold and talk to the "female" baby in softer, quieter ways than we do with the "male" baby.

Our perceptual set also influences how we make sense of people, circumstances, and events. Deeply religious individuals may talk about healings as miracles or answers to prayer, whereas others may describe them as natural responses to medication.[34] Highly homophobic people are more likely than others to perceive affectionate communication between men as sexual in nature.[35]

In summary, perception is a complex process, susceptible to many different biases and patterns. As we'll discover in the next section, we are vulnerable to mistakes not only when we form perceptions but also when we try to explain what we perceive.

How We Explain Our Perceptions

Moments into her speech accepting the 2009 MTV Video Music Award for Best Female Video, country singer Taylor Swift—along with her audience—was stunned when rapper Kanye West suddenly appeared onstage, grabbed the microphone from her hands, and declared that a video from pop singer Beyoncé should have won the award instead. "Taylor, I'm really happy for you," West said. "I'll let you finish, but Beyoncé had one of the best videos of all time. One of the best videos of all time!" Visibly shaken, Swift walked offstage moments after West's outburst, leaving viewers to wonder why he had so rudely interrupted Swift's acceptance speech.

When we perceive social behavior, especially behavior we find surprising, our nearly automatic reaction is to try to make sense of it.[36] We need to understand what is happening to know how to react to it. Think about it: if you perceive that someone is communicating out of anger or jealousy, you'll likely react to that behavior differently than if you perceive it is motivated by humor or sarcasm. The ability to explain social behavior—including our own behavior—is therefore an important aspect of how we perceive our social world. In this section, we'll see that we explain behaviors by forming attributions for them, and we'll discover how to avoid two of the most common errors people make when formulating attributions for communication behavior.

• **attribution** An explanation for an observed behavior.

WE EXPLAIN BEHAVIOR THROUGH ATTRIBUTIONS

An **attribution** is an explanation, the answer to a "why" question.[37] You notice your brother ignoring his girlfriend, for instance, and you wonder what to attribute his behavior to. Although we can generate countless attributions for a given behavior, they vary along three important dimensions: locus, stability, and controllability.[38]

Locus  Locus refers to where the cause of a behavior is "located," whether within or outside ourselves.[39] Some of our behaviors have *internal* loci (the plural of locus); they're caused by a particular characteristic of ourselves. Other behaviors have *external* loci, meaning they're caused by something outside ourselves. If your boss is late for your 9 A.M. performance review, an internal attribution you might make about her is that she has lost track of time or she's making you wait on purpose. An external attribution you might form about her is that the traffic is heavy that morning or an earlier meeting she is attending has run long.

Stability A second dimension of attributions is whether the cause of a behavior is stable or unstable.[40] A *stable* cause is one that is permanent, semipermanent, or at least not easily changed. Why was your boss late? Rush hour traffic would be a stable cause for lateness, because it's a permanent feature of almost everyone's morning commute. The attribution that she is rarely punctual would likewise be stable, because it identifies an enduring aspect of her behavior. In contrast, a traffic accident or an overly long morning meeting would be an *unstable* cause of your boss's lateness, because those events occur only from time to time and are largely unpredictable.

Controllability Finally, causes for behavior vary in how controllable they are.[41] You make a *controllable* attribution for someone's behavior when you believe the cause of the behavior was under that person's control. In contrast, an *uncontrollable* attribution identifies a cause that was beyond the person's control. If you perceive that your boss is late for your appointment because she has spent too much time socializing with other coworkers beforehand, that is a controllable attribution because socializing is under her control. Alternatively, if you perceive she's late owing to a car accident on the way to work, that is an uncontrollable attribution because she couldn't help but be late if she wrecked her car.

AVOIDING TWO COMMON ATTRIBUTION ERRORS

Although most of us probably try to generate accurate attributions for other people's behaviors, we are still vulnerable to making attribution mistakes.[42] Those errors can create communication problems because, as noted above, our responses to other people's behaviors are often based on the attributions we make for those behaviors.

We can attribute a person's lateness to either internal or external causes. Was your boss late because she lost track of time—or because she got caught in heavy traffic?

Let's say that Maggie and her stepson Craig argue one night about whether Craig can go on a school-sponsored overnight trip. After their argument, they both go to bed angry. When Maggie gets up the following morning, she finds that Craig hasn't done the dishes or taken out the trash, two chores he is responsible for doing every night before bed. It turns out that Craig was so upset by the argument that his chores slipped his mind. Maggie makes a different attribution, however: she perceives that Craig didn't do the chores because he was deliberately disobeying her. On the basis of her attribution, she tells Craig he's grounded for a week and is definitely not going on the trip. Her actions only prolong and intensify the conflict between them. Had Maggie correctly attributed Craig's behavior to an honest oversight, she might have been able to overlook it instead of making it the basis for additional conflict. In other words, recognizing a common attribution error might have equipped Maggie to avoid a mistake that made a bad situation worse.

We might think we always explain behavior objectively and rationally, but the truth is that we're all prone to taking mental shortcuts when generating attributions. As a result, our attributions are often less accurate than they should be. Two of the most common attribution errors—which we can better prepare ourselves to avoid by understanding them—are the self-serving bias and the fundamental attribution error.

Self-Serving Bias The **self-serving bias,** which relates primarily to how we explain our own behaviors, refers to our tendency to attribute our successes to stable, internal causes while attributing our failures to unstable, external causes.[43] For instance, if you gave a great informative speech in your class, you say it was great because you were well prepared, but if your speech went poorly, you say the assignment was unfair or other students were distracting you. Such attributions are self-serving, because they suggest that our successes are deserved but our failures are not our fault.

- **self-serving bias** The tendency to attribute one's successes to stable internal causes and one's failures to unstable external causes.

Although the self-serving bias deals primarily with attributions we make for our own behaviors, research shows that we often extend this tendency to important people in our lives.[44] In a happy relationship, for instance, people tend to attribute their partner's positive behaviors to internal causes ("She remembered my birthday because she's thoughtful") and negative behaviors to external causes ("He forgot my birthday because he's been very preoccupied by his job"). In a distressed relationship, the reverse is often true: people attribute negative behaviors to internal causes ("She forgot my birthday because she's completely self-absorbed") and positive behaviors to external causes ("He remembered my birthday only because I reminded him five times").

Many people have a self-serving bias when it comes to explaining their own behaviors.

• **fundamental attribution error** The tendency to attribute others' behaviors to internal rather than external causes.

Fundamental Attribution Error Think about how you reacted the last time someone cut you off in traffic. What attribution did you make for the driver's behavior? You might have thought "She must be late for something important" or "He must have a car full of noisy children," but you probably didn't. "What a jerk!" may be closer to your reaction.

The reason for that response is the human tendency to commit the **fundamental attribution error,** in which we attribute other people's behaviors to internal rather than external causes.[45] The high school student ran the pledge drive because he's a caring, giving person, not because he earned extra credit for doing so. The cashier gave you the wrong change because she doesn't know how to count, not because she was distracted by an announcement over the store's audio system.

As a student of communication, you should bear in mind that people's behaviors—including your own—are often responses to external forces. For instance, when the new doctor you're seeing spends only three minutes diagnosing your condition and prescribing a treatment before moving on to the next patient, you might perceive that she's not very caring. That would be an internal attribution for her communication behavior, which the fundamental attribution error makes more likely. To judge the merits of that attribution, however, ask yourself what external forces might have motivated the doctor's behavior. For example, might she have rushed through your consultation because another doctor's absence that day left her with twice as many patients as usual? Good communicators recognize the tendency to form internal attributions for people's behaviors, and they force themselves to consider external causes that might also be influential.

Like other forms of perception, attributions are important but prone to error. That observation doesn't imply that we *never* make accurate attributions for people's behaviors (including our own). It simply acknowledges that the self-serving bias and the fundamental attribution error are easy mistakes to commit. The more we know about those processes, therefore, the better we can base our communication behaviors on accurate perceptions of ourselves and others.

SHARPEN Your Skills: *Attribution-making*

Working with a partner or in a small group, generate as many attributions as you can for Kanye West's interruption of Taylor Swift's acceptance speech. Identify whether each attribution is internal or external, and note which type is easier to generate. Finally, narrow your list to the three external attributions you believe are most plausible.

How We Perceive Ourselves

As much as your communication's effectiveness depends on your ability to perceive others, it also depends on your ability to perceive yourself. Ask yourself: Who am I? How do I relate to others? What is the *self* in *myself*? Grappling with those challenging questions will allow you to communicate and to form relationships with a sure understanding of who you are and what you have to offer.

In this section, we'll discover that each of us perceives our self through our self-concept, and we'll examine the characteristics of a self-concept. We'll also learn how self-concept influences communication behavior and relates to self-esteem.

SELF-CONCEPT DEFINED

Let's say you are asked to come up with 10 ways to answer the question "Who am I?" What words will you pick? Which answers are most important? Each of us has a set of ideas about who we are that isn't influenced by moment-to-moment events (such as "I'm happy right now") but is fairly stable over the course of our lives (such as "I'm a happy person"). Your **self-concept** is composed of those stable ideas about who you are. It is your **identity,** your understanding of who you are. As we'll see in this section, self-concepts are multifaceted and partly subjective.

Self-Concept Is Multifaceted We define ourselves in many different ways. Some of these ways rely on our name: "I'm Sunita" or "I'm Darren." Some rely on physical or social categories: "I am a vegan" or "I am Australian." Others make use of our skills or interests: "I'm artistic" or "I'm a good cook." Still others are based on our relationships to other people: "I am an uncle" or "I do volunteer work with homeless children." Finally, some rely on our evaluations of ourselves: "I am honest" or "I am impatient." You can probably think of several other ways to describe who you are.

Which of those descriptions is the *real* you?

The answer is that your self-concept has several different parts, and each of your descriptions taps into one or more of those parts. What we call *the self* is a collection of smaller *selves.* If you're female, that's a part of who you are, but it isn't everything you are. Asian, athletic, agnostic, or asthmatic may all be parts of your self-concept, but none of those terms defines you completely. All the different ways you would describe yourself are pieces of your overall self-concept.

One way to think about your self-concept is to distinguish between aspects of yourself that are known to others and aspects that are known only to you. In 1955, U.S. psychologists Joseph Luft and Harry Ingham created the **Johari window,** a visual representation of the self as composed of four separate parts.[46] According to this model, which is illustrated in Figure 3.2, the *open area* consists of characteristics that are known both to the self and to others. Those probably include your name, sex, hobbies, academic major, and other aspects of your self-concept that you are aware of and freely share with others. In contrast, the *hidden area* consists of characteristics that you know about yourself but choose not to reveal to others, such as emotional insecurities or traumas from your past that you elect to keep hidden.

An innovative aspect of the Johari window is that it recognizes dimensions of our self-concept of which we may be unaware. For instance, others might see us as impatient or moody even if we don't recognize these traits in ourselves. Those characteristics make up the third part of the model, the *blind area.* Finally, the *unknown area* comprises aspects of our self-concept that are not known either to us or to others. For example, no one—including you—knows what kind of parent you will be until you actually become one.

- **self-concept** The set of perceptions a person has about who he or she is; also known as *identity.*

- **identity** The set of perceptions a person has about who he or she is; also known as *self-concept.*

- **Johari window** A visual representation of components of the self that are known or unknown to the self and to others.

FIGURE 3.2
JOHARI WINDOW

	Known to Self	Unknown to Self
Known to Others	OPEN	BLIND
Unknown to Others	HIDDEN	UNKNOWN

In the Johari window, the open area represents what you know and choose to reveal to others, and the hidden area depicts what you know but choose not to reveal. The blind area reflects what others know about you but you don't recognize in yourself, and the unknown area comprises the dimensions of yourself that no one knows.

Self-Concept Is Partly Subjective

Some of what we know about ourselves is based on objective facts. For instance, I'm 5′8″ tall and have brown hair, I was born in Seattle but now live in Phoenix, and I teach college for a living. Those aspects of my self-concept are objective—they're based on fact and not on someone's opinion. That doesn't mean I have no choice about them. I chose to move to Arizona and to take a teaching job, and although I was born with brown hair, I could change my hair color if I wanted to. Referring to those personal characteristics as "objective" simply means that they are factually true. Many aspects of our self-concept are subjective rather than objective, however. "Subjective" means that they're based on the impressions we have of ourselves rather than on objective facts.

It is often difficult for people to judge themselves accurately or objectively. Sometimes our self-assessments are unreasonably positive. For instance, you might know individuals who have unrealistic ideas about their intelligence, talents, or understanding of the world or other people. In one study, the College Board (the company that administers the SAT college entrance examination) asked almost a million American high school seniors to rate their ability to get along with others. *Every single student* in the study responded that he or she was "above average"—a result that is mathematically impossible! Moreover, 60 percent claimed their ability to get along with others was in the top 10 percent, and a whopping 25 percent rated themselves in the top 1 percent, both of which are highly improbable.[47]

In contrast, sometimes our judgments of ourselves are unreasonably negative. That is especially true for people with low self-esteem. Several studies have shown that such individuals tend to magnify the importance of their failures.[48] They often underestimate their abilities, and when they get negative feedback, such as a bad evaluation at work or a disrespectful remark from someone they know, they are likely to believe it accurately reflects their self-worth.

Several studies have also suggested that people with low self-esteem have a higher-than-average risk of clinical depression, a condition that impairs not only mental and emotional well-being but also physical health and the ways people communicate in their social relationships.[49] We return to self-esteem a little later in this chapter.

AWARENESS AND MANAGEMENT OF THE SELF-CONCEPT

Part of being a competent, skilled communicator is being aware of your self-concept and managing its influences on your communication with others. Two pathways by which self-concept can shape communicative behavior are self-monitoring and the self-fulfilling prophecy.

Self-Monitoring Recall from Chapter 1 that *self-monitoring* is an awareness of how you look and sound

SHARPEN Your Skills: *Your Johari window*

Select three people who are important to you. Considering your relationship with each person separately, draw a Johari window that reflects your self-concept with that person, making the *open, hidden, blind,* and *unknown* portions of the window appropriately larger or smaller. Then write a short paragraph explaining why the panes of your Johari window differ in size for each relationship and how they reflect your communication behaviors with each of those people.

It is difficult for many people to judge themselves accurately or objectively. Self-assessments are often subjective.

and how your behavior is affecting those around you. The tendency toward self-monitoring ranges along a continuum from high to low. People on the high end of the scale pay attention to how others are reacting to their own behaviors, and they have the ability to adjust their communication as needed. People on the low end express whatever they are thinking or feeling without paying attention to the impression they're creating.

To understand how self-monitoring operates, imagine that you've fixed up your friends Caleb and Keith to go out. As a high self-monitor, Caleb pays a great deal of attention to his clothes and grooming to make sure he looks and smells good. In contrast, as a low self-monitor, Keith doesn't spend much time thinking about those things. During their date, Caleb is aware of what he's saying, so he comes across as nice, easygoing, and funny. Keith, however, says whatever is on his mind, without considering what Caleb might think. Caleb notices if his behavior seems to make Keith uncomfortable, and he adjusts his actions accordingly. In contrast, Keith doesn't tune in to what he's doing and how he's affecting Caleb.

From that example, you might get the impression that it's best to be a high self-monitor. Self-monitoring certainly has its advantages. High self-monitors tend to be better at making whatever kind of impression they want to make, because they are aware of their communication behaviors and others' responses to them. They often find it easier than low self-monitors to put other people at ease in social situations. High self-monitors also tend to be good at figuring out what others are thinking and feeling, and that skill gives them a clear advantage in many social settings.

Being a low self-monitor also has advantages, however. Low self-monitors spend less time and energy thinking about their appearance and behavior, so they are probably more relaxed than high self-monitors in many situations. In addition, because they are less aware of, or concerned with, the impressions they make, they are often more straightforward communicators. They may even be seen as more genuine and trustworthy than high self-monitors.

• **self-fulfilling prophecy**
An expectation that gives rise to behaviors that cause the expectation to come true.

Self-Fulfilling Prophecy

Imagine meeting a new coworker whom you've heard other people describe as painfully shy. Because you don't want to make her uncomfortable, you spend little time talking to her when you meet her, and you don't invite her to join you and your friends for lunch. Consequently, she says little to you all day and eats lunch alone at her desk. You think to yourself, "I guess everyone was right about her; she *is* really shy." Why did your expectation about a shy coworker come true? Most likely, the cause is a phenomenon called a **self-fulfilling prophecy**—a situation in which a prediction causes people to act and communicate in ways that make that prediction come true.

How do self-fulfilling prophecies affect how we communicate? Sometimes our expectations influence our communication behavior, as when we're talking to someone we think is shy so we treat her as if she were shy. Similarly, when we expect our relationships to succeed, we behave in ways that strengthen them, and when we expect to be socially rejected, we perceive and react to rejection even when it isn't really there.[50]

There is one very important clarification here. For a prophecy to be self-fulfilling, it's not enough that you expect something to happen and then it does. Rather, it has to be the case that your expectation *causes* it to happen. To illustrate that point, let's say that yesterday morning you expected it to rain, and later it did rain. That isn't a self-fulfilling prophecy, because your expectation didn't cause the rain: it would have rained regardless of whether you thought it would. In other words, your expectation was fulfilled, but it was not *self*-fulfilled. A self-fulfilling prophecy is one in which the expectation itself causes the behaviors that make it come true.

COMPETENT COMMUNICATOR

Are You Happy with You? Measure Your Self-Esteem

How much do you agree with each of the following statements? On the line before each statement, record your level of agreement on a 1 to 7 scale. A higher number means you agree more; a lower number means you agree less.

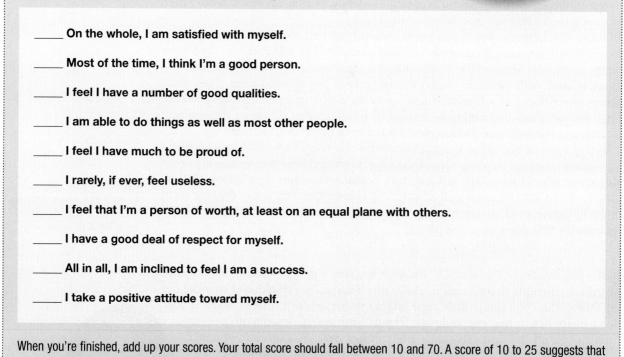

_____ On the whole, I am satisfied with myself.

_____ Most of the time, I think I'm a good person.

_____ I feel I have a number of good qualities.

_____ I am able to do things as well as most other people.

_____ I feel I have much to be proud of.

_____ I rarely, if ever, feel useless.

_____ I feel that I'm a person of worth, at least on an equal plane with others.

_____ I have a good deal of respect for myself.

_____ All in all, I am inclined to feel I am a success.

_____ I take a positive attitude toward myself.

When you're finished, add up your scores. Your total score should fall between 10 and 70. A score of 10 to 25 suggests that your self-esteem is relatively low right now. If you scored between 25 and 55, you have a moderate level of self-esteem. A score above 55 suggests that your self-esteem is relatively high.

SOURCE: Rosenberg, M. (1965). _Society and the adolescent self-image._ Princeton, NJ: Princeton University Press.

VALUING THE SELF: SELF-ESTEEM

Knowing your self-concept and _being happy with_ your self-concept are two different things. How do you feel about yourself? Are you satisfied with your looks? Your accomplishments? Your personality? Your relationships? Do you feel confident about and proud of who you are? Such questions concern your **self-esteem,** your subjective evaluation of your value and worth as a person.

Like self-monitoring, your level of self-esteem ranges along a continuum from high to low. If you evaluate yourself positively and feel happy about who you are, you probably have high self-esteem. In contrast, if you are pessimistic about your abilities and dissatisfied with your self-concept, you probably have low self-esteem. Take a minute to respond to the questions in "The Competent Communicator" to evaluate your level of self-esteem.

Maintaining a positive image of ourselves does appear to have its advantages when it comes to communication behavior. Individuals with higher self-esteem are generally more outgoing and more willing to communicate and build relationships with others.[51] They are more comfortable initiating relationships, and they're more likely to believe that their partners' expressions of love and support are genuine.[52]

• **self-esteem** One's subjective evaluation of one's value and worth as a person.

Despite its advantages, high self-esteem also has some drawbacks, particularly for adolescents and young adults. Although several researchers have speculated that having low self-esteem promotes aggressive and antisocial behavior, they found the reverse is true. Aggressive people tend to have higher self-esteem, not lower.[53] Adolescents with higher self-esteem are also more prone to be sexually active and to engage in risky sexual behaviors than teens with lower self-esteem.[54] Finally, when their relationships run into problems, people with high self-esteem are more likely than their low self-esteem counterparts to end those relationships and seek out new ones.[55]

In this section, we've considered that we perceive ourselves through our self-concepts, which are multifaceted and partly subjective. We've seen how we exercise awareness of our self-concepts through self-monitoring and self-fulfilling prophecies, and we've examined self-esteem and learned about its benefits and drawbacks. All those concepts help people to form and modify their perceptions of themselves. As we'll discover in the next section, people use a variety of communication behaviors to express their desired self-perceptions to others.

Managing Our Image

Our self-concept is related to *the way we see ourselves*. When we communicate with other people, we are also interested in *the way we want them to see us*. In some situations, we might want others to regard us as friendly, outgoing, and fun. In other situations, we might want people to view us as reliable, competent, and serious. Our concern is the kind of **image** we want to project—that is, the personal "face" we want others to see. In this section, we examine what scholars call image management, and we look into research that has shed light on that process.

In many situations, we carefully consider how we want others to perceive us. That is the process of image management.

COMMUNICATION AND IMAGE MANAGEMENT

The film *The Help* (2011) is set in Jackson, Mississippi, during the early 1960s. Minny Jackson (played by Octavia Spencer) is an African American maid who works for several upper-class white families. When her daughter, Sugar (played by Kelsey Scot), is forced to quit school and go to work as a maid to help support the family, Minny gives her several explicit lessons about managing her image with her employer. For instance, she teaches Sugar to serve coffee by setting the cup down in front of the person and pouring it—rather than handing the person a cup of coffee—"cause your hand can't touch." She advises Sugar to use the same cup and plate for her own meals every day, so she doesn't give the impression of having used her employer's china and silverware. And most important, says Minny, "No sass mouth." Those lessons come from Minny's years of experience managing her own image in the racially segregated South of the Civil Rights era.

The process of behavioral adjustment to project a desired image is known as **image management.** In the following discussion, we consider that image management is collaborative, that we manage multiple identities, and that managing an image is complex.

Image Management Is Collaborative To some extent, managing your image is an individual process. After all, your image is yours. Yet you also get a lot of help managing your image from the people around you. As psychologist Dan McAdams has suggested, each of us develops a **life story,** a way of presenting ourselves to others that is based on our self-concept but is also influenced by other people.[56]

• **image** The way one wishes to be seen or perceived by others.

• **image management** The process of projecting one's desired public image.

• **life story** A way of presenting oneself to others that is based on one's self-concept but is also influenced by other people.

Mental Illness: Would You Tell?

Experiencing a mental illness can be frightening, debilitating, and confusing. It can also cause patients and their families great shame, because people so frequently misunderstand mental illness and stigmatize those who have it.

Although mental illnesses vary substantially in their effects, many patients have difficulty deciding whether to disclose their condition to others. On the one hand, disclosing may help them acquire both medical and emotional support, and it may help others to become better educated about mental health. Disclosure can be risky, however. People suffering from mental illness may have several reasons for choosing not to disclose their condition:

- *Stigma:* They worry about others rejecting or even hurting them.
- *Privacy:* They are concerned that information about their illness will be shared without their consent.

- *Communication difficulties:* They don't know how to tell others about their condition.
- *Fear of discrimination:* They fear that employers, landlords, or others will discriminate against them.
- *Protection of others:* They don't want others to worry about them.

Despite those risks, talking about mental illness can be useful in many ways. Beyond helping individuals get the necessary medical attention and emotional support, disclosure can also help to reduce the fear and stigma associated with mental disease. It may also strengthen relationships, particularly with others who also struggle with mental health issues.

If others accept the image you portray, they'll tend to behave in ways that encourage that image. Let's say you see yourself as a confident person, and you project that image when you interact with others. If other people see you as confident, they'll treat you as though you are—and their behavior will strengthen that part of your identity in your own mind. If others don't accept the image of yourself that you portray, however, they may treat you as less credible or as untrustworthy.

Perhaps you have encountered people who seem as though they are trying to be someone they aren't, or who are portraying an image that you don't accept as genuine. Many of us find it hard to take such people seriously, and we react to them accordingly. In May 2011, New York Congressman Anthony Weiner came into the national spotlight amid allegations that he had sent sexually explicit photos of himself to a Twitter follower. For several days, Weiner publicly denied that he had sent the images and said that his office was investigating how his Twitter account could have been hacked. Finally, he admitted to sending the photos, apologized for his earlier denials, and announced his resignation from Congress. After more than a decade in the House of Representatives, Weiner left office ridiculed not only for tweeting explicit photos but also for denying his actions.

We Manage Multiple Identities If you think of all the people who know you, you'll probably realize that most of them know you only in certain contexts. You have your circle of friends, who know you as a friend. You have your family members, who might know you as a mother, a son, an aunt, a brother, a cousin, or a grandchild. Your boss and coworkers know you as an employee.

Each of those contexts carries its own distinctive role expectations, so you probably enact a somewhat different identity in each one. In fact, we all manage multiple identities. That is, we show different parts of ourselves to different people in our lives.

The challenge of managing multiple identities is especially pronounced for individuals with "invisible" medical conditions—illnesses or disorders that are not necessarily apparent to others. Conditions such as Down syndrome, stuttering, developmental disabilities, and confinement to a wheelchair are relatively visible in the sense that many people will notice those conditions after seeing or listening to someone who has them. However, individuals can, to varying degrees, hide the fact that they have other kinds of conditions, such as cancer, diabetes, asthma, and depression, if they don't want others to know. Most people can't identify someone with diabetes or asthma, for example, simply by observing the person.

People with invisible conditions have both the responsibility and the ability to determine how to incorporate their conditions into the image they project. Many individuals with such conditions must continually decide whom to tell about their conditions, when to make those disclosures, and how to do so. That decision can be particularly agonizing for individuals suffering from invisible conditions that are also socially stigmatized, such as mental health disorders and HIV-positive status, because of the fear of how others will react to their disclosures. "The Dark Side of Communication" addresses this issue as it pertains to individuals who are mentally ill.

getCONNECTED
Managing Multiple Identities Online

In the virtual world of the Internet, a person can create and maintain as many different identities as he or she chooses, simply by generating multiple e-mail addresses or web pages or participating in various virtual communities.[57] For instance, you might have one e-mail address associated with your college or university that indicates both your name and the school (mine is kory.floyd@asu.edu). You might have another address from a free e-mail server, such as Yahoo or Gmail, containing no identifying information about yourself (for example, mybro4816@gmail.com). Perhaps you use such an anonymous address when you want to communicate online without revealing your identity. In virtual communities, such as chat rooms and Second Life, you can even manipulate your identity to appear as though you are of a different gender, different ethnicity, or even a different species.[58] Some people may create multiple online identities to protect themselves when interacting with strangers; others may do so for amusement or to explore various aspects of their personalities.

One online venue in which portraying multiple identities is surprisingly *un*common is the blog, a website that features running commentary, news, and/or personal thoughts about one or more topics. Although some blogs belong to companies or organizations, many are created and maintained by individuals—most frequently adolescents—who often use them as a type of online diary. A 2004 study of communication on personal blogs found that 67 percent of bloggers provided their real names on their blogs, whether their full names (31 percent) or just their first names (36 percent). In contrast, only 29 percent used a fake name, with the remainder providing no name whatsoever. Further, more than half the bloggers in the study provided explicit demographic information about themselves, such as their age, occupation, or geographic location.[59]

More recent research has found that male bloggers are more likely than their female counterparts to provide information about their location, to use emoticons that indicate sadness or flirtatiousness, and to reveal their sexual identity as homosexual. In comparison, female bloggers are more likely to include links to their personal web pages.[60]

Image Management Is Complex Image management is often complicated and may generate competing goals for our interactions with others. Let's say you need to ask your parents to lend you money. You want them to think of you as a responsible adult who will pay them back in a timely manner. You therefore have to present your request in a way that projects your image as a mature person who makes good decisions. At the same time, though, you want to persuade them that you really need the money. That goal may prompt you to project the image that you need help. Thus, you may find your image needs in conflict: you want to appear responsible but also in need of assistance. Managing those competing image needs—while still persuading your parents to lend you money—can be complex.

Research indicates that people rarely manage multiple blog identities. Instead, most bloggers provide their real name and reveal true demographic information about themselves.

• **face** A person's desired public image.

• **facework** The behaviors people use to establish and maintain their desired public image with others.

• **face needs** Important components of one's desired public image.

In relationships, people try to project a desired public image, known as *face*.

Communication researcher Myra Goldschmidt found that when people ask others for favors, they often create narratives—ways of telling their stories—that help them to maintain their image while still being persuasive.[61] To your parents, you might make such statements as "I'll be able to pay you back as soon as I get my financial aid check" and "I'll even pay interest on the loan." Such strategies can help preserve your image as a responsible individual even in a situation where that image might be threatened.

We've seen that managing your image is a collaborative process that often requires you to negotiate several identities in a complex way. How do we determine what our image needs are in the first place?

COMMUNICATION AND FACE NEEDS

Helping someone "save face" means helping that person to avoid embarrassment and preserve dignity in a situation where that dignity is threatened. The very reason we hate getting embarrassed is that it threatens the image of ourselves we're trying to project, and that threat is a function of our need to save face. Sometimes we associate the concept of saving face with collectivistic cultures such as Korea and Japan. In reality, saving face is important in many cultures.[62] Let's consider what happens when our desired public image is threatened.

Face and Face Needs Each of us has a desired public image—a certain way that we want others to see and think of us—and we work to maintain that image through the ways we communicate. For instance, if you want others to see you as intelligent and competent, you will likely communicate in ways that nurture that impression and will try to avoid situations that would make you look uninformed or incompetent. Sociologist Erving Goffman coined the term **face** to describe our desired public image and the term **facework** to describe the behaviors we use to project that image to others.[63]

Researchers believe our face is made up of three different **face needs,** or important components of our desired public image.[64] You might find it easy to remember those face needs by noting that the first letters of their names—fellowship, autonomy, and competence—are also the first three letters in the word *face*.

Fellowship face refers to the need to have others like and accept us. That is the part of our identity that motivates us to make friends, join clubs and social groups, and communicate pleasantly with others. **Autonomy face** refers to our need to avoid being imposed on by others. It's our autonomy face that motivates us to be in control of our time and resources and to avoid having other people make decisions for us. Finally, **competence face** is our need to be respected—to have others acknowledge our abilities and intelligence. That need drives us to seek careers and hobbies in which we can excel and to avoid situations that will embarrass us.

Face Threats Each of us has a different desired public image, so our face needs vary. Some people have a very strong fellowship face need, meaning it is extremely important that others like them. Other people much prefer to be respected rather than liked. Similarly, one person may have a very high need for autonomy, whereas another person doesn't mind having decisions made for him or her. Those differences are part of what makes everyone's identity unique.

We often become consciously aware of our face needs only when they're threatened. Let's say you apply to join an honor society but are not accepted. The decision not to include you could threaten your fellowship face. It could also threaten your competence face by making you feel you aren't smart enough to get into the group. The rejection of your application, therefore, is a **face-threatening act** because it hinders the fulfillment of one or more of your face needs.

Face-threatening acts often lead people to behave in ways that help them restore their face. In the case of the honor society, you might say to others, "I didn't really want to be in that group anyway."[65] In truth, you probably *did* want to be in the honor society, or you wouldn't have applied. So, you would likely make such a statement as a way of managing your image with others—that is, you want it to *appear* that your face needs have not been threatened. Your statement is thus a type of *defense mechanism*—a response that minimizes the effects of a face-threatening act.

Face Threats in Socially Marginalized Groups Face threats are common in many socially marginalized populations. For example, many elderly people experience threats to their autonomy face as a result of physical and cognitive limitations associated with aging.[66] Similarly, people with certain disabilities may perceive threats to their autonomy face if they are unable to do activities that others can do, such as driving a car. Still other groups may feel their autonomy is jeopardized when they don't have the legal authority to make certain decisions for themselves, as in the case of lesbian and gay adults who (in most states) cannot choose to marry their romantic partners.

Being marginalized also leads many people to feel disrespected and shamed. Such feelings can threaten both their fellowship face and their competence face. In U.S. society, for example, there are stigmas associated with being homeless, poor, unemployed, old, disabled, lesbian, gay, mentally ill, and (in some circles) divorced, even though a person may have no choice about belonging to any of these groups.[67] Stigmatized people might feel that they don't fit in with those around them, and those perceptions threaten their fellowship face by making them feel unaccepted. They may also perceive that others judge them not on the basis of their intelligence or abilities but because of their stigmatized condition. Such perceptions threaten their competence face by causing them to feel disrespected.

Whether we're aware of it or not, each of us is constantly managing our public image, hoping that others perceive us the way we want them to. Through communication behavior, we manage multiple identities in multiple ways, and we protect our face needs and respond to situations that threaten them.

- **fellowship face** The need to be liked and accepted by others.

- **autonomy face** The need to avoid being imposed on by others.

- **competence face** The need to be respected and viewed as competent and intelligent.

- **face-threatening act** Any behavior that threatens one or more face needs.

SHARPEN Your Skills: *Minimizing face threats*

With others in your class, role-play a conversation in which you have to criticize someone else's work. Practice delivering your critiques to one another in ways that minimize face threats for the recipients.

- **How do we form perceptions of others?** Perceiving others is a process whereby we select information for attention, organize that information according to a perceptual schema, and then interpret it to give it meaning.

- **What influences our perceptions?** Our cultural background, stereotypes, primacy and recency effects, and perceptual sets are among the most potent influences on our perceptions. Our attributions for behavior are also influenced by the self-serving bias and the fundamental attribution error.

- **How do we manage our image?** Over the course of life, we create and refine a self-concept. Our communication behavior reflects our self-concept through the way we manage our image, both in person and online.

POP QUIZ

Multiple Choice

1. Noticing that someone is a communication major is an example of the schema for classifying information about people known as

   a. physical.

   b. interaction.

   c. psychological.

   d. role.

2. When Jacob makes attributions about his roommate's communication behaviors, his attributions might include all the following dimensions *except*

   a. locus.

   b. stability.

   c. controllability.

   d. self-serving bias.

3. The predisposition to perceive only what we want or expect to perceive is known as

   a. interpretation.

   b. perceptual set.

   c. attribution.

   d. perceptual schema.

4. The Johari window is a representation of self that consists of all the following parts *except*

   a. open.

   b. hidden.

   c. visual.

   d. unknown.

5. The need to avoid being imposed on by others is known as

   a. fellowship face.

   b. competence face.

   c. saving face.

   d. autonomy face.

Fill in the Blanks

6. The first of the three stages of perception is the _____ stage.

7. According to the _____, first impressions are crucial because they set the tone for future interactions.

8. The _____ causes us to attribute others' communication behaviors more to internal causes than to external causes.

9. The subjective evaluation of one's value and worth as a person is known as one's _____.

10. A _____ is a behavior that threatens one's face needs.

ANSWERS: 1. d; 2. d; 3. b; 4. c; 5. d; 6. selection; 7. primacy effect; 8. fundamental attribution error; 9. self-esteem; 10. face-threatening act

KEY TERMS

perception 56
selection 58
organization 58
perceptual schema 58
interpretation 59
stereotype 61
primacy effect 62
recency effect 63
perceptual set 63
attribution 64
self-serving bias 65
fundamental attribution error 66
self-concept 67
identity 67
Johari window 67
self-fulfilling prophecy 69
self-esteem 70
image 71
image management 71
life story 71
face 74
facework 74
face needs 74
fellowship face 75
autonomy face 75
competence face 75
face-threatening act 75

HOW WE USE LANGUAGE

What's in a Word?

"Hi. I'm Dr. Patti McCarver, and I'm your nurse." That's how McCarver, a registered nurse who recently returned to school to earn a doctorate, introduces herself to patients. Her words are fueling a national controversy over use of the word "doctor." Technically, a doctor is anyone who has a doctorate degree, including many college professors—yet physicians claim that most patients automatically equate "doctor" with "physician," and for decades only physicians used the title. As more nurses, pharmacists, physical therapists, and other health care providers gain doctorate degrees in their respective fields, however, they earn the right to use that title as well, which physicians claim will only confuse patients. Some states forbid non-physicians to call themselves "doctor"—regardless of their education—unless they immediately specify their profession, as McCarver did. What do you think? Should nurses with doctorate degrees call themselves "Doctor," or should that word be reserved for physicians?

▶ As You READ

- What are the defining characteristics of language?
- For what reasons do people use language?
- How can you use language more effectively?

Words can shape our lives in extraordinary ways. By announcing in 1776 that "all men are created equal," Thomas Jefferson and the Second Continental Congress declared to the world the emergence of a new sovereign nation founded on the principle of individual liberty. Nearly two centuries later, Martin Luther King, Jr., described his vision for civil rights and racial equality by proclaiming, "I have a dream." In those and many other cases throughout history, powerful words have inspired women and men to enact dramatic social change.

Because language can be so consequential, we have to choose our words carefully in many situations. Using the right words in a job interview, a political campaign, and a marriage proposal may make the difference between failure and success. Being a competent communicator therefore requires us to use language in a deliberate and informed way.

The Nature of Language

Abraham Lincoln was reportedly fond of asking people, "How many legs does a dog have if you call its tail a leg?" Think about how you would respond to that question. Many replied that if you call the dog's tail a leg, then a dog has five legs. Lincoln answered that dogs have only four legs, because calling a tail a leg doesn't make it one.

Some would say the former U.S. president was correct and that simply changing the way we talk about an object doesn't change the nature of the object itself. Others, however, would observe that Lincoln's assessment was incorrect, that words have only the meanings we choose to assign them. Thus the term *leg* means what it does only because English language speakers give that meaning to it—so, if we call a tail a leg, it is therefore a leg. Lincoln's riddle illustrates one reason why it's so important for us to understand language: We use words to refer to objects, events, ideas, and other entities in the real world, but most words have only the meanings that we, as the users of a language, give them.

• **language** A structured system of symbols used for communicating meaning.

What is language in the first place? **Language** is a structured system of symbols used for communicating meaning. You can probably think of many behaviors and items that represent or symbolize some type of meaning. A smile often symbolizes happiness, for instance; a red traffic light symbolizes the need to stop. Many gestures also have symbolic meaning, in that they represent a particular concept or idea. For example, you probably wave to say "hello" and shrug your shoulders to indicate "I don't know." Although facial expressions, traffic lights, and gestures all symbolize meaning, however, none qualifies as language. Why? The answer is that language is characterized by the use of a specific type of symbol: words.[1]

Words are the building blocks of language and verbal communication. As we'll see in this chapter, we use them to represent ideas, observations, feelings, and thoughts. Words—whether we speak or write them—can have a profound influence on how we relate to others. In this section, we'll see that language is symbolic, is usually arbitrary, is governed by rules, has layers of meaning, varies in clarity, and is bound by context and culture.

LANGUAGE IS SYMBOLIC

When we say language is symbolic, we mean that each word represents a particular object or idea, but it does not constitute the object or idea itself. For example, the word *textbook* represents a bound or online collection of printed material to be read as a supplement for lectures and in-class activities in a course. The word itself is not the object, though; it merely symbolizes it. Similarly, the word *five* represents a specific quantity of something (one more than four, and one fewer than six), yet the word itself is not the quantity; it simply represents it.

One way to understand the symbolic nature of language is to remember that different languages often have different words for the same object. The English word *textbook*, for instance, is *läromedel* in Swedish, 教科書 in Japanese, учебник in Bulgarian, and *kitabu* in Swahili. Those are completely different symbols, but they all represent the same entity, a textbook. If you were to invent your own language, you could create any term you wanted to represent the concept of a textbook.

We often acquire new words, and new meanings for older words, as technology advances. The widespread use of computer-mediated communication, for instance, has added new terms to our everyday conversations, such as *blog*, *e-mail*, and *instant messaging*. In addition, it has generated new meanings for existing words, such as *web*, *crash*, *tweet*, and *net*. As computer technology continues to develop, new words will likely be added to our vocabulary to help us communicate about it.

LANGUAGE IS USUALLY ARBITRARY

Why do words symbolize the particular objects and ideas they do? For the most part, words have only an arbitrary connection to their meanings. Think of the word *car*. That word doesn't look or sound like a car, so why does it make us think of one? The only reason is that speakers of English have agreed to give the word *car* that particular meaning. They could just as easily have called cars "hanners" or "steeks" or "rayverts." Those words don't mean anything to speakers of English, but they would if we were to assign them a meaning. The point is that the meaning of almost all words is arbitrary: words literally mean whatever we, as users of a language, choose for them to mean.

Language can be arbitrary precisely *because* it is symbolic. As we saw above, words only symbolize their meanings; they don't constitute their meanings themselves. For that reason we can select almost any word to symbolize a particular meaning, and so the connection between language and meaning is arbitrary.

In that sense, then, Abraham Lincoln was wrong when he said that calling a tail a leg doesn't make it one. It's true that calling a tail a leg doesn't change any of its physical properties, but because of the arbitrary nature of language, we can choose to make *leg* the appropriate term to describe a tail . . . or a rainbow, a fishing boat, a salt shaker, or any other object or idea we wish to describe.

LANGUAGE IS GOVERNED BY RULES

We have said that language is symbolic and that the meaning of most words is arbitrary. If those statements are both true, then how do we all understand one another? The answer is that every language is governed by rules.

You already know many of the rules that frame your native language. Even if you can't explain them, you usually take notice when they're violated. To a native speaker of English, for instance, the statement "I filled the bottle with water" sounds correct, but "I filled water into the bottle" does not. Even if you aren't quite sure *why* the second sentence sounds wrong, you probably still recognize that it does. Along the same lines, when you learn a new language, you don't learn just the words; you also learn the rules for how the words work together to convey meaning.

New words are constantly being added to our language. In 2005, comedian Stephen Colbert coined the word *truthiness* as a way to describe something that feels true, despite any reliable evidence.

Why do we call a car a car?

Researchers distinguish among four different types of language rules:

- *Phonological rules* deal with the correct pronunciation of a word, and they vary from language to language. If you speak French, for example, you know that the proper way to pronounce *travail* is "trah-VYE." According to English phonological rules, however, the word looks as though it should be pronounced "trah-VALE."

- *Syntactic rules* govern the order of words within phrases and clauses. The question, "What is your name?" makes sense to an English speaker because the words are in the proper order. To ask the same question in American Sign Language, a system of visual signs used by hearing-impaired people to communicate, we would sign "your – name – what?" Signing "what – your – name?" is incorrect because it violates the syntactic rules of American Sign Language.

- *Semantic rules* have to do with the meaning of individual words. Those meanings may be arbitrary, as we saw above, but speakers of a language agree on them. When you hear the word *lawyer*, for instance, you think of an attorney, not a paper mill or a cell phone or a Caribbean vacation. It is a semantic rule that connects *lawyer* with *attorney* and not with one of those other meanings.

- *Pragmatic rules* deal with the implications or interpretations of statements. "Nice to meet you" is a common greeting among speakers of English. Depending on the context and the speaker's tone of voice, you might think the speaker really *is* happy to meet you, or you might infer that he or she is just saying so to be polite. If there's a sarcastic tone in the speaker's voice, you might even infer that he or she is *unhappy* to meet you. In each instance, pragmatic rules lead you to your conclusion.

As children acquire a language, they gain an almost intuitive sense of its phonological, syntactic, semantic, and pragmatic rules. That knowledge allows native speakers of a language to speak and write fluently. In contrast, people who are less familiar with the language are more likely to violate those rules by mistake.[2] You'll read about one career that requires mastery of the rules of the English language in the "Putting Communication to Work" box.

- **denotative meaning** The literal meaning of a word.

- **connotative meaning** The ideas or concepts a word suggests in addition to its literal definition.

No matter how we communicate verbally, we observe phonological, syntactic, semantic, and pragmatic rules for language.

LANGUAGE HAS LAYERS OF MEANING

Many words imply certain ideas that are separate from their literal meanings. The literal meaning of a word—the way a dictionary defines it—is its **denotative meaning.** Think of the word *home*, for instance. Its denotative meaning is "a shelter used as a residence." When you hear the word *home*, however, you may also think along the lines of "a place where I feel safe, accepted, and loved" or "a space where I am free to do whatever I want." Those are examples of the word's **connotative meaning,** the ideas or concepts the word suggests in addition to its literal definition.

The Semantic Triangle To illustrate the relationship between words and their denotative and connotative meanings, psychologist Charles Ogden and English professor Ivor Richards developed the *semantic triangle* (Figure 4.1).[3] In its three corners, the semantic triangle portrays three necessary elements for identifying the meaning in language. The first element is the *symbol*, which is the word being communicated. In the second corner is the *reference*, which is the word's connotative meaning. Finally, there's the *referent*, which is the denotative meaning.

If several listeners hear the same word, they might attribute the same denotative meaning to it even if they have different connotative meanings. For instance, if I say the word *euthanasia*, the word itself is the symbol, and its referent is a medically assisted death. To one listener, the word evokes images of a merciful end to someone's pain and suffering. To another person, it evokes images of homicide. It makes other listeners think of an unfortunate but sometimes justified component of the death experience. Those are all differences in the word's reference, or connotative meaning, rather than in its denotative meaning. The semantic triangle therefore illustrates how people can hear the same words yet derive quite different meanings from them.

Loaded Language In February 2009, President Barack Obama signed into law the American Recovery and Reinvestment Act of 2009, an economic stimulus package authorizing the federal government to spend nearly $800 billion to improve infrastructure and education and expand unemployment benefits and other social welfare programs. The law was highly controversial, and the controversy was reflected in the language people used to describe it. For those who favored it, the Recovery and Reinvestment Act was a "rescue plan," but for many who opposed it, it was a "bailout." Both those terms are examples of **loaded language,** words with strongly positive or negative connotations. Notice that the term *rescue plan* sounds positive because

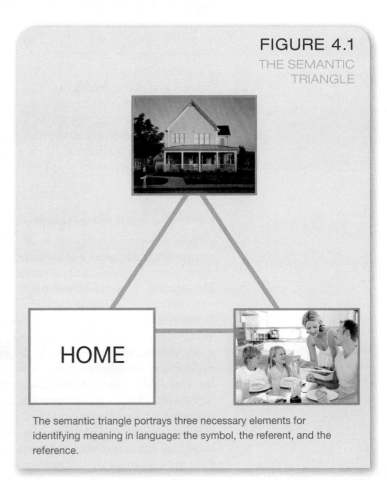

FIGURE 4.1
THE SEMANTIC TRIANGLE

The semantic triangle portrays three necessary elements for identifying meaning in language: the symbol, the referent, and the reference.

it conjures images of a hero saving the innocent victims of a crisis. The term *bailout*, however, sounds negative because it connotes begrudgingly helping people deal with problems they themselves have created.

Loaded language reflects the fact that denotations and connotations represent different layers of meaning. At a denotative level, for instance, the word *cancer* simply refers to a malignant growth or tumor in the body. For many people, however, the term connotes any evil condition that spreads destructively. For instance, you might hear someone describe conditions such as poverty and bigotry as "cancers on society." That example illustrates that people can use the word *cancer* as a loaded term when they wish to evoke feelings of fear, disgust, or anger on the part of listeners. People can also use loaded words to evoke positive emotions. Terms such as *family* and *freedom* have emotionally positive connotations even if their denotative meanings are emotionally neutral.[4]

LANGUAGE VARIES IN CLARITY

Josh is driving his brother Jeremy to a doctor's appointment, and Jeremy has the directions. As they approach an intersection, they have the following conversation:

> **Josh:** *I need to turn left at this next light, don't I?*

> **Jeremy:** *Right.*

Which way should Josh turn? Was Jeremy saying that Josh was accurate in thinking that he should turn left, or was he correcting Josh by instructing him to turn right? We don't really know, because Jeremy has used **ambiguous language** by making a statement that we can interpret to have more than one meaning.

A certain amount of ambiguity is inherent in our language. In fact, according to the *Oxford English Dictionary*, the 500 most frequently used words in the English language have an average of 23 different meanings each. The word *set* has so many different meanings—nearly 200, more than any other English word—that it takes the *Oxford English Dictionary* 60,000 words to define it![5] One reason language varies in clarity is that some words are more *concrete* than others. A word that is concrete refers to a specific object in the physical world, such as a particular laptop computer, a specific restaurant, or an individual person. In contrast, a word that is *abstract* refers to a broader category or organizing concept of objects. According to English professor Samuel Hayakawa, words can be arrayed along a "ladder of abstraction" that shows their progression from more abstract to more concrete.[6]

Figure 4.2 gives an example of Hayakawa's ladder of abstraction. At the bottom of the ladder is a reference to all living beings, which is a broad, abstract category. As we move upward in the diagram, the concepts become more and more concrete, referencing all animals and then all mammals, all primates, all *Homo sapiens*, and all females before reaching the most concrete reference to a specific individual.

LANGUAGE IS BOUND BY CONTEXT AND CULTURE

Finally, meaning in language is affected by the social and cultural context in which people use it. Societies and cultures differ in their degree of individualism and their use of communication codes. Many of those differences are evident in verbal messages. For instance, "I'm looking out for Number One" is a very individualistic message that would be relatively uncommon in a collectivistic society. In fact, a common saying in Japan, and one that reflects that nation's collectivistic culture, states, "It is the nail that sticks out that gets hammered down."[7]

In what became known as the **Sapir-Whorf hypothesis,** anthropologist Edward Sapir and linguist Benjamin Whorf proposed that language shapes our views of reality. Their notion was that language influences the ways members of a culture see the world—and that a society's attitudes and behaviors are reflected in its language.[8] The Sapir-Whorf hypothesis embodies two specific principles. The first, *linguistic determinism*, suggests that the structure of language determines how we think. In other words, we can conceive of something only if we have a term for it in our vocabulary.[9] Imagine a language that includes no term describing the emotion of envy. According to the principle of linguistic determinism, people who speak that language would not experience envy because they have no words to describe it.

The second principle, *linguistic relativity*, suggests that because language determines our perceptions of reality, people see the world differently depending on which language they speak. Whorf discovered, for instance, that the language of the Hopi Indians of the American Southwest makes no distinction between nouns and verbs. Whereas English uses nouns to refer to *things* and verbs to refer to *actions*, the Hopi language describes just about everything as an action or a process. Compared to English speakers, then, the Hopi tend to see the world as being constantly in motion.[10]

The Sapir-Whorf hypothesis is provocative, but is it true? Check out the "Fact or Fiction?" box for insight into this question.

Appreciating the Power of Words

English writer Rudyard Kipling, author of *The Jungle Book*, once called words "the most powerful drug used by mankind." To understand his point, think about how you feel when someone you love expresses affection to you, or when you listen to a speech by a politician you dislike, or when you comfort a friend who is grieving the loss of a family member. Words can literally change a person's day—or a person's life—in positive or negative ways.

Entire books have been written about the power of language. Here we focus on four important functions that language serves in our daily lives. Specifically, we'll discover that language expresses who we are, connects us to others, separates us from others, and motivates action.

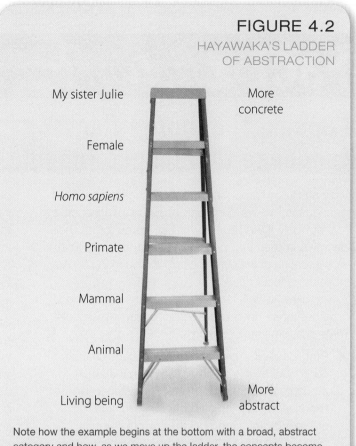

FIGURE 4.2
HAYAWAKA'S LADDER OF ABSTRACTION

My sister Julie — More concrete

Female

Homo sapiens

Primate

Mammal

Animal

Living being — More abstract

Note how the example begins at the bottom with a broad, abstract category and how, as we move up the ladder, the concepts become more and more concrete and specific.

LANGUAGE EXPRESSES WHO WE ARE

Think about playing a game in which you have to select one word to represent your identity. Should you pick an adjective, such as *adventurous, conservative,* or *shy?* Maybe you should choose a verb instead, such as *think, sing,* or *run.* That game is challenging because any word we choose might represent a part of who we are but may not represent us fully. As humans, we express our identities in many ways—by our clothes, jobs, preferred leisure activities, and the language we use to communicate with others.

Language expresses who we are in at least two ways: by naming and identifying us and by enhancing our credibility. Let's take a look at each.

Names Define and Differentiate Us What's something that belongs to you yet is constantly used by others? The answer is *your name.* By itself, a name is simply a linguistic device that identifies something or someone. Your name does more, however, than differentiate you from others—it's also an important component of your sense of self. Naming is therefore one way you gain information about other people and represent yourself to the world.

Fact or *fiction*?

I Speak, Therefore I Think: Language Determines Thought

Sapir and Whorf proposed that our thoughts are rooted in language, so we can think about or experience a concept only if we have a word or words for it. Their idea also implies that people will see the world differently *because of the differences in their languages.* Are those ideas fact or fiction?

It's hard to tell for certain, but the Sapir-Whorf hypothesis has been widely criticized by researchers. Three criticisms are common:

- First, although it proposes that language shapes our thoughts, it is equally possible that our thoughts shape our language. For instance, an experienced fashion designer might look at four different jackets and label their colors "scarlet," "ruby," "crimson," and "vermilion." You might look at the same jackets and call them all "red." Does the designer think of the four colors as different because she has more terms for them than you do? Or does she have more terms because she has more experience thinking about differences among colors? Both ideas are possible.

- Second, not having a word for a particular experience doesn't necessarily mean that people don't have that experience. English speakers may occasionally feel pleasure at the misfortunes of others, for instance, even if they don't have a word to describe that feeling, which is called *Schadenfreude* in German.

- Third, as linguist Steven Pinker has pointed out, even people who don't acquire language, perhaps because of mental deficiencies, are able to think, count, and interact with others; they would not be able to do those things if language determined thought.

Those criticisms don't necessarily mean that the Sapir-Whorf hypothesis is entirely wrong. They do suggest, however, that language doesn't shape and constrain our ways of thinking to the extent that Sapir and Whorf believed.

ASK YOURSELF

- What did you think of the Sapir-Whorf hypothesis when you first read about it? Did it seem reasonable or unreasonable to you at first? Why?
- Do you think only in words? Do you ever think in numbers or colors or sounds?

SOURCE: Pinker, S. (1994). *The language instinct*. New York: HarperCollins.

A person's first name, for instance, can suggest information about the person's characteristics. One such characteristic is the person's sex. In Western societies, we usually assign names such as Jacob, Michael, and Caleb only to males and names such as Emma, Savannah, and Nicole only to females. Names can also provide clues about a person's ethnicity. You might infer that LaKeisha is African American, Huong is Asian, and Santiago is Latino. Because names go in and out of style over time, some names even suggest a person's age group, so you might assume that Jennifer, Emily, and Hannah are younger than Edna, Mildred, and Bertha.

In addition to demographic information, names can suggest information about our disposition and sense of self. For instance, we might perceive an adult man who goes by the name Richard differently from one who goes by Ricky, even though those are two forms of the same name. Indeed, research shows that we do make assumptions about people—accurately or not—on the basis of their names.[11] In one study, people made more positive evaluations of men named David, Jon, Joshua, and Gregory than they did of men named Oswald, Myron, Reginald, and Edmund, even though they were given no other information about the men.[12] Other studies have shown that people whose names strongly suggest a nonwhite ethnicity sometimes experience discrimination based only on their names.[13]

Language Enhances or Diminishes Credibility A second way in which words express who we are is by reflecting our credibility. **Credibility** is the extent to which others perceive us to be competent and trustworthy. Some speakers have credibility on certain topics because of their training and expertise. You'll probably have more confidence in medical advice if you hear it from a doctor, for instance, than from the barista at your local coffee shop. If the advice is about making a great latte, however, you'll probably trust your barista more than your doctor. In either case, you are assigning credibility on the basis of the speaker's specific expertise.

Language is intimately tied to issues of credibility. Irrespective of our training or credentials, our words can portray us as confident, trustworthy communicators, or they can make us appear unsure of ourselves. In either situation, our ability to get what we want is affected by the credibility our language use gives us. As we'll see next, several specific forms of language have the potential to enhance or diminish our credibility.

Clichés *Clichés* are words or phrases that were novel at one time but have lost their effect owing to overuse. When politicians talk about "making a difference" or business leaders refer to "thinking outside the box," they may lose credibility with their audiences; those phrases are clichés that can make speakers sound uninformed or out-of-touch. Even if a cliché expresses the point you want to make, you will usually be more persuasive if you use different words. Encouraging someone to "evaluate your situation from a new perspective" can be more powerful than telling the person to "think outside the box," because the latter phrase is so overused.

Dialects We can also enhance or diminish our credibility by using *dialects*, language variations shared by people of a certain region or social class. For instance, whether you call a soft drink a "soda," a "pop," a "coke," or something else depends largely on where you grew up. As Figure 4.3 shows, "pop" is the favored term in the U.S. northwest and midwest, whereas "coke" is used mostly in the south, and "soda" is favored in the southwest and northeast. According to *communication accommodation theory*, developed by communication scholars Howard Giles and John Wiemann, we may be able to enhance our credibility by speaking in a dialect that is familiar to our audience.[14] In contrast, when we use a dialect different from that of our listeners, they may see us as an outsider and question our credibility.

Equivocation Another form of language that sometimes influences a speaker's credibility is *equivocation*, language that disguises the speaker's true intentions through strategic ambiguity. We often choose to use equivocal language when we're in a dilemma, a situation in which none of our options is a good one. Suppose, for example, that you're asked to provide a reference for your friend Dylan, who is applying for a job on your town's police force. One of the questions you're asked is how well Dylan handles pressure. Even though Dylan is your friend, you can immediately think of several occasions when he hasn't dealt well with pressure. Now you're in a bind. On the one

• **credibility** The extent to which others perceive us to be competent and trustworthy.

A barista has credibility when it comes to making great coffee but not when it comes to giving medical advice.

FIGURE 4.3

DIALECT DIFFERENCES IN NAMES FOR SOFT DRINKS

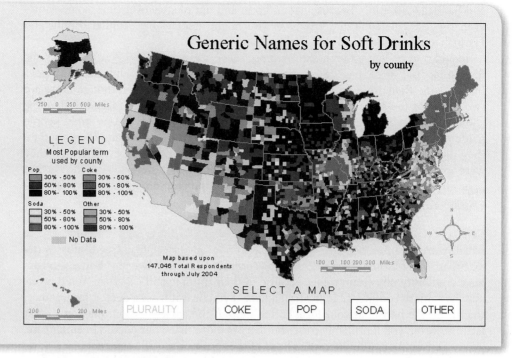

Generic Names for Soft Drinks
by county

LEGEND
Most Popular term used by county

Pop
30% - 50%
50% - 80%
80% - 100%

Coke
30% - 50%
50% - 80%
80% - 100%

Soda
30% - 50%
50% - 80%
80% - 100%

Other
30% - 50%
50% - 80%
80% - 100%

No Data

Map based upon 147,046 Total Respondents through July 2004

SELECT A MAP

PLURALITY | COKE | POP | SODA | OTHER

SOURCE: "Generic Names for Soft Drinks By County," Matthew Campbell and Prof. Greg Plumb, East Central University, Oklahoma, retrieved via http://popvssoda.com/countystats/total-county.html on June 8, 2012.

hand, you want Dylan to get the job because he's your friend. On the other hand, you don't want to lie to the police lieutenant who's phoning you for the reference.

Several studies have shown that when we're faced with two unappealing choices we often use equivocal language.[15] You might tell the lieutenant, "Well, it depends; there are different kinds of pressure." As you can probably tell, that statement doesn't give the lieutenant much information at all. Instead, it might imply that you don't know how well Dylan deals with pressure, but you don't want to admit that you don't know. It might also imply that you do know how well Dylan handles pressure but don't want to say. In either case, you are likely to come across as less credible than if you had answered the question directly.[16] Researchers John Daly, Carol Diesel, and David Weber have suggested that those sorts of conversational dilemmas are common and that we frequently use equivocal language in them.[17]

Weasel Words A form of language related to equivocation is *weasel words*, terms or phrases intended to mislead listeners by implying something they don't actually say. Advertisers often use weasel words when making claims about their products. When you hear that "four out of five dentists prefer" a certain brand of toothpaste, the implication is that 80 percent of *all* dentists prefer that brand. That level of preference would be really impressive—but the statement does not actually make that specific claim. For all we know, only five dentists were surveyed. If that were the case, the support of "four out of five" would appear much less impressive.

Allness Statements One specific form of weasel words is an *allness statement*, a statement implying that a claim is true without exception. For instance, when you hear someone claim that "experts agree that corporal punishment is emotionally damaging to children," the implication is that *all* experts agree. Note, however, that the speaker provides no evidence to back up that implication. Likewise, when someone says, "There's no known cure for depression," the implication is that no cure exists. All the statement *actually* means, however, is that no cure is known to the speaker.

Naming and enhancing our credibility aren't the only ways language reflects who we are, but they are among the most noticeable. We also use language to form positive connections with others, as we'll consider next.

LANGUAGE CONNECTS US TO OTHERS

For many years, the telecommunications company AT&T ran an advertising campaign whose slogan was, "Reach out and touch someone." The phrase was meant to suggest that by calling someone on the telephone, we could establish or reinforce a personal bond with that person. Today, many of us use social networking sites such as Facebook for the same purposes: to meet new people and to stay connected with those we already know. Even texting and tweeting help us to reinforce relational bonds with others, as some of the abbreviations in Table 4.1 illustrate.

Language can help us to connect with others; it allows us to express affection, provide comfort and support, and share social information. Let's look at each of those primary social functions of language.

Language Expresses Affection Think about the people in your life to whom you feel the closest. How do you convey your feelings of love and appreciation to them? Although you probably use some nonverbal behaviors—such as smiling, hugging, and kissing—chances are you also express your feelings verbally.

Language has a profound ability to communicate affection. Some statements express our fondness for another person, such as "I like you." Others reinforce the importance of our relationship with the person, such as "You're my best friend." Still others convey hopes or dreams for the future of the relationship, including "I can't wait until we get married." Finally, some statements express the value of the relationship by noting how we would feel without it, such as "My life would be empty without you." Statements such as those are characteristic of our closest personal relationships.

Research indicates that communicating affection is good both for relationships and for the people in them. Family studies researcher Ted Huston and his colleagues found that the more affection spouses communicated to each other during their first 2 years of marriage, the more likely they were to remain married 13 years later.[18] Other studies have found that expressing and receiving affection can produce several health benefits, including lower stress hormones,[19] better cardiovascular health,[20] lower cholesterol,[21] an improved ability to recover from stress,[22] lower average blood sugar (a risk factor for diabetes),[23] better mental health,[24] and lesser risk of developing clinical depression and anxiety.[25]

Language Provides Comfort From time to time, you probably need to comfort someone in distress. Your spoken exchanges with the individual can be mundane, as when you soothe a child with a stubbed toe, or they can occur in extraordinary circumstances, as when you offer support to someone grieving the death of his or her romantic partner. Perhaps you can recall situations when you have been in distress yourself and another's comforting words calmed you.

We also use written messages to convey support to others. Consider that the U.S. greeting card industry is a $10 billion-a-year business. Although people send cards to acknowledge birthdays and communicate good wishes for holidays, they also use get-well and sympathy cards to extend verbal messages of comfort.[26] Cards can also express gratitude or convey hope. Bluemountain.com, a website from which people can send free electronic greeting

TABLE 4.1
CONNECTING BY TEXT AND TWEET

When communicating by text or tweet, many people use abbreviations for common phrases to connect to others efficiently. Here are some popular abbreviations and their meanings.

WRUD	What are you doing?
FYEO	For your eyes only
UG2BK	You've got to be kidding
TTYL	Talk to you later
HAND	Have a nice day
LOL	Laugh out loud
PCM	Please call me
KUTGW	Keep up the good work
LMIRL	Let's meet in real life
^5	High five

Research shows that communicating affection with our loved ones helps to keep us happy and healthy.

Language provides comfort to individuals in distress.

• **gossip** Informal, and frequently judgmental, talk about people who are not present.

cards, offers e-cards in several special categories related to comfort and healing, including cards for the families of deployed military personnel and for the remembrance of victims of the September 11 attacks.[27]

Language Conveys Social Information A third way in which language connects people is by allowing us to share social information, which includes facts and opinions we have of others. We often do so by engaging in **gossip,** which is informal—and frequently judgmental—talk about people who are not present during the conversation. Gossip is a common communicative behavior in all sorts of social group settings, from neighborhoods to offices to churches and synagogues.[28]

Many people frown on gossip—even those who engage in it themselves—because it frequently consists of spreading negative information about others. Although we sometimes gossip about people's positive qualities, such as talking about a coworker's new promotion, research shows that we are far more likely to gossip about a person's negative features or behaviors.[29] Moreover, studies indicate that most people enjoy hearing negative gossip more than positive gossip.[30] Mean-spirited gossip can embarrass people, however, by damaging their reputations and revealing personal, private information about them to others.

How, then, does engaging in gossip help us connect with others? The answer is that gossip serves to strengthen the social bonds between those who exchange it.[31] Like sharing secrets, sharing gossip with someone requires us to trust that person to handle the information sensitively. Thus, we don't typically share gossip with strangers or people we don't like; rather, we do so with people we trust and feel close to, reinforcing our personal relationships with them.

The utility of gossip has spurred a proliferation of gossip websites on the Internet, most of which provide gossip about celebrities and their lives and are extraordinarily popular. One such site—omg.yahoo.com—boasts over 29 million visitors per month, a testament to how much people enjoy engaging in gossip about others.[32]

As we've seen, we can use language to express feelings of love and affection, provide comfort and support, and reinforce our social bonds through gossip. In these ways, language can serve to connect us to others. Language can also separate us from others by causing hurt, as the following discussion reveals.

• **criticism** The act of passing judgment on someone or something.

Although gossip is frequently judgmental, sharing gossip can reinforce our social bonds to others.

LANGUAGE SEPARATES US FROM OTHERS

During election years, it is common for political candidates to run negative campaign advertisements that focus on the shortcomings of their opponent. Such ads make misleading claims about the opponent's position on issues, or derogatory statements about his or her character and values. Although viewers often perceive negative campaign ads as distasteful, these appeals can strongly influence voters by mobilizing them around their candidate of choice[33] and encouraging them to vote accordingly.[34] In these ways, the negative language in such advertisements is effective not in bringing people together but in separating them—ideologically, at least—from one another.

You may have grown up hearing that "sticks and stones might break my bones, but words can never hurt me." According to this common proverb, language has no power to cause people pain. Your own experiences, however, have probably taught you that the opposite is true: Words can hurt us in profound and enduring ways. Two forms of language that can be especially harmful are criticisms and threats.

Criticisms **Criticism** is the act of passing judgment on someone or something. When you say what you dislike about an organization's public relations campaign, a coworker's new reading glasses, or your grandmother's cooking, you're expressing criticism.

THE DARK SIDE OF COMMUNICATION

Crossing the Line: When Criticism Becomes Abuse

In personal relationships, when one person continually criticizes another in destructive rather than constructive ways, that behavior can qualify as *verbal abuse.* Verbal abuse can produce long-term psychological and emotional damage and can also be accompanied by physical aggression or violence.

"Laura," a 33-year-old mother of two, suffered verbal abuse at the hands of her ex-husband for years. "I could never do anything right, in his opinion," she explains. "The food was never good enough, the house was never clean enough. I'm not thin enough. He calls me 'fat' and 'bitch' in front of our children and now my little boy has started calling me 'fat.' How am I supposed to react to that? He tells me I'm worthless. He won't give me money when I need it, says I don't pay the bills so why should he give me anything?"

Laura is the fictitious name of a real verbal abuse victim. As she explains, she was constantly put down and demeaned by her husband, even in front of others. She was made to feel inadequate, unimportant, and worthless. Unfortunately, those are common experiences for people who endure verbal abuse.

Verbal abuse is especially damaging to children, who depend on their parents and loved ones for protection and who lack the ability to process criticism cognitively rather than emotionally. According to the organization Prevent Child Abuse America, verbally abused children are likely to become depressed and socially withdrawn and to have difficulty making and keeping friends. That organization strongly encourages parents to seek help if they have difficulty managing stress so that they won't take their stress out on their children in the form of critical language.

Criticism is often difficult to hear. Especially when it comes from people whom we respect or love, criticism can make us feel hurt, unappreciated, and incompetent. These reactions are magnified when we receive *destructive criticism*, which occurs when we feel that someone is criticizing us to put us down or destroy our self-confidence. As "The Dark Side" box describes, destructive criticism that is too frequent or harsh can constitute verbal abuse. Most of us would likely prefer to receive *constructive criticism*, as we do when we feel that someone is criticizing us to help us to improve.

Threats A second form of language that can cause hurt is a **threat,** a declaration of the intention to harm someone if the receiver does or doesn't do something specific ("If you touch my car, I'll break your neck"). Statements such as those are intended to motivate or to prevent particular actions. Instead of using persuasion to accomplish those goals (a topic we'll take up later in this chapter), threats telegraph the promise of harm and cause fear. Threats of physical harm to another person, a person's family, or a person's property violate the law in most jurisdictions in the United States, even if the threatened harm is never enacted.

• **threat** A declaration of the intention to harm someone.

Criticisms and threats can separate us from others by causing emotional pain and fear. Those negative feelings are probably magnified when the person criticizing or threatening us is someone with whom we have close emotional ties, such as a family member, a good friend, or a romantic partner.

Thus far, we've seen how language can express who we are, connect us to others, and separate us from others. Words can also motivate us to behave in certain ways, a topic we explore next.

LANGUAGE MOTIVATES ACTION

One of marketing's most powerful tools for selling a product or a service is the *slogan*, a short and memorable phrase that will motivate people to become customers. Effective slogans become ingrained in our subconscious, causing us to recall them

SHARPEN Your Skills: *Constructive criticism*

Recall the last time someone criticized you in a harsh manner. Taking that person's perspective, write out how he or she could have delivered the criticism more constructively. What could your critic have said differently to make the message easier for you to accept? Recall this exercise the next time you have to deliver criticism to someone else, and consider how you can make it constructive rather than destructive.

• **persuasion** The process of convincing people to think or act in a certain way.

with minimal effort. How many times have you heard "Red Bull—it gives you wings," "L'Oréal—because you're worth it," and "What happens in Vegas stays in Vegas"? The purpose of an advertising slogan isn't just to be memorable, however: It's also to motivate you to buy the advertised product or service.

Just as advertisers use language in the form of slogans to motivate buying behavior, we can use various forms of language to motivate others to think or act in particular ways. Words can be powerfully persuasive if we choose them correctly. **Persuasion** is the process of convincing people that they should think or act in a certain way. Every time we watch a TV commercial, read a pop-up ad on the Internet or our smart phone, or listen to a political speech, someone is trying to influence what we believe or how we will behave.

Let's say you've decided to run in a 10-kilometer race to benefit the local children's hospital, and you're trying to persuade your relatives, friends, and coworkers to make pledges to sponsor you. What are some ways of asking for their sponsorship that would encourage them to agree?

• **anchor-and-contrast approach** A persuasion technique by which one precedes a desired request with a request that is much larger.

Anchor and Contrast One strategy is to use what researchers call an **anchor-and-contrast approach.** First you draft a request so ambitious that few people will agree to do it. That sweeping request is the *anchor*. After people reject the anchor, you ask for what you actually want, the *contrast*, which will seem reasonable to most people by comparison to the anchor and thus encourage them to comply. To solicit sponsors for your 10K run, for instance, you could write a letter giving people the following sponsorship options:

- $40 per kilometer, or $400 in total
- $20 per kilometer, or $200 in total
- $10 per kilometer, or $100 in total
- $5 per kilometer, or $50 in total

If you simply asked people to pledge $50 or even $100, many probably would decline on the grounds that those amounts are too costly. But $50 doesn't seem like so much when it is contrasted with anchors of larger amounts, such as $200 and $400. In fact, it appears quite reasonable by comparison, and the fact that your potential sponsors will see it as such will likely increase the persuasive success of your appeal.[35]

• **norm of reciprocity** The expectation that favors are reciprocated.

Norm of Reciprocity You may have heard the old saying, "One good turn deserves another." This idea suggests that when someone gives you some type of gift or resource, you are expected to return the favor. Sociologist Alvin Gouldner called that expectation the **norm of reciprocity.**[36] Because of the norm of reciprocity, we should feel a sense of duty to help people who have helped us in the past.[37] Businesses and organizations appeal to reciprocity any time they offer you free samples of their products. You might employ that persuasive technique when soliciting sponsorships for your 10K race by reminding people of ways in which you have helped them in the past.

• **social validation principle** The idea that people will comply with requests if they believe that others are also complying.

Social Validation A third persuasive strategy is to invoke the **social validation principle,** which maintains that people will comply with requests if they believe others are also complying.[38] Whenever advertisers say that "four out of five people preferred" a certain brand of car, refrigerator, or toilet bowl cleaner, they are hoping you will want to buy the same brand that most people are buying. The idea is that you gain social approval by acting the way others act. So, to the extent that social approval is important to you, the quest for approval can influence the decisions you make. When soliciting sponsors for your 10K race, you could invoke the social validation principle by pointing out how many others have already sponsored you.

Expressing our identities, connecting us to others, separating us from others, and motivating action aren't the only functions that language serves. However, they are among the most relevant to our day-to-day lives as communicators.

Ways We Use and Abuse Language

We've seen that language serves a wide variety of functions. Now let's survey the ways in which language also varies in its form. Some forms, including humor, are generally positive and can produce good outcomes, such as entertaining others, strengthening relationships, and even contributing to healing. Other forms, such as hate speech, can cause devastating hurt. In this section, we explore several different forms of language—humor, euphemism, slang, defamation, profanity, and hate speech—and discover that many are neither entirely good nor entirely bad.

HUMOR: WHAT'S SO FUNNY?

A few years ago, psychologist Richard Wiseman designed a study on the Internet with an ambitious goal: to discover the world's funniest joke. More than 2 million people from around the world visited his website and rated some 40,000 jokes for their level of humor. Here was the winning entry—the funniest joke in the world:

> *Two hunters are out in the woods when one of them collapses. He doesn't seem to be breathing, and his eyes are glazed. The other guy takes out his phone and calls the emergency services. He gasps: "My friend is dead! What can I do?" The operator says: "Calm down, I can help. First, let's make sure he's dead." There is a silence, then a gunshot is heard. Back on the phone, the guy says: "Okay, now what?"*[39]

Not everyone finds that joke funny, and some may even find it offensive. Regardless, you can probably recognize the humor in it. The joke contains what researchers believe to be the most important aspect of humor: a violation of our expectations.[40] Most of us would interpret the operator's statement ("Let's make sure he's dead") as a suggestion to check the hunter's vital signs, not as a recommendation to shoot him. It's that twist on our expectations that makes the joke funny. In fact, researchers have discovered that specific parts of the brain process humor, and that without the violation of expectations—the punch line—those neurological structures don't "light up" or provide the mental reward we associate with a good joke.[41]

Humor can enhance our communication and associations with others in many ways. It can bring us closer to people and make social interaction more pleasant and enjoyable.[42] It can defuse stress, such as the tension that occurs when people are in conflict with one another.[43] Within relationships, "inside jokes" can reinforce people's feelings of intimacy. Humor can provide so many personal and social benefits, in fact, that a good sense of humor is a strongly desired characteristic that both women and men seek in a romantic partner.[44]

Not all effects of humor are positive, however. Humor can also demean individuals and social or cultural groups, as in the case of racial jokes and gags about elderly people or persons with disabilities. Moreover, even when they are made without the intention to offend, jokes told at another's expense can cause embarrassment or distress and might even qualify as harassment.[45]

When using humor, it's therefore essential to take stock of your audience to make certain that your jokes will amuse rather than offend.

Humor can enhance the closeness of our social and personal relationships. It can also demean or offend others if used inappropriately.

adaptability Practicing Persuasion

The Scene: You're in charge of signing up volunteers for a community cleanup day in your neighborhood, which has a diverse population. As you prepare to knock on your neighbors' doors to ask for their participation, you consider what you might say to persuade them to volunteer. You recognize that the same message might not persuade everyone, so you plan to draft more than one.

Your Task: Construct three separate messages you could use to persuade your neighbors to volunteer. How could you craft a persuasive message to

- Employ the anchor-and-contrast method?
- Invoke the norm of reciprocity?
- Appeal to social validation?

EUPHEMISMS: SUGAR COATING

• **euphemism** A vague, mild expression that symbolizes and substitutes for something blunter or harsher.

Some topics are difficult or impolite to talk about directly. In those cases, we might use a **euphemism,** a vague, mild expression that symbolizes and substitutes for something that is blunter or harsher. Instead of saying that someone has died, for instance, we might say that he has "passed away," and rather than mentioning that she is pregnant, a woman might say that she's "expecting." You can probably think of many different euphemisms, including to "let go" (instead of to "fire") and to "sleep together" (instead of to "have sex"). In June 2009, when North Carolina governor Mark Sanford claimed to be hiking along the Appalachian Trail while he was actually visiting his mistress in Argentina, "hiking the Appalachian Trail" became a euphemism for having an extramarital affair.

Typically, the euphemistic term sounds less harsh or less explicit than the term it stands for, and that's the point. We use euphemisms when we want to talk about sensitive topics without making others feel embarrassed or offended.[46] Yet euphemisms require more than just a technical understanding of the language (English, French, Japanese, and so on) in which they are made; they also require an understanding of cultural idioms. That understanding is necessary because euphemisms often have a literal meaning that differs from their euphemistic meaning. For example, at a literal level, the phrase "sleep together" simply means to engage in sleep while together. If you didn't realize that is a cultural euphemism for "have sex," then you wouldn't understand the meaning when it is used in that way.

• **slang** Informal and unconventional words often understood only within a particular group.

SHARPEN Your Skills: *Slang*

Many groups of people have their own slang. Pair up with a classmate whose hobbies and interests are very different from yours, and learn some of the slang common to groups that pursue such interests. In a blog or journal entry, report on three such words.

SLANG: THE LANGUAGE OF CO-CULTURES

Closely related to euphemism is **slang,** the use of informal and unconventional words that often are understood only by others in a particular group. Slang can serve an important social function by helping people to distinguish between those who do and don't belong to their particular social networks. If you grew up in Boston, for instance, you probably know that "Rhodie" is a slang term for people from nearby Rhode Island. In Australia, "snag" is slang for "sausage." If you don't know that "geggy" means "mouth," you're probably not from Scotland, and if you don't know whether you're in "T Town" (Texarkana) or "Big T" (Tucson), you're probably not a trucker.

A form of informal speech closely related to slang is **jargon,** the technical vocabulary of a certain occupation or profession. Jargon allows members of that occupation or profession to communicate with one another precisely and efficiently. For example, many law enforcement officers in North America talk to one another using *ten-codes*, or number combinations that represent common phrases. In that jargon, "10-4" means that you've received another person's message. Health care providers also use jargon specific to their profession—for instance, referring to a heart attack as a "myocardial infarction." Other occupations and professions that have their own jargon include attorneys, engineers, dancers, airplane pilots, television producers, and the military.

• **jargon** Technical vocabulary of a certain occupation or profession.

Like humor and euphemisms, slang and jargon are neither inherently good nor inherently bad. As we've considered, those forms of language serve many positive purposes, among them reaffirming our membership in a particular social community. Whether you're into surfing or wine tasting, doing calligraphy or restoring vintage cars, learning and using the slang appropriate to those interests serves as a type of membership badge that connects you with others like you.

By the same token, however, using slang and jargon around people who don't understand it can make them feel like outsiders. If you're a police officer, saying that you're "10-7" instead of "done for the day" might make civilians around you feel excluded from the conversation. For that reason you should consider how your use of slang and jargon might come across to others around you.

• **defamation** Language that harms a person's reputation or image.

DEFAMATION: HARMFUL WORDS

In May 2011, San Diego attorney Rhonda Holmes filed a lawsuit against rock singer Courtney Love. Love believed that Holmes had accepted bribes in a case involving money stolen from the estate of Love's former husband, the late rocker Kurt Cobain. In her lawsuit, Holmes claimed that Love posted a message on Twitter that not only was untrue but that also had damaged Holmes's professional reputation.

In 2011, Courtney Love's former attorney sued her for defamation.

Holmes's claim was that Love had engaged in **defamation,** language that harms a person's reputation or gives that person a negative image. Defamation comes in two forms. The first, *libel,* refers to defamatory statements made in print or some other fixed medium, such as a photograph or a motion picture. The second, *slander,* is a defamatory statement made aloud, within earshot of others.

For instance, let's say that Aliyah wants to open a day care center in a town where Toni also operates one. To discourage parents from using Aliyah's center, Toni circulates rumors that Aliyah has been charged with child molestation. That statement is defamatory because it harms Aliyah's reputation and could cause her financial damage in the form of lost business.

Does it matter whether Toni's accusation is true? Usually the answer is yes: under most legal systems, a statement must be false to be considered libel or slander. There are situations, however, when even a true statement can qualify as defamation. Those cases often involve public figures, such as politicians and celebrities, and they hinge on the importance of the information for the public. Disclosing in print that a senator has tested positive for HIV, for example, might qualify as libel even when it is true, *if* disclosing the information serves no prevailing public interest.

PROFANITY: OFFENSIVE LANGUAGE

Profanity is language that is considered vulgar, rude, or obscene in the context in which it is used. We sometimes call profane terms *swear words* or *curse words*, and they come in many forms. Some profane terms are meant to put down certain groups of people, as in calling a person a "bitch" or a "fag." (Many of those also qualify as instances of hate speech, our next topic.) Other terms attack religious beliefs or figures considered sacred by followers of a particular religion. Still others describe sexual acts or refer to people's sexual organs or bodily functions. Finally, some are general expressions of anger or disappointment, such as "Damn!"

Like other forms of language, profanity is context-specific: What makes a word profane is that it is considered rude or obscene in the language and context in which it is used. For instance, calling a woman a "bitch" might be profane, but using the same term to describe a female dog is not. In the United States, "fag" is a derogatory expression for gay men, but to the British, it refers to a cigarette. Some swear words translate across languages; for example, the expression "Damn" in English is "Zut" in French and "Verflucht" in German and can be profane in all of them. Other words appear to be unique to certain languages; for instance, a Dutch speaker might say "Krijg de pest!" which translates to, "Go get infected with the plague!" Profanity has many different effects on social interaction. Often, it makes people feel uncomfortable or insulted. In recent years, some social groups have recognized that they can negate the effect of certain profane terms that refer to them by making the terms more commonplace, thus reducing or eliminating their shock value. That practice is called *re-claiming* the term. For instance, when homosexuals call one another "queers," their intent is not to offend but rather to remove the word's power to insult. Other social groups have supported efforts to eliminate certain insulting words from everyday speech. The movement "Spread the Word to End the Word," for example, encourages people to pledge never to call people with intellectual disabilities "retarded," since that term has derogatory implications.

Still, not all effects of profanity are negative. In certain contexts, the use of profanity can act as a social lubricant by maintaining an informal social atmosphere. Profanity is a common element in comedy, for instance, partly because it creates an expectation that nothing is taboo in that context and that ideas can flow freely. In addition, for someone to use profanity within his or her own social network can reinforce interpersonal bonds by sending the metamessage that "I feel comfortable enough with you to use profanity in your presence."

HATE SPEECH: PROFANITY WITH A HURTFUL PURPOSE

Hate speech is a specific form of profanity meant to degrade, intimidate, or dehumanize people based on their sex, national origin, sexual orientation, religion, race, disability status, or political or moral views.[47] Calling people derogatory names, intimidating them, and advocating violence against groups of individuals might all qualify as hate speech. For instance, the terms *bitch* and *fag* can be used not only as profanity but also as hate speech if they're directed at women or homosexuals with the intent to degrade or intimidate them.

Particular groups have brought widespread public attention to the issue of hate speech. Members of the Westboro Baptist Church in Topeka, Kansas, for instance, are notorious for desecrating U.S. flags, picketing the funerals of fallen service members, and protesting in support of their extreme anti-Jewish and antihomosexual beliefs. The church is monitored by antidefamation organizations as a hate group and was banned from entering the United Kingdom for a planned antigay demonstration. After members picketed the funeral of Marine Lance Corporal Matthew Snyder in 2006, the church was sued for defamation, invasion of privacy, and intentional infliction of emotional distress. In March 2011, the U.S. Supreme Court ruled 8-1 in favor of the church, finding that its speech acts—although distressing—are protected as acts of free speech by the First Amendment of the U.S. Constitution.

getCONNECTED............................
Hate Speech Online

As communication professor Michael Waltman and his colleagues have noted, the use of hate speech is increasingly common online.[48] In 2006, the Federal Bureau of Investigation (FBI) arrested Randall Ashby in Delaware for allegedly sending hate speech by e-mail to the National Association for the Advancement of Colored People (NAACP).[49] In his message, Ashby had told NAACP members that "you are no match for our numbers and our power" and suggested that they would be victimized in their sleep. The FBI determined that the e-mail violated a federal law prohibiting the interstate communication of a threat. Several laws and regulations in the United States and Canada restrict hate speech and other acts of intimidation against minority groups and punish people who engage in them.

Many instances of hate speech have incited violence, particularly when they have touched on sensitive issues such as race.

In summary, language comes in many forms, including humor, euphemism, slang, libel and slander, profanity, and hate speech. Some, such as humor, generally have positive effects but can also produce unwanted negative outcomes. Other forms, such as profanity, are generally negative even though they can have positive effects on the people using them. Understanding the positive and negative aspects of these diverse forms of language helps us to appreciate the power and complexity of verbal communication.

Improving Your Use of Language

This section presents three pieces of advice for improving verbal communication. Some may be more relevant to one situation than another, but collectively they can serve as a useful road map for fine-tuning your language use. Specifically, we will explore how to separate opinions from factual claims, speak at an appropriate level, and own your thoughts and feelings.

SEPARATE OPINIONS FROM FACTUAL CLAIMS

Many communicators have a tendency to confuse factual claims with personal opinions. Doing so can be especially problematic when listening to a political speech or even a news report, since speakers may disguise opinions as factual claims. If we're unable to tell the difference, we risk supporting positions or voting for ideas based on faulty, untrustworthy data.

A factual claim makes an assertion that we can verify with evidence and show to be true or false ("I live in the United States"). An opinion expresses a personal judgment or preference that we could agree or disagree with but that is not true or false in an absolute sense ("I live in the greatest country on Earth"). Competent communicators know how to keep opinions and factual claims separate in verbal communication. Unfortunately, distinguishing factual claims from opinions is easier said than done, especially when we're dealing with strong opinions on emotionally heated issues.

Let's say you and several friends are discussing an upcoming election in which you're choosing between two candidates. Half of you prefer Candidate C, the conservative, and the other half prefer Candidate L, the liberal. One of your friends makes the following statements:

- "Candidate C has more experience in government." That is a factual claim because we can show it to be true or false by looking at the candidates' records.

- "Candidate L is the better choice for our future." That is an opinion because it expresses a value judgment (this candidate is *better*) that we cannot objectively validate.

- "Candidate C is immoral." That is an opinion because the truth of the claim depends on the speaker's (in this case, your friend's) morals. Morals are subjective; therefore, the statement can't be proved true or false in an absolute sense.
- "Candidate L accepted bribes." That is a factual claim because it is possible to examine the evidence to discover whether it's true.

Opinions and factual claims require different types of responses. Suppose you tell me, "Candidate C has never held an elective office," and I reply by saying, "I disagree." That isn't a competent response. You have made a factual claim, which by definition is either true or false. Therefore, whether I agree with it is irrelevant. I can agree or disagree with an opinion, but a factual claim is either true or false no matter how I feel about it. If I had responded to your statement by saying "I think you're incorrect," that would be a competent reply because we would now be discussing the *truth* of your statement rather than my agreement with it.

How good are you at distinguishing opinions from factual claims? Check out "The Competent Communicator" box to find out.

As you develop that skill, keep two principles in mind. First, *opinions are opinions whether you agree with them or not.* If you believe abortion should be illegal in the United States, for instance, you might be inclined to call that statement a fact. It isn't, though. It is still a statement of opinion because it expresses an evaluation about what "should be." Second, *factual claims are factual claims whether they are true or not.* If you think it's untrue that men talk as much as women do, you might be inclined to call that statement an opinion, but it isn't. Even if it isn't true, however, it is still a factual claim because it expresses something that can be verified by evidence.

Although it's probably more difficult to separate opinions from facts when you feel strongly about an issue, that's often when it is most important to do so. Instead of telling others that their positions on sensitive issues are right or wrong, state that you agree or disagree with them. That language expresses your own position and acknowledges that different—even contradictory—opinions may also exist.

SPEAK AT AN APPROPRIATE LEVEL

Another part of being an effective verbal communicator is knowing how simple or how complex your language should be for your audience. A competent instructor, for instance, knows to use simpler language when teaching an introductory course than when teaching an advanced course because students in each class will have different levels of understanding. When you use language that is too complex for your listeners, you are *talking over their heads*. If you have been in a situation where someone has talked over your head, you know how hard it can be to understand what the speaker is trying to say.

The opposite problem is *talking down* to people, or using language that is inappropriately simple. Talking down often happens by mistake. You might provide unnecessary detail when giving someone driving directions, for example, because you don't realize that he or she is familiar with the area. At other times, overly simple language is used on purpose. That behavior can make listeners feel patronized, disrespected, or even insulted.

SHARPEN Your Skills: *Speaking at an appropriate level*

Select a topic about which you know quite a bit, and imagine you were explaining that topic to two different groups. Write one paragraph representing how you would explain the topic to people who also have a sophisticated understanding of it. Write a second paragraph representing how you would explain it to people who know nothing about it. Then, in a blog or journal entry, describe how you used language differently in each paragraph.

OWN YOUR THOUGHTS AND FEELINGS

People often use language that shifts responsibility for their thoughts and feelings onto others. Perhaps, for example, when your academic adviser doesn't understand you, she typically says "You're not being clear," but when you don't understand her,

COMPETENT COMMUNICATOR

How Well Can You Distinguish Opinions from Factual Claims?

The ability to separate opinions from factual claims is an essential skill for effective verbal communication. How well can you spot the difference? Read each of the following statements. Assuming nothing more than what the statement tells you, indicate whether you think the statement is an opinion or a factual claim by placing a checkmark in the appropriate column.

	Opinion	Factual Claim
1. Lady Gaga is the best singer in the world.	_____	_____
2. Television was invented in the 1920s.	_____	_____
3. Religious people are happier than nonreligious people.	_____	_____
4. The United States is better off with a Republican as president.	_____	_____
5. Men talk as much as women do.	_____	_____
6. Same-sex couples should be allowed to marry.	_____	_____
7. Children should be required to learn a foreign language.	_____	_____
8. Neil Armstrong was the first person to walk on the moon.	_____	_____
9. Dogs have a keener sense of smell than people do.	_____	_____
10. Abortion should be illegal in the United States.	_____	_____

Statements 1, 4, 6, 7, and 10 are all opinions. Statements 2, 3, 5, 8, and 9 are all factual claims. How well did you do? If you missed some of the answers, don't worry—distinguishing opinions from factual claims can be harder than it seems.

she says "You're not paying attention." By using that language pattern, your adviser blames you for misunderstandings but takes no responsibility for her own role in the communication process. The real problem may be that she is not paying attention herself or is not using clearly understandable language.

Good communicators take responsibility for their thoughts and feelings by using I-statements rather than you-statements. An **I-statement** claims ownership of what a communicator is feeling or thinking, whereas a **you-statement** shifts that responsibility to the other person. Instead of saying "You're not being clear," your adviser might say "I'm having a hard time understanding you." Rather than saying "You make me mad" you might say "I'm angry right now." Table 4.2 provides examples of you-statements and I-statements.

I-statements don't ignore the problem; instead, they allow the communicator to claim ownership of his or her feelings. That ownership is important, because it acknowledges that the individual controls how he or she thinks and feels. Remember that other

• **I-statement** A statement that claims ownership of the communicator's feelings or thoughts.

• **you-statement** A statement that shifts responsibility for the communicator's feelings or thoughts to the other party in the communication.

TABLE 4.2

EXAMPLES OF YOU-STATEMENTS AND I-STATEMENTS

You-Statement	I-Statement
You're making me mad.	I'm mad right now.
You're not listening to me.	I'm feeling ignored.
You don't know what you're doing.	I don't think this task is getting done right.
You hurt my feelings.	My feelings are hurt.
You're not making any sense.	I'm having trouble understanding you.

Learning how to communicate better is an ongoing process.

people can't control our thoughts and feelings unless we let them. Effective communicators therefore speak in ways that acknowledge responsibility for and ownership of the ways they feel and think.

You were not born using language. Rather, you had to *learn* how to use it. You can also learn to use it better. By distinguishing opinions from statements of fact, speaking at a level that is appropriate for your audience, and taking ownership of your thoughts and feelings, you will be empowered to express yourself effectively in a broad range of social and professional situations.

For REVIEW

- **What are the defining characteristics of language?** Language is a structured system of symbols used for communicating meaning. Language is symbolic, usually arbitrary, and rule-governed; it has layers of meaning and varies in clarity; and it is bound by context and culture.

- **For what reasons do people use language?** People use language to express who they are, to connect to others, to separate themselves from others, and to motivate action. Common uses and abuses of language include humor, euphemism, slang, defamation, profanity, and hate speech.

- **How can you use language more effectively?** You can improve your language skills by separating opinions from factual claims, speaking at an appropriate level for your audience, and owning your thoughts and feelings.

POP QUIZ

Multiple Choice

1. The dictionary definition of a word is its _____ meaning, whereas the implication of that word is its _____ meaning.

   a. denotative; connotative
   b. connotative; denotative
   c. denotative; relational
   d. connotative; relational

2. The term for the type of rule that governs the order of words within phrases is

   a. phonological.
   b. syntactic.
   c. semantic.
   d. pragmatic.

3. The idea that language shapes our views of reality by influencing how various cultures see the world is reflected in

   a. the semantic triangle.
   b. the ladder of abstraction.
   c. the Sapir-Whorf hypothesis.
   d. communication accommodation theory.

4. A vague, mild expression that symbolizes something that is blunter or harsher is

   a. a euphemism.
   b. an equivocation.
   c. euthanasia.
   d. an ambiguity.

5. Reminding others of favors you have done for them in the past can constitute the persuasive tactic known as

   a. anchor and contrast.
   b. norm of reciprocity.
   c. social validation.
   d. pragmatic rules.

Fill in the Blanks

6. Because language is _____, each word represents a particular object or idea, but it does not constitute the object or idea itself.

7. A statement that we can interpret to have more than one meaning is an example of _____.

8. _____ rules allow an individual to connect the word *lawyer* with the meaning "attorney."

9. The idea that we can conceive of something only if we have a word for it is known as _____.

10. Terms or phrases that are intended to mislead listeners by implying something that they don't actually say are known as _____.

KEY TERMS

5

COMMUNICATING NONVERBALLY

Silent Gestures Can Speak Volumes

Not many people can claim to have a gesture named after them, but Tim Tebow can. After three years as starting quarterback for the University of Florida, the Heisman Trophy winner joined the Denver Broncos in 2010. Despite his notable skill at rushing and passing the football, however, what attracted the most attention were Tebow's frequent expressions of religious belief. On the field, he has become known for kneeling and praying—a gesture now widely known as "Tebowing." His religious expressions have brought him adulation from many fans and conservative media groups, yet criticism from many other fans and liberal media groups. Tebowing has also prompted a national dialogue about the proper role of religious communication in professional athletics. In December 2011, the life-sized wall sticker company Fathead released a Tebowing sticker that became its hottest-selling product in two days. Whether people's perceptions of Tim Tebow are positive or negative, there's no denying the influence of his nonverbal behavior.

▸ As You READ

- How do people communicate nonverbally?
- How do culture and sex influence nonverbal behavior?
- In what ways can you improve your nonverbal communication skills?

Nonverbal communication is powerful stuff. Sometimes the smallest gesture—a glance, a warm vocal tone, a prayer-like kneel to the ground—can send unmistakable messages about ourselves to others. Moreover, so much of what we learn about other people's thoughts and feelings comes not through listening to their words but through observing their body language—watching their facial expressions, seeing how they move and gesture, and taking note of their eye contact. Those and other behaviors can "speak" volumes about people in efficient and sometimes subtle ways.

The Nature and Functions of Nonverbal Communication

On the animated TV show *Family Guy*, Stewie is seldom shy about expressing frustration with his mother Lois or his siblings Chris and Meg. He frequently communicates his feelings through his facial expressions, posture, and tone of voice when he's annoyed. What makes nonverbal behavior such an effective form of communication? We'll find out in this section, first by differentiating nonverbal from verbal communication and then by examining six of its most important characteristics.

WHAT IS NONVERBAL COMMUNICATION?

Nonverbal means just what it sounds like—not verbal. Nonverbal communication requires neither words nor language. How do we communicate with others, if not with words and language?

The answer is, in many ways. We can tell a great deal about people by watching their facial expressions, for instance, or by listening to the tone of their voice. Think about it: when you listen to your doctor tell you the results of your recent blood tests, you might hear tension in her voice and determine that something is wrong, or you might see a pleasant look on her face and conclude that everything is fine. We also interpret people's gestures and the way they carry themselves: you see two teenage boys punching each other and determine from their behaviors that they are playing rather than genuinely fighting.

Sometimes we even perceive others based on the way they use their time and the space around them. Perhaps you try talking with your boss about your recent evaluation and you feel ignored because she keeps looking at her iPhone. People routinely communicate more information through their nonverbal behaviors than they do through spoken language. So when it comes to communication, actions often do speak louder than words.

We can define **nonverbal communication** as those behaviors and characteristics that convey meaning without the use of words. Nonverbal communication behaviors sometimes *accompany* verbal messages, to clarify or reinforce them. For instance, if someone asks you which direction to go to find the bookstore, and you point and say, "It's that way," your nonverbal behavior (pointing) clarifies the meaning of your verbal message. If you just say, "It's that way" without pointing, your verbal message is ambiguous—and not especially helpful. At other times, however, nonverbal communication behaviors convey meaning on their own. If you ask me where the bookstore is and I shrug my shoulders, you will probably infer from my behavior that I don't know, even though I never actually said so.

Nonverbal behavior is a powerful way of communicating, and it comes naturally to many of us. In fact, we often engage in nonverbal behavior so effortlessly that you might wonder why you need to study it. The truth is, even though we frequently enact nonverbal behaviors and encounter them in others, there's a lot more to interpreting them than you might think.

- **nonverbal communication** Behaviors and characteristics that convey meaning without the use of words.

SIX CHARACTERISTICS OF NONVERBAL COMMUNICATION

It's difficult to imagine life without nonverbal communication. The capacity to communicate without words is critical for those lacking in language ability. Such individuals include infants, who haven't yet learned how to speak, and people with certain neurological problems, like the effects of a stroke, that might limit their language use. But even people with language ability depend immensely on nonverbal communication. Because she had only a limited knowledge of Spanish, for instance, Bergitta relied heavily on nonverbal behaviors while traveling through Bolivia, Uruguay, and Argentina after graduation. She was frequently amazed at how well she could understand others simply by observing their gestures and facial expressions. Her communication was more challenging than it would have been if she had known the language, but she was still able to understand—and to be understood by others—through nonverbal behaviors.

Let's take a look at some of the most compelling reasons why nonverbal communication plays such an important role in human interaction.

On the basis of nonverbal behaviors, we interpret the behavior of others as playful rather than aggressive.

Nonverbal Communication Is Present in Most Communication Contexts Whether you talk with people one-on-one or in a group, you have access not only to their spoken words but also to several dimensions of nonverbal communication. For instance, you might tell from his facial expression that your supervisor is bored at a business lunch and eager to go home. At a party, you can judge from the tone of her voice when your host is being serious and when she's kidding. Even the way people dress and smell can send you information. Glancing around the auditorium at a large business event, you might be able to guess which people are managers and which are staff members by the formality of their clothing. We are flooded with nonverbal signals in many kinds of social situations.

In other communication contexts, such as talking on the telephone and sending e-mail, we don't have access to as many nonverbal cues as we do in face-to-face conversation. We still make use of what's available, however. Even if we haven't met those to whom we're speaking on a two-way radio, we can make judgments about them from certain qualities of their voices—noticing, for example, how fast they're talking, how loudly, with what tone, and with what type of accent. In electronically mediated communication—such as e-mail, instant messaging, and text messaging—we can introduce nonverbal cues through the use of **emoticons,** the familiar textual representations of facial expressions (Figure 5.1). Other cues that help us make judgments in electronic media are pauses and the use of all capital letters.

Most human communication includes at least some form of nonverbal behavior, and when we have only a few nonverbal signals to go on, we pay extra attention to those cues. For example, vocal characteristics, such as the tone and sound of someone's voice, are important nonverbal cues in face-to-face conversation, but they are even more important on the telephone, where so many other nonverbal signals are unavailable. By the same token, when we lose the ability to use one of our senses in our communications, we typically compensate by relying more heavily on the remaining ones. People who are deaf pay extra attention to visual cues when communicating with others because they are unable to interpret vocal characteristics. Similarly, individuals with impaired vision often rely more heavily on hearing and touch to help them communicate, because they are unable to see gestures and facial expressions.

• **emoticons** Textual representations of facial expressions.

FIGURE 5.1
EMOTICONS

Communication in computer-mediated formats, such as e-mail, instant messaging, and text messaging, relies heavily on language. Even in these environments, however, people can still introduce nonverbal facial expressions through the use of emoticons (a word that means *emotional icons*). Here are some of the most common emoticons:

Smiles	:)	
Laughs	:D	
Frowns	:(	
Winks	;)	
Kisses	:X	
Confusion	:/	
Sticking out tongue	:P	

Nonverbal Communication Often Conveys More Information Than Verbal Communication

Go to the self-help section of almost any bookstore, and open up such titles as *How to Read a Person Like a Book* and *The Power of Nonverbal Communication: What You Do Is More Important Than What You Say*.[1] You'll probably get the impression that nearly all the information we get by communicating with others comes through nonverbal behavior. In fact, some unreliable but frequently cited studies have estimated that as much as 93 percent of meaning is transmitted nonverbally, leaving only 7 percent to be accounted for by the words we use.[2] Nonverbal communication isn't quite that powerful, however. More realistic estimates from nonverbal communication scholar Judee Burgoon suggest that 65 to 70 percent of meaning comes from nonverbal clues, with 30 to 35 percent coming from language.[3] In many situations, therefore, we do communicate more information through nonverbal behavior than we do through our words.

• **nonverbal channels** The various behavioral forms that nonverbal communication takes.

The most likely reason that nonverbal communication adds up to such a significant percentage is its use of many **nonverbal channels,** or behavioral forms of expression. The interpretation of some of those channels, including facial expressions, gestures, and personal appearance, relies on our sense of vision. Vocal characteristics—such as loudness, pitch, and tone of voice, engage our sense of hearing. We often express different messages with touch, such as a handshake and a hug, and we convey subtle messages about attraction to others through our use of smell.

We sometimes rely on clues from nonverbal channels to make sense of a situation when talking isn't a good option. Rick has learned that his alcoholic mother, Claudia, has very unpredictable mood swings. When he gets home from school each day, he's never sure how she'll be feeling. Some days she's happy and outgoing; other days she's sullen and withdrawn. Occasionally, she'll start yelling at the slightest provocation. Over time, Rick has noticed that he can determine Claudia's mood without even talking to her: He needs only to look at her posture and facial expression to tell whether she's cheerful, depressed, or angry.

Nonverbal Communication Is Usually Believed over Verbal Communication

It's not uncommon to get conflicting messages from what a person says and what he or she does. Most of the time, we believe the nonverbal clues.[4] Let's say you're waiting for your friend Joel at your favorite coffee shop. When he walks in, Joel slumps into the seat next to you, rolls his eyes, and sighs heavily. You ask him how he's doing, and he says "It's been a *great* day." Joel's verbal behavior is sending you one message ("I'm having a great day"), but his nonverbal behavior is suggesting something quite different ("I'm having a lousy day"). Which of these contradictory messages do you believe? Most of us would put more stock in what Joel is *doing* than in what he is *saying*. In other words, as multiple studies have shown, we believe his nonverbal message.

Why do we put our trust in nonverbal communication? Experts think we do so because most of us believe people have a harder time controlling nonverbal signals than verbal ones, so we think nonverbal behaviors more accurately reflect what a person is really thinking or feeling. It's easy for Joel to *say* he's having a great day, but if he feels frustrated or depressed, it's probably tougher for him to *act* as if his day is going well. When he slumps, rolls his eyes, and sighs, you probably conclude that his day is going poorly, despite what he says.

• **deception** The act of leading others to believe something the speaker knows to be untrue.

The human preference for believing nonverbal signals even when they conflict with words is especially critical for detecting **deception**—the act of leading someone to believe something one knows to be untrue—because people often have inconsistent verbal and nonverbal behaviors when they're lying. Imagine that Olivia spends the afternoon with her ex-boyfriend Greg but tells her current boyfriend Ethan that she spent the afternoon reading at Starbucks. Olivia might feel nervous telling such a lie, especially because she knows how upset Ethan would be if he found out she were lying. Chances are that her nervousness will affect her nonverbal behavior. She might perspire, get dry in the mouth, sound unusually tense, and appear especially rigid in her posture. If Olivia really had been at Starbucks as she said, there's probably no reason she would be nervous telling Ethan about it. She would be able to explain her afternoon's activities calmly. So, if she looks or sounds nervous, those nonverbal messages will contradict her verbal message and may give Ethan reason to think she's not telling the truth.

Nonverbal Communication Is the Primary Means of Expressing Emotion

We have a large verbal vocabulary for describing our emotions, but our nonverbal behaviors do it much more efficiently. How many times have you been able to tell how someone is feeling just by looking at him or her? We might not always be right about the emotions we sense—and some of us are better than others at interpreting people's emotions—but research shows that humans are acutely sensitive to nonverbal emotion cues.[5] As we saw in the example above about Rick and his mother Claudia, Rick has developed the ability to interpret Claudia's emotional state accurately with just a glance, by paying attention to her facial expressions and posture.

We can often interpret a person's emotional state from his or her nonverbal signals.

Reality television shows often capture images of intense emotional expressions.

Emotion is a powerful influence on our behavior, and our primary way of communicating how we feel is through our nonverbal behaviors. Two channels of nonverbal behavior that are particularly important in the communication of emotion are facial expressions and vocal behaviors.

Humans are highly visual beings, meaning that we tend to pay a lot of attention to people's facial expressions when we want to figure out their emotional state. We take close note of these expressions whether we're talking with them face to face, listening to them speak to a group, or even watching them on television. On reality TV shows such as *The Amazing Race*, *Dancing with the Stars*, and *Keeping Up with the Kardashians*, producers often shoot close-ups of people's faces during critical moments, to capture their facial expressions of emotion. Most of us can easily think of the type of facial expression that connotes happiness: the eyes tend to be wide and bright, and the person tends to be smiling. That look of happiness differs notably from the facial expressions we associate with anger, sadness, surprise, and disappointment. The distinctive patterns we perceive for each are keys to helping us interpret other people's emotions. In fact, several studies suggest that facial expressions of these basic emotions are interpreted similarly across cultures.[6] Psychologist Paul Ekman took photographs of people communicating six basic emotions through their facial expressions: happiness, fear, disgust, anger, sadness, and surprise. He then showed the photos to participants in five different countries—Chile, Brazil, Argentina, Japan, and the United States—and asked them to match each photograph with the emotion they believed it displayed. When Ekman compared the responses from different countries he found that the participants were equally accurate at matching emotions to the photographs.[7]

Similar studies have repeated those results using groups from a range of cultures—including Greek, Chinese, Turkish, Malaysian, Ethiopian, Swedish, Italian, Sumatran, Estonian, and Scottish[8]—and found that interpretations of emotional displays do differ from culture to culture. They also differ from emotion to emotion, with happiness, for instance, being interpreted more consistently than fear.[9] Overall, however, it appears that facial expressions of our most basic emotions are understood similarly around the world.

We also pay attention to vocal cues to understand a person's emotional state. When someone is yelling and using harsh vocal tones, we usually infer that the person is angry, whereas laughter and lots of pitch variation suggest happiness or excitement. It turns out that we may be even more accurate at interpreting emotions through vocal cues than through facial expressions.[10] This situation appears to be particularly true when the vocal channel is the only accessible channel, such as when we're speaking with someone on the phone. We don't necessarily get *more* information about individuals' emotional states from their voices than we do from their facial expressions, but we may get *more accurate* information.

Nonverbal Communication Metacommunicates As we discussed in Chapter 1, metacommunication is communication *about* communication, and we often metacommunicate verbally. When we use statements such as "Let me tell you what I think," "Don't take this the wrong way," and "I'm just kidding," we are sending messages related to our other messages—that is, we're communicating about our communication. Usually, we do so to avoid misunderstandings and to provide listeners with greater clarity about the meaning of our statements. Communicating clearly is a very important feature of social interaction, and several nonverbal behaviors also help us to achieve this goal.

• **immediacy behaviors**
Nonverbal signals of affection and affiliation.

Nonverbal behavior can metacommunicate. For instance, we can use non-verbal signals to indicate the metamessage that "this is a secret."

Suppose, for example, that you're sitting at the dinner table with your brother and he leans over to you, lowers his voice to a whisper, and cups his mouth with his hand. That combination of nonverbal behaviors sends you the message "What I'm about to say is meant for only you to hear." In other words, your brother's nonverbal behavior metacommunicates his intentions to you. We often use nonverbal behaviors such as facial expressions and gestures to indicate how someone else should interpret our messages. For instance, we might smile and wink to indicate that we're being sarcastic, or raise our eyebrows to signal that what we're saying is very serious.

Nonverbal Communication Serves Multiple Functions Beyond its role in emotional expression, nonverbal communication serves several additional functions that help us interact effectively with others. Let's take a quick look at some of them.

• *Nonverbal communication helps us manage conversations.* We can use nonverbal signals—such as raising a hand in class—to indicate that we wish to speak. We can also use eye contact to convey that we understand what a speaker is saying.[11]

• *Nonverbal communication helps us maintain relationships.* We reinforce many of our important relationships through the use of **immediacy behaviors,** nonverbal signals of affection and affiliation. In many relationships, such behaviors include smiling, engaging in affectionate touch, using warm vocal tones, and standing or sitting close to each other.[12]

- *Nonverbal communication helps us form impressions.* By observing how another person looks, sounds, dresses, and carries himself or herself, we can form impressions about that individual's personality, education level, cultural and ethnic background, economic status, political affiliation, and sexual orientation.[13] Our impressions may not always be accurate, but we rely heavily on nonverbal cues when we form them.

- *Nonverbal communication helps us influence other people.* When we attempt to cause others to think or act in a certain way, we can manipulate some visual cues, such as our clothing, to appear more authoritative.[14] We can also use nonverbal immediacy behaviors to enhance our affiliation with others; in this way, we might lead them to be more open to our suggestions than they otherwise might be.[15]

- *Nonverbal communication helps us conceal information.* Several nonverbal behaviors coincide with our attempts to deceive other people. When we try to conceal the truth, we often speak in a higher voice than normal,[16] and our smile looks more fake or forced.[17] We also use fewer gestures and adopt a more rigid posture, probably because we're trying to control signs of nervousness.[18]

Ten Channels of Nonverbal Communication

Nonverbal communication engages nearly all our senses, so it's probably no surprise that we experience it in so many different forms, or channels. Those channels are facial displays, eye behaviors, movement and gestures, touch behaviors, vocal behaviors, the use of smell, the use of space, physical appearance, the use of time, and the use of artifacts.

FACIAL DISPLAYS

It's difficult to overstate the importance of **facial displays,** or facial expressions, in nonverbal communication. Indeed, according to the *principle of facial primacy*, the face communicates more information than any other channel of nonverbal behavior.[19] That communication power is especially evident in three important functions of facial displays: revealing identity, signaling attractiveness, and expressing emotion.

• **facial displays** Facial expressions that are an important source of information in nonverbal communication.

1. *Identity.* First, the face is the most important visual clue that humans use to identify one another.[20] After all, most of us don't display photos of our loved ones' hands, legs, or feet—we display pictures of their faces, because the appearance of the face is our most reliable clue to identity.

2. *Attractiveness.* Second, the face plays a large role in attractiveness. Two properties that appear to be especially important are symmetry and proportionality. **Symmetry** is the similarity between the left and right sides of your face (Figure 5.2). **Proportionality** refers to the relative size of your facial features. It may seem odd to identify symmetry and proportionality as primary contributors to facial attractiveness, because we so often think of attractiveness as a highly individual assessment. However, as you'll learn in the "Fact or Fiction?" box, we're much more similar than dissimilar when it comes to judging a person's attractiveness.

• **symmetry** The similarity between the left and right sides of a face or body.

• **proportionality** The relative sizes of facial or body features.

3. *Emotion.* Finally, as noted above, facial behavior is our primary means of communicating emotion. Our facial muscles give us the ability to make hundreds of different expressions. We use those expressions to convey a host of emotions—from happiness, surprise, and determination to anger, fear, sadness, and contempt.

Facial expressions are also extremely useful for those who communicate through sign language. In sign language, facial expressions are sometimes called *nonmanual signals* because they work alongside hand signs to help express a particular meaning. For instance, when someone asks a yes or no question using sign language, the eyes are wide open, the eyebrows are raised, and the head and shoulders are pushed forward. Sometimes a person can change the entire meaning of a sign just by changing the facial expression that goes with it (Figure 5.3).[21]

FIGURE 5.2 ASYMMETRICAL AND SYMMETRICAL FACES

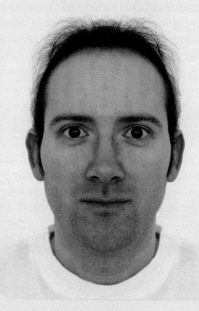

All else being equal, symmetrical faces are more attractive than asymmetrical faces. When researchers study facial symmetry, they often do so by taking a photograph of a face and modifying it with computer software to make it appear more symmetrical. For instance, the image on the left is an original, unretouched photo of an adult man's face, and the image on the right is a modified version of the same face that increases its symmetry. Research indicates that most people would find the face on the right to be more attractive.

FIGURE 5.3 FACIAL EXPRESSION IN AMERICAN SIGN LANGUAGE

Facial expression plays a vital role in communicating ideas in American Sign Language (ASL). In some instances, the same hand sign is associated with different meanings when it is accompanied by different facial expressions. Both photographs in the figure feature the hand sign for "you," but with different facial displays. The photo on the left represents a question, such as "Are you?" or "Did you?" The photo on the right, however, is interpreted as an exclamation, such as "It's you!" Although the hand signal is the same in both photographs, the meaning differs because of the accompanying facial expression.

In the Eye of Which Beholder?—Cultures Vary Widely in Perceptions of Beauty

Most of us have heard the cliché that "beauty is in the eye of the beholder," meaning that what one group finds attractive may not be appealing to another. Surprisingly, this idea dates back at least to the third century B.C., indicating that humans have long considered beauty to be subjective, a matter of individual taste. If that were the case, then we would expect to find little agreement from person to person, and from culture to culture, about what is physically attractive. Exactly how true is that idea, though?

Not very, according to research. In fact, a host of studies has shown just the opposite: people are remarkably consistent when it comes to judging attractiveness. Researcher Judith Langlois and her colleagues have reviewed 130 of those studies and found that within cultures, people showed 90 percent agreement with one another when judging someone's attractiveness. Moreover, people from different cultures agreed in their judgments of attractiveness 94 percent of the time. Thus, although we sometimes think of beauty as being culturally specific, Langlois and her team found that there was substantial agreement both *within* cultures and *across* cultures in assessing attractiveness.

These findings indicate that people are much more similar than different when it comes to judging looks. Therefore, people who are considered attractive by one social group are also likely to be considered attractive by other groups.

ASK YOURSELF

- Why does the idea that "beauty is in the eye of the beholder" persist?
- What do you find most physically attractive in members of the other sex? How about in members of your own sex?

SOURCE: Langlois, J. H., Kalakanis, L. E., Rubenstein, A. J., Larson, A. D., Hallam, M. J., & Smoot, M. T. (2000). Maxims or myths of beauty: A meta-analytic and theoretical review. *Psychological Bulletin, 126,* 380–423.

EYE BEHAVIORS

Because the eyes are part of the face, it may strike you as odd that researchers study eye behavior separately from facial behavior. Just as facial behavior communicates more than any other nonverbal channel, however, the eyes communicate more than any other part of the face—thus, we treat **oculesics**, the study of eye behavior, as a separate nonverbal channel.

When many people think about eye behavior, eye contact first comes to mind, for good reason. Eye contact plays a role in several important types of relational interaction. We use eye contact to signal attraction to someone and to infer that someone is attracted to us. We use it to gain credibility and to come across as sincere or trustworthy. We use it to persuade others, as well as to signal that we are paying attention and understanding what others are saying. We can even use eye contact when we want to intimidate someone or take a dominant or an authoritative position in a conversation or a group discussion. Indeed, there are few times when we feel as connected to another person—in either positive or negative ways—as when we are looking each other in the eye. As we'll see later in the chapter, however, those functions of eye contact often vary by culture.

• **oculesics** The study of eye behavior.

Another eye behavior with communicative value is pupil size. The pupil is the dark spot right in the center of each eye, which you can see in a mirror. Your pupils control how much light enters your eyes; as a result, they continually change in size. In darker environments, they dilate, or open wider, in order to take in all available light. In brighter environments, they contract, or become smaller, to avoid taking in too much light at once. What communication researchers find interesting, however, is that your pupils also dilate when you look at someone you find physically attractive and when you feel arousal, whether it is a positive response, such as excitement or sexual arousal, or a negative response, such as anxiety or fear. Watching how a person's pupils react to different social situations or conversational partners can therefore tell us something about the individual's interest and arousal.

MOVEMENT AND GESTURES

Think about the different ways you walk. When you're feeling confident, you hold your head high and walk with smooth, consistent strides. When you're nervous, you probably walk more timidly, stealing frequent glances at the people around you. Your *gait*, or the way you walk, is one example of how your body movement can communicate various messages about you to others, such as "I feel proud" or "I feel scared." The study of movement, including the movement of walking, is called **kinesics.**

Now consider how you use your arms and hands to communicate. Perhaps it's to wave at your neighbor when you see her at the grocery store. Maybe it's to hold up two fingers to signal that you want two hot dogs at the football game concession stand. The use of arm and hand movements to communicate is called **gesticulation.** Research indicates that most people—even those who are born blind—use gestures even before they begin speaking.[22]

Communication scholars divide gestures into several forms, including emblems, illustrators, affect displays, regulators, and adaptors.

- **Emblems** are any gestures that have a direct verbal translation. Whenever you see an emblematic gesture, you should be able to translate it into words. Examples include the wave for "hello" or "goodbye" and the upright extended palm for "stop."
- **Illustrators** are gestures that go along with a verbal message to clarify it. If you hold up your hands a certain distance apart when you say the fish you caught was "this big," your gesture serves as an illustrator to clarify what you mean by "this big."

• **kinesics** The study of movement.

• **gesticulation** The use of arm and hand movements to communicate.

• **emblems** Gestures that have a direct verbal translation.

• **illustrators** Gestures that go along with a verbal message to clarify it.

We often infer people's emotional state from the way they walk.

- **Affect displays** are gestures that communicate emotion (*affect*). You probably know people who wring their hands when they're nervous or cover their mouth with their hands when they're surprised. Those are both affect displays because they coincide with particular emotions.

- **Regulators** are gestures that control the flow of conversation. One regulator with which you're probably very familiar is raising your hand when you're in a group and wish to speak. Gestures such as that help regulate who is speaking, and when, so communication can flow smoothly.

- **Adaptors** are gestures you use to satisfy some personal need, such as scratching an itch or picking lint off your shirt. When we do those behaviors to ourselves, we call them *self-adaptors*. When adaptors are directed at others (say, picking lint off someone else's shirt), they're called *other-adaptors*.

TOUCH BEHAVIORS

Touch is the first of our five senses to develop. Even before an infant can see, hear, taste, or smell, his or her skin can respond to stimuli in the environment. Touch is also the only sense without which we cannot survive. Consider that no matter how much we may cherish our other senses, it's entirely possible to survive without being able to see, hear, taste, or smell. Without touch, however, we would constantly be susceptible to burn, frostbite, and other potentially life-threatening forms of injury.

Haptics is the study of how we use touch to communicate. In terms of human communication, there are five major areas in which touch plays a critical role in conveying meaning: affection, caregiving, power and control, aggression, and ritual.

- *Affectionate touch.* Behaviors such as hugging, kissing, and handholding communicate love, intimacy, commitment, and safety and are commonplace in many romantic relationships, parent-child relationships, and friendships.[23] One reason affectionate touch is so important is that it contributes to our physical and mental well-being. Infants who are regularly cuddled, for instance, experience faster physical development than those who are not.[24]

- *Caregiving touch.* We often receive touch from others while receiving some form of care or service. When you get your hair cut, have your teeth cleaned, or work with a personal trainer, for instance, you're touched in ways that correspond to those activities. Caregiving touch is distinguished from affectionate touch because although it *can* reflect positive emotion for the person being touched, it does not necessarily do so.

- *Power and control touch.* Still other touches are used to exert power over people's behavior. We sometimes touch people merely to suggest a certain course of behavior, as when the host of a party puts his hand on a guest's back to guide her in a certain direction. In other cases, we touch people to control their behavior against their wishes, such as when police officers hold a suspect on the ground while applying handcuffs.

- *Aggressive touch.* Behaviors done to inflict physical harm—such as punching, pushing, kicking, slapping, and stabbing—are all forms of aggressive touch. Using touch behaviors to inflict

Research indicates that physical affection—including affectionate touch—is essential for our physical and mental health.

- **affect displays** Gestures that communicate emotion.

- **regulators** Gestures that control the flow of conversation.

Ritualistic touch does not necessarily convey relational meaning, but it often involves skin-to-skin contact, which can spread germs. Before the 2012 Olympic Games in London, British athletes were warned not to shake hands with other athletes, visitors, or dignitaries to avoid contracting an illness that could affect their athletic performance.

physical harm on others almost always constitutes a criminal act. Despite the legal constraints on such behaviors, incidents of violence and abuse using aggressive touch are unfortunately still common in North America and many societies around the world.

- *Ritualistic touch.* Some touches are ritualistic, meaning that we do them as part of a custom or tradition. In North America, shaking hands is one such example; when we shake hands with people as part of a greeting ritual, we understand that the handshake does not convey any particular meaning about the relationship (the way that, say, holding hands would).

VOCAL BEHAVIORS

Perhaps you have a high, breathy voice or a deep, booming voice. Maybe you usually talk very fast or quite loudly. Perhaps you have an accent that indicates to others where you grew up. And there are times when you speak with a particular tone in your voice, to suggest that you are irritated, amused, or bored. Those and other characteristics of the voice are referred to, collectively, as **vocalics.** We also refer to them as **paralanguage** (meaning "beside language") to indicate that they go along with the words we speak to convey meaning.

   Some people are surprised to learn that the voice is a channel of nonverbal communication. After all, we speak with our voices, and spoken communication is verbal, right? That statement is true, but the only verbal aspect of spoken communication is *what we say*—the words themselves. Everything else about our voices, including the following characteristics, is nonverbal.

- *Pitch.* The pitch of your voice is an index of how high or deep your voice sounds. On average, women's voices have a higher pitch than men's voices, and adults have deeper voices than children.

- *Inflection.* When we talk about the inflection in your voice, we're referring to your variation in pitch. Voices that have a lot of inflection are usually described as very expressive; those with little inflection are said to be monotone.[25]

- *Volume.* Volume is an index of how loud or quiet your voice is. Most of us alter our vocal volume as the social context demands, such as by speaking quietly in a library and more loudly at a crowded reception.

- *Rate.* Vocal rate refers to how fast or slowly you speak. The average adult speaks at a rate of approximately 150 words per minute,[26] but we might speak faster when we're excited or slower when we're unsure of ourselves.

- *Filler words.* Filler words are nonword sounds such as "umm" and "er" that people often use to fill the silence during pauses. If we have to pause while speaking— say, to remember the word we want to use—we can use filler words to indicate that we intend to continue speaking.

- *Pronunciation.* Pronunciation reflects how correctly you combine vowel and consonant sounds to say a word. For example, how would you pronounce the word *victuals?* Although it looks as though it should be pronounced "VIK-tules," its correct pronunciation is "VIT-tles."

- *Articulation.* Articulation, also known as enunciation, describes how clearly you speak. People who mumble their words or speak with their mouth full demonstrate poor articulation. In contrast, individuals whose words are clear and easily understandable are good articulators.

- *Accent.* An accent is a pattern of pronouncing vowel and consonant sounds that is representative of a particular language or geographic area. Everyone speaks with an accent—even you—although we typically notice only accents that are different from ours.

- *Silence.* Silence is the absence of sound. We frequently use silence to convey meaning in conversations.[27] For instance, we often become silent when we are unsure how to respond to a question or when we have said as much as we wish to about a topic.

THE USE OF SMELL

Of all the channels of nonverbal behavior, the hardest one to associate with human communication is smell. It turns out that your sense of smell, which we call **olfactics,** operates subtly but powerfully to influence your reactions to other people. In fact, two phenomena central to the human experience and to communication—memory and sexual attraction—are profoundly affected and regulated by smell.

Memory Smells can affect our communication behavior by influencing our memories and moods. Have you ever smelled a particular scent—maybe a certain food or cologne—and instantly remembered a particular person, event, or place? Maybe the aroma of banana bread makes you think of your grandmother's kitchen, or the smell of a particular cologne or perfume makes you think of a close friend. Those connections are examples of *olfactic association*, the tendency of odors to bring up specific memories. Why do olfactic associations matter for communication? It happens that memories often come with specific emotions, so when a smell reminds us of a particular person or place, it has the potential to affect our mood and behavior.

Sexual Attraction Smell also affects our communication by playing a role in determining to whom we are sexually attracted. That connection between smell and attraction may surprise you, because chances are you think of sexual attraction as being driven mostly by visual cues—whether you think an individual *looks* attractive. In fact, your judgments about a person's sexual attractiveness are strongly affected by the way he or she smells to you. More specifically, research tells us that when we are looking for opposite-sex romantic partners, we are drawn to people whose natural body scent is most different from our own. Why?

If two people have very similar scents, scientists have determined that their genes are also very similar, and this similarity can increase their probability of producing genetically abnormal children. People produce much healthier children when they mate with partners who are genetically dissimilar to them. A person's natural body scent sends a signal to your brain that tells you how similar his or her genes are to yours. The more dissimilar a person's body odor is to yours, therefore, the more sexually attractive you will instinctively judge that individual to be. Of course, not all instances of sexual attraction coincide with the desire to reproduce. Nonetheless, nature has connected smell to sexual attraction to help motivate healthy mate choices when procreation is our goal. We don't sniff out a person's scent profile consciously, however; rather, our brain is adapted to pick up on those olfactic signals subconsciously.

THE USE OF SPACE

When we interact socially, we constantly negotiate our use of space. That negotiating process becomes particularly apparent when our personal space is limited; think of being in a crowded elevator or on a full airplane. Many of us find such situations uncomfortable, but why? The scientific study of spatial use, known as **proxemics,** tells us that we each have a preferred amount of personal space that we carry like an invisible bubble around us. How much personal space we prefer depends on our temperament, the situation we're in, and our level of familiarity with those around us.

Anthropologist Edward T. Hall discovered that in Western cultures, people use four different spatial zones, or levels of personal distance, when interacting with one another.[28] **Intimate distance,** which ranges from 0 to approximately 1½ feet, is the zone we willingly occupy with only our closest and most intimate friends, family members, and romantic partners. With other friends

Many smells invoke specific memories. The smell of freshly baked bread might make you think of your grandmother's kitchen.

• **olfactics** The study of the sense of smell.

• **proxemics** The study of the use of space.

• **intimate distance** The zone of space willingly occupied only with intimate friends, family members, and romantic partners.

We each prefer a certain amount of personal space. As a result, we often feel uncomfortable in crowded conditions.

- **personal distance** The zone of space occupied with close friends and relatives.

and relatives, we typically maintain a **personal distance,** which Hall defined as extending from 1½ to about 4 feet. With customers, casual acquaintances, or others whom we don't know very well, we occupy a **social distance.** That ranges from about 4 to 12 feet and conveys more formal, impersonal interaction. Finally, **public distance** typically applies when someone is giving a speech or performing in front of a large audience. The purpose is to keep the presenter far enough away from the group that he or she is safe and visible to everyone. Public distances are usually 12 to 25 feet or greater, depending on the circumstance.

PHYSICAL APPEARANCE

- **social distance** The zone of space occupied with casual acquaintances.

- **public distance** The zone of space maintained during a public presentation.

- **halo effect** A predisposition to attribute positive qualities to physically attractive people.

We place extraordinary importance on physical appearance. Whether we intend to or not, we make all sorts of judgments about people based on their looks. In particular, we have a strong predisposition to attribute positive qualities to physically attractive people, a tendency that researchers refer to as the **halo effect.** In other words, when a person *looks* good, most of us subconsciously assume he or she *is* good. Indeed, research has shown that we think attractive people are friendlier, more competent, and more socially skilled than less attractive people.[29] Those perceptions translate into some real advantages for attractiveness. For instance, attractive people have higher self-esteem and more dating experience than less attractive people.[30] We are also nicer and more cooperative toward attractive people and more lenient toward attractive criminal defendants.[31] So if it seems at times that good-looking people get all the breaks, research tells us that is often the case. Much as we may like to claim otherwise, most of us are strongly influenced by physical appearance when making assessments about other people. That preference for beauty has a dark side, however. Because physical attractiveness is so highly valued, some people go to dangerous extremes to achieve it. As you'll see in "The Dark Side of Communication," one of the unfortunate effects of the quest for beauty is the prevalence of eating disorders.

SHARPEN Your Skills: *Adapting your appearance*

Dress in conservative attire and visit a restaurant, department store, bank, or other business. Take note of how friendly the employees are toward you and how quickly they help you. Now repeat the experiment in casual or run-down clothing. What differences do you notice in other people's behaviors toward you? What differences do you notice in your own behaviors? Write up your results in a brief report.

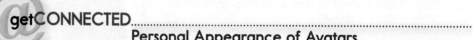

getCONNECTED
Personal Appearance of Avatars

As a nonverbal channel, personal appearance is influential not only in face-to-face interaction but also online. When interacting in cyberspace, many people use avatars as representations of themselves. Although avatars are not "real" people, they signify real people, and so we become accustomed to perceiving them in many of the same ways we perceive the people around us. Including an avatar alongside an e-mail message or chat room posting can make our words seem more personal to others—but how does the appearance of an avatar matter? To find out, communication researchers Kristine Nowak and Christian Rauh had college students evaluate a series of avatars and report on their perceptions.[32] They discovered that

- Avatars should look as human as possible, rather than looking like animals or inanimate objects.
- Avatars should have a defined gender, rather than appearing androgynous.
- Communicators prefer avatars that look like themselves.

We often feel powerless and frustrated when forced to wait for others. Many waiting areas even lack clocks to reduce complaints about the passage of time.

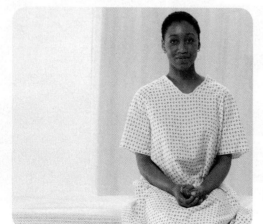

THE USE OF TIME

Chronemics is the way we use time. You might not immediately think of time usage as nonverbal behavior, but the way we give (or

THE DARK SIDE OF COMMUNICATION

Eating Disorders and the Pressure to Be Attractive

There's little question that being physically attractive is an advantage in everyday life. Because of the halo effect, we think attractive people are nicer, smarter, friendlier, more honest, and more competent than unattractive people, and we treat them accordingly. Most of us grow up learning that physical attractiveness is prized. That lesson can create enormous social and psychological pressure on people to look as attractive as possible.

Particularly in Western societies, people see thin, slim bodies as attractive and overweight bodies as unattractive. Because of the pressure to be attractive and because being attractive means being thin, an alarming number of people suffer from eating disorders. According to the U.S. National Institute of Mental Health, eating disorders are of two major types. *Anorexia nervosa* derives from the desire to be as thin as possible. Individuals with anorexia pursue thinness relentlessly through excessive dieting and exercise, self-induced vomiting, and the abuse of laxatives or diuretics. *Bulimia nervosa* is a disorder characterized by binging on large quantities of food and then compensating for overeating by vomiting, abusing laxatives or diuretics, or fasting. Whereas people with anorexia are often excessively thin, those with bulimia are often of normal weight for their age and height. Like those with anorexia, though, individuals with bulimia fear gaining weight and are intensely unhappy with their body. Both anorexia and bulimia elevate the risk of several health problems, including low blood pressure, cardiac arrest, clinical depression, gastrointestinal disorders, and suicide.

ASK YOURSELF

- Why do you suppose thinness is considered attractive in so many cultures, particularly for women?
- Besides developing eating disorders, what are some other examples of the dangerous extremes to which people will go in their quest for attractiveness?

SOURCES: National Institute of Mental Health: www.nimh.nih.gov/health/publications/eating-disorders/what-are-eating-disorders.shtml; National Eating Disorders Association: www.nationaleatingdisorders.org; both accessed May 14, 2012.

---

refuse to give) our time to others can send them important messages about how we feel about them. Because most of us spend our time on the people and activities that matter to us, for instance, the way we use time communicates messages about what we value. When we give our time to others, we imply that we value those people. Our use of time also sends messages about power. When you go to see someone who is in a position of power over you, such as your supervisor, it is not uncommon to be kept waiting. However, you would probably consider it bad form to make a more powerful person wait for you. Indeed, the rule seems to be that the time of powerful people is more valuable than the time of less powerful people.

• **chronemics** The use of time.

THE USE OF ARTIFACTS

Each of us inhabits and controls certain physical environments, such as a house or apartment, a dorm room, or an office. **Artifacts** are the objects and visual features within an environment that reflect who we are and what we like. One office you routinely visit, for instance, may be plush and opulent, with an oak desk, leather furniture, soft lighting, and expensive paintings on the walls. Another office may be plain and basic, featuring a metal desk and chairs, fluorescent lighting, and bare walls. What messages might those different artifacts send you about the occupants of those two offices?

• **artifacts** Objects and visual features that reflect a person's identity and preferences.

The way artifacts such as furniture are placed within an environment can facilitate or inhibit communication. For example, teachers at Phillips Exeter Academy, a private preparatory school in New Hampshire, practice the Harkness method of teaching, arranging up to 12 students and a teacher around an oval table. That arrangement is meant to diminish the separation between students and teachers and encourage everyone to interact in an open, engaging way. In contrast, people who wish to discourage conversation in their office or work environment might place their desk so their back is to others.

The 10 different channels by which we communicate with others nonverbally encompass almost all our senses, making nonverbal communication a truly engaging experience. Not everyone enacts nonverbal behavior in the same ways, however. As we'll see in the next section, culture and sex are both powerful influences on our styles of communicating nonverbally.

Culture, Sex, and Nonverbal Communication

Suppose you've won an Olympic gold medal. Imagine the immense joy you feel as you stand atop the podium listening to your national anthem, with your friends and family beaming with pride from the stands. In that scenario, what nonverbal behaviors would you likely engage in? How would you stand? What expression would be on your face? What gestures might you make? If you can picture yourself in that situation, it's easy to imagine that everyone would behave the same way you would. Research tells us, however, that our ways of communicating nonverbally are affected not only by our individual emotions and the demands of the situation, but also by two major influences on nonverbal communication: culture and sex. We'll take a look at each in this section.

CULTURE INFLUENCES NONVERBAL COMMUNICATION

When they watch the Olympic Games on television, many American fans are surprised by some of the nonverbal behaviors of athletes from different cultures. They may greet each other differently than is the norm in the United States. They may stand closer to—or farther from—each other than is typical in U.S. culture. The reason is that these and many other nonverbal behaviors are shaped by the cultural practices with which people are raised. To learn about a career in which knowledge of cultural variation in nonverbal behavior is helpful, see "Putting Communication to Work."

Consider these many ways in which culture influences nonverbal communication:

Differences in greeting behaviors are one way in which athletes in international competitions display cultural differences.

- *Emblems:* The specific messages that an emblem symbolizes often vary by culture. The "come here" gesture commonly used in the United States means "goodbye" in China, Italy, and Columbia.[33] Gestures such as A-OK, thumbs up, and crossed fingers have sexual or obscene meanings in many parts of the world.[34]

- *Affect displays:* Some displays of affect (emotion) are specific to certain cultures. In China, for example, women express emotional satisfaction by holding their fingertips over their closed mouths. Similarly, a man in Uruguay will hold his fists together and turn them in opposite directions, as if wringing out a wet cloth, to express anger.

- *Personal distance:* People from Arab countries generally converse with each other at closer distances than do people in the United States.[35] One study

Job Title >

Work Responsibilities >

Overseas teacher of English

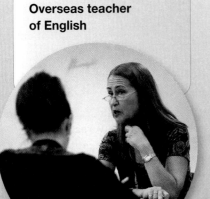

Native English speakers with a bachelor's degree are often hired to teach English as a foreign language in other countries. Some work with young children, others with adolescents, and others with adult learners. In each case, the ability to adapt to the nonverbal customs of the host culture is an enormous advantage. For instance, those who teach in high-contact cultures, where people touch each other frequently, must learn to adapt to their lack of personal space. Those who teach in polychronic cultures must remember that their students may have quite different norms with respect to time. Although the teacher may be discussing U.S. customs along with teaching the English language, he or she should also be ready to adapt to the local nonverbal norms.

found that because of differences in their preferred conversational distance, Arab college students regarded those from the United States as aloof, whereas the U.S. students regarded the Arab students as overbearing.[36]

- *Eye contact:* In many Western cultures, direct eye contact signifies that someone is sincere, trustworthy, and authoritative, whereas the lack of eye contact elicits negative evaluations from others.[37] In comparison, some Asian, Latin American, and Middle Eastern cultures emphasize the lack of eye contact as a sign of deference or respect for authority.[38]

- *Facial displays of emotion:* As noted above, decades of research indicate that people around the world express emotions—particularly primary emotions such as happiness, sadness, fear, anger, surprise, and disgust—in highly similar ways.[39] What tends to differ across cultures is how expressive people are of emotion, with those in individualistic cultures routinely being more emotionally expressive than those in collectivistic cultures.[40]

- *Greeting behavior:* People in Western countries typically greet social acquaintances with a handshake, whereas people in Mediterranean countries usually kiss each other on both cheeks. In Asian countries, it is common to greet others by bowing, with the longest and lowest bows reserved for the most respected individuals.[41]

- *Time orientations:* Recall from Chapter 2 that some cultures—including those in the United States, Canada, Finland, Great Britain, and Germany—are *monochronic*, meaning that they see time as a tangible commodity, expect events to begin "on time," and dislike having their time wasted.[42] Other cultures—including those in France, Brazil, Mexico, and Saudi Arabia—are *polychronic*, meaning they see time as flexible and diffused and don't necessarily expect punctuality.[43]

Greeting behaviors vary significantly from culture to culture. Some people shake hands, some kiss each other on the cheek, and others bow when meeting someone new.

- *Touch:* People in *high-contact cultures*, which include France, Mexico, and Greece, touch each other significantly more often than do people in *low-contact cultures*, such as Japan, Sweden, and Finland.[44] Research indicates that the United States is most accurately classified as a *medium-contact culture*.[45]
- *Vocalics:* Besides their readily noticeable differences in accents, cultures also differ in their use of filler words.[46] Although "umm" and "er" are common filler words for English speakers, Chinese speakers often say "zhege zhege zhege"—which translates to "this this this"—as filler words.

Before we proceed, it's important to acknowledge that not *every* nonverbal behavior differs by culture. People around the world interpret a smile as an expression of joy.[47] Parents in every known culture speak *babytalk*—soft, high-pitched vocal tones and highly simplified language—to their infants.[48] The fact that two people come from different cultures doesn't mean they can't communicate with each other nonverbally. It simply means they should be aware of the many ways in which each of their cultural backgrounds is influencing the way they do so.

SEX INFLUENCES NONVERBAL COMMUNICATION

A second major influence on our nonverbal communication is our sex. Perhaps you've noticed that women and men sometimes react with different nonverbal behaviors—or to different degrees—to the same situation. The question *why* sex influences nonverbal communication has intrigued researchers for decades.

One explanation is that beginning in early childhood, boys and girls are socialized to communicate in gender-specific ways (masculine for boys, feminine for girls).[49] Another explanation is that anatomical and physiological differences between the sexes cause them to behave in different ways.[50] Both possibilities have received extensive support from research, but not always for the same behaviors. In other words, sex differences in some nonverbal behaviors appear to be more influenced by socialization than biology, whereas others are more affected by biology than socialization.

No matter what the reason, sex influences several forms of nonverbal communication, including

- *Emotional expressiveness:* Several studies document that women are more expressive than men with respect to a variety of emotional states, including joy,[51] affection,[52] sadness,[53] and depression.[54] Some research indicates that men are more expressive than women of anger,[55] although other studies have found no sex difference in anger expression.[56]
- *Eye contact:* When communicating with others of their same sex, women engage in more eye contact than do men,[57] a difference that has been demonstrated in both the United States and Japan.[58] In fact, female pairs use higher amounts of gaze than do male pairs when speaking, while listening, and even during silence.[59] Research indicates that male–female pairs are similar to female–female pairs in terms of eye contact.[60]
- *Personal space:* In comparison to men, women are approached more closely, give way more readily to others, stand and sit closer to each other, and tolerate more violations of their personal space than do men.[61] In opposite-sex interactions, men are also more likely to violate women's personal space than women are to violate men's.[62]
- *Vocalics:* On average, men's voices have a lower pitch than do women's. The primary reason is that men have a larger voice box and longer vocal cords—which produce the sound of the voice—than women do, as a result of physiological changes that occur during puberty.[63] Research indicates that men also use more filler words and pauses while speaking than do women.[64]
- *Touch:* Among adults, men are more likely to touch women than women are to touch men, unless the touch is occurring as part of a greeting (such as a handshake).[65] In same-sex pairs, however, women touch each other more than men do, although that sex difference is smaller in close friendships than among acquaintances.[66]

- *Appearance:* Sex differences in appearance are also influenced by culture. Moreover, women and men typically adorn themselves in notably different ways. In Western cultures, for example, cosmetic use is significantly more common for women than for men.[67] Also, women and men usually wear different styles of clothing and jewelry and adopt different hairstyles, and those conventions further accentuate the differences in their appearance.

As with culture, it's important to note that not every nonverbal behavior differs by sex. Perhaps more important is to acknowledge that sex differences, even when they're present, aren't always substantial. Popular author John Gray, who wrote the highly successful book *Men Are from Mars, Women Are from Venus,*[68] has suggested that women and men communicate so differently that they might as well be from different planets. Although many communication behaviors do differ by sex, research tells us that those sex differences are often relatively small, not nearly as significant as Gray proposed. Indeed, communication scientist Kathryn Dindia has suggested a more modest metaphor for sex differences: "Men are from North Dakota, women are from South Dakota."[69]

Culture and sex aren't the only important influences on nonverbal communication. Another significant influence—and one in which our ability to communicate nonverbally is continually evolving—is computer-mediated communication. Table 5.1 highlights some of the ways in which changes in technology—and in our use of it—have influenced our nonverbal behavior.

Improving Your Nonverbal Communication Skills

In the CBS comedy series *The Big Bang Theory,* Sheldon Cooper is a theoretical physicist at Caltech who shares an apartment with his friend and colleague, Leonard Hofstadter. Despite having two doctoral degrees and being at the top of his professional field, Cooper is inept in most social situations. He does not understand many social conventions, such as the rules of politeness, and has little ability to interpret other people's emotions. Similarly, he shows near distain for human contact. He maintains a social network, although even his closest friends find him annoying and complain that he is difficult to be around. In all, Cooper is not a particularly skilled nonverbal communicator.

Sheldon Cooper would be well advised to read this section, in which we'll explore some ways of improving two particular types of nonverbal communication skills: interpreting nonverbal communication and expressing messages nonverbally.

INTERPRETING NONVERBAL COMMUNICATION

As we've seen in this chapter, people use nonverbal communication to express many types of messages, including those related to emotions and attitudes, power and dominance, persuasion, and deception. An important skill for communicators, therefore, is the ability to decode, or interpret, the nonverbal behaviors of others. That ability requires two separate but interrelated skills, as we'll now consider.

TABLE 5.1

CYBEREXPRESSIONS: COMPUTER-MEDIATED NONVERBAL COMMUNICATION

Although early computer-mediated communication relied exclusively on text, people eventually developed ways of expressing themselves nonverbally online. These include:

- **Emoticons:** As we noted earlier in this chapter, textual representations of a facial expression can help to convey a person's emotional state :)
- **Capitalization:** When you type something in all capital letters, IT IS OFTEN INTERPRETED AS YELLING.
- **Random symbols:** Instead of using obscenities in an e-mail message, a series of random keyboard symbols will often do the %#@&* trick.
- **Images:** You can incorporate both still pictures and video clips in computer-mediated communication to add a visual dimension to your message.

Learning how to communicate better is an ongoing process.

Be Sensitive to Nonverbal Messages

One skill useful in interpreting nonverbal communication is being sensitive to others' nonverbal messages. When your daughter grimaces after learning you're serving broccoli for dinner, or your son has an excited tone in his voice when talking about his last fencing match, do you notice those nonverbal emotion cues? When a competitor at work intentionally keeps you waiting for an appointment or seems unusually tense during your conversation, do you pick up on those potential signs of dominance or deception?

Sensitivity to nonverbal behaviors is essential because we can't interpret messages unless we first take note of them. Although research indicates that some of us are naturally more nonverbally sensitive than others, it is possible to increase our nonverbal sensitivity through mindful awareness—that is, by tuning in closely to what's happening around us.[70] When you're interacting with someone, try these approaches:

- Pay particular attention to facial expressions for signs of what the person is feeling. Remember that the face communicates more emotion than all other nonverbal channels.
- Take note of his or her tone of voice and body movements, because these are particularly relevant for signaling dominance and deception.

Decipher the Meaning of Nonverbal Messages

Nonverbal messages sometimes carry multiple meanings. If you notice a young man smiling as he interacts with another person, it might mean he's happy. Alternatively, it might mean that he's persuading a customer to make a purchase, comforting a relative who has just shared bad news, or flirting.[71] If you hear him speaking loudly, it might mean he's excited, or it may mean he's angry, surprised, or talking with someone who's hard of hearing.

An essential part of interpretation, therefore, is deciphering the meaning of nonverbal behaviors that others enact. Accurately deciphering a nonverbal behavior means taking it to mean what the sender intended.[72] Suppose that while you are describing your grandmother's failing health, your friend Vanessa squeezes your hand to convey her support. If you take her behavior as a gesture of support, then you have accurately deciphered her nonverbal message. If you take it to mean she's trying to persuade you or is interested in you romantically, however, then you have deciphered her message inaccurately.

To improve your skill at deciphering nonverbal messages, try the following strategies:

When we communicate across cultures, we cannot assume that a nonverbal gesture has the same meaning to us as it does to other societies. In many cultures, the "thumbs-up" gesture is considered obscene.

- Consider both the social situation a person is in and the other nonverbal behaviors he or she is enacting. If you notice a man crying, your first instinct might be to conclude that he's sad. Perhaps you also notice, however, that he is surrounded by smiling people who are hugging him and patting him on the back. You even hear him laugh, although tears are running down his face. Armed with these additional pieces of information, you might take his crying to mean that he is happy or relieved rather than sad.

- Keep in mind that cultural differences sometimes influence the meaning of a nonverbal message—particularly for gestures and eye behaviors. Using the thumbs-up gesture or failing to make eye contact while talking with someone can have different meanings in different cultures. The more you learn about cultural variation in nonverbal behavior, the more accurately you'll be able to decipher it.

- When you're unsure how accurately you've deciphered someone's nonverbal message, ask the person. Let's say you're relating the details of a new product to a client and her facial expression suggests confusion. Instead of assuming you've deciphered her expression accurately, you might ask her directly, "Did my description make sense?" If she replies that she found it confusing, you can explain the product again, using simpler language. If she instead replies that she is developing a headache, you will learn that the expression you deciphered as confusion was actually one of discomfort. Asking is a way to check your interpretation of someone's nonverbal message and to make sure you have deciphered it correctly.

As you practice your sensitivity and deciphering skills, you should be able to improve your ability to interpret the meaning of nonverbal behaviors.[73]

EXPRESSING NONVERBAL MESSAGES

Some of us are good at interpreting the nonverbal behaviors of others but not particularly good at expressing ourselves nonverbally. Yet as we've seen, we communicate more information nonverbally than verbally. If you're skilled at expressing nonverbal messages, you'll therefore be able to communicate with others more effectively and more efficiently than someone who is less skilled.

Just as with interpretation skills, some people are naturally more expressive, charismatic, and outgoing than others.[74] To improve your own skill at expressing nonverbal messages, try the following ideas:

- Spend time with highly expressive people. Some researchers have suggested that we can learn how to become more nonverbally expressive by being around extroverted and charismatic people.[75] Research also suggests that highly expressive people are attracted to certain professions, which include teaching and lecturing, acting and singing, politics, sales, diplomacy, customer service, counseling and therapy, and religious ministry.[76] Each of these requires an ability to communicate clearly and competently with others, which is served by being nonverbally expressive.

- Take part in games and activities that exercise your nonverbal expression skills. A good example is playing charades, in which you act out a word or phrase without speaking, while members of your team try to guess the answer based on your depiction. Another example is role playing, in which you act out the roles of characters in a specific but hypothetical situation the way you would if you were actually in that situation.

You can take a first step toward improving your skills at nonverbal interpretation and expression by assessing how skilled you are now. Complete the exercise in "The Competent Communicator" to evaluate your current interpretation and expression abilities.

adaptability Enacting Expressiveness

The Scene: One of your work responsibilities is to deliver sales presentations about vacation homes for sale. Because your audiences vary, you must make some of your presentations face-to-face, some over the telephone, and some in the form of e-mail messages. As a sales professional, you know how important effective nonverbal communication is. You also realize that communication channels vary in the types of nonverbal behaviors they allow.

Your Task: Practice a short sales pitch as you would deliver it face-to-face and by telephone, and then write an example of that sales pitch delivered as an e-mail message. Afterward, describe

- How you express yourself nonverbally in a face-to-face context.
- How your voice becomes more expressive over the telephone.
- How you incorporate nonverbal cues into an e-mail message.

Nonverbal Know-How: Rate Your Interpretation and Expression Skills

How much do you agree with each of the following statements? On the line before each statement, record your level of agreement on a 1 to 7 scale. A higher number means you agree more; a lower number means you agree less.

1. _____ When I feel depressed, I tend to bring down those around me.

2. _____ It is nearly impossible for people to hide their true feelings from me.

3. _____ I have been told that I have expressive eyes.

4. _____ In social settings I can instantly tell when someone is interested in me.

5. _____ Quite often I tend to be the life of the party.

6. _____ People often tell me that I am a sensitive and understanding person.

When you're finished, add up your scores from items 1, 3, and 5. That is your score for expressiveness. Next add up your scores for items 2, 4, and 6. That is your score for interpretation. Both scores should range from 3 to 21.

If your scores on both scales are between 16 and 21, then you are already quite good at nonverbal interpretation and expressiveness. If your scores are between 9 and 15, you have a moderate ability to interpret and express nonverbal behavior, and the suggestions offered in this chapter may help you sharpen those abilities. If your scores are between 3 and 8, then you especially can benefit from the guidance provided in this chapter for improving your skills. You may also find that one of your scores is considerably higher than the other. If that's the case, then you know which skill you're already good at and which skill could benefit from more practice.

SOURCE: Riggio, R. E. (1986). Assessment of basic social skills. *Journal of Personality and Social Psychology, 51,* 649–660.

For REVIEW

- **How do people communicate nonverbally?** Nonverbal communication comprises those behaviors and characteristics that convey meaning without the use of words. People communicate nonverbally via several channels, including facial displays, eye behaviors, movement and gestures, touch, vocal behaviors, smell, use of space, physical appearance, use of time, and use of artifacts.

- **How do culture and sex influence nonverbal behavior?** Culture and sex affect multiple nonverbal communication behaviors, including gestures, personal distance and touch, eye contact, time orientation, vocalics, and emotional expression.

- **In what ways can you improve your nonverbal communication skills?** You can improve your nonverbal communication skills by being sensitive to the nonverbal messages you encounter, learning to decipher their meanings accurately, and practicing your nonverbal expressiveness.

POP QUIZ

Multiple Choice

1. The two characteristics that contribute most to facial attractiveness are

    a. symmetry and proportionality.

    b. symmetry and expressiveness.

    c. proportionality and diameter.

    d. proportionality and expressiveness.

2. Diane announces that she is doing a study of oculesics. The form of nonverbal communication she is studying is

    a. the use of smell.

    b. the influence of attractiveness.

    c. emotional expressiveness.

    d. eye behaviors.

3. A manicurist touches Suzi's hands while giving her a manicure. The type of touch Suzi is receiving is

    a. affectionate.

    b. caregiving.

    c. ritualistic.

    d. power and control.

4. How high or low a voice sounds is an index of the vocal characteristic known as

    a. inflection.

    b. volume.

    c. rate.

    d. pitch.

5. Because she's from this type of culture, Laila sees time as flexible and diffused and doesn't necessarily expect punctuality.

    a. monochronic culture

    b. high-contact culture

    c. polychronic culture

    d. low-contact culture

Fill in the Blanks

6. _____ is the first of the five senses to develop in humans.

7. The study of smell is called _____.

8. Nonword sounds such as "umm" and "uh" are called _____.

9. People in _____ cultures touch each other significantly more than do people in other cultures.

10. The _____ is the idea that the face communicates more information than any other nonverbal behavior channel.

ANSWERS: 1. a; 2. d; 3. b; 4. d; 5. c; 6. touch; 7. olfactics; 8. filler words; 9. high-contact; 10. principle of facial primacy

KEY TERMS

nonverbal communication 104

emoticons 105

nonverbal channels 106

deception 106

immediacy behaviors 108

facial displays 109

symmetry 109

proportionality 109

oculesics 111

kinesics 112

gesticulation 112

emblems 112

illustrators 112

affect displays 113

regulators 113

adaptors 114

haptics 114

vocalics 114

paralanguage 114

olfactics 115

proxemics 115

intimate distance 115

personal distance 116

social distance 116

public distance 116

halo effect 116

chronemics 117

artifacts 117

LISTENING EFFECTIVELY

Listening and Forgiving

No one could blame Mary Johnson for hating Oshea Israel. As a teenager in Minneapolis, Israel shot and killed Mary's only son, Laramiun Byrd, during a fight at a party. As he neared the end of his prison sentence, Israel met with Johnson and listened as she described her profound sorrow at the loss of her son and her anger and animosity at Israel for ending his life. Israel says that listening to Johnson made her son "become human to me." That conversation paved the way for Johnson not only to forgive Israel but also to form a close, lasting relationship with him. The two now live next door to each other, and Johnson treats Israel as if he were her own son. Because they made the effort to listen to each other, Johnson and Israel have moved beyond their horrific past and have built a future together.

As You READ

- What does it mean to listen effectively?
- Why is listening effectively so challenging?
- How can you improve your listening skills?

You've probably had the frustrating experience of feeling as though someone was *hearing* you but not really *listening*. If so, you know that effective communication involves more than understanding the words that another person is speaking. You must also make sense of the speaker's intended message.

As you might imagine, problems with listening are fairly common in many types of relationships, from marriages and families to relationships in the workplace.[1] In addition, students often struggle to listen effectively to lectures and class presentations. Why? The reason is that proficient listening is a challenging skill you have to learn and practice. When you do it properly, listening adds much to the quality of your learning and your relationships, just as it did for Mary Johnson and Oshea Israel. When you don't listen effectively, your communication, relationships, and learning suffer.

What It Means to Listen

You probably don't give much thought to how well you listen. You can take classes to become a better speaker or a better writer, but few schools offer courses on improving listening skills. Yet if you're like most people, you spend much more time listening than you do speaking, writing, or engaging in other communicative behaviors. That's one reason why listening effectively is such a valuable skill.

WHAT IS LISTENING?

Listening is one of the most important concepts in human communication, yet many people find effective listening hard to define. When someone says, "You're not listening to me!" what exactly does that statement mean?

We can think of **listening** as the active process of making meaning from another person's spoken message.[2] Several details about that definition are important to note. First, listening is an active process. That means it isn't automatic; you have to *make* yourself listen to someone. Second, listening isn't just about **hearing,** which is the sensory process of receiving and perceiving sounds—listening is about creating meaning from what you hear. It is about **attending** to someone's words, or paying attention well enough to understand what that person is trying to communicate.

Even if people are hearing the same message, they may construct different meanings for it, an indicator that they are listening differently. For instance, you might listen to your brother's description of his new officemate and conclude that he finds her competent and likable. After listening to the same description, however, your mother might conclude that your brother feels threatened by his officemate's intelligence and self-confidence. You and your mother both heard the same description, but you listened to it differently.

Finally, listening deals with spoken messages. We certainly pay attention to written messages, as well as to nonverbal messages, which influence our interpretation of people's behaviors. But we can engage in listening only when someone is speaking.

Listening to someone doesn't automatically mean listening *effectively*. Effective listening requires listening with the conscious and explicit goal of understanding what the speaker intends to communicate. You might never know for certain whether you have understood a speaker's meaning *exactly* as he or she intended. If you're listening with the goal of understanding the speaker's meaning as best you can, however, you're listening effectively.

As we consider in this chapter, several barriers exist that make effective listening difficult, and different situations call for different types of listening. Understanding those dimensions of listening can help each of us to improve our ability to listen effectively. That's a worthwhile goal, as we'll now see.

THE IMPORTANCE OF LISTENING EFFECTIVELY

How much of your day do you think you spend listening? In one study, researchers Kathryn Dindia and Bonnie Kennedy found that college students spend more time listening than doing any other communication activity. As depicted in Figure 6.1, participants spent 50 percent of their waking hours listening.[3] In contrast, they spent only 20 percent

• **listening** The active process of making meaning out of another person's spoken message.

• **hearing** The sensory process of receiving and perceiving sounds.

• **attending** Paying attention to someone's words well enough to understand what that person is trying to communicate.

of their time speaking, 13 percent reading, and 12 percent writing. Other studies have found similar results, at least with college students, suggesting that most of us spend a similar percentage of our communication time listening.[4]

The ability to listen effectively is important to our success in a variety of contexts. Good listening skills are essential in the workplace. Suppose, for instance, that your employees don't listen when you tell them the alarm they will soon be hearing signals a fire drill, not a real fire. Some might panic at the sound of the alarm, and some might injure themselves as they rush frantically from their workspaces. Now suppose your manager at work doesn't listen to the staff's warnings about problems with the company's equipment. As a result, a critical production line breaks down, stalling operations for a week.

Those examples illustrate how consequential effective listening can be in the workplace. In one survey, a thousand human resource professionals ranked listening as the single most important quality of effective managers.[5] In other research, listening also topped the list of the most important communication skills in families and personal relationships.[6] Being a good listener is vital to just about every social and personal bond we have.[7]

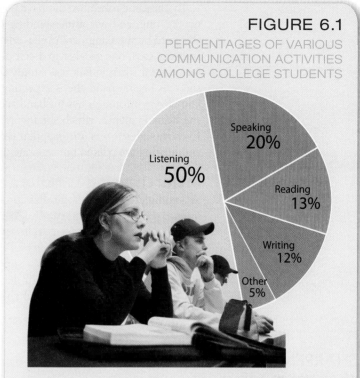

FIGURE 6.1
PERCENTAGES OF VARIOUS COMMUNICATION ACTIVITIES AMONG COLLEGE STUDENTS

Listening 50%
Speaking 20%
Reading 13%
Writing 12%
Other 5%

College students spend more time listening than communicating in other ways.

Despite the importance of listening skills, many of us nevertheless overestimate our listening abilities. In one study, 94 percent of corporate managers rated themselves as "good" or "very good" at listening, whereas not a single one rated himself or herself as "poor" or "very poor." Their employees told quite a different story, however; several rated their managers' listening skills as weak.[8] There appears to be very little association, in other words, between how good *we* think we are at listening and how good *others* think we are.[9]

As we'll soon see, many obstacles can get in the way of our ability to listen well. The good news, though, is that listening is a skill we can improve, and in this chapter we look at some ways to do just that.[10]

MISCONCEPTIONS ABOUT LISTENING

Are you surprised to learn that people often overestimate their listening abilities? Here are some other misunderstandings about the listening process.

Myth: Hearing Is the Same as Listening Some people use the terms *hearing* and *listening* interchangeably, but they aren't the same activity. Hearing is merely the perception of sound. Most people hear sounds almost continuously—you hear your roommate's music, the neighbor's dogs barking, the car alarm that wakes you in the middle of the night. Hearing is a passive process that occurs when sound waves cause the bones in your inner ear to vibrate and send signals to your brain.

Unlike hearing, listening is an active process of paying attention to a sound, assigning meaning to it, and responding to it. Hearing is a part of that process, but listening requires much more than just perceiving the sounds around you.

By the same token, we can have the relatively infrequent experience of listening without hearing, and our understanding can be impaired as a result. A series of television ads aired by the Cingular/AT&T telephone company illustrated this point humorously. In every case, one speaker in a cell phone conversation interprets the other's silence as meaningful when in fact it is simply the result of a dropped call. For instance, just after she tells her husband she is expecting a baby, one woman's call is dropped without her knowledge. Although her husband is exclaiming his excitement about the pregnancy, all she hears is silence, which she incorrectly interprets as indifference or fear on his part. Even though she was *listening*, that is, she wasn't *hearing*. As those ads illustrate, listening and hearing are related but separate processes.

Myth: Listening Is Natural and Effortless

It's easy to think of listening as a completely natural, mindless process, much like breathing. In reality, listening is a *learned skill*, not an innate ability. We have to acquire our listening abilities. Just as we are taught to speak, we have to be taught to listen—and to listen effectively.

We learn from our experiences. Perhaps, for example, you can recall instances when you didn't listen effectively to a supervisor's instructions about how to accomplish a work project and you made poor decisions as a result. Maybe you have been in a situation with a romantic partner when you didn't listen as effectively as you could have, and the consequence was an unnecessary argument. Those types of unhappy experiences have probably taught you about the importance of effective listening, because good communicators learn from their mistakes. We also learn through instruction, such as the instruction you are receiving in your introductory communication course. The more you learn about what makes listening effective and what barriers to watch out for, the better equipped you'll be to listen effectively to others.

The fact that listening is a skill also means that people vary in their listening abilities. Just as some people are better than others at drawing or singing or writing, some are better listeners than others. Finally, like most other skills, your listening ability can improve with education and training.[11]

Counselors and social workers, for instance, are trained to listen effectively to clients, a skill that improves the quality of their work. In recent years, medical schools around the United States have added course work on effective listening and other interpersonal skills to their curricula for training new physicians. People in many professions, from education and ministry to customer service and politics, can benefit from training in effective listening.

HOW CULTURE AFFECTS LISTENING BEHAVIOR

Cultural messages shape many communication behaviors, and listening is no exception. Research indicates that culture affects listening behavior in at least three ways: expectations for directness, nonverbal listening responses, and understanding of language.

SHARPEN Your Skills: *Listening rather than responding*

Have a conversation with someone about a topic on which you disagree. During your talk, focus your attention on what the other person is saying rather than on how you're going to respond. Check your ability by repeating the person's claims back to him or her after your conversation.

Effective listening is an essential skill for health workers. Many medical schools now teach new physicians how to listen effectively to patients.

Culture Affects Listeners' Expectations for Directness
Listening behavior is influenced by how people in a given culture think about the importance of time. Reflecting their monochronic culture, American speakers commonly say that "time is money" and conceive of time as something that can be saved, spent, and wasted. Listeners in a monochronic culture value direct, straightforward communication and become impatient with speakers who don't get to the point.[12] In contrast, people in polychronic cultures such as China and Korea emphasize social harmony over efficiency. These listeners often pay close attention to nonverbal behaviors and contextual cues to determine the meaning of a speaker's message.[13]

Culture Affects Nonverbal Listening Responses
Cultural expectations can also influence what individuals consider to be appropriate listening responses, particularly with respect to nonverbal behavior. For instance, people in U.S. culture typically expect listeners to maintain eye contact with them while they're speaking. Listeners who look down or away usually seem as though they aren't listening. Within Native American culture, however, looking down or away while listening is a sign of respect rather than a signal that someone is not listening.[14]

Culture Affects Understanding of Language
When people speak a language in which listeners aren't fluent, listeners can have a hard time understanding what is being said for at least two reasons. One reason, which we examined in Chapter 4, is that many languages include idioms—phrases often understandable only to native speakers of that language. For instance, you might tell an overseas visitor that you're "on Cloud 9"about to your upcoming graduation, but if English isn't her first language, she may not understand that you mean you're very happy. Consequently, she would have difficulty listening effectively to you.

The second reason language differences can lead to listening challenges is that listeners may not comprehend the words being spoken. When I have foreign exchange students in my classes, I try to be aware of terms and phrases they may be unable to interpret because of their limited knowledge of English, and I provide an explanation for those words. That approach is especially helpful when I'm using highly technical terms with which non-native listeners may be unfamiliar.

Listeners for whom English is a non-native language can improve their listening abilities online by visiting http://wiki.vec.hku.hk/index.php/listening. This virtual English Wiki site offers links to a wide variety of other websites providing listening materials, songs, television links, and exercises for those whose native language is other than English.

Ways of Listening

Until now, we've been talking about listening as though it were a single activity. In truth, listening *effectively* has *several* stages, all of which are equally important.

STAGES OF EFFECTIVE LISTENING

Judi Brownell, an expert on listening, developed the **HURIER model** to describe the stages of effective listening.[15] The six stages, from whose first letters the model is named, are hearing, understanding, remembering, interpreting, evaluating, and responding. We don't necessarily have to enact those stages in order; sometimes listening effectively requires us to go back and forth among them. Nonetheless, when we listen effectively, those are the behaviors we adopt.

• HURIER model A model describing the stages of effective listening as hearing, understanding, remembering, interpreting, evaluating, and responding.

Hearing
Hearing, the physical process of perceiving sound, is where listening begins. Yet, as we've seen, we can certainly hear someone without listening to that person. Hearing without listening is common when we're tired or uninterested in

what a person is saying, or when we're hearing multiple voices at once, as in a crowded restaurant. However, we can't really listen effectively to someone unless we can first hear the person.

The sensory task of hearing may be difficult for individuals with hearing impairments. Some read lips, and others use sign language to communicate. For individuals without hearing problems, though, hearing is the first step in effective listening.

Understanding It's not enough simply to hear what someone is saying—you also have to understand it. That means comprehending the meanings of the words and phrases.[16] If someone is speaking in a language you don't comprehend, you might be able to hear, but you won't be able to listen effectively. The same is true when you hear technical language or jargon with which you're unfamiliar: Even if the speaker is speaking your language, you can't effectively listen if you do not understand the words. If you're uncertain whether you understand what a speaker is saying, the most effective course of action is usually to ask the person questions so you can check your understanding.

Remembering The third stage of the HURIER model of effective listening is remembering, or being able to store something in your memory and retrieve it when needed.[17] Remembering what you hear is often important for interpersonal communication, because it can help you to avoid awkward situations with others. For instance, you might have had the embarrassing experience of running into someone whose name you can't remember, even though you have met the person before. In such an encounter, the ability to remember what you heard previously—the person's name in this instance—can help you communicate more effectively.

As a student, you probably have your memory skills tested on an ongoing basis. If you're particularly good at remembering the details of a conversation, you're in the minority. Research shows that most people can recall a mere 25 percent of what they hear—and even then, they remember only about 20 percent of it accurately.[18] The average person is therefore not especially good at remembering. Fortunately, short-term memory is a skill you can practice and improve.

• **mnemonics** Devices that can aid short- and long-term memory.

Mnemonics are tricks that can aid our short- and long-term memory. Such devices come in several forms. If you've ever studied music, for instance, perhaps you learned  to recall the lines of the treble staff—EGBDF—by treating the letters as an acronym for a phrase such as "Every good boy does fine." You might also develop rhymes to help you remember certain rules, such as the spelling convention "*I* before *E*, except after *C*." In another mnemonic device, you might treat an acronym as if it were a word. For instance, if you remember the elements of Brownell's effective listening model by learning the word HURIER, you are employing that type of mnemonic device. Research suggests that using mnemonic devices can significantly enhance our memory of what we hear.[19]

Interpreting Besides hearing, understanding, and remembering, an effective listener must interpret the information he or she receives. Interpreting has two parts. The first part is paying attention to all the speaker's verbal and nonverbal behaviors so you can assign meaning to the person's message. Suppose your friend Maya says, "It's a beautiful day outside!" Based on her facial expressions and tone of voice, you might interpret her message as sincere—meaning that Maya thinks today's weather *is* beautiful—or as sarcastic—meaning she thinks the weather is lousy. Those are very different interpretations of Maya's message, even though her words are the same.

The second part of interpreting is signaling your interpretation of the message to the speaker. If you interpret Maya's statement as sincere, you might smile and say you're looking forward to getting outside to enjoy the great weather. If you interpret her statement as sarcastic, however, you might laugh or respond with a cynical remark of your own. Signaling, in other words, not only lets the speaker know we're following along with the message but also allows us to check our interpretations. Suppose, for instance, that Maya intended her comment to be sarcastic but you interpreted it as sincere. If you smiled and said you were looking forward to getting outside, you would probably be signaling to Maya that you have misinterpreted the intent of her statement. She might then say "I was just kidding" to correct your interpretation.

Evaluating Several things happen at the evaluation stage, another crucial step for effective listening. For one thing, you're judging whether the speaker's statements are accurate and true. You might base those judgments on what you already know, or you might seek out information that verifies or challenges their accuracy. Second, you're separating factual claims from opinions. As Chapter 4 explains, opinions assert *what should be*, whereas factual claims assert *what is*, and each statement calls for a different type of response. Finally, you're considering the speaker's words in the context of other information you have from that speaker, such as his or her actions or previous statements. You might note, for instance, that the speaker is making a different claim today than he or she made last week, which would call the accuracy of the claim into question. All those processes help you to be an active, engaged listener rather than a passive recipient of information.

Responding The last stage of effective listening is responding, or indicating to a speaker that we are listening. We sometimes refer to that process as "giving feedback." We respond both verbally and nonverbally using a variety of strategies.[20]

Below are seven types of listening responses you might use, arranged in order from the most passive to the most active strategies:

- *Stonewalling:* Responding with silence and a lack of expression on your face. Stonewalling often signals a lack of interest in what the speaker is saying.
- *Backchanneling:* Using facial expressions, nods, vocalizations such as "uh-huh" and verbal statements such as "I understand" and "that's very interesting" to let the speaker know you're paying attention.
- *Paraphrasing:* Restating in your own words what the speaker has said, to show that you understand.
- *Empathizing:* Conveying to the speaker that you understand and share his or her feelings on the topic being discussed.
- *Supporting:* Expressing your agreement with the speaker's opinion or point of view.
- *Analyzing:* Providing your own perspective on what the speaker has said.
- *Advising:* Communicating advice to the speaker about what he or she should think, feel, or do.

Depending on the situation, some of those responses may be more useful or appropriate than others. For instance, if you are listening to a friend who has just lost her favorite uncle to cancer, empathizing and supporting responses are probably the most fitting. Stonewalling, backchanneling, or paraphrasing might make it seem as though you don't care about your friend, whereas analyzing or advising might seem insensitive. In contrast, if you're listening to a client who is wondering how she can make the most of her stock portfolio, then analyzing and advising are probably called for.

To summarize, the stages of effective listening are hearing, understanding, remembering, interpreting, evaluating, and responding. (Keep in mind that mnemonic word *HURIER*.) A brief recap appears in Table 6.1. According to Brownell's model, those

stages characterize effective listening no matter why we are listening in the first place. As you probably know, we listen to others for several different reasons. We'll take a close look at three of the most common types of listening next.

TYPES OF LISTENING

When we talk about different *types* of listening, we're referring to the different *goals* we have when we listen to other people. Sometimes we listen to learn, sometimes to evaluate, and sometimes to empathize. Those goals aren't necessarily exclusive; sometimes we listen with more than one goal in mind. When we distinguish among types of listening, we are considering what our *primary* listening goal is at a given time.

Informational Listening
Much of the listening you do in class or at work is **informational listening,** or listening to learn. Whenever you watch the news or listen to driving directions or pay attention to a professor's lecture, you're engaged in informational listening.

Informational listening is one of the most important ways we learn. It is also a relatively passive process. When we engage in informational listening, we're simply taking in information. That is, although we may be listening effectively and even taking notes, we are listening primarily to learn something new rather than to critique what we're hearing or to support the person saying it.

Critical Listening
When our goal is to evaluate or analyze what we're hearing, we are engaged in **critical listening.** You listen carefully to a television commercial to see whether you want to buy the product being advertised. You listen to a sales presentation or a political speech and evaluate the merits of what you're hearing. You listen critically to your mother's description of her recent medical appointment to determine how worried she is about the results of her blood test.

Critical listening doesn't necessarily mean criticizing what you're hearing. Instead, it means analyzing and evaluating the merits of a speaker's words. Compared to informational listening, critical listening is therefore a more active, engaging process. It requires not only taking in information but also evaluating and judging it. As you will see at the end of this chapter, practicing critical listening skills is one of the best ways of becoming a better listener.

Empathic Listening
The most challenging form of listening is often **empathic listening,** which occurs when you are trying to identify with the speaker by understanding and experiencing what he or she is thinking or feeling.[21] When talking to a friend who has just lost a beloved pet, you can use empathic listening to give comfort and support.

Responding to a speaker with silence and a lack of expression is known as stonewalling.

• **informational listening** Listening to learn.

• **critical listening** Listening to evaluate or analyze.

• **empathic listening** Listening to experience what the speaker thinks or feels.

TABLE 6.1 HURIER MODEL OF EFFECTIVE LISTENING	Brownell's model suggests that effective listening has six elements, represented by the acronym HURIER.	
	Hearing	Physically perceiving sound
	Understanding	Comprehending the words we have heard
	Remembering	Storing ideas in memory
	Interpreting	Assigning meaning to what we've heard
	Evaluating	Judging the speaker's believability and intentions
	Responding	Indicating that we are listening

Effective empathic listening requires two separate skills. The first, *perspective taking*, is the ability to understand a situation from another's point of view.[22] The second skill, *empathic concern*, is the ability to identify how someone else is feeling and to experience those feelings yourself.[23] When listening to a co-worker describing his recent diabetes diagnosis, for instance, you can practice perspective taking by trying to think about the situation as he would think about it. You can practice empathic concern by imagining how he must feel and by sharing in those emotions.

Empathic listening is different from *sympathetic listening*, which involves feeling sorry for another person. If your neighbors lost their young grandson to leukemia, for instance, you might be able to sympathize with them even if you can't truly understand their grief. With empathic listening, however, the goal is to understand a situation from the speaker's perspective and to feel what he or she is feeling. You might be listening to a friend who didn't get into her first-choice graduate school and trying to convey that you feel and share her disappointment. Listening empathically can be a challenge, because our own perceptions can cause us to focus on how *we* would be feeling in the same situation, when our goal is to understand the *speaker's* feelings.

When you listen to an instructor for the purpose of learning something, you are engaged in informational listening.

Other Types of Listening Informational, critical, and empathic listening aren't the only types of listening. For example, sometimes we engage in *inspirational listening*, which is listening to be inspired by what someone is saying. That type of listening is common when we're taking in a sermon or a motivational speech. Other times, we engage in *appreciative listening*, which is listening for pure enjoyment. We adopt that style when listening to someone telling a funny story or singing one of our favorite songs. When it comes to interacting with others, however, informational, critical, and empathic listening are among the most common and most important types.

In addition to engaging in different *types* of listening, many of us also differ in our *styles* of listening. Check out "The Competent Communicator" to see what listening style best describes you.

Common Barriers to Effective Listening

In the 2006 movie *The Break Up*, Brooke Meyers (played by Jennifer Aniston) asks her boyfriend Gary Grobowski (played by Vince Vaughn) to bring home a dozen lemons for a dinner party she is throwing for their families. Gary doesn't listen and ends up bringing home only three lemons. Brooke finds Gary's goof distressing because their company is arriving shortly, so she expresses her concern to Gary—who watches television while talking to her:

Brooke: *You got three lemons.*

Gary: *What my baby wants, my baby gets; you know that.*

Brooke: *I know, but I wanted 12, baby wanted 12.*

Gary: *Why would you want 12 lemons?*

Brooke: *Because I'm making a 12-lemon centerpiece.*

Gary: *So no one's actually even eating them, they're just show lemons?*

Brooke: *Yeah, they're just show lemons. To go in the center of the table. I'm glad you find that amusing, but I cannot fill a vase with only three lemons.*

People, Action, Content, Time: What's Your Listening Style?

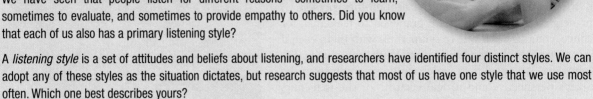

We have seen that people listen for different reasons—sometimes to learn, sometimes to evaluate, and sometimes to provide empathy to others. Did you know that each of us also has a primary listening style?

A *listening style* is a set of attitudes and beliefs about listening, and researchers have identified four distinct styles. We can adopt any of these styles as the situation dictates, but research suggests that most of us have one style that we use most often. Which one best describes yours?

- **People-oriented style:** This style emphasizes concern for other people's emotions and interests. Someone with this style tries to find common interests with others. For example, when listening to his middle-school students, Lorenzo tries to understand what they think and feel so that he can relate to them effectively.

- **Action-oriented style:** This style emphasizes organization and precision. Someone with this style likes neat, concise, error-free presentations. For instance, Monica loves it when her interns fill her in on the week's activities in a clear, straightforward way, and she gets frustrated when she can't understand them.

- **Content-oriented style:** This style emphasizes intellectual challenges. Someone with this style likes to attend to details and think things through. Emma really enjoys listening to political commentators, for example, because they make her think about her own social and political views.

- **Time-oriented style:** This style emphasizes efficiency. Someone with this style prefers conversations that are quick and to the point. As an emergency room physician, for instance, Ben relies on short and fast reports on a patient's condition from paramedics and nurses, and he gets impatient when they give him irrelevant information.

Each listening style has its strengths and weaknesses, and none is inherently better than the others. If you're primarily a people-oriented listener, you're likely to get to know others well, but you may not be able to work as efficiently as a time-oriented listener. If you're an action-oriented listener, you might do best in a major that emphasizes clarity and precision, such as engineering or computer science, whereas a content-oriented listener might prefer a major that tolerates greater ambiguity and room for debate, such as fine arts or political science.

SOURCE: Watson, K. W., Barker, L. L., & Weaver, J. B. (2005). The listening styles profile (LSP-16): Development and validation of an instrument to assess four listening styles. *International Journal of Listening, 9,* 1–13.

Brooke isn't upset in this scene just because she doesn't have the right number of lemons. She's also upset because Gary didn't listen to her when she asked him to bring home a dozen lemons, and she gets increasingly frustrated because he continues watching television during their conversation instead of paying attention to her.

Why are so few of us good listeners? The answer is that various factors can get in our way, acting as barriers to our ability to listen well. We will take a look at several of those obstacles next, beginning with noise.

NOISE

How many different stimuli are competing for your attention right now—or perhaps at work, where your boss, customers, and coworkers may all be trying to talk to you at once? In the context of listening, **noise** is anything that distracts you from listening to what you wish to listen to. That distraction could be *physical noise*, which consists of actual sound, or *psychological noise*, which is anything else we find distracting.

Most of us find it tougher to listen to a conversational partner when there are other sounds in the environment, such as a TV or loud music.[24] These are examples of physical noise. However, it isn't just sound that can distract us. If we're hungry or tired, or if we're in an especially hot or cold environment, those influences qualify as psychological noise because they distract us and thus reduce our ability to listen effectively.[25]

When faced with such distractions, focus your attention on your conversational partner and listen intently to what he or she is saying. That strategy requires being conscious of noise in your environment and identifying the factors that are drawing your attention away from your conversation. If you can eliminate or ignore these, such as by turning off your car radio or disregarding your ringing cell phone, you will better focus attention on your partner. If you're being distracted by noise you can't ignore or reduce, it may be best to reschedule your conversation for a time when fewer stimuli are competing for your attention.

• noise Anything that distracts people from listening to what they wish to listen to.

PSEUDOLISTENING AND SELECTIVE ATTENTION

At one time or another, you've probably pretended to pay attention to someone when you weren't really listening, a behavior called **pseudolistening.** When you are pseudolistening, you use feedback behaviors that make it *seem* as though you're paying attention, even though your mind is elsewhere. A variation of pseudolistening is **selective attention,** which means listening only to what you want to hear and ignoring the rest.[26] With selective attention, you are actually listening to some parts of a person's message but pseudolistening to other parts. In her job as an insurance adjustor, for instance, Sue-Ann receives an evaluation from her supervisor every January. Most of her supervisor's comments are usually positive, but some suggest ways in which Sue-Ann could improve. The problem is, Sue-Ann doesn't listen to those suggestions. Instead, she listens selectively, paying close attention to her supervisor's praise but only pretending to listen to his critiques.

• pseudolistening Pretending to listen.

• selective attention Listening only to what one wants to hear and ignoring the rest.

People engage in pseudolistening and selective attention for many different reasons. Think about your own experiences. Maybe you're bored with what a speaker is saying, but you don't want to seem rude. Maybe you don't understand what you're hearing, but you're embarrassed to say so. Maybe you're paying attention to something else while someone is talking to you, or maybe you simply don't like what is being said. Whatever the reason, pseudolistening and selective attention are not only barriers to effective listening; they can also be a source of frustration for those you're pretending to listen to, because (as you probably know from your own experience) people are often aware when others aren't listening to what they're saying.

INFORMATION OVERLOAD

A third barrier to effective listening is **information overload,** the state of being overwhelmed by the huge amount of information each of us takes in every day. We talk to people, watch television, listen to the radio, surf the Internet, get text messages, thumb through magazines, read newspapers and college textbooks, and observe a variety of advertisements. At times, the sheer volume of information we have to attend to can seem overwhelming. When it is, we find it hard to listen effectively to new information.

• information overload The state of being overwhelmed by the enormous amount of information encountered each day.

Sources and Effects of Information Overload Consider how many advertising messages you see or hear on a daily basis. We view ads on television, in magazines and newspapers, on billboards, on people's clothing, in junk mail, and in movie previews. We receive ads by fax and cell phone, hear them on the radio, and find them in product inserts. We see and hear them at gas pumps, at automated

teller machines, on banners flying behind airplanes, and on the stickers we peel off apples and other fruits. We also receive them in the form of e-mail spam and pop-up announcements on the Internet.

It might seem as though information overload is a product of the digital age, as massive amounts of information have become so easily and immediately available at the stroke of a key. In fact, the term *information overload* was coined in 1970 by sociologist Alvin Toffler, in a book discussing the downsides of rapid technological change.[27] Thus, people were experiencing the distracting effects of information overload long before computer-mediated communication was widely used.

One of the biggest problems with information overload is that it can interrupt our attention. If you're e-mailing with an important client, for instance, your ability to pay attention to her messages can be compromised repeatedly by each new radio advertisement you hear, each new faxed announcement you receive, and each new pop-up ad you see. In fact, the average young person in the United States is exposed to more than 3,000 advertisements every day on television, on billboards, in magazines, and online.[28] Those interruptions might seem small and inconsequential when considered individually, but when you think about their effects on the entire population over time, they become a significant distraction. An analysis by a New York–based management research firm estimated the annual cost to U.S. companies of unnecessary interruptions from information overload to be a staggering $650 billion.[29]

Information overload can be particularly troubling for people with *attention-deficit hyperactivity disorder (ADHD)*, a developmental disorder. Individuals with ADHD are often easily distracted and have trouble focusing their attention for very long at a time. They are often also overly active and restless.[30] Although ADHD symptoms usually appear during childhood, a majority of children diagnosed with ADHD will continue to suffer from it as adults.[31] Because of their impaired ability to focus and susceptibility to distraction, individuals with ADHD may have an especially difficult time coping with the volume of information most of us encounter every day.

 getCONNECTED

Avoiding Information Overload from Computer-Mediated Sources

You can employ several strategies to reduce the distracting effects of information overload. For example:

- During meetings and important conversations, turn off the ringer on your cell phone or smartphone so you won't be distracted by incoming calls, text messages, and e-mails.
- Set the filters on your e-mail system to reduce spam, and use a pop-up blocker to eliminate ads when you're online.

- Contact the Direct Marketing Association to have your address removed from junk mail lists.
- Use your DVR (digital video recorder) to record your favorite TV shows so you can watch them at your convenience and skip the commercials.

Employing such strategies will help you to focus more of your attention on others and less on the blitz of information emanating from computer-mediated and other communication sources.

GLAZING OVER

A fourth reason effective listening is challenging is that the mind thinks much faster than most people talk. Most of us are capable of understanding up to 600 words per minute, but the average person speaks fewer than 150 words per minute.[32] That gap leaves a lot of spare time for the mind to wander, during which we can engage in what researchers call **glazing over,** or daydreaming.

For instance, Rochelle picks up her 6-year-old daughter and 9-year-old son every afternoon, and during the drive home the children describe what they did in school that day. Although she listens to what they say, Rochelle allows her mind to wander as they talk. She thinks about the novel she's reading and ponders her grocery list. Because her children speak more slowly than she can listen, and because the reports of their school activities are similar every day, Rochelle often glazes over when listening to them.

Glazing over is different from pseudolistening, which, as you'll recall, means only pretending to listen. When you're glazing over, you actually *are* listening to the speaker. It's just that you're allowing your mind to drift while doing so.

Glazing over can lead to at least three different problems. First, it can cause you to miss important details in what you're hearing. If you're glazing over while listening to a lecture in your communication course, for instance, you might fail to hear a critical piece of information about the term paper assignment. Second, glazing over might lead you to listen less critically than you normally would. For example, if your mind is wandering while you're listening to a salesperson describe the terms of a car loan, you might not realize that the deal isn't as good as it seems. Finally, glazing over can make it appear to a speaker that you aren't listening to what he or she is saying, even though you are. In those instances, you can come across as inattentive or dismissive. An effective listener will work to keep his or her focus on what the speaker is saying, instead of daydreaming or thinking about other topics.

REBUTTAL TENDENCY

Regan has recently started work as a customer service representative for an electronics retailer, but his first two weeks on the job have not gone well. He knows he should listen nonjudgmentally to customers as they describe their frustrations with the products they bought and then offer them his assistance and advice. Instead, Regan begins arguing with customers in his mind while they're still speaking. Rather than listening carefully to their concerns, he jumps to conclusions about what they have done wrong, and he formulates his response even before they have stopped talking.

Regan is enacting a **rebuttal tendency,** the propensity to debate a speaker's point and formulate a reply while that person is still speaking.[33] According to research by business professor Steven Golen, the tendency to think of how you're going to respond to a speaker, arguing with the speaker in your mind, and jumping to conclusions before the speaker has finished talking are all barriers to effective listening.[34] There are two reasons why.

First, the rebuttal tendency requires mental energy that should be spent paying attention to the speaker. That is, it's difficult to listen effectively when all you're thinking about is how to respond. Second, because you're not paying close attention to the speaker, you can easily miss some of the details that might change your response in the first place. Regan had that very experience when a woman returned a wireless Internet router she was having trouble installing. Regan concluded too quickly that she hadn't

• **glazing over** Daydreaming or allowing the mind to wander while another person is speaking.

• **rebuttal tendency** The propensity to debate a speaker's point and formulate a reply while that person is still speaking.

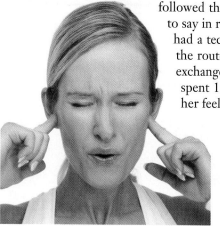

followed the instructions, and he got sidetracked thinking about what he was going to say in response. Consequently, he didn't hear the customer say that she'd already had a technician guide her through the installation procedure and advise her that the router was defective. If Regan had heard that important detail, he could have exchanged the product efficiently and sent the customer on her way. Instead, he spent 10 minutes telling the customer to do what she had already done, leaving her feeling frustrated.

CLOSED-MINDEDNESS

We're closed-minded when we refuse to listen to anything with which we disagree.

Another barrier to effective listening is **closed-mindedness,** the tendency not to listen to anything with which we disagree.[35] Perhaps you know people whom you would describe as closed-minded: they typically refuse to consider the merits of a speaker's point if it conflicts with their own views. They also tend to overreact to certain forms of language, such as slang and profanity, and stop listening to speakers who use them.[36]

• **closed-mindedness**
The tendency not to listen to anything with which one disagrees.

Many people are closed-minded only about particular issues, not about everything. For example, as an educator, Bella prides herself in being open to diverse opinions on a range of topics. When it comes to her own religious beliefs, however, she is so thoroughly convinced of their merits that she refuses to listen to religious ideas that she doesn't already accept. It's as if Bella is shutting her mind to the possibility that any religious ideas besides her own can have value. Many of her teaching colleagues find this reaction off-putting. It prevents Bella not only from learning more about their religious traditions but also from teaching others about her beliefs, because she refuses to talk about religion with anyone who doesn't already share her views.

Bella should remember that we can listen effectively to people even if we disagree with them. As the Greek philosopher Aristotle (384–322 B.C.) wrote: "It is the mark of an educated mind to be able to entertain a thought without accepting it." When we refuse even to listen to ideas with which we disagree, we limit our ability to learn from other people and their experiences. If you find yourself feeling closed-minded toward particular ideas, remind yourself that listening to an idea doesn't necessarily mean accepting it.

SHARPEN Your Skills: *Open-mindedness*

Listen to a politician or talk-radio host with whose viewpoints you strongly disagree. Take note of the discomfort you might feel, but listen carefully to the arguments being made and the evidence being offered to support them. Afterward, choose one of the speaker's arguments and write a paragraph defending it. You needn't agree with the argument; only listen with an open enough mind to defend that speaker's position.

COMPETITIVE INTERRUPTING

Normal conversation is a series of speaking "turns." You speak for a while, and then you allow another person to have a turn, and thus the conversation goes back and forth. Occasionally, though, people talk when it isn't their turn. We call that behavior *interrupting,* and there are many reasons people do it. Sometimes they interrupt to express support or enthusiasm for what the other person is saying ("Yeah, I agree!"); sometimes they do so to stop the speaker and ask for clarification ("Wait, I'm not sure what you mean"); and sometimes they talk out of turn to warn the speaker of an impending danger ("Stop! You're spilling your coffee!").

• **competitive interrupting**
The practice of using interruptions to take control of the conversation.

For some people, however, interrupting can be a way to dominate a conversation. Researchers use the term **competitive interrupting** to describe the practice of using interruptions to take control of the conversation. The goal in competitive interrupting is to make sure that you get to speak more than the other person does and that your ideas and perspectives take priority. You can probably think of people who engage in that behavior—individuals with whom you feel you "can't get a word in edgewise."

Although research shows that most interruptions *aren't* competitive, talking with a competitive interrupter can be frustrating.[37] Some people respond by becoming competitive themselves, turning the conversation into a battle of wits; others simply withdraw from the interaction. Some studies suggest that on average, men interrupt more often than women, although other studies have found no sex difference in the use of interruptions.[38]

How else do women and men differ in their listening behaviors? Check out the "Fact or Fiction?" box to find out.

Table 6.2 summarizes the barriers to effective listening. Bear in mind that each of them can be overcome. Specifically, with training and practice, most of us can improve our abilities to listen well, as we'll now consider.

Honing Your Listening Skills

In this chapter we've explored several examples of ineffective listening. We've seen that in the movie *The Break Up*, Gary doesn't listen to Brooke when she says she needs a dozen lemons. We've witnessed that Regan doesn't listen effectively to his customers' complaints and that Rochelle glazes over when listening to her children describe their day at school.

Listening effectively to others can be challenging. Fortunately, effective listening is a skill rather than an innate ability, so it is possible to become a better listener through education and practice. In this section, we'll look at various strategies you can use to improve your skills for informational, critical, and empathic listening.

BECOME A BETTER INFORMATIONAL LISTENER

When you engage in informational listening, your goal is to understand and learn from the speaker's message. For instance, you might be participating in a videoconference about saving for retirement or asking a nurse practitioner over Skype about your medications. How can you make the most of those opportunities?

Separate What Is and Isn't Said One important strategy for improving your informational listening skills is to beware of the tendency to "hear" words or statements that aren't actually said. Think about the last time you saw a TV commercial for a pain reliever, for instance. A common tactic for advertisers is to claim that "nothing is more effective" than their product. What do you learn from hearing that statement? In other words, how would you restate the message in your own words?

The advertisers are hoping you learn that their particular pain reliever is the strongest one available—but that's not really what they said, is it? All they said is that nothing is more effective, a statement that could mean that there may be several other products *just as effective* as theirs. It may also mean that all the products are equally ineffective! If you listened to that type of ad and concluded that the product was the most effective one available, you arrived at that conclusion on your own. When you are engaged in informational listening, practice being aware of what is actually being said versus what you are simply inferring.

Perhaps the most effective way to determine whether you have understood a speaker's message is to paraphrase it. As we saw earlier in the chapter, paraphrasing means restating a speaker's message in your own words in order to clarify its meaning. If you paraphrase a statement in a way that accurately reflects its meaning, the speaker will usually confirm your understanding.

Let's suppose that while leaving a theater after a movie, your roommate Dean and you have the following exchange:

> **Dean:** *I think we should swing by that new barbecue place on the way home.*
>
> **You:** *You want to pick up some dinner?*
>
> **Dean:** *Yeah, I'm starving.*

Fact or *fiction*?

Sex Matters: Men and Women Listen Differently

In this book we examine several stereotypes about how women and men communicate. Some are outright false, others are true, and some are true but highly exaggerated. One idea that relates to listening is that women and men have different listening styles: women are more interested in people, whereas men are more interested in facts. Are those distinctions fact or fiction?

Research suggests these assumed differences are true. In a study of adults' listening styles, researchers Stephanie Sargent and James Weaver found that women rated themselves higher on people-oriented listening than men did, suggesting that women use their listening skills to learn about people and make connections with others. In contrast, men rated themselves higher on content-oriented listening, an outcome suggesting that men use their listening skills to take in content and solve intellectual challenges. Those findings do not mean women don't engage in content-oriented listening and men don't engage in people-oriented listening—they certainly do in both cases. Rather, the study results show that women and men—overall—have different approaches to listening, just as the stereotype suggests.

You might recall reading earlier in this chapter that people often overestimate their listening abilities, so you may wonder how you can have confidence in the result of a study that relies on self-reports. Because virtually every study of listening styles uses a self-report method for collecting data, that's a critical question. The answer is that reporting on *how* you listen is different from reporting on *how well* you listen. Many of us do have a tendency to exaggerate how well we listen, but research suggests that we are much more accurate at reporting the style of listening we use.

Research shows that women and men have different styles of listening. Women are more likely than men are to say they use their listening skills to learn about people and make personal connections. Men are more likely to say they use their listening skills to solve intellectual challenges.

How can we apply the information about sex differences in listening styles to improve our communication abilities? When communicating with members of the other sex, we can consider their listening tendencies and formulate our messages accordingly. Let's say you're describing to different friends a recent conflict you had with your romantic partner. Because you know that men tend to focus on the content of what they're hearing, you might tailor your description to male friends to highlight what the conflict was about and what each person's position was. Because you know that women tend to focus on the interpersonal aspects of what they're hearing, you might adapt your description to female friends to focus on what the conflict taught you about your relational partner and yourself. Although sex differences in listening preferences are just tendencies, they can still give you clues for communicating effectively with members of each sex.

ASK YOURSELF

- How do the general sex differences described above compare to the listening behavior of women and men you know?

- Is one style of listening better than another, in your opinion? How might men's and women's styles of listening be appropriate in different situations?

SOURCE: Sargent, S. L., & Weaver, J. B. (2003). Listening styles: Sex differences in perceptions of self and others. *International Journal of Listening, 17*, 5–18.

TABLE 6.2
BARRIERS TO
EFFECTIVE LISTENING

noise—Anything that distracts you from listening to what you wish to listen to

pseudolistening—Using feedback behaviors to give the false impression that you are listening

selective attention—Listening only to points you want to hear, while ignoring all other points

information overload—Being overwhelmed with the large amount of information you must take in every day

glazing over—Daydreaming when you aren't speaking or listening during a conversation

rebuttal tendency—Propensity to argue inwardly with a speaker and formulate your conclusions and responses prematurely

closed-mindedness—Refusal even to listen to ideas or positions with which you disagree

competitive interrupting—Interrupting others to gain control of a conversation

You conclude that Dean is implying he's hungry and wants to get some food, but that isn't actually what he said. To check your understanding, you therefore paraphrase his statement by putting it into your own words. Because you understood his statement correctly, he replies by confirming your interpretation.

If you paraphrase a statement in a way that changes its meaning, many speakers will reply by correcting your understanding. Let's say the exchange with Dean goes like this:

> **Dean:** *I think we should swing by that new barbecue place on the way home.*
>
> **You:** *You want to pick up some dinner?*
>
> **Dean:** *No, I want to see if my friend Blake is working tonight.*

In that instance, your interpretation of Dean's statement was inaccurate. By paraphrasing his statement, you invited him to correct your understanding, and he did. Paraphrasing is a simple but very efficient way to determine whether you have correctly separated what a speaker has and has not said.

Avoid the Confirmation Bias

The **confirmation bias** is the tendency to pay attention only to information that supports our values and beliefs, while discounting or ignoring information that doesn't.[39] This tendency becomes a problem for listening when it causes us to make up our minds about an issue without paying attention to all sides.

Suppose you're turning to talk radio for perspective on U.S. immigration policies. If you favor a conservative approach to immigration laws, including deportation of illegal immigrants, then you may be more inclined to consider Rush Limbaugh or Glenn Beck a credible source than Rachel Maddow or Keith Olbermann. If your preference is for a more liberal immigration policy, including a guest-worker program, then you'll probably listen more to what Maddow or Olbermann have to say. In either case, by seeking a perspective that already aligns with your point of view, you avoid exposing yourself to alternative viewpoints.

Good informational listeners are aware, however, that their beliefs are not necessarily accurate. Thus, another strategy for improving your informational listening skills is to ask yourself whether you have listened to all sides of an issue before you form a conclusion—or whether, instead, you are simply avoiding information that would lead you to question your beliefs.

Listen for Substance More Than Style

The psychological principle called the **vividness effect** is the tendency of dramatic, shocking events to distort our perceptions of reality.[40] We watch news coverage of a deadly plane crash, for instance, and we worry about flying even though we have heard from reliable sources that the probability of dying in a plane crash is only about 1 in 8 million.[41] The vividness effect was also in evidence when, two days after the 1999 massacre at Columbine High

• **confirmation bias** The tendency to pay attention only to information that supports one's values and beliefs, while discounting or ignoring information that does not.

• **vividness effect** The tendency of dramatic, shocking events to distort one's perceptions of reality.

School, 63 percent of U.S. parents surveyed said they thought a shooting at their own child's school was likely, even though only 10 percent of all public schools report even one episode of violent crime in an entire year.[42] The same effect can occur in relationships. If your parents went through a traumatic divorce when you were a child, that experience might make you think marriage is more likely to fail than it actually is. The reason for all these mistaken conclusions is that dramatic events are more vivid and memorable than everyday events, so we pay more attention to them.

We can experience much the same problem during informational listening if we focus only on what's most vivid. Let's say that your history class yesterday included dramatic stories and flashy PowerPoint slides you found highly entertaining, but in today's class the lecture was comparatively dry and lacked those bells and whistles. You shouldn't conclude that the flashy presentation contained better information than the dry one did, or that you necessarily learned more from it. Similarly, you might love being in classes with engaging, humorous teachers, but that doesn't necessarily mean you'll learn more from them than from more serious teachers. Being a good informational listener means being able to look past what is dramatic and vivid to focus on the *substance* of what you're hearing. That skill starts with being aware of the vividness effect and remembering that vivid experiences can distort your perceptions. The next time you go through a dramatic event or listen to a particularly engaging speaker, ask yourself whether you are listening and paying attention to accurate information instead of being swayed by the event's drama or the speaker's charisma.

BECOME A BETTER CRITICAL LISTENER

Many interpersonal situations require you to assess the reliability and trustworthiness of what you're hearing. Here are three ways to hone that ability.

Be a Skeptic Being a good critical listener starts with being skeptical of what you hear. **Skepticism**—an attitude that includes raising questions or having doubts—isn't about being cynical or finding fault; it's about evaluating the evidence for a stated claim. As we noted above with respect to the confirmation bias, some people pay attention only to evidence that supports what they already believe. Being skeptical means setting aside your biases and being willing to be persuaded by the merits of the argument and the quality of the evidence. A good critical listener doesn't accept claims blindly but questions them to see whether they're valid.[43]

Suppose your coworker Fahid has come up with a business opportunity, tells you about his plan, and asks you to consider investing in it. Poor critical listeners might make their decision based on how they feel about Fahid or how excited they are at the prospect of making money. If you're a good critical listener, though, you'll set aside your feelings and focus on the merits of Fahid's idea. Does he have a sound business plan? Is there a genuine market for his product? Has he budgeted for advertising? Did he explain how he would use your investment? Being a critical listener doesn't mean criticizing his plans—it means evaluating them to see whether they make sense.

Evaluate a Speaker's Credibility Besides analyzing the merits of an argument, a good critical listener pays attention to the credibility of the speaker. As we've seen, *credibility* refers to the reliability and trustworthiness of someone or something. All other things being equal, you can generally presume that information from a credible source is more believable than information from a noncredible source.

Several qualities make a speaker more or less credible. One is expertise. It makes more sense for us to trust medical advice we receive from a physician than from a professional athlete, for instance, because the doctor is a medical expert and the athlete is not. At the same time, it doesn't make sense to trust a physician for legal or financial advice, because he or she isn't an expert in those realms.

It's sometimes easy to confuse *expertise* with *experience*. Having experience with something may give a person credibility in that area, but it doesn't necessarily make the individual an expert. Consider Hannah, the mother of six children. In the course of raising her kids, Hannah has become a very experienced parent, so she has sufficient

• **skepticism** An attitude that involves raising questions or having doubts.

credibility to give advice to other moms insofar as she can draw on her many experiences. Yet Hannah isn't an expert on parenting, because her only source of credibility is her individual experience. For example, she isn't a recognized authority on parenting issues, nor does she have a degree in child development.

Conversely, people can be experts on topics and areas with which they have no direct personal experience. As a board-certified obstetrician and gynecologist, Tyrell is an expert on pregnancy and women's health, even though, as a man, he has not personally experienced a pregnancy or a disease to which women are vulnerable. Similarly, Young Li is an outstanding marital therapist who has helped countless couples even though she has never married. How can a man be a good obstetrician and a single person be a good marital therapist? The answer is that they draw on their training and expertise to help others, not on their individual experiences.

Another characteristic that affects a speaker's credibility is bias. If a speaker has a special interest in making you believe some idea or claim, that bias tends to reduce his or her credibility. For instance, if a tobacco company executive claimed publicly that smoking has health benefits, a good critical listener would be highly skeptical because the executive is a biased source. That bias might seem obvious, because we know the executive makes a living from the sale of tobacco products—but sometimes you have to dig below the surface to evaluate someone's credibility. For example, you might be intrigued to hear about a research report claiming that using your cell phone while driving does not increase your risk of being in a collision. You might assume the study was conducted by a reputable source, such as a research team at a major university, and that assumption would enhance the report's credibility in your mind. You decide to investigate further, however, and you discover that the study was funded by a group that lobbies on behalf of the telecommunications industry. Given its purpose, such a group would have a vested interest in research results favorable to cell phone use. That doesn't necessarily mean the study's conclusions are wrong. It does mean, though, that you should be more skeptical when thinking about the results.

Understand Probability Evaluating the merits of a claim means speculating about the likelihood that the claim is true. Such speculation can be tricky, however, because we sometimes confuse what's possible with what's probable and what's probable with what's certain. An event or fact is *possible* if there's even the slightest chance, however small, that it might be true. In contrast, to be *probable*, a statement has to have greater than a 50 percent chance of being true. Finally, a statement is *certain* only if its likelihood of being true is 100 percent and nothing less.

adaptability Considering Candidates

The Scene: You're attending a debate between two candidates for governor of your state. The election is only two weeks away, so you are hoping the debate will inform you about the candidates and their positions. You notice that one candidate speaks in a poised, confident manner, using inspiring language to describe lofty goals for "securing a better tomorrow." In contrast, the other candidate speaks in a less dramatic way, focusing attention on specific plans, policies, and strategies instead of more abstract goals.

Your Task: Consider how you should adapt both your informational and your critical listening skills to decide which candidate to support. What strategies could you use in this situation to

- Listen for substance more than for style?
- Evaluate the speaker's credibility?
- Be skeptical of what each speaker says?

SHARPEN Your Skills: *Critical listening*

Television commercials offer ample opportunity to sharpen your critical listening skills. During the next TV show you watch, choose three commercials and think about the claims they are making. For each, write a paragraph addressing these questions: How credible are the sources? How probable are the claims? What inferences, unsupported by evidence, do the commercials encourage you to make?

Consider a claim such as "I can survive without water for a month." There's a possibility that assertion could be true, but the likelihood is pretty small. The claim certainly isn't probable, and a good critical listener wouldn't treat it as though it were. The statement "I will get married someday" is not only possible, it's also probable, because a very large majority of people marry at least once in their lives. Is that claim therefore certain? No, because there's a chance, however small, that it might not happen. For a claim to be certain, there can be *absolutely no chance* that it isn't true. A claim such as "I will die someday" is certain, because every living being eventually dies. Good critical listeners understand the differences among possibility, probability, and certainty. They bear in mind that a claim that is possible isn't necessarily one that is worth believing.

BECOME A BETTER EMPATHIC LISTENER

Within our relationships, a common goal for listening is to provide empathy and support. Being a good empathic listener can be challenging at times, but it's not impossible.

Listen Nonjudgmentally When we listen to learn, and especially when we listen to evaluate, we often make judgments about the information we're taking in. But good empathic listening is about being open-minded and nonjudgmental.

Two strategies are particularly helpful here. First, listen without interrupting. Being empathic means letting the other person say what he or she needs to say without jumping into the middle of the message. Fight the urge to interrupt, and simply listen to the other person. Second, think twice before offering unsolicited advice. When other people tell us their problems, our tendency is often to respond with advice on solving those problems.[44] A good empathic listener remembers that people aren't always looking for advice—they often just want someone to listen to them.

Acknowledge Feelings Empathizing is about understanding how someone else is feeling and trying to relate to those feelings. It's *not* the same as sympathizing, which is feeling sorry for the other person. An important strategy for good empathic listening, therefore, is to acknowledge a speaker's feelings and allow him or her to continue expressing them.

We do so by responding to speakers with *continuer statements*, phrases that identify the emotions a person is experiencing and allow him or her to communicate them further. In contrast, it is important to avoid *terminator statements*, phrases that fail to acknowledge a speaker's emotions, shutting down his or her opportunity to express them. After listening to a patient describe her concerns about the progress of her illness, for instance, empathic physicians can use continuer statements such as "That must make you feel very uncertain" and "I can imagine how scary this must be" to convey to the patient that they understand and appreciate her feelings. Physicians with less empathic ability will be more likely to use terminator statements such as "We're doing everything we can" and "You just need to give this some time." Those types of responses imply to the patient that her feelings are unimportant.

In a recent study, researchers, with permission, recorded nearly 400 conversations between advanced cancer patients and their oncologists[45] and listened for times when patients expressed negative emotions such as sadness, fear, and anxiety. When those moments arose, doctors replied with continuer statements only 22 percent of the time. Younger physicians were more likely than older ones to use continuers, and female physicians were more likely than male doctors to do so. That doesn't mean oncologists lack empathy. Rather, it illustrates that they may have trouble communicating their empathy through emotionally supportive listening responses, which are particularly important for individuals struggling with a terminal illness such as advanced cancer.

There are times when it may be difficult to empathize with others. For example, if you haven't experienced a great deal of grief in your life, it can be hard to understand the power of that emotion. "The Dark Side of Communication" box suggests some ways of practicing effective empathic listening during times of grief.

Communicate Support Nonverbally One of the most important aspects of being a good empathic listener is communicating your support nonverbally. When you're listening rather than speaking, your nonverbal behaviors convey your interest, understanding, and empathy to the speaker.

Perhaps the most important nonverbal behavior in this situation is eye contact. Others often watch your eye behaviors to see whether you're paying attention to what they're saying. If you allow yourself to be distracted by your environment, you can convey the message that you aren't really listening. Other important empathic behaviors are your use of facial expressions and touch. A reassuring smile and a warm touch can make people feel as though you understand, support, and empathize with them.[46]

Times of Grief: Providing Effective Empathic Listening

Dealing with grief—as we do, for instance, when we lose a loved one—is among life's most traumatic experiences. When someone you care about is grieving, one of the ways you can be most supportive is to be a good listener, even though it means actively attending to something that is difficult to hear. Here are some tips for listening empathically during times of grief:

- Appreciate that everyone grieves differently, and there is no right or wrong way to go through a loss.

- Avoid telling the grieving individual "I know exactly how you feel" unless you have been through the same type of loss.

- Encourage the person to take care of his or her needs, especially physical needs. If you're close

to the person and feel it's appropriate, suggest that major life decisions be put off until the person is in a better frame of mind.

- Don't try to diminish the person's grief by using a statement such as "You have to be strong" or "Look how much you still have." Such imperatives can make people feel ashamed of their grief.

- Remind the person that you are willing to listen and to help.

SOURCE: Adapted from St. Mary's College Counseling Center Grief and Loss Guidelines: www.stmarysca.edu/prospective /undergraduate_admissions/student_life_and_services/student_support/counseling_center/grief.html

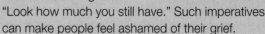

For REVIEW

- **What does it mean to listen effectively?** We listen effectively when we hear, understand, remember, interpret, evaluate, and respond to what someone has said. Cultural messages shape listening, just as they influence many communication behaviors.

- **Why is listening effectively so challenging?** Many barriers exist to effective listening, including noise, pseudolistening, selective attention, information overload, glazing over, rebuttal tendency, closed-mindedness, and competitive interrupting.

- **How can you improve your listening skills?** You can be a better informational listener by separating what is and isn't said, avoiding the confirmation bias, and listening for substance. You can improve your critical listening skills by being skeptical, evaluating credibility, and understanding probability. You can become better at empathic listening by listening nonjudgmentally, acknowledging a speaker's feelings, and communicating support nonverbally.

POP QUIZ

Multiple Choice

1. Which of the following statements most accurately reflects how culture affects listening behavior?

   a. In monochronic cultures, people tend to think of time as something that can be saved or spent, and listeners tend to be impatient when speakers do not get to the point.

   b. In polychronic cultures, people tend to think of time as something that can be saved or spent, and listeners tend to be impatient when speakers do not get to the point.

   c. When listening, people in individualistic cultures pay close attention to nonverbal behaviors to determine the meaning of a speaker's message.

   d. When listening, people in collectivistic cultures pay close attention to nonverbal behaviors to determine the meaning of a speaker's message.

2. The type of listening in which we try to understand a situation from a speaker's perspective is

   a. informational listening.   c. critical listening.

   b. appreciative listening.   d. empathic listening.

3. Marilyn's listening style, which emphasizes organization and precision, is best described as

   a. people-oriented.   c. time-oriented.

   b. action-oriented.   d. content-oriented.

4. In class, Charyn cannot keep her mind off her problems at work. Instead of skipping class, she attends and pretends to listen to the professor's lecture. This behavior is known as

   a. information overload.   c. pseudolistening.

   b. closed-mindedness.   d. competitive interrupting.

5. Understanding probability is crucial for being a good critical listener. Evaluate these messages and identify which one is true.

   a. For a message to be probable, it has to have at least a 1 percent chance of being true.

   b. For a message to be certain, it must be true 99 percent of the time.

   c. For a message to be possible, it need have only the slightest chance of being true.

   d. For a message to be certain, it has to have a 51 percent chance of being true.

Fill in the Blanks

6. Using facial expressions and verbal statements such as "I understand" to let the speaker know you are paying attention is called _____.

7. Jack's tendency to daydream when he isn't listening increases his chances of _____.

8. The _____ style of listening emphasizes efficiency.

9. The tendency to pay attention only to information that supports our values and beliefs, while discounting or ignoring information that does not, is called the _____.

10. _____ is anything that distracts you from listening to what you wish to listen to.

ANSWERS: 1. a; 2. d; 3. b; 4. c; 5. c; 6. backchanneling; 7. glazing over; 8. time-oriented; 9. confirmation bias; 10. Noise

KEY TERMS

COMMUNICATING IN SOCIAL AND PROFESSIONAL RELATIONSHIPS

FRIENDSHIP IN UNEXPECTED PLACES

Ann Atwater and C. P. Ellis were never destined to become friends. In the 1970s, Atwater—a poor African American welfare mother—was a civil rights activist in Durham, North Carolina. That's where Ellis was a leader in the Ku Klux Klan, a violent white supremacist organization. The two were the fiercest of enemies. During 10 days of community talks about school desegregation, Ellis came to believe that both whites and minorities would benefit from attending racially integrated schools—and he and Atwater became partners in the civil rights movement. They also became close personal friends. Together, they struggled against oppression and social stereotypes, and they leaned on each other heavily for support. From the diversity of their life experiences, a solid and enduring bond had formed.

When Ellis died of Alzheimer's disease in 2005, Atwater, having lost a dear—and most unlikely—friend, gave the eulogy at his funeral.

►As You READ

- Why do social relationships matter so much to us?
- Which characteristics of friendships make them vital to our social experience and well-being?
- How do we manage social relationships in the workplace?

Imagine what life would be like without friends. Families and romantic relationships are important to us, but our friends and acquaintances also contribute significantly to our well-being. Sometimes we look to friends for social and emotional support. Sometimes we seek out our friends when we just want to hang out and relax, and sometimes we do so when we need help making a decision or talking through a problem. Just as Ann Atwater and C. P. Ellis did for each other, friends lift our spirits and remind us we're not alone in the world.

This chapter probes the importance of social and professional relationships, such as those with our friends and coworkers, and focuses on how we use interpersonal communication to manage them. All relationships are social to some extent. Because romantic and familial relationships often meet different social needs than friendships and workplace relationships do, we examine them in the next chapter.

Why Social Relationships Matter

Each of us can probably think of many friends who support us through life's ups and downs. Having strong social ties with friends, neighbors, coworkers, and others improves the quality of our life in multiple ways. In this opening section, we'll see that we form social relationships because we have a strong need to belong. We'll also examine some benefits of our social relationships, as well as certain costs we incur by maintaining them.

WE FORM RELATIONSHIPS BECAUSE WE NEED TO BELONG

• need to belong theory
A psychological theory proposing a fundamental human inclination to bond with others.

In his book *Personal Relationships and Personal Networks* (2007), communication scholar Mac Parks wrote: "We humans are social animals down to our very cells. Nature did not make us noble loners."[1] He's right. One reason social relationships matter is that it's in our nature to form them. In fact, evolutionary psychologists argue that our motivation toward social relationships is innate rather than learned.[2]

That fundamental human inclination to bond with others is the idea behind psychologist Roy Baumeister's **need to belong theory**.[3] This theory says each of us is born with a drive to seek, form, maintain, and protect strong social relationships. To fulfill that drive, we use communication to form social bonds with others at work, at school, in our neighborhoods, in community and religious organizations, on sports teams, in online communities, and in other social contexts. According to the theory, each of those relationships helps us feel we aren't alone because we belong to a social community.

Strong social relationships improve the quality of our life in many ways.

What We Need from Social Relationships The need to belong theory suggests that for us to satisfy our drive for relationships, we need social bonds that are both interactive and emotionally close. For example, most of us wouldn't be satisfied if we had emotionally close relationships with people with whom we never got to communicate. Being cut off from social interaction can be physically and psychologically devastating. That's one of the reasons solitary confinement is considered such a harsh punishment for prisoners.[4] Women and men who are deployed for military service,[5] and many elderly individuals who live alone,[6] also experience loneliness when they don't see their families or friends for extended periods.

By the same token, interacting only with people for whom we have no real feelings is unrewarding as well. Imagine moving to a large city where you don't know anyone. Even though you'd have plenty of interactions with people—taxi drivers, grocery store clerks, an eye doctor, the neighborhood dry cleaner—you might not initially encounter anyone to whom you feel close. Although task-oriented relationships help you to accomplish various needs, such as getting from one place to another and having your vision checked, they don't fulfill your need to belong, because they usually aren't emotionally close.

People don't just *enjoy* social interaction—they truly *need* it.

Top Eight Reasons for Using Instant Messaging	Percentage of Respondents
1. Keep in touch with friends	92%
2. Make plans with friends	88%
3. Play games with IM software	62%
4. Play a trick on someone	60%
5. Ask someone out on a date	44%
6. Write something you wouldn't say in person	42%
7. Send nontext information	39%
8. Break up with someone	24%

TABLE 7.1

MEET ME IN CYBERSPACE: RELATING BY INSTANT MESSAGE

SOURCE: Bryant, J. A., Sanders-Jackson, A., & Smallwood, A. M. K. (2006). IMing, text messaging, and adolescent social networks. *Journal of Computer-Mediated Communication, 11,* article 10, http://jcmc .indiana.edu/vol11/issue2/bryant.html.

get**C**ONNECTED
Meeting Our Social Needs Online

We develop many of our important relationships in face-to-face contexts. However, we form others online—and research shows that those relationships are often just as emotionally close and include just as frequent interaction as do our face-to-face relationships.[7] Many of us therefore meet our need to belong partially via electronically mediated communication channels such as e-mail, Facebook, text messaging, and Twitter.

In a study of adolescents' use of text messaging and instant messaging (IM), researchers found that participants used IM as a primary means of communicating with their social networks. In particular, adolescents used IM and text messaging to enhance their sense of social belonging and to manage their self-disclosures with friends.[8] Table 7.1 lists the top eight reasons for using IM, as identified by a separate study.

Who forms social relationships online? Only a decade or so ago, people who developed relationships online were stigmatized as lacking the self-confidence and social

skills to form face-to-face bonds.[9] Today, online relationships are so common that it is difficult to distinguish people who form them from those who don't. Research finds no differences in self-esteem, social skills, loneliness, anxiety, or number of face-to-face relationships between college students who have and have not formed social relationships online.[10]

Despite being common, social relationships formed online differ from face-to-face relationships in some important ways. One study found that friendships started on the Internet were less interdependent and less committed, and they resulted in less understanding than friendships formed offline.[11] Over time, however, the differences in those relationship qualities decreased, meaning that online and face-to-face friendships became more similar. A separate study confirmed that ties to online friendships are weaker, at first, than ties to offline friends, but the strength of the relationship depended on certain factors. For example, women reported weaker ties to their online friends than did men, and frequent Internet users reported stronger ties than did occasional users. Most important, those who shared personal information with their online friends reported stronger ties than did those who shared only impersonal information.[12]

Just as the Internet provides multiple opportunities for forming positive social relationships, it unfortunately also allows people to offer their friendship in a deceptive, self-serving way. As "The Dark Side of Communication" explains, such behavior can have devastating effects on its victims.

Whether formed online or in person, many social relationships fulfill our needs for interaction and emotional closeness and can help us feel connected to others in meaningful and significant ways. The natural "need to belong" is not the only reason social relationships matter to human beings, but Baumeister's need to belong theory suggests it's one of the biggest.

SHARPEN Your Skills: *Discouraging cyberbullying*

Create a blog entry or webpage for young adolescents in which you explain what cyberbullying is, why it is so harmful, and what to do if you're a victim. Draw your information from a reputable source, such as the National Bullying Prevention Center or the Anti-Defamation League, but write it for a middle school audience. Make sure to include links to online resources for bullying victims, such as a suicide prevention hotline. When you're finished, share your blog or webpage with the adolescents in your life and encourage them to share it with their friends.

SOCIAL RELATIONSHIPS BRING REWARDS

Besides fulfilling our need to belong, social relationships matter because they bring us rewards. We'll now look at three types of rewards—emotional, material, and health—and find they are often intertwined in our social relationships.

Social Relationships Bring Emotional Rewards Friends provide at least two types of emotional rewards. One is emotional support, or encouragement during times of emotional turmoil. Whether you're going through a serious crisis or just having a bad day, friends can provide comfort and empathy to help you make it through.[13] When Atwater and Ellis struggled with the emotional trauma of the civil rights movement, for instance, they supported and listened to each other. Although their struggles were enormously challenging, their strong friendship helped them cope.

The second emotional reward of having friends is happiness. We enjoy interacting with friends because it's fun and relaxing and because our friends entertain us. One of Erin's favorite ways to spend a Friday night, for example, is to invite her good friends over to cook dinner, watch DVDs, and talk about what's going on in their lives.

THE DARK SIDE OF COMMUNICATION

Cyberbullying

Cyberbullying means using the Internet to inflict emotional or psychological harm on someone, and it often has devastating consequences. In September 2010, for example, 13-year-old Seth Walsh from Tehachapi, California committed suicide after enduring relentless harassment from friends online because of his sexual orientation. Cyberbullying reflects the dark side of forming and maintaining friendships online. According to research:

- Among adolescents, 43 percent have experienced some form of online harassment.

- The most common cyberbullying acts are posting messages on semipublic spaces (such as social networking pages) that make fun of another person, distributing gossip to an individual's social network via e-mail or text message, and posting or distributing embarrassing photos of someone without his or her permission.

- Girls are twice as likely as boys to be the victims of cyberbullying. They are also twice as likely as boys to be the perpetrators of cyberbullying.

- Cyberbullying affects all age groups that interact online, but it is most prevalent among individuals 15 to 16 years old.

- The most common reason people give for perpetrating cyberbullying is to get revenge on the victim.

- Online victims of cyberbullying are 8 times as likely as nonvictims to have carried a weapon to school in the previous 30 days.

California teen Seth Walsh committed suicide in 2010 at age 13 after enduring merciless online harassment about being gay.

SOURCES: Hinduja, S., & Patchin, W. J. (2009). *Bullying beyond the schoolyard: Preventing and responding to cyberbullying.* Thousand Oaks, CA: Sage; Kowalski, R. M., Guimetti, G. W., Schroeder, A. N., & Reese, H. H. (2012). Cyberbullying among college students: Evidence from multiple domains of college life. In L. A. Wankel & C. Wankel (Eds.), *Misbehavior online in higher education* (pp. 293–321). Bingley, England: Emerald Group Publishing.

Hanging out with her close friends always makes Erin feel good. Indeed, many of our happiest times are spent with our close friends around us.[14]

Social Relationships Bring Material Rewards
A second way social relationships benefit us is by helping to meet our material needs, such as our needs for money, food, shelter, and transportation. People tend to share those types of resources with others to whom they feel close. When you need help moving, or a place to stay for the weekend, or a few extra dollars to tide you over until payday, you're more likely to have those material needs met if you have strong social relationships to draw on than if you don't. You're also more likely to offer those material rewards to your close friends than to strangers or people you don't know well.

Social Relationships Bring Health Rewards
Positive social relationships also promote good health. A study by psychologist Sheldon Cohen and his colleagues found, for instance, that the more social relationships people had, the better able they were to fight off the common cold.[15] Another study reported that people with a strong social network were twice as likely as others to survive a heart attack.[16] In fact, after reviewing more than 60 published studies on the topic, sociologist James House and his colleagues determined that the lack of

strong, positive social relationships is as big a risk factor for premature mortality as cigarette smoking, obesity, and elevated blood pressure.[17] Research suggests that close relationships help people to manage the negative effects of stress[18] and maintain a healthy lifestyle.[19]

SOCIAL RELATIONSHIPS CARRY COSTS AS WELL AS BENEFITS

It's relatively easy to think of the benefits of social relationships—they bring us emotional support, help us during times of need, and even make us healthier. However, friendships and other social relationships carry costs as well as rewards. Think about what it "costs" you to be friends with someone. A friendship takes time that you might spend doing something rewarding by yourself. It requires an emotional investment, particularly when your friend is in need of your support. There can be material costs associated with doing things together, such as the expenses you incur in taking road trips and going out to dinner. Friendships often require physical investments as well—you may not *want* to help your friend move into her new apartment, but you do it anyway because she's your friend.

Much of the time, we decide that the benefits of friendship are well worth the costs. Some social relationships, however, eventually reach the point where the costs of staying in the relationship outweigh the benefits. As we'll see in the next section, a social exchange orientation suggests that being in that kind of "under-benefited" state can motivate people to end relationships—or at least make them feel unsatisfied in them.

Forming and Maintaining Social Bonds

We've examined why social relationships matter and how we are rewarded by them. In this section, we look at several theories that explain the various interpersonal forces at work in the formation and development of social relationships. Some of those theories help us to understand with whom we choose to form social relationships, including

- Attraction theory, which describes why we are drawn to others
- Uncertainty reduction theory, which indicates why we initially interact with others

Other theories explain why and how we maintain social relationships once we form them, including

- Social exchange theories, which indicate how we compare our current relationships with our alternatives and how we count our costs and benefits
- Relational maintenance behaviors theory, which concerns the communication behaviors we use to sustain our relationships

ATTRACTION THEORY

Attraction theory explains why individuals are drawn to others. The process of forming most relationships begins with **interpersonal attraction,** the force that draws people together.

You're probably already familiar with the concept of **physical attraction,** or being drawn to someone because of his or her looks, but there are at least two other ways to be attracted to another person. A second type of interpersonal attraction is **social attraction,** which means being attracted to someone's personality. For example, you might like your new officemate at work because of her positive attitude or great sense of humor. A third kind of interpersonal attraction is **task attraction,** or being attracted to someone's abilities and dependability.[20] You might feel positive toward your new carpool partner because he shows up on time every day, rain or shine, or toward your suitemate because of her excellent karaoke technique. Any or all of those types of attraction can draw you to others and make you want to get to know them.

• **attraction theory**
A theory that explains why individuals are drawn to others.

• **interpersonal attraction**
The force that draws people together.

• **physical attraction**
Attraction to someone's appearance.

• **social attraction**
Attraction to someone's personality.

• **task attraction** Attraction to someone's abilities or dependability.

To consider how physical, social, and task attraction play a role in your own social relationships, think of your closest friend and then respond to the items in "The Competent Communicator."

A variety of qualities in a new acquaintance can spark interpersonal attraction, but four are especially powerful: personal appearance, proximity, similarity, and complementarity. Let's look at each and then consider the role culture plays in what we find attractive about others.

We Are Attracted by Appearance When we say a person is attractive, we often mean that he or she *looks* attractive. Humans are very visually oriented, so finding someone physically attractive often motivates us to get to know that person better. There are at least two reasons for this attraction. One is that we value and appreciate physical attractiveness, so we want to be around people we think are attractive.[21] Another reason is that throughout history, humans have sought others who are physically attractive as mates.[22] Because attractive people often have very healthy genes, their children are likely to have especially good health because they will inherit those genes.[23]

We Are Attracted by Proximity Another important predictor of attraction is **proximity,** or closeness, including how closely together people live or work and thus how often they interact. We're more likely to form attraction—particularly social and task attraction—with people we see often than with those we see rarely.[24] For example, we tend to know our next-door neighbors better than the neighbors down the road, and we're more likely to become friends and maintain friendships with classmates and coworkers than with people we seldom see, such as other students at school or other employees at work.

• **proximity** Closeness, as in how closely together people live or work.

We Are Attracted by Similarity We've all had the experience of getting to know someone and marveling at how much we have in common with that person. When we meet people with backgrounds, experiences, beliefs, and interests that are similar to our own, we find them to be comfortable and familiar. Sometimes it's almost as if we already know them.

We find similarity to be very attractive, particularly with respect to social attraction. Research shows we're more likely to form social relationships with people who are similar to us.[25] We often find social validation in those who are familiar to us. In other words, being attracted to people who are similar to us is, in a way, like being attracted to ourselves. We might be especially drawn to individuals who share our hobbies, sense of humor, or worldview, because those people make us feel good about who we are.[26] We don't necessarily think about that effect at a conscious level, but it may nonetheless be one of the reasons we find similarity attractive.

We Are Attracted by Complementarity As the "Fact or Fiction?" box confirms, similarity is often more attractive than difference. Still, opposites can sometimes attract. Specifically, we can be attracted to those who are unlike us if we see their differences as providing **complementarity**—a beneficial supplement by another person of something we lack in ourselves. Many people also benefit from the diversity of their friends' experiences. Thus, we might enjoy having friends whose religious, political, economic, or sexual orientations differ from our own, because they bring us new ideas and help us learn to communicate with a wider range of people.

• **complementarity** The beneficial provision by another person of a quality that one lacks.

Culture Sometimes Influences Our Perceptions of Attractiveness Culture influences so many of the ways we interact with others that it shouldn't be a surprise to learn it influences our perceptions of attractiveness as well. We see the effects of culture most directly on perceptions of physical attractiveness. Consider weight, for example. In North America and Western Europe, a thin, physically fit body type is generally considered most attractive. In many African and Australian tribal cultures, however, a fuller figure is viewed as most attractive, at least for women.[27]

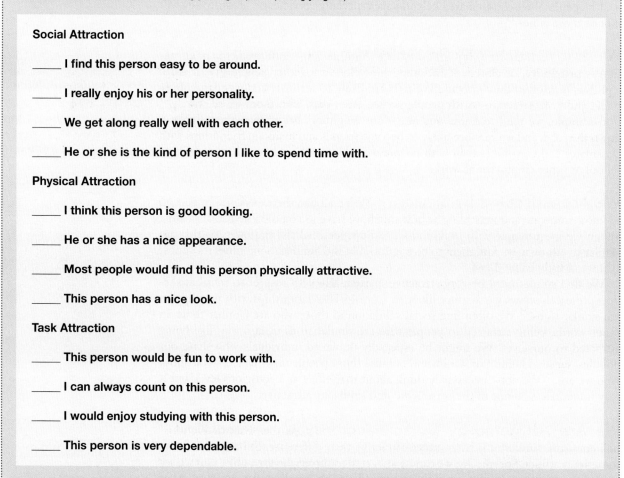

What Draws You? Attraction in Your Closest Friendship

Close friendships always include one or more forms of interpersonal attraction. We might be attracted to someone's personality. We might find the person physically attractive. We might also be drawn to someone as a work partner. Think about your current closest friendship, and note how much you agree or disagree with each of the following statements, using a scale of 1 (strongly disagree) to 7 (strongly agree).

Social Attraction

_____ I find this person easy to be around.

_____ I really enjoy his or her personality.

_____ We get along really well with each other.

_____ He or she is the kind of person I like to spend time with.

Physical Attraction

_____ I think this person is good looking.

_____ He or she has a nice appearance.

_____ Most people would find this person physically attractive.

_____ This person has a nice look.

Task Attraction

_____ This person would be fun to work with.

_____ I can always count on this person.

_____ I would enjoy studying with this person.

_____ This person is very dependable.

Add up your scores for each scale. For each type of attraction, a score of 4–12 indicates that you don't perceive that type of attraction very strongly for your friend. A score of 13–20 suggests you have a moderate level of that form of attraction. A score of 21–28 indicates that you perceive a good deal of that form of attraction for your friend.

Your scores for each scale might differ quite a bit. If so, that simply means your friendship is based more heavily on some forms of attraction than on others. In any event, this exercise will give you a chance to reflect on what you find most attractive about your closest friendship.

SOURCE: Items adapted from McCroskey, J. C., & McCain, T. A. (1974). The measurement of interpersonal attraction. *Speech Monographs, 41,* 261–266.

Fact or *fiction*?

Magnetic Force: When It Comes to Forming Friendships, Opposites Attract

You've probably heard the expression "opposites attract." It suggests that we find differences attractive and will be drawn most strongly to people who are different from us. Is that idea fact or fiction?

According to research, it is largely fiction. When we're forming friendships, difference *can* be attractive to us, but only if we see the difference as complementary—that is, if it benefits us in some way, such as by reflecting a positive personality trait that we lack. Study after study has shown, however, that we find similarity to be much more attractive.

In one study, researchers paired up college students at the beginning of a semester with strangers of their same sex and ethnicity. Both people in each pair reported on their individual attitudes, personalities, and ways of seeing the world. Over the next eight weeks, they also reported how much they liked each other. The researchers found that having similar attitudes was the strongest predictor of initial attraction. If their attitudes were highly dissimilar, the students tended not to like each other. The study also found that having similar personalities and ways of seeing the world was the strongest predictor of whether students remained friends after being initially drawn to each other. The results of this and dozens of other studies suggest that when it comes to forming friendships, the more accurate statement would be "similars attract."

ASK YOURSELF

- Have you tended to believe that opposites attract? Why do you suppose that idea persists?
- Why do we find similarity to be rewarding in a friend?

SOURCE: Neimeyer, R. A., & Mitchell, K. A. (1988). Similarity and attraction: A longitudinal study. *Journal of Social and Personal Relationships, 5,* 131–148.

Cultural diversity also exists in the ways people manipulate or mutilate the body to achieve physical attractiveness. Girls in the Mursi ethnic group of southern Ethiopia and among the Mebêngôkre Indians of Brazil have their lips pierced at a young age, and a large wooden or clay plate is inserted into the hole. As the girls grow older, their lip plates are increased in size, and individuals with the largest plates are considered the most desirable as mates.[28] In a different kind of body manipulation, women in the Padaung tribe of Myanmar often wear metal rings around their necks to make their necks appear longer than they are. The longest-necked women are considered the most attractive and most desirable as mates.[29]

Other perceptions of attractiveness are largely cross-cultural. For instance, people around the world prefer bodies and faces that are symmetrical and proportional (two concepts we reviewed in Chapter 5). Across cultures, men are also attracted to women who appear healthy and young, because those characteristics signal their ability to produce healthy offspring.[30] Similarly, women across cultures are attracted to men who look powerful and appear to have resources, because those characteristics signal

their ability to provide for a family.[31] We may not consider these factors at a conscious level when we're assessing another person's attractiveness, but research demonstrates that people around the world are nonetheless attracted to such qualities in others.[32]

UNCERTAINTY REDUCTION THEORY

A second major theory about why we form relationships focuses not on attraction but on the uncertainty we feel when we don't know others very well. Let's say you meet someone and want to get to know the person better. What does it *mean* to get to know that individual? According to communication scholars Charles Berger and Richard Calabrese, it means you're reducing your level of uncertainty about the person.[33]

When you first meet a new coworker, for instance, you don't know much about her, so your uncertainty about her personality and her likes and dislikes is high. Berger and Calabrese's **uncertainty reduction theory** suggests that you will find uncertainty to be unpleasant, so you'll be motivated to reduce it by using communication behaviors to get to know your new coworker. At first, you probably talk about basic information, such as where she lives and what she does outside work. As you get to know her better, she will probably disclose more personal information about herself. You might also learn about her by paying attention to nonverbal cues, such as her personal appearance, the sound of her voice, and her use of gestures.

Cultures vary significantly in how they manipulate or mutilate the body to make it physically attractive.

Communication researcher Dale Brashers found that people routinely use a variety of sources when collecting information to reduce their uncertainty.[34] Each new piece of information you gain further reduces your uncertainty.

Uncertainty reduction theory also proposes that the less uncertain we are, the more we will like a new acquaintance. The relationship between liking and uncertainty, as reflected in uncertainty reduction theory, is shown in Figure 7.1.

• **uncertainty reduction theory** Theory suggesting that people find uncertainty to be unpleasant, so they are motivated to reduce their uncertainty by getting to know others.

But does reducing your uncertainty about a person *guarantee* that you'll like him or her? Theories developed since uncertainty reduction theory say no. In his *predicted outcome value theory,* Michael Sunnafrank explained that we consider the merits of what we learn about other people when forming opinions of them.[35] In contrast to uncertainty reduction theory, Sunnafrank's theory suggests that when we dislike the information we learn about others, that information can cause us to like them less, not more.[36]

Research has also revealed cultural diversity in the way people deal with uncertainty. Recall from Chapter 2 that some cultures accept uncertainty as a normal part of life, whereas others tend to avoid it whenever possible. Some studies have compared participants from Japan—an uncertainty-avoiding society—and the United States—an uncertainty-accepting society. Compared to U.S. adults, Japanese adults are less engaged and less likely to reveal information about themselves when they know little about the person with whom they're interacting. That cultural difference emerges whether people are communicating online[37] or in simulated face-to-face conversations.[38]

Even if we do form a social relationship with someone, that doesn't guarantee that we'll want to maintain it. For instance, some friendships grow and flourish, while others start strong but fade over time. We'll look next at two sets of ideas that help us understand why and how we maintain the social relationships we have formed: theories of cost/benefit calculations and theories of relational maintenance behaviors.

SOCIAL EXCHANGE AND EQUITY THEORIES: WEIGHING COSTS AND BENEFITS

Suppose you're drawn to someone, you get to know that person, and now the two of you are friends. You've formed a social relationship—but how will you decide whether you want to stay in it? One way to understand why we maintain certain friendships while letting others fizzle out is to examine the give-and-take of relational costs and benefits.

Earlier in this chapter, we saw that relationships carry costs as well as rewards. We give certain things to a friendship, such as our time, attention, and money, and we get certain benefits from it, such as emotional support, entertainment, and help. Two specific theories help us understand how those costs and benefits influence which relationships we are most likely to maintain: social exchange theory and equity theory.

Social Exchange Theory The guiding principle of **social exchange theory** is that people seek to maintain relationships in which their benefits outweigh their costs.[39] Think of your relationship with a neighbor. There are costs involved in being neighborly: You have to be willing to help when needed, and there might be a loss of privacy if your neighbor is aware of your comings and goings. There are also benefits to a neighborly relationship, including knowing your neighbor is there to watch your place when you're away and having someone close by whom you enjoy being around. The question, according to social exchange theory, is whether you think the benefits outweigh the costs. If you do, then you're likely to stay in that relationship; if not, then you're less inclined to maintain it.

An important concept in social exchange theory is **comparison level,** our realistic expectation of what we want and think we deserve from a relationship. That expectation comes both from experience with social relationships and from cultural norms for such relationships. For example, perhaps you think neighbors should be friendly and should offer help when you need it but should otherwise mind their own business. Those ideas form part of your comparison level for your own neighborly relationships. Perhaps you believe friends should care about your well-being, always keep your secrets, and support you even when they disagree with your decisions. Those desires and expectations will be part of your comparison level for your own friendships.

Equally important is our **comparison level for alternatives,** which measures how much better or worse our current relationship is than other options. Are you satisfied with your neighborly relationships, or do you think you could find better neighbors if you moved? Likewise, are you happy with your current friendships, or do you think you'd be better off ending them? Social exchange theory suggests that we maintain relationships when we think doing so is better than our alternatives, such as ending them and developing new ones. The theory also indicates we are most likely to end relationships if we believe staying in them is worse than our alternatives.

In some relationships, our comparison level for a particular relationship strongly influences *how satisfied we are in that relationship*.[40] Significantly, though, our comparison level for alternatives more strongly influences *whether that relationship will last*. Even satisfying friendships can end if the alternatives are more appealing. However, sometimes unsatisfying friendships endure. The association between the comparison level and the comparison level for alternatives is depicted in Figure 7.2.

Social exchange theory therefore provides a rationale for why people maintain relationships that appear to be costly, such as an abusive friendship. Any type of abuse—whether physical, psychological, or emotional—represents a cost rather than a benefit of being in a relationship. For the person being abused, however, the choice

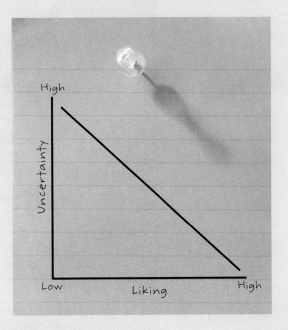

This theory says that as uncertainty about a person goes down, liking for that person goes up.

• **social exchange theory** Theory suggesting that people seek to maintain relationships in which their benefits outweigh their costs.

• **comparison level** A realistic expectation of what one wants and thinks one deserves from a relationship.

• **comparison level for alternatives** An assessment of how much better or worse one's current relationship is than one's other options.

- **over-benefited** A state in which one's relational benefits outweigh one's costs.

- **under-benefited** A state in which one's relational costs outweigh one's benefits.

- **equity theory** Theory that a good relationship is one in which a person's ratio of costs and benefits is equal to his or her partner's.

between maintaining and ending the abusive relationship is rarely as simple as it seems to outsiders. Some victims of abuse perceive that an abusive friend's positive qualities make up for his or her negative characteristics; thus, they have a favorable comparison level. Others believe the costs of ending the relationship—which might include loneliness, loss of other friends, or even the threat of violence—exceed the costs of staying in the relationship. In that case, their comparison level exceeds their comparison level for alternatives because they believe that even if the relationship is bad, ending it would be worse.

Equity Theory If we think of social relationships as having costs and rewards, then it's easy to see that both people in a given relationship might not benefit equally. Imagine that your friend Chandra is always texting you about her problems but never seems to have time to listen to you communicate about yours. She's getting the benefit of your time and attention without the cost of giving her own time and attention to you. You, however, are putting more into the friendship than you're getting from it.

In that situation, Chandra is **over-benefited** and you are **under-benefited.** According to equity theory, such inequality will lead to trouble.[41] **Equity theory** borrows the concepts of cost and benefit from social exchange theory and extends them, stating that a good relationship is one in which our ratio of costs and benefits is equal to our partner's. It's fine if you're working harder on your relationship than your friend is, as long as you're getting more out of it than she does. For example, if you're doing all the cooking every night but Chandra is letting you share her apartment for free, you're probably getting more out of the friendship than Chandra is, even though you might also be putting more effort into it.

However, if both partners get the same level of benefit but one partner's costs are greater than the other's, equity theory predicts that the partner with the greater costs won't want to maintain that relationship. That doesn't mean relationships have to be equitable every moment or in every instance—just in the long run. In many long-term friendships each friend may be over-benefited at some points and under-benefited at others, but as long as they experience equal costs and rewards in the long run, equity theory predicts that their friendship will be stable.

Our costs and benefits in friendships aren't just a matter of tangible goods. We also invest

FIGURE 7.2

COMPARISON LEVEL AND COMPARISON LEVEL FOR ALTERNATIVES IN SOCIAL EXCHANGE THEORY

		Comparison Level	
		High	**Low**
Comparison Level for Alternatives	**High**	Your relationship is satisfying, but you may be inclined to end it if an even more satisfying relationship looks probable.	You're likely to be dissatisfied with this relationship and will probably look for opportunities to end it.
	Low	You'll probably be satisfied with this relationship and won't be likely to end it.	Although you won't find your relationship satisfying, you are unlikely to end it.

Social exchange theory says that four outcomes are possible when we cross our comparison level with our comparison level for alternatives.

time, attention, and care in our friends; in an equitable relationship, we reap those rewards back from them. In some situations, however, we may go through prolonged periods when our investments far outweigh our returns, such as when we provide substantial care for someone suffering a significant health problem.

RELATIONAL MAINTENANCE BEHAVIORS THEORY

Social exchange theory and equity theory both explain *why* we choose to maintain relationships. In contrast, **relational maintenance behaviors theory** explains *how* we maintain them—specifically, it focuses on the primary behaviors we use to do so.

Let's imagine you've made friends with someone, and you're both satisfied with the costs and benefits of your friendship. You'll therefore want to maintain your relationship so it grows and thrives. How do you do so? Communication researchers Laura Stafford and Dan Canary have found that people use five primary relational maintenance behaviors:[42]

• **relational maintenance behaviors theory** Theory specifying the primary behaviors people use to maintain their relationships.

1. *Positivity* includes behaviors such as acting friendly and cheerful, being courteous to others, and refraining from criticism. Individuals who engage in positivity behaviors smile a lot, express affection and appreciation for others, and don't complain—in other words, they're pleasant and fun to be around. Those types of behaviors tend to make people well liked.[43]

2. *Openness* describes a person's willingness to discuss his or her relationship with a friend or other relational partner. People who use this relational maintenance strategy are likely to disclose their thoughts and feelings, to ask how their friend feels about the relationship, and to confide in their friend. Although it's certainly possible to have too much openness in a relationship, an optimal amount will help maintain the relationship and keep it strong.[44]

3. *Assurances* are verbal and nonverbal behaviors that people use to stress their faithfulness and commitment to others. A statement such as "Of course I'll help you; you're my best friend" sends the message that someone is committed to the relationship, and it reassures the friend or partner that the relationship has a future.[45]

4. *Social networks* include all the friendships and family relationships you have. An important relational maintenance behavior is to share your social networks with another. You and a close friend, for instance, are likely to know each other's family, coworkers, and other friends. When you do, we say that your and your friend's social networks have *converged*. Convergence is an important way to keep relationships stable and strong.[46]

5. *Sharing tasks* means performing your fair share of the work in a friendship. If your friend gives you a ride to the airport whenever you need it, for example, then it's only fair that you help her paint her apartment when she asks. As we've seen, being in a social relationship requires investments of energy and effort—so, one way of maintaining a relationship is to make sure you're both contributing equally.[47]

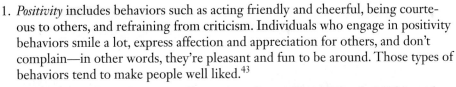

SHARPEN Your Skills:
Relational maintenance behaviors

Choose one of your friendships and make a point of practicing positivity, openness, and assurances with that friend over the next few weeks. What changes in your friendship do you notice in that time?

You may have additional ways of maintaining your social relationships, such as doing favors for a friend and always asking about his or her day. Many friends also maintain their relationships by participating in their shared interests, such as watching sporting events, going to movies, and trying out new recipes.[48] In various ways, each of those behaviors conveys the message that you appreciate and value your friend and enjoy his or her company. Because friendships are largely voluntary, feeling appreciated and valued can motivate you to stay in them.

Revealing Ourselves in Relationships

Now that we've explored why and how we form social relationships, let's examine how we communicate about ourselves in those relationships. **Self-disclosure** is the act of intentionally giving others information about ourselves that we believe is true but that we think they don't already have. From intimate conversations about our hopes and dreams to mundane chats about our favorite restaurants, self-disclosure reveals a part of us to someone else through communication. In this section, we'll first look at several characteristics of self-disclosure and review some of the benefits it can bring to us and our relationships. We'll then survey some risks of self-disclosure—and thereby gain insight into avoiding them.

CHARACTERISTICS OF SELF-DISCLOSURE

Most of us engage in some form of self-disclosure on an ongoing basis. It has several important attributes.

Self-Disclosure Is Intentional and Truthful For an act of communication to qualify as self-disclosure, it must meet two conditions. First, we must deliberately share the information about ourselves. Second, we must believe the information is true.

Let's say that through a momentary lapse in attention, your friend Dean accidentally mentions his financial problems to you. That incident would not constitute an act of self-disclosure according to the definition provided above, because Dean did not share the information deliberately. This is an example of verbal "leakage"—information unintentionally shared with others.

Now let's say you tell a coworker you've never traveled outside your home country. That statement qualifies as self-disclosure if you believe it to be true. It's your belief in the truth of the information that matters, not the absolute truth of the statement. Perhaps you traveled outside the country when you were too young to remember. If you believe the information you're providing is true, however, then it qualifies as self-disclosure.

Self-Disclosure Varies in Breadth and Depth **Social penetration theory,** developed by researchers Irwin Altman and Dalmas Taylor and depicted in Figure 7.3, illustrates how self-disclosing over time is like peeling away the layers of an onion: Each self-disclosure helps us learn more and more about a person we're getting to know.[49]

According to social penetration theory, peeling away the layers to get to know someone requires sharing disclosures that vary along two dimensions: breadth and depth.

Breadth describes the range of topics we discuss with various people. With some people, our self-disclosure has little breadth, because we disclose about only a limited range of topics. With close friends and coworkers, however, we probably talk about several different aspects of our life, such as our work and school experiences, financial concerns, professional ambitions, health, spiritual or religious beliefs, political opinions, and desires for the future, giving our disclosure in those relationships greater breadth.

The second dimension, **depth,** measures how personal or intimate our disclosures are, reflecting how carefully we feel we must guard the information we might give out. Let's say Ramona and her romantic partner are having problems. Ramona might describe her difficulties in detail with her mother, not only because she values her mother's opinion but also because she trusts her to keep the information private. Because she doesn't feel the need to guard the information from her mother, Ramona can engage in disclosure that has great depth. With her assistant, however, Ramona

• **breadth** The range of topics we self-disclose to various people.

• **depth** The degree of intimacy of our self-disclosures.

FIGURE 7.3
SOCIAL PENETRATION THEORY

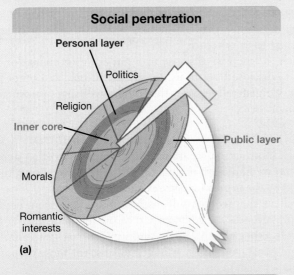

(a)

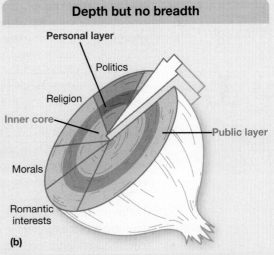

(b)

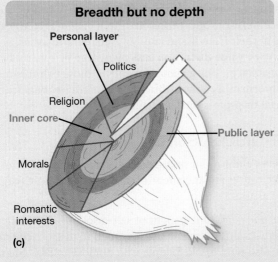

(c)

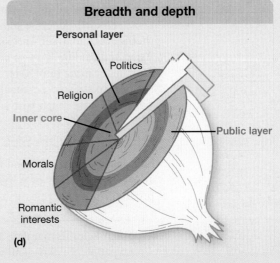

(d)

Researchers use the image of a multilayered onion to represent the process of social penetration in a relationship. The outer layer represents breadth of self-disclosure, and the inner layers reflect depth of self-disclosure. Our close relationships are usually characterized by both breadth and depth.

discloses that she is having difficulty, but she doesn't go into detail because she doesn't feel comfortable entrusting her assistant with the specifics. In that instance, Ramona engages in self-disclosure of less depth.

Self-Disclosure Varies among Relationships

Not every relationship is characterized by the same breadth and depth of self-disclosure. With your accountant, for instance, you might disclose in depth about financial matters but not about anything else. See the representation of this type of relationship in Figure 7.3b.

Other relationships are characterized by breadth of disclosure but very little depth. With casual friends at school or work, for example, you might disclose a little about several areas of your life—family, hobbies, political ideas, career ambitions—but not provide intimate details about any of them. See Figure 7.3c.

In still other relationships, such as close friendships, people typically share both public and private information about multiple aspects of their lives. You can see that higher degree of depth and breadth depicted in Figure 7.3d.

Self-Disclosure Is Usually Reciprocal

The adage "One good turn deserves another" suggests that when someone gives you a gift or shares a resource, you should return the favor. Sociologist Alvin Gouldner called that expectation the **norm of reciprocity**.[50] In North American cultures, among others, the norm of reciprocity usually extends to self-disclosure; that is, when we disclose to other people, we typically expect them to disclose to us in return.[51]

There are exceptions, such as when we disclose to a physician or counselor. We don't expect that individual to disclose back to us. In our friendships and other personal relationships, however, we generally expect that others will share information with us as we share it with them.

Self-Disclosure Is Influenced by Cultural and Gender Roles

Many factors affect how much information we are willing to disclose to other people, such as the type of relationship we have with them and how long we've known them. Self-disclosure is also affected by the norms for our sex and culture.[52]

Many people probably believe that women self-disclose more than men, because disclosure and emotional expressiveness are a bigger part of the feminine gender role than the masculine gender role, especially in North America.[53] Is that generalization true? The evidence does suggest that women, on average, self-disclose more than men, although the difference is smaller than many believe.[54]

Diversity in cultural norms can also affect self-disclosure. In some cultures, such as those in North America and northern Europe, people are often encouraged to express themselves and to self-disclose to their friends and family. Other cultures, such as most Asian and Middle Eastern cultures, value discretion and encourage people to disclose only under more limited circumstances. For instance, people in those cultures may be inclined to disclose personal information only within their families or romantic relationships, rather than with social or professional acquaintances.[55]

BENEFITS OF SELF-DISCLOSURE

Self-disclosure can be good for us and for our relationships. Here we take a brief look at four key benefits of self-disclosure: enhancement of relationships and trust; reciprocity; emotional release; and assistance to others.

1. *Enhancement of relationships and trust.* One benefit of self-disclosure is that it often helps us maintain high-quality relationships. We tend to disclose the most to people we like—and we also tend to like people who disclose to us.[56] Sharing appropriate self-disclosure in close relationships helps us to maintain those relationships and to reinforce the trust we share with those individuals.[57]

2. *Reciprocity.* As noted above, many of us follow a norm of reciprocity when it comes to self-disclosure: When others disclose to us, we tend to disclose back to them.[58] Thus, one way to get to know other people is to tell them about ourselves, so they feel more comfortable doing the same in return.

• **norm of reciprocity** The social expectation that favors should be reciprocated.

3. *Emotional release.* Sometimes the best part of self-disclosing is the feeling of getting something "off your chest." Perhaps you've had the experience of holding on to a secret of yours that you felt you just had to talk to someone about. Appropriate self-disclosures can often bring emotional release.[59] Also, as several studies have shown, self-disclosures can reduce the stress of holding on to a secret. That stress reduction is an important benefit because it can improve our mental and physical health.[60]

4. *Assistance to others.* We can also self-disclose in ways that help other people, particularly when we are consoling individuals who are going through hard times. If your friend is having difficulty handling his father's death, you might disclose how you managed traumatic situations in your own life. That disclosure can provide comfort and signal to your friend that he's not alone. Many self-help programs, among them Alcoholics Anonymous, encourage such disclosures to help their members realize they are all going through a similar struggle.[61] Although enhanced relationships, reciprocity, emotional release, and assistance to others are not the only benefits provided by self-disclosure, they're among the most important for social relationships.

Whereas people in North America and northern Europe are often encouraged to express themselves, people in Asian and Middle Eastern cultures are frequently taught to value discretion.

RISKS OF SELF-DISCLOSURE

Like many communication behaviors, self-disclosure isn't always a positive action; it has both good and bad aspects. Here we'll look at four potential risks of self-disclosure: being rejected, obligating others, hurting others, and violating privacy.

1. *Rejection.* What if the people to whom we're disclosing don't like what we tell them? Let's say your coworker decides to confide to you that he's gay. His disclosure might bring you closer together. If his sexuality is a problem for you, however, his disclosure could lead you to reject him. Often, the way a person reacts to a disclosure will determine whether its outcome is positive or negative.

2. *Obligations in others.* The reciprocity of self-disclosure can be a very good thing if we are trying to get to know someone better. However, it can make the other person feel put on the spot and uncomfortable about disclosing something back. Even worse, it could encourage the person to avoid us in the future.

3. *Hurt to others.* It's possible to hurt others with disclosures that are too critical or too personal. Despite the idea that honesty is the best policy, uncensored candor can lead to wounded feelings and resentment. Especially when sharing highly

The Scene: While inebriated one night, your close friend confides in you that she is contemplating suicide—and she makes you promise not to share that information with anyone. She has never seemed suicidal to you before, so you wonder whether she was exaggerating, owing to her intoxication. Given that her threat of suicide might be real, however, you feel a duty to warn someone who can help. At the same time, you did promise to keep her secret, and you worry about upsetting her further if she is already suicidal.

Your Task: Consider how you should adapt your disclosure behavior to the competing demands of this situation. What strategies could you use in this situation to

- Assist your friend?
- Honor her desire for privacy?
- Enhance her trust in your friendship?

sensitive disclosures, consider how receivers will react to the information. If necessary, preface your statement by saying "I know this is a sensitive topic" or "I understand this may be hard to hear." By doing so, you help to prepare your listener for a critical or personal disclosure, reducing the chances that he or she will feel harmed.

4. *Violation of other people's privacy.* Inappropriate disclosures can even hurt people who aren't participating in the conversation. People in many relationships—including families, friendships, and workplace relationships—disclose private information that is not meant to be shared, sometimes unintentionally by forwarding an e-mail or text without permission. When we do so, we risk hurting our loved ones and damaging their trust in us.

Although these poor outcomes *can* occur when we self-disclose, they aren't inevitable. When managed with care and sensitivity, self-disclosure can reinforce the most positive aspects of our social and professional relationships.

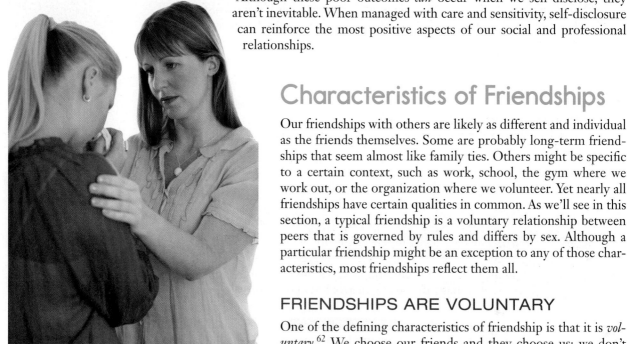

Self-disclosure can help us console others during difficult times.

Characteristics of Friendships

Our friendships with others are likely as different and individual as the friends themselves. Some are probably long-term friendships that seem almost like family ties. Others might be specific to a certain context, such as work, school, the gym where we work out, or the organization where we volunteer. Yet nearly all friendships have certain qualities in common. As we'll see in this section, a typical friendship is a voluntary relationship between peers that is governed by rules and differs by sex. Although a particular friendship might be an exception to any of those characteristics, most friendships reflect them all.

FRIENDSHIPS ARE VOLUNTARY

One of the defining characteristics of friendship is that it is *voluntary.*[62] We choose our friends and they choose us; we don't *have to* be friends with anyone. Part of what makes a friendship so special is that both friends are in the relationship by choice.

When we meet someone we want to be friends with, initiating a friendship requires communication behaviors. Not only do we need to interact with that person to form the friendship in the first place, we also must use relationship maintenance behaviors such as positivity, openness, assurances, network convergence, and sharing tasks to maintain our friendship.

FRIENDSHIPS USUALLY DEVELOP BETWEEN PEERS

A second important characteristic of friendship is that it is usually a relationship between equals. A **peer** is someone similar to us in power or status. We aren't a peer of our professors, boss, or parents, because they all exercise some measure of control over us, at least temporarily. Most of us conceive of friendship as a relationship between peers—people who are our equals, no more or less powerful than we are.

• **peer** A person similar to us in status or power.

We *can* have satisfying friendships with others who have some type of power over us. Those relationships can be complicated, however, because people in power sometimes have to make decisions that conflict with the friendship. A supervisor might want to share news about an upcoming layoff with a friend who works for her, for instance, but may feel she cannot because of her supervisory position. In such friendships, it is often best to discuss these competing expectations directly and agree on ground rules for addressing them.

FRIENDSHIPS ARE GOVERNED BY RULES

In some ways, a friendship is like a social contract to which both parties agree. By being someone's friend, we acknowledge—at least implicitly—that we expect certain things from that person and that he or she can expect certain things from us. Those expectations are possible because friendships follow rules. Even if the rules aren't explicitly stated, most people within a given society usually know and understand them.[63]

As Table 7.2 shows, researchers have studied many of the rules of friendship. Some relate to a specific behavior, such as practicing self-disclosure or including friends in your activities. Others relate to the qualities we should exhibit in our friendships, such as loyalty and authenticity. Perhaps you've been in a friendship in which one or more of those implicit rules were broken. For example, maybe you have a friend who rarely makes time for you or often excludes you from his plans. Most people agree there are ways to treat our friends that are simply right or wrong.[64] Like communication rules in general, these friendship rules often become explicit only when somebody violates them.

FRIENDSHIPS DIFFER BY SEX

You have probably noticed differences between your friendships with women and those with men. Researchers have written volumes about sex differences and similarities in friendships and friendship behaviors. Let's examine those separately for same- and opposite-sex friendships.

SHARPEN Your Skills: *Friendship rules*

Survey some of your closest friends to determine what rules they follow in their friendships. Ask specifically about any differences in their rules for same- and opposite-sex friendships. Document your findings in a blog or journal entry.

TABLE 7.2 FRIENDSHIP RULES	One way to understand a relationship is to think about the rules or expectations that govern it. Communication researcher Jeff Hall examined 36 studies of friendship expectations. Here are some of the most important friendship rules he found. What rules would *you* add to this list?

- Be loyal to your friends.

- Provide support when needed.

- Be authentic and trustworthy.

- Practice self-disclosure with your friends.

- Include friends in your activities.

- Make time to spend together.

- Offer money or other resources when needed.

SOURCE: Hall, J. A. (2011). Sex differences in friendship expectations: A meta-analysis. *Journal of Social and Personal Relationships, 28,* 723–747.

Same-Sex Friends For same-sex friends, one of the most consistent findings in research is that women and men value different aspects of their friendships. Friendships between women often emphasize conversational and emotional expressiveness more than do friendships between men.[65] Best friends Juanita and Linsay, for instance, frequently get together just to talk and catch up. Their visits often include sharing their feelings about what's going on in their lives. They would say their ability to share, disclose, and express feelings with each other is what makes their friendship so close.

Men's friendships tend to place a heavier emphasis on shared activities and common interests.[66] For instance, the time Alex spends with his best friend Jake almost always revolves around some activity. It might be playing a round of golf and then having nachos and beer at a sports bar, or working together on Jake's vintage car. For Alex and Jake, it's the *doing*, not the *talking*, that makes their friendship close.

Two aspects of those sex differences are important to note. First, like nearly all sex differences in behavior, differences in same-sex friendships are just averages. They don't characterize all friendships. Some women's friendships focus more on shared activities than conversation, and some men routinely share personal conversations with their male friends even if they aren't engaged in an activity together. Second, those differences don't mean friendships are any more important to one sex than the other. Some people believe women's friendships are closer and more satisfying than men's because women self-disclose more to each other than men do. Research has instead shown that women and men report equal levels of closeness in their same-sex friendships.[67] What differs between the sexes is simply the characteristics that make those friendships close. For women, it's often shared conversation; for men, it's frequently shared activity.

Many lesbian, gay, bisexual, and transgendered adults form important same-sex friendships with heterosexuals.[68] As communication professor Lisa Tillmann-Healy describes in her book, *Between Gay and Straight: Understanding Friendship across Sexual Orientation*, such friendships can be both inherently challenging and richly rewarding.[69] Heterosexual and nonheterosexual adults manage the challenges of their same-sex friendships in a variety of ways. A study of gay male-straight male friendships found that some friends embrace and celebrate the differences in their sexual orientation. Others struggle with those differences, and others ignore them completely.[70] A similar study of women found that sexual tension and discomfort with self-disclosure are common barriers to same-sex friendships between straight women and lesbians.[71]

Many opposite-sex friends communicate in ways that resemble romantic relationships, such as by flirting with each other and sharing sexual humor.

Despite their challenges, however, same-sex friendships between heterosexuals and nonheterosexuals can promote understanding and sensitivity, provide emotional support, and discourage harmful stereotypes.[72]

Opposite-Sex Friends What about opposite-sex friendships, then? Research suggests that both men and women value them as a chance to see things from each other's perspective.[73] Opposite-sex friendships can provide opportunities for men to be emotionally expressive and for women to enjoy shared activities that their same-sex friendships do not.[74] In addition, many opposite-sex friends feel some degree of physical or romantic attraction toward each other,[75] and they often communicate in ways that resemble romantic relationships, such as flirting with each other[76] and sharing sexual humor.[77]

In a study of 324 U.S. college students, in fact, communication scientists Walid Afifi and Sandra Faulkner found that half the students reported having engaged in sexual activity in a nonromantic opposite-sex friendship.[78] Some researchers have suggested that sexual activity changes the fundamental nature of an opposite-sex friendship from platonic to romantic.[79] Yet more than half the students in Afifi and Faulkner's study who had engaged in sexual activity with an opposite-sex friend reported no such change in the nature of their relationship. Research by communication scholars Mikayla Hughes, Kelly Morrison, and Kelli Jean Asada suggests that such relationships are more positive if the friends observe certain rules, such as not getting emotionally attached and always practicing safe sex.[80]

Whether they are attracted to each other or not, many opposite-sex friends have specific reasons for not wanting their friendship to evolve into a romantic relationship. In surveys of more than 600 U.S. college students, communication scholars Susan Messman, Dan Canary, and Kimberly Hause discovered that people avoid romance in their opposite-sex friendships for six primary reasons:[81]

1. They aren't physically attracted to their friend.
2. Their relatives and other friends wouldn't approve of a romantic relationship with the friend.
3. They aren't ready to be in a romantic relationship.
4. They want to protect their existing friendship.
5. They fear being disappointed or hurt.
6. They are concerned about a third party, such as a sibling who is romantically interested in the friend.

Very little research has examined the qualities of opposite-sex friendships in which one of the friends is lesbian, gay, bisexual, or transgendered. One study examined the friendships of gay men and straight women that formed through workplace contact. The researcher found that gay men and straight women had rewarding but complex friendships.[82] Many participants in that study said they felt there were few "models" for such friendships, so they made up their own friendship rules. Other research has found that straight women who maintain friendships with gay men often feel stigmatized by other straight women.[83]

Studies show that same- and opposite-sex friendships each offer unique rewards. Both women and men report that their same-sex friends are more loyal and helpful than their opposite-sex counterparts.[84] Opposite-sex friendships, however, allow women and men to enjoy those aspects of friendship most valued by the other sex.

Social Relationships in the Workplace

Nearly all of us will be employed at some point in life, and many jobs will require us to interact with other people. It's therefore realistic to assume that we will have to relate to and communicate with people we know from work, whether they're coworkers, superiors, subordinates, or customers. Further, many public agencies and private corporations expect specific behaviors from their employees, which likely include communicating honestly, treating people with dignity, listening attentively, and being open to others' opinions. All those communication behaviors contribute to a civil and respectful work environment, and they can also facilitate the formation of workplace friendships.[85]

Friendships at work can be a dual-edged sword. On the one hand, having friends at work can make the workday fun and pleasant and provide us with help and support when we need it. On the other hand, friendship roles and work roles sometimes conflict. For instance, your friends may want to visit with you at work, but if you have tasks to complete by a deadline, you may not have time to socialize.

Workplace friendships may also be more challenging to control than regular friendships. If you have an argument with a regular friend, you can choose to avoid him or her until you both cool down. Because of your work obligations, however, you may not have that option with workplace friends.

For all the foregoing reasons, it is particularly useful to understand the dynamics of workplace friendships, so we can deal with the challenges they present. Let's examine those dynamics in three specific workplace relationships: between coworkers, between superiors and subordinates, and with clients.

Social relationships in the workplace can bring both support and frustration.

SOCIAL RELATIONSHIPS WITH COWORKERS

Perhaps the most likely opportunity for forming friendships at work arises with respect to our immediate coworkers. One reason is that coworkers are usually peers rather than superiors or subordinates, so they tend to have levels of power and responsibility similar to ours.[86] Another reason is that by virtue of being coworkers, they share some common experiences with us, such as working in the same organizational culture and perhaps for the same department and supervisor. On top of that, we typically spend a great deal of time with our coworkers, perhaps even more than we spend with friends outside work. Thus, there is a ready-made basis for friendship with coworkers.[87]

The quality of people's friendships with their coworkers affects their job satisfaction.[88] That is, the closer we are to our coworkers, the happier we are at work. Yet as beneficial as they are, friendships with coworkers can be challenging. They have both a *social* or personal dimension and a *task* or professional dimension, and those can come into conflict.

Let's say you're friends with your coworker Tonya, who's up for a promotion. *As her friend*, you want her to have the promotion. *As her coworker*, however, you don't think she deserves it, because in your opinion she hasn't earned it. It's easy to see how your opinion might be troublesome for your friendship, but being friends with your coworkers means having to balance the personal and professional sides of the relationship at all times.

In that situation, you might decide it's important to tell Tonya you support her, to voice enthusiasm if she receives the promotion, and to express disappointment if she doesn't, because she's your friend. Even though you don't feel she's earned the promotion, your friendship with Tonya may motivate you to be supportive of her anyway. However, you might remind Tonya that the promotion is very competitive, that employees with more experience and seniority than she has are competing for it, and that she shouldn't be surprised if she doesn't get it. You might even say "I'm telling you this as your coworker," to make it clear you are speaking from the perspective of your professional rather than personal relationship. Which approach you choose will probably depend on the closeness of your friendship and on the outcomes of similar situations you have experienced.

One career requiring the ability to manage social relationships in the workplace is affirmative action officer. Check out "Putting Communication to Work" to learn more about that job.

SOCIAL RELATIONSHIPS BETWEEN SUPERIORS AND SUBORDINATES

Even though they can be tricky, friendships among coworkers are fairly common. Friendships between superiors and subordinates are considerably more complicated because they include a power differential.[89] When two friends are a supervisor and an employee, the power difference between them introduces a task dimension that friendships between coworkers usually don't have.

Genuine friendships between superiors and subordinates certainly aren't impossible to form or maintain. Indeed, being friends with the boss usually adds to a person's job satisfaction.[90] That effect makes sense: if we like our supervisor, we'll probably enjoy working for him or her. The challenge is that what's best for the superior–subordinate relationship isn't always what's best for the friendship. If you're the employee, for instance, you may find yourself disliking decisions your boss makes about the company's policies or future direction, particularly when those decisions might significantly affect you. If you're the supervisor, you may agonize about such decisions, realizing that what's best for the organization is not always what's best for each individual employee.

To save money, for instance, your supervisor may announce that the company will reduce the office support staff on whom you depend to get your work done. Or, to

Job Title >

Work Responsibilities >

Affirmative Action Officer

Affirmative action officers usually work for the human resources division of a company, organization, or institution. They help to recruit and retain a diverse workforce that includes women, ethnic minorities, and persons with disabilities. They also advise executives, administrators, or government officials of their rights and obligations to affirmative action, and they may help to mediate disputes between supervisors and employees. The position requires not only a thorough understanding of affirmative action laws but also an ability to communicate sensitively with a wide variety of people.

accommodate a new business strategy, your boss may decide to cancel a promotional campaign you've been developing. In those cases, it may be hard not to take your boss's actions personally, and they can strain your friendship.[91] In a study of superior–subordinate friendships, communication scholar Theodore Zorn found that superiors commonly experienced those types of tensions between their work responsibilities and their friendships with subordinates.[92] Still, friendships between superiors and subordinates aren't necessarily doomed.

Often it's best if both parties in a power-imbalanced friendship acknowledge that their friendship and their work relationship might conflict and if they agree to keep those relationships separate. It's helpful, too, if the two can discuss the potential for conflicts directly, particularly if they started their relationship as peers and one of them was later promoted. By acknowledging the possibility of conflicts and establishing their expectations for how to address clashes of interests *before they occur*, a supervisor and an employee can lay the groundwork for a successful friendship. Although doing so doesn't mean they'll avoid all the tensions that often accompany that type of relationship, they will be better able to handle them when they arise.

SHARPEN Your Skills: *Communicating with a superior*

Suppose you're good friends with your supervisor, Kyle, whose quarterly sales figures have been dismal. Kyle asks you to let him take credit for some of your sales so he has a chance of getting a satisfactory performance review from his superiors. On the one hand, you recognize the value of making your supervisor look good, and you know Kyle will repay your generosity. On the other hand, you are uncomfortable lying, and you resent the idea of Kyle's taking credit for your hard work. With a friend or classmate, role-play a conversation in which you discuss this situation with Kyle and try to reach agreement on how to resolve it.

SOCIAL RELATIONSHIPS WITH CLIENTS

In most professions, you'll also interact with customers. For instance, you might work for a financial or technology firm that offers ongoing consulting services to a number of long-term business clients. Depending on the nature of your job, you may have clients you see or talk to on a regular basis, so it's reasonable to expect that you may form social relationships with some of them.[93] Those relationships can be highly rewarding personally, and they can also benefit your organization because they may be a large part of the reason why your customers continue to buy from you or your company.[94] After all, most of us prefer dealing with a service provider or a salesperson with whom we can develop a comfortable and trusting relationship.

Friendships with customers can run into some of the same task-versus-social tensions that occur in friendships between co-workers and between superiors and subordinates. Our customers may be our friends, but they still expect us to furnish a high-quality product or service, and we still expect them to provide full and prompt payment. If either party doesn't uphold its end of the bargain, the customer–provider relationship can be disrupted and the friendship can suffer.

Perhaps to avoid those tensions, some companies discourage their employees from developing personal friendships with customers. Although *friendliness* is critical in customer relations, many businesses recognize that the feelings of loyalty and favor we often have for friends can interfere with the professional relationship. When he took a position as a sales representative for a cable television company, for instance, Deion became close friends with several clients. Because he liked them, he began giving them discounts on their cable service that other customers didn't receive. Because his client-friends liked Deion, they consistently gave him the highest possible scores on customer satisfaction surveys. Those special deals and preferential treatments continued for almost a year before Deion's regional manager realized what was happening. She reprimanded Deion for allowing his friendships with clients to compromise his professional relationships with them.

The separation of personal and professional relationships is particularly important in the health care setting. In the United States, ethical guidelines of the American College of Physicians discourage doctors from treating friends, relatives, intimate partners, or others with whom they have close personal relationships.[95] A doctor's professional judgment and objectivity could be compromised by his or her personal feelings for the patient. If objectivity is lost, then the doctor might not make proper decisions about the patient's condition or treatment and might put the patient's health at risk.

If you do become friends with customers, be especially clear with them about the boundaries between your personal and professional relationships. While conducting business, treat them as you would treat any other customer, and ask them to treat you as they would any other provider.

A personal friendship with customers can be successful if the friends agree that their professional relationship is separate and should be treated professionally.

In both our professional and our personal lives, having friends and other social relationships enriches us. English poet Samuel Taylor Coleridge once called friendship a "sheltering tree" to point out how friends can shield and protect us from many of the stresses of life. Friends make our life safer, happier, and more meaningful.

- Why do social relationships matter so much to us? We have a natural need to belong that motivates us to seek, form, and maintain social relationships. Those relationships in turn provide us with emotional, material, and health rewards.

- Which characteristics of friendships make them vital to our social experience and well-being? Friendships are voluntary relationships, usually among peers, that are governed by rules and differ by sex.

- How do we manage social relationships in the workplace? In relationships with coworkers, superiors, subordinates, and clients, it is important to separate the social dimension of the relationship from its task dimension and to be aware of power differences.

POP QUIZ

Multiple Choice

1. When she meets her neighbor Carma for the first time, Patrice is immediately attracted to her personality. Patrice is experiencing

   a. task attraction.

   b. physical attraction.

   c. role-limited attraction.

   d. social attraction.

2. Uncertainty reduction theory states that

   a. uncertainty about someone creates mystery and facilitates attraction toward him or her.

   b. we like uncertainty because what we do not know cannot hurt us.

   c. uncertainty is unpleasant, and through communication we seek to reduce it.

   d. we dislike uncertainty but there is not much we can do about it.

3. Jake and Peter are best friends who both invest heavily in their friendship. According to equity theory, the best scenario for Jake is that

   a. his rewards outweigh his costs.

   b. his costs outweigh his rewards.

   c. his ratio of costs to rewards is the same as Peter's.

   d. none of these.

4. The theory illustrating how self-disclosure over time is like peeling away the layers of an onion is

   a. attraction theory.

   b. social penetration theory.

   c. predicted outcome value theory.

   d. social exchange theory.

5. Workplace relationships can be challenging because they contain both a social dimension and

   a. task dimension.

   b. complementarity dimension.

   c. role-limited dimension.

   d. network convergence dimension.

Fill in the Blank

6. The theory that says that each of us is born with a desire to seek, form, and maintain social relationships is _____.

7. We can be attracted to others who are different from ourselves if we perceive their differences as _____, or beneficial to ourselves.

8. _____ describes the range of topics we discuss with other people.

9. Because friendships are _____, we choose our friends and they choose us.

10. Relationships between subordinates and superiors can be complicated because they include a _____ difference that coworker relationships generally do not include.

KEY TERMS

need to belong theory 152
attraction theory 156
interpersonal attraction 156
physical attraction 156
social attraction 156
task attraction 156
proximity 157
complementarity 157

uncertainty reduction theory 160
social exchange theory 161
comparison level 161
comparison level for alternatives 161
over-benefited 162
under-benefited 162
equity theory 162

relational maintenance behaviors theory 163
self-disclosure 164
social penetration theory 164
breadth 165
depth 165
norm of reciprocity 166
peer 169

COMMUNICATING IN INTIMATE RELATIONSHIPS

In Sickness and In Health

When Rachelle Friedman imagined her wedding, she never dreamed of coming down the aisle in a wheelchair. At her bachelorette party in August 2010, however, she was pushed into a swimming pool by one of her bridesmaids as a joke. After hitting her head on the bottom of the pool, Friedman suffered a spinal cord injury that left her unable to walk or to feel any sensation below her collarbone. Despite the physical and emotional trauma of the accident, Friedman has maintained a decidedly positive outlook on life—and so has her fiancée, Chris Chapman, who never wavered in his devotion to his bride. Demonstrating his commitment, Chapman says he never thought "What am I going to do?" but only "What are *we* going to do?" Public support for the couple was so overwhelming that the costs of their wedding and honeymoon, as well as Friedman's rehab therapy, were fully covered by donors. Friedman and Chapman were married in June 2011, in Pittsboro, North Carolina.

▶ As You READ

- What makes some relationships intimate?
- How do we form, maintain, and dissolve romantic relationships?
- What makes a family, and how do we communicate in families?

It's difficult to overstate the importance of our intimate relationships. We may have many close friends, coworkers, and other acquaintances, but our relationships with romantic partners and family members are special. Those are the people whose lives affect us the most and with whom we share our deepest sorrows and greatest joys. Most of us invest more in, and feel more committed to, those relationships than any others. The intimate relationships we develop with our families and romantic partners truly shape our lives in unique and important ways.

Family life and romantic relationships also influence each other. Growing up in a family gives most of us our first exposure to the concept of personal relationships and our first examples of romantic unions. Moreover, when we form romantic relationships in adulthood, those often provide the basis for starting new families. Thus, although romantic and familial relationships are different in some notable respects, there is often an intimate connection between the two.

The Nature of Intimate Relationships

Many people think specifically of romantic relationships when they hear the word *intimate*, but intimacy is about more than just romance. **Intimacy** means significant emotional closeness that we experience in a relationship, whether romantic or not. As we'll see in this section, intimate relationships require deep commitment, foster interdependence, require continuous investment, and spark dialectical tensions.

• **intimacy** Significant emotional closeness experienced in a relationship, whether romantic or not.

INTIMATE RELATIONSHIPS REQUIRE DEEP COMMITMENT

Chris Chapman demonstrated unwavering commitment to his fiancée—and now wife—Rachelle Friedman. Despite Friedman's long and challenging ordeal, Chapman adapted to her changing physical and emotional needs without ever once hinting a desire to call off their wedding.

Like Chapman, most of us are more committed to our intimate relationships than we are to other relationships in our lives. For instance, we may be more willing to put aside minor differences and make compromises to preserve our intimate relationships. **Commitment** is our desire to stay in a relationship no matter what happens. When people are committed to each other, they assume they have a future together. That assumption is important because most intimate relationships—such as families and romantic relationships—experience conflict and distress from time to time. What allows us to deal with those difficult times is the belief that our relationship will survive them.

• **commitment** The desire to stay in a relationship no matter what happens.

How do we commit ourselves to others? Intimate relationships usually include some level of *emotional commitment*, or a sense of responsibility for each other's feelings and emotional well-being. For example, it's your emotional commitment to

Parents often provide the social, emotional, and financial commitments that help their children succeed.

your sibling that leads you to listen to his or her problems, even if they seem trivial to you. Our intimate relationships also include a level of *social commitment*, which motivates us to spend time together, to compromise, to be generous with praise, and to avoid petty conflict. In some romantic relationships, social commitment takes the form of spending time with a partner's friends or family members even if we don't enjoy their company. Finally, some intimate relationships are bound by *legal* and *financial commitments*, which are more formal expressions of people's obligations to each other. Parents have a legal responsibility to provide housing, food, clothing, health care, and education for their children who are minors, and family members often take on

THE DARK SIDE OF COMMUNICATION

When Commitment Becomes Obsession

Although deep commitment is necessary in intimate relationships, an excessive level can turn into an unhealthy obsession with another person. According to communication scholars William Cupach and Brian Spitzberg, intimate relationships are healthy and satisfying only if both partners desire approximately the same level of connection and interaction with each other. When one expresses a substantially higher level of interest in the relationship than the other, the result can be what Cupach and Spitzberg call *obsessive relational intrusion,* or ORI. (ORI sometimes also occurs between strangers.)

ORI can prompt an individual to enact several specific behaviors aimed at increasing intimacy with the target of his or her affections. Those include spying on the target or invading his or her privacy, sending the person unwelcome expressions of attraction or love, and engaging in sexually harassing behaviors. They can also include demanding that the target curtail communication with others and commit to an exclusive relationship with the obsessed person.

Although relational intrusion can occur in face-to-face contexts, it is also becoming increasingly common online. Using the Internet, e-mail, or other electronic means to intrude on another person's life is called *cyberstalking.* Intrusive behaviors can have various negative effects on the recipients, including physical and psychological stress, disruptions in everyday routines, loss of sleep or appetite, and diminished trust in others.

SOURCES: Cupach, W. R., & Spitzberg, B. H. (2004). *The dark side of relationship pursuit: From attraction to obsession and stalking.* Mahwah, NJ: Lawrence Erlbaum Associates; Spitzberg, B. H., & Hoobler, G. (2002). Cyberstalking and the technologies of interpersonal terrorism. *New Media & Society, 4,* 71–92.

financial obligations to care for relatives who are aging or who have specific physical or mental needs. No matter what form it takes, commitment is one of the foundations of intimate relationships.

Although deep commitment is important for many relationships, people can take it too far. At an extreme level, commitment can turn into obsession, a topic explored in "The Dark Side of Communication."

Interdependence means that an event or a decision that affects one person in a relationship—such as taking a job or moving—affects everyone else in the relationship.

INTIMATE RELATIONSHIPS FOSTER INTERDEPENDENCE

Another hallmark of intimate relationships is that they include high degrees of **interdependence.** Because people in families and romantic relationships depend on one another, what happens to one person, or what one person does, affects everyone else in the relationship. For instance, the way parents use their time and money depends not only on themselves but also on their children's needs. Likewise, how children perform in school and the way they treat their siblings also affect their parents. Parents and children are therefore interdependent. So are romantic partners: If a woman is offered a job promotion that requires her to relocate, for example, her decision will affect her romantic partner as much as it will affect her. The essence of interdependence is the idea that our actions influence other people's lives as much as they influence our own.

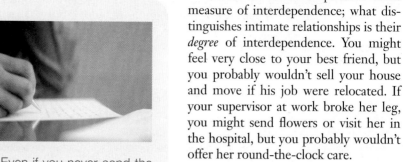

Almost all relationships have some measure of interdependence; what distinguishes intimate relationships is their *degree* of interdependence. You might feel very close to your best friend, but you probably wouldn't sell your house and move if his job were relocated. If your supervisor at work broke her leg, you might send flowers or visit her in the hospital, but you probably wouldn't offer her round-the-clock care.

Like most social relationships, friendships and professional relationships are interdependent to a degree. What typically sets our romantic and familial relationships apart, however, is their *higher* level of interdependence.

• **interdependence**
The state in which what happens to one person affects everyone else in the relationship.

That often motivates us to engage in greater relational maintenance behaviors than we do with friends or coworkers.

INTIMATE RELATIONSHIPS REQUIRE CONTINUOUS INVESTMENT

Compared to other relationships, intimate relationships usually also exhibit a higher degree of **investment**—that is, the commitment of our energies and other resources, particularly time, energy, and attention. We also expect to benefit from our investment—think of our expectations from financial investments, for instance—but we know we cannot retrieve the resources we've dedicated to the relationship if it comes to an end. For example, if we drift apart from our siblings during adulthood, we may retain memories of our relationships, but we cannot get back the time, attention, and material resources we invested in them.

People in romantic relationships are often especially aware of how much—and how equitably—they are each investing in the relationship. Research shows that romantic partners are happiest when they feel they are both investing in their relationship to the same degree.[1] If you think you are putting more into your relationship than your partner is, it's easy to feel resentful. The most satisfying intimate relationships appear to be those in which both parties are investing equally.

• **investment**
The commitment of one's energies and resources to a relationship.

INTIMATE RELATIONSHIPS SPARK DIALECTICAL TENSIONS

Have you ever felt as though you wanted to be closer to someone but also wanted to maintain your individuality? In your relationships, have you wished to have more self-disclosure but still desired to keep some thoughts private? Maybe you enjoy novelty and surprise in your relationships but you also like them to be stable and predictable. If you can relate to any of those feelings, you have experienced what relationship researchers call **dialectical tensions**—conflicts between two important but opposing needs or desires. Dialectical tensions are common in intimate relationships.[2] Within families, romantic relationships, and even friendships, three dialectical tensions in particular often arise.

• **dialectical tensions**
Conflicts between two important but opposing relational needs or desires.

Autonomy versus Connection A common tension in intimate relations is between *autonomy*—the desire to be your own person—and *connection*—the desire to be close to others. People often observe that tension in their children, especially entering adolescence. After all, adolescence is a period of life when teenagers begin to develop independent identities and make decisions for themselves.[3] Many, however, still want to be emotionally close to their parents. They continue to need and crave the security of family closeness even as they are learning to behave like adults. In fact, it's not uncommon for parents and children to experience that dialectical tension for some time, even as the children grow into adulthood.

Openness versus Closedness A second dialectical tension in intimate relationships is the conflict between *openness*—the desire for disclosure and honesty—and *closedness*—the desire to keep certain facts, thoughts, or ideas to yourself. Suppose your mother asks you how your new relationship is going. On the one hand, you might want to confide in her as a way of reinforcing your closeness to her. On the other hand, you may feel it's best to keep some of the details to yourself, out of respect for your partner's privacy. In other words, part of you desires openness, and another part desires closedness.

Predictability versus Novelty Finally, many intimate relationships experience conflict between *predictability*—the desire for consistency and stability—and *novelty*—the desire for fresh new experiences. After nearly 20 years of marriage, for instance, Pauline and Victor were so settled in their routines that their relationship had become highly predictable. Such predictability can be comforting, but at times it made their marriage feel stale and left them longing for something new. They found that trying new activities—such as taking a foreign language class together and volunteering at a soup kitchen—provided a refreshing change from the predictability of their married life. By the same token, however, they recognized that predictability gave their relationship an orderliness and certainty they both appreciated.

Researchers believe that dialectical tensions are a normal part of any close, interdependent relationship and that they become problematic only when people fail to manage them constructively. At the end of this chapter we'll look at several strategies relational partners use to manage dialectical tensions.

Characteristics of Romantic Relationships

The most intimate of intimate relationships is often with a romantic partner. Forming romantic relationships is a nearly universal human experience. Some 95 percent of us will marry at least once in our lifetime, and many who don't will have at least one significant, marriage-like romantic relationship.[4]

Marriages and long-term relationships are very important to our health and well-being. Multiple studies have shown, for instance, that married people live longer[5] and healthier[6] lives than those who never marry. One reason is that being married reduces a person's likelihood of engaging in risky health behaviors. Married people drink less[7] and are less likely to use an illicit drug such as marijuana than their unmarried counterparts.[8] They are also less likely to suffer from a mental disorder such as depression.[9] Several studies have shown that the health benefits of marriage are greater for men than for women.[10] Women are also healthier if married than if single, however, particularly if they are unemployed and lack the social support and financial resources employment provides.[11]

People in every known society form romantic unions, and although many romantic relationships share certain characteristics, there is also diversity among them. Let's look at variations in the extent to which romantic relationships are exclusive, voluntary, based on love, and composed of opposite-sex partners.

ROMANTIC RELATIONSHIPS AND EXCLUSIVITY

One common expectation for romantic relationships is that they are exclusive. Usually, exclusivity takes the form of **monogamy,** which means being in only one romantic relationship at a time and avoiding romantic or sexual involvement with others outside that relationship. Exclusivity is an expression of commitment and faithfulness that romantic partners share and trust each other to uphold. As a result, relational

• **monogamy** The state of being in only one romantic relationship at a time and avoiding romantic or sexual involvement with others outside that relationship.

infidelity, which means having romantic or sexual interaction with someone outside the romantic relationship, is often an emotionally traumatic experience for the partner who is wronged.

Not all romantic partners expect their relationship to be exclusive, however. Instead, some choose to have "open" relationships in which romantic and/or sexual involvement with people outside the relationship is accepted.[12] Although it's difficult to know how common open relationships are, research indicates that they are observed between heterosexuals,[13] bisexuals,[14] gay men,[15] and lesbians alike.[16]

ROMANTIC RELATIONSHIPS AND VOLUNTARINESS

Another common expectation for romantic relationships is that they are voluntary, meaning that people choose for themselves whether to be romantically involved—and if they decide to, they get to select their romantic partner. That expectation presumes that a relationship is satisfying only if both partners have freely chosen to participate in it. One indicator of this belief in the United States is the abundance of online and in-person dating services, which allow customers to browse the profiles of prospective partners and choose the ones with whom they want to make contact. One such service—Match.com—boasts over 23 million unique site visitors every month.[17]

Even if people enter into romantic relationships voluntarily, they do not always stay in them voluntarily. Indeed, research shows that many people are unhappy in their relationships but stay in them anyway.[18] According to relationship scholars Denise Previti and Paul Amato, the most common reasons people stay in relationships involuntarily are

- They want to provide stability for their children.
- Their religious beliefs disallow separation or divorce.
- They are concerned about the financial implications of separating.
- They see no positive alternatives to their current relationship.[19]

Individuals may also have their own reasons for staying in relationships they find dissatisfying. As this research makes clear, relationship stability does not necessarily imply relationship satisfaction.

ROMANTIC RELATIONSHIPS AND LOVE

In much of the Western world, people think of marriage and other romantic relationships as being based on love. In individualist societies such as the United States and Canada, that is, people tend to believe not only that they should get to choose their romantic partner but that their choice should be based on love and attraction.[20] Indeed, the typical U.S. wedding ceremony (whether religious or civil) emphasizes the importance of love in the marital relationship, whereas a lack of love is frequently cited as a reason relationships fail.[21]

Some cultures endorse the practice of arranged marriage, in which individuals are expected to marry the partner their parents select for them.

Whether or not they love each other, however, some people enter into romantic relationships for other reasons. Some do so for financial stability.[22] Others form relationships to gain, consolidate, or protect power,[23] such as when members of royal or politically powerful families intermarry.

ROMANTIC RELATIONSHIPS AND SEXUALITY

In many ways, people communicate similarly in same- and opposite-sex romantic relationships.[24] Both kinds of relationships value intimacy and equality between relational partners.[25] They both experience conflict,[26] and over similar topics.[27]

They both seek emotional support from family members and friends.[28] Further, they both negotiate how to accomplish mundane (or "instrumental") needs such as everyday household chores.[29] People in same-sex romantic relationships report levels of relationship satisfaction equal to those of opposite-sex dating, engaged, and married couples.[30]

Despite those similarities, same- and opposite-sex romantic relationships in most parts of the world differ with respect to the legal recognition of their relationships. In the United States and abroad, the question whether same-sex romantic partners should be allowed to marry has been socially and politically controversial for decades. People in many same-sex relationships live as *domestic partners*, often jointly owning property and raising children together, so many have demanded that they be allowed to legally marry. Supporters of same-sex marriage argue that people should be permitted to marry whomever they love and that it is discriminatory to deny marriage rights to people based on their sex. Opponents say that marriage is inherently a reproductive relationship and that allowing same-sex couples to marry threatens the sanctity of marriage and the family. The issue is likely to remain controversial for some time.

Same-sex marriage is a controversial issue in the United States and abroad.

ROMANTIC RELATIONSHIPS AROUND THE WORLD

As we've seen, every common expectation for romantic relationships has exceptions. Each expectation is also subject to cultural diversity, as we'll discover next.

Culture Affects Expectations for Exclusivity Although exclusivity is often expected for romantic relationships in the Western world, people in many other cultures don't share that expectation. In fact, many countries—primarily in Africa and southern Asia—allow the practice of **polygamy,** in which one person has two or more spouses at once. Some people in a polygamous relationship report that they appreciate the closeness and intimacy they share with multiple partners. Others indicate that feelings of jealousy and resentment can lead to increased conflict in such relationships.[31]

• **polygamy** The state of having two or more spouses at once.

Culture Affects Expectations for Voluntariness People in Western cultures usually expect to be able to choose their own romantic partners. In much of the world, however, it is common for other people—usually one person's parents—to choose that individual's romantic partner. In fact, according to the practice of *arranged marriage* (which is most common in the Middle East, Asia, and Africa), many people are expected to marry the partner their parents select. Sometimes children can reject their parents' selection of a spouse, in which case the parents look for someone else. In other cases, children may be pressured to marry their parents' choice. In either situation, an arranged marriage is not entirely voluntary.

Culture Affects Expectations for Love Would you marry someone you didn't love? Although many people in individualistic Western cultures would say no, many in collectivistic societies would say yes. For example, in China and India, the choice of a spouse often has more to do with the wishes and preferences of family and social groups than it does with love, even if the marriage isn't arranged. One study found that only half the participants in India and Pakistan felt love was necessary for marriage, whereas 96 percent of the U.S. participants did.[32] Sociologist Frances Hsu explained that when considering marriage "an American asks 'How does my heart feel?' A Chinese [person] asks, 'What will other people say?'"[33]

Culture Affects Expectations for Sexuality Social and legal acceptance of same-sex romantic relationships varies dramatically among different cultures. Currently, same-sex partners can marry with full legal recognition in 10 countries: Argentina, Belgium, Canada, Iceland, the Netherlands, Norway, Portugal, South Africa, Spain, and Sweden. Several other countries—including Colombia, Denmark, Slovenia, and Switzerland—recognize civil unions or domestic partnerships. In sharp contrast, many other nations prohibit people of the same sex from being romantically or sexually involved at all. In some countries—such as Guyana, Uganda, Pakistan, and Tanzania— people convicted of engaging in same-sex relations face life in prison. Other nations— including Iran, Nigeria, Sudan, United Arab Emirates, Mauritania, Yemen, and Saudi Arabia—impose the death penalty on those who violate laws banning same-sex relations.

Whatever their form, romantic relationships are clearly among the most significant of all human relationships. To examine your own expectations for romantic relationships, see "The Competent Communicator."

Forming and Communicating in Romantic Relationships

Romantic relationships don't form overnight. Instead, like many important relationships, they evolve. In this section, we'll see that people follow some fairly consistent steps when they develop a romantic relationship. They also vary in how they handle several common communication tasks, and they tend to end their relationships in stages.

GETTING IN: STAGES OF RELATIONSHIP DEVELOPMENT

Communication scholar Mark Knapp has suggested that relationship formation has five separate stages: initiating, experimenting, intensifying, integrating, and bonding.[34] Let's first take a brief look at each stage:

1. *Initiating.* The **initiating stage** occurs when people meet and interact for the first time. For instance, you might make eye contact with someone on the first day of class and decide to introduce yourself, or you might find yourself sitting next to someone on an airplane and strike up a conversation. "What's your name?" and "Where are you from?" are common questions people ask at this initial stage.

2. *Experimenting.* When you meet someone in whom you're initially interested, you might move to the **experimenting stage,** during which you have conversations to learn more about that person. Individuals in the experimenting stage might ask questions such as "What movies do you like?" and "What do you do for fun?" to gain basic information about a potential partner. This stage helps individuals decide whether they have enough in common to move the relationship forward.

* **initiating stage** The stage of relationship development at which people meet and interact for the first time.

* **experimenting stage** The stage of relationship development at which people converse to learn more about each other.

So, What Do You Expect? Your Expectations for Romantic Relationships

People come into romantic relationships with a variety of expectations. What are yours? Read the statements below and circle the numbers for each statement with which you agree. You can take this quiz whether you are currently in a romantic relationship or not.

1. I expect my romantic partner to be my best friend.

2. I expect my romantic relationship to be only one of several important relationships in my life.

3. I expect my romantic relationship to be problem-free.

4. I expect any romantic relationship to have its share of problems.

5. I think the most important aspects of a good romantic relationship are love and attraction.

6. I think a romantic relationship can be successful and satisfying even without high degrees of love and attraction.

7. I expect that once I get married or enter into a significant relationship, I will remain in that relationship until one of us dies.

8. I don't necessarily expect to spend the rest of my life with the same romantic partner.

9. I think living together before marriage sets up the marriage to fail.

10. I think living together before marriage is realistic and wise.

When you're finished, count how many odd-numbered statements you circled. Then count how many even-numbered statements you circled. Which number is greater? If you circled more odd-numbered statements, your expectations for romantic relationships are mostly *idealistic.* You believe in the ideal version of romantic relationships and want that for yourself. If you circled more even-numbered statements, your expectations are mostly *pragmatic.* You may want a good romantic relationship for yourself, but you don't necessarily expect it to be perfect or permanent.

3. *Intensifying.* During the **intensifying stage,** people move from being acquaintances to being close friends. They spend more time together and might begin to meet each other's friends. They start to share more intimate information with each other, such as their fears, future goals, and secrets about the past. They also increase their commitment to the relationship and may express it verbally through statements such as "You're really important to me."

- **intensifying stage** The stage of relationship development at which people move from being acquaintances to being close friends.

4. *Integrating.* The **integrating stage** occurs when a deep commitment has formed, and the partners share a strong sense that the relationship has its own identity. At that stage, the partners' lives become integrated, and they also begin to think of themselves as a pair—not just "you" and "I" but "we." Others start expecting to see the two individuals together and begin referring to them as a couple.

- **integrating stage** The stage of relationship development at which a deep commitment has formed, and the partners share a strong sense that the relationship has its own identity.

5. *Bonding.* The final stage in Knapp's model of relationship development is the **bonding stage,** in which the partners make a public announcement of their commitment to each other. That might include moving in together, getting

engaged, or having a commitment ceremony. Beyond serving as a public expression of a couple's commitment, bonding also allows individuals to gain the support and approval of people in their social networks.

Individual and Cultural Variations in Relationship Formation

Not every couple goes through the stages of relationship development in the same way. Some may stay at the experimenting stage for a long time before moving into the intensifying stage. Others may progress through the stages very quickly. Still others may go as far as the integrating stage but put off the bonding stage. Furthermore, research shows the stages of relational development to be similar in same-sex and opposite-sex relationships.[35]

Relationship formation is not necessarily the same in all cultures. In countries that practice arranged marriage, for instance, the process of forming a marital relationship would look much different and include negotiation and decision making by the parents, with less input (if any) from the children. In countries where polygamy is common, the integration and bonding stages would also look different, because one person may be joining multiple spouses at once. As we noted earlier in this chapter, cultures vary in their expectations about romantic relationships—and as their expectations differ, so do their ways of forming relationships.

Forming Relationships Online

The Internet provides a wide range of options for meeting people and developing relationships, including dating sites, social networking sites, chat rooms, bulletin boards, and massively multiplayer online role-playing games (MMORPGs). As a result, online communication has become one of the primary means of establishing romantic relationships.[36] Because communication capabilities on the Internet differ from those in face-to-face interaction, we might expect that relationships would develop quite differently online than in real life. Yet several studies indicate that individuals follow largely the same steps whether forming relationships online or in face-to-face contexts.[37]

Many forms of computer-mediated communication pose particular challenges for communicating with potential dating partners, however. Suppose, for instance, that Jake has posted a profile on a dating website. He browses the profiles of other users to see whether anyone sparks his interest, and other users do the same with his profile. One challenge is that Jake's pool of prospective dating partners is limited to those with Internet access. Although Internet availability is relatively high in middle-class urban areas, it remains low in many poorer rural areas and among ethnic minority populations.[38] In the United States today, 20 percent of adults don't use the Internet at all.[39] Online access is lower still in much of the developing world, a phenomenon known as the *digital divide*.[40] How significant a challenge that will likely pose for Jake therefore depends largely on where he lives.

A second challenge is that the information offered in online profiles may be inaccurate. Indeed, more than 80% of online dating participants worry that others misrepresent themselves.[41] Male daters usually add an inch or two to their height, whereas female daters subtract a few pounds from their weight as a way to enhance their attractiveness.[42] In face-to-face contexts, such deceptions might easily be discovered; even if Jake claims to be 5'11", it will likely be evident to any date he meets that he is only 5'8". On the Internet, however, prospective dating partners may have only a photograph by which to judge a person's claims about appearance—and photographs are easy to alter. Communication researchers Jeffrey Hancock and Catalina Toma found that approximately a third of photographs in online dating profiles are inaccurate representations of the person's appearance.[43] Women's photographs were judged to be less accurate than men's photographs, because they were more likely to be older and retouched.

Despite these and other challenges, the Internet continues to grow as a venue for relationship formation. In 1999, only around 2 million single U.S. adults had used some form of online dating service,[44] while nearly 25 million unique users accessed an online dating site in April 2011 alone.[45] It appears, therefore, that many individuals are able to overcome the limitations of online communication and to follow similar trajectories for relationships formed online and offline.[46]

Romantic relationships are as individual as the people in them. Several of the ways people differ are related to their communication behaviors within the relationship, as we consider next.

COMMUNICATING IN ROMANTIC RELATIONSHIPS

We can learn a lot about the quality of romantic relationships by looking at the way the partners communicate with each other. Although couples engage in many forms of communication, four communication behaviors have particular influence on their satisfaction with their relationship: conflict, privacy, emotional communication, and instrumental communication.

"I can't wait to see what you're like online."

Romantic Relationships Vary in How They Handle Conflict

Conflict is a common characteristic of many romantic relationships. Communication scholars William Wilmot and Joyce Hocker define **conflict** as "an expressed struggle between at least two interdependent parties who perceive incompatible goals, scarce resources, and interference from the other party in achieving their goals."[47] Partners in a romantic relationship can have conflicts about many issues, including how they spend their time and money, raise their children, manage their personal and professional obligations, and enact their sex life. Although conflict isn't fun, it isn't necessarily bad for a relationship. The way couples handle it—rather than the amount of conflict they have—is what influences the success of their relationship.

- **conflict** An expressed struggle between at least two interdependent parties who perceive incompatible goals, scarce resources, and interference from the other party in achieving their goals.

Much of what we know about how romantic partners handle conflict comes from research on marriage. For instance, social psychologist and marital therapist John Gottman has spent many years studying how spouses communicate during conflict episodes.[48] His work suggests marital couples can be classified into four groups, depending on how they handle conflict:[49]

1. *Validating couples* talk about their disagreements openly and cooperatively and communicate respect for each other's opinions even when they disagree with them. They stay calm when discussing hotly contested topics. They also use humor and expressions of positive emotion to defuse the tension that conflict can create.

2. *Volatile couples* also talk about their disagreements openly, but in a way that is competitive rather than cooperative. Each spouse tries to persuade the other to adopt his or her point of view, and their conflicts tend to be marked with expressions of negative rather than positive emotion. Those conflicts, however, are often followed by intense periods of affection and "making up."

3. *Conflict-avoiding couples* talk about their disagreements covertly rather than openly. To avoid the discomfort of engaging in conflict directly, they try to defuse negative emotion and focus on their similarities, believing that most problems will resolve themselves. They often "agree to disagree," a position that can side-step conflict but can also leave their points of disagreement unresolved.

4. *Hostile couples* have frequent and intense conflict. They use negative emotion displays, such as harsh tones of voice and facial expressions of anger or frustration. They also engage in personal attacks, insults, sarcasm, name calling, blaming, and other forms of criticism with each other.

More recent work by researchers Thomas Holman and Mark Jarvis has indicated that the same categories also apply to unmarried heterosexual couples.[50]

Less research has examined the conflict communication of lesbian and gay couples, but Gottman's studies have identified some differences between the conflict styles of homosexual and heterosexual couples. Specifically, gay and lesbian couples

- Use more humor and positive emotion during conflict conversations
- Are less likely to become hostile after a conflict
- Use fewer displays of dominance and power during a conflict episode
- Are less likely to take conflict personally
- Stay calmer emotionally and physiologically during conflict

For many romantic relationships, conflict is an unpleasant but unavoidable fact of life. We will learn more about strategies for managing conflict later in this chapter.

Romantic Relationships Vary in How They Handle Privacy

In every romantic relationship, the partners must choose for themselves how to manage information they consider to be private. When Kali and Neal were having difficulty conceiving a child, for instance, they carefully considered whom they were going to tell. Neal felt the information was no one's business but theirs and preferred to keep it private. Kali wanted to tell her family and close friends because she needed their emotional support. Their problems conceiving were causing enough stress in their relationship already; disagreeing about whether to keep the problems private was only making matters more stressful.

Communication scientist Sandra Petronio believes we all experience tensions between disclosing certain information and keeping it private. She developed **communication privacy management (CPM) theory** to explain how individuals and couples manage those tensions.[51] CPM theory would say Kali and Neal *jointly own* the information about their problems. The information belongs to them, so they must decide whether to keep it to themselves or share it with others.

Individuals and couples vary in their approach to privacy. Some of us are "open books"—that is, uninhibited about disclosing private information to others. Others are discreet, sharing private information with only a select few. Research indicates that some of us are simply more inclined than others to disclose private information. In most cases, however, we adapt our disclosure to the people to whom we are disclosing, to how much we trust them, and how much they have disclosed to us.[52] No matter what our reasons for disclosing to others, we should always be aware of information that a romantic partner expects us to keep private.

- **communication privacy management (CPM) theory** A theory explaining how people in relationships negotiate the tension between disclosing information and keeping it private.

Romantic Relationships Vary in How They Handle Emotional Communication

Emotional communication is an important part of most romantic relationships. The way romantic partners express emotion to each other can say a lot about the quality of their relationship.[53] Specifically, it reflects how satisfied the partners are with each other.[54]

Suppose Anita and her husband Jonah have been together for 8 years. They co-own a home where they run a small pottery studio and raise Jonah's twin girls from a previous marriage. They have their challenges just like any couple, but they are both highly satisfied with their relationship. Now suppose Brad and Lynne live across the street from Anita and Jonah. They have been together almost 10 years but have separated twice in that time. Their most recent separation lasted 7 months and would have ended their relationship permanently were it not for pressure from Lynne's family for the couple to work out their difficulties. Both Brad and Lynne would describe their relationship as very unsatisfying.

According to research, one of the most noticeable differences between the communication patterns of those two couples will be in their expression of emotion. Over the course of several studies, social psychologists John Gottman and Robert Levenson have identified two patterns of emotional communication that differentiate happy from unhappy couples.

First, happy partners such as Anita and Jonah communicate more positive emotion and less negative emotion with each other than do unhappy partners such as Brad and Lynne.[55] In particular, people in satisfying relationships express more affection, use more humor, and communicate more assurances (that is, verbal expressions of their commitment to the relationship). In comparison, people in unsatisfying relationships express more negative emotion in the form of anger, contempt, sadness, and hostility.[56] Gottman's work has found, specifically, that people in satisfied couples maintain a ratio of approximately five positive behaviors for every one negative behavior.[57]

The second pattern of emotional communication Gottman and Levenson identified is that unhappy couples are more likely than happy couples to reciprocate expressions of negative emotion.[58] When Lynne criticizes or expresses anger toward Brad, for example, he often reciprocates her behavior by expressing criticism or anger back at her. That type of response escalates the negativity in their conversation. As a result, they often find it difficult to address the issues underlying their conflict because they are so focused on the negative emotion they're each communicating. In comparison, people in happy couples are more likely to respond to negative expressions with positive or neutral ones.

Romantic partners must communicate about several instrumental tasks, such as making dinner and taking children to soccer practice.

Romantic Relationships Vary in How They Handle Instrumental Communication

People in most romantic relationships communicate with each other about instrumental (day-to-day) topics such as who's making dinner and who's taking the children to soccer practice.[59] The fact that instrumental communication addresses the necessary daily tasks couples face explains why it is one of the most common forms of communication among romantic partners.[60] It can also be one of the most contentious issues couples face, because romantic partners often disagree over the division of responsibilities for instrumental tasks.[61]

Romantic partners don't always divide instrumental tasks along traditional gender lines. Thus, a woman may elect to take responsibility for both child care and home maintenance.

The way partners negotiate the division of everyday tasks matters for their relationship for at least two reasons. First, day-to-day tasks such as cleaning, cooking, and childcare *need* to be completed, so most couples cannot leave decisions about who will do them to chance. Second, the way in which partners divide mundane, everyday tasks often reflects the balance of power in their relationship.[62] If one partner assumes greater power and control than the other, that partner is in a greater position to dictate how tasks will be divided. If instead both partners see themselves as equally powerful, the division of instrumental tasks can be more equitable.[63]

Romantic relationships vary greatly in how the partners communicate about the division of day-to-day tasks. In opposite-sex relationships, partners who believe in traditional gender role behaviors will often divide instrumental tasks along stereotypical gender lines.[64] Thus, men perform tasks such as yard maintenance and auto repair, whereas women take responsibility for meal preparation and childcare. In contrast, partners who do not necessarily adopt traditional gender role behaviors frequently have a conflict over how instrumental tasks should be divided.[65]

Specifically, women often wish their partners would take greater responsibility for household tasks and childcare than they actually do.[66] Compared to men, women are more likely to feel that the division of instrumental tasks is unfair, and those feelings reduce their relational satisfaction.[67]

With regard to same-sex relationships, recent research has speculated that homosexual partners may divide instrumental tasks more equally than opposite-sex couples do, with each partner sharing in both stereotypically masculine and stereotypically feminine responsibilities. In a survey of 113 same-sex romantic couples from around the United States, communication researcher Justin Boren discovered that a pattern of sharing was common, particularly among those who were highly satisfied with their relationships.[68]

GETTING OUT: ENDING ROMANTIC RELATIONSHIPS

Just as romantic relationships develop over time, they also come apart over time. Communication researcher Mark Knapp has described five stages relationships go through when they end: differentiating, circumscribing, stagnating, avoiding, and terminating.[69]

• **differentiating stage** The stage of relationship dissolution at which partners begin to view their differences as undesirable or annoying.

1. *Differentiating.* Partners in any romantic relationship are similar to each other in some ways and different in other ways. In happy, stable relationships, partners see their differences as complementary. At the **differentiating stage,** however, partners begin to view their differences as undesirable or annoying.

2. *Circumscribing.* When romantic partners enter the **circumscribing stage,** they begin to decrease the quality and quantity of their communication with each other. Their purpose in doing so is to avoid dealing with conflicts.[70] They start spending more time apart,[71] and when they're together, they usually don't talk about problems, disagreements, or sensitive issues in their relationship. Instead they focus on "safe" topics and issues about which they agree.

• **circumscribing stage** The stage of relationship dissolution at which partners begin to decrease the quality and quantity of their communication with each other.

3. *Stagnating.* If circumscribing progresses to the point where the partners are barely speaking to each other, the relationship enters the **stagnating stage,** in which it stops growing and the partners feel as if they are just "going through the motions." Partners avoid communicating about anything important because they fear it will only lead to conflict. Many relationships stay stagnant for long periods of time.

• **stagnating stage** The stage of relationship dissolution at which the relationship stops growing and the partners feel as if they are just "going through the motions."

4. *Avoiding.* When partners decide they are no longer willing to live in a stagnant relationship, they enter the **avoiding stage,** during which they create physical

and emotional distance from each other. Some partners take a direct route to creating distance, such as by moving out of the house or saying "I can't be around you right now." Others create distance indirectly, for example by making up excuses for being apart ("I have company in town all next week, so I won't be able to see you") and curtailing their availability by screening phone calls or not responding to texts or messages.

• **avoiding stage** The stage of relationship dissolution at which partners create physical and emotional distance from each other.

5. *Terminating.* The last stage in Knapp's model of relationship dissolution is the **terminating stage,** at which point the relationship is officially judged to be over. In nonmarital relationships, that usually means one or both partners' moving out if the couple shared a residence. It

• **terminating stage** The stage of relationship dissolution at which the relationship is officially deemed to be over.

also includes dividing property, announcing to friends and family that the relationship has ended, and negotiating the rules of any future contact between the partners. For legally married partners, relational termination means getting a **divorce,** which is the legal discontinuation of the marriage. In the United States today, approximately 40 percent of all marriages end in divorce.[72]

• **divorce** The legal discontinuation of a marriage.

The decision to terminate a romantic relationship is a significant one. It often requires a substantial reorganization of the family, and it can take an enormous mental and emotional toll, particularly on children of the couple. Children can be negatively affected by divorce or relationship dissolution well into their own adulthood.[73] That isn't always the case, though. When the romantic relationship is highly conflicted, neglectful, or abusive, children and their parents are often better off after the relationship ends.[74]

@getCONNECTED

Predicting Breakups on Facebook

In August 2011, television personality and socialite Kim Kardashian made headlines when her marriage to NBA player Kris Humphries lasted a mere 1,728 hours before she filed for divorce. Although short celebrity marriages are hardly unusual, summer is an uncommon time to break up, according to British journalist David McCandless. In July 2009, McCandless and a colleague surveyed 10,000 Facebook status updates for the terms "breakup" and "broken up." After plotting their nonscientific findings along a time graph, they discovered two periods in the year when relational dissolution is especially likely: the two weeks after Valentine's Day and the two weeks before Christmas Day. Summer and fall saw the fewest breakups—and Christmas Day was the single least likely day of the year for a relationship to fall apart.[75]

Communicating in Families

The first relationships most of us have are with our family members. Familial relationships can provide us with a feeling of belonging, a sense of our own history, and a measure of unconditional love and support we cannot find anywhere else. Growing up in a family also introduces us to the concept of relationships and can help us form mental models of ways to engage in friendships and romantic relationships in adolescence and adulthood. Families can be a source of great frustration and heartache—and many family relationships bring both peace and conflict. The depth of our engagement with families, and the fact that they can be so positive *and* so negative, make families one of our most important intimate relationships.

In this section, we examine what makes a family a family and what characteristics familial relationships often share. We'll also survey types of family structures and discover what communication issues are common in family relationships.

WHAT MAKES A FAMILY?

If you were asked to draw a picture of your family, whom would you choose to include? Some people might be obvious options,

such as your parents, spouse, siblings, and children. How about your grandparents? Nieces and nephews? In-laws? What about your stepsiblings? Maybe there are close friends or longtime neighbors you think of as family—would you include them?

Even researchers have difficulty defining exactly what makes a family a family, yet many scholars agree that most family relationships have one or more of three important characteristics: genetic ties, legal obligations, and role behaviors. Let's briefly examine each.

Genetic Ties Many family members are related "by blood," meaning they share a specified proportion of their genetic material. For instance, you share about 50 percent of your genes with your biological mother, biological father, and each full biological sibling (or 100 percent if you're an identical twin or triplet). With your grandparents, aunts and uncles, and any half-siblings, you share about 25 percent of your genes, and with cousins, about 12.5 percent.

However, a genetic link isn't the only characteristic that defines family relationships. Consider that we typically share zero percent of our genes with our spouses, steprelatives, and adopted relatives, yet we generally consider them to be family. Moreover, although sharing a genetic tie makes two people biological relatives, it does not necessarily mean they share a social or an emotional relationship.

Legal Obligations Another aspect of many family relationships is that they include legal bonds. For example, parents have many legal obligations toward their minor children; neglecting to house, feed, educate, and care for them is a crime.[76] Furthermore, marriage is the most heavily regulated family relationship from a legal perspective—in the United States, well over a thousand different federal laws govern some aspect of marriage.[77]

The law also regulates adoptive relationships, domestic partnerships, and even some aspects of stepfamilies. The existence of a legal familial bond is therefore another characteristic of many family relationships. Family members may feel they have responsibilities to one another even without the law's saying so, but laws formalize those responsibilities and help ensure they are met.

Role Behaviors Regardless of whether a relationship is bound by genetic or legal ties, many people believe the most important characteristic that defines a family is that the people in it *act* like family. According to that idea, family members are expected to enact **roles,** patterns of behavior that define a person's function in a group. These may include living together, taking care of and loving one another, and representing themselves as a family to outsiders. People who enact such behaviors and who think of themselves as family therefore *are* family, according to that definition.

These elements—genetic, legal, and role—are not mutually exclusive. Rather, they are characteristics that often help to define a

• **role** A pattern of behavior that defines a person's function within a group, such as a family.

Identical twins are called "identical" because they share 100 percent of their genetic material with each other. Fraternal twins share only 50 percent of their genes—the same as other biological siblings.

relationship as familial, and some relationships, such as parental relationships, include all three. How researchers define family is important because that determines, in part, which relationships family scholars study and which they do not. How *you* define family is also important because that can influence whom you invite to significant occasions in your life, with whom you share resources, and to whom you entrust secrets or sensitive information.

TYPES OF FAMILIES

The ABC television series *Modern Family* depicts a large and diverse family structure headed by Jay Pritchett (played by Ed O'Neill). Pritchett lives with his much younger wife and his stepson. His daughter Claire and her husband Phil have three biological children, whereas his son Mitchell is raising an adopted Vietnamese baby with his partner Cameron. The diversity of relationships in Pritchett's extended family illustrates the point that families come in many forms.

We examine some of the diversity of family types in this section. Let's begin by distinguishing between what researchers call family of origin and family of procreation. **Family of origin** is the family we grew up in, so it typically consists of our parents or stepparents and any siblings we have. **Family of procreation** is the family we start as an adult, and it consists of our spouse or romantic partner and/or any children we raise as our own. Most adults would say they belong to both a family of origin and a family of procreation; others, however, may identify with only one type of family or with neither.

Families of origin and families of procreation develop in many forms. Perhaps the most traditional profile consists of a married woman and man and their biological children. Researchers often call that configuration a *nuclear family*, and it is the traditional family form in the United States. Is the nuclear family still the most common type today? See the "Fact or Fiction?" box to find out.[78] One family type that is becoming increasingly common is the *blended family*, with two adult partners (who may be married or cohabiting and of the same or opposite sex) raising children who are not the biological offspring of both partners. The children might be adopted, or they might be the biological offspring of one of the parents and the stepchildren of the other.

A third family form is the *single-parent family*, in which one adult raises one or more children. As in blended families, the children may be the parent's biological offspring or they may be adopted or stepchildren. According to the U.S. Census Bureau, 20.2 million U.S. children lived in a single-parent family in 2009, 86 percent of them in households headed by a single mother.[79]

• **family of origin** The family in which one grows up, usually consisting of parents and siblings.

• **family of procreation** The family one starts as an adult, usually consisting of a spouse or romantic partner and children.

Fact or *fiction?*

Still Going Nuclear: The Average American Family Remains a Nuclear Family

In the 1950s TV show *Leave It to Beaver,* the Cleaver family was like most American families at the time: a legally married husband and wife and their biological children living together in the same household. For decades, people have referred to that arrangement as the "average American family," and in the 1950s, almost two-thirds of families in the United States fit that description. The Simpsons, from the much later animated series of the same name, represent the same family configuration. Is the average American family of today still nuclear in form?

The answer is no. According to the U.S. Census Bureau, fewer than 50 percent of families in the United States are now headed by a married couple. That statistic doesn't mean fewer people are marrying—rather, it means more U.S. families are now headed by single adults, cohabiting opposite-sex couples, and cohabiting same-sex couples than at any point in the country's history.

Furthermore, typical family arrangements vary around the country. According to the Census Bureau's American Community Survey, the highest percentage of families headed by a married couple is in Utah County, Utah, at nearly 70 percent. The lowest, at just 26 percent, is in Manhattan, New York.

Families come in many forms.

ASK YOURSELF

- Do you consider your family of origin to be average or typical? If so, in what ways?
- How do you think changes in the family structure affect the ways family members communicate?

SOURCE: U.S. Census Bureau. (2006). American community survey, www.census.gov/acs/www/

COMMUNICATION ISSUES IN FAMILIES

As in all significant relationships, communication plays a big part in making or breaking family relationships. We'll examine four communication issues families commonly encounter: roles, rituals, stories, and secrets.

Family Roles Family roles embody the functions people serve in the family system. One person might be the problem solver; another might act as the jokester or the peacemaker. One sibling may be the troublemaker, whereas another is the caregiver or the helpless victim. Notice that roles are different from family positions, so we wouldn't talk about the "role of the father," for instance, or the "role of the daughter."

Positions such as father and daughter are based on the structure of our relationships with others, but *roles* are based on the social and emotional functions our behavior serves within the family.

Family roles often become particularly relevant when the family is in conflict. Family therapist Virginia Satir has suggested that four roles are especially common during conflict episodes.[80] The first is the *blamer*, who holds others responsible for whatever goes wrong but accepts no responsibility for his or her own behaviors. A second role is the *placater*, the peacemaker who will go to any lengths to reduce conflict. That person may simply agree with whatever anyone says to keep others from getting angry. A third role is the *computer*, who attempts to use logic and reason—rather than emotion—to defuse the situation. Finally, there's the *distracter*, who makes random, irrelevant comments so the rest of the family will forget about the conflict. Each role leads people to communicate in different ways. Some role behaviors, such as computing and placating, can be useful for resolving conflict or at least preventing it from escalating. The behavior of blamers and distracters, on the other hand, might make conflict worse by taking attention away from the topic of the conflict.

SHARPEN Your Skills: *Family roles*

Considering either your family of origin or your family of procreation, create a diagram in which you depict each family member and name and describe his or her family role(s). Use lines to connect family members with the same or similar roles. Place those members with the most dissimilar roles farthest apart on your diagram. Don't forget to include yourself.

• **family rituals** Repetitive activities that have special meaning for a family.

Family Rituals Many families have their own important traditions. One family's tradition might be to spend every Thanksgiving serving turkey dinners at a shelter for homeless veterans. Another's might be to attend drag races together every summer. We call those behaviors **family rituals,** or repetitive activities that have special meaning for a family. Rituals serve a variety of functions in family interactions, among them reinforcing a family's values and providing a sense of belonging. A family ritual such as an annual road trip isn't just about the trip; it's also about spending time together, creating memories, and emphasizing the importance of family relationships.

According to communication scholars Dawn Braithwaite, Leslie Baxter, and Anneliese Harper, rituals can be especially important in blended families of stepparents and stepchildren. These researchers found that people often "import" into their blended family rituals from their original family[81] that are sometimes retained or adapted. For instance, Braithwaite and her colleagues described one family in which a widowed mother and her children would have a pizza "picnic" in the living room on a regular basis. The children would cuddle with the mother on the couch, eat pizza, and talk, and all considered it to be a special time. When the mother remarried and acquired stepchildren, however, the ritual stopped, perhaps because the stepchildren would have been uncomfortable taking part. Braithwaite and colleagues also found that it's important for blended families to develop their own rituals. In one such family, a young man described how his new stepfather began a ritual of watching the Super Bowl with his brother and him. According to this young man, that ritual served as a means of promoting communication with his stepfather.[82]

Family Stories Many of us can think of particular stories we've heard over and over again from members of our family. Maybe your grandparents were fond of describing how they overcame hardships when they were first married, and your parents have a favorite story about your childhood antics. Even events that were stressful or unpleasant at the time but turned out well, such as fixing a flat tire while on vacation, can serve a reassuring or cautionary function when they become part of the family lore. Stories are common in families, and communication scholar Elizabeth Stone suggests that they do more than provide entertainment. Family stories, she says, give

families a sense of their history, express what family members expect of one another, and reinforce connections across different generations.[83]

Family stories are as varied as families are, but they all tend to have at least two characteristics in common. First, they're told and retold, often over long periods of time. In that way, they become part of a family's collective knowledge: after a while, most everyone in the family has heard each story over and over. Second, family stories convey an underlying message about the family, such as "We are proud," "We overcome adversity," or "We stick together no matter what."

These days, many families choose to tell parts of their family stories on family web pages. As Table 8.1 notes, the Internet provides several resources for families to do so.

Family Secrets Many families have secrets they intentionally keep hidden from others. These often contain information the family considers private and inappropriate for sharing with outsiders, such as details of religious practices, health or legal issues, family conflicts, or financial information. When you were growing up, you may remember your parents telling you not to talk about such issues with people outside your family. Keeping family secrets doesn't just protect private family information, though; it also reinforces the family's identity and exclusivity, because only family members are allowed to know the secrets.[84]

Secrets can also be kept *within* families. For instance, Marco may not want his parents to know that he has moved in with his girlfriend, so he swears his sister to secrecy. Erin and Tammy may not want their kids to know that Tammy has breast cancer, so they agree to keep it secret. People might choose to keep secrets from other family members for many reasons, such as avoiding embarrassment or conflict, protecting another's feelings, and maintaining a sense of autonomy and privacy.

Improving Communication in Intimate Relationships

Because romantic and familial relationships are so important to us, it's in our best interests to communicate within them as competently as we can. In this section, we look at four strategies for improving communication within your intimate relationships: emphasizing excitement and positivity, handling conflict constructively, having realistic expectations, and managing dialectical tensions.

GO FOR FUN: EMPHASIZE EXCITEMENT AND POSITIVITY

You might have heard the saying "The family that plays together, stays together." That bit of folk wisdom has some truth to it. Research by relationships scholar Art

TABLE 8.1 THE ONLINE FAMILY: RESOURCES FOR CREATING FAMILY WEB PAGES	Creating a family web page is easy, thanks to several Internet resources. Here are a few sites designed to help families to do so:
	• www.yourfamily.com
	• www.myfamily.com
	• www.familylobby.com
	• www.familydetails.com
	• www.mygreatbigfamily.com

Aron and his colleagues has shown that partners who engage together in exciting or exhilarating forms of play—such as rollerblading, riding a roller coaster, and going to a suspenseful movie—increase their level of relationship satisfaction.[85] Less exhilarating activities such as playing cards and going out to dinner, even if they are pleasant, don't have the same effect. Why? Aron suggests that when partners engage in activities that elevate their physical arousal—the way riding a roller coaster or watching a thriller movie can—they may attribute their elevated arousal to each other instead of to the activity. Subconsciously, that is, people may notice their physical arousal and conclude that their partner, rather than the activity, is causing it. Sharing exhilarating play activities together can therefore help partners keep a level of positivity and freshness in their relationship that might otherwise fade with time.

You can use the knowledge gained from the Aron research to improve your own relationships. With your romantic partner, family members, and even your friends, make opportunities to share exciting and novel experiences. You may well find that your relationships become closer as a result.

Another important way to emphasize positivity in family relationships is to use **confirming messages,** behaviors that indicate how much we value another person.[86] Those are the opposite of **disconfirming messages,** behaviors that imply a lack of respect or value for others. Several decades ago, researcher Jack Gibb observed that people can communicate confirming and disconfirming messages in several ways.[87] Table 8.2 identifies and explains six types of supportive, confirming messages people use in their close relationships. Table 8.3 summarizes six types of disconfirming messages that Gibb believed created a defensive, unsupportive climate in relationships.

Research shows that confirming messages are particularly important in marital relationships. Psychologist John Gottman has spent much of his career looking at why marriages succeed or fail. As we considered earlier in this chapter, stable, satisfied couples have a 5-to-1 ratio of positive to negative communication. In other words, spouses who are happy with their marriages enact at least five positive behaviors (such as confirming messages) for every negative one. Gottman has found that couples with lower positive-to-negative ratios have an elevated risk of divorce.[88]

• **confirming messages** Behaviors that convey how much another person is valued.

• **disconfirming messages** Behaviors that imply a lack of respect or value for others.

DEAL WITH THE DARK SIDE: HANDLE CONFLICT CONSTRUCTIVELY

Even the happiest, most stable relationships experience conflict from time to time when partners have competing goals. How can we manage conflict in a constructive way?

TABLE 8.2
SIX TYPES OF CONFIRMING MESSAGES

Descriptive Messages that communicate support clearly and specifically, without judgmental words: "There are a few opportunities for improvement in the yardwork you've done."

Inquiry Orientation Messages that invite others to work cooperatively to solve problems or understand issues: "Why don't we see if there's a way we can both go to Stephanie's soccer match?"

Spontaneity Messages that are unplanned and free of hidden motives: "I'm planning a birthday party for Derrick; want to come?"

Empathy Messages that express understanding of, and interest in, another's thoughts and feelings: "I'm sorry you didn't get the promotion you wanted at work; you must be so disappointed."

Equality Messages that seek others' viewpoints and express value for others' ideas: "You have a very nice way of responding to solicitors who come to our door; I've never thought of taking the approach you do."

Provisional Messages that convey points of view but invite alternative views: "What leads you to the opinion that Proposition 40 is unfair to families like ours? Is it possible that the source of your information is wrong?"

TABLE 8.3

SIX TYPES OF
DISCONFIRMING
MESSAGES

Evaluative Messages that convey judgments of what's right and wrong, good and bad: "That was the worst job of cutting the lawn you've ever done."

Control Messages that attempt to impose ideas on others and coerce others to agree: "You can't use the laptop right now; I'm using it."

Strategy Messages that suggest the speaker is trying to direct others' behaviors: "Are you busy tomorrow?"

Neutrality Messages that imply indifference or a lack of interest in others: "Life's unfair sometimes; better get used to it."

Superiority Messages that imply the speaker is superior to his or her listeners: "I can't imagine why you organized our family vacation this way; you don't know what you're doing."

Certainty Messages that convey that the speaker's ideas are absolutely true and no other viewpoints are valid: "You're wrong."

It turns out that handling conflict constructively is more about what we *don't do* than what we *do*. That is, couples who manage conflict in a positive manner do so by avoiding certain problematic behaviors. To identify those behaviors, Gottman has spent years studying how romantic partners interact with each other during conflict episodes. We might expect that couples who fight frequently are most likely to split up. In fact, Gottman's research found otherwise: The *way* couples argue, not how frequently, predicts their chances of staying together.[89] Gottman identified four specific warning signs for separation or relational dissolution: criticism, contempt, defensiveness, and stonewalling. He refers to them as the "Four Horsemen of the Apocalypse" to indicate that they signal distress.[90] Let's take a close look at each.

Criticism According to Gottman, the first warning sign occurs when partners engage in **criticism** or complaints about each other. Criticism isn't always bad, but it becomes counterproductive when it focuses on people's personality or character rather than on their behavior. Statements such as "You always have to be right" and "You never care about my feelings" focus on attacking the person and assigning blame.

Criticisms also tend to be global statements about a person's value or virtue instead of specific critiques about the topic of the conflict. For example, a distressed partner might say, "You never think of anyone but yourself" rather than, "You should be more attentive when I describe my feelings to you." Because criticisms often come across as personal attacks instead of accurate descriptions of the sources of conflict, they tend to inflame conflict situations. At that point, criticism becomes a sign of a distressed relationship.

Contempt A second warning sign occurs when partners show **contempt** for each other—hostile behavior in which they insult each other and attack the other's self-worth. That behavior can include calling names ("You stupid idiot!"), using sarcasm or mockery to make fun of the other person, and engaging in nonverbal behaviors that suggest a low opinion of the partner, such as sneering and eye rolling. It can also include ridiculing the person in front of others and encouraging others to do the same. Contempt functions to put down and degrade the other person. Responding to conflict with contempt often increases the partners' stress, and elevated stress in turn can impair physical health as well as relational satisfaction.[91]

Defensiveness A third danger sign is that partners become defensive during their conflict. **Defensiveness** means seeing yourself as a victim and denying responsibility for your behaviors. Instead of listening to their partners' concerns and acknowledging that they need to change certain behaviors, defensive people whine ("It's not fair"), make excuses ("It's not my fault"), and respond to complaints with additional

• **criticism** Complaints about another person or the person's behaviors.

• **contempt** Hostile behavior in which people insult each other and attack the other's self-worth.
• **defensiveness** Seeing oneself as a victim and denying responsibility for one's behaviors.

complaints ("Maybe I spend too much money, but you never make time for the kids and me"). People are particularly prone to defensiveness when they recognize that the criticisms have merit but they don't want to accept the responsibility of changing their behavior.

Stonewalling The last of Gottman's "Four Horsemen" is **stonewalling,** or withdrawing from the conversation. People who engage in stonewalling often act as though they are "shutting down." They stop looking at their partners, stop speaking, and stop responding to what their partners are saying. In some cases, they physically leave the room to end the conversation. The reason for their departure isn't to calm down, which might be an effective strategy. Rather, it is to shut down the conversation entirely.

• **stonewalling** Withdrawing from a conversation.

Gottman's research has suggested that people stonewall when they feel emotionally and psychologically "flooded," or incapable of engaging in the conversation any longer. Unfortunately, when one partner stonewalls, it becomes almost impossible for the couple to resolve their disagreements. Research has also shown that when men stonewall during a conflict, women often experience significant increases in stress hormones.[92]

Gottman's research therefore tells us that *constructive* conflicts are characterized not by the behaviors that are present but by those that are absent. When we are able to engage in conflict without criticizing, showing contempt, becoming defensive, and stonewalling, we stand a much better chance of preserving the quality of our relationship even as we work with our partner to resolve our differences.

GET REAL: HAVE REALISTIC EXPECTATIONS

Another way to improve communication in intimate relationships is to make sure that *everyone* in those relationships has realistic expectations for them. When expectations are unrealistic, relationships are likely to fail, causing the individuals to feel disappointed, hurt, or betrayed. Only through open communication can everyone's expectations come to light and the partners reach agreement on how realistic they are.

Six months after marrying Carla, for instance, Gregory stopped spending time with his parents, brother, and even his close friends. He wanted to spend all his time with Carla and began feeling anxious when they were apart. Carla started to feel smothered, and she explained to Gregory that they both needed other people in their lives besides each other. She encouraged him to reconnect with his family and friends. Gregory in turn explained that spending time with Carla helped him feel secure about their relationship. Eventually, they agreed on a new expectation for spending time together that seemed more reasonable to both of them. By communicating about their different expectations for their marriage and coming to an agreement on what they both considered realistic, Carla and Gregory were able to strengthen their feelings of satisfaction with each other.

As in Gregory's case, it's common to want to spend a lot of time with a romantic partner. However, it is important to be realistic about what we expect from our relationships. No one person—not even a spouse—can meet *all* our social and emotional needs. Expecting someone to do so places an unfair burden on that person and may lead to disappointment.

A better approach is to appreciate each relationship individually and to remember that the important people in our lives are important for different reasons. For example, you might talk to your romantic partner about most issues, but maybe you feel more comfortable discussing your dad's health or your daughter's financial difficulties with your sibling. Further, just as no single person can meet all *your* needs, you cannot meet someone else's every need. Being realistic about your expectations helps you appreciate the most positive aspects of each of your relationships.

The Scene: For the fifth time this month, your romantic partner has neglected his or her chores around the house. You're getting extremely irritated, not only because you have to do the extra work but also because your partner seems to be ignoring you. When you ask about the chores, your partner becomes angry, and you begin a heated argument with each other.

Your Task: Consider how you can adapt your conflict behavior to be constructive rather than destructive. What strategies could you use in this situation to

- Keep from criticizing your partner?
- Avoid showing contempt or defensiveness?
- Refrain from stonewalling?

PUSH AND PULL: MANAGE DIALECTICAL TENSIONS

As we saw earlier in this chapter, people in romantic and familial relationships often experience dialectical tensions—conflicts between two opposing needs. Managing dialectical tensions can help improve communication in intimate relationships. Researchers have identified eight different strategies to manage dialectical tensions.[93] None of these is inherently positive or negative. Whether they work depends on our goals for the relationship and the context in which we are using them.

Let's suppose Moira is engaged to Albee and has been spending a lot of time with him. She is experiencing the tension between autonomy and connection. She strongly desires to retain her own individuality and autonomy but also passionately wants to be connected to Albee. Different strategies she might use to manage that tension include denial, disorientation, alternation, segmentation, balance, integration, recalibration, and reaffirmation. Table 8.4 explains each strategy and shows how Moira can apply it to her situation.

Individuals in families and romantic relationships commonly try several of those strategies, and they may find some more effective than others. Improving your communication in intimate relationships doesn't require you to adopt specific strategies and ignore others. Rather, if you're aware of the options for managing dialectical tensions, you can use the ones that work best for you.

SHARPEN Your Skills: *Dialectical tensions*

Identify a dialectical tension you are currently experiencing in a romantic or familial relationship. Have a conversation with the other person in which you describe how those two needs oppose each other, and he or she describes how they complement each other. In your conversation, work to recalibrate the dialectical tension by discussing how both sides of the tension are useful for your relationship.

Denial—entails responding to only one side of the tension and ignoring the other. Were Moira to adopt this strategy, she might deny her desire for autonomy and focus all her attention on being connected with Albee.

Disorientation—means ending the relationship in which the tension exists. Moira may feel so disoriented by the tension between her desires for autonomy and connection that she calls off her engagement to avoid it.

Alternation—means going back and forth between the two sides of a tension. On some days, Moira might act in ways that enhance her autonomy and individuality. On other days, she might act in ways that strengthen her connection to Albee.

Segmentation—is dealing with one side of a tension in some aspects of a relationship and with the other side of the tension in other aspects of that relationship. Moira might emphasize her connection to Albee by sharing intimate disclosures, but she might stress her autonomy by keeping her finances separate from his. Rather than going back and forth between the two sides of the tension, as in alternation, she addresses one side of the tension in some segments of her relationship and the other side in other segments.

Balance—means trying to compromise, or find a middle ground, between the two opposing forces of a tension. For instance, Moira may disclose most but not all of her feelings to Albee. She may not feel as autonomous as she wants *or* as connected as she wants, but she may feel she is satisfying each desire to some degree.

Integration—entails developing behaviors that will satisfy both sides of a tension simultaneously. Moira feels connected to Albee when they spend their evenings together, but she also likes to choose how she spends her time. To integrate those needs, she reads or does crossword puzzles while Albee watches television in the same room, an option that allows her to feel autonomous and connected at the same time. Unlike the balance strategy, which focuses on compromising each desire, integration finds ways to satisfy both without compromising either.

Recalibration—means reframing a tension so the contradiction between opposing needs disappears. By communicating about their needs and expectations for their relationship, Moira and Albee might realize that autonomy and connection are both desirable. As a result, they may come to see autonomy and connection as complementary rather than opposing needs.

Reaffirmation—means simply embracing dialectical tensions as a normal part of life. Moira may come to realize that she will always feel torn between being autonomous and being connected. Instead of fighting the tension or struggling to resolve it, she accepts it as a normal feature of her relationship. Whereas recalibration means eliminating the tension by seeing the opposing needs as complementary, reaffirmation means accepting the tension as normal.

TABLE 8.4
STRATEGIES FOR MANAGING DIALECTICAL TENSIONS

- **What makes some relationships intimate?** Intimate relationships require deep commitment, foster interdependence, require continuous investment, and spark dialectical tensions.

- **How do we form, maintain, and dissolve romantic relationships?** Forming romantic relationships involves initiating, experimenting, intensifying, integrating, and bonding. We maintain our relationships by the way we handle conflict, privacy, emotional communication, and instrumental communication. Ending romantic relationships involves differentiating, circumscribing, stagnating, avoiding, and terminating.

- **What makes a family, and how do we communicate in families?** Family relationships typically involve some combination of genetic ties, legal obligations, and role behaviors. We use family roles, rituals, stories, and secrets to maintain communication in our familial relationships.

POP QUIZ

Multiple Choice

1. Johann and his partner Cris go out to dinner and see a movie every Friday night. That routine bores Johann but provides stability that Cris values. The dialectical tension Johann and Cris are experiencing is
   a. openness versus closedness.
   b. autonomy versus connectedness.
   c. presence versus absence.
   d. predictability versus novelty.

2. The idea that romantic relationships occur between individuals who choose to be together reflects the characteristic that romantic relationships are
   a. exclusive.
   b. voluntary.
   c. composed of opposite-sex partners.
   d. based on love.

3. The stage of Knapp's relational model that helps individuals decide whether they have enough in common to move the relationship forward is
   a. initiating.
   b. intensifying.
   c. differentiating.
   d. experimenting.

4. The practice in which one person has two or more spouses at a time is called
   a. monogamy.
   b. infidelity.
   c. polygamy.
   d. annulment.

5. Doug's family has a tradition of calling his grandmother every Sunday morning. That practice exemplifies a family
   a. ritual.
   b. role.
   c. secret.
   d. story.

Fill in the Blank

6. Connectedness is in dialectical tension with _____.

7. Discussions about topics such as who's doing the laundry and who's taking out the paper and glass for recycling are examples of _____ communication.

8. According to Gottman, couples who talk openly about disagreements and stay calm throughout conflict episodes are called _____ couples.

9. According to _____ theory, partners in a romantic relationship jointly own information about their problems.

10. A romantic relationship is _____ when the partners are going through the motions of a relationship that is no longer satisfying.

KEY TERMS

intimacy 180
commitment 180
interdependence 182
investment 182
dialectical tensions 182
monogamy 183
infidelity 184
polygamy 185
initiating stage 186
experimenting stage 186
intensifying stage 187

integrating stage 187
bonding stage 188
conflict 189
communication privacy management (CPM) theory 190
differentiating stage 192
circumscribing stage 192
stagnating stage 192
avoiding stage 192
terminating stage 192
divorce 193

role 194
family of origin 195
family of procreation 195
family rituals 197
confirming messages 199
disconfirming messages 199
criticism 200
contempt 200
defensiveness 200
stonewalling 201

COMMUNICATING IN SMALL GROUPS

Adapting Communication "On the Fly"

For actors doing improv, success depends on communication and cooperation. Improvisational theater—*improv*—is a form of performance art in which actors create content, setting, and dialogue spontaneously, often in response to audience suggestions. Much improv is performed in small groups called *comedy troupes* composed of 3 to 8 members. When training to do improv, actors learn that their success depends as much on their fellow troupe members as it does on themselves. To facilitate smooth, coordinated interaction, actors agree on some basic communication rules, such as "Offer statements instead of questions" and "Never say no." Observing those rules helps to ensure that each actor's words provide opportunities for other actors to respond, thus allowing the scene to develop. Suppose during an improv scene, I say "I'm getting really hungry; let's grab some dinner." Replying to my idea with the words, "No, I just ate a huge meal" shuts down the opportunity for a scene to develop around our shared dinner. But observing the "never say no" rule, you might instead offer the reply, "Sounds great; I hear that Cuban restaurant in the mall is excellent." That response offers us the opportunity to develop our scene by discussing the Cuban food and décor of the restaurant or reacting to the events at the mall. As in any small group, success for an improv comedy troupe requires adapting effectively to each member's communication behaviors.

As You READ

- What are small groups, and what do they do?
- Why and how do people join small groups?
- How can you communicate better in a small group?

We humans have lived, worked, and communicated in small groups for thousands of years. Archeologists tell us our prehistoric ancestors lived in small groups of hunters and gatherers and may have interacted with only a couple of dozen people over their entire lives.[1] Although the world is considerably different today, our tendency to interact in small groups endures.

Communicating in small groups can be difficult, however. People often have strikingly different ideas about what decisions a group should make and how they should be implemented. Coming together over ideas can therefore be a challenging process. For that reason, it's beneficial to know how small group communication operates and how we can excel at it. We can apply that knowledge to almost any small group to which we belong.

What Is a Small Group?

In 1942, a small group of farmers near Americus, Georgia, began discussing a concept they called "partnership housing." Their idea was that people in need of safe, adequate shelter would work alongside volunteers to build simple, affordable houses. The homes would be sold—at no interest and for no profit—to those who needed them. As the group communicated its ideas with others, it received the help and capital it required to launch its mission. What began nearly seven decades ago as a small group of farmers grew into today's Habitat for Humanity, an international charitable organization that has built more than 500,000 homes, providing affordable shelter for more than 2 million people in over 3,000 communities around the world.[2]

In this and countless other instances, people communicating in a small group have had a positive influence on the lives of others. That success doesn't mean small group communication is without its problems. Indeed, working in small groups can be stressful and even frustrating. Further, as we'll see, small groups don't always make the smartest, most informed decisions, despite their best efforts. If we know how to conduct small group communication effectively, however, and we learn what problems to avoid, we stand a better chance of making our small group experiences positive and productive.

We can define a **small group** as a collection of 3 or more people working cooperatively and interdependently to accomplish a task.[3] Small groups address a broad range of tasks, whether it's creating a dramatic presentation, organizing a fundraiser, making a policy recommendation, or providing affordable housing. Although small

• small group A collection of people working interdependently to accomplish a task; small groups typically include 3 to 20 members.

Habitat for Humanity, which has built more than 500,000 homes, began as a small group.

groups have diverse missions, they share important similarities that distinguish them from other social units. In this section, we'll see that

- Small groups are distinguished by their size.
- Small groups are interdependent.
- Small groups are cohesive.
- Small groups enforce rules and norms.
- Small groups include individual roles.
- Small groups have their own identities.
- Small groups have distinctive communication practices.
- Small groups often interact online.

INSOMNIACS ANONYMOUS~

SMALL GROUPS ARE DISTINGUISHED BY THEIR SIZE

An important part of what distinguishes a small group is its size. A 1,500-person church, a 90-piece orchestra, and the 435-member U.S. House of Representatives are all groups, but most researchers wouldn't classify any of them as a small group. Rather, communication scholars consider small groups to include at least 3 members (as noted in the formal definition above) but no more than about 15 or 20.[4]

The size of a small group matters because most of us communicate differently in larger and smaller collections of people. When we interact with only one other person, we are engaged in interpersonal rather than small group communication. Interpersonal communication usually focuses on the development and maintenance of a personal relationship, whereas small group communication is concerned with the performance of tasks. When we interact with *larger* groups of people, our communication can become impersonal because we may not know the other group members very well. Indeed, if the group is too large, we might feel as though our input won't be heard. However, interpersonal communication and large group communication each have their functions.

Many of us form and maintain interpersonal relationships *within* groups. We use our understanding of interpersonal communication in those relationships. Yet communicating effectively with a small group utilizes a distinct set of skills.[5]

A small group's size depends on its purposes. If the small group is a barbershop quartet, it needs exactly four people. If it's a jury, it will usually have 12 members plus a couple of alternates. Focus groups, committees, support groups, sports teams, and other small groups vary in size according to the tasks they have to accomplish. If there are too few members, the group may not have sufficient help to complete its goals. Likewise, if there are too many members, scheduling and coordinating the group's activities can be cumbersome. For those reasons, each small group must evaluate for itself what the best number of members will be.[6]

- **interdependence** With respect to groups, a state in which each member of a group affects, and is affected by, every other member.

SMALL GROUPS ARE INTERDEPENDENT

When professional chefs create new recipes, they keep in mind that each ingredient will affect, and be affected by, each of the others. Too little salt leaves a soup tasting bland; too much salt overpowers the individual flavors of the chicken and the vegetables. The appropriate amount of water—essential for a good broth—depends on the volume of the soup ingredients. Because each ingredient influences and is influenced by every other in the composition of a tasty finished product, we say the ingredients are **interdependent.**

According to *systems theory*, members of a small group are also interdependent in the sense that each one affects and is affected by every other member in some way.[7] Whenever the National Aeronautics and Space Administration (NASA) launched a mission into space, for

instance, a group of 16 flight controllers monitored every aspect. Each individual controller oversaw specific dimensions, such as communication with the crew, deployment and retrieval of the spacecraft's payload, flight navigation, electrical generation, and the execution of spacewalks. To ensure the success of the mission and the safety of the crew, the flight controllers had to work interdependently. Although each person's responsibilities were different, everyone's actions influenced, and were influenced by, everyone else's. For instance, communication with the crew was impaired if electrical generation malfunctioned. Spacewalks were safe only if the flight navigation was accurate. In this interdependent group of flight controllers, the members had to communicate to understand how their behaviors and decisions affected the others.

Interdependence doesn't necessarily mean that each member's influence on all other members is always positive. Perhaps you can recall attending small group gatherings in which two or three people expressed a disagreement that soon escalated into a full-scale argument within the group. In that instance, group members were influencing one another in a *negative* way by letting a conflict get out of hand. They were still demonstrating interdependence, however, because the moods and behaviors of some members affected, and were affected by, those of others.

SMALL GROUPS ARE COHESIVE

If you've ever studied music, you know that a song's melody is its primary tune and that other pitches are added to the melody to create harmonies. Most melodies aren't quite as beautiful without harmonies, and most harmonies are incomplete without the melodies. When melodies and harmonies work together, though, they can produce something truly special. The same principle applies in small groups.

• **cohesion** The force by which the members of a group work together in the service of a common goal.

To be effective, small groups must have **cohesion,** which means the members work together—as melodies and harmonies do—in the service of a common goal.[8] Cohesion takes interdependence a step farther: Groups are interdependent if the members all influence one another, but they are cohesive only if the members work together toward the same goal.[9]

Two types of cohesion are particularly important for small groups. The first is what researchers call *task cohesion*, the extent to which everyone in the group is working together toward the same objectives.[10] Task cohesion is high when all the group members know their specific tasks and follow through on them. When only some members do so while others neglect their responsibilities, then task cohesion is low. If you've taken part in small groups in which only a few members did the majority of the work, you know that being in such groups is often unsatisfying.

The second important type of cohesion is *social cohesion*, which refers to the level of positive regard group members have for one another.[11] In groups with high social cohesion, the members generally get along well and maintain positive relationships among themselves. They trust and listen to one another, they adapt their communication behaviors to one another, and they respect one another's opinions even when they disagree. In contrast, members of groups with low social cohesion are often distrustful of the other members. They disregard one another's opinions and don't seem to care much about one another. In some groups, low social cohesion causes members to argue frequently; in others, it causes them to ignore one another. Not surprisingly, most people are more satisfied participating in groups with high social cohesion than in those with low social cohesion.[12]

When members act contrarily to a group's goals, the group can become dysfunctional and counterproductive. Take a closer look at group dysfunction in "The Dark Side of Communication."

SMALL GROUPS ENFORCE RULES AND NORMS

In the 2004 movie *Mean Girls*, Cady Heron (played by Lindsay Lohan) enrolls in a public high school for the first time. There, she meets and befriends a small group

THE DARK SIDE OF COMMUNICATION

Working at Odds: Dysfunctional Groups

A cohesive group is effective because everyone is contributing to the group's collective goals. When cohesion breaks down and some members behave in ways that inhibit the group's goals, the group becomes *dysfunctional* because it is no longer operating to pursue a collective purpose. According to researchers who study small groups, four behaviors in particular can cause a group to become dysfunctional.

The first dysfunctional behavior, *parasitism,* occurs when some group members persuade or coerce others to do their work for them. The second behavior, *interpersonal aggression,* refers to actions that undermine the physical or psychological well-being of others, such as bullying and intimidation. Third, *boastfulness* exaggerates the value of your own contributions in relation to those of other group members. Finally, *misuse of resources* occurs when group members waste important materials or misuse equipment, reducing their availability for the rest of the group.

Dysfunction does not just cause groups to become unproductive. It also increases stress and impairs the psychological well-being of the individuals in the group. As you communicate within small groups, it is therefore helpful to watch out for parasitism, interpersonal aggression, boastfulness, and misuse of resources. If everyone is aware that those behaviors are problematic, your group stands a better chance of avoiding dysfunction.

SOURCE: Aubé, C., Rousseau, V., Mama, C., & Morin, E. M. (2009). Counterproductive behaviors and psychological well-being: The moderating effect of task interdependence. *Journal of Business and Psychology, 24,* 351–361.

---

known as the Plastics, comprising the school's most popular girls. She soon realizes that, like all small groups, the Plastics have both rules and norms. A group's *rules* are its explicitly stated principles for governing what its members can and cannot do. Shortly after she joins the Plastics, for instance, Cady receives instruction in some of its rules by fellow member Gretchen Wieners (played by Lacey Chabert):

Small groups, such as the Plastics in the movie *Mean Girls*, enforce rules and norms that their members are expected to observe.

> **Gretchen:** *You can't wear a tank top two days in a row, and you can only wear your hair in a ponytail once a week, so I guess you picked today. Oh, and we only wear jeans or track pants on Fridays. If you break any of these rules, you can't sit with us at lunch. I mean, not just you . . . any of us. Okay look, if I was wearing jeans today, I'd be sitting over there with the art freaks. Oh, we always vote before we ask someone to eat lunch with us, because you have to be considerate of the rest of the group. I mean, you wouldn't buy a skirt without asking your friends first if it looked good on you.*
>
> **Cady:** *I wouldn't?*
>
> **Gretchen:** *Right. Oh, and it's the same with guys. I mean, you may think you like someone, but you could be wrong.*

The guidelines Gretchen explains in this scene constitute rules because they are explicitly communicated.

Other principles for how group members should behave are never officially stated, however, but seem to be understood implicitly within the group. Those are called the group's *norms,* and even though they aren't expressly communicated, they nonetheless affect behavior. While in the Plastics, for instance, Cady realizes she is expected to talk only to certain people, attend specific parties, keep other group members' secrets, and gossip about other students. Although these expectations are never communicated to her explicitly, she infers them from observing how others in the group behave.

Nearly every small group has both rules and norms that its members are expected to follow. Some govern how group members should interact with one another, such as "we stick together no matter what." Others dictate how the group should function, such as "we always vote before asking someone to have lunch with us." Still other rules and norms focus on the nature of the group's mission, such as "everything we do must be done with the utmost professionalism." Table 9.1 gives additional examples of small group rules and norms. As we'll see later in this section, introducing new members to the rules and norms is an important part of socializing them into the group.

SMALL GROUPS INCLUDE INDIVIDUAL ROLES

Most small groups have one or more collective goals or purposes. Tennis teams exist to compete with other teams in tennis matches. Jazz bands exist to create and perform music. In each case, everyone is expected to work together toward the group's collective mission, but that doesn't mean everyone contributes in the same way. Rather, individual members of the group often take on specific roles, patterns of behavior that define a person's function within a group or a larger organization.[13]

As captain of the Mexican women's soccer team, Monica Gonzales fulfills a formal role.

Some roles in small groups are *formal roles*, meaning they are specifically assigned to people to help the group to fulfill its mission. On a tennis team, for instance, one person usually plays the role of captain, the individual in charge of organizing team meetings and boosting players' morale. Because they are specifically assigned, formal roles usually receive official recognition both inside and outside the group. For example, all the players on a team know who the captain is because someone selected him or her and officially bestowed that title.

Other roles are better described as *informal roles*, meaning they are not formally assigned and anyone in the group can choose to take them on.[14] Unlike formal roles, which often ensure that important group assignments get fulfilled, informal roles more frequently relate to how well or poorly the group functions while carrying out its mission, and members take on whichever one fits their personality. In a jazz band, for instance, one member might play the role of humorist, always making funny observations to lighten the mood. Another might enact the role of mediator, helping members to find common ground when conflicts arise. A third might play the nurturer, attending to everyone else's emotional and physical needs. An individual member might have more than one informal role, and a given informal role might be fulfilled by more than one member at a time.

TABLE 9.1	Behavior in most small groups is influenced by explicit rules and implicit norms. Here are some that a college study group might use.
EXAMPLES OF RULES AND NORMS IN A SMALL GROUP	**Rules** Study sessions always start at 8 P.M. Members always share study materials. Everyone produces a weekly reading outline. One person brings snacks each week. No music is played during meetings. **Norms** Send a text message if you're going to be late. Don't discuss the group with others. Come to each meeting prepared. Always cooperate with one another. If one person falls behind, help that person to catch up.

Because formal roles are assigned and officially recognized, it's tempting to conclude that they're more important to a group's success than informal roles. That's not always the case, however. Although a team captain can keep a group organized and on task, members who enact helpful informal roles might make equally important contributions to a satisfying and productive group atmosphere.[15] Formal and informal roles can therefore complement each other, together creating a positive small group experience.

SMALL GROUPS HAVE THEIR OWN IDENTITIES

When two people get married or enter a committed relationship, it's often as if their relationship takes on a life of its own. They may say to each other: "There used to be you and me, but now there's you, me, and *us.*" That sentiment reflects the idea that the relationship has become an entity unto itself, one with its own identity. Many small groups have the same experience: once people come together to form a small group, the group takes on its own identity. When that happens, people begin referring to "the group" as well as to individual members, and they start to think about the group's needs and desires, reflecting the idea that the group has become an entity unto itself.

One reason group identities are important is that they set boundaries around a group's membership by defining who belongs and who does not. Some groups establish and maintain their boundaries in elaborate ways. For instance, members of the Freemasons, an international fraternal organization, are thought to use secret knocks, hand signals, passwords, and other covert signs to differentiate true members from individuals posing as members.[16] Likewise, fraternities and sororities often put new pledges through highly involved initiation rituals, during which they may teach them secret handshakes or code words by which they can signify their membership.[17] Similarly, many gangs require new members to get specific tattoos to signify their affiliation with and allegiance to the gang.[18]

Other groups establish and maintain their boundaries in less dramatic ways. For example, the Red Hat Society is a social organization for women over 50 whose members wear red hats and purple clothing whenever they meet in groups.[19] Their attire therefore serves as a marker of membership, distinguishing those who belong to the group from those who do not. In the same vein, Alcoholics Anonymous members attending small group meetings recite the "serenity prayer," which symbolizes their inclusion in the group. Membership cards, lapel pins, member jackets, and similar tokens also signify who belongs to a group and who does not. In each of these ways, groups express and reinforce their identity both to those in the group and to outsiders.

SMALL GROUPS HAVE DISTINCTIVE COMMUNICATION PRACTICES

Central to accomplishing any group's mission is the practice of communication.[20] Can you imagine any small group that could meet its goals if its members couldn't communicate with one another? They wouldn't be able to share ideas, encourage one another, make collective decisions, assign individual tasks, or stay informed about what other members are doing.

Researchers have discovered four specific types of communication that characterize small groups.[21] The first type, *problem-solving communication*, focuses on the details of how a small group can accomplish its tasks. *Role communication*, the second type, relates to the formal and informal roles each member plays within the group. *Consciousness-raising communication*, the third type, strengthens the group's identity and the morale of its members. Finally, *encounter communication* describes the interpersonal interactions among group members.

To illustrate each type of communication, let's say you're on an advisory board charged with reviewing the policies of the student health center on your campus. At your first meeting, you and the other board members will probably identify each of your specific tasks, discuss how often you need to meet, and determine how you'll communicate with one another about your progress between meetings. Those are all examples of problem-solving communication because they relate to your goals and your strategies for meeting them. You might also talk about who's going to be in charge of your board, who's going to keep the records of your meetings, and who will be responsible for communicating with the health center administrators. That conversation is an example of role communication because it concerns the individual roles that board members will play.

Suppose the advisory board experiences several challenges while attempting to complete its mission, and you and the other board members are feeling overwhelmed and discouraged. Perhaps the leader of your group gives everyone a pep talk about the importance of your task, stressing that you'll be successful if you all stick together and work as a team. That is an example of consciousness-raising communication because it is meant to raise morale and reinforce your identity as a group. Let's say you've been particularly discouraged lately because of the stresses of school and your part-time job, and you confide in another group member about your feelings. That is an example of encounter communication because it is an interpersonal conversation that occurs within the group.

SMALL GROUPS OFTEN INTERACT ONLINE

An increasing number of small groups interact either primarily or exclusively online.[22] Some do so because their members are located in different cities or countries, so face-to-face communication is impractical.[23] Other groups interact online because computer-mediated communication can be more efficient than face-to-face conversation. Technologies such as e-mail, instant messaging, message boards, texting, and video-conferencing allow group members to interact whenever—and wherever—they choose.

Nonetheless, online groups pose challenges. Compared to people in face-to-face groups, individuals who interact with other group members online report being less committed to the group and less happy while working with it. Small group researchers Stefanie Johnson, Kenneth Bettenhausen, and Ellie Gibbons found negative outcomes are particularly likely in groups that interact via computer-mediated communication more than 90 percent of the time.[24] Other research has found that regardless of their culture, people feel less confident in their ability to be productive in virtual groups compared to face-to-face groups.[25]

SHARPEN Your Skills: *Online group communication*

Join an online group—such as through Google Groups or Yahoo Groups—that reflects one of your interests. For a week, interact online with other group members, and examine how the members communicate with one another. Pay particular attention to the forms of messages they encourage and what forms, if any, they discourage or prohibit. Then, in a blog or journal entry, describe the communication rules of the group, based on your experience. Compare and contrast your experiences with those of your classmates.

getCONNECTED
Success in Online Groups

What makes an online small group successful? Researchers Ann Majchrzak, Arvind Malhotra, Jeffrey Stamps, and Jessica Lipnack offer the following suggestions:[26]

- *Take advantage of diversity.* In communicating electronically, groups can find it difficult to ensure that everyone's input is heard when a decision must be made. By actively seeking and considering divergent opinions, online groups can make decisions that better reflect their members' needs.

- *Simulate reality.* One of the downsides of technologies such as e-mail is that it doesn't allow group members to interact with one another in *real time*, as they would in a face-to-face conversation.

Consequently, members can feel disengaged or left out of the dialogue. Successful groups use computer-mediated technologies that simulate real-life interactions, such as videoconferencing and virtual workspaces (websites where people can talk and share documents or graphics in real time).

- *Keep the team together.* The lower commitment virtual groups often feel (relative to face-to-face groups) increases the chance that members will become bored with the group and decide to leave. Communicating with group members on a daily basis may help to reduce that possibility by keeping everyone engaged in the group's business.

Communicating online—as in a videoconference—is often more efficient than interacting in person, particularly for groups whose members are geographically dispersed.

As we've seen in this section, several characteristics define the small group experience: group size, interdependence, cohesion, rules and norms, individual roles, unique identities, and communication practices. In addition, people in many small groups interact—either primarily or exclusively—online. Why might someone choose to take part in the small group experience at all? We'll probe some of the most important reasons in the next section.

Functions of Small Groups

Once a month, community members in towns and cities across the United States come together for a dinner in which they eat locally grown foods and discuss ways to make food production more sustainable. They are members of the Slow Food movement, an organization that began in Italy in 1986 to promote long, leisurely dining experiences that encourage conversation and an appreciation of the food being eaten. The movement, which opposes the quick consumption of mass-produced food, now has 100,000 worldwide members. Yet despite the organization's size, Slow Food members meet in small groups to enjoy and celebrate their good meals. Whether we're talking about a Slow Food group, a service organization, a committee, or a sports team, we'll discover in this section that small groups can serve several different functions.

Members of the Slow Food movement meet in small groups to enjoy leisurely dining experiences.

SMALL GROUPS HAVE MANY FUNCTIONS

Groups don't come together by accident. Rather, we form them when we believe they'll help us in some way. In this section, we'll see that small groups

- Focus on discrete tasks.
- Evaluate and advise.
- Create art and ideas.
- Provide service and support.
- Promote social networking.
- Compete.
- Help us to learn.

FIGURE 9.1
SOME FUNCTIONS OF SMALL GROUPS

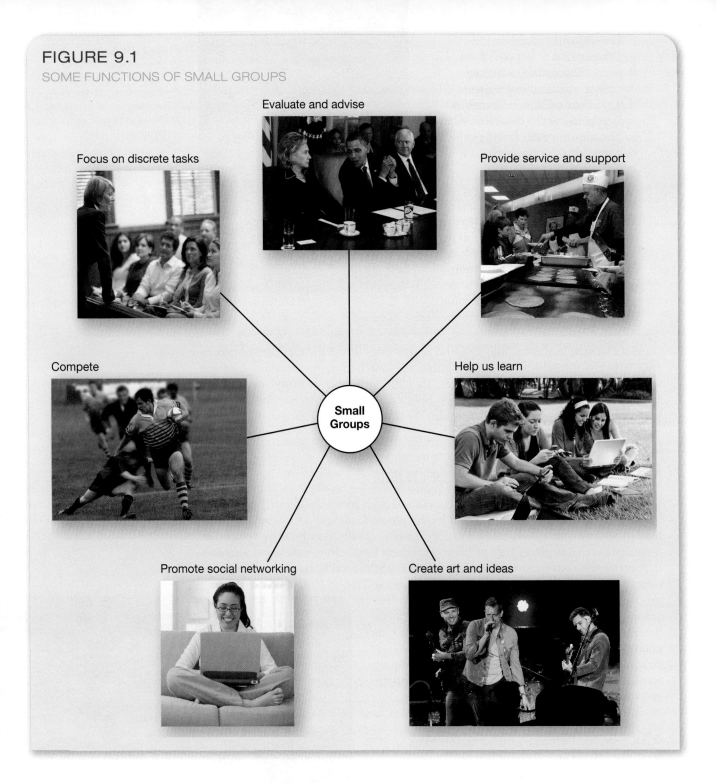

Evaluate and advise

Focus on discrete tasks

Provide service and support

Compete

Small Groups

Help us learn

Promote social networking

Create art and ideas

Figure 9.1 illustrates the functions small groups can serve. As you read and examine these functions, bear in mind that they aren't mutually exclusive. Any given group can serve multiple functions at once.

Some Small Groups Focus on Discrete Tasks One function of some groups is to accomplish specific assigned tasks. In 2002, for example, a small group was appointed in Washington, D.C., to "prepare a full and complete account of the circumstances surrounding the September 11, 2001 terrorist attacks, including preparedness for and the immediate response to the attacks."[27] The group, which came to be known as the 9/11 Commission, was composed of 10 individuals, most of whom were attorneys and former politicians. They investigated the September 11 attacks for more than a year and a half, interviewing over 1,200 people and reviewing some 2.5 million pages of documents.[28] In 2004, the group completed its assigned task by releasing a 604-page report detailing its findings.

Similarly, whenever a jury is assembled for a criminal or civil trial, it hears evidence, takes part in deliberation, and then fulfills its mission by communicating a verdict. Like a jury or the 9/11 Commission, most small groups that focus on discrete tasks usually disband after their tasks have been completed.

Some Small Groups Evaluate and Advise

The purpose of some small groups is to discuss and evaluate particular issues and give advice on how they should be addressed. The president of the United States, for instance, appoints a cabinet of 15 individuals who head major governmental agencies, such as the departments of State, Justice, Defense, Homeland Security, Education, and Commerce. The cabinet meets regularly to advise the president on issues related to domestic and foreign policy.[29] Although its individual members change, the cabinet has been a permanent group since the presidency of George Washington in the late eighteenth century.

Other small groups evaluate and advise on an as-needed basis. To evaluate the merits of a new product and how best to market it, for instance, many companies turn to *focus groups*.[30] Focus groups are usually composed of 6 to 10 typical consumers who may use and provide their feedback on a new product before it is available to the public. They may also give input on the new product's name or packaging. Other small groups that evaluate and advise are an award selection committee, an advisory board, and an employee performance evaluation committee.

Some Small Groups Create Art and Ideas

Coldplay is a small group whose purpose is to create, perform, and record rock music. Composed of four musicians, the Grammy Award–winning band has sold over 55 million albums worldwide and is one of the most successful creative small groups in history.[31]

Like Coldplay, many small groups exist primarily to create forms of art. A string quartet, a sculpting class, and the cast of *Saturday Night Live* are all small groups that produce artistic expressions. Other groups are charged with creating ideas instead of art. Many companies and organizations, for instance, use *brainstorming groups*, small groups of people assembled to generate innovative ways of thinking. When a county hospital needed a more efficient way of processing patients in the emergency room, it brought together a small group of nurses, medical technicians, paramedics, and volunteers to compile a list of suggestions. After listening to one another's experiences and concerns, the members of the brainstorming group were able to generate ideas for improving efficiency that hospital administrators had not previously considered.

Some Small Groups Provide Service and Support

Many small groups focus on providing community service to those who need it. For instance, local chapters of Kiwanis International serve their local communities through such activities as building playgrounds, running food drives, and raising money for pediatric medical research.[32]

Similarly, local chapters of the Lions Club raise funds to aid victims of natural disasters and to support screening for blindness and hearing loss.[33] Although Kiwanis and the Lions Club are international organizations, their members frequently work in small groups to accomplish community service missions. Many colleges, universities, and religious organizations also sponsor groups whose purpose is to provide community services.

Other small groups provide social and emotional support for people dealing with difficult circumstances. Some *support groups* aid those battling health concerns, such as diabetes, alcoholism, depression, and acne. Others help people to cope with the prejudice and discrimination they experience because they are mentally or physically disabled or sexual minorities. People in support groups often benefit by communicating with others whose circumstances are similar to theirs.[34] A woman addicted to gambling, for instance, may feel the only people who understand her are others battling the same addiction. Listening to others' stories in a support group may help the individual feel less alone and better able to control the problem behavior. Research has shown, in fact, that taking part in support groups for health conditions can improve physical and mental health.[35] Although some support groups meet in person, many now meet online, providing emotional encouragement and support to members worldwide.[36] An estimated 1.2 million support groups currently exist online.[37]

Some Small Groups Promote Social Networking At one point or another, many of us have joined small groups simply to meet other people. Groups with this purpose, known as *social networking groups*, allow people to meet, communicate, and get to know each other.[38] On the day she moved into her new residence hall, for instance, Lindsay and her fellow residents were divided into groups of 10 and given time to get to know one another. Taking part in that type of social networking group ensured that Lindsay knew at least 9 other people when she began the year in her new campus home.

Although social networking groups sometimes meet in person, as in Lindsay's case, they are particularly common on the Internet. For instance, chat rooms allow people to communicate online in real time, via text or web cams. Chat rooms often focus on a particular shared interest (such as pop culture or video gaming) or appeal to a specific demographic (such as single fathers or women over 40). Their primary purpose, however, is typically to allow people to communicate and to get to know one another.[39] Social networking websites, such as foursquare and Facebook, also allow users to interact with others in groups. Like chat rooms, many of these groups are organized to appeal to a specific population, such as fans of a certain celebrity or alumni of a particular high school. Although some groups and chat rooms can get quite large—growing to several hundred members—they often include only small numbers of people interacting at a given time.[40]

Some Small Groups Compete Many small groups are organized to take part in team competitions. For instance, colleges and universities around the United States sponsor groups of 8 to 12 students who compete in Quiz Bowl.[41] Quiz Bowl is an academic competition in which students respond to questions posed by a moderator about a wide range of subjects. The team that correctly answers the most questions in the shortest time wins the match, so members of a Quiz Bowl team must work interdependently to accomplish their mission.

Similarly, the teams organized for many athletic competitions are small groups. Your school may have a wrestling, diving, or crew team, for example, that has 20 or fewer members and therefore functions as a small group. The purpose of competitive groups is to train and practice a particular set of skills and then to compete with similar groups to win material prizes (such as trophies) or recognition.

Some Small Groups Help Us to Learn Finally, we join some small groups because they help us to learn. You may have taken part in *study groups*, which

usually include a small number of students who help one another to understand the material and prepare for the exams in a specific course. Workshops and Bible studies are also small groups that help us to learn. Participating in learning groups enhances critical thinking skills, such as the ability to analyze and evaluate ideas,[42] and lets us contribute our own understanding of the material for the benefit of others as well as take advantage of what others can teach us.

As we've seen, small groups can enact several different functions, including accomplishing discrete tasks, evaluating and advising, creating, providing service and support, promoting social networking, competing, and helping us to learn. These functions are not mutually exclusive; many groups focus on more than one of them at once. A nonprofit organization might form a committee to evaluate its public relations efforts, for instance, but the committee might also create new ideas, implement those ideas in the form of a new public relations campaign, and provide an opportunity for social networking among its members. A support group might provide encouragement for people suffering from arthritis, but in the process its members might learn more about their condition and the options available for treatment. As these examples illustrate, participating in small groups often helps people in many different ways.

Joining Small Groups

The first group to which most of us belong is a family—and because we're either born or adopted into our family, we have little say over our membership. Over the course of our life, however, we may join and leave a wide variety of small groups. Although each one is different, we can understand the process of joining them by considering why and how we do so. We begin this section by exploring some of the major reasons people have for joining small groups. We then look at the process by which people become socialized into groups.

WE JOIN SMALL GROUPS FOR MANY REASONS

Thinking back on your own small group experiences, you'll likely realize that you joined different groups for different reasons. Perhaps you joined some enthusiastically, primarily for social reasons, whereas you might have taken part in others because you felt compelled to. People join because they need to belong, because groups provide protection, because group membership can improve their performance, and because they feel pressure to join.

We Join Small Groups Because We Need to Belong In the 1999 comedy *Never Been Kissed*, Drew Barrymore plays Josie Geller, a 25-year-old newspaper copy editor assigned to pose as a high school student and write an undercover story about adolescent life. During her own high school years, Josie was an intelligent but socially awkward teenager who yearned for acceptance and popularity. As she begins her undercover assignment, she is inhibited by insecurity. On her first day of school, however, her classmate Aldys (played by Leelee Sobieski) invites her to join the Denominators, a small group of students who excel in math and compete in math competitions. The Denominators wear matching sweatshirts, sit together during lunch, and provide Josie with an immediate group of friends who give her a sense of belonging.

Humans are highly social beings. We don't just *want* to belong to social networks; we *need* to. Friendships and families can meet many of our social needs, but small groups can also give us a sense of social belonging. Especially in situations where we feel out of place or unsure of ourselves—as Josie did when she began her undercover assignment—having a group to belong to and identify with can be comforting.

We Join Small Groups for Protection The expression "There's safety in numbers" suggests we are better protected against threats or problems when we're part of a group than when we're alone. The reason is that group members can take care of one another, and those who are stronger can protect those who are weaker.

In some instances, the protection we gain from groups is physical. You and your immediate neighbors might form a neighborhood watch group, for example, in which you agree to look out for one another's safety and property. Belonging to the group provides you the assurance of knowing that if something goes wrong, neighbors will seek help on your behalf. Religious and community groups may also come together to provide aid when a member is sick and unable to care for himself or herself. In those

cases, being in a small group gives some measure of protection for someone's physical health and well-being.

We can also gain social or emotional protection from groups. Many people facing chronic or life-threatening illnesses find comfort in support groups, gaining emotional sustenance from others experiencing the same trial that can encourage them and remind them they aren't alone in their struggles. In support groups for addiction to alcohol, drugs, or gambling, members are routinely assigned a sponsor to whom they are accountable for their behavior. When they feel the urge to gamble or use alcohol or drugs, they can call on their sponsor for the support necessary to resist those behaviors.

We Join Small Groups to Improve Our Effectiveness

A third reason people join small groups is to improve their skills or to become more effective at some task.[43] Contestants on the NBC series *The Biggest Loser* form small groups led by personal trainers who help them to lose weight. The members of each group work out together, offer mutual encouragement, and hold one another accountable for maintaining their diet and exercise regimens. Participating in their small groups often makes contestants much more effective at losing weight than they could be alone. In fact, many individuals trying to lose weight seek support and encouragement from small groups because they believe it will help them. Will it? Check out the "Fact or Fiction?" box to find out.

Membership in various other kinds of small groups can also help us to improve particular skills. Joining an investment group may teach you things you didn't know about money and help you to become a more effective investor. Joining a golf team may expose you to the skills of other players and give you opportunities to sharpen your own skills through competition. Joining a small standup comedy group might make you a better, more confident performer on stage.

We Join Small Groups Because We Feel Pressure to Join

Although we often join small groups by choice, we sometimes join because we feel pressured into doing so. Perhaps you've been enrolled in college courses that required you to participate in a group project. In such cases, your group participation wasn't voluntary. Similarly, if many of your friends at work are joining a small group to support a certain political candidate, you might feel pressured to do the same, even if that wouldn't have been your choice.

Feeling pressure to join a small group doesn't necessarily mean your experience in it will be negative. After being assigned to a group for a class project, for example, you might develop a friendship with some of the other members. Whether you join a group by choice or for another reason, your experience will be as positive or negative as you make it.

Now that we've identified some of the reasons we join small groups, let's take a look at how we become socialized into them.

WE ARE SOCIALIZED INTO SMALL GROUPS

Think back to your first day of college. You can likely remember the anticipation, some uncertainty about your courses, and the excitement about being part of a campus community. You probably found these feelings faded as you learned what to expect and became accustomed to your college routine. The process by which you gained greater certainty about the college experience is called *socialization*, and the same occurs when you join a small group.

Researchers believe we are socialized into small groups in five phases—the antecedent phase, the anticipatory phase, the encounter phase, the assimilation phase, and the exit phase (Figure 9.2). Let's review each.

Antecedent Phase
The first phase of socialization begins before we even enter a new group, when we develop certain beliefs, attitudes, and expectations about it in the *antecedent phase*.

Fact or *fiction*?

Losing Weight Is Easier in Groups

Individuals who want to shed weight often join a small weight-loss group. Many believe the support and accountability they receive from the group will help them to lose more weight than they could on their own. Is that belief fact or fiction?

Taking part in a weight-loss group is more effective than trying to reduce weight individually. In one study, overweight adults worked with a weight-loss counselor for 26 weeks, either on their own or in groups of 8 to 12. During each group session, participants reported on their progress, and the counselor led a group discussion focused on rewarding progress and overcoming obstacles. Participants were also weighed and instructed in proper diet and exercise strategies. Those who worked with a counselor individually received all the same information and encouragement, just not in a group setting. By the end of the study, the participants who worked in groups had reduced their weight and body mass significantly more than had the participants who worked individually.

Other studies have produced similar results. For instance, people are more successful at giving up nicotine and cocaine when they take part in small groups designed to help them than when they try to quit on their own.

ASK YOURSELF

- Why do you suppose working in small groups helps people to improve their health more than working alone?

- What health problems, if any, do you think most people would resolve more effectively alone than in groups?

SOURCES: Renjilian, D. A., Perri, M. G., Nezu, A. M., McKelvey, W. F., Shermer, R. L., & Anton, S. D. (2001). Individual versus group therapy for obesity: Effects of matching participants to their treatment preferences. *Journal of Consulting and Clinical Psychology, 69*, 717–721; Schmitz, J. M., Oswald, L. M., Jacks, S. D., Rustin, T., Rhoades, H. M., & Grabowski, J. (1997). Relapse prevention treatment for cocaine dependence: Group vs. individual format. *Addictive Behaviors, 22*, 405–418; Stead, L. F., & Lancaster, T. (2005). Group behaviour therapy programmes for smoking cessation. *Cochrane Database of Systematic Reviews, 10*, OD001007.

Let's say that in the last three classes in which you've worked on a group project, you ended up doing the bulk of the work while other members shirked their responsibilities. As a result, you've come to believe that group work is never fair. You've developed a negative attitude about small groups and the expectation that you will always have to do more than your share. The next time you decide to join a small group, you therefore approach it less optimistically than you might if your previous experiences had been more positive.[44]

FIGURE 9.2

THE FIVE PHASES OF SOCIALIZATION INTO SMALL GROUPS

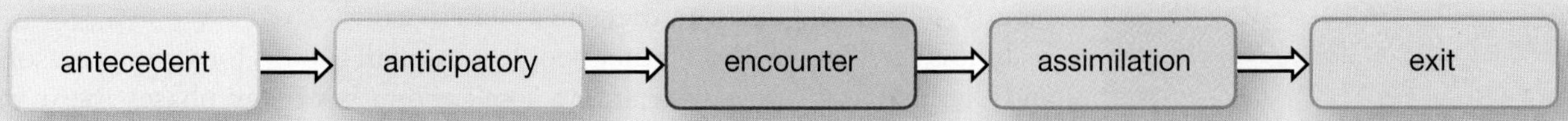

antecedent → anticipatory → encounter → assimilation → exit

Anticipatory Phase When we first decide to join a group, we make judgments about what we expect from that group and its members. The process of forming those judgments is called the *anticipatory phase*. Some of our judgments might be based on the beliefs, attitudes, and expectations we formed from previous experiences with small groups. Others may be influenced by what we've heard about the particular group's objectives or traditions.

The anticipatory phase can be stressful if our expectations for a group are unrealistic.[45] For instance, you might join a study group expecting it will help you to understand the course material, only to discover that the group's primary purpose is social, not academic. You may then alter your expectations for the group or you may decide to join a different group instead.

Encounter Phase The *encounter phase* occurs the first time we meet with others as a group. For some groups, that meeting will occur face-to-face. For others, it may occur in electronically mediated formats, such as teleconferencing, or in virtual reality, by which the group interacts online.

At least three important tasks are typically addressed during the encounter phase. First, groups often use their initial meeting to establish their mission and define their goals. A committee might identify its specific tasks, while a support group might discuss its members' needs. Second, groups often assign roles and responsibilities during the encounter phase, such as leader or record keeper for the group. Finally, groups may use the encounter phase to remind members of expectations for their behavior. Those expectations form part of the group's culture, and they often take the form of statements such as "Everyone in this group is expected to do his or her fair share of the work" and "In this group, no one is more important than anyone else."

Assimilation Phase Once the expectations for a group's culture are known, individual members must decide whether to accept them. If they do, they enter the *assimilation phase*. It's at this stage of socialization that the group acquires its own identity. Members begin to identify with the group and to think of themselves not as "you and I" but as "we."

During the assimilation phase, group members may begin enacting specific rituals or communication behaviors that signify their membership in the group. Those might include wearing specific signs of membership, such as matching sweatshirts or lapel pins, or conforming to the group's traditions by greeting other members with a secret handshake or reciting a specific pledge at every group meeting. Some members may accept a group's culture outright; others may accept it but attempt to change it over time.[46] Members who do not accept a group's culture or who find themselves at odds with a group's purpose often enter the final stage of group socialization by leaving.

In a small group such as a Little League team, new members are socialized into the group's norms and expectations.

Exit Phase Membership in most small groups has a life span. Individual members may leave voluntarily or involuntarily in the final stage of socialization, the *exit phase*. For instance, you might grow dissatisfied with the advisory board you're on at work after its new leader changes the group's mission significantly, so you may choose to leave it voluntarily. If instead you were to be laid off from your job, you would have to leave the advisory board whether you wanted to or not.

Members also exit groups when the groups themselves cease to exist.[47] Many small groups meet only long enough to accomplish a specific task, such as studying for exams in a college course, painting a mural in a neighborhood park, or drafting a policy on yard maintenance for a homeowners' association. When they have completed the task, they disband. Other small groups stop meeting because members lose interest or because they can no longer count on the resources they require. Whatever the reason, most small groups disband at some point, causing their members to exit.[48]

In this section, we've seen that people join small groups for various reasons and that becoming socialized into a small group has many phases. Next we explore some of the advantages and challenges of communicating in small group settings.

Advantages and Challenges of Small Group Communication

On the CBS drama *NCIS*, the group of special agents at the Naval Criminal Investigative Service experiences many of the benefits and the trials of small group communication. Although the closeness of their group provides the agents with emotional support and assistance with their jobs, it can also invite conflict and cause them to wear on one another's nerves. *NCIS* is fictional, but the advantages and challenges of communicating in small groups are not. In this section, we explore some of the benefits we can accrue and some of the tribulations we can encounter when participating in a small group.

COMMUNICATING IN SMALL GROUPS HAS ADVANTAGES

Participating in small groups confers some specific benefits. In this section, we examine three: small groups provide resources, they experience synergy, and they expose us to diversity.

Small Groups Provide Resources

Accomplishing almost any task requires the availability of **resources,** or assets that enable us to be productive. Some resources are tangible, such as money, space, materials, and equipment. Others are intangible, such as time, information, talent, and expertise. Each of us has different resources at our disposal. When we come together with people in a small group, we gain access to the resources of others.[49]

• **resources** Assets that enable a group to be productive.

Suppose you're on a committee to raise funds for a renovation of your local high school's computer facilities. As a busy college student, you don't have much free time to go door to door or make phone calls soliciting donations, but your training in communication allows you to draft good persuasive messages for others to use. Other committee members can provide materials for making signs, cars to use for canvassing neighborhoods, or money to cover expenses. In this small group, as in many small groups, each of you can take advantage of the resources of other members.

Small Groups Experience Synergy

In many small groups, members can accomplish more by working together than they could by working individually. When they do, researchers say they are experiencing **synergy,** a collaboration that produces more than the sum of its parts.

• **synergy** A collaboration that produces more than the sum of its parts.

Let's say you and two friends are each running for separate seats on your county's board of supervisors. By campaigning as individuals, each of you might generate approximately 25,000 votes, for a total of 75,000 votes. Instead, however, you decide to campaign as a group by publicly endorsing one another, representing yourselves as three running mates, and encouraging people to vote for all three of you. By adopting that strategy, you are able to pool your money to buy more advertising time and post more campaign signs around your county than your individual opponents can afford. As a result, each of you generates 40,000 votes. That's a total of 120,000 votes, or 45,000 more than you would have generated by working individually. Can you think of occasions when you have taken part in a small group that experienced synergy?

The special agents depicted in *NCIS* are subject to both the advantages and the challenges of small group communication.

Small Groups Expose Us to Diversity

The expression, "Two heads are better than one" reflects the idea that getting input from others can help us to make better, more informed decisions than we would make on our own. The reason is that each person brings a different set of ideas, experiences, insights, and values to bear on the choice. Listening to the perspectives of other people often makes us consider aspects of a decision that hadn't occurred to us before. Thus, one important advantage of participating in a small group is exposure to ways of thinking that are different from our own.[50]

Suppose two "juries" were to hear the same fictitious criminal case in a law school's mock trial exercise. Jury A is composed of 12 people with highly diverse work experience, cultural background, educational level, and socioeconomic status. Jury B consists of 12 people with highly similar characteristics. After hearing the case, Jury B quickly arrives at a unanimous verdict. Because the members of this jury are so similar, they paid attention to the same pieces of evidence, were persuaded by the same arguments, and brought similar biases and prejudices to bear on their decision. In contrast, Jury A takes much longer to arrive at a unanimous verdict. Because of their diversity, the members each paid attention to different aspects of the case. Whereas some found the physical evidence persuasive, others listened more carefully to the eyewitness accounts or watched the defendant's facial expressions while testimony was being presented.

When it came time to reach a verdict, the members of Jury A drew from a much more diverse set of ideas, arguments, and biases. Even though arriving at a unanimous decision was a long and difficult process for this group, its verdict was better informed because it was fully considered from many different points of view. Although working in diverse groups can present challenges, it can also help us to think in more open-minded ways—and thereby to come to better decisions.

COMMUNICATING IN SMALL GROUPS POSES CHALLENGES

Taking part in small groups can be extremely rewarding, but it isn't always easy. At least three challenges are common to small groups: they require sacrifices, they can experience conflict, and they can be difficult to coordinate.

Small Groups Require Sacrifices Belonging to a small group sometimes requires making sacrifices for the benefit of the group. Let's say you're on a committee at work that is charged with selecting a new marketing slogan. Your deadline is fast approaching, so the group decides to hold a meeting on Sunday afternoon, a time you usually spend with your family. As a result, you may have to sacrifice your family time for the sake of the group's mission.

Besides sacrificing time, group members sometimes find they have to do more work than their fellow members to make sure tasks get completed. The reason is that some group members may engage in **social loafing,** meaning they contribute less to the group than the average member, which is particularly easy as the group grows in size.[51] Perhaps you've been in small groups at school in which one or two people did the bulk of the work and others hardly did any. If so, you know that can be a frustrating experience for those who take responsibility for the group's productivity.[52] In effect, members who do more than their share of work are sacrificing their time and effort so the group can accomplish its goals. Table 9.2 presents some strategies for reducing social loafing in small groups.

Small Groups Can Experience Conflict Whenever small groups have to make decisions, they are likely to experience some measure of conflict. As we considered in Chapter 8, conflict arises when two or more parties perceive that their goals are incompatible and their resources are limited. This situation is probable in many group decision-making contexts.

Suppose you and some close friends are trying to decide on a graduation gift for another friend in the group. You intend to pool your money to purchase one item on behalf of the group, but you're undecided about what to buy and how much to spend. One person thinks you should get your friend a Kindle Fire. Another thinks a gift card for her favorite Mexican restaurant would be a better idea. Two people in the group think you should just give your friend money, and you think it would be

• **social loafing** The tendency of some members of a group to contribute less to the group than the average member does, particularly as the group grows in size.

TABLE 9.2
WAYS TO REDUCE
SOCIAL LOAFING

When group members engage in social loafing, the group's productivity suffers and other members can become resentful. Here are some strategies for reducing social loafing.

- *Name names.* Make every member's specific contributions to the group known to the rest of the group, so that if a specific person is being unproductive, others will know; research shows that naming reduces social loafing by up to 29 percent.[53]

- *Be specific about goals.* Social loafing is easier when the group's goals are ambiguous; make sure each person knows exactly what he or she is meant to do.

- *Make the consequences clear.* People are less likely to engage in social loafing if they understand how their individual behaviors contribute to the group's goal.

best to buy her some work clothes for the job she is about to begin.

Because you have a finite amount of money to spend, your group has to choose just one gift, and because different people prefer different outcomes, members may experience conflict in the process of making a decision. As we saw in Chapter 8, conflict is a normal part of human communication, and it isn't necessarily problematic. What matters is how groups handle conflict when it arises. If it is managed inappropriately, conflict can be a destructive force in a group, leading to resentment and hurt feelings and a general lack of productivity for the group. If managed constructively, however, it can lead groups to make more informed and more creative decisions than they otherwise would. We'll examine strategies for managing group conflict appropriately in Chapter 10.

SHARPEN Your Skills: *Group conflict*

With a few students from your class, role-play a conversation in which you must decide on a policy for a controversial issue, such as stem cell research or the use of torture during interrogations. Encourage your fellow students to voice their opinions even if others disagree. If conflict arises during the discussion, take note of when it occurs and how the group deals with it. After the conversation, allow time for each student to assess how the group handled conflict.

Small Groups Can Be Difficult to Coordinate If you've ever been in charge of coordinating a group's meetings or activities, you know how challenging that task can be. Even in groups with only three or four members, finding dates and times to meet that fit everyone's schedule can be difficult. That challenge is even more pronounced in groups with 15 or more members. These days, online group scheduling

Many small groups experience conflict. As a normal part of human communication, conflict isn't necessarily problematic. What matters is how groups handle it.

programs such as Doodle.com help to facilitate the coordination of schedules. Some groups may even find it necessary to divide their work, assigning specific tasks to pairs of people who can more easily coordinate their schedules rather than trying to get the entire group together.

Scheduling isn't the only challenge for small groups. Particularly as groups grow in size, members often find it increasingly difficult to communicate efficiently with one another. As a result, larger groups tend to communicate less about their tasks than do smaller groups.[54] People in larger groups also encounter more challenges when trying to maintain their relationships with one another.[55]

Although small groups require sacrifice, can experience conflict, and can be tough to coordinate, those realities don't mean that participating in them isn't worth the effort. On the contrary, belonging to a small group can be a positive and rewarding experience. That outcome is all the more likely if we are aware of the challenges of small group communication and can manage them productively.

Becoming a Better Small Group Communicator

If you've participated in many small groups, some of your experiences were probably more favorable than others. Although your future experiences in groups will also vary, you can use your knowledge of small group communication to make them positive. Two particularly important communication skills for small groups are socializing new members constructively and maintaining positive group relationships.

SOCIALIZE NEW MEMBERS CONSTRUCTIVELY

Becoming part of a small group requires more than signing your name to a membership roster. New members must also be socialized into the group. They must be informed about the group's expectations, roles, ways of working, and culture. New members who are not properly socialized may feel unwelcome or unenthusiastic about having joined the group. They may also unintentionally disrupt activities because they aren't aware of the group's norms and expectations. Part of communicating competently in small groups therefore is helping to socialize new members.

Experts point out that two sets of skills are necessary for proper socialization.[56] As we'll now consider, the first set consists of skills the group must have, and the second set encompasses skills of the new member.

Socialize New Members to the Group When new members join a group, it is important to welcome them. Four behaviors in particular help to socialize new members positively and constructively:

- *Recruit good members.* Seek out potential members who will contribute to the group's mission. Be on the lookout for individuals who fit the group's personality, and encourage them to consider joining.

- *Create a group orientation.* Spend time with new members and teach them about the group's history, norms, expectations, and procedures. Knowing about these aspects of the group will aid them in being positive contributors.[57]

- *Include new members in activities.* Ensure that new members are included in group functions and activities. If, for example, the work team meets every Wednesday morning for breakfast, invite the new members. They will feel welcomed and encouraged to participate when they are included.

- *Be a mentor.* An experienced group member can be a mentor for a new member.[58] A *mentor* is someone who serves as a trusted friend, counselor, or teacher for another person. Even if new members are properly initiated when they first join a group, they may benefit from having a seasoned mentor. How good are you at mentoring? Take the quiz in "The Competent Communicator" to find out.

One on One: Mentoring a New Group Member

One of the most important skills for socializing new members to groups is mentoring. How good a mentor are you already? Indicate how well each of the following statements describes you by assigning it a number between 1 ("not at all") and 7 ("very well").

_____ I enjoy helping people.

_____ People frequently turn to me for advice.

_____ I like to take someone "under my wing" and help him or her to succeed.

_____ I feel bad if a new person in my group seems uncomfortable.

_____ I am a good listener.

_____ Supporting people intellectually and emotionally makes me feel good.

_____ People tell me I am good at giving guidance.

_____ I like to "show people the ropes" when they are new to a group or situation.

_____ I try to be the kind of person that others can trust.

_____ I take my responsibilities toward other people seriously.

When you're finished, add up your scores. A score of 10–25 suggests that mentoring is a skill you can build, and learning about small group communication is one way to do so. If you scored between 25 and 55, you are fairly good at mentoring, and as you have more opportunities to be a mentor, you can improve that skill. If you scored above 55, you are probably an experienced mentor. You are well poised to help socialize new members into the small groups to which you belong.

These behaviors are useful ways of socializing new members into groups to which you already belong. What if *you* are the new member, however? Let's look at four ways you can help to ensure successful socialization for yourself.

Join a Group When you join a new group, you can aid your own process of socialization by following four steps:

- *Embrace the group's culture.* If you've made the effort to join a small group, you probably already support that group's goals, norms, values, and behaviors. Thus, part of socializing yourself into a new group is communicating in ways that reflect the group's culture.

- *Acquire appropriate skills.* If you are to become an active member of a group, you'll need to develop the skills to carry out your role and responsibilities. If you've joined a community outreach group, for instance, you may need to brush up on your conversational skills so you can interact with the public. Think about the skills you'll need to contribute to the group's mission, and look for ways to acquire or improve them.

- *Learn what matters.* Groups often have multiple goals that require members to juggle several demands on their time and attention. Usually, however, some of these goals are more important than others. Learn how the group prioritizes competing demands. If you understand what matters most, you will be well positioned to work toward the group's most valued goals.

- *Contribute to the group.* Like most people, as a new member you probably require a period of adjustment during which you learn about the group's mission and culture. Once you are socialized into the group, take responsibility for contributing to it and its members.[59]

Joining a group can be intimidating for anyone. Whether you're helping to socialize a new member into your group or attempting to join a new group yourself, you can contribute to a more positive socialization experience by following the steps we've examined.

MAINTAIN POSITIVE GROUP RELATIONSHIPS

Your experiences in almost any small group will be more productive and meaningful if you develop and maintain positive relationships within the group. That doesn't necessarily mean you have to become a friend with every member. Indeed, you can establish positive relationships in two other specific ways: by contributing to the creation of a constructive group environment and by helping to build group cohesion.

Contribute to a Constructive Group Environment Maintaining positive relationships within a group is easiest if an optimistic, constructive attitude prevails. When group members believe they have the resources to achieve their tasks and deal successfully with challenges, they feel better about themselves and others. Here are a few tips to help you to contribute to a constructive group environment:

- *Celebrate success.* When someone in the group receives good news or achieves success in a task, ask that person if you can share the news with the group. Many people are uncomfortable telling others of their own good fortune for fear they will be seen as bragging, but they appreciate when others relate their good news for them. That way, everyone can celebrate members' successes.

- *Defuse stress.* It's normal for groups to experience stress from time to time. When interactions among group members become tense, try to defuse the stress. Suggest a group outing, such as going on a hike or taking in a movie. Use humor to reduce tensions and help people relax. When group members feel less stressed, they will likely get along better and be more productive.

- *Respect others.* In almost any group, there are people whose perspectives are at odds. Creating a positive group environment doesn't mean everyone has to agree or individuals have to give up their own viewpoints. Rather, group members show respect for others by listening to different perspectives. Acknowledge the positive aspects of others' ideas and then present your own. When group members treat one another respectfully, their diversity can benefit them by helping them to consider all the possibilities in a given situation.

The ability to build and maintain positive relationships in groups is a particular asset in the workplace. To explore one career in which small group communication skills are especially useful, check out "Putting Communication to Work."

Help to Build Group Cohesion Recall from earlier in this chapter that group cohesion is the extent to which everyone in the group works together toward a common goal. Cohesive groups are more productive and have happier, more satisfied

putting**communication**to**work**

Search

Job Title >

Work Responsibilities >

Jury Coordinator for Superior Court

Jury coordinators are responsible for organizing small groups of citizens who report to the superior court each day for jury duty. They welcome and conduct briefings for jurors to help to prepare them for service. They work with judges to administer jury selection questionnaires. Most important, whenever a new jury is paneled, they orient the jurors to their responsibilities and help them select a leader. This career requires excellent small group communication skills and the ability to help people from very different backgrounds work together.

members than groups lacking cohesion.[60] Contributing to group cohesion is therefore an important way to build positive group relationships. You can promote cohesion in the groups to which you belong in the following ways:

- *Emphasize collective goals.* Encourage the group to identify its shared goals clearly. Some goals will be broad, such as "Support economic development in the community." Others will be specific, such as "Plan a rally for next Thursday evening." Whatever the group's goals, cohesion suffers when members lose sight of their collective goals. Take opportunities to remind others in the group of the common goals. When members concentrate on their shared objectives, group cohesiveness often increases.

- *Keep track of progress.* When a goal takes longer to achieve than a group planned, or when members encounter unanticipated problems along the way, those who are working toward a common goal can get discouraged. You can help by acknowledging your group's progress so far. Stress what members have already accomplished, not what they haven't yet achieved. When they are raising funds, for instance, some groups create a large drawing of a thermometer, which they post in a visible place and fill in with color to indicate how much money they have collected. When group members pay attention to what they have achieved, they may focus more on their collective goals than on the challenges of meeting those goals.

- *Remind others of their value to the group.* Almost everyone has a need to belong and appreciates feeling valued. Therefore, another way you can contribute to group cohesion is to point out the reasons you value others in the group. Some reasons might directly relate to the group's task; for instance, you might value one member because of her skill at generating publicity or her knack for organizing efficient workspaces. More generally, you might value a member's empathy or sense of humor. In either case, people are often more committed to groups or causes if they feel valued than if they don't, so reminding people of the ways in which you appreciate them can increase the cohesiveness of the group.

adaptability Promoting Positivity

The Scene: You have a group project due in your communication course in two weeks. Your group is far behind on its progress because of disagreements over what to do. Some members feel their ideas have been ignored and everyone seems to lack enthusiasm about working together. If you don't complete the project, however, you and the rest of your group will probably fail the course.

Your Task: Consider how you can adapt your communication behavior to promote a more positive atmosphere in the group. What strategies could you use in this situation to

- Defuse stress and soothe hurt feelings?
- Emphasize the group's collective goals?
- Get the group's work back on track?

For REVIEW

- **What are small groups, and what do they do?** Small groups are collections of 3 to 20 people who focus on discrete tasks, evaluate and advise, create art and ideas, provide services and support, promote social networking, compete, and/ or help their members to learn.

- **Why and how do people join small groups?** People join small groups because they need to belong, they seek protection, they want to improve their effectiveness at a skill, and/ or they are pressured into joining. Whatever the reason, people are socialized into small groups in several stages.

- **How can you communicate better in a small group?** You can contribute to a positive socialization experience for new members, and you can maintain good group relationships by contributing to a constructive environment and helping to build group cohesion.

POP QUIZ

Multiple Choice

1. The term for the ability of group members to work together in the service of a common goal, much as do melodies and harmonies in music, is

   a. cohesion.

   b. independence.

   c. formal roles.

   d. introversion.

2. The phase of group socialization that occurs when individual members decide to accept the expectations for the group's culture is the

   a. anticipatory phase.

   b. assimilation phase.

   c. encounter phase.

   d. antecedent phase.

3. While working in a group to complete a class project, Ron contributes far less than anyone else in the group. Ron is engaging in

   a. synergy.

   b. role communication.

   c. social loafing.

   d. the need to belong.

4. Greta has been elected president of her homeowners' association. Being president is an example of a(n)

   a. group role.

   b. formal role.

   c. norm.

   d. informal role.

5. On a NASA flight crew, each member affected, and was affected by, every other member. That is an example of the crew's

   a. interdependence.

   b. social cohesion.

   c. task communication.

   d. resources.

Fill in the Blank

6. A fan club on Facebook is a group that serves the function of _____.

7. The assets that enable us to be productive—such as money, equipment, and expertise—are known as _____.

8. Quiz Bowl teams exemplify groups that _____.

9. A collaboration that produces more than the sum of its parts is creating _____.

10. In the _____ phase of group socialization, you meet with a small group for the first time.

KEY TERMS

small group 208	cohesion 210	synergy 223
interdependence 209	resources 223	social loafing 224

DECISION MAKING AND LEADERSHIP IN GROUPS

Making Critical Decisions Requires Communication

For the nine justices of the U.S. Supreme Court, making difficult decisions is a way of life.   The Supreme Court serves as the highest judicial body in the nation, handing down final decisions on controversial cases that often require interpretation of the U.S. Constitution. Because their cases can be so hotly contested and have such far-reaching effects on the country, Supreme Court justices, who are appointed for life, must learn to work together productively despite frequent differences of opinion. They do so by communicating with one another regularly, both in writing and in face-to-face conferences. When they meet to discuss the merits of a case, they follow rules and traditions that protect everyone's right to be heard. Those procedures help the Court to make decisions even when the justices' positions are strongly divided, as they were in a 2005 case, *McCreary County v. ACLU of Kentucky.* In that case the Court ruled that two Kentucky counties could not display copies of the Ten Commandments in courtrooms, because doing so violated the separation of church and state. Then, as in many other controversial cases, the justices were narrowly divided by a vote of 5 to 4.

As You READ

- How do groups generate ideas and make decisions?
- How do leaders enact leadership and exercise power?
- What communication skills improve group decision making?

No matter what its primary functions are, almost every group makes decisions. A criminal jury decides whether a defendant is guilty. A faculty committee may have decided to select this textbook for your class. From time to time, the justices of the U.S. Supreme Court decide on a case with far-reaching implications for Americans. Those decisions are all very different, but as you'll discover in this chapter, they have more in common than you might think.

Whether groups make good or bad decisions often depends on how their members interact. The quality of a group's choices can also be influenced by who leads the group and how that leader exercises power. Because so many groups make decisions that affect the lives of others—often in significant ways—learning about leadership and decision making can help you contribute more productively in the groups to which you belong.

Generating Ideas and Making Decisions

In the wake of the economic recession plaguing much of the United States, small businesses are fighting to survive. Increased competition from large retail chains and reduced disposable income among consumers have forced many merchants to lay off employees or shut their doors altogether. Rather than give up, however, several small retailers in the city of Hanford, California, came together to generate ideas for adapting to and surviving the recession. So far, the group has devised several business-boosting plans, which include sponsoring community events and improving the landscaping downtown, where most of the retailers are clustered. The group hopes these and other ideas will help the city's small businesses to weather the economic downturn.[1]

For many groups—such as the Hanford merchants—the ability to make wise decisions is essential to their livelihood and quality of life. Fortunately, groups have several good options for generating and choosing among ideas, as we'll see in this section. We also consider that several cultural and social characteristics can influence which decision-making options are best.

GROUPS GENERATE IDEAS THROUGH VARIOUS METHODS

A human resources committee may need to decide how to advertise the three new positions it must fill. A musical group may need to choose a repertoire of songs to perform for an upcoming concert series. In both cases, generating a list of possible options is an important first step in the decision-making process. Here we'll examine

A musical group can use a variety of decision-making methods to choose its repertoire of songs for an upcoming performance.

three of the most common methods groups use to generate ideas: brainstorming, the nominal group technique, and ideawriting.

Groups Can Brainstorm

A technique popularized in the 1950s to stimulate creative decision making,[2] **brainstorming** allows group members to freely offer any ideas they wish and create a list of all the proposed ideas before any are evaluated. The concept behind brainstorming is that if people feel free to think in unorthodox ways without fear of being ridiculed, they may generate better and more creative ideas.[3]

Groups usually begin a brainstorming session by identifying the question to be answered or the problem to be solved. During the session, group members are encouraged to pose ideas, no matter how outlandish they might seem at first. All ideas are added to a master list, and the process continues until no one expresses any new ideas. At that point, the group considers the merits of each idea, discarding some and possibly combining others, with the goal of selecting the best one or more. Finally, the group may decide which idea or ideas to adopt. We will consider various methods of group decision making later in this chapter.

To brainstorm productively, groups should observe four general rules that are clearly communicated to group members before the brainstorming session begins. That way, everyone knows what to expect. Those rules are[4]

- *Focus on quantity:* Generate as many different ideas as possible in the allotted time.
- *Don't criticize:* While ideas are being generated, don't criticize them. Put all discussion about the merits of ideas on hold until later.
- *Encourage creativity:* Welcome unusual ideas, even those that may sound crazy or nonsensical at first.
- *Piggyback:* Allow members to build on each other's ideas or combine ideas.

Researchers suggest that brainstorming sessions last no longer than about 30 minutes so the group's energy and creativity don't wane.[5] When done properly, brainstorming can lead a group to generate useful and innovative ideas.

Groups Can Use the Nominal Group Technique

Brainstorming works well when all members of the group feel comfortable offering ideas and sharing opinions. Members who are shy or who fear being ridiculed may be unlikely to participate, however. In that situation, a more productive option may be the **nominal group technique (NGT).**[6] NGT calls for group members to generate their initial ideas silently and independently and then combine them and consider them as a group.

Like brainstorming, NGT begins with the identification of a question to be answered or a problem to be solved. Instead of contributing their initial ideas aloud in front of the group, however, members each make a list of ideas on their own, working silently. Afterward, a group facilitator asks each member to read his or her ideas aloud, one at a time, while the facilitator writes them on a master list. The facilitator can also collect the ideas and compile the master list on his or her own so no one knows who came up with each idea.[7]

Once the master list is in place, NGT follows essentially the same process as brainstorming. The group considers the merits of each idea on the list, discarding some and debating or modifying others. Finally, the group selects whichever idea it believes to

• brainstorming
An idea-generating process in which group members offer whatever ideas they wish before any are debated.

Brainstorming can be a very effective method of generating ideas.

• nominal group technique (NGT) An idea-generating process in which group members generate their initial ideas silently and independently and then combine them and consider them as a group.

be the best. The major advantage of NGT over brainstorming is that it can encourage participation from members who might be uncomfortable contributing their ideas aloud.[8]

• **ideawriting** An idea-generating process in which each member adds three or four ideas to a pile and then offers comments on others' ideas. Afterward, members respond to comments made about their ideas and generate a master list of ideas worthy of consideration.

Groups Can Ideawrite A third method groups can use to generate ideas is ideawriting.[9] **Ideawriting** encourages members to generate and evaluate ideas in writing while working independently.

Like brainstorming and NGT, ideawriting starts with the description of a specific question to be answered or problem to be solved. The ideawriting process then proceeds in four steps. In the first step, each member creates a list of three to four ideas including the reasons why each idea has merit. Members put their individual lists in a pile. In the second step, each member chooses a list from the pile that is not his or hers. Working alone, members read all the ideas and reasons shown on the list they select and add their own comments about the strengths and weaknesses of each idea. When they're done, they return the list to the pile, select another list, and do the same. The second step continues until every member has read and commented on every other member's ideas.

In the third step, members retrieve the list of ideas they originally created, which now contains written comments from everyone else in the group. Each member reads and responds in writing to the comments made about his or her ideas, which allows everyone to react to feedback and potential criticism of their ideas in a nonthreatening way. Finally, in the fourth step, group members come together to create a master list of ideas they think are worthy of additional discussion. They then work toward selecting the best idea, as they would in brainstorming and NGT.

Of the three idea-generation methods we've surveyed, ideawriting is the least collaborative, because group members accomplish most of the steps individually rather than as a group. The major advantage of ideawriting is that it allows each member to offer ideas, respond to others' ideas, and react to criticisms of his or her own ideas in a private manner.[10] Privacy can help to shield group members from the feelings of resentment or defensiveness that might arise in a public process.

Having used a technique such as brainstorming, NGT, or ideawriting to generate ideas, groups usually must choose the best idea from among the various options. That process requires them to use a decision-making method, our next point of focus.

SHARPEN Your Skills: *Brainstorming*

With a small group of students from your class, spend 15 minutes brainstorming to generate a list of actions you could take to address a social problem in your community. First, identify the problem you want to address—such as homelessness, unequal access to health care, hunger, inadequate child care, or low adult literacy. Next, follow the principles of brainstorming to list various actions your group could take to improve the lives of those affected. Afterward, spend a few minutes discussing what you found most enjoyable and most challenging about brainstorming. Present your final list of ideas to the rest of the class as a way to encourage community involvement.

GROUPS MAKE DECISIONS IN MANY WAYS

To illustrate the various methods by which groups can make decisions, let's imagine you're an employee of Star Bank. You are assigned to a team charged with choosing a marketing slogan for the bank's new account options, which were designed to meet the needs of senior citizens. Your team has generated several ideas for slogans and has narrowed the list to three:

- *Star Bank: Where Seniors Reach for the Stars*
- *Star Bank: The Right Choice for Your Active Lifestyle*
- *Protect Your Golden Years with Star Bank*

Your team must select one slogan from this list. Let's examine five methods by which the team members might arrive at their decision: consensus, majority rule, minority rule, expert opinion, and authority rule.

Some Groups Decide by Unanimous Consensus One option for making a decision is to try to get everyone to agree about which slogan is best. Once you begin discussion, for instance, you might find that all the members of your team prefer the first marketing slogan to the other two. If everyone in the group prefers the same slogan, then the group has **unanimous consensus,** which is uncontested support for a decision. In some instances, unanimous consensus is the only option for group decision making. A jury hearing a criminal case, for example, must arrive at a unanimous verdict about the defendant's innocence or guilt. Verdicts on which not all jurors agree are considered invalid. Even if it isn't required, however, unanimous consensus can be advantageous because group members are likely to support more enthusiastically a decision on which they all agree.

Achieving unanimous consensus isn't always easy, though. Particularly if the decision is controversial, group members may vary dramatically in the outcomes they prefer. In that case, arriving at a decision may require the group to engage in long, often frustrating discussions. Even so, such discussions may end in a **stalemate,** an outcome where members' opinions are so sharply divided that unanimity is impossible to achieve. In the event of a stalemate, a group may have to resort to one of the other forms of decision making *if* it has the option of doing so.

When trying to decide by unanimous consensus, groups must also be careful not to achieve **false consensus,** which occurs when some members say they support the decision even though they do not. These members may feel pressure to support the majority's wishes so unanimity can be reached, but the resulting false consensus reduces the chance that everyone will be enthusiastic about the decision. Groups often discover false consensus after the fact, when members who felt pressured to vote with the majority begin voicing their concerns about the decision. The likelihood of false consensus is diminished if group members feel safe expressing their opinions, even those that contradict the views of their fellow members.

Some Groups Decide by Majority Rule Instead of choosing a marketing slogan by unanimous consensus, your team might reach its decision by **majority rule,** a decision-making process that follows the will of the majority. If someone says, "Let's take a vote" when a group decision is looming, he or she is probably recommending majority rule. To select among your marketing slogans, therefore, each member of your team might cast a vote for one of the slogans. The slogan receiving the fewest votes will be discarded, and each member will then vote for one of the remaining two. The slogan that now receives more votes has been chosen by majority rule.

Majority rule operates on the democratic principle that decisions should reflect what most people want, not what a smaller number of more powerful people prefer. The primary advantage of majority rule is that, by definition, it ensures that most people in the group support the decision being made. People raised in democratic societies are used to majority rule as a form of decision making, and under most circumstances, they accept that the will of the majority should be followed even if they themselves voted with the minority.

When a vote is particularly close, however, the minority can feel the decision was arbitrary. For instance, if one marketing slogan received eight votes from your team and the other received seven, those who favored the second slogan might feel the decision was unfair because the margin of victory was so small. They may then be less inclined to support the team's decision than if the winning slogan had won by more votes. When using majority rule to make decisions on controversial issues, everyone in the group should remember the importance of supporting the majority decision, whatever it is.

Majority rule can be problematic in groups that have an even number of members, because of the possibility of a tied vote. If each marketing slogan wins 50 percent of

• **unanimous consensus** Uncontested support for a decision—sometimes the only option in a group's decision-making process.

• **stalemate** An outcome where members' opinions are so sharply divided that consensus is impossible to achieve.

• **false consensus** An outcome where some members of a group say they support the unanimous decision even though they do not.

• **majority rule** A decision-making process that follows the will of the majority.

the vote, neither has received a majority. Whenever an even number of votes will be cast, groups should determine ahead of time what procedures to follow in the event of a tie. For example, perhaps the leader will cast a vote only if it is necessary to break a tie. To prevent the possibility of a tied vote, some groups—including the U.S. Supreme Court—decide ahead of time to have an odd number of members.

Some Groups Decide by Minority Rule

A third form of decision making is **minority rule,** a process in which a small number of members makes a decision on behalf of the group. Decision makers often use minority rule for the sake of efficiency.

Let's say your Star Bank team wants to host a reception to unveil its new marketing slogan. Instead of having the entire team discuss where and when to hold the event, the leader might delegate that responsibility to two or three team members. Those members then have the ability to make decisions about the reception on the team's behalf. The minority rule strategy saves the team's time for discussing more important decisions, such as which marketing slogan to adopt.

By definition, minority rule excludes the input of most members of the group. For that reason, it is rarely a good option for making decisions that are controversial or consequential.

Some Groups Decide by Expert Opinion

Some groups include people whose training or experience makes them experts on the type of decision the groups are making. Such groups may reach their decisions by deferring to **expert opinion,** or the recommendations of individuals with expertise in a particular area. Let's assume your Star Bank team includes someone with a master's degree in marketing. Because of that person's expertise, your team might ask his or her advice on which marketing slogan to adopt, instead of taking a vote or trying to achieve unanimous consensus.

Expert opinion works on the principle that certain people have better judgment or more informed opinions on specific topics that enable them to make better decisions than nonexperts. Bear in mind, however, that expertise is always specific to particular topics or matters. No one is an expert on everything. If the group is going to rely on expert opinion, members should make certain they're listening to someone with appropriate expertise.

Some Groups Decide by Authority Rule

Suppose that instead of building unanimous consensus, taking a vote, assigning the decision to a minority, or consulting an expert, your team at Star Bank leaves the choice of a slogan to the team leader. That approach is an example of **authority rule,** a process by which the leader of the group makes the decisions. Authority rule is a common method of decision making in some groups. In a class or workshop, for instance, a teacher usually makes decisions about the group's activities, and others adapt to those decisions. In a group of firefighters responding to a blaze, the senior commander makes the decisions and issues the orders.

Authority rule is best when someone in the group has legitimate authority over other members. Teachers and fire commanders make decisions on behalf of their groups because it's their responsibility and their prerogative to do so. Authority rule is also very efficient. If firefighters had to meet to consider and vote on all possible approaches to dealing with an emergency, lives would be lost in the time their discussions took. If the commander makes the decisions, however, the group can act more quickly, and this consideration is critical when time is short.[11]

Authority rule can be problematic, however, when exercised in groups that have no legitimate authority figure. If someone on your work team were to say "I've decided we should choose the second slogan," the other members would likely resent that person's attempt to exercise authority over the team. When no one in the group is a legitimate authority figure, other methods of decision making are likely to be more effective.

- **minority rule** A decision-making process in which a small number of members makes a decision on behalf of the group.

- **expert opinion** Recommendations of individuals who have expertise in a particular area that are sometimes the basis of a group's decision-making process.

- **authority rule** A decision-making process in which the leader of the group makes the decisions.

Authority rule is best if one person has the experience and responsibility to make decisions for everyone else in the group.

The Choice of Method Depends on Various Factors The method of making decisions that is best depends on several factors that vary from decision to decision. One factor is the importance of the decision itself. Relatively unimportant decisions may be best made by authority or minority rule because those methods are efficient. More important decisions—those that will affect many people or require a great deal of money to implement—might be better made by unanimous consensus, majority rule, or expert opinion, because those methods often entail a closer, more critical consideration of the options.

A second factor in determining the right decision-making method is whether the decision requires expert knowledge. Expert opinion is often the most effective method of making decisions that require specialized knowledge not shared by everyone in the group. Authority rule can also be effective in such situations if the leader has authority *because of his or her expertise*, as, for example, a fire commander usually does.

A third factor influencing the choice of decision-making method is how quickly the decision must be made. Authority rule is often the fastest way of making decisions, whereas building unanimous consensus is frequently the most time-intensive. When selecting its method of decision making, a group might consider the time constraints on the decision.

CULTURAL CONTEXT AFFECTS DECISION MAKING

Diversity in the cultural and social characteristics of its members also can influence the decision-making method a group prefers. These characteristics include individualism, power distance, and time orientation. We examined them in Chapter 2; now let's see how they can affect group decision making.

Individualism Affects Decision Making People in individualistic cultures are taught that their primary responsibility is to themselves. Competition, self-reliance, and individual achievement are valued in highly individualistic cultures. In contrast, people in collectivistic cultures believe their primary responsibility is to their families, their communities, and their employers. Collectivistic cultures value collaboration, harmony, and solidarity rather than competition and individual achievement.

Whether a group hails from an individualistic or a collectivistic culture can influence how that group makes decisions. Groups in collectivistic cultures, for instance, may place great emphasis on reaching group consensus. Because collectivistic cultures stress collaboration, group members value what's best for the group, even if that means having to compromise on their individual preferences. In contrast, groups in individualistic cultures are more likely to encourage members to voice their opinions on decisions, even if those opinions differ. Because individualistic cultures emphasize competition, group members may be less interested in reaching consensus than in persuading others to agree with their position.

Power Distance Affects Decision Making Recall that cultures vary in how they expect power to be distributed within a society. In high-power-distance cultures, certain groups of people have great power and the average citizen has much less. In low-power-distance cultures, people value equality and believe no one person or group should have excessive power over others.

A culture's power distance can influence how groups within that culture arrive at decisions. Groups in high-power-distance cultures may be particularly deferential to authority, for instance. Consequently, they may prefer to make decisions by authority rule or by following expert opinion. In contrast, groups in low-power-distance cultures are more likely to prefer majority rule as a decision-making method, given that majority rule treats everyone's vote as equal to everyone else's.

Time Orientation Affects Decision Making Cultures differ with respect to their norms and expectations concerning the use of time. Monochronic cultures view time as a tangible commodity. As a result, people in monochronic cultures enjoy "saving" time and try to avoid "wasting" it. In contrast, polychronic cultures conceive of time as more fluid. People don't prioritize efficiency and punctuality to the same extent that people do in monochronic cultures. Instead, they attach greater value to the quality of their lives and their relationships with others.

A group's preferred decision-making method may depend on whether its culture is monochronic or polychronic. Groups from monochronic cultures may opt for majority rule, minority rule, or authority rule because those methods often use time efficiently. However, groups from polychronic cultures, which have less incentive to make decisions quickly, may be more likely to try achieving unanimous consensus if they believe that method will produce a better decision.

In summary, groups have many options for making decisions. Individualism, power distance, and time orientation can each influence the decision-making methods a group *prefers*, but they do not necessarily determine the methods that group will *use*. As we've seen, a group's method of decision making is also affected by the nature of the decision to be made. Nonetheless, cultural influences can be powerful, shaping not only how groups make decisions but also how satisfied they are with them.

Being a Leader

Mary Ellen Diaz knows about effective leadership. A world-class chef who trained at the famed Le Cordon Bleu in Paris, Diaz has worked in exclusive restaurants, including at the Ritz-Carlton hotel in Chicago. Although she prepared gourmet meals for her restaurants' clients, she felt personally drawn to the cause of providing food for the hungry. She didn't want to feed people leftover scraps or second-rate food but the same high-quality meals she prepared in Chicago's restaurants. With a small group of staff members, Diaz founded First Slice, an organization that distributes fresh, expertly prepared food to the needy. Because of her leadership and the decisions her group has made, First Slice delivers more than 1,400 meals each month to the hungry, homeless, and disenfranchised in Chicago.

With effective leadership and constructive decision-making techniques, groups of people can achieve great things. What does it mean to be a leader, however? In this section, we'll examine the characteristics and behaviors of effective leaders, and we'll discover that leaders enact distinct leadership styles.

LEADERS OFTEN SHARE SPECIFIC TRAITS

• traits Defining characteristics of a person that are often relatively enduring and not easily changeable.

One way to understand leadership is to look at some common traits of leaders. **Traits** are distinguishing personal characteristics that are often relatively enduring and not easily changeable. Each of us has certain physical traits, such as our eye color, sex, and height. We also have psychosocial traits, such as our self-esteem, temperament, and level of anxiety when faced with a communication task. Physical traits tend to be more enduring than psychosocial traits.

None of these traits, however, necessarily determines who's going to be a good leader and who isn't. Rather, most of us can learn to be an effective leader no matter what physical and psychosocial traits we possess. In fact, sometimes the responsibilities of leadership are assigned to us whether or not we want them. Still, researchers have discovered that leaders often share particular traits, as we'll now consider.

Physical Traits The body's attributes are referred to as its **physical traits.** Three physical traits in particular can influence who is likely to become leaders and how effective they are perceived to be.

One such trait is sex. Some studies have reported that people perceive women less favorably than men as potential leaders and that they evaluate the work of female leaders less positively than the work of male leaders.[12] These findings don't mean that men actually *are* more effective leaders, only that they are sometimes perceived to be. Other research has found that people in groups express more negative nonverbal reactions, such as facial expressions and gestures, toward female leaders than male leaders,[13] particularly when female leaders enact stereotypically masculine behaviors such as dominance and aggression.[14] Other studies have not found that difference.[15] Although people may respond to male and female leaders differently, they appear to judge female and male leaders as being equally competent.[16]

A second physical trait that can affect leadership is height.[17] In Western cultures, people often associate height with dominance, competence, and power.[18] It therefore may not surprise you to learn that taller people are more likely than shorter people to be nominated or elected to leadership positions.[19] For example, 29 of the 44 U.S. presidents have been taller than the average U.S. adult man, and since 1990, the taller candidate for president has won the popular vote 66 percent of the time.[20] Perhaps because the average adult man is taller than the average adult woman, however, height is a stronger predictor of leadership success for men than it is for women.[21]

Finally, physical appearance influences leadership. Studies have shown, for instance, that leaders with masculine-looking faces are judged as more competent than are leaders with feminine-looking faces.[22] Masculine faces typically feature a wide, square jaw and small eyes, whereas feminine faces feature large eyes and a small, rounded jaw. Researchers speculate that people associate masculine faces with competent leadership because they think of men as being more dominant and powerful than women.[23]

Regardless of whether they appear masculine or feminine, however, leaders are more likely to be physically attractive than unattractive.[24] As you might know from your own experience, people associate physical attractiveness with a range of positive qualities, including intelligence, honesty, and competence. It should therefore come as no surprise that physically attractive people are *perceived* to be better leaders than less attractive individuals.

It's worth repeating that although sex, height, and physical appearance are *related to* leadership, none of those traits determines who will be a good leader and who will not. Leadership is a skill you can develop and nurture over time, regardless of your physical traits.

Psychosocial Traits Many effective leaders share particular **psychosocial traits,** which are characteristics of their personality and ways of relating to others. Much of the research has focused on three particular traits: self-esteem, self-monitoring, and outgoingness.

Recall from Chapter 3 that self-esteem is a person's subjective evaluation of his or her value and worth. Because having self-esteem gives us confidence in ourselves, it seems likely that people are better leaders if their self-esteem is higher rather than lower. In line with that idea, research tells us that people with high self-esteem rate themselves as better leaders than do those with low self-esteem.[25] Surprisingly, though, a leader's self-esteem doesn't predict how *other people* rate his or her leadership abilities.[26] Although having high self-esteem improves how leaders perceive themselves, it doesn't improve how others perceive them.

• **physical traits** The body's physical attributes.

• **psychosocial traits** Characteristics of one's personality and ways of relating to others.

Your Self-Monitoring— High, Low, or No?

Self-monitoring is your awareness of your behaviors and their effects on others. How high a self-monitor are you? Read each of the following statements and indicate whether you think it is true or false with respect to yourself. There are no right or wrong answers. Simply respond to each statement in whatever way seems to best represent you.

	True	False
I find it easy to imitate the behavior of other people.	____	____
I can argue in favor of ideas even if I don't believe in them.	____	____
I guess I put on a show to impress or entertain people.	____	____
When I am uncertain how to act in a social situation, I look to the behavior of others for cues.	____	____
I would probably make a good actor.	____	____
I laugh more when I watch a comedy with others than by myself.	____	____
In groups of people, I am often the center of attention.	____	____
I often act differently in different situations or when I'm around different people.	____	____
I'm good at making other people like me.	____	____
I rarely feel awkward in social settings.	____	____

When you're finished, add up the number of statements you marked as true. If your total was 7 or above, you are a high self-monitor. You are highly aware of your own behavior and of how other people perceive you. If your total was between 4 and 6, you are a moderate self-monitor. You're aware of yourself and your effect on others, but not to a substantial degree. If your total was 3 or lower, you are a low self-monitor. You tend not to direct your attention to your own behavior or to your interactions with others.

SOURCE: Items adapted from Snyder, M. (1974). Self-monitoring of expressive behavior. *Journal of Personality and Social Psychology, 30*, 526–537.

A second psychosocial trait that has been studied with reference to leadership is self-monitoring. Recall that self-monitoring is our awareness of our own behavior and its effects on others. Some researchers have suggested that people who are high self-monitors are able to perceive the needs of others in a group and adapt their own behavior to meet those needs. In line with that idea, several studies have found that self-monitoring is strongly related to leadership emergence in groups.[27] Curiously, some research has shown that self-monitoring predicts leadership only for men,[28] but most research indicates that both female and male leaders are likely to be high self-monitors. How high a self-monitor are you? Take the quiz in "The Competent Communicator" to find out.

Finally, several studies have indicated that leaders are more likely to be outgoing and expressive rather than shy and withdrawn. One project examined the findings of 73 different studies and found that people are more apt to become leaders—and more apt to be *effective* leaders—if they are extroverted rather than introverted.[29] **Extroversion** is a personality trait shared by people who are friendly, assertive, and outgoing with others. Leadership is inherently social, so extroverts tend to excel at leadership because they are comfortable interacting socially with others. In contrast, **introversion** characterizes people who are shy, reserved, and aloof. Because of their more reserved nature, introverts often experience **communication apprehension,** anxiety or fear about communicating with others. Apprehensive communicators often have difficulty leading. One study found that people who scored high on a test of communication apprehension perceived themselves—and were perceived by others—as less likely to be good leaders than were people who scored low on communication apprehension.[30]

Just as not every effective leader is male, tall, and physically attractive, not every effective leader scores high on self-esteem, self-monitoring, and extroversion. Examining traits that many leaders share tells us only part of the story about effective leadership. To understand leadership more fully, we must look not only at *who leaders are* but also at *how leaders behave*, our next topic.

LEADERS ENACT DISTINCT STYLES

Think about the leaders of groups to which you've belonged. How would you describe their leadership styles? Regardless of his or her physical or psychosocial traits, chances are each leader had a specific way of enacting leadership responsibilities. Many years ago, a team of social psychologists determined that most leaders enact one of three distinct styles in the way they lead others—democratic, autocratic, and laissez-faire. Let's take a quick look at each.

Some Leaders Are Democratic
One of the underlying principles of a democracy is that every citizen has the right to participate in decision making. Group leaders who enact a **democratic style** reflect that principle in their leadership.[31]

Let's say Taylor chairs the committee overseeing the adult literacy outreach program at her community center. When the committee needs to generate ideas about how to raise community awareness, Taylor strives to get everyone's input. She cultivates a nonjudgmental environment in which committee members feel free to express their ideas. She makes sure the committee considers every opinion, even ideas that may conflict with her own views. When it's time for the committee to make a decision, she counts everyone's vote equally, and she supports the will of the majority even if it doesn't reflect her own preferences. As a leader with a democratic style, Taylor sees herself as a facilitator for the group's mission.

Some Leaders Are Autocratic
As the organizer of his calculus study group, Adya believes it's his responsibility to make decisions on behalf of his group. He sets the schedule for group meetings and decides where each one will be held. Whenever the group gets together, Adya takes charge and controls how the study session proceeds. Adya is enacting an **autocratic style** of leadership.[32] That is, he sees himself as having both the authority and the responsibility to take action on his group's behalf. When decisions need to be made, he makes them, usually without asking others in the group what they want. When tasks need to be done, he assigns them to individuals in the group instead of soliciting volunteers. Unlike Taylor, Adya considers himself to be the most important member of his group.

Most U.S. presidents—including Bill Clinton and George W. Bush—have been taller than the average U.S. man.

• **extroversion** A personality trait shared by people who are friendly, assertive, and outgoing with others.

• **introversion** A personality trait shared by people who are shy, reserved, and aloof.

• **communication apprehension** Anxiety or fear about communicating with others.

• **democratic style** A leadership style in which every member of a group has the right to participate in decision making.

• **autocratic style** A leadership style in which leaders see themselves as having both the authority and the responsibility to take action on a group's behalf.

Some Leaders Are Laissez-Faire

Meghan has just been promoted to lieutenant in charge of eight patrol officers in her police precinct. Her philosophy is that patrol officers should work independently, with little direction or personal involvement from her. She rarely interacts with her officers, and she gives them little feedback on their job performance. When she is forced to oversee decisions or mediate conflicts, she involves herself only as long as is necessary. Afterward, she resumes her general lack of engagement in the operations of her division. All these characteristics reflect Meghan's **laissez-faire style** of leadership.[33] It's not that she doesn't care about her patrol officers; she simply thinks they function at their best with minimal supervision. Thus, unlike Taylor and Adya, Meghan often sees herself as the person who is least important to the success of her group.

• **laissez-faire style** A leadership style in which leaders offer minimal supervision.

Each Leadership Style Has Its Strengths

Which type of leader—democratic, autocratic, or laissez-faire—would you prefer? If you were raised in a country with a democratic style of government, such as the United States, you might be inclined to say democratic leaders are best because they value everyone's input equally. You might also like laissez-faire leaders because they allow you to work autonomously. If you value equality and autonomy, you might say that autocratic leaders are least preferable because they give you neither equality nor autonomy.

Preferences aside, each style of leadership is best under certain circumstances. When it's important that everyone in a group believes that he or she has an equal voice in decision making, the democratic style of leadership is the most likely to accomplish that goal.[34] Even if everyone doesn't agree with the group's decision, the democratic style helps ensure that no one feels neglected or unimportant.

If the group's priority is to accomplish its tasks quickly, however, the autocratic style is best because only one person needs to make the decisions. The autocratic style is also the most effective when the leader has knowledge or expertise that the group members at large lack. If a senior physician is leading a group of interns in a complicated surgery, for instance, it's best for everyone if the physician takes charge and gives orders rather than taking a vote about how to proceed with the surgery, because the surgeon's experience confers knowledge the interns don't yet have.

In groups composed of people who are proficient at working on their own, the laissez-faire style can be best because it provides group members with the greatest autonomy to do their work. Although most leaders need to provide some level of oversight, a laissez-faire leader lets his or her group members work independently, giving direction only when absolutely necessary. That approach backfires when group members lack the skills or training to work autonomously, but it can be very effective when group members are proficient at working on their own.

SHARPEN Your Skills: *Leadership styles*

In a small group, discuss and identify the primary leadership styles of several leaders with whom you're familiar, such as the U.S. President, the governor of your state, the mayor of your city, the president of your college, and your student body president. Identify the behaviors and characteristics that lead you to make each assessment. Afterward, compare your assessments with those of other groups in your class.

@getCONNECTED
Leadership in Online Groups

Many people take part in online groups, such as support groups and ongoing discussion boards. What does it take to be a successful group leader on the Internet? To find out, media scholar David Huffaker analyzed 632,622 messages from 33,450 participants across 16 Google Groups over a 2-year period.[35] He wanted to find out how leaders communicated in influential ways in online settings. His analyses showed that influential leaders communicate more often than other group members and with greater diversity in the types of words they use. He also found that leaders used more assertive and more emotional language than other members and that they communicate with a broader range of people. By adopting those communication patterns, leaders in online groups influence other group members just as leaders in face-to-face groups.

Exercising Power

Regardless of which styles of leadership they enact, leaders rely on the exercise of power to achieve their goals. **Power** is the ability to influence or control people or events.[36] Being an effective leader requires having some form of power.

• **power** The ability to influence or control people or events.

People exercise influence or control over others in many ways. In this section, we explore the various forms of power that leaders can possess. We will observe that power resides not in leaders themselves but in their relationships with the people they lead.

LEADERS EXERCISE MANY FORMS OF POWER

Exercising power over people may seem relatively straightforward: A leader tells people what to do and they do it. The important question, however, is *why* they do it. Some people might follow instructions because they are being paid to do so. Others might follow along because they want to please the leader or because they fear the consequences of disobeying.

In their now classic studies, social psychologists John French and Bertram Raven determined that the reason *why* a leader is followed constitutes the form of power that leader has. French and Raven proposed that power comes in six specific forms: reward, coercive, referent, legitimate, expert, and informational.[37] As we take a close look at these forms, keep in mind that they aren't mutually exclusive. Rather, one person may exercise multiple forms of power in different situations or even within the same situation.

Leaders Exercise Reward Power As its name implies, **reward power** operates when a leader has the ability to reward another for doing what the leader says. The supervisor of your work team has power over you, for instance, because she pays you and can promote you for following her instructions. In this case, your pay and the possibility of advancement are the rewards. If your supervisor loses the ability to pay or promote you (say, if your company goes bankrupt or she leaves her job), she also loses her power over you.

• **reward power** A form of power based on the leader's ability to reward another for doing what the leader says.

Leaders can exercise many different forms of power over others.

Having reward power requires you not only to provide a reward to those who follow your instructions but to provide a *sufficient* reward. People who feel they are not rewarded adequately for following someone are likely to eventually stop. When employees perceive that they are not receiving fair wages in exchange for their work, for instance, their willingness to follow the company leadership decreases.[38]

Leaders Exercise Coercive Power The opposite of reward power is **coercive power,** or power that comes from the ability to punish. When you go to court, for example, the judge has power over you because he or she can punish you with fines or imprisonment for not doing what you must. Throughout history, dictators have exercised coercive power over their populations by ordering imprisonment or even death for those who don't follow their orders.

Just as reward power requires the ability to provide a *sufficient* reward, coercive power requires the ability to issue a *sufficient* punishment. For instance, most of us would follow the directions of a university administrator who had the power to expel us. If the worst punishment that administrator could dole out were a memo of reprimand that would get buried in some file drawer, however, we might feel less obligated to follow his or her directions.

Although exercising coercive power can be an effective way of achieving our goals, it entails certain disadvantages. One study, for example, found that the more often a manufacturing company exercised coercive power over its dealers, the fewer other forms of power the dealers perceived it to have.[39] So the company's ability to control its dealers through those other forms was diminished. As "The Dark Side of Communication" explains, excessive use of coercive power can also constitute emotional abuse.

Leaders Exercise Referent Power French and Raven used the term **referent power** to refer to the power of attraction, the idea being that we tend to comply with requests made by people we like, admire, or find attractive in some way. It's human nature to desire their approval. In contrast, gaining the approval of people we don't like or admire is usually not a high priority. In a volunteer group, for instance, you might work harder for a group leader you like than for one you dislike.

In a similar vein, many of us are persuaded to buy products or services endorsed by celebrities we like or find attractive.[40] Because we usually don't know the celebrities personally, we aren't trying to gain their approval when we follow their recommendations. Instead, we are trying to *be* like them. Researchers have shown that we have a strong tendency to emulate—or act like—people we find attractive.[41] Therefore, when a handsome singer or a glamorous actress endorses a particular brand of shampoo, protein bar, or cable TV service, we are often persuaded to buy those brands from our desire to be like that individual.

Leaders Exercise Legitimate Power People exercise **legitimate power** when their status or position gives them the right to make requests with which others must comply. When the president of the United States meets with the Cabinet, for instance, members of that group follow the president's directives because the president is in a position of legitimate authority.

Because legitimate power is granted by people's status or position, it is no longer effective when they lose their status or leave their position. Suppose you have been promoted to interim department head at your company to fill in for someone who is on maternity leave. During the time you fill that position, you have legitimate power to issue instructions, make purchasing decisions, conduct employee evaluations, and hire and fire at your discretion. Each of those abilities is a legitimate exercise of the position you hold. When the permanent department head returns from maternity leave, however, you will return to your previous position. At

• coercive power A form of power that comes from the ability to punish.

• referent power A form of power that derives from attraction to the leader.

• legitimate power A form of power in which leaders' status or position gives them the right to make requests with which others must comply.

We tend to comply with requests made by people we like, admire, or find attractive. That type of power is known as referent power.

THE DARK SIDE OF COMMUNICATION

When Coercion Becomes Abuse

Any form of power can be put to positive or negative uses. Coercive power is a positive force if it encourages people to act in their best interests, as when a parent threatens to withhold cell phone privileges if her teenage son breaks curfew. However, those who are threatened with excessive consequences—especially when they are encouraged to act contrary to their best interests—are often the victims of emotional abuse. In 2012, for instance, Sheriff Paul Babeu of Arizona's Pinal County was

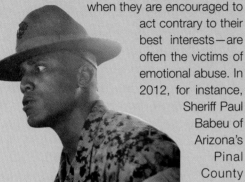

sued by his former boyfriend—Mexican immigrant Jose Orozco—after Orozco claimed that Babeu threatened to have him deported if he publicly revealed the sheriff's sexuality.[38] In that and similar cases, someone in a leadership position induces extreme fear to elicit the behaviors he or she desires from others. The exercise of coercive power can intimidate or even terrorize the victim and thus constitutes emotional abuse.

Sustained emotional abuse often has many negative effects on its victims, including severe anxiety and depression, low self-esteem, diminished physical health, and even heightened risk of suicide. Like many other forms of abuse, it is most commonly perpetrated on the most vulnerable people in a society, such as the poor, the disabled, the elderly, women, children, and minorities. To help someone you suspect of being victimized by excessive coercion, identify sources of aid, such as a company's human resources office and a county abuse hotline.

SOURCE: National Clearinghouse on Family Violence Information

that point, you will no longer have the powers you exercised as the interim department head because you will no longer have legitimate claim to them.

Leaders Exercise Expert Power The fifth form of power on French and Raven's list is **expert power,** power that stems from having expertise in a particular area. In a chamber orchestra, for instance, the musicians follow the instructions of the conductor because he or she has the musical expertise to make the orchestra sound as good as possible. In many cases, we perceive that it is in our best interests to comply with the directions of experts, because their experience or training gives them specialized knowledge we lack.

It can be tricky to identify exactly what constitutes expertise. For the most part, we recognize expertise through agreement: A person is an expert if the right people consider him or her to be so. For instance, a physician is considered a medical expert because he or she graduated from medical school, completed a residency, and was certified to practice medicine by other medical professionals. That individual's doctoral degree and medical license indicate a consensus about his or her qualifications as an expert. Other people may have the same level of medical knowledge as the doctor but may not exercise expert power because their expertise is not formally recognized. Later in this section, we will further discuss the importance of recognizing power.

Leaders Exercise Informational Power A final form of power is **informational power,** power that stems from the ability to control access to information. Many socialist and communist governments exercise informational power over their populations, for example, by controlling all the media in their countries. Citizens in

• **expert power** A form of power that stems from having expertise in a particular area.

• **informational power** A form of power that stems from the ability to control access to information.

those societies are exposed only to news their governments want them to know, and thus they become dependent on their government leaders for information.

A similar situation can occur in smaller groups if one person has news or information that others want. This person has power over the others until he or she releases the information. Informational power is usually greatest when the information is valuable and cannot be obtained elsewhere.

Table 10.1 summarizes the six forms of power leaders can exercise.

POWER RESIDES IN RELATIONSHIPS, NOT IN PEOPLE

As we saw in the last section, people wield many forms of power in many different situations. Because some people seem to have more power than others, we might think of them as being *powerful people*, as though their power resides within them. In truth, however, power doesn't exist within people—it exists within relationships. As we'll see in this section, we have power only over particular people and only when our power is recognized. In other words, power is an inherently social experience.

Power Is Relative One characteristic of power is that it is *relative*, meaning that people have power only *in relation to* other people. No person has absolute power. Regardless of what forms of power we possess, each of us exercises power only over particular people in particular situations. Your manager may have some power over you, but that doesn't mean she also has power over your friends and neighbors. She is powerful only relative to the people who work for her.

We often acknowledge the relative nature of power when people overstep their boundaries by attempting to exert power they don't have, as when a child rejects direction from an older sibling with the response "You're not the boss of me!" Similarly, adults may feel defensive when they receive direction from people who have no reward, coercive, referent, legitimate, expert, or informational power over them.[42]

Power Requires Recognition In groups and organizations, powerful people have only the power their followers recognize in them. A charismatic religious leader may exercise referent power over her followers, but she does not have that power over others who don't share her followers' desire to please her and gain her approval.

SHARPEN Your Skills: *Applying referent power*

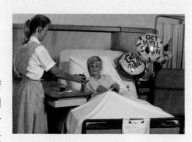

Suppose you supervise a group of high school volunteers at a local children's hospital. One of your responsibilities is to ensure that they clock in and out properly when they start and end their shifts. With another student, brainstorm ways you could use referent power to influence the volunteers' behavior. Offer your ideas in a journal entry or short presentation to your class.

TABLE 10.1 FORMS OF POWER	According to French and Raven, leaders exercise six forms of power in their relationships with others.
	1 Reward Power based on the ability to reward for compliance
	2 Coercive Power based on the ability to punish for noncompliance
	3 Referent Power based on liking, admiring, and being attracted to the leader
	4 Legitimate Power based on rightfully granted status or position
	5 Expert Power based on knowledge, training, experience, and/or expertise
	6 Informational Power based on access to valued information

The Scene: You've been placed in charge of organizing a group of volunteers for a hospital fund-raising drive. You must get some volunteers to agree to go door to door asking for donations and others to staff a 24-hour telephone pledge line. Because most of the volunteers are full-time students or working adults, you know this is asking a lot.

Your Task: Consider how you can adapt your communication behavior to exercise appropriate forms of power in this context. How could you construct your requests in this situation to

- Invoke legitimate power?
- Appeal to referent power?
- Exercise reward power?

Recognizing that someone has power does not necessarily mean we give our consent to be governed. If a police officer stops you while you're driving, for instance, you would likely recognize the power he has over you even if you don't want to be subject to that power. In other words, we don't always enjoy having others tell us what to do, even though we may still recognize their right to do so. We can therefore say that a person can have power over others only if others recognize that power.

We've seen that leaders can exercise many different forms of power, that all power is relative, and that power requires recognition. To end this section, let's also acknowledge that power itself is neither positive nor negative. Rather, it's the way we *use* power that makes it good or bad. When we abuse the power we have over others or exercise it unwisely, we can cause harm and heartache; in such instances, we may not hold on to power for long. As former U.S. senator Elizabeth Dole observed, however: "Power is a positive force if it is used for positive purposes." Using power in a positive way can improve the lives of those who follow us.

Many of us resent illegitimate attempts to exert power over us.

Leadership and Decision-Making Skills

Effective leadership and decision making are not always easy to achieve or sustain. Many factors can inhibit the ability of leaders and groups to function at their best. The more we understand about leadership and decision-making skills, the better equipped we are to contribute positively to the groups to which we belong. As we'll see in this section, three particular skills that are useful for groups and their leaders are their ability to

- Manage conflict constructively
- Avoid groupthink
- Listen carefully

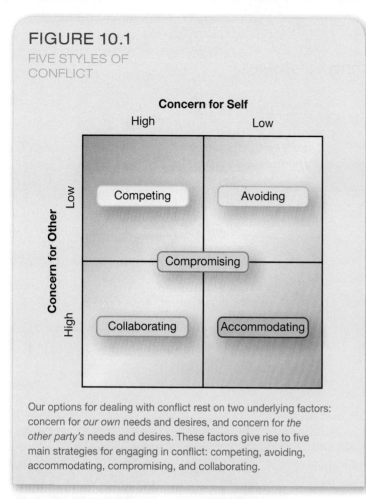

FIGURE 10.1
FIVE STYLES OF CONFLICT

Concern for Self

High | Low

Low

| Competing | Avoiding |

Compromising

High

| Collaborating | Accommodating |

Concern for Other

Our options for dealing with conflict rest on two underlying factors: concern for *our own* needs and desires, and concern for *the other party's* needs and desires. These factors give rise to five main strategies for engaging in conflict: competing, avoiding, accommodating, compromising, and collaborating.

SOURCE: Adapted from Blake, R. R., & Mouton, J. S. (1984). *The managerial grid III* (3rd ed.). Houston: Gulf.

MANAGE CONFLICT CONSTRUCTIVELY

Because the members of a group are interdependent, they are bound to experience conflict from time to time. Recall that conflict occurs when two or more interdependent parties enact a struggle over goals they perceive to be incompatible. Especially when groups are faced with making decisions, conflict can arise because of perceived differences in the goals of individual members. Conflict is not necessarily problematic. In fact, it can motivate groups to make more creative decisions than they otherwise might. What matters is the way groups manage conflict when it arises.

According to researchers Robert Blake and Jane Mouton, our options for dealing with conflict are based on two underlying dimensions: our concern for our own needs and desires, and our concern for the other party's needs and desires.[43] When plotted on a graph (Figure 10.1), these dimensions give rise to five major strategies for engaging in conflict: competing, avoiding, accommodating, compromising, and collaborating. These strategies are behaviors rather than personality types, so we can learn to use any of them. Some may seem more appropriate or more desirable than others. As we examine them, however, consider that each may be best under certain circumstances.

Competing The *competing* style represents a high concern for our own needs and desires and a low concern for those of the other party. The goal is to win the conflict while the other party loses. Engaging in conflict in this style is much like playing football. There are no tied games—rather, one team's win is the other team's loss.

Competing might be appropriate when there is a concrete outcome that cannot be shared, such as when two people are vying to become a committee chair. People may also see ongoing competition as a positive aspect of their relationship if it motivates each to perform at his or her best.[44] The competing style of managing conflict becomes problematic, however, when it leads to resentment or a desire to get even with people who win.[45]

Avoiding A very different approach to conflict is the *avoiding* style, which demonstrates low concern for both the self and the other party. Adopting this style means ignoring the conflict and hoping it will go away on its own. Some people choose avoidance because they are uncomfortable engaging in conflict. Others choose it because they don't care enough about the outcome of the conflict to bother. Avoiding conflict isn't always the wrong choice; many people in groups opt to ignore or avoid certain points of contention among themselves to maintain harmony.[46] When avoidance becomes a group's primary way of managing conflict, however, it often leaves important matters unresolved. In this situation, the result can be dissatisfying relationships within the group.[47]

Accommodating *Accommodating* is the opposite of competing and reflects a high concern for the other party but a low concern for the self. The goal of accommodating is

In collectivistic societies, accommodating in response to conflict is often expected and is viewed as respectful or noble.

to sacrifice so the other party wins. People in a group sometimes accommodate to keep the peace, which may work well in the short term. In the long run, however, continually accommodating the other party can lead to resentment.

Cultural ideas play an important role in the use of accommodation. In collectivistic societies, accommodating in response to conflict is often expected and is viewed as respectful or noble.[48] In contrast, in individualistic societies, people may be seen as weak or spineless if they consistently accommodate others.

Compromising *Compromising* reflects a moderate concern for everyone's needs and desires. In this strategy, both parties in the conflict give up something in order to gain something. No one gets exactly what he or she wants, but everyone leaves the conflict having gained something valuable.

Let's say you're negotiating a job offer with a new work group, and you want a higher salary than the group leader wants to pay. Through your negotiation, you agree to accept a lower salary than you originally wanted, and the group leader agrees to give you an extra week of vacation in return. Neither of you got exactly what you wanted, but you each got something you valued in return for giving up something else. Compromising takes time and patience, but it often leads to more satisfying outcomes than do competing, avoiding, or accommodating.

Collaborating The *collaborating* style represents a high concern for the needs of both sides in a conflict. The goal is to arrive at a win–win situation that maximizes both parties' gains.

After they unexpectedly had a third child, for example, Mick and Laura felt the strain of paying for day care while Mick worked and Laura went to school. Their other children, Tara and Tana, were excited about having a younger sibling but upset about the reduced attention they would get. Soon, the tensions gave rise to conflict within the family. After collaborating on a solution, the family decided that Mick would cut his work hours and Laura would enroll in online courses so that at least one of them would be home every day. The money they saved in day care expenses more than made up for Mick's reduced income. Moreover, both Laura and Mick felt better because they were able to care for their new child themselves, and Tara and Tana got to spend more time with their parents than they had before.

Work at It: Groups Can Resolve Any Conflict If They Try Hard Enough

The fact that there are many ways to manage conflict in groups might suggest that if you have the right skills and try hard enough, your group can eventually resolve any conflict it might encounter. That outcome would be great, but the truth is that some conflicts are simply irresolvable.

Let's say you're part of a jury hearing a lawsuit brought against a pharmaceutical company. The plaintiff has alleged the company was negligent when it failed to warn consumers that its prescription pain relievers should not be given to animals. During your deliberations, you discover that some jurors steadfastly believe the company is negligent. Others believe just as strongly

that reasonable people should know not to give animals medications prescribed for humans. The longer your deliberations go, the more entrenched jurors become in their opposing viewpoints. As a result, you report to the judge that the jury is hopelessly deadlocked, and the case is dismissed.

This scenario illustrates that when people hold diametrically opposed opinions they are unwilling or unable to change, they are unlikely to resolve their conflicts no matter how hard they try. In such cases, the only real option is to avoid the conflict, agree to disagree, or try to minimize the effects of the conflict on other aspects of the group's relationship.

ASK YOURSELF

- What conflicts have you experienced that seemed impossible to resolve?
- When should a group give up trying to resolve a conflict? When should a group continue trying to resolve a conflict, even if it seems irresolvable?

SHARPEN Your Skills: *Conflict resolution*

With two or three other people, generate a topic of conflict and then role-play resolving it using each of Blake and Mouton's conflict styles. Afterward, discuss which style or styles seemed most appropriate for the conflict you were having, and consider how other styles might have been more appropriate for a different type of conflict.

In many situations, collaborating is the best way for groups to handle conflict. Yet collaborating can require a great deal of energy, patience, and imagination. Even when it is the ideal approach to managing conflict, it can therefore also be the most time-consuming and laborious solution.

Managing conflict appropriately can be very beneficial for groups, but can *every* conflict be resolved? Take a look at the "Fact or Fiction?" box to find out.

AVOID GROUPTHINK

Let's suppose you're part of a group of engineers designing a new toy for children. The toy is colorful and fun to play with, and the manufacturer is pressuring your group to approve the toy's design so it can go into production in time for the holiday shopping season. Although you like the toy, you are concerned that the paint on its exterior could be unsafe for children. When the group meets to consider approving the design, however, you feel pressured to keep your concerns to yourself. You sense that some other engineers are also concerned about safety, but most don't speak up. When someone asks whether the paint is safe for children, the group leader says, "Yes, it's safe; now let's move on." Soon, you hear people say it's important that the group approve the toy's design unanimously so consumers will have confidence in the product. Although you have serious doubts about the toy's safety, you feel pressured to ignore your misgivings—and, along with everyone else in the group, you vote to approve the design.

That example illustrates the problem of **groupthink,** which occurs when group members seek unanimous agreement despite their individual doubts.[49] According to psychologist Irving Janis, a pioneer of groupthink research, there are eight major warning signs that a group has fallen victim to groupthink:[50]

- *Illusion of invulnerability:* Group members are overly confident in their position, ignoring obvious problems.
- *Collective rationalization:* Members "explain away" any ideas that are contrary to the group's position.
- *Illusion of morality:* Members believe the decisions they make are morally correct, ignoring any arguments to the contrary.
- *Excessive stereotyping:* Members construct negative stereotypes of anyone who disagrees with them.
- *Pressure for conformity:* Members feel pressure to conform to the group's decision and are branded as disloyal if they do not.
- *Self-censorship:* Members don't speak up if they have dissenting viewpoints.
- *Illusion of unanimity:* Members falsely perceive that everyone agrees with the group's decision, because they don't hear anyone offering counterarguments.
- *Mindguards:* Some members actively prevent the group from hearing about arguments or evidence against the group's position.

Groupthink is particularly likely to occur when a group has a strong, authoritarian leader, is composed of members with similar backgrounds, and is isolated from outside influence.[51] Under those conditions, groups can produce decisions that appear both unanimous and well informed but are actually neither. Indeed, decisions produced by groupthink tend to be problematic because they have not been subjected to critical thought. In fact, group members are nearly 200 percent more likely to voice disagreement if groupthink is not occurring than if it is.[52] Groupthink discourages all attempts to consider a decision critically, because critical analysis might prevent members from reaching consensus.

Decisions reached by groupthink can have disastrous effects, such as exposing thousands of children to potentially unsafe paint on a new toy. In fact, groupthink has been identified as a contributing factor in several national disasters, including the attack on Pearl Harbor, the Cuban Missile Crisis, the Watergate scandal, and the 1986 explosion of the space shuttle *Challenger.*[53] What is most troubling about those examples is that some of them might have been avoided if the groups in charge had thought critically about their decisions instead of falling victim to groupthink.

Avoiding groupthink is therefore an important aspect of communicating competently in groups.[54] Group members can take several specific steps to prevent groupthink from occurring:

Groupthink played a role in the fatal explosion of the space shuttle *Challenger*.

- *Be aware of the potential for groupthink.* Teach others in the group about what groupthink is, why it is so problematic, and what its warning signs are. If you detect any of the warning signs, speak up and remind others how important it is to avoid groupthink.

- *Make sure the group has sufficient time to make decisions.* Groupthink can occur when members feel pressured to arrive at a decision quickly. If your group is making an important decision, remind members to allow sufficient time for discussion. If the process feels rushed, say "It might be better to put off making this decision until we have more time."

- *Encourage dissenting viewpoints.* When it appears that most members have the same position on an issue, ask, "What are some alternate ideas?" Encourage members to play devil's advocate by questioning the merits of each another's positions. Remind the group to examine each idea critically and not accept any at face value.

- *Seek input from outside the group.* Suggest that group members consult with people outside the group who might offer useful input on the group's decision. Look up relevant research and bring it to the group's attention.

- *Give important decisions a second chance.* Even after the group has made its decision, recommend that members meet once more to reconsider it. Encourage members to express any doubts or second thoughts they have about the decision. Listen to all arguments, whether they are for the decision or against it. Then ask the group to vote on its decision again.

It might seem that these recommendations will discourage a group from reaching any decision at all. Their purpose, however, is to help the group to make a *good* decision by avoiding the problems of groupthink.

LISTEN CAREFULLY

When we interact with others, our ability to communicate effectively relies heavily on how well we listen. That observation is especially true when we interact within groups, a setting where multiple ideas or positions are often discussed at the same time. One way to become a better group communicator is to build listening competence. Particularly useful strategies are knowing how to recognize barriers to effective listening and practicing listening skills.

Recognize Barriers to Effective Listening in Groups A starting point for honing your listening skills is to acknowledge factors that might be inhibiting your ability to listen attentively. Barriers to effective listening common in many groups include these:

- *Noise:* Noise is anything in the physical environment (such as sound) or in your individual experience (such as hunger) that distracts you from listening effectively. Try to identify what is causing the noise and do what you can to reduce its effect.

- *Boredom:* When you're bored, effective listening becomes difficult because your mind wanders. If you find that boredom is preventing you from listening effectively, suggest to the group that members take a break and come back to the discussion later. If a break isn't possible, try to identify some aspect of what's being said that you find interesting, and focus on that.

- *Information overload:* Many of us have difficulty listening effectively when we feel we're being bombarded with information. If a member of your group is overloading you with information, politely suggest that he or she identify the most critical pieces of information and focus specifically on those.

- *Rebuttal tendency:* We saw in Chapter 6 that the rebuttal tendency is the propensity to debate a speaker's point and formulate your reply while the person is still speaking. The rebuttal impulse can be a particularly common barrier to effective listening in groups that evaluate or analyze—such as juries, focus groups, and advisory boards—because members of such groups may disagree on the merits of the various ideas they're discussing. If you notice the rebuttal tendency in

Boredom makes it difficult to listen effectively.

yourself, remember to listen to everything a speaker says *before* you formulate your response. Doing so may help you overcome your boredom and allow you to listen more actively.

Practice Listening Listening is a skill, not an innate ability. Thus, you can hone your ability to listen through practice. Perhaps you're unsure about how you can *practice* listening. If so, remember that people listen with various goals in mind. As we considered in Chapter 6, people sometimes engage in informational listening, which is listening to learn. At other times, they engage in critical listening, which is listening to evaluate and analyze what they hear. Individuals also engage in empathic listening, when the goal is to experience what another person is thinking or feeling. These goals are quite different from one another. You can therefore practice your listening skills by paying attention to the specific listening goals that are most useful to you in a given situation.

Informational listening skills are particularly important when you need to understand and retain what you're hearing, such as when you take part in a study group. To ensure you have understood what you've heard, try paraphrasing the speaker's message. Paraphrasing is restating the speaker's message in your own words to clarify its meaning. If you paraphrase a statement in a way that accurately reflects its meaning, the speaker will usually reply by confirming your understanding. If you paraphrase in a way that changes the meaning of a statement, however, the speaker will generally correct your misunderstanding. Paraphrasing can therefore help you to understand a speaker's message more accurately.

Critical listening skills are especially important in groups that have to make important decisions, such as a state legislature and a corporate board of directors. To improve your critical listening skills, remind yourself not to accept what you hear at face value. Instead, question what you hear. Start by considering the credibility of the speakers. Are they experts on the topic about which they're speaking? Are they biased toward one point of view? If you find the speakers to be credible, ask yourself whether their statements have merit. Are their assertions logical and well thought out, or do they seem inconsistent? Do the speakers make claims that are improbable? Keep in mind, too, that it's relatively easy to listen critically when you are hearing ideas or claims you don't like, because you may already be inclined to discredit such information. It's when you *approve* of the speakers or their message that it is most important to listen critically. Doing so will help to ensure you accept ideas on their merits rather than at face value.

Finally, empathic listening skills are most important in groups that provide comfort, such as support groups. In such groups, people often listen to understand how others are thinking or feeling. If that's your goal, practice listening without interrupting. As you probably know from your own experience, being interrupted while you're speaking is frustrating. Particularly when people are sharing personal or sensitive information—as they often do in a support group—they appreciate being able to speak without interruption. Also, practice listening without offering advice. Unless they specifically ask for your advice, many people would prefer that you simply listen to what they have to say.

The effectiveness of communication in many groups depends on members' ability to listen to one another. By acknowledging the barriers to effective listening and practicing the listening skills appropriate to the situation, you can improve your own ability to communicate effectively in groups.

▸ For REVIEW

- **How do groups generate ideas and make decisions?** Groups can use brainstorming, nominal group technique, and ideawriting to generate ideas, and they can make decisions by unanimous consensus, majority rule, minority rule, expert opinion, and authority rule. The preferred decision-making technique depends on the nature of the decision and on the cultural context of the group.

- **How do leaders enact leadership and exercise power?** Leaders can enact democratic, autocratic, or laissez-faire leadership styles, each of which has its strengths. Leaders exercise several forms of power—including reward, coercive, referent, legitimate, expert, and informational power—over the people they lead.

- **What communication skills improve group decision making?** Group members should learn to manage conflict appropriately, avoid groupthink, and listen carefully to contribute positively to group decision making.

POP QUIZ

Multiple Choice

1. To choose a theme for next year's conference, a student group votes on three possible themes and selects the one that receives the most votes. The group's decision-making process is

   a. unanimous consensus.

   b. majority rule.

   c. minority rule.

   d. authority rule.

2. The style of managing conflict that represents a high level of concern for the needs of the self and the needs of the other party is

   a. competing.

   b. avoiding.

   c. accommodating.

   d. collaborating.

3. The style of leadership that reflects the philosophy that group members should work independently, with minimal involvement from the leader, is

   a. democratic.

   b. autocratic.

   c. laissez-faire.

   d. legitimate.

4. Everyone in Arianne's group follows her suggestions because they all admire her and want to please her. Arianne's form of power is

   a. reward power.

   b. referent power.

   c. legitimate power.

   d. informational power.

5. The eight major warning signs that a group has fallen victim to groupthink include all of the following *except*

   a. illusion of anonymity.

   b. illusion of morality.

   c. illusion of invulnerability.

   d. illusion of unanimity.

Fill in the Blank

6. Leaders who score high on _____ are highly aware of their own behavior and how it affects others.

7. When using _____ to make a decision, group members generate their initial ideas silently and independently and then combine them and consider them as a group.

8. A(n) _____ leader believes it is his or her right and responsibility to make decisions on behalf of the group.

9. Leaders who exercise _____ power punish people for not doing what the leaders want them to do.

10. To avoid groupthink, groups should encourage members to play _____ by questioning the merits of one another's positions.

ANSWERS: 1. b; 2. d; 3. c; 4. b; 5. a; 6. self-monitoring; 7. nominal group technique or NGT; 8. autocratic; 9. coercive; 10. devil's advocate

KEY TERMS

brainstorming 235
nominal group technique (NGT) 235
ideawriting 236
unanimous consensus 237
stalemate 237
false consensus 237
majority rule 237
minority rule 238
expert opinion 238

authority rule 238
traits 240
physical traits 241
psychosocial traits 241
extroversion 243
introversion 243
communication apprehension 243
democratic style 243
autocratic style 243

laissez-faire style 244
power 245
reward power 245
coercive power 246
referent power 246
legitimate power 246
expert power 247
informational power 247
groupthink 253

SPEAKING INFORMATIVELY

Dangers of Misinformation Online

Sexually active adolescents often seek information about sexual health online, especially if they feel uncomfortable talking to a parent or doctor. The Internet can be a rich source of medical information, but it can also spread misinformation. Do most websites offer teenagers accurate data about sexual health? To find out, Dr. Sophia Yen, a professor of medicine at Stanford University, surveyed 35 of the most popular websites that adolescents consult for sexual health information. She looked specifically at what each site said about issues such as birth control, emergency contraception, and sexually transmitted diseases. Her analysis uncovered incorrect or incomplete information on 41 percent of the sites. In particular, she found that many sites perpetuate myths about sexual health, such as that emergency contraception triggers spontaneous abortion, that hormonal contraceptives cause weight gain, and that herpes cannot be transmitted through kissing. Dr. Yen warns that such misinformation can hurt adolescents by encouraging them to adopt unsafe sexual practices. She recommends that anyone seeking medical information online steer toward websites associated with university medical centers, because experts will have reviewed the information on those sites to ensure its accuracy.[1]

As You READ

- What methods can we use to inform?
- In what ways should we frame an informative speech?
- Through what strategies can we hone our informative-speaking skills?

We rely on accurate information from websites, newspapers, interpersonal encounters, and many other sources to make decisions in our personal and professional lives. Having good information can empower us to make wise choices. Often, however, the manner in which information is presented matters as much as the information itself. If the information we receive from others isn't accurate, complete, or understandable, or if it doesn't grab our attention, it may lead us to make poor decisions. The same is true when we have occasion to speak informatively to others. Unless we convey our message clearly and completely and in a way that engages our listeners' attention, their decision making might be compromised.

In this chapter, we explore the various methods for informing an audience and ways to frame the speech topic for maximum effectiveness. We'll also examine several techniques for presenting successfully and peruse an award-winning informative speech.

Choosing a Method of Informing

In the past two decades, more than 24,000 college graduates have participated in Teach for America, a nonprofit organization that recruits individuals to teach for two years in low-income communities throughout the United States.[2] Unlike traditional teachers who have earned undergraduate degrees in education, most Teach for America instructors have no training in teaching practices when they apply for the program. However, many recruits quickly learn that there are several ways to impart knowledge to their students and that although one method may be ineffective, another often works well. The same can be said for any type of informative speaking.

- **informative speaking**
Publicly addressing others
to increase their knowledge,
understanding, or skills.

We can approach **informative speaking**—publicly addressing others to increase their knowledge, understanding, or skills—in several different ways. The techniques available to us include defining, describing, explaining, and demonstrating. The method or methods we choose depend on our speech topic and audience.

INFORMATIVE SPEECHES CAN DEFINE

- **defining** Providing the
meaning of a word or concept.

One method of informing an audience is **defining:** providing the meaning of a word or concept. Let's say you want to educate your listeners about the credit industry. You might focus part of your speech on defining the term *FICO score*, a widely used personal credit score calculated by the Fair Isaac Corporation. An individual's FICO score strongly influences his or her ability to obtain credit, so knowing what a FICO score is can help your audience to understand how the credit industry works.

Teach for America
instructors learn to try
various strategies for
imparting knowledge to
their students.

Defining a term may sound like a straightforward task because it requires only that you connect the term to its meaning. Meanings can be highly contested, however. The way a society defines the word *marriage*, for instance, differentiates those who can enjoy the benefits of such a relationship from those who cannot. Likewise, the way a government defines the word *torture* dictates what methods its military personnel can use in combat and interrogations. Individuals often have dramatically different perspectives on how words such as *marriage* and *torture* ought to be defined, largely because the definitions have consequences for so many people.

If defining a word or concept will help you to inform your listeners, you can choose from several methods:

- *Identify the denotative meaning.* You may recall from Chapter 4 that a term's denotative meaning is its dictionary definition. In a speech about global warming, for instance, you could define *greenhouse gases* as "atmospheric gases that absorb and emit radiation."

- *Explain the connotative meaning.* A term's connotative meaning is its socially or culturally implied meaning. One connotative meaning of the word *home*, for example, is "a place where you feel safe and secure."

- *Provide the etymology.* The **etymology** of a term is its origin or history. In a speech about affectionate communication, you could explain that the word *affection* derives from the Latin word *affectio*, meaning "an emotion of the mind."

  • **etymology** The origin or history of a word.

- *Give synonyms or antonyms.* You can define a word by identifying **synonyms,** words that have the same meaning as your word, or **antonyms,** words that have the opposite meaning. Synonyms for the term *normal* include *usual, ordinary,* and *typical,* whereas antonyms include *abnormal, irregular,* and *odd.*

  • **synonyms** Words that have the same meaning.

  • **antonyms** Words that have opposite meanings.

- *Define by example.* You may help your audience to understand a concept by providing examples that illustrate its meaning. In a speech about the immune system, you might define the term *pathogen* by giving examples of types of pathogens, such as viruses, bacteria, fungi, and parasites.

- *Use compare-and-contrast definitions.* You can discuss similarities and differences between two or more definitions of a term. To some people, the definition of *family* is limited to legal and biological relationships; to others, it includes anyone to whom they feel emotionally close. If you were speaking about the concept of family, you could compare and contrast those two definitions of the term.

SHARPEN Your Skills: *Defining a term in multiple ways*

Select one word or concept and define it according to its denotative and connotative meanings, etymology, synonyms, antonyms, and examples. Write a brief paragraph or journal entry commenting on which approaches seemed to work best for your word, and why.

INFORMATIVE SPEECHES CAN DESCRIBE

A second way to inform your audience about something is to describe it. **Describing** means using words to depict or portray a person, a place, an object, or an experience. You might describe the arrangement of rooms in the campus student center or the experience of having your eyes dilated by an optometrist, using language that creates a mental image for your listeners.

• **describing** Using words to depict or portray a person, a place, an object, or an experience.

Two forms of description are common in informative speeches. With the first, **representation,** you describe something in terms of its physical or psychological attributes. You could represent the Great Wall of China by telling your audience what it looks like or what kind of awe it inspires when people see it. When you describe by representation, you are helping your listeners to imagine their physical or emotional experiences if they were to encounter what you are describing.

• **representation** Describing something in terms of its physical or psychological attributes.

The second form of description common in informative speeches is **narration,** with which you describe a series of events in sequence. You can think of narration

• **narration** Describing a series of events in sequence.

as storytelling. In an informative speech about the field of veterinary medicine, for instance, you could describe what your aunt went through to become a veterinarian or tell a story about your first visit to an animal hospital.

Many speakers combine representation and narration. Let's say you wanted to teach your audience about the life of singer and actress Jennifer Hudson. You could use representation to describe some of the memorable characters she has played in her movies, such as Effie White in *Dreamgirls*, her Academy Award-winning performance. You could use narration to describe how Hudson competed in *American Idol* in 2004 or how she tragically lost her mother, brother, and nephew in 2008. Incorporating both forms of description can produce a richer mental image for your listeners than either form can evoke on its own.

An informative speech about the Great Wall of China could describe its physical dimensions or detail the awe it inspires in visitors.

• **explaining** Revealing why something occurred or how something works.

INFORMATIVE SPEECHES CAN EXPLAIN

In many informative presentations, the speaker explains something to the audience. **Explaining** means revealing why something occurred or how something works. For example, you might explain how Larry Page and Sergey Brin, then Ph.D. students at Stanford University, developed the search engine Google. You could also explain how cancer cells spread through the body or why people in Great Britain drive on the left side of the road.

When offering an explanation, speakers must use clear, concrete language and avoid jargon that will be unfamiliar to listeners. Suppose that in an informative speech about statistics, you hear a speaker explain: "Mean scores are considered significantly different only if the p-value is smaller than the critical alpha." Although that explanation would make perfect sense to a statistician, it won't make sense to you unless you already understand what mean scores, p-values, and critical alphas are and why they matter. It is always useful to assess how much your listeners already know about your speech topic and then adapt your words to their current knowledge. That consideration is particularly crucial when you are explaining something, to ensure that your audience will understand all the elements of your explanation.

In Chapter 11 we examined the various goals a speaker might have in planning a public presentation, and we differentiated between speaking to inform and speaking to persuade. Of all the techniques speakers can use to inform an audience, explaining most often risks crossing the line from informing to persuading. The reason is

• **objective** Based on facts rather than opinions.

that people's opinions and perspectives frequently influence their explanations of events or processes. In February 2012, for instance, 17-year-old Trayvon Martin was shot and killed by George Zimmerman, coordinator of the neighborhood watch program in the community where Martin was visiting his father. Zimmerman told police that the African American teenager had attacked him and that he had responded in self-defense. After the discovery that Martin had been unarmed, many in the community called Zimmerman's actions an example of overt racism. Either explanation—justified self-defense or unjustified racism—may have merit, but the explanation you believe may be influenced by your own attitudes about race or your own experiences with law enforcement. An informative speaker who explained Martin's shooting as the product of either self-defense or racism would implicitly be persuading the audience to believe the explanation being offered.

You can avoid crossing the line from informative to persuasive speaking by keeping your remarks **objective**—that is, based on facts rather than opinions. When you speak objectively, you avoid trying to convince

TABLE 14.1
TO INFORM OR
TO PERSUADE?

Avoid turning an informative speech into a persuasive speech by keeping in mind these fundamental differences.

	Persuasive Speech	Informative Speech
Focus	What should be	What is
Evidence	Facts and opinions that support the predetermined conclusion	Facts and information relevant to the topic
Goal	To convince listeners to adopt a particular belief or action	To educate listeners about the speech topic

listeners of a particular point of view. In comparison, remarks in a persuasive speech are **subjective**—that is, biased toward a specific conclusion. Consult Table 14.1 for some key differences between informative and persuasive speaking.

• **subjective** Biased toward a specific conclusion.

INFORMATIVE SPEECHES CAN DEMONSTRATE

Many people learn better by *seeing* how to do something rather than by simply hearing how to do it. Therefore, one way to maximize the effectiveness of an explanation is to incorporate a demonstration. **Demonstrating** means showing how to do something by doing it as it is explained. For instance, you could teach listeners how to play Angry Birds, clean a camera lens, or stretch properly before exercise by demonstrating those activities during your speech.

• **demonstrating** Showing how to do something by doing it as it is explained.

When you're demonstrating a process, it's important to describe each step as you do it. Let's say your informative speech is about how to prepare a Caprese salad. You might start by identifying each of the ingredients you'll be using: tomato, mozzarella cheese, basil, black pepper, and balsamic vinegar. Then, as you slice the tomatoes and mozzarella, tell your audience what you're doing ("I am slicing the tomato and cheese into equal-size pieces so they'll be easier to eat"). When you chop the basil, describe how you're doing it ("First I'm going to cut the stem off each basil leaf; then I'll roll the leaves together and give them a rough chop"). Explain how you are arranging the tomatoes, cheese, and basil on a plate ("I'm interspersing slices of tomato and cheese on the plate in a vertical pattern and then sprinkling the chopped basil over the top"). Describe seasoning the salad with black pepper and balsamic vinegar as you do so. In this way, your audience will both *see* and *hear* every step of the process.

Does demonstrating while giving a speech enhance listeners' ability to learn? Check out the "Fact or Fiction?" box to find out.

If you want to include a demonstration in your informative speech, take note of the advice offered in Chapter 13 about using presentation aids. In particular, make sure you will have everything you need to run your demonstration, such as adequate space, the right equipment, and access to a power supply if you require one. Ensure that you can conduct the demonstration safely and that it won't pose a threat to anyone in your audience. Be certain you can complete the demonstration within the time allocated for your speech, and have a backup plan in case any elements of your demonstration fail.

Selecting and Framing the Topic

Students who compete in speech and debate know the importance of choosing a compelling topic and framing it appropriately for their listeners. They put their speaking skills on the line in every tournament, so they can't afford to bore their audiences.

Imagine that *you* are taking part in an informative-speaking competition with undergraduates from around the country. How will you choose an intriguing topic? How can you frame your presentation in such a way that your listeners will care about and pay attention to the content? In this section, we explore eight categories of topics for informative speeches, and we'll see that effective informative speakers frame their

Fact or *fiction*?

Show and Tell: People Learn Best by Seeing *and* Hearing

Speech instructors often encourage students to use demonstrations on the assumption that listeners learn best by seeing *and* hearing rather than by just seeing *or* just hearing. Is that assumption fact or fiction?

Research suggests that it is a fact. Let's say that in addition to describing how to download applications on the iPad, you also *demonstrate* by downloading applications during your speech. Some of us seem to be primarily *visual learners,* who learn best by seeing. Others seem to be primarily *auditory learners,* who learn best by hearing. Yet studies show that students who encounter both visual and auditory stimuli accurately recall 11 percent more of what they learn than do students exposed only to visual stimuli, and 8 percent more than students exposed only to auditory stimuli. The explanation may be that we process verbal

and visual information separately, so when we are presented with both types of information, they reinforce each other and enhance our ability to learn.

ASK YOURSELF

- How do you learn best? In what ways is your own learning influenced by verbal and visual stimuli?
- Based on the research described here, how do you think listeners' learning would be affected if a speaker engaged an additional sense—such as their sense of touch or smell—in addition to using visual and auditory stimuli?

SOURCE: See Berk, R. A. (2009). Multimedia teaching with video clips: TV, movies, YouTube, and mtvU in the college classroom. *International Journal of Technology in Teaching and Learning, 5,* 1–21.

presentations in two connected ways: first by relating themselves to their topic and then by relating the topic to their audience.

SELECT A CAPTIVATING TOPIC

When planning an informative speech, many people have difficulty selecting a topic that will capture and hold their listeners' attention. That decision needn't be a challenge, however, because the list of potential topics for an informative speech is virtually unlimited. Communication scholars Ron Allen and Ray McKerrow have identified eight categories of topics that work particularly well for informative speeches:[3]

- *Issues:* According to Allen and McKerrow, *issues* are problems or points of controversy about which people desire resolution. You could choose to speak on a contemporary issue facing the United States, such as unemployment, immigration, or the war in Afghanistan. You might also select an issue that has been controversial for some time, such as affirmative action or sex education in public schools. When you focus your informative speech on an issue, your purpose isn't to persuade your listeners to adopt any particular point of view but rather to give them the facts necessary to form their own opinions.

- *Events:* *Events* are occurrences that are noteworthy for the meanings they represent. You may choose to speak about an event that was publicly experienced, such as the 2012 London Olympics or the death of football coach Joe Paterno. You might also elect to speak about a significant event in your personal life, such as a visit to a foreign country or a religious conversion. In each instance, you can educate your audience about the event and communicate the significant meaning it has, either for your listeners or for you.

- *People:* Many informative speakers focus their presentations on other people. You might choose to discuss an individual who made history, such as Keith Ellison, the first Muslim elected to the U.S. Congress. You could talk about someone who is noteworthy for acts of charity, such as the late Mother Teresa of Calcutta. You might talk about the life of a person in the public spotlight, such as golfer Phil Mickelson or pop singer Shakira. You could also focus your remarks on a group, such as the Amish or the Apollo 11 astronauts.

- *Places:* Cable television's Travel Channel is popular because it informs viewers about interesting and exotic places. You can do the same by focusing your speech on a place you find significant or intriguing. It might be a place you have personally visited, or it could be a locale where daily life is substantially different than it is for your listeners, such as Cuba, Iceland, or Yemen. You can even focus on a place in a specific historical period, such as China during the Shang Dynasty or Moscow before the breakup of the former Soviet Union.

- *Objects:* Allen and McKerrow have categorized as *objects* any entities that are nonhuman, including living or animate objects, such as the California giant redwoods and the endangered Great White Shark, and inanimate objects, such as the guillotine and the Empire State Building. Effective speeches about an object often educate listeners about the object's evolution and development or its significance in history, culture, politics, or ecology.

- *Concepts:* Whereas objects are tangible items, *concepts* are abstract ideas. Oppression, compassion, integrity, bias, and forgiveness are all examples of concepts because each is a notion or an idea rather than a concrete object. Some powerful speeches have focused on concepts that were significant to their audiences. In January 2012, for instance, Washington governor Christine Gregoire delivered a speech supporting equality in marriage laws for same-sex couples. Equality isn't an object that can be seen or felt; it's a complex idea and one that affects millions of lives as a social concept.

- *Processes:* As we saw earlier in the chapter, many informative speeches describe or demonstrate a *process*, a series of actions that culminates in a specific result. For instance, you might focus on a natural process, such as how coal becomes diamond or how a canyon forms from water erosion. Or you might choose a human-created process, such as the design of currency or the functions of a CT scanner. You can also use your informative speech to teach your listeners a process, such as how to tie a bowline knot or crop a digital photo.

- *Policies:* Finally, informative speeches can focus on *policies*, that is, programs that aim to guide future decision making or to achieve some goal. For instance, you might inform your listeners about policies that existed in the past but were overturned, such as school segregation in the United States and apartheid in South Africa. You might also speak on current policies, such as those that regulate interrogation tactics in the military. Some humorous informative speeches focus on bizarre policies and laws, such as the New Jersey prohibition against frowning at police officers and the Nevada law against riding a camel on public highways.

As we've seen, a wide range of topics is available for an informative speech, so be creative! Consider issues, events, people, places, objects, concepts, processes, or policies you feel are well suited to yourself and your audience. As you do so, however, remember that your listeners' cultural background can influence what topics are appropriate. Although to U.S. audiences few topics are considered *taboo*—or inappropriate for public discussion—listeners from other cultures may be surprised or even offended by certain topics. Table 14.2 presents some examples of culturally taboo topics.

Once you have selected your topic, you will want to frame it for your listeners in a compelling way, as we'll see in the next two sections.

RELATE YOURSELF TO YOUR TOPIC

Recall the discussion in Chapter 11 of the advantages of choosing a speech topic you know and care about. By choosing a topic you care about, you ensure you'll have both the knowledge and the enthusiasm to speak in a way that engages and informs. In some instances, your personal connection to the topic may be evident to your audience when you begin speaking. For example, if everyone in your public speaking class knows that you come from abroad, your listeners will understand why you have chosen to speak informatively about international students' experiences. On some occasions, however, your personal connection to your topic may not be immediately evident. In such cases, it is important to explain why your topic is meaningful to you. For example, one student expressed her personal connection to the topic of the children of deaf adults in this way:

> Unlike most of you, I didn't speak my first word. Rather, I communicated my first word— mother—in American Sign Language. You see, I'm what is commonly referred to as a "CODA," a child of deaf adults. As the only person in my immediate family who can hear, I learned to sign before I learned to speak. I'd like to tell you today about what it's like to grow up as a CODA, straddling the fence between the deaf and hearing worlds.

To make her connection to the topic of CODAs more evident to her audience, this student augmented parts of her speech with sign language. By explaining her background and demonstrating her fluency in signing, she made clear to her listeners why the topic of CODAs and their experiences was relevant to her.

Relating yourself to your topic is advantageous for two reasons. First, it establishes for your audience that you have the credibility to speak with authority about the topic.

TABLE 14.2	Teachers of English as a second language (ESL) are taught to avoid particular topics when speaking to certain groups around the world. If your audience consists largely of listeners from one of these societies, you, too, may find it prudent to avoid certain speech topics—or at least to exercise sensitivity when discussing them. What topics, if any, would you consider taboo in *your own* culture?
CULTURAL DO'S AND DON'TS: MANAGING TABOO TOPICS	

Country	Topics to Avoid
China	Tibet and the Dalai Lama; the Falun-Gong movement
France	Jobs, financial success, and wealth; immigration
India	Poverty; religious beliefs; India's relationship with Pakistan
Muslim countries	Sex and sexual practices
Japan	World War II
Korea	Politics; personal family matters; the relationship between North and South Korea
Mexico	Pollution; illegal immigration; sexuality
Taiwan	Politics; Taiwan's relationship with mainland China
Thailand	National security; criticisms of the monarchy

If you have training, personal experience, or a vested interest in what you're discussing, you are likely to be knowledgeable about it. Explaining your connection to the topic establishes you as a qualified speaker whose words can be trusted. The second advantage is that your listeners will care more about the topic if they believe it matters personally to you than if they do not. You may

know from your own experience that it is difficult to get excited about a speech when not even the speaker seems to care about the topic. In contrast, when you make clear to your listeners that you are enthusiastic about or deeply invested in the topic of the speech, they are more likely to care about what you have to say.

RELATE YOUR TOPIC TO YOUR AUDIENCE

Seeing that *you* know and care about your topic will matter to your listeners. What will matter to them even more, however, is seeing why *they* should know and care about it. To frame an informative speech effectively, you must therefore make clear how the topic is relevant to your audience.

Establish Listeners' Vested Interest in Your Topic

Some topics will be easy to relate to your listeners' current experiences. Suppose you are speaking to a group of college-bound high school students about strategies for getting financial aid. That topic will matter to your listeners because many of them will require financial assistance to get a college education. They therefore have a **vested interest** in your topic—an inherent motivation to pay attention to it—and you need only point that out to relate it to them successfully.

Establish Your Topic's Relevance to Listeners
In other instances, it's necessary to tell your listeners why they should care about your topic. Even if your audience doesn't have direct experience with the topic of your speech, you can often make it relevant by asking your listeners to imagine themselves in a hypothetical situation. Notice how the following introduction accomplishes that goal:

> *Imagine this: You're spending the holidays with family and you've just gotten up from a delicious dinner when you see your dad stumble and fall to the floor. At first, you think he just tripped, but his eyes are closed and he isn't moving. Your mom runs to call 911, but it could be several minutes before anyone arrives. Would you know what to do to keep your father alive until help gets there? You would if you'd been trained in cardiopulmonary resuscitation, or CPR. Today, I'm going to tell you what CPR is, how it works, and where you can learn to perform it. If you know how to administer CPR properly, you may be able to save the life of someone near and dear to you.*

In this introduction, the speaker makes clear why the topic of CPR is relevant to the listeners. The speaker relates the topic to listeners, even if they have no direct experience with it. Check out "The Competent Communicator" to practice framing topics for an informative speech.

Honing Your Informative-Speaking Skills

Even if you have chosen a compelling topic and successfully framed it for your audience, you must still deliver your speech in a way that will draw—and hold—your listeners' attention. In this section, we'll explore several strategies for delivering an informative speech effectively, including creating information hunger, being organized, making learning easy, involving your audience, and being ethical.

SHARPEN Your Skills: *Generating informative speech topics*

Generate a list of eight topics—one representing each of Allen and McKerrow's categories—about which you could speak informatively.

Children of deaf adults, or CODAs, often learn to communicate through sign language even before they can speak.

• **vested interest** An inherent motivation to pay attention.

It's All Relative: Framing Your Informative Topic

When selecting the topic of your informative speech, consider how you can relate yourself to your topic and how you can relate your topic to your audience. Doing so with a few different topics can help you to decide which topic is best for your presentation. In this exercise, select three potential informative-speaking topics, each of which represents a different category in Allen and McKerrow's list. List two ways you could relate yourself to each topic and two ways you could relate the topic to your audience.

	Topic	How the Topic Relates to Me	How the Topic Relates to My Listeners
1.	_____	_____	_____
	_____	_____	_____
2.	_____	_____	_____
	_____	_____	_____
3.	_____	_____	_____
	_____	_____	_____

Based on your responses, which of the three topics you chose do you think you could frame most effectively? Why?

CREATE INFORMATION HUNGER

Perhaps you've had the experience of taking a high school or college course that you thought would be boring, only to be surprised by how interesting the instructor made the material. The instructor inspired your interest by creating **information hunger,** the desire to learn. As an informative speaker, you can do the same with your listeners by sparking their curiosity and giving them reason to want the information you have. In short, you can show your listeners "what's in it for them" if they pay attention to your speech.

Recall from Chapter 1 the five types of needs—physical, relational, identity, spiritual, and instrumental—that communication helps us meet. An excellent way to generate information hunger is to connect your topic to one or more of those needs. By doing so, you imply the benefits of listening to the information you have to share, creating a desire for that information among your listeners.

Imagine that you're preparing a speech about food. Let's look at some examples of how you might connect that topic to each of the five needs:

- *Physical needs:* Teach listeners to cook a meal that is healthy and flavorful.
- *Relational needs:* Discuss the importance of cooking rituals—such as preparing a Thanksgiving dinner—in maintaining family relationships.
- *Identity needs:* Explain how individuals with an eating disorder view their consumption of food as a central component of their identity.
- *Spiritual needs:* Explore various real and symbolic uses and meanings of food and drink in religious ceremonies, such as Christian communion.
- *Instrumental needs:* Teach your listeners how to find the best deals on food staples, such as fresh fruit, vegetables, and milk.

• **information hunger**
The desire to learn.

By connecting the information in your speech to one or more of your listeners' needs, you make that information relevant to *them* and thereby motivate the audience to pay attention to your words and message.

BE ORGANIZED

Studies confirm what you probably already know: We learn better from presentations that are well organized.[4] That may be so because most of us process information best in a limited number of segments at a time; thus, a speech that presents easily identified "chunks" of information in a coherent order is easiest for listeners to follow.[5] Just *appearing* organized, in fact, is enough to boost your listeners' retention of what you say—that's how powerful organization is.[6]

Creating a well-organized informative speech is easy. Recall the different components of a speech—introduction, body, conclusion, and transitions—and the role each component plays in making your presentation coherent. As you prepare your informative speech, work on each component individually to ensure that it is serving its necessary functions. If each component does its job, your speech will have a logical, organized structure, and you will be poised for success.

Use the checklist in Table 14.3 to make certain that your informative speech includes all the elements necessary for an organized presentation.

MAKE IT EASY TO LISTEN

We've all encountered speakers who seem oblivious to their listeners' needs and desires—for example, presenters who talk too long or use unfamiliar technical jargon. It is difficult to pay attention to such speakers or to care about what they're saying. To avoid that reaction from your own audience, make it easy for them to listen to you by keeping your message short, using clear language, starting with familiar concepts, repeating your key points, and sprinkling in humor when it's appropriate.

Keep It Short In most instances, you will have a specific time slot for your informative speech. Your time frame will limit the amount of material you can effectively discuss in your presentation, so make sure you include only as much information as you can reasonably cover.

Keep It Simple It might seem obvious that your listeners must understand what you're saying before they can learn from it, but many speakers forget that crucial

TABLE 14.3

As you prepare an informative speech, remember your priorities for each component of your presentation.

Section	Priorities
Introduction	**1.** Generate interest in your topic.
	2. Present your thesis statement.
	3. Relate your topic to yourself and to your listeners.
	4. Preview your main points.
Body	**1.** Present each of your main points, with appropriate transitions between them.
	2. Make sure you have at least three main points and that they are sufficiently related to each other.
Conclusion	**1.** Reinforce your central idea by reviewing your main points.
	2. Create a memorable moment for your audience.
Transitions	**1.** Use transitions to review the material you've presented already.
	2. Use transitions to preview material yet to be presented.

consideration. A common mistake for informative speakers is to use technical language or jargon that they erroneously assume their audience understands. A better approach—particularly if you're unsure whether certain words will be familiar to your listeners—is to use plain, simple language that everyone will understand.

Start with What's Familiar Many of us feel uneasy when we're asked to learn a new skill or understand new information. To reduce that anxiety among your listeners, begin your informative speech by describing something that is familiar to them. Then discuss how that familiar concept is related to the new information or skill you intend to describe. For instance, being "psychologically flooded" means experiencing thoughts and feelings so intense that you become unable to continue interacting with others. To describe that phenomenon, you might begin by reminding your listeners what happens to a car engine when it gets flooded. As most drivers know, a flooded engine won't start. You can then make comparisons between that familiar concept and the new knowledge you wish to impart.

Repeat Key Points Research shows that repetition of critical points will help your listeners to remember more of what you say.[7] Take advantage of that fact by repeating your most important points during your speech. To use repetition effectively, however, repeat only the important points, not trivial ones, and do not repeat them so many times that your audience tunes out.[8]

Make It Fun Like repetition, humor can also enhance your presentation and increase your listeners' retention if you use it appropriately. Humor in informative presentations promotes relaxation that allows listeners to understand and assimilate the information.[9] Remember to consider who your listeners are and what they are likely to find funny. Humor that is distasteful, obscene, or disrespectful of others is never appropriate in an informative speech *unless* the humor itself is the topic.

INVOLVE THE AUDIENCE

Many of us learn better when we're somehow engaged in the lesson than when we're passively receiving it. Skillful informative speakers use several techniques to involve listeners in their presentations.

Invite Direct Participation In this method, you ask your listeners to perform some action that helps them understand your topic. In an informative speech about relaxation techniques, you might instruct your listeners to close their eyes, let their facial muscles go slack, and breathe slowly and deeply, to help them grasp how the techniques work.

Ask for Volunteers If your lesson is too complex for everyone in the audience to participate in it, ask for one or more volunteers with whom you can demonstrate it for the rest of the listeners. In a speech about self-defense, you could ask for a volunteer on whom to demonstrate ways of fending off an attacker.

Poll the Audience A good way to gauge your listeners' opinions or experiences is to take an informal poll related to your topic. You might say "Raise your hand if you've ever known anyone who has suffered from asthma." If you're speaking in a room with a classroom response system—commonly known as *clicker technology*—your audience can respond to your questions anonymously.

@getCONNECTED
Use Online Resources

When you're speaking in a venue that has Internet access, consider incorporating audio-visual material from online sources into your speech. In a speech about the justified use of police force, for instance, show your listeners a YouTube video of police interacting aggressively with a suspect and then ask your listeners whether they thought the officers used excessive force. If you select a video clip from a case with which you're familiar, you can end your speech by revealing whether the officers were charged and/or convicted of excessive aggression.

Pose a Hypothetical Situation A technique similar to polling your audience is to ask your listeners to consider a hypothetical situation. For example: "Imagine you're driving late at night along a back road, hit a patch of ice, and end up in a ditch with no way to get out. You're alone, the temperature is below freezing, and there's no cell phone coverage where you are. What would you do?" Asking listeners to picture themselves in such a situation can spark their interest in your speech. The difference between that technique and polling your audience is that you are not asking your listeners to respond.

Refer to Individual Listeners Particularly if your audience is small, an excellent way to connect to your listeners is to refer to them individually during your speech when appropriate. For instance, "Last week we heard Tariq describe his life-changing experience of visiting Mecca. Today, I'd like to tell you about the two major denominations of Islam: the Sunni and the Shi'a." Even though you're referring only to one specific listener, the technique connects all your listeners to you and to your presentation.

Effective speakers make it easy for the audience to listen to their presentations.

Invite Questions At the end of some informative speeches, presenters involve listeners by inviting and responding to their questions. If you have the time and wish to use that technique, it's often helpful to tell your audience early in your speech that you'll be taking questions at the end. That way, you encourage listeners to think of questions as you speak. During a question-and-answer period, be mindful of the time allotted so you don't run over.

BE ETHICAL

Finally, treat your listeners ethically. In the context of an informative speech, one of the most important requirements of ethical behavior is truthfulness. Because your purpose is to impart information to your audience, you have a responsibility as an ethical speaker to ensure that your information is true and accurate. Specifically, you should:

- *Use information only from reputable sources.* Scientific journals and major newspapers are more reputable sources than tabloids and Wikipedia pages, for instance, because information in journals and large mainstream newspapers is checked for accuracy before being published.
- *Understand the information you're reporting.* If you're unsure how to interpret the meaning of a report or a statistic, ask an instructor for help. If you don't, you risk drawing conclusions from your information that are unwarranted.

The Scene: Halfway through your informative speech about the various forms of yoga, you perceive that your listeners are growing restless and bored. You still have half your speech to go, but you fear you are losing their attention.

Your Task: Consider how you could adapt your presentation as you start to perceive listeners' boredom. What strategies would you use to

- Make it easy to listen?
- Involve your listeners?
- Make your audience want to hear what you have to say?

SHARPEN Your Skills: *Audience involvement*

Take a specific informative speech topic and generate a list of five or six concrete ways you could involve your audience in a presentation about that topic.

- *Incorporate verbal footnotes.* When you use information in your speech from another source, identify that source while you're speaking. For example, you might say: "According to the U.S. Bureau of Labor Statistics, occupational therapy is one of the fastest-growing professions."

- *Be clear about when you're speculating.* Many sources of information allow us to infer ideas or speculate about possibilities, and it is fine to include those inferences or speculations in an informative speech as long as you make it clear that they aren't facts. Ethical speakers also avoid using offensive language, exposing their audience to sensitive sights and sounds, and engaging in behaviors that would make their listeners uncomfortable—*unless* they have specifically warned their listeners in advance.

One highly unethical use of informative speaking is to coerce your audience into believing or doing something. If your purpose is to persuade individuals to adopt a particular belief, opinion, or behavior—a topic we'll examine in Chapter 15—you owe it to your listeners to be upfront about that objective. Speakers who hide their persuasive intentions in seemingly objective informative speeches often cross an ethical boundary by engaging in propaganda. Read more about propaganda—and learn how to identify it—in "The Dark Side of Communication."

Inviting and responding to questions can be an excellent way to draw listeners into your presentation.

A Sample Informative Speech

When we're learning or polishing a skill such as informative speaking, it's often helpful to study excellent examples

THE DARK SIDE OF COMMUNICATION

Listener Beware: When "Information" Becomes Propaganda

It's easy to think of informative speeches as offering only objective details and facts. Some speakers, however, use "informative" speeches to disguise their attempts to persuade or coerce their listeners. When they do, they are no longer simply informing but engaging in propaganda.

Informative speeches whose true purpose is coercive often contain one or more of the following elements. How many political speeches have you recently heard that included these elements?

- *Moral labeling:* Using terms with negative connotations to refer to your opponent. Politicians denounce "special-interest groups," for instance, to put down those whose priorities contradict their own. They may use words such as *radical* and *extremist* to describe people with whom they disagree. In recent years, it has become fashionable to call one's opponents "Nazis," drawing comparisons to the fascist German group responsible for killing millions of Jews, Gypsies, homosexuals, and others in the twentieth century. The problem with such labeling is that calling someone a "radical," an "extremist," or a "Nazi" doesn't mean the person actually has any of the characteristics of such groups. Therefore, the labels are meaningless, although highly provocative.

- *Glowing generalizations:* Using positive terms to refer to yourself or your allies. While applying negative terms to their opponents, lawmakers might refer to people and policies in their own parties as "patriotic," "loyal," "democratic," and "fair to working families." Likewise, food and drug companies might describe their products as "100 percent natural" to highlight their quality, even though many 100 percent natural substances are poisonous! Just as denouncing an opponent with negative terms doesn't mean those terms are accurate, referring to yourself or your products with positive terms doesn't necessarily make them any more positive in reality.

- *False dichotomy:* Conveying the idea that "if you aren't *for* us, you're *against* us" to cast anyone with a different opinion as an opponent. Such a ploy categorizes everyone into one of two groups: us or them. It separates people and discourages attempts at reaching compromise or finding common ground.

- *Ordinary folk:* Describing yourself as "of the people" while depicting your opponent as "out of touch with the average citizen." A particularly common tactic among U.S. politicians is to campaign on the premise that the federal government is "broken" and "out of touch with" the realities of U.S. life and that the candidate is a "Washington outsider" who will "fix" the system once he or she is elected. That approach garners support because it casts the speaker as "one of us."

Keep in mind that propaganda does not mean everything you disagree with when you're listening to a speech. Rather, propaganda is a speaker's deliberate attempts to make coercive messages sound like objective information. Knowing the common techniques of propaganda can help you to resist its influence when you encounter it.

SOURCES: Caplan, A. L. (2005). Misusing the Nazi analogy. *Science, 309,* 535; for further information see Jowett, G. S., & O'Donnell, V. (2006). *Propaganda and persuasion.* Thousand Oaks, CA: Sage.

provided by others. Below is the text of an informative speech by Eric Dern, an economics major at Arizona State University and a member of the school's speech and debate team. The speech describes the Golden Shield surveillance project in China. In April 2009, Eric tied for first place in informative speaking with this speech at the national tournament of the American Forensics Association, a teachers' association dedicated to cultivating excellence in public speaking and debate. Alongside the text are comments about what makes each section of his speech—the introduction, body, and conclusion—so effective. Figure 14.1, which precedes the speech, provides the formal outline for Eric's speech and helps you to appreciate its organizational structure.

TITLE: China's Golden Shield Surveillance Project

General purpose: To inform

Purpose statement: Inform audience about the Golden Shield surveillance project in China.

INTRODUCTION

I. The Chinese fishing community of Shenzen has been transformed into a metropolis and a unique lab for Golden Shield, history's largest surveillance project.

II. Golden Shield's more than 2 million cameras watch the population's every move.

Thesis: The Golden Shield surveillance project has far-reaching implications regarding U.S. foreign policy, privacy rights, and the role of government in individual lives.

Transition: To understand Golden Shield's impact, we first examine its technology, then its applications, and finally its implications.

BODY

I. Golden Shield stands out due to its technological sophistication.
   A. *Brunei Times:* Golden Shield has advanced camera technology.
      1. Subjects' facial features and walking mannerisms can be tracked.
      2. *Blink:* Detection of involuntary facial microexpressions allows authorities to read motives and predict behavior.
   B. Golden Shield can listen in on every cell phone signal in the city.
      1. *China's Golden Shield:* Voice recordings are saved in a huge database.
      2. Surveillance is constant and exceeds the level of most countries.

Transition: Now that we know how Golden Shield works, we can see its applications in the world.

II. Golden Shield has applications related to crime prevention and security in China and the United States.
   A. *Shenzen Daily:* Golden Shield is extremely effective in preventing crime.
      1. Shenzhen's crime rate has fallen by nearly 14 percent.
      2. The city is much safer and more secure.
   B. Several U.S. companies are investors in Golden Shield.
      1. *International Herald Tribune:* American hedge funds paid for 91 percent of Golden Shield's face- and behavior-recognition software in the last year.

2. Golden Shield has an excellent relationship with major U.S. firms.
   C. *New York Times:* Thousands of the same high-tech cameras used by Golden Shield have been installed in New York and Chicago.

Transition: There are three far-reaching implications for Golden Shield.

III. Golden Shield has three far-reaching implications.
   A. By affecting the foundation on which the United States advances democracy, Golden Shield may alter U.S. foreign policy.
      1. *American Prospect:* American investment is helping China suppress internal political activism.
      2. U.S. policymakers must rethink the long-held notion that capitalism and democracy go hand in hand.
   B. MSNBC: Golden Shield may redefine privacy as Americans understand it.
      1. *United States v. Dionisio:* The Fourth Amendment does not protect Americans against Golden Shield's ability to read emotions and motives.
      2. Golden Shield has prompted a redefinition of "probable cause."
   C. *Discipline and Punish:* Promotion of citizen self-policing could free governments to suppress political opponents.
      1. A precedent for self-enforcement among Chinese citizens implies that Golden Shield could be turned off and citizens would police themselves.
      2. The state would thus be freed to carry out repressive agendas.

Transition: After examining Golden Shield's technology, applications, and implications, we better understand the system's worldwide effects.

CONCLUSION

I. Review of main points
   A. Golden Shield is unique in its size and technological sophistication.
   B. Golden Shield has applications related to crime prevention and security.
   C. Golden Shield has implications for U.S. foreign policy, the meaning of privacy rights, and the intrusion of government into individual affairs.

II. Final remarks
   A. Golden Shield has profound implications for how U.S. democratic society functions.
   B. It seems inevitable that a population control system such as Golden Shield will become a larger reality in the United States.

FIGURE 14.1

FORMAL SPEECH OUTLINE: CHINA'S GOLDEN SHIELD SURVEILLANCE PROJECT

COMMENTARY	SPEECH

This introduction opens with a short story introducing listeners to the topic of the speech, the Golden Shield.
 	
Notice here how the speaker relates his topic to his audience.
 	
Here, the speaker previews the topics to be covered in the body of the speech.
	Southeastern China's Shenzhen was once a simple fishing community, only truly notable for its proximity to the border of Hong Kong. In 1979, the Chinese Communist Party stepped in and chose Shenzhen as the first of four Special Economic Zones, areas where capitalism would be allowed on a trial basis. Today, this Gotham-like metropolis, widely known as China's organized crime capital, is home to 12.4 million people—twice the size of Los Angeles—and is a city of pure commerce.
	
	    But this rags-to-riches story has its own interesting twist. *Rolling Stone,* on May 29, 2008, reports that it's only fitting that this concoction of crime and capitalism should once again serve as a laboratory, this time for the largest surveillance project in history. Golden Shield, a system of over 2 million cameras, not only watches every move of the city's population but also detects emotion and predicts thoughts. And surprisingly, the communist country's best imitation of George Orwell is far more American that some would like to admit. *Rolling Stone* reports $30 billion of the $33-billion Golden Shield system consists of American investments, so just like everything else made in China with American parts, "Police State 2.0" is ready for export to a neighborhood near you.
	
	    Golden Shield not only is significant for its giant leaps in human tracking technology, but also has implications for how our democratic society functions as a whole. To understand the impact Golden Shield will have on the world, we will first examine the technology of Shenzhen's Golden Shield, next understand its applications, and finally draw some implications from China's massive social experiment.

In the body of the speech, the speaker uses transitions to indicate when he is beginning a new topic.
 	
The speaker is careful throughout the speech to cite his sources properly.
 	
By saying "second," the speaker signals that he is shifting to a new dimension of his topic.
 	
Here, the speaker uses a quote from an expert as supporting material for the point he is making.
	What separates Golden Shield from London's famous security set-up or the surveillance of the Patriot Act is the system's sheer size and sophistication. To get a full picture of Golden Shield, let's first examine the technology that makes up the system, which is intended to be able to "see" and "hear."
	
	    First, if I were to stand at the corner at Shenzhen's Civic Centre, the area of the city where most security and government buildings are located, I would be watched by 38 different cameras. The *Brunei Times* of August 30, 2008, details the cameras' technology that allows subjects' eyes, facial features, and walking mannerisms to be checked against a database containing names, photos, and even reproductive information. Additionally, Malcolm Gladwell's 2002 book *Blink* chronicles the exploration of involuntary facial "microexpressions," explaining "When we experience a basic emotion, a corresponding message is sent to the muscles in our face." Golden Shield's software is so advanced that it is capable of reading these involuntary microexpressions within a millisecond, giving authorities the ability to instantly read motives and predict behavior. "The smallest thing could give you away. A nervous tic, a look of anxiety, a habit of muttering to yourself—anything that carries with it the suggestion of having something to hide is itself a punishable offense." This may sound familiar. George Orwell wrote this prediction of a dystopian future in his novel *1984.* Orwell's fantasy may certainly become a reality.
	
	    Second, Golden Shield has been equipped to "hear" the sounds of the city. According to the 2006 essay *China's Golden Shield,* the system is capable of listening in on every cell phone signal in the city and saving these voice recordings in a huge database. So, if I were standing on that same corner in the Civic Centre, my cell phone would be constantly tracked and recorded, and my voice could be immediately recognized if I uttered a single word on the street. By utilizing the system's ability to both see and hear, China has reached a state of constant surveillance that few countries can rival.
	
	    Now that we know how Golden Shield works, we can see its applications in the world. Golden Shield has applications on crime and security not only in China but also right here in the United States. But first, let's admit it, 2 million cameras spying on every move you make sounds pretty wrong. And creepy. But in a post-9/11 era, when terrorism and mass attacks are very real possibilities, China doesn't necessarily seem so out of line in installing Golden Shield. In fact, Golden Shield is devastatingly effective at preventing crime in Shenzhen. According to the January 24, 2007, *Shenzhen Daily,* in the very first week of Golden Shield's installation, robberies in the city dropped by 15 percent. Since then, the city's crime rate, once 9 times higher than Shanghai and 3 times higher than New York City, has fallen by nearly 14 percent. Golden Shield has time and time again proved its ability to make Shenzhen a much safer and more secure city.
	
	    But Golden Shield is not simply a Chinese security system. It is a cooperative effort between Chinese communism and American investment. The *International Herald Tribune* of September 10, 2008, reveals that 91 percent of Golden Shield's face- and behavior-recognition software was paid for by American hedge fund money in the last year. Robin Huang, chief operating officer of China Public Security, stated that Golden Shield has "a very good relationship with U.S. companies like Google, Honeywell, IBM, Cisco, HP, and Dell." *Rolling Stone* speculates that "these global corporations currently earning profits from Golden Shield are unlikely to be content if the lucrative new market remains confined to Shenzhen." And, accordingly, this technology is already being applied by these companies in the United States. The *Huffington Post* of August 7, 2008, reports that the same Golden Shield backers are also the companies invested in a Defense Department project auspiciously named "Operation Noble Shield." This virtual database can create constantly updated dossiers and surveillance footage for every U.S. citizen. The July 9, 2008, *New York Times* reports that the first 3,000 of these high-tech cameras were installed in New York, while another 2,200 were installed in Chicago in the past year.
	
	    There is a good chance that half of everything you own was made in Shenzhen: iPods, sneakers, maybe your car, and almost certainly your cell phone. And now population surveillance devices. There are three far-reaching implications for Golden Shield, related to American involvement in foreign policy, the meaning of privacy rights, and the intrusion of government into individual affairs.
	
	    First, Western powers claim that by doing business in China, they are spreading democracy. But the September 20, 2007, *American Prospect* points out, "We are now seeing the reverse: investment is helping China . . . actively repress a new generation of activists." This means America must disenthrall itself from one of its most cherished cornerstones in foreign policy: the idea that capitalism and democracy go hand in hand. As Naomi Klein states, "Remember how we've always been told that free markets and free people go hand in hand? That was a lie. It turns out that the most efficient delivery system for capitalism is actually a communist-style police state, fortressed with American 'homeland security' technologies, pumped up with 'war on terror' rhetoric." By changing the foundation on which the United States spreads democracy, the existence of Golden Shield may very well alter the course of American foreign policy.

COMMENTARY	SPEECH
	Next, privacy rights. Mike Sullivan, a police technology consultant, states in a November 24, 2008, MSNBC interview that "the difference between the Noble Shield and Golden Shield is the Supreme Court. We have the ability as U.S. citizens to cry foul. In China, citizens do not." However, in the 1973 decision *United States v. Dionisio,* the Supreme Court found a person's physical characteristics, like the eyes or face, are not protected by constitutional privacy rights. This means that while the Fourth Amendment protects us from searches and seizures without probable cause, it does not protect us against Golden Shield's ability to read one's emotions and motives. Golden Shield is redefining the term "probable cause" and may even redefine what we all consider to be privacy.
	Finally, in his book *Discipline and Punish,* philosopher Michel Foucault examines Jeremy Bentham's panopticon, a prison layout where prisoners are allowed to roam freely under the permanent visibility of guards in a central tower. Foucault further explains that these guards do not even have to be in the tower for the panopticon to work; the very potential of visibility traps prisoners into disciplining themselves. Golden Shield works in the same way, using cameras instead of towers to ensure the automatic functioning of power.
	However, *Rolling Stone* details the repression of Tibetan protestors by everyday Chinese citizens who aided authorities in the capture of political activists. This self-enforcement among Chinese citizens implies that Golden Shield could be turned off completely and citizens would police themselves. Traditionally, governments have always been responsible for the security of their citizens. But when citizens begin to check themselves, instead of the government, that frees the state to carry out oppressive agendas. For China, a country that has multiple regional conflicts, this could provide the final silencing of opposition to the cultural extermination of Tibet and Taiwan.
In his conclusion, the speaker reiterates the main points he has made in the speech. He ends with a quote that will make his conclusion memorable.	When Beijing was awarded the Olympic games, the theory was that international scrutiny would force China's government to grant more rights to its people. Instead, the Olympics opened up a back door for the regime to massively upgrade its systems of population control. After examining how Golden Shield works, its applications, and finally its implications, we better understand how the system affects China and the world. No longer is Golden Shield confined to distant and unfamiliar worlds where most of us have probably never been. With the Olympics potentially coming to Chicago in 2016, it seems like only a matter of time before Operation Noble Shield brings this reality closer to home. Maybe George Orwell was right when he wrote, "Big Brother is watching."

For REVIEW

- **What methods can we use to inform?** In an informative speech, we can define, describe, explain, and demonstrate.

- **In what ways should we frame an informative speech?** We should begin by relating ourselves to the topic of the speech. We should then relate the speech topic to our listeners.

- **Through what strategies can we hone our informative-speaking skills?** We can create information hunger, present a speech that is well organized, make it easy for our audience to listen, involve our listeners in our presentation, and communicate in an ethical manner.

POP QUIZ

Multiple Choice

1. Caroline's informative speech reveals how the Federal Reserve System works. Her speech is an example of one that

   a. defines.

   b. describes.

   c. explains.

   d. demonstrates.

2. In his informative speech, Jake defines the word *romance* by detailing the word's origin and history. Jake's method of definition is

   a. providing etymology.

   b. identifying denotative definition.

   c. defining by example.

   d. explaining connotative definition.

3. Tara wants to focus her speech on a problem or a point of controversy. In Allen and McKerrow's list of categories, that focus exemplifies a(n)
   a. event.
   b. concept.
   c. process.
   d. issue.
4. Compared to those who listen to lectures that are not humorous, people who listen to lectures that include humor do all the following *except*
   a. evaluate the lecture more positively.
   b. more accurately recall the material.
   c. perceive the lecture to be shorter.
   d. make more positive assessments of the lecturer.
5. When speaking to a group of Japanese businesspeople, Lance would do well to remember that a taboo topic for this audience is
   a. immigration.
   b. World War II.
   c. pollution.
   d. criticisms of the monarchy.

Fill in the Blank

6. Describing a series of events in sequence, as you would when telling a story, is called _____.
7. _____ are words that have opposite meanings.
8. A person's _____ is his or her inherent motivation to pay attention to something.
9. A series of actions that culminates in a specific result is called a _____.
10. When you create _____, you spark your listeners' desire to learn.

ANSWERS: 1. c; 2. a; 3. d; 4. c; 5. b; 6. narration; 7. Antonyms; 8. vested interest; 9. process; 10. information hunger

KEY TERMS

informative speaking 338
defining 338
etymology 339
synonyms 339
antonyms 339
describing 339
representation 339
narration 339
explaining 340
objective 340
subjective 341
demonstrating 341
vested interest 345
information hunger 346

15

SPEAKING PERSUASIVELY

PERSUASION CAN PRESERVE A LIFE

The A&E television series *Intervention* chronicles stories of young adults with dependencies on alcohol or drugs, or with other destructively compulsive behaviors, who have put themselves at serious physical, emotional, and social risk. Each episode includes a real-life intervention—a structured conversation in which the young person's family and friends try to persuade the individual to get professional help. Such was the experience of Brooks, a 21-year-old man who became addicted to drugs after an automobile accident left him paralyzed from the waist down. When Brooks's family intervened, his younger brother Chace pleaded with him to enter a treatment facility: "Brooks, I have seen your drug addiction affect your life negatively in the following ways. By destroying the close relationships that you and I once had. You sleep all day and party all night. It is not all right for me to keep enabling you to live like this. I can support your life only if you are willing to help yourself. Will you go to treatment today?" As a result of his family's persuasive efforts, Brooks agreed to begin rehabilitation. Although his recovery was long and painful, he finally became sober.

As You READ

- What does it mean to persuade?
- In what ways can we craft a persuasive message?
- Through what strategies can we hone our persuasive-speaking skills?

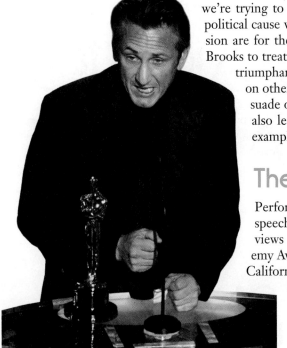

We have many occasions to persuade others for our own personal gain. Perhaps we're trying to convince someone to buy the car we wish to sell or to support a political cause we care about. In some situations, however, our attempts at persuasion are for the benefit of others. Had his relatives not succeeded in persuading Brooks to treat his drug addiction, his story could have ended tragically instead of triumphantly. Our ability to persuade can therefore have significant effects on other people's lives. In this chapter, you'll discover what it means to persuade others and how you can craft a successful persuasive message. You'll also learn several techniques for presenting effectively, and you'll see an example of an award-winning persuasive speech.

The Meaning and Art of Persuasion

Performers who win major awards frequently use their acceptance speeches as an opportunity to persuade their audiences to adopt their views on politically controversial issues. Upon winning the 2009 Academy Award for best actor for his role in *Milk*, Sean Penn sharply attacked California's Proposition 8, outlawing same-sex marriage in that state. In his speech, Penn remarked: "For those who saw the signs of hatred as our cars drove in tonight, I think that it is a good time for those who voted for the ban against gay marriage to sit and reflect, and anticipate their great shame, and the shame in their grandchildren's eyes if they continue that way of support. We've got to have equal rights for everyone." By expressing those sentiments, Penn wasn't merely conveying his own viewpoint—he was trying to persuade others to share that viewpoint and to act accordingly. Although the occasion may not have called for it, Penn was using **persuasive speaking**—public speech that aims to influence listeners' beliefs, attitudes, and actions.

We can think of **persuasion** as an attempt to motivate others, through communication, to adopt or to maintain a specific manner of thinking or doing. Some persuasion—including national advertising campaigns and Sean Penn's speech in front of a television audience of millions—occurs on a broad scale and seeks to motivate large numbers of people at once. Other persuasion—including the types most of us undertake in our daily interactions—occurs one-on-one or with small groups, such as a family or a work staff. In this section, we'll see that persuasion can influence beliefs, opinions, and actions. We'll also discover that good persuasive speakers support their arguments with appeals to integrity, emotion, and reason.

Actor Sean Penn used the occasion of winning the Academy Award for best actor in 2009 to make a persuasive statement about same-sex marriage.

• **persuasive speaking**
Public speech that aims to influence listeners' beliefs, attitudes, and actions.

• **persuasion**
An attempt to motivate others, through communication, to adopt or to maintain a specific manner of thinking or doing.

WHAT IT MEANS TO PERSUADE

When we try to motivate people to adopt a specific manner of thinking or doing, we usually have one of three concrete goals in mind:

- To persuade them to believe that a claim we're making is true.
- To convince them to share our opinion on a particular issue.
- To get them to do something.

We may also be working toward more than one of those goals at a time. Let's take a close look at how we can use persuasion to influence others' beliefs, opinions, and actions.

• **belief**
Perception about what is true or false, accurate or inaccurate.

Some Persuasion Affects Beliefs Our **beliefs** are perceptions about what is true or false, accurate or inaccurate. When others attempt to persuade us to believe something, they are trying to convince us that their words are a valid reflection of reality.

Suppose that several weeks after having a traffic accident, you and the other driver appear before a judge. Each of you tells the judge, in your own words, what led to your collision. You indicate that the other driver made an illegal turn, hitting your car.

The other driver claims the collision occurred because you failed to stop completely at a stop sign. Each of you is trying to convince the judge that your description of the events is true in an objective sense—that is, an accurate depiction of what *really* happened.[1] To help your case, you might offer evidence that supports your description, such as photos from the collision scene or statements from witnesses.

Some Persuasion Affects Opinions Whereas our beliefs are our perceptions of what's true and false, our **opinions** are our evaluations about what's good and bad. Opinions reflect what we think *should be*, not necessarily what *is*. When people use persuasion to influence our opinions, they want us to evaluate something in the same way they do.

• opinion
Evaluation about what is good and bad.

Perhaps you've attended rallies at your school where the speakers are voicing an opinion on a specific issue, such as unemployment or government-funded healthcare. Although they may present facts in support of their position, their goal is not simply for you to accept the facts as true. Rather, it's to cause you to agree with their position on the issue—that is, to arrive at the same evaluation of the facts that they hold. To help their case, the speakers might appeal to your morals or your sense of fairness.

SHARPEN Your Skills: *Analyzing opinion appeals*

Find and examine five examples of attempts to persuade an opinion. They could be from a political speech, a television advertisement, a magazine column, a website, or from many other sources. For each, identify the opinion being advocated, and list the arguments offered in support of it.

Some Persuasion Affects Actions Our beliefs and opinions are what we think, but our actions are what we do. **Actions** are the behaviors we undertake, and many persuasive messages attempt to influence them.

• action
A behavior someone undertakes.

Suppose you see a television commercial advertising a Bluetooth headset that you can use to make cell phone calls while driving. The commercial first shows drivers who are frustrated and distracted when using their cell phone; then they appear happy and unencumbered while using the Bluetooth headset. The advertisement claims that similar devices are more expensive or poorly manufactured, implying that the featured product is a good value. By suggesting that the device is both convenient to use and reasonably priced, the commercial's producers are attempting to motivate you to take a specific action—to buy the product.[2]

People attending rallies in support of controversial issues often try to persuade others to accept their position.

FIGURE 15.1
CYBERPERSUASION:
WHAT MAKES US
CLICK THROUGH?

Internet advertisements—such as the boxes and banners that pop up on websites—persuade people to spend billions of dollars annually on the products or services they tout. The ads are usually effective, however, only if people click on them to get the details of the advertised product or service. What persuades us to click through? According to research, three features of an Internet advertisement draw us:

- *Size matters.* We are more likely to click on large ads than small ones.
- *Specificity matters.* Online ads that describe their products or services specifically, rather than vaguely, are more effective.
- *Amount of text matters.* We favor online ads with lots of text over ads with little text.

SOURCES: Brettel, M., & Spilker-Attig, A. (2010). Online advertising effectiveness: A cross-cultural comparison. *Journal of Research in Interactive Marketing, 4,* 176–196; Robinson, H., Wysocka, A., & Hand, C. (2007). The effect of design on click-through rates for banner ads. *International Journal of Advertising, 26,* 527–541.

Today, many companies use the Internet as a major channel for advertising their products or services. What characteristics make Internet advertisements persuasive? Check out Figure 15.1 to find out.

THREE FORMS OF RHETORICAL PROOF

In one of his major writings, *Treatise on Rhetoric,* the Greek philosopher Aristotle (384–322 B.C.) described three **forms of rhetorical proof,** which are ways to support a persuasive argument. These proofs are appeals to ethos, pathos, and logos.

Ethos Imagine listening to a speaker about whom you know nothing as he makes a persuasive appeal for money to help the victims of the devastating floods that claimed more than 800 lives in Thailand in summer 2011. He says that if you donate your funds to him, he will use them directly for the benefit of the Thai people instead of deducting a large proportion of the money to fund his operating costs. Moreover, he claims to know where the needs in Thailand are most dire, and he assures you that he will fund those needs first. Do you donate?

Many people, although inclined to help the victims of natural disasters, would want to know more about the speaker before they decided whether to give him their money. The reason is that a speaker who's respectable and trustworthy is generally more persuasive than one who isn't.[3] Aristotle recognized that, to be persuaded, people needed to have positive regard for the person whose message they were considering. He used the term **ethos** to refer to a speaker's respectability, trustworthiness, and moral character.[4]

Speakers can establish ethos with listeners by displaying these specific qualities:

- *Knowledge, experience, and wisdom with respect to the topic:* Does the speaker have adequate expertise with the issue to be persuasive? The individual appealing for your donations to Thailand could establish knowledge, experience, and wisdom by describing his extensive experience working in Thailand and his many professional connections in Bangkok, its capital.

- *Integrity and virtue:* Is the speaker honest and trustworthy, or do you have reason to doubt his of her integrity? The fundraiser for Thailand could establish integrity and virtue by mentioning his moral standards and his intolerance for individuals who cheat or steal.[5]

- *Goodwill toward the audience:* Does the speaker care about the welfare of listeners, or is he or she only trying to use them? The speaker asking for donations could establish goodwill by acknowledging his audience's concerns about giving money and addressing them to his listeners' satisfaction.

Note that judgments about ethos belong to the audience. Listeners decide for themselves how much experience, integrity, and goodwill a speaker has. Good persuasive speakers therefore establish and reinforce their ethos with every audience, knowing it will enhance their persuasive abilities.

Pathos Many compelling persuasive appeals are memorable and effective because they stir people's emotions. Although it's helpful for a speaker to convince listeners

• forms of
rhetorical proof
Ways to support a persuasive argument, including ethos, pathos, and logos.

• ethos
A speaker's respectability, trustworthiness, and moral character.

Fact or *fiction*?

Hooked on a Feeling: Emotion Persuades

From advertisers to political candidates to addiction counselors, many people appeal to emotion based on Aristotle's idea that feeling can affect beliefs, opinions, and behaviors. Is it fact or fiction that emotion has this effect?

A wide variety of experiments indicates that it's a fact. When researchers examine the findings of multiple studies, they conclude that appeals to positive emotion are often most effective at persuading people to change their attitudes or opinions, whereas appeals to negative emotion (particularly fear) are frequently most

effective at inducing behavioral change. Some persuasion scientists believe we are most likely to change our mind about something when we feel good, because then we don't scrutinize the arguments very closely, but are most likely to change our behavior when we feel bad, because we want to end the bad feelings. You can use the findings from this research to compose your own persuasive messages, depending on whether you are trying to change someone's beliefs, opinions, or actions.

ASK YOURSELF

- Besides happiness or joy, to what other positive emotions could you appeal?
- Which emotions most strongly affect your own behaviors?

SOURCES: Dillard, J. P., & Meijnders, A. (2002). Persuasion and the structure of affect. In J. P. Dillard & M. W. Pfau (Eds.), *The persuasion handbook: Developments in theory and practice* (pp. 309–328). Thousand Oaks, CA: Sage; Witte, K., & Allen, M. (2000). A meta-analysis of fear appeals: Implications for effective public health campaigns. *Health Education & Behavior, 27*, 591–615.

of his or her integrity, it's often much more powerful if the speaker can generate a strong emotional reaction from the audience. The reason is that when people are emotionally aroused, their receptivity to new ideas is enhanced. Aristotle used the term **pathos** to refer to listeners' emotions, and he understood that emotion can be a significant persuasive tool. Was he right? Check out "Fact or Fiction?" to find out.

Consider the experience of Brooks in the vignette at the start of the chapter. Many people had tried to persuade him over the years to seek treatment, but he never did. Reasoning with drug or alcohol addicts that they should end their harmful behaviors is often ineffective, because that approach

Advertisements try to persuade us to buy a product or a service.

• **pathos** Listeners' emotions.

underestimates the powerful force of addictions.[6] Even if addicts rationally understand *why* they need help, they may not be sufficiently persuaded to seek it until they have had a significant emotional experience. In a typical intervention such as the one Brooks received, the letters and other testimony of friends and relatives describe how the addict's behaviors have negatively affected them. They also explain the potential

TABLE 15.1

SOME EXAMPLES OF EMOTIONAL APPEALS

Suppose you were designing a message to persuade people to stop smoking. Here are examples of appeals to pathos that you might use.

Type of Appeal	Example Statement
Appeal to fear	Thousands of people die from lung cancer every year; you could be next.
Appeal to guilt	Think about how many children you're hurting with second-hand smoke.
Appeal to joy	Imagine how happy you'd be if you were free of your nicotine addiction.
Appeal to disgust	See this charred skin tissue? That's what your lungs look like right now.
Appeal to shame	You're an embarrassment to your family when you smoke.
Appeal to anger	If you're sick and tired of nicotine controlling your life, then kick the habit.
Appeal to sadness	Imagine saying goodbye to your kids because smoking is claiming your life.

• **logos**
Listeners' ability to reason.

• **reason**
To make judgments about the world based on evidence rather than emotion or intuition.

• **inductive reasoning**
A form of reasoning in which one considers evidence and then draws general conclusions from it.

consequences if the person does not accept help, including their ending contact with the addict and cutting off sources of money or shelter.

When friends and family members read their letters aloud during the intervention, their intent is to elicit emotional reactions in the addict that are strong enough to persuade him or her to get medical help. To generate sorrow and guilt, they describe the negative effects of the addict's behavior on their own lives. To generate fear, they spell out the consequences of continued drug or alcohol use. And to generate hope, someone at the intervention, usually a professional counselor, describes the treatments available to the addict. The emotions of sorrow, guilt, and fear about current behavior—and hope for changing it—can often persuade the individual to modify his or her behavior significantly, where reasoning alone did not work.

Although stirring virtually any emotion can be persuasive, emotional appeals often focus on generating negative emotions such as fear, guilt, disgust, anger, and sadness.[7] The reason is that we generally dislike experiencing such emotions, so we are motivated to respond to the persuasive appeal as a way of reducing them. Table 15.1 presents examples of emotional appeals that might be used in a campaign to encourage people to quit smoking.

Logos A third way to persuade people is to appeal to their sense of reason. If a particular belief, opinion, or behavior makes good sense, then people will be inclined to adopt it if they have the capacity to do so. As we saw in the preceding example, appealing to reason doesn't always work, particularly if some other force—such as an addiction—influences a person's behavior. When people are free to choose their beliefs, opinions, and behaviors, however, they are frequently persuaded by a solidly logical argument. Aristotle used the term **logos** to refer to listeners' ability to reason.

To **reason** means to make judgments about the world based on evidence rather than emotion or intuition. When we appeal to logos, we provide our listeners with certain evidence, hoping they will arrive at the same conclusion we have reached. People can engage in the reasoning process in two ways: inductively and deductively.

Inductive Reasoning In **inductive reasoning,** we first consider the specific evidence and then draw general conclusions from it. As the evidence changes or as new evidence becomes available, we modify our conclusions accordingly.

For example, when you get sick and visit the doctor, she asks you about your symptoms, runs diagnostic tests, and examines your medical record. Each of those sources provides evidence. Let's say your symptoms are a rash, fever, and persistent headache. After considering those symptoms, looking at results of your blood tests, and noticing from your records that you haven't had chicken pox, the doctor diagnoses your condition as chicken pox.

To apply inductive reasoning, that is, the doctor started with the specific evidence and drew her general conclusion from it. It is possible, of course, that her conclusion is incorrect. Even though your symptoms are consistent with a diagnosis of chicken pox, they may also be consistent with another diagnosis, such as meningitis or Rocky Mountain spotted fever. When making an inductive claim, your doctor considers the evidence available to her and draws the conclusion she believes that evidence best supports. If you later developed symptoms inconsistent with a diagnosis of chicken pox, she would have to reconsider her conclusion based on the new evidence.

Deductive Reasoning In **deductive reasoning,** we start with a general conclusion and then use it to explain specific individual cases. Deductive claims often make use of a **syllogism,** a three-line argument consisting of a major premise, a minor premise, and a conclusion. In a valid syllogism, if both the major and minor premises are true, then the conclusion logically *must* be true.

Consider the following example:

Major premise:	All fruits contain seeds.
Minor premise:	Tomatoes are fruits.
Conclusion:	Therefore, tomatoes contain seeds.

Let's consider the logic of that argument. If it is true that all fruits contain seeds, and if it is true that tomatoes are fruits, then logically it must be the case that tomatoes contain seeds. There is no logical way the major and minor premises could be true and the conclusion false. We therefore say the conclusion *follows* from the premises, producing a valid syllogism.

When using a syllogism to persuade, we must first establish the accuracy of the premises. Listeners may not be convinced by the logic of your argument if they don't believe both premises are true. Suppose everyone in your audience accepts that all fruits contain seeds, but some listeners believe tomatoes are vegetables, not fruits. They may not find your argument persuasive unless you first convince them the tomato is a fruit. To do so, you might quote an authority on botany or plant biology to support that claim.

Establishing the truth of the premises is necessary, but it isn't sufficient for producing a valid argument. Consider the following syllogism:

Major premise:	All mothers are women.
Minor premise:	Lucy is a woman.
Conclusion:	Therefore, Lucy is a mother.

That syllogism is not valid. The reason is that, even if both premises are true, the conclusion could still be false. Just because Lucy is a woman and all mothers are women, it doesn't follow that Lucy is a mother, because even though all mothers are women, not all women are mothers.

A second way we can reason deductively is with an enthymeme. An **enthymeme** is a syllogism in which one of the premises is already so widely known and accepted that it isn't mentioned.[8] Consider the now-famous statement made by seventeenth-century French philosopher René Descartes: *I think, therefore I am.* If we were to state his argument in the form of a syllogism, it would look like this:

Major premise:	Anyone who thinks must exist.
Minor premise:	I think.
Conclusion:	Therefore, I exist.

Descartes may have believed the major premise ("Anyone who thinks must exist") was so obviously true that it didn't require articulating. If so, then he could safely construct his argument based only on the minor premise and the conclusion, which results in an enthymeme. Enthymemes can be just as persuasive as full syllogisms, but only if listeners accept the validity of both the omitted premise and the stated one.

Whether we do it inductively or deductively, appealing to reason provides our audience with the evidence and explains how it led us to our conclusions. Our goal in doing so is to persuade our listeners to adopt the same conclusions we have.

• **deductive reasoning**
A form of reasoning in which one starts with a general conclusion and then uses it to explain specific individual cases.

• **syllogism**
A three-line argument consisting of a major premise, a minor premise, and a conclusion.

• **enthymeme**
A syllogism in which one of the premises is already so widely known and accepted that it is omitted.

Creating a Persuasive Message

In 2009, Montana became the most recent U.S. state to permit physicians to help terminally ill patients to end their own lives. Such doctor-assisted suicide is highly controversial. Supporters argue that people with terminal illnesses deserve to die with dignity and that a doctor's primary role should be to relieve suffering. Opponents say that the practice undermines society's respect for human life and transforms doctors from healers into killers.

Suppose you had the opportunity to persuade citizens to vote one way or the other on the legality of doctor-assisted suicide. Your success would rely not only on the strength of your convictions but also on your ability to communicate them in a compelling way. In this section, we'll consider the types of persuasive propositions you can employ, the options you have for organizing your persuasive message, and the logical fallacies you should avoid.

TYPES OF PERSUASIVE PROPOSITIONS

As we saw in Chapter 12, preparing a speech includes drafting a thesis statement, a one-sentence version of your message. In persuasive speaking we sometimes call the thesis statement a **proposition,** because we are proposing something we want our audience to accept. Recall that some persuasive messages influence beliefs, others influence attitudes, and others influence actions. As we'll see next, we use different types of propositions to achieve these different persuasive goals.

We Influence Beliefs with Propositions of Fact
When we ask people to believe a statement, we are also asserting that it is true. To achieve our persuasive goal, we use a **proposition of fact,** a claim that a particular argument is supported by the best available evidence and should therefore be taken as factual. Some examples of propositions of fact are

- Barack Obama was born in Hawaii.
- Flying is the safest mode of transportation.
- Solar power alone is not capable of meeting the energy demand in the United States.

Notice that the first and second examples make a claim about *what is*, whereas the third example makes a claim about *what is not*. All three are propositions of fact, however, because in each case we are asking our listeners to accept what we say as true. If it's true that flying is the safest mode of transportation, then that's our proposition, and our speech must provide the evidence to support that claim. Similarly, if it's true that solar power cannot meet U.S. energy demand, we would give the evidence necessary to support that argument.

Propositions of fact are claims about reality. It isn't a matter of opinion whether Barack Obama was born in Hawaii—either he was or he was not. When we assert propositions of fact, our persuasive goal is to make our listeners believe in the objective truth of what we're saying. That goal requires us to support propositions of fact with credible—that is, believable—evidence.

We examine what makes evidence credible and strong later in this chapter.

We Influence Opinions with Propositions of Value
Whereas propositions of fact are statements about what is objectively true, **propositions of value** are claims that evaluate the worth of a person, an object, or an idea. When we assert propositions of value, our persuasive goal isn't to make someone *believe* us—it's to make someone *agree with* us. Some examples of propositions of value are

- Fathers are just as important as mothers.
- Animal cloning is immoral.
- Our country is right to do anything it can to protect its citizens.

Notice that all three statements make claims, but they are not claims about facts. Rather, they are judgments that reflect the speaker's opinions about what is important,

---

• **proposition**
That which a persuasive speech attempts to convince an audience to accept.

• **proposition of fact**
A claim that a particular argument is supported by the best available evidence and should therefore be taken as factual.

• **proposition of value**
A claim that evaluates the worth of a person, an object, or an idea.

moral, and right. Unlike facts, opinions are never true or false in an absolute sense—they are only correct or incorrect in the minds of the people who discuss them. Therefore, we can't *prove* an opinion in the way we prove a factual claim. We might use facts to establish a basis for advocating a specific opinion—for instance, we may quote evidence about threats of terrorism and the safety of U.S. citizens—but the facts themselves will never settle the issue. One person might interpret that evidence as justifying our nation's right to defend itself against its enemies. Another person might interpret the same evidence as proof of our failed foreign policy and the need for greater diplomacy. Who is right? That's a matter of opinion.

We Influence Actions with Propositions of Policy Closely tied to propositions of value are **propositions of policy,** claims about *what we should do.* Speakers offer propositions of policy to suggest a specific course of action for listeners to follow or to support. Some examples of propositions of policy are

• **proposition of policy**
A claim about what should be done.

- The federal government should ban the use of human stem cells in medical research.
- Hate crimes against ethnic, religious, and sexual minorities should be capital offenses.
- Everyone should eat only locally grown, organic foods whenever possible.

Notice that each statement contains the word *should,* a characteristic that makes it closer to a proposition of value than a proposition of fact. Whereas propositions of value suggest what we should *think,* however, propositions of policy suggest what we should *do.* Each of the examples, that is, suggests a specific course of action, either for individuals ("eat only locally grown, organic foods") or for the government ("ban the use of human stem cells"). When advocating for individual action, speakers attempt to persuade listeners to adopt the action themselves. When advocating for government action, speakers are usually trying to persuade listeners to support the action, such as by voting for it or encouraging their elected officials to do the same.

Some Persuasive Speeches Include More Than One Type of Proposition Although each type of proposition can be persuasive on its own, many persuasive speeches integrate two or even all three types to support their message. Let's say, for instance, that you wanted to advocate expanding affirmative action laws that help members of minority groups to get jobs. You might begin your speech with a proposition of value, such as "Diversity in the workplace is important," and persuade your listeners to adopt that opinion. Next, you might introduce a proposition of fact, such as "Affirmative action laws have increased workplace diversity by 27 percent in the past three decades," and provide the evidence for your listeners to believe that factual claim. Finally, you might assert a proposition of policy, such as "The U.S. government should expand affirmative action laws to increase workplace diversity even further," and use your earlier claims about values and facts to persuade listeners to support that action. In this speech, each new proposition you introduce is supported by the propositions that preceded it, and the result can add up to a powerfully persuasive argument.

getCONNECTED..
Computer-Mediated Persuasion

In a face-to-face speech, you can incorporate propositions of fact, value, and/or policy to achieve your persuasive ends. Research shows that the same strategies work in computer-mediated persuasive messages. Several recent studies, for instance, have found that value appeals and fact appeals sent by text message can influence recipients' health behaviors, including their attitudes toward smoking[9] and the amount of physical exercise they achieve.[10] Given how commonly people use text messaging and other forms of computer-mediated technologies to communicate with each other, persuasive messages are likely to be increasingly frequent.

Some persuasive speakers include propositions of fact, value, and policy in their presentations.

SHARPEN Your Skills:
Propositions of value, fact, and policy

Write a proposition of value, a proposition of fact, and a proposition of policy you would use if you were persuading lawmakers how to vote with respect to doctor-assisted suicide.

FOUR WAYS TO ORGANIZE A PERSUASIVE MESSAGE

The way you organize a persuasive message often matters as much as the message itself. Even good arguments can lose their persuasive appeal if they aren't presented in a meaningful sequence. In this section, we look at four options for organizing a persuasive message.

Problem-Solving Pattern One way to organize a persuasive speech is to use a **problem-solving pattern,** in which you establish the existence of a problem and then propose a solution to it. The problem-solving approach requires you persuade your listeners on two separate points. First, you must show that the problem exists and is serious enough to warrant intervention. Second, you must establish that your proposed solution is possible and practical and will be effective at reducing or eliminating the problem.

• **problem-solving pattern**
A way of organizing a persuasive speech in which the speaker establishes the existence of a problem and then proposes a solution to it.

Suppose your persuasive speech is about slowing the loss of family farms. You might begin by pointing out how many family farms in the United States have gone out of business in the last 50 years because of competition from corporate mega-farms. Next you need to explain why that's a problem worth solving. For instance, you could show it has eliminated thousands of jobs and required stores to buy food grown hundreds of miles away, decreasing its nutritional value.

Perhaps your proposed solution is that the government increase its subsidies to family farms to help to keep them in business. You then need to provide evidence that such a solution is *possible* (the government has the money to fund the subsidies), *practical* (an infrastructure exists to dispense the subsidies to family farmers), and *effective* (providing the subsidies will keep more family farms in business).

Refutational Approach A problem-solving pattern can work well when your audience is open-minded about the problem and solution you describe. Sometimes, however, your audience may be predisposed toward a certain position you plan to refute. Let's say, for instance, that you're speaking in favor of capital punishment, and you already know some of your listeners oppose it. In this instance, you might use a **refutational approach,** whereby you begin by presenting the main arguments against your position and then immediately refute them.

One common argument against capital punishment is that it won't bring crime victims back. That statement is often persuasive because it's true, and many people use it to argue that capital punishment is therefore futile. If you plan to advocate the death penalty in your speech, you might begin by acknowledging that statement and admitting that it is true. You could then point out, however, that *no* form of punishment will bring the victims back. The fact that the victims won't come back is therefore not a valid argument against capital punishment.

In the refutational method, after you've acknowledged and responded to the main arguments against your position, you then state your own position and argue for it. The refutational approach is designed to dispense with the arguments against your position first—or at least to weaken them—so your own position looks stronger by comparison.[11]

Comparative Advantage Method On occasion, you may find yourself speaking to people who already agree that a problem exists—they just can't agree on the best way to solve it. In that situation, it's often best to use the **comparative advantage method,** in which you explain why your point of view is superior to others on the same topic.

Imagine you're speaking to a group of schoolteachers on the topic of teacher evaluations. Your listeners all agree that evaluations are important, but they have little consensus about how evaluations should be done. To persuade the audience to adopt *your* suggestion, you begin by reminding everyone of the importance of the problem: "Although teacher evaluations are critical to school success, there's no fair way of conducting them."

Next, you identify the various alternative viewpoints and explain why each one is deficient:

> *Evaluating teachers on the basis of student test scores is unfair because that rewards the teachers who "teach to the test." Having principals evaluate teachers is unfair because principals can play favorites. Evaluating teachers based on student feedback is unfair because only popular teachers receive good evaluations.*

After identifying the shortcomings of the alternatives, you propose your own solution to the problem:

> *The only fair way to evaluate teachers is by using expert evaluators from other school districts. Because they won't know the content of student exams, they cannot reward teachers for "teaching to the test." Because they don't know the teachers they're evaluating personally, they won't be inclined to play favorites. Finally, because they are experts, their evaluations won't be swayed by teacher popularity.*

By using the comparative advantage method, you acknowledge that other viewpoints exist, but you give your listeners reason to discount them in favor of the viewpoint you are advocating.

Monroe's Motivated Sequence A final way of organizing a persuasive speech is with **Monroe's motivated sequence,** a problem-oriented structure for persuasive arguments. The sequence, developed by former Purdue University professor Alan Monroe, has proved to be particularly effective at motivating listeners to adopt a specific *action,* such as buying a product or giving money to a charity.

• **refutational approach**
A way of organizing a persuasive speech in which the speaker begins by presenting the main arguments against his or her position and then immediately refutes those arguments.

• **comparative advantage method**
A way of organizing a persuasive speech in which the speaker explains why his or her point of view is superior to others on the same topic.

• **Monroe's motivated sequence**
A way of organizing a persuasive speech consisting of appeals to attention, need, satisfaction, visualization, and then action.

Let's say you must give a speech persuading people to donate blood. Monroe's motivated sequence has five stages you address in order:

- *Attention:* The attention stage arouses people's interest and sparks their desire to listen, often by making the topic personally relevant to them. Your message at the attention stage is: *Please listen!*

Example

Imagine you're badly injured in a head-on car crash, and you're quickly losing blood. After you arrive by ambulance at the emergency room, the doctor says you need an immediate blood transfusion to save your life. The only problem is, they don't have enough blood to give you.

- *Need:* Once you've aroused your listeners' attention, your next priority is to identify the need or problem that requires their action. Your message at the need stage is: *Something must be done.*

Example

In the past few years, community blood drives have been less and less successful at collecting enough blood to meet our area's medical needs. Our supply of healthy, usable blood is drying up fast.

- *Satisfaction:* After you've established the problem at the need stage, you use the satisfaction stage to propose your solution. Your message at the satisfaction stage is: *This is what should be done.*

Example

We need an association of healthy, committed volunteers who will donate blood on a regular basis and will encourage their friends, relatives, coworkers, and acquaintances to do the same. That will ensure an ongoing supply of blood to meet our needs.

- *Visualization:* At the visualization stage, you ask your audience to imagine how much better their situation will be if they do what you're proposing. Your message at this stage is: *Consider the benefits.*

Example

With a continuous supply of blood on hand, our area hospitals will be well equipped to respond to a wide range of medical situations, ensuring the health and welfare of the people in our community.

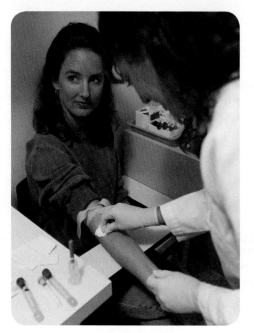

- *Action:* Finally, at the action stage, you tell your listeners what you want them to do. Your request could be that they change their opinions or their beliefs, but often it's that they change their actions. Your message at the action stage is: *Act now!*

Example

You can make a difference by filling out the blood donor cards I'm passing around and dropping them in the cardboard box at the back of the room as you leave.

Each of the four options for organizing a persuasive speech that we've reviewed in this section has its strengths. Every situation is different, and you will need to choose the best option for the specific circumstances. As you consider ways to organize your presentation, think about what you are trying to accomplish and how sympathetic you expect your audience to be. You can use that information to select the organizational approach that will work best for you.

No matter how you organize your persuasive appeal, it's critical that you use valid arguments. Many arguments that seem valid when you first hear them may actually be problematic on closer inspection, as we consider next.

AVOIDING LOGICAL FALLACIES

A **logical fallacy** is a line of reasoning that, even if it makes sense, doesn't genuinely support a speaker's point. Competent speakers avoid logical fallacies because they offer invalid or incomplete evidence for claims. Instead, good speakers focus on providing valid logical arguments and evidence to support their points.

Some logical fallacies are easy to spot; others are subtle and more difficult to identify. The most common fallacies are these:

- Ad hominem *fallacy:* A common but illogical way to counter arguments is to criticize the person who makes them—for instance, "I wouldn't believe anything Senator Rodgers says about fiscal responsibility; the man's an idiot." That line of reasoning, called an **ad hominem fallacy,** implies that if a person has shortcomings, his or her arguments must therefore be deficient. That implication is a fallacy, however; consider that, in our example, even if the speaker doesn't respect Senator Rodgers, the lawmaker's arguments about fiscal responsibility aren't necessarily wrong. To show they are, the speaker must attack the arguments themselves.

- *Slippery slope:* A **slippery slope fallacy**—also called a *reduction to the absurd*—unfairly tries to shoot down an argument by taking it to such an extreme that it appears ludicrous. An activist advocating a ban on same-sex marriage might state: "If we allow gay marriage, pretty soon we'll be legalizing polygamy and allowing people to marry animals." Such a method tries to persuade people not to adopt an argument by extending it to a ridiculous and undesirable extreme.

- *Either/or fallacy:* An **either/or fallacy** identifies two alternatives and falsely suggests that if we reject one, we must accept the other. Take the statement, "Either we make condoms available in public schools or we prepare for an epidemic of sexually transmitted infections among our teenagers." That statement argues for providing condoms by identifying an epidemic of infections as the only possible alternative. The reasoning is invalid—a fallacy—because it ignores the possibility that there may be other ways to keep sexually active adolescents infection-free.

- *False-cause fallacy:* A **false-cause fallacy**—also known as the *post hoc ergo propter hoc* fallacy—asserts that if an event occurs before some outcome, the event therefore caused that outcome. Consider the claim "I started taking ginseng and fish oil supplements three years ago, and I haven't gotten sick once during that time." That claim implies that because the speaker's streak of wellness *followed* her use of supplements, it was therefore *caused by* her use of supplements. Her reasoning is a fallacy, however, because she has no way of knowing whether she would have been free of illness even if she hadn't taken the supplements. The fact that one occurrence preceded the other doesn't mean it caused the other.

- *Bandwagon appeal:* **Bandwagon appeal** suggests that a listener should accept an argument because many other people have. Think about the assertion "Over 15 million people buy Vetris motor oil each month, and you should too—15 million satisfied customers can't be wrong!" The implication is that if an argument (such as to use a particular brand) is popular, it therefore has merit. That may well be true—good products are often popular *because* they are good—but it isn't necessarily true. Can 15 million people be wrong? Absolutely—so the popularity of an argument is no guarantee of its merit.

- *Hasty generalization:* A **hasty generalization** is a broad claim based on insufficient evidence, usually one or two isolated examples. Suppose you were to claim in your speech that it is unsafe to travel in Turkey. To support your claim, you tell of having had your passport stolen from your hotel room during your study-abroad experience in Turkey last year. Your argument is a hasty generalization because your evidence is limited to one incident in one hotel.

- **logical fallacy**
A line of reasoning that, even if it makes sense, does not genuinely support a speaker's point.

- *ad hominem* fallacy
A statement that attempts to counter an argument by criticizing the person who made it.

- slippery slope fallacy
A statement that attacks an argument by taking it to such an extreme that it appears ludicrous.

- either/or fallacy
A statement that identifies two alternatives and falsely suggests that if one is rejected, the other must be accepted.

- false-cause fallacy
A statement asserting that if an event occurs before some outcome, the event therefore caused that outcome.

- bandwagon appeal
A claim that a listener should accept an argument because of how many other people have already accepted it.

- hasty generalization
A broad claim that is based on insufficient evidence.

- *Red herring fallacy:* When people are unable to respond legitimately to an argument, they sometimes introduce an irrelevant detail—thus committing what is known as the **red herring fallacy**—to divert attention from the point of the argument. Suppose you hear someone say "We shouldn't prosecute people for smoking marijuana when there are so many more dangerous drugs out there." Smoking marijuana is still illegal even if other drugs are more dangerous, so the danger of other drugs is irrelevant to the claim that marijuana users shouldn't be prosecuted.

- *Straw man fallacy:* A speaker uses a **straw man fallacy** when he or she refutes a claim that was never made. Let's say the governor of your state proposes to reduce the drinking age in your state to 19 for beer and wine. A legislator responds in a televised interview by saying "Our governor thinks kids should be able to sit in bars drinking martinis! I doubt most parents in this state want to see children getting hammered with hard liquor after school." In that instance, the legislator is trying to refute an argument that the governor hasn't made. After all, the governor's proposal is about 19-year-olds, not children, and about beer and wine, not hard liquor.

- *Begging the question:* **Begging the question** means supporting an argument using the argument itself as evidence. Suppose a speaker says "The use of cell phones while driving should be banned because people shouldn't talk on the phone while driving." That statement presents a claim—cell phone use while driving should be banned—but then supports that claim simply by restating it in another way. No evidence is offered in support of the claim beyond the claim itself.

- *Appeal to false authority:* An **appeal to false authority** uses as evidence the testimony of someone who is not an expert on a given topic. In a persuasive speech about the benefits of a vegan diet, for instance, a student might say "According to an interview with Ellen DeGeneres, a vegan diet is the healthiest way to eat." The problem is that although DeGeneres is a vegan, she is not a physician, nutritionist, or medical scientist. Therefore, despite her high public profile, she is unqualified to comment with authority on the health benefits of veganism or any other diet.

The lines of reasoning described above are fallacies because they each represent an illogical way of supporting an argument. Two important caveats are worth noting, however. First, *arguments supported by logical fallacies may still be true.* Although Ellen DeGeneres is not a medical authority, that fact does not mean, by itself, that she's inaccurate in saying a vegan diet is healthful. It simply means she does not have the credibility (about which we will read shortly) to make that claim. Knowing whether the claim is true or false would require more believable evidence.

Second, *even though they are illogical, fallacies may still be persuasive.* Consider that politicians frequently use *ad hominem* attacks during campaigns, pointing out, say, that an opponent has failed in her business or his marriage. Although such a statement doesn't logically mean the individual is unfit for public office, people aren't persuaded only by logic, as you'll recall from the earlier discussion of rhetorical proof. They are also persuaded by emotion. If politicians can arouse negative emotion about their opponents, even with illogical arguments, they can be—and often are—persuasive in discrediting their rivals. That practice, known as *negative campaigning* or *mudslinging*, is highly controversial

Name That Fallacy!

It's time to put your understanding of logical fallacies to the test. Match each of the fallacies listed below with the statement that exemplifies it.

Fallacy	Statement
_____ 1. bandwagon appeal	A. If we restrict oil drilling in Alaska, then eventually we won't be able to drill for oil anywhere and we'll be back in the Stone Age.
_____ 2. either/or argument	B. You should get an LCD television because that's the type 9 of 10 consumers prefer.
_____ 3. *ad hominem* attack	C. Joining a fraternity made my son an alcoholic. He never drank before he moved into that frat house.
_____ 4. red herring	D. My pediatrician overcharged me for some tests last year. Doctors are crooks!
_____ 5. slippery slope	E. Richard Jones would make a terrible mayor; his daughter's in rehab, for goodness' sake!
_____ 6. hasty generalization	F. You should try acupuncture; Michael Phelps swears by it, and he's won 22 Olympic medals.
_____ 7. appeal to false authority	G. Grading on a curve is unfair because teaching shouldn't be a popularity contest; it's about educating our students.
_____ 8. false cause	H. If you're not pro life, then you're in favor of killing millions of innocent babies.

Spotting logical fallacies can be tricky, but it's a skill you can improve with practice. Answers for this exercise appear at the end of the chapter. Not all fallacies addressed in the chapter are included here, because some are impossible to identify without knowing the arguments that preceded them.

and often considered unethical, particularly when politicians make misleading statements about each other. Although the practice is an example of the dark side of communication, research indicates that negative campaign ads can be just as persuasive as positive ads.[12]

Those caveats aside, however, good persuasive speakers know how to avoid committing logical fallacies. To do so, they first have to be able to spot them accurately. Check out "The Competent Communicator" to see how well *you* can identify some of the most common fallacies.

Honing Your Persuasive-Speaking Skills

Just as an exceptional salesperson can sell almost anything to almost anyone, an outstanding persuasive speaker has the skills to persuade even the most resistant audiences. In this section, we'll explore several strategies for delivering a persuasive speech effectively, including adapting to your audience, building rapport, and establishing your credibility.

ADAPT TO YOUR AUDIENCE

As we've discussed in earlier chapters, it's always important to know who your listeners are and adapt to their needs. Accommodating listeners' needs is useful when you give an informative speech because it helps to ensure that you present information your listeners can understand and don't already know. It is equally important when you are speaking persuasively, because it gives your message the best chance for acceptance. Adapting to your audience requires identifying its general disposition and neutralizing hostility when you encounter it.

Identify Your Audience's Disposition Before presenting a persuasive speech you should know how your audience is likely to react. Some audiences will be receptive to your message, others will be neutral, and still others will be hostile. Connecting with each type of audience requires a different presentational style:

- A **receptive audience** is composed of people who already accept and agree with all or most of what you plan to say. We sometimes use the phrase "preaching to the choir" to describe speaking to a receptive audience. When you have such an audience, your persuasive task is relatively easy because your listeners are likely to respond favorably to whatever you say.

- A **neutral audience** doesn't have strong feelings for or against the topic of your speech. Perhaps such listeners don't know enough about your topic to have formed a strong opinion on it, or maybe they don't care enough about your topic—or see enough of a personal connection to themselves—to bother forming a strong opinion. When speaking to a neutral audience, you should thus inform listeners about what your topic is and why it should matter to them. Once you make it relevant to them, you'll find it easier to persuade them to adopt your viewpoint on the topic.

- The most difficult group to persuade is a **hostile audience,** whose members are predisposed to disagree with you. Their hostile disposition may reflect that they already have a viewpoint on the issue that conflicts with yours, or it may be that they dislike you personally. Whatever the reason, hostile audiences are challenging because they are against you even before you start speaking. Good persuasive speakers can neutralize hostility, however, as we will see later.

Your audience's disposition—and the kinds of persuasive appeals to which it will respond—can also depend on your listeners' cultural background. Research shows that people from different cultures are persuaded by different types of messages. See Table 15.2 for specific examples.

Neutralize Hostility Many people find it difficult to listen to—let alone to be persuaded by—someone toward whom they feel hostility. If a portion of an audience already is disapproving of a speaker, his or her ideas, or the occasion on which the person is speaking, it is challenging to convey the message effectively. Many speakers are so uncomfortable with such situations that they ignore the hostility, hoping their message will be enough to persuade their listeners. Skilled persuasive speakers, however, acknowledge the listeners' negative feelings and then identify points on which they and their listeners agree.

• receptive audience
An audience composed of people who already accept and agree with all or most of what a speaker plans to say.

• neutral audience
An audience lacking strong feelings for or against the topic of a speech.

• hostile audience
An audience in which listeners are predisposed to disagree with the speaker.

TABLE 15.2
CULTURE MATTERS:
CULTURAL
DIFFERENCES IN
PERSUASION

Cultural background can influence the persuasive strategies to which listeners respond. In one study, researchers from Stanford University observed employees of the same international corporation in four different countries. Each employee was asked to comply with a request from another employee. The researchers found noteworthy cultural differences in what persuaded the employees. How might you use this information to understand your audience better?

Culture	Most Effective Persuasive Strategy
Chinese	Authority: Chinese employees complied with requests made by higher-status individuals.
Spanish	Liking: Spanish employees complied with requests made by people they liked.
German	Consistency: German employees complied with requests if such requests were consistent with the organization's rules.
U.S.	Reciprocity: U.S. employees complied with requests made by people who had recently done something for them.

SOURCE: Morris, M. W., Podolny, J. M., & Ariel, S. (2000). *Innovations in international and cross-cultural management.* Thousand Oaks, CA: Sage.

When President Barack Obama delivered the commencement address at the University of Notre Dame in May 2009, he faced just such a situation. As a Catholic institution, Notre Dame opposes abortion, as do many of its students, so they protested the selection of pro-choice Obama as speaker. Instead of shying away from their concerns, the president acknowledged them respectfully and focused on points on which he and his audience could agree:

> *When we open up our hearts and our minds to those who may not think precisely like we do or believe precisely what we believe, that's when we discover at least the possibility of common ground. That's when we begin to say, "Maybe we won't agree on abortion, but we can still agree that this heart-wrenching decision for any woman is not made casually, it has both moral and spiritual dimensions. So let us work together to reduce the number of women seeking abortions, let's reduce unintended pregnancies. Let's make adoption more available. Let's provide care and support for women who do carry their children to term. Let's honor the conscience of those who disagree with abortion, and draft a sensible conscience clause, and make sure that all of our health care policies are grounded not only in sound science, but also in clear ethics, as well as respect for the equality of women." Those are things we can do.*

By giving voice to his opponents' views on abortion, Obama made his critics feel respected instead of maligned. Further, by identifying points on which he and his critics agreed, he provided a way for people on all sides of this divisive issue to communicate with one another, neutralizing much of the opposition that surrounded his selection as commencement speaker.

To read about one career in which you could use your audience analysis skills, check out the "Putting Communication to Work" box.

During his commencement speech at the University of Notre Dame in May 2009, President Barack Obama respectfully acknowledged differences of opinion regarding the controversial issue of abortion.

• **build rapport**
Create the perception that listeners and the speaker see things similarly.

BUILD RAPPORT WITH YOUR LISTENERS

Knowing your audience will also help you to build rapport with your listeners. To **build rapport** is to create the perception that your listeners and you see things similarly. It establishes trust and encourages audience members to listen even if they disagree with you.

SHARPEN Your Skills: *Establishing common ground*

Suppose you were speaking on a controversial topic to a hostile audience. Select a topic on which you and your audience would disagree, and then outline at least three ways you could establish common ground with your listeners on the topic.

Job Title >

Work Responsibilities >

Sales Associate for Financial Services Firm

Financial services firms often offer a broad range of products geared toward diverse audiences, such as first-time investors, parents saving for college costs, and retirees. A sales associate meets with various groups of people and must determine which products would appeal to each crowd. He or she then explains what the financial services firm can do and persuades listeners to buy the firm's products. Besides requiring good public speaking skills, this position also benefits from a keen ability to analyze audiences and ascertain how best to appeal to each group of listeners.

Several behaviors can help you to build rapport with your audience:

- *Interact with listeners before your speech.* Particularly when you're speaking to people you don't know well, spend time talking to them—and listening to them—before your speech. Not only will you get information about who your listeners are and what they're thinking; you will also signal to your audience that you care about them.

- *Maintain eye contact while you speak.* According to research, most people believe a lack of eye contact indicates the speaker is being deceptive.[13] If you don't look at your audience while you speak, you're likely to come across as untrustworthy—an undesirable effect when you're trying to persuade. Practice establishing and maintaining eye contact with each person in your audience for three to four seconds at a time.

- *Open with a story.* Because everyone loves a good story, an excellent way to build rapport with your audience is to open with one. Stories are especially effective when they include information to which your audience can relate. If you live in a cold climate but are speaking in a hot one, for instance, you could describe your experience of dealing with the heat, because your listeners will be able to relate to it themselves.

- *Use humor when appropriate.* It's difficult not to like people who make us laugh. Therefore, a particularly effective way to establish rapport is to use humor in your presentation. Humor can consist of short jokes or one-liners and can also be reflected in the stories you tell. Incorporating humor can help your listeners to relax and enjoy your presentation—and be receptive to your message. When considering the use of humor, however, think carefully about what your audience is likely to find funny and in good taste. It is best to stay away from jokes that risk offending listeners and that your audience may not understand or appreciate.

adaptability Defusing Discord

The Scene: You are giving a persuasive speech on the topic of government-sanctioned torture in the interrogation of suspected terrorists. You predict that your audience will be mostly neutral on the issue, but as you begin to describe your point of view, you perceive that many of your listeners are becoming hostile to your ideas. You fear you will fail to persuade them and will lose their respect.

Your Task: Consider how you could adapt your presentation as you start to perceive listeners' hostility. What strategies would you use to

- Neutralize hostility?

- Build rapport?

- Repair your credibility?

ESTABLISH YOUR CREDIBILITY

Earlier in this chapter, we considered the value of appealing to ethos, which is the integrity, trustworthiness, and goodness of the speaker. Knowing that ethos is important, good persuasive speakers work to establish credibility with their audiences. **Credibility** means believability—if you're credible, people will believe what you have to say. If you have a good deal of credibility, audiences will take your words seriously and be open to new ideas. If your credibility is low, however, you will find it hard to persuade, even if your evidence is strong. Establishing credibility is thus vital for persuasive speakers. Researchers believe credibility has three different components: competence, character, and charisma.[14]

• credibility
A speaker's believability.

Demonstrate Your Competence People have *competence* when they have the required skills, knowledge, and organization to perform a task well. Think back to the first day of this class. What impressions did you have of your instructor? Did he or she seem knowledgeable, organized, well prepared, and professional? If so, those characteristics probably gave you confidence in what your instructor had to say. By comparison, when you've had instructors who appeared ignorant, disorganized, unprepared, and unprofessional, you probably lacked confidence in their abilities.

Just as you have more confidence in a competent instructor, listeners will have more confidence in you if you come across as a competent speaker. Describing the experience and knowledge you have of your topic, and speaking in a polished, well-organized manner, will demonstrate your competence.

Accent Your Character A person's *character* is his or her degree of honesty. People who appear honest are more credible than those who appear dishonest because we can have greater confidence that what honest individuals say is accurate and true. In jury trials, for example, lawyers frequently cast doubt on the testimony of their opponents' witnesses by questioning their character. If an attorney can establish that an opposing witness has been caught lying in the past, that history makes the witness appear to be of questionable character and can lead the jury to doubt his or her testimony.

Misleading to Persuade: A Threat to Credibility

High fuel prices and concerns about the global environment have combined in recent years to boost sales of hybrid cars. By using electricity as well as gasoline, hybrid cars can dramatically reduce fossil-fuel consumption. One of the most popular models of hybrid car is the Honda Civic, which the auto manufacturer advertised as getting 50 miles per gallon of gas.

Honda customer Heather Peters found that claim unpersuasive, however. After purchasing a 2006 Civic hybrid, Peters experienced fuel economy closer to 30 miles per gallon than the advertised 50. She therefore took Honda to small claims court, asserting that the manufacturer had made misleading claims about the Civic's fuel efficiency.

In February 2012, the small claims division of Los Angeles County Superior Court awarded Peters $9,867 after finding merit in her claim of false advertising. Although small, the award (and the media coverage of the controversy) may have cast doubt on Honda's credibility in the minds of its customers and perhaps served as an example for other companies wishing to protect their own credibility.

Good persuasive speakers establish their character by incorporating stories and anecdotes about themselves that demonstrate their honesty. In addition, speakers who enact *high-immediacy behaviors*—such as standing close to others, leaning forward, using eye contact, and maintaining an open posture—are judged to be of more positive character than speakers who do not enact those behaviors.[15]

Communicate with Charisma A final component of credibility is *charisma*, which is a speaker's enthusiasm. As you know, it's much easier to listen to—and be persuaded by—someone who speaks dynamically and energetically than by someone who seems bored by his or her own words. So, when you're giving a persuasive speech, approach your topic and your audience with enthusiasm. Smile! Use gestures and vary your tone of voice to keep your presentation interesting. Look at your audience and use facial expressions that reflect the mood of your message. Bringing energy and excitement to your presentation will encourage your listeners to pay attention and make them receptive to your words.

Table 15.3 provides a brief summary of the three components of credibility.

The Bottom Line: Credibility Matters In the business world, a company's credibility often directly affects its profits. Corporations therefore go to great lengths to establish and maintain their credibility.

In late 2009 and early 2010, for instance, Toyota recalled thousands of its cars because of problems with the accelerator

Charismatic speakers are often more persuasive than speakers who lack energy and excitement.

Competence—Competent speakers appear knowledgeable, organized, professional, and prepared.	**TABLE 15.3**
Character—Speakers of good character appear honest and trustworthy.	THAT'S CREDIBLE! THREE COMPONENTS OF CREDIBILITY
Charisma—Charismatic speakers are energetic, dynamic, and excited about their message.	

and brakes. After months of denying that any problems existed, Toyota placed advertisements on U.S. television and in major publications reinforcing its commitment to stand by its products and fix the problems.[16] By taking that action, the company tried to restore consumer confidence and repair damage to its credibility that could have resulted in lost sales and reduced profits.

In contrast, companies found to use false or misleading statements to persuade customers often lose credibility and suffer decreased profits as a result. Consumers find deceptive practices in advertising to be unethical. To read about the problems one company encountered after losing credibility due to misleading statements, see "The Dark Side of Communication."

A Sample Persuasive Speech

A good way to develop persuasive-speaking skills is to study excellent examples. Below is the text of a persuasive speech by Jennifer Wells, a communication studies major at the University of Alabama and a member of the school's speech and debate team. Jennifer's speech advocates expanding laws that protect people from sexual harassment in the workplace. Jennifer was a quarter-finalist in persuasive speaking with this speech at the American Forensics Association National Tournament in April 2009. Alongside the text are comments about what makes each section of her speech so effective. The formal outline for Jennifer's speech appears in Figure 15.2.

CLOSING THE LOOPHOLE ON SEXUAL HARASSMENT

COMMENTARY	SPEECH
This introduction opens with a compelling story introducing listeners to the problem described in the speech, same-sex sexual harassment in the workplace.	Joseph Oncale is not a household name . . . at least, not yet. After taking a job as a roughneck on an oil rig with Sundowner Offshore Services, Oncale's outgoing personality was incorrectly perceived as stereotypically homosexual behavior by his coworkers. They verbally and physically abused Oncale, culminating in an episode in which Oncale's arms were pinned behind his back in the shower while cheering coworkers looked on as a Sundowner supervisor simulated raping Oncale with a bar of soap.
	Certain that he would be protected against such unrestrained subjugation and cruelty, Oncale sued Sundowner for sexual harassment. According to the *Labor Law Journal* of April 1, 2005, the Louisiana Supreme Court found that the atrocities committed against the heterosexual Oncale by Sundowner Services were perfectly excusable under the law. After all, boys will be boys. A loophole in Title 7—the federal safeguard protecting against sexual harassment and discrimination—permits heinous same-sex sexual harassment.
Here, the speaker makes her persuasive appeal. Notice that she offers a proposition of value: *we should protect people from same-sex sexual harassment.* Later, she will advocate changing the law, which is a proposition of policy.	The starkest ramifications of this loophole can be seen in discriminatory practices between men. According to a report from the Equal Employment Opportunity Commission, or EEOC, between 1997 and 2007, 1 out of every 6 reports of sexual harassment was filed by a man. While significant, the scope of the issue is blurred by the fact that, according to the *Mondaq Legal News Network* on July 31, 2008, of those incidents, only a few make it to the verdict stage of a trial, and even fewer survive the appellate proceedings.
	Regardless of one's moral, ethical, or religious views on sexuality, everyone deserves the protection of a safe workplace. Therefore, it is our duty as a vigilant society to ensure that we recognize the extent of this social injustice, identify the sources allowing this backwater practice to persist, and unite to protect those whose fundamental human rights have been ignored.

COMMENTARY	SPEECH
Notice how the speaker effectively previews the topics she plans to address.

The speaker is careful throughout the speech to cite her sources. These citations help to give her words credibility. | To understand this problem better, let's first examine the ramifications of a hostile work environment, and second, the loophole in the law. First, men deciding to report harassment risk escalating a hostile work environment into an openly discriminatory work environment. Servers who filed suit against the Cheesecake Factory stated in the July 11, 2008, *Los Angeles Times,* "It's just different when it happens to a guy; there's always the fear that they're going to question your manhood." The fact that the servers reported anything is unusual, because on top of the vulnerability involved in reporting harassment, coworkers and companies often make it even harder. *PR Week* of May 2, 2008, reports a case in which a finance director assaulted his male assistant during a trip. When the assistant reported it, he was forced to leave his job, but the finance director remains unpunished. |
	Second, those brave enough to report sexual harassment often do so without the support of the law. The protection of Title 7 of the Civil Rights Act of 1964 extends only to individuals who are discriminated against on the basis of race, color, religion, sex, or national origin. This wording means that the law provides no protection from harassment based on sexual orientation or assumed sexual orientation, or from a member of one's own sex. Therefore, if you are a man and another man sexually harasses you in some way, you have no federally secured recourse. Contending that it is impossible for a man to sexually harass another man, the courts and Congress have repeatedly refused to acknowledge same-sex sexual harassment as an actionable discrimination, especially harassment based on sexual orientation. The December 2006 *Journal of Individual Employment Rights* succinctly explains that, as a federally unprotected class, homosexuals remain extremely exposed to discrimination in the form of sexual harassment.
Here, the speaker offers another brief preview of points she plans to make. By doing so, she helps her listeners to follow the organization of her speech.	The same misconceptions that permitted the Title 7 loophole in 1964 perpetuate today. To better understand why, we must first understand the motivations behind sexual harassment and then examine the short-sighted view many take of it. First, although most people blame sexual desire for demeaning behavior, more often than not desire has nothing to do with motivating perpetrators. The *Journal of Individual Employment Rights* asserts that same-sex sexual harassment usually cannot be attributed to the sexual orientation of the victim or the perpetrator. Instead, it is a "power issue." A 2004 *Journal of Sex Roles* study clarifies that hostile sexism results from the belief that heterosexual men are superior to women and effeminate or homosexual men. That motivation means that the loophole in Title 7 not only permits heinous discrimination but also perpetuates behaviors that invoke heterosexual as the "normal" or "superior" lifestyle. This desire to maintain the status quo propels perpetrators to exploit positions of power, resulting in increasingly hostile work environments.
Here, the speaker uses a quote from an attorney involved in the lawsuit as a way of supporting her point.	The second reason why same-sex sexual harassment is so often overlooked is because of general attitudes toward interpersonal relationships between men. When the law was written over 40 years ago, the sexual harassment tenet was included solely to safeguard women from men. That concentrated focus kept lawmakers from realizing that sexual harassment may occur in ways outside of their hetero-normative viewpoint. As the attorney in the lawsuit against the Cheesecake Factory stated in the *Los Angeles Times,* "There's this expectation that this doesn't happen to men. It's almost this boys-will-be-boys attitude of 'Oh, it's just hazing, it's just teasing, you can't take it seriously.'" The servers of the Cheesecake Factory restaurant in the lawsuit reported harassment that included simulated gang rape. The managers—who were fully aware of the problem—seemed amused and took no action to prohibit the offensive behavior. Their attitude of amusement carried into the court proceedings where, according to the previously cited article from *Mondaq Legal News Network,* in the appeal of *EEOC v. Harbert-Yeargin, Inc.,* the court furthered the "horseplay" excuse and overturned the original guilty verdict by asking, "What's next? Towel slapping in the locker room?"
The speaker introduces her proposition of policy, which is a change in Title 7.	This shamefully outdated view of sexual harassment provides a breeding ground for hostility and degradation. However, solutions exist on the government and personal levels. We as citizens must petition our government officials, letting them know that we do not agree with the loophole in Title 7 but we do agree that action must be taken. I have with me a petition. At the end of this speech round, please add your name to the list alongside those who disagree with allowing a law that permits discrimination to stand. At the end of the year I will send this petition to the EEOC, the organization spearheading the movement to close the loophole in Title 7. This petition will show our support of their activism and our willingness to add our names to the cause. In an open letter released on February 28, 2008, President Obama told the LGBT [lesbian, gay, bisexual, and transgender] community that he would end workplace discrimination based on sexual orientation or gender identity. Hopefully, our outpouring of support will further encourage the president to make good on his promise and move toward equality for all by closing the loophole.
	A mandate on the national level would force corporations to update and streamline their policies in accordance with federal law. On a personal level, we can all take a stand against sexual harassment in any form. Most important, we must reshape our paradigms regarding what constitutes harassment. If you see something that would be considered harassment were it to take place between a man and a woman, it is harassment. Teasing is never an excuse. After all, as a community that generally prides itself in promoting acceptance, if change does not begin with us, where will it begin?
In her conclusion, the speaker reminds her listeners of her opening story, a technique that personalizes the issue.	Anytime sexual harassment occurs it is disgraceful, yet when sexual harassment is all but sanctioned under the law it is despicable. Fortunately, Joseph Oncale took his case before the U.S. Supreme Court, who decided that what happened to Oncale was indeed sexual harassment. The decision read by Justice Antonin Scalia laid the foundation to eventually protect the rights of all workers. Hopefully, the name Joseph Oncale will eventually be remembered as a pioneer in defending those whom the government had left to defend themselves.

TITLE: Closing the Loophole on Sexual Harassment

General purpose: To persuade

Purpose statement: Persuade my audience that it is the duty of a vigilant society to protect individuals from same-sex sexual harassment in the workplace.

INTRODUCTION

I. Joseph Oncale was subjected to simulated rape by his fellow male oil rig workers.

II. Despite his protests, no punishment ensued because same-sex sexual harassment is not recognized under the law.

III. **Thesis:** Regardless of one's moral, ethical, or religious views on sexuality, everyone deserves the protection of a safe workplace.

Transition: Describe ramifications of hostile work environment; identify loophole in sexual harassment law; offer solutions.

BODY

I. What is same-sex sexual harassment?
   A. Reporting same-sex harassment risks escalating hostility.
      1. Reporting harassment can turn a hostile work environment into an openly discriminatory one.
      2. *PR Week:* Financial director accused of assault of a male subordinate was allowed to keep his job.
   B. Those brave enough to report sexual harassment often do so without the support of the law.
      1. Title 7 of the Civil Rights Act of 1964 provides no protection from same-sex sexual harassment.
      2. *Journal of Individual Employment Rights:* As a federally unprotected class, homosexuals remain exposed to discrimination.

Transition: To understand why same-sex harassment is permitted by the loophole, we must understand the nature of sexual harassment.

II. The law overlooks same-sex sexual harassment.
   A. Power is a motivator of demeaning behavior.
      1. *Journal of Sex Roles:* Hostile sexism results from the belief that heterosexual men are superior to women and homosexual men.

2. The loophole therefore perpetuates the stereotype of heterosexuality as "normal."
   B. Outdated attitudes and beliefs persist about interpersonal relationships between men.
      1. Sexual harassment laws were originally intended to protect women from men.
      2. *Mondaq Legal News Network:* Courts accept the "boys will be boys" explanation for same-sex harassment.

Transition: Obsolete views of sexual harassment encourage hostility and degradation. Solutions exist, however.

III. Solutions exist at government and personal levels.
   A. The Title 7 loophole needs to be closed.
      1. Sign petition to the Equal Employment Opportunity Commission.
      2. Obama: I will end workplace discrimination based on sexual orientation or gender identity.
   B. People should take individual stands against sexual harassment.
      1. We must reshape our ideas about what constitutes sexual harassment.
      2. Any sexual harassment should be reported to authorities.

Transition: Any sexual harassment is disgraceful, but when sexual harassment is all but sanctioned under the law, it is despicable and must be legally prohibited.

CONCLUSION

I. Review of main points
   A. People deserve protection from sexual harassment, whether same-sex or opposite-sex.
   B. Sexual harassment that is sanctioned by law is despicable.

II. Final remarks
   A. Joseph Oncale's case has been heard by the U.S. Supreme Court.
   B. His case hopefully will prompt changes to federal sexual harassment laws in the United States.

FIGURE 15.2

FORMAL SPEECH OUTLINE: CLOSING THE LOOPHOLE ON SEXUAL HARASSMENT

- **What does it mean to persuade?** Persuasion is an attempt to motivate others to adopt a specific belief, opinion, or behavior. We persuade others by appealing to ethos, pathos, and/or logos.

- **In what ways can we craft a persuasive message?** Persuasive messages can propose facts, values, or policies. They are organized in a compelling manner and avoid the use of logical fallacies.

- **Through what strategies can we hone our persuasive-speaking skills?** We can adapt to our audience, build rapport with our listeners, and establish our credibility.

POP QUIZ

Multiple Choice

1. Kellie tries to convince her instructor that she did her homework but left it in her car. Kellie is trying to influence her instructor's

   a. belief.
   b. opinion.
   c. evaluation.
   d. action.

2. Which statement constitutes a proposition of fact?

   a. English should be the official language of the United States.
   b. College tuition should be made fully tax-deductible.
   c. National security is more important than individual rights.
   d. Platinum is three times as heavy as gold.

3. In Monroe's motivated sequence, the message "consider the benefits" would occur at the stage called

   a. need.
   b. satisfaction.
   c. visualization.
   d. action.

4. Mac suggests that you should accept his argument because many other people already have. Mac is using the logical fallacy known as

   a. false cause.
   b. straw man.
   c. red herring.
   d. bandwagon appeal.

5. The aspect of credibility that reflects a speaker's honesty is

   a. competence.
   b. character.
   c. charisma.
   d. enthusiasm.

Fill in the Blank

6. Aristotle used the term _____ to refer to listeners' emotions.

7. _____ reasoning starts with a general conclusion and then applies it to individual cases.

8. A _____ approach to persuasion begins by presenting, and then arguing against, the main objections to your position.

9. A "reduction to the absurd" is also called a _____.

10. When you build _____, you create the perception that you and your listeners see things similarly.

ANSWERS FOR THE COMPETENT COMMUNICATOR EXERCISE: 5-A; 1-B; 8-C; 6-D; 3-E; 7-F; 4-G; 2-H

ANSWERS: 1. a; 2. d; 3. c; 4. d; 5. b; 6. pathos; 7. Deductive; 8. refutational; 9. slippery slope; 10. rapport

KEY TERMS

persuasive speaking 358
persuasion 358
belief 358
opinion 359
action 359
forms of rhetorical proof 360
ethos 360
pathos 361
logos 362
reason 362
inductive reasoning 362
deductive reasoning 363
syllogism 363

enthymeme 363
proposition 364
proposition of fact 364
proposition of value 364
proposition of policy 365
problem-solving pattern 366
refutational approach 367
comparative advantage method 367
Monroe's motivated sequence 367
logical fallacy 369
ad hominem fallacy 369
slippery slope fallacy 369

either/or fallacy 369
false-cause fallacy 369
bandwagon appeal 369
hasty generalization 369
red herring fallacy 370
straw man fallacy 370
begging the question 370
appeal to false authority 370
receptive audience 372
neutral audience 372
hostile audience 372
build rapport 373
credibility 375

Appendix

WORKPLACE COMMUNICATION AND INTERVIEWING

················▶ As You READ

- What communication processes are important in the workplace?
- What communication challenges do workplaces face today?
- In what ways can we improve our interviewing skills?

Nearly all of us will be employed at some point in our lives. Whether we work for a large multinational corporation or a small business with only a few employees, our ability to communicate effectively in the workplace can matter greatly to those whose lives are affected by our work. In this appendix, we explore **workplace communication**, the interactions people have as part of their employment.

Communicating in the Workplace

Many popular television shows—from dramas such as *NCIS* and *Criminal Minds* to comedies such as *30 Rock* and *Community*—focus their storylines on how the characters communicate in the workplace. Most viewers can relate to the communication behaviors and challenges depicted in such shows. Building and maintaining workplace relationships is often difficult, although it can be highly rewarding. In this section, we survey the challenges and benefits of communicating within the workplace, look at employees' communications with people outside the workplace, and examine some key dimensions of creating a positive workplace culture.

COMMUNICATING WITHIN THE WORKPLACE

Much of workplace communication is **internal communication**, that is, the messages people within the workplace convey to one another. A face-to-face or virtual meeting of managers, a companywide e-mail message, and an employee intranet are all examples of internal communication. Internal workplace communication can be either formal or informal.

Formal Workplace Communication
Formal communication consists of messages from the work organization that relate to its operations. Whether written or electronic, memos, official announcements, company newsletters, mission statements, and employee evaluations are all types of formal communication that members of many organizations regularly encounter.

The tone and content of formal workplace communication vary according to the relative status of the sender and the audience. For instance, few of us would speak in the same way to our boss as to our peers. We can understand the effects of relative status on formal workplace communication by differentiating among communication that is upward, downward, and lateral.

- **Upward communication** consists of messages we send to people at higher levels of the organizational hierarchy than ours. These include messages to immediate supervisors as well as to higher-level employees, such as an e-mail we might send to the company president. When communicating upward, we're most likely to be taken seriously if our statements are clear, concise, and respectful.

- **Downward communication** describes messages we send to people at lower levels of the organizational hierarchy, such as subordinates, interns, and staff members who report to us. Although such messages are often instructions regarding work assignments, they may also be general announcements, explanations of policy, or notes of encouragement. When communicating downward, avoid specialized jargon and use language that anyone—regardless of his or her job—can understand. If your message contains criticism, choose your words tactfully and avoid embarrassing people by singling them out.

- **Lateral communication** consists of messages we share with peers, coworkers, and anyone who occupies the same position or level of power in the workplace hierarchy that we do. Effective communication with peers contributes to a positive work environment and makes the work experience more satisfying. Good lateral communication treats people as equals and helps them to accomplish the goals we share.

Informal Workplace Communication

Formal communication—whether upward, downward, or lateral—is critical to any organization's ability to manage its image and conduct its operations. However, much of the communication in workplaces is informal. Unlike formal communication, **informal communication** is not necessarily sanctioned by the employer but arises from the social interactions of its members.

Many people say that informal communication travels along a **grapevine**, a metaphor indicating that informal messages are often conveyed in upward, downward, and lateral directions simultaneously. Just as a grapevine twists and turns in seemingly unpredictable ways as it grows, in many workplaces informal messages take a similarly unpredictable path.

Regarding communication grapevines, research tells us that:

- *Grapevines use multiple communication channels.* Much communication along the grapevine is accomplished face to face, as people visit informally (and perhaps even secretly) to share information and gossip. Workplace grapevines also make use of telephone, e-mail, text messaging, instant messaging, and other forms of electronically mediated communication, allowing people to participate who aren't physically present.[1]

- *People rely heavily on the grapevine during a crisis.* When employees feel threatened by a situation, such as the announcement of upcoming layoffs, they can spend as much as 70 percent of their workplace communication time on the grapevine, listening to what others know and speculating about what they've heard. Particularly when a situation is ambiguous, we seem to crave the comfort of our informal communication networks.[2]

- *Communication along the grapevine can be remarkably accurate.* The informality of grapevine communication doesn't mean it's inaccurate. Studies show that grapevine messages are substantially accurate 75 to 95 percent of the time. Equally important, employees tend to *believe* grapevine messages are accurate, maybe even more accurate than the employer's formal communication.[3]

COMMUNICATING TO EXTERNAL AUDIENCES

Nearly all organizations also communicate regularly with external audiences. When conducted effectively, **external communication**—that is, messages people within the workplace convey to others outside the organization—can significantly enhance the company's reputation, productivity, community support, and economic success. In contrast, poorly managed external communication can cause a workplace irreparable harm.

Among the many external audiences with whom companies must communicate are these:

- *Consumers*, or anyone who buys or might buy a company's products or services. For many organizations, a primary vehicle for communicating with consumers is advertising. Companies advertise their goods or services in multiple ways, including television and radio commercials; print advertisements and inserts in newspapers and magazines; electronic ads posted on the Internet or sent via e-mail or smart phone; corporate web pages and social media pages and Twitter feeds; signs and billboards visible to drivers; unsolicited sales calls made in person or by telephone; and booths at fairs, trade shows, and sporting events. To explore one career requiring frequent communication with consumers, check out "Putting Communication to Work."

- *Potential members*, or anyone who might come to work for the organization as either a paid employee or a volunteer. Corporations, nonprofit groups, and the military frequently recruit employees or volunteers through television, radio, and social network and Internet ads.

puttingcommunicationtowork

[Search]

Job Title >

Work Responsibilities >

Account manager for telecommunications company

The primary responsibility of an account manager is to communicate with customers and ensure their satisfaction with the company's products and services. Account managers intervene to solve problems when consumers are dissatisfied, and they describe new products and services in which consumers may be interested. The position requires excellent listening skills as well as an ability to anticipate what customers want or need.

- *Stockholders*, or people who own shares of a publicly traded company. Companies communicate with their stockholders primarily through their annual reports, which detail the financial gains and losses of a company's endeavors over the course of a year.

- *The media*, which include broadcast, print, and electronic forms of mass communication. Many organizations have spokespersons or media relations managers who accommodate reporters' requests for informational interviews or statements to include in news features.

- *Lawmakers*, including local elected officials, state legislators, and members of Congress. In January 2012, for instance, the chief executive officer of General Motors testified before a committee of the U.S. House of Representatives to discuss the safety of electric cars.

- *The general public*, which includes current or potential customers and employees and anyone else to whom an employer's reputation matters. Many large companies employ public relations experts who use communication to shape their public image.

WORKPLACE CULTURE

Pixar Animation Studios in Emeryville, California, is an unconventional place to work. To stimulate innovative, outside-the-box thinking, company president Ed Catmull instituted Pixar University. This professional-development program encourages risk taking and invites irrational thought as avenues to creativity. To minimize stress, Catmull makes a physician and a massage therapist available to Pixar employees several times a month, and he requires animators to get special permission to work more than 50 hours in a single week. The animation studio boasts a café, break rooms with pool and foosball tables, and an open area for concerts and lectures. At the urging of former

Pixar CEO Steve Jobs, Catmull even created one giant bathroom for the company's 700 employees so people across the organization would regularly interact and talk. Its innovations have put Pixar on the map as a company with a remarkable workplace culture.

Throughout this book, we have talked about culture as the collective values, customs, and communication behaviors shared among people in a particular country or social group. Communication researchers believe that workplaces have their own cultures. We can think of **workplace culture** as the values, customs, and communication behaviors that workplace members share and that reflect their organization's distinct identity. We can understand workplace culture by examining its rites, rituals, and roles.

• workplace culture The values, customs, and communication behaviors that workplace members share and that reflect their organization's distinct identity.

• rites Ceremonial acts and practices that convey one or more characteristics of a workplace's culture.

Workplaces Have Rites
Rites are ceremonial acts and practices that convey one or more characteristics of a workplace's culture. Organizational behavior scholars Harrison Trice and Janice Beyer identified six types of workplace rites:[4]

- *Rites of passage* signify people's advancement to a higher status or level in a workplace. Ceremonies to celebrate an employee's promotion are examples of rites of passage.
- *Rites of integration* enhance feelings of inclusion and community in the workplace. Participation in a company's annual picnic, for instance, can reinforce employees' sense of belonging to the group.
- *Blaming rites* are concerned with consequences for poor or unethical performance. For example, attorneys who violate client confidentiality might be reprimanded, demoted, or fired and may lose their license to practice law.
- *Enhancement rites* relate to consequences for superior performance. Excellent salespeople might receive plaques, cash bonuses, trips, or recognition as Salesperson of the Year in acknowledgment of outstanding achievement.
- *Renewal rites* update and revitalize a workplace. After a particularly disappointing year of collecting donations, a nonprofit group, for example, might organize a retreat to boost morale and refresh its employees' solicitation skills.
- *Conflict resolution rites* aim to manage disagreements and discord. To resolve conflicts between management and employees, a large corporation might use a mediator to help representatives from each group reach consensus on their disagreements.

• rituals Repeated behaviors that provide a familiar routine to a workplace's experiences.

Workplaces Have Rituals
Whereas rites occur when circumstances call for them, **rituals** are repeated behaviors that provide a familiar routine to a workplace's experiences.[5] In workplaces, three types of rituals are especially common:

1. *Personal rituals* are routine behaviors through which individuals convey their workplace identity.[6] On the first day of each fiscal year, a manager might personally greet each arriving employee as a way of communicating her interest in their well-being.
2. *Social rituals* are recurring events that reinforce personal relationships among workplace members.[7] The custodial staff at a government agency might meet every other Thursday for happy hour, for example, in a ritual that allows them to socialize, share information, and affirm their personal bonds.
3. *Task rituals* are repeated activities that enhance people's abilities to do their jobs. For example, when greeting a patient at a clinic, a medical assistant typically performs a series of ritualized tasks, such as asking about symptoms, current medications, and drug allergies and then taking the patient's vital signs.

SHARPEN Your Skills: *Workplace rites*

Identify a rite that is common in your workplace. Observe the communication behaviors that rite affects, and in what ways. Notice especially how it influences your own communication. Write up your observations in a short paragraph or journal entry.

Many rites and rituals reinforce a workplace's current cultural practices. As a workplace culture evolves, however, its rites and rituals often follow suit. In response to various threats to traveler safety, for instance, the U.S. Transportation Security Administration has changed its task rituals for screening airline passengers. Those changes include requiring passengers to remove their shoes for X-ray screening and limiting the types and amounts of liquid that passengers can bring aboard an airplane.

Workplaces Have Roles As we saw in Chapter 8, people in families enact different *roles*, which embody their functions within the family system. The same can be said of people in workplaces. Each employee has certain responsibilities to the group that reflect his or her role.

Some workplace roles are **formal roles**, functions that are prescribed by the employer itself. The formal role of a receptionist, for instance, may be to greet visitors, provide directions to specific company facilities, issue visitor passes, and answer incoming telephone calls. Formal roles are interconnected in a system that fulfills all necessary functions of the workplace. Organizational charts, such as the one in Figure A.1, specify the connections among various roles in a fictitious manufacturing company.

Formal roles are tied to *positions* within the workplace rather than to particular individuals. The formal role of a receptionist is the same no matter who has that job. In contrast, **informal roles** are functions adopted by specific people rather than being dictated by the workplace. Whereas formal roles serve the organization's professional needs, informal roles often evolve to serve social and interpersonal needs. At his advertising agency, for instance, Jay is known as someone with an exceptional sense of humor who can always be counted on to bring comic relief to stressful situations. We might say that Jay has assumed the informal role of company comedian. No one

• **formal roles** Responsibilities and functions that are prescribed by the employer.

• **informal roles** Responsibilities and functions adopted by specific people rather than being dictated by the workplace.

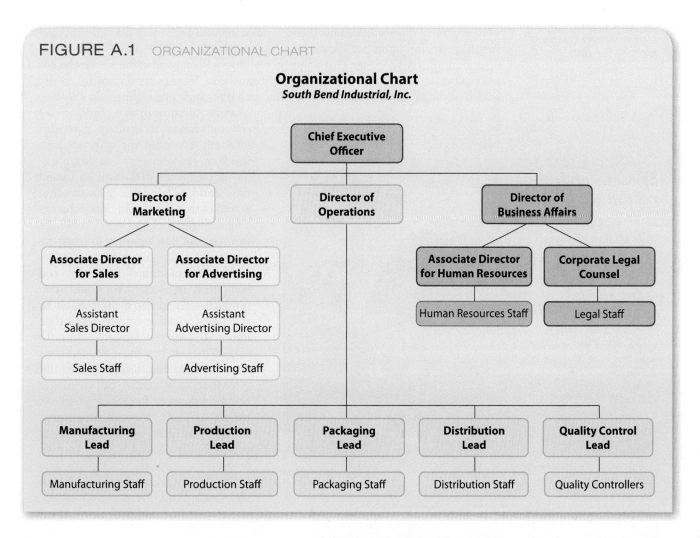

FIGURE A.1 ORGANIZATIONAL CHART

Organizational Chart
South Bend Industrial, Inc.

formally assigned him that responsibility; it wasn't included in his job description or detailed in his contract. Moreover, that role is tied specifically to Jay because of his personality and sense of humor; it would not necessarily be expected of the next person to occupy Jay's position. For those reasons, company comedian is an informal role.

An informal role isn't necessarily any less important than a formal role. Indeed, research shows that sharing humor in the workplace—as Jay does informally—can reinforce company culture,[8] alleviate tension,[9] foster creativity,[10] and enhance interpersonal relationships.[11] Many informal roles employees might play—including conflict mediator, confidante, or social event organizer—are seen by others as indispensable to the group's success.

Managing Workplace Communication Challenges

Everyone in workplace organizations—large and small—encounters communication challenges from time to time. Although no list can enumerate every possible challenge, we can appreciate the communication trials that employees face by examining four issues: globalization, communication technology, work/life conflict, and diversity.

GLOBALIZATION AND CROSS-CULTURAL CHALLENGES

• **globalization** The increasing interconnectedness of societies and their economies as a result of developments in transportation and communication.

The world has shrunk considerably—figuratively speaking, at least—in the past hundred years. Almost unbelievably, travel time between continents used to be measured in weeks rather than hours. Only a few decades ago, telephone calls to other countries were extremely expensive, and mail service was unreliable and slow. Consequently, only very large organizations had the means to communicate and do business with overseas organizations. Today, we can chat online in real time with anyone in the world who has a computer or smartphone and an Internet connection. We can fax documents to any corner of the globe in minutes, and we can send a package overnight to virtually any country. Advances in transportation and communication technology have significantly expanded the audience with which we can interact and made it possible for companies to do business around the world. The term **globalization** describes the increasing interconnectedness of societies and their economies as a result of developments in transportation and communication.

Millions of items—from cars and computers to clothes, toys, and food products—are either manufactured or assembled in other countries and then imported into the United States for sale. When we buy those products, we are affecting, and being affected by, globalization. When we call to receive technical support for a new purchase, we are as likely to speak with someone in New Delhi as in New York. As companies have expanded to include employees, suppliers, customers, and members around the world, they have had to adapt to a diversity of languages, customs, and ways of doing business.

SHARPEN Your Skills: *Intercultural communication*

Interview two or three people who travel extensively as part of their job. Ask them to identify the communication challenges they most commonly encounter when interacting with people from other cultures and to describe how they overcome those challenges. Based on what you discover, generate a list of recommendations for ways people can improve their intercultural communication skills. Document your findings in a short paper or journal entry.

COMMUNICATION TECHNOLOGY CHALLENGES

Few organizations today could operate as they do without communication technology. E-mail, videoconferencing, text messaging, telephone and fax machines, and workplace websites allow individuals to work together without *being* together and to communicate with unprecedented efficiency. A large majority of U.S. workers use electronically mediated forms of communication, such as e-mail and the Internet, on a daily basis at their jobs.[12] Such technologies have significantly expanded the audience a workplace can reach, while simultaneously making communication faster and more cost-effective. Like many innovations, however, communication technology has also presented new challenges.

Choosing a Communication Channel One challenge of using communication technology in the workplace is deciding which technology to employ in a given situation. Recall from Chapter 1 that some communication contexts are *channel-rich*, meaning they allow people to perceive several communication behaviors at once. The most channel-rich context is the face-to-face conversation, because it provides communicators access to each other's words, gestures, facial expressions, vocalic behaviors, touch, and scent. When face-to-face meetings are not feasible, however, a web cam conversation provides the next most channel-rich context. In a web cam conversation, participants can see and hear one another in **real time**, that is, while they are communicating.

Other communication technologies provide *channel-lean* contexts, meaning they restrict the number of communication channels people can perceive. Texting and instant messaging, for instance, allow people to communicate in real time but with only words and emoticons that approximate facial expressions. The communicators cannot feel one another's touch, smell their scent, or see their gestures and facial expressions as they can in contexts that offer more communication channels. E-mails and posts to an electronic bulletin board, blog, or Facebook or other social media wall are even more channel-lean than text and instant messages because they normally do not constitute real-time communication and may not be read for hours or even days.

Ensuring Security A second challenge for workplaces—and for many individuals—is ensuring the security of information they communicate, particularly online. Because companies rely so heavily on e-mail to communicate with their internal and external audiences, concerns over the security of e-mail messages have become paramount. In 1986, the U.S. Congress enacted the Electronic Communications Privacy Act (ECPA) to protect the privacy of electronic communication. The ECPA prohibits intercepting a person's private e-mail messages without consent and prevents the government from requiring electronic communication providers (such as Google and Yahoo) to disclose their subscribers' identity except in a narrow range of circumstances. Some workplaces add an addendum to outgoing e-mails notifying the recipient that the messages are protected by the law. Figure A.2 provides an example of one such addendum.

Reducing Distraction A third challenge posed by communication technology is the time it takes to keep up with it. According to one survey, the average person sends and receives approximately 105 e-mail messages per day.[13] Although some of those messages are related to work, others are personal messages or unsolicited advertisements. Attending to all that e-mail during work hours can be distracting and can reduce productivity.

Distraction is an even bigger danger when employees use the Internet during work hours for personal activities such as shopping, banking, blogging, and social networking. A 2011 survey found that 61 percent of office workers send non-work-related e-mail message from the office, and 56 percent check Facebook or other social networking sites during the workday.[14] At least half of all U.S. companies monitor their employees' Internet and e-mail use, and 22 percent of employers have fired someone for inappropriate Internet use during work hours.[15] Know your employer's policy on using the Internet for personal business, and be mindful of the ways it can reduce your own productivity.

• **real time** At the actual time ("live") when a communication or an event takes place.

FIGURE A.2 E-MAIL MESSAGE ADDENDUM REGARDING PRIVACY

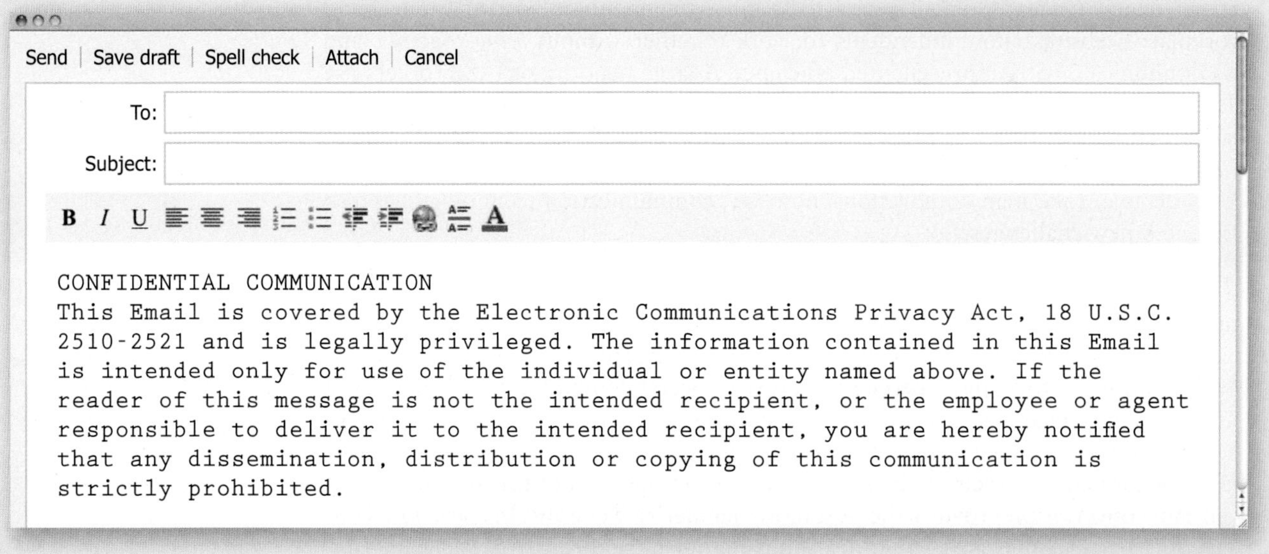

Send | Save draft | Spell check | Attach | Cancel

To:

Subject:

B *I* U

```
CONFIDENTIAL COMMUNICATION
This Email is covered by the Electronic Communications Privacy Act, 18 U.S.C.
2510-2521 and is legally privileged. The information contained in this Email
is intended only for use of the individual or entity named above. If the
reader of this message is not the intended recipient, or the employee or agent
responsible to deliver it to the intended recipient, you are hereby notified
that any dissemination, distribution or copying of this communication is
strictly prohibited.
```

WORK/LIFE CONFLICT

• **work/life conflict** Conflict created by the pressure of balancing the demands of work with the rest of one's activities.

The typical U.S. family of the 1950s was supported financially by only one parent, usually the father, working full-time. In the twenty-first century, however, *dual-career families*—in which both adults work full-time—are the norm.[16] The pressure of balancing the demands of work with the rest of life's activities creates a **work/life conflict** for many people that can be highly problematic for them and their employers if not managed constructively.

Two types of work/life conflict occur. The first is *life interference with work*, which happens when people's life responsibilities impede their job performance. If Ramon's elderly mother falls ill and requires his help, for instance, he may miss work or important deadlines. The second type is *work interference with life*, which happens when people's job responsibilities hinder their ability to fulfill personal obligations. If Simone's position requires her to travel frequently, for example, her repeated absences may make it difficult to maintain close friendships.

• **burnout** A chronic sense of exhaustion or apathy that can come from long-term frustration and stress.

Studies have shown that individuals with significant work/life conflict are at elevated risk of health problems such as clinical depression[17] and sleep disorders.[18] They also experience increased job stress and reduced satisfaction with life,[19] marriage,[20] and family relationships.[21] Finally, individuals with substantial work/life conflict aren't very happy.[22] One of the most harmful effects of work/life conflict is **burnout**, a chronic sense of exhaustion or apathy that can come from long-term frustration and stress. Burnout isn't a component of work/life conflict; it's a result of it. When their employees experience burnout, workplaces suffer in the form of increased absenteeism,[23] lost productivity,[24] and decreased communicative effectiveness.[25]

Individuals can also feel conflicted about their work lives when they experience sexual harassment in the workplace. See "The Dark Side of Communication" to explore this problem.

WORKPLACE DIVERSITY

In many workplaces, employees represent a mix of different cultures, religious beliefs, mental and physical abilities, educational achievements, ages, genders, and political orientations.[26] It's therefore likely that workplace experiences will expose us to people with backgrounds, customs, and ways of thinking that are quite different from our own.[27] Many organizations regard such diversity as an essential asset because it may produce more innovative ideas than a homogeneous staff.

THE DARK SIDE OF COMMUNICATION

Sexual Harassment in the Workplace

A serious problem arises in the workplace when employees feel they have been sexually harassed by their superiors. In the United States, the federal Equal Employment Opportunity Commission (EEOC) defines sexual harassment as unsolicited, unwelcome behavior of a sexual nature in the workplace.[28] You might intend to be friendly or supportive by putting your arm around a subordinate, for instance, but if the subordinate feels uncomfortable by your behavior, it may constitute harassment.

According to the EEOC, sexual harassment can occur in two forms. The first, *quid pro quo* (Latin for "this for that") *harassment,* happens when a supervisor offers an employee rewards in exchange for sexual favors. A statement such as "I'll give you tomorrow off if you have a drink with me tonight" can qualify as *quid pro quo* harassment if it is directed at a subordinate. The second form, *hostile work environment harassment,* occurs when work conditions are sexually offensive or intimidating. Telling sexually suggestive jokes when both men and women are present, or making derogatory comments about a person's sexual orientation, can qualify as hostile work environment harassment.

Sexual harassment is a serious and pervasive problem in some workplaces, and its victims often suffer long-term emotional and psychological harm. If you ever feel you are being sexually harassed, it can be hard to speak up, but ignoring the situation won't make it go away. Remember that sexual harassment is illegal and you have a right not to be victimized.

Sometimes, all it takes to stop harassment is for you to speak up and tell another person that his or her behavior offends you. If you're uncomfortable doing so, or if the offensive behavior continues afterward, report the situation to your organization's human resources department or affirmative action office.

Yet diversity can pose challenges for communication and interpersonal interaction. Working with people whose capabilities, beliefs, and life experiences differ dramatically from our own can be frustrating. Our personal background leads each of us to take certain ideas and experiences for granted that others may not. For instance, when scheduling a meeting of a work team, it may not occur to you that the date you set is an important religious holiday for some in the group. Recognizing and adapting to people's differences can improve our ability to work harmoniously and productively with others.

You can improve your adaptability to workplace diversity if you:

- *Check your assumptions.* When you send an e-mail to coworkers, for instance, do you tend to assume everyone will understand your terminology? Do you assume the recipients will all share the priorities your message conveys? If there's a chance your assumptions may not be valid, adjust your message before sending it.

- *Remember that being different doesn't mean being wrong.* If, say, your religious beliefs are very important to you, you might tend to see alternative ideas as wrong. That tendency can make it difficult to communicate openly and respectfully with people whose beliefs differ from yours. There are many ways to think about religion, and your beliefs are "right" to you only because *you* believe them. Others see their beliefs as right because they believe them. Having a different orientation from you doesn't make someone else wrong, only different. Just as you want others to treat your beliefs respectfully, you should extend that courtesy to them.

- *Help others to adapt.* Being adaptable to diversity doesn't mean only respecting and accommodating others—it also means informing others when they're ignoring your needs or beliefs. Through your honest input, they can learn to be more adaptable as well. When someone doesn't acknowledge your uniqueness, point out—tactfully and respectfully—that your background gives you experiences, beliefs, priorities, and needs he or she may not be recognizing.

Interviewing Successfully

People conduct interviews for various reasons, many of which are related to the workplace. Your ability to participate successfully in interviews can therefore be an asset when communicating in the workplace. We'll begin this section by exploring the diverse purposes of interviewing. We'll then consider how you can land, and subsequently prepare for, a successful job interview and how you should respond to discriminatory questions if you encounter them.

WHAT IS AN INTERVIEW?

- **interview** A structured conversation that focuses on questions and answers.

A useful and versatile component of workplace communication is the **interview**, a structured conversation that focuses on questions and answers.[29] When we hear the word *interview*, many of us think immediately of a job interview. The job interview—which we will examine below as an example of a *selection interview*—is critical in the workplace; after all, most of us won't be hired in the first place unless we succeed at the job interview. There are, however, *many* forms of interviewing, some of which occur commonly in the workplace.

TYPES OF INTERVIEWS

Interviews are of different types and have varying purposes, including these:

- **appraisal interview** A discussion focused on an employee's performance and goals for the future.

- *The appraisal interview:* Whenever you sit down with someone to discuss your performance and your goals for the future, you're taking part in an **appraisal interview**. In many lines of work, managers and supervisors conduct appraisals of all their employees on a yearly basis. The appraisal interview can encourage you to continue what you're doing well and guide you in ways to improve.[30]

- **problem-solving interview** A discussion conducted to identify solutions to a problem or conflict.

- *The problem-solving interview:* A **problem-solving interview** occurs to understand the nature of a problem and identify potential solutions. You take part in problem-solving interviews, for instance, when you discuss treatment options for an illness with your physician or financial options for a mortgage with your banker.[31]

- **exit interview** A conversation about an employee's experiences with an organization that he or she is leaving.

- *The exit interview:* If you've resigned from an organization to take a job elsewhere, you may be asked to complete an **exit interview**, a conversation about your experiences with the organization you're leaving. During an exit interview, you usually would describe both positive and negative aspects of your job, your supervisors, and the organization.

- **counseling interview** An interaction aimed at supporting an individual through a personal problem.

- *The counseling interview:* When you go through a difficult time, you might reach out to close friends, relatives, or a professional therapist. With those people, you can express your feelings, receive empathy, and gain an outside perspective on your situation. That type of conversation—whether conducted with a therapist or a loved one— constitutes a **counseling interview**, an interaction aimed at supporting an individual through a personal problem.

- **service-oriented interview** A conversation oriented toward helping people with a product or service they have purchased.

- *The service-oriented interview:* A **service-oriented interview** is a conversation oriented toward helping you with a product or service you have purchased. When you tell the customer service representative at the clothing store that you've discovered a torn lining in a jacket you just bought, he may examine the jacket and offer either to refund your money or to exchange your damaged jacket.

- **persuasive interview** A conversation intended to affect beliefs, opinions, or behaviors.

- *The persuasive interview:* If you've ever received a telephone call asking you to support a political candidate or vote a certain way on a proposition, you've participated in a **persuasive interview**, a conversation intended to affect your belief, opinion, or behavior. During elections, it's common for campaign workers to call or visit registered voters to encourage them to vote in a particular way. You also take part in persuasive interviews when people try to convince you to donate money or volunteer your time.

- *The survey interview:* Each decade, the federal government conducts a *census*, a survey to count and gather information about the U.S. population. To collect census data, government workers may visit or call households and businesses. If you were to be visited by a census surveyor, you would likely be asked a variety of questions, including "How many people live in your household?" and "How many of you are employed full-time?" Your conversation with the census worker constitutes a **survey interview**, an interaction aimed at gathering information.

- *The selection interview:* A **selection interview** is a conversation intended to help the interviewer to choose the most appropriate person for a position, an assignment, a promotion, or an award. When you interview for a job, you are taking part in a selection interview. The ability to succeed in selection interviews is critical to your chances for employment.

LANDING A JOB INTERVIEW

Your first conversation with a potential employer is likely to occur during a selection interview in which you're competing for a specific job. Only rarely do jobs come looking for you. Landing a job interview typically requires identifying employment opportunities in your field of interest and preparing a professional résumé and cover letter to submit for those vacancies. This section contains tips for accomplishing those tasks and also for ensuring that your hard work is not undermined by your online persona.

Conduct a Job Search The first step in landing a job interview is to identify positions for which to apply. An excellent place to start is with your friends, family members, instructors, and anyone you know who works in your field of interest. Tell those people the kind of work you want to do, and ask for ideas about where to look. They may be able to put you in touch with employers in your field who are looking for people to hire and also give you pointers for connecting with other potential employers.

Most colleges and universities also have job placement centers where employers can post announcements of vacancies. Because those centers exist specifically to help students find jobs, they can be a valuable resource for identifying opportunities. Get to know the staff at your placement office and find out about the resources available to you there.

You can also search for job openings on your own. Websites such as Monster.com and SimplyHired.com allow you to search for jobs by location, field, or company. Those sites will describe available openings and allow you to apply for the jobs online. Some websites specialize in advertising positions with a specific field. For instance, TeacherJobs.com posts vacancies for educators, and Firefighter-Jobs.com lists openings for positions in the fire service. You can also identify vacancies at specific companies by looking at their individual websites.

Prepare a Cover Letter and Résumé When you find job postings that catch your interest, the next step is to communicate that interest to the employers. In many cases, you will make your first contact with an employer in the form of a cover letter and résumé. Because many employers receive dozens or even hundreds of applications for each available position, you need to ensure that your cover letter and résumé make a positive first impression.

The Cover Letter A **cover letter** is a one-page letter in which you formally apply for a specific position. In your cover letter, you have the opportunity to express your interest in the job and describe how your education, skills, and experience would benefit the employer.

Some applicants write long, detailed cover letters describing their every qualification for the position. That approach is almost never a good strategy. The reason is

- **survey interview** An interaction aimed at gathering information.

- **selection interview** A conversation intended to help the interviewer to choose the most appropriate person for a position, an assignment, a promotion, or an award.

- **cover letter** A one-page letter in which a person formally applies for a specific position.

that your potential employer will likely have stacks of cover letters to read and may not have the time to peruse yours in depth. Remember that the goal of your cover letter isn't to land you the job—it's to land you the job *interview*. Cover letters shouldn't contain your life story; they should hit the highlights and make the employer want to know more about you.

Figure A.3 contains a sample cover letter. Notice how the writer expresses his interest in the job, mentions his qualifications, and then says he looks forward to discussing the position further. For most positions, a brief and direct letter such as the sample is best.

The Résumé A **résumé** is a short document listing your employment qualifications. When you're applying for an entry-level position, it is usually best to keep your résumé to one page. As you progress in your career, your résumé may grow in length, but you should always strive to keep it straightforward and clear.

There are several ways to compile a résumé. You'll generally want to include the following details:

- *Name and contact information:* Be certain that your name appears at the top of your résumé and is followed by your mailing address, telephone number, and e-mail address. Ensure that the telephone number you provide has an answering machine or voice mail that contains a clear, professional message.

- *Employment objective:* Briefly describe the type of position you are seeking and the kind of employer for whom you wish to work. If you will be applying for several different types of jobs, create different versions of your résumé so you can keep your employment objectives as specific as possible.

- *Education:* Identify the schools you have attended and the degrees or certificates you have earned (or are expecting to earn) at each. Note your academic major and areas of concentration, and list your grade point average if you think it will help to make your application competitive.

- *Employment experience:* Starting with your current or most recent job, list the jobs you have had that are relevant to the type of employment you are seeking. For each job, identify your job title, employer, dates of employment, and primary responsibilities. Even if you worked on a volunteer basis in some cases, include the positions most relevant to the work you are seeking now.

- *Skills and interests:* In this section, tell your potential employer about any special skills you have and about your major interests. If you're fluent in sign language, certified in CPR, or proficient at computer programming, say so. Potential employers may find your skills and interests to be particularly attractive.

- *References:* Your employment references should be individuals who can attest to your skills, work ethic, and character. They typically include current or former employers, college instructors, coaches, and others who can verify that you are responsible and proficient. It is usually best not to include relatives, romantic partners, and others whose assessments of you would seem biased by their personal feelings. You can either list your references and their contact information on your résumé or indicate that you will provide those details on request. Be sure to ask permission from your references before including their contact information on your résumé.

Figure A.4 illustrates a sample résumé. You might consult the placement office at your college or university for additional examples.

@getCONNECTED
Check Your Online Persona

In your job search, you have carefully crafted your résumé and cover letter to portray yourself as competent, professional, and responsible. However, don't make the mistake of believing those documents constitute all the information a potential employer could find about you. What would a human resources director learn about you if she

---

• **résumé** A short document listing a person's employment qualifications.

1001 Main Street
Seattle, WA 98195
(206) 555–4844
d.shaffer@gmail.com

May 2, 2012

Dr. Ellen Hurston, Sales Manager
Chrysalis Publishing
342 Eighth Avenue, Suite 11
Chicago, IL 60603

Dear Dr. Hurston:

In response to your advertisement in the April 28, 2012 issue of *The Chicago Sun-Times,* enclosed is my resume for the position of sales associate with Chrysalis Publishing. I am currently a senior majoring in communication at the University of Washington and have a strong interest in using my sales experience and interpersonal skills in the field of academic publishing.

Currently I am the Sales Manager for *The Daily,* the student newspaper at the University of Washington, which has a daily circulation of nearly 30,000. In my position, I coordinate the sale of classified advertising for both campus and corporate clients, and I oversee a staff of 12 part-time student salespeople. This position has given me valuable experience with building and maintaining professional relationships and ensuring high-quality customer service for the newspaper's clients. I would love the opportunity to put those skills to use for Chrysalis Publishing.

My publishing experience also includes work as a copyeditor for Grand Systems Publishing, a producer of technical writing textbooks, and as a sales associate for Borders Books. Both of those positions have helped me to hone my communication, sales, and customer service skills, which I believe would be advantageous in the academic publishing industry.

I am fluent in both English and Spanish and have experience working with people from diverse ethnic and cultural backgrounds. I am also proficient in Microsoft computer programs, including Word, Excel, PowerPoint, and Pages. If you would like a list of personal and professional references, I would be glad to furnish it.

Thank you for the opportunity to apply for the position of sales associate with Chrysalis Publishing. I will look forward to discussing my skills and experience with you in person.

Sincerely yours,

David Shaffer

David Shaffer

Googled your name? Would she find overly personal comments on Twitter? Would she read on Facebook that your interests include "getting smashed every weekend"?

There's a simple way to find out. Google your own name, and see what comes up. Whatever information you can find about yourself online will be easily accessible to any potential employer. You may consider it an invasion of your privacy for employers to consult the Internet for information about you. Once you post something online, however, it becomes accessible not only to your friends but also to anyone seeking information about you, including a prospective employer.

If your Google search on your name returns anything that you wouldn't want a potential employer to see, take that information down or make it accessible to authorized viewers only (such as your closest Facebook friends). The last thing you want is to lose a job opportunity because a human resources manager sees your spring break pictures online and concludes that you don't have the character or the maturity to perform competently in the job.

SUCCEEDING IN A JOB INTERVIEW

Now that you've landed a job interview, how can you ensure that you're ready to negotiate the interview successfully? Job selection interviews can be stressful and even daunting, but you can manage those challenges if you're prepared. In this section, we survey some crucial strategies for winning the job.

Research Your Potential Employer One of the best ways to prepare for a successful job selection interview is to learn as much as you can about your potential employer. Let's say you are interviewing for a marketing position at a major sportswear retailer. Before your interview, you will want to find out about the company's size, the location of its headquarters and major divisions, its top officers, and its past and recent history. Explore the company's website and other sites that discuss the firm for that information, or look for it in the company's annual report, which you may be able to download.

In addition, learn as much as you can about the specific position for which you're applying, such as the facility where you would be working, the size of the marketing division, and the manager to whom you'd be reporting. Carefully reading the job description and searching the website for information about the marketing division—if there is one—should give you some clues.

Anticipate Likely Questions A major reason job selection interviews are stressful is that you don't usually know beforehand what questions the interviewer will ask. However, you can anticipate many and prepare for them. Let's first briefly examine the most common types of questions and identify successful responses to each.

- *Open-ended questions* invite a broad range of answers. Examples include "Tell me about yourself," and "What are your goals for the future?" An open-ended question gives you the opportunity to reply in a way that reflects positively on you. In response to a question about your goals, for instance, you can focus on two or three that are relevant to the job and explain how you are already working toward attaining them.

- *Closed-ended questions* prompt brief, specific answers. Some call for a simple yes or no, such as "Can you work weekends?" Others elicit particular pieces of information, such as "What was your college major?" When you're asked closed-ended questions, it is best to provide short, direct answers. If the interviewer wants you to elaborate on your answer, he or she will ask you to do so.

- *Hypothetical questions* describe a realistic situation and ask you to speculate about how you would react if you encountered it. An interviewer might ask "Suppose a customer asked you to refund an item without a receipt. How would you handle that?" By posing such a question, the interviewer assesses how you would analyze and approach the situation.

David Shaffer

1001 Main Street, Seattle WA 98195
206.555-4844 • d.shaffer@gmail.com

Employment Objective
To obtain an entry-level sales position for an academic publishing company.

Education
Bachelor of Arts, Communication, University of Washington   May 2012
    Cumulative GPA: 3.69/4.00
    Dean's List five out of six quarters

Associate of Arts, Liberal Studies, Seattle Community College   May 2010
    Cumulative GPA: 3.80/4.00
    Graduated *magna cum laude*

Employment Experience
Sales Manager, *The Daily,* University of Washington   April 2011–present
    Coordinate sales of advertising for major university student newspaper. Maintain business
    relationships with nearly 100 corporate accounts. Provide customer service and editorial support.
    Responsible for increasing advertising revenue by 15%.

Copyeditor, Grand Systems Publishing, Seattle WA   February 2008–April 2011
    Edited technical writing book produced for undergraduate and graduate students in engineering, city
    planning, and design. Developed software to reduce copyediting errors.

Sales Associate, Borders Books, Seattle WA   September 2005–January 2008
    Assisted customers with locating books. Conducted sales transactions. Stocked book shelves.
    Provided assistance for publication deliveries. Responsible for closing store at night.

Skills and Interests
Computer skills: Word, Excel, PowerPoint, Pages.

Language skills: Fluent in English and Spanish.

Other interests: Writing, software design, cross-country skiing.

References
Furnished upon request.

Tell me about yourself.

What are your primary strengths?

What do you consider your most serious weaknesses?

Why are you interested in this particular job/company?

Describe a difficult situation you've been in and how you handled it. Would you handle it differently today?

Who have been the biggest influences in your life? Why?

What can you do for this company? Why should we hire you instead of someone else?

What are your professional goals for the next five years? Ten years?

What do you value in a coworker?

Are you willing to relocate if necessary?

How is your academic background/work experience relevant for this job?

Do you have any questions for me?

- *Probing questions* request more detail on answers you have already provided. Let's say you are asked why you left your previous job, and you cite the lack of opportunities for advancement as the reason. A probing question will ask "What opportunities for advancement make a job more appealing to you?" Use probing questions as your chance to elaborate on what you've said.

Most job selection interviews include a mix of general and position-specific questions. Interviewers commonly begin with broad, open-ended questions, such as "Tell me a little about yourself." From there, they typically move to more specific, closed-ended, hypothetical, and probing questions about the candidate's education, work history, skills and talents, and qualifications for the job. Many interviewers end by asking whether the applicant has any questions. Although it is impossible to anticipate every question, you can prepare for your interview by formulating answers to commonly asked questions such as those in Table A.1.

Generate Questions of Your Own Always prepare at least three or four questions to ask if given the opportunity. Some strategies for formulating good questions are these:

- *Ask questions that allow the interviewer to reflect on his or her own experiences.* An excellent question to ask the interviewer is "What have you most enjoyed about working here?" That type of question allows the interviewer to tell you about himself or herself and also to identify the aspects of the employer he or she most appreciates.

- *Ask questions that indicate your long-term interest in the job.* A question such as "What opportunities would this position offer for someone who is interested in growing with this company?" suggests you are thinking about your career in the long term and will be serious about your commitment to your employer.

- *Don't ask for details about the company that you should already know.* Recall that part of preparing for a job selection interview is researching your potential employer. Therefore, you don't want your questions to reveal ignorance about the company, such as "Where is this company's headquarters located?"

- *Never ask about salary or benefits unless the interviewer has brought up those subjects.* Some interviewers may ask you about your salary requirements. However, unless the interviewer introduces the topic, don't inquire about the salary, vacation time, or medical benefits. Those are questions to be posed after you have a job offer.

Follow Up after the Interview Finally, send your interviewer a thank-you note shortly after your interview. As illustrated in Figure A.5, indicate that you appreciate the interviewer's having taken time to speak with you, note how you benefited from the interview experience, and express you are excited about the position. You might want to close by saying you look forward to hearing back. Sending a

SHARPEN Your Skills:
Preparing for a job interview

Think of a job you would like to have when you graduate. Review the questions in Table A.1, and write out a short answer for each. Afterward, ask a trusted relative or advisor to go through your answers and offer you feedback about how you might improve them.

thank-you note requires only a few moments but may be the one gesture that sets you apart from equally qualified competitors. After you send your note, however, resist the urge to call or e-mail the interviewer with a question such as "When do you expect to make a hiring decision?" Although the temptation to do so can be great, you run the risk of annoying the interviewer and reducing—or eliminating—whatever goodwill you created during your interview.

Table A.2 provides quick tips on some interviewing do's and don'ts.

IDENTIFYING AND RESPONDING TO ILLEGAL QUESTIONS

In the United States, the Equal Employment Opportunity Commission (EEOC) is the federal agency that monitors unfair discrimination in hiring and firing decisions. For the last four decades, the EEOC has enforced guidelines that specify what an employer may and may not ask prospective job candidates during employment interviews and on application forms. The guidelines are intended to ensure that employers ask only for information relevant to the position being sought.

During a job selection interview, you might be asked a question that violates federal employment discrimination laws, often as the result of an honest mistake reflecting the interviewer's lack of awareness of the EEOC guidelines. On occasion, however, it represents an intentional attempt to gain information about you that the prospective employer doesn't need. When faced with an illegal question, many job candidates feel caught in an impossible position. They may recognize the question as discriminatory but feel compelled to answer anyway. If you find yourself in such a situation, you can respond effectively by knowing the law and dealing with the question tactfully.

Be Aware of Employment Law Companies can make employment decisions based only on information that is relevant to job performance. In most cases, the law prohibits employers from considering factors such as a person's sex, age, ethnicity, sexual orientation, religion, marital status, political orientation, or disability status in decisions to hire, promote, or fire. Exceptions are allowed only when there is a *bona fide*, or legally legitimate, reason for them. For instance, if the position legitimately requires someone of a certain sex (such as a men's locker room attendant), a certain ethnicity (such as an actress playing an ethnic-specific movie role), or a certain physical ability (such as a firefighter, who must be able to walk and carry loads of a certain weight), these factors may be considered in employment decisions.

Most jobs, however, require only the skills and training necessary to perform the assigned tasks. If there is no bona fide reason to require applicants to fit a specific demographic profile (such as being of a particular age, marital status, or political orientation or a member of a particular religion), employers cannot legally ask about those characteristics during a job selection interview. Even if one characteristic, such as ethnicity or physical ability, is a bona fide job requirement, the employer can ask only about *that* attribute, not the others.

As a job applicant, you benefit by knowing the laws regarding employment and illegal discrimination. Table A.3 offers a list of questions that are generally illegal for employers to ask in an interview, alongside similar, job-related questions that *are* legal to ask.

FIGURE A.5
SAMPLE THANK-YOU NOTE

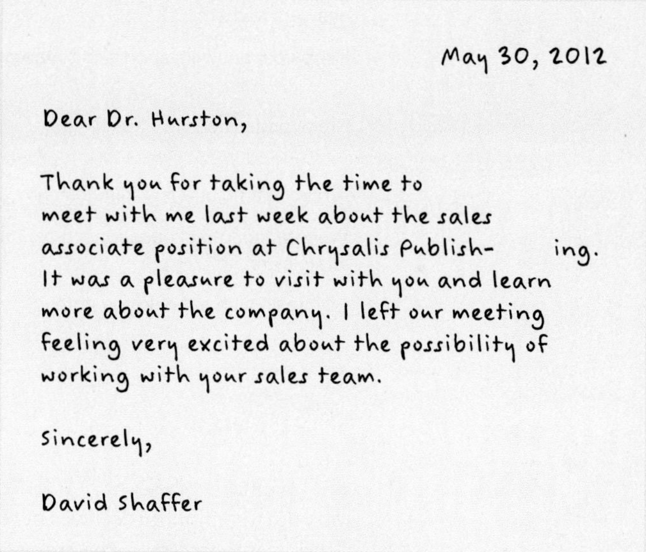

May 30, 2012

Dear Dr. Hurston,

Thank you for taking the time to meet with me last week about the sales associate position at Chrysalis Publishing. It was a pleasure to visit with you and learn more about the company. I left our meeting feeling very excited about the possibility of working with your sales team.

Sincerely,

David Shaffer

Do	Don't
Find out as much about the company as you can.	Ask questions about the company to which you should already know the answer.
Anticipate likely questions and practice your answers to them.	Go into a job interview intending to "wing it."
Keep your answers short and to the point.	Monopolize the conversation by giving long, rambling answers.
Dress professionally.	Look as if you gave no thought to your appearance.
Arrive on time or a few minutes early.	Arrive late.
Prepare thoughtful questions to ask of your interviewer.	Indicate a lack of interest in the position by asking no questions about it.
Follow up with a thank-you note.	Think a thank-you note won't make any difference.

Respond Tactfully to Illegal Questions If you are asked illegal questions during a job interview, there are ways you can provide the necessary information without embarrassing the interviewer and causing everyone's discomfort to escalate. Communication professors Charles Stewart and William Cash suggest five potential ways of responding effectively to illegal questions:[32]

- *Answer directly but briefly.* "Do you go to church?" "Yes, I do."
- *Pose a tactful inquiry.* "What is your political orientation?" "Why do you ask?"
- *Tactfully refuse to answer.* "Do you plan to have children?" "My family plans won't interfere with my ability to do this job."

Legal to Ask	Illegal to Ask
Are you authorized to work in the United States?	Are you a citizen of the United States?
What languages do you speak, read, or write fluently?	What is your native language?
Are you available to work on the days this job requires?	What religious holidays or days of worship do you observe?
Are you 18 years of age or older?	How old are you?
Have you worked or earned a degree under another name?	Is this your maiden name?
What is your experience with such-and-such an age group?	Do you have children?
Are you able to perform the specific duties of this position?	Do you have any disabilities?
Do you have upcoming events that would require extensive time away from work?	Are you a member of the National Guard or military reserves?
Are you willing to relocate if necessary?	Do you live nearby?
Tell me about your experience managing others.	How do you feel about supervising men or women?

SOURCE: hrworld.com/features/30-interview-questions-111507

adaptability Averting Awkwardness

The Scene: You're interviewing for a job you really want. You have prepared three questions to ask at the end—but the interviewer answers all of them during your interview, leaving you with nothing new to ask. Therefore, you're already flustered when the interviewer asks, "How do you feel about supervising women?"

Your Task: Role-play this scenario with a parent or instructor. How could you adapt your verbal and nonverbal communication to

- Respond tactfully to the illegal question?

- Generate new questions to ask?

- Avoid letting your discomfort become obvious?

- *Neutralize the question.* "What happens if your spouse gets called for military duty?" "My spouse and I would discuss the logistical requirements of any change in our circumstances."

- *Take advantage of the question.* "Do you have any disabilities?" "As someone with mild dyslexia, I've learned to treat people with a wide range of abilities empathically and respectfully."

   Although you may feel uncomfortable or even offended when asked an illegal question, it is seldom best to respond defensively ("You can't ask me that; it's none of your business"). Instead, use one of Stewart and Cash's strategies to defuse the tension and show that you can react tactfully and professionally in an uncomfortable situation.

- **What communication processes are important in the workplace?** In the workplace, people must communicate in upward, downward, and lateral ways to others within the organization, and to multiple constituencies outside of the organization. Organizational culture is reflected in an organization's rites, rituals, rules, and roles.

- **What common communication challenges do workplaces face today?** Many workplaces struggle with the communication challenges of globalization, communication technology, sexual harassment, work/life conflict, and diversity.

- **In what ways can we improve our interviewing skills?** We can succeed at job selection interviews by researching a potential employer, anticipating likely questions, formulating questions of our own, and writing a thank-you note after an interview.

POP QUIZ

Multiple Choice

1. Tara sends an e-mail to her interns at the accounting firm where she works. Her message is an example of

   a. informal communication.

   b. lateral communication.

   c. upward communication.

   d. downward communication.

2. Research tells us that grapevine communication

   a. usually uses only one communication channel.

   b. is typically ignored by those who receive it.

   c. can be remarkably accurate.

   d. is an example of formal workplace communication.

3. Peter is leaving his current position to take a job at another company. To learn more about his experiences in the job he is leaving, his supervisors might conduct

   a. an exit interview.

   b. a counseling interview.

   c. a problem-solving interview.

   d. a service-oriented interview.

4. An example of *quid pro quo* sexual harassment is

   a. work conditions that are sexually offensive or intimidating.

   b. an employee's confiding in her peer about her sexual attraction to her boss.

   c. a supervisor's offer of rewards to an employee in exchange for sexual favors.

   d. an employee telling a sexually obscene joke in mixed company.

5. The question "What was your college major?" is an example of a(n)

   a. open-ended question.

   b. closed-ended question.

   c. hypothetical question.

   d. probing question.

Fill in the Blank

6. A structured conversation that focuses on questions and answers is called a(n) _____.

7. Rites of _____ enhance feelings of inclusion and communication in the workplace.

8. _____ is the increasing connectedness of societies and their economies as a result of developments in transportation and communication.

9. E-mail, electronic bulletin boards, blogs, and social media site are considered channel-_____ contexts.

10. A _____ job requirement is one that is legally legitimate.

KEY TERMS

workplace communication A-2
internal communication A-2
formal communication A-2
upward communication A-2
downward communication A-2
lateral communication A-2
informal communication A-3
grapevine A-3
external communication A-3
workplace culture A-5

rites A-5
rituals A-5
formal roles A-6
informal roles A-6
globalization A-7
real time A-8
work/life conflict A-9
burnout A-9
interview A-11
appraisal interview A-11

problem-solving interview A-11
exit interview A-11
counseling interview A-11
service-oriented interview A-11
persuasive interview A-11
survey interview A-12
selection interview A-12
cover letter A-12
résumé A-13

A

action   A behavior someone undertakes.

action model   A model describing communication as a one-way process.

ad hominem **fallacy**   A statement that attempts to counter an argument by criticizing the person who made it.

adapt   To change one's behavior to accommodate what others are doing.

adaptors   Gestures used to satisfy a personal need.

advertising   Communication intended to promote the purchase of a product or service.

affect displays   Gestures that communicate emotion.

agenda-setting theory   The theory that media tell people what to think about by determining what they watch, read, and hear.

alternative media   Media channels that give voice to a wider range of viewpoints than mainstream media.

ambiguous language   Words that can have more than one meaning.

American Medical Association (AMA)   A professional association for physicians and medical students in the United States.

anchor-and-contrast approach   A persuasion technique by which one precedes a desired request with a request that is much larger.

anticipatory anxiety   The worry people feel when looking ahead to a speech.

antonyms   Words that have opposite meanings.

anxiety   A psychological state of worry and unease.

appeal to false authority   A claim that uses as evidence the testimony of someone who is not an expert on the topic.

appraisal interview   A discussion focused on an employee's performance and goals for the future.

articulation   The extent to which a speaker pronounces words clearly.

artifacts   Objects and visual features that reflect a person's identity and preferences.

attending   Paying attention to someone's words well enough to understand what that person is trying to communicate.

attraction theory   A theory that explains why individuals are drawn to others.

attribution   An explanation for an observed behavior.

audience analysis   Carefully considering the characteristics of one's listeners when preparing a speech.

authority rule   A decision-making process in which the leader of the group makes the decisions.

autocratic style   A leadership style in which leaders see themselves as having both the authority and the responsibility to take action on a group's behalf.

autonomy face   The need to avoid being imposed on by others.

avatars   Graphic representations of people.

avoiding stage   The stage of relationship dissolution at which partners create physical and emotional distance from each other.

B

bandwagon appeal   A claim that a listener should accept an argument because of how many other people have already accepted it.

bar chart   A graphic display of numbers as bars on a graph.

begging the question   Supporting an argument using the argument itself as evidence.

belief   Perception about what is true or false, accurate or inaccurate.

bibliography   A list of the sources used in preparing a speech.

blockbusters   Films that are highly successful financially.

blog   Short for *web logs*, blogs are websites providing news, commentary, and personal diary entries from the user—the *blogger*—often along with comments from visitors.

bonding stage   The stage of relationship development at which partners make a public announcement of their commitment to each other.

brainstorming   An idea-generating process in which group members offer whatever ideas they wish before any are debated.

breadth   The range of topics we self-disclose to various people.

build rapport   Create the perception that listeners and the speaker see things similarly.

burnout   Chronic sense of exhaustion or apathy that can come from long-term frustration and stress.

C

caregivers   People with the responsibility of tending to the mental and physical health needs of others.

catalytic theory   The theory that watching violence in the media can encourage real-life violence, but only if other influences are also present.

cause-and-effect pattern A pattern of organizing the main points of a speech so that they describe the causes of an event and then identify its consequences.

centralized power structure Occurs when a small number of people—such as a company president and board of directors—holds the majority of the decision-making ability.

channel A pathway through which messages are conveyed.

channel-lean contexts Communication environments involving few channels at once.

channel-rich contexts Communication environments involving many channels at once.

chart A graphic display of numeric information.

chronemics The use of time.

circumscribing stage The stage of relationship dissolution at which partners begin to decrease the quality and quantity of their communication with each other.

closed-mindedness The tendency not to listen to anything with which one disagrees.

closed systems Organizations that interact little with people or groups outside the organization.

co-cultures Groups of people who share values, customs, and norms related to mutual interests or characteristics besides their national citizenship.

coercive power A form of power that comes from the ability to punish.

cognitive complexity The ability to understand a given situation in multiple ways.

cohesion The force by which the members of a group work together in the service of a common goal.

collaborative communication A model that encourages patients and providers to interact as partners or peers in their communication.

collectivistic culture A culture in which people believe that their primary responsibility is to their families, their communities, and their employers.

commitment The desire to stay in a relationship no matter what happens.

communication The process by which people use signs, symbols, and behaviors to exchange information and create meaning.

communication apprehension Anxiety or fear about communicating with others.

communication codes Verbal and nonverbal behaviors whose meanings are often understood only by people from the same culture.

communication competence Communication that is effective and appropriate for a given situation.

communication privacy management (CPM) theory A theory explaining how people in relationships negotiate the tension between disclosing information and keeping it private.

comparative advantage method A way of organizing a persuasive speech in which the speaker explains why his or her point of view is superior to others on the same topic.

comparison level A realistic expectation of what one wants and thinks one deserves from a relationship.

comparison level for alternatives An assessment of how much better or worse one's current relationship is than one's other options.

competence face The need to be respected and viewed as competent and intelligent.

competitive interrupting The practice of using interruptions to take control of the conversation.

complementarity The beneficial provision by another person of a quality that one lacks.

confirmation bias The tendency to pay attention only to information that supports one's values and beliefs, while discounting or ignoring information that does not.

confirming messages Behaviors that convey how much another person is valued.

conflict An expressed struggle between at least two interdependent parties who perceive incompatible goals, scarce resources, and interference from the other party in achieving their goals.

connotative meaning The ideas or concepts a word suggests in addition to its literal definition.

constraint The limitations imposed on creativity by the context in which you are working.

contempt Hostile behavior in which people insult each other and attack the other's self-worth.

content dimension Literal information that is communicated by a message.

context The physical or psychological environment in which communication occurs.

coping Efforts to eliminate or reduce the effects of a stressful situation.

counseling interview An interaction aimed at supporting an individual through a personal problem.

coupons Documents a consumer can exchange for discounts or rebates on a product or service.

cover letter A one-page letter in which a person formally applies for a specific position.

creativity The freedom to make independent choices.

credibility (in public speaking) A speaker's believability.

credibility   The extent to which others perceive us to be competent and trustworthy.

critical listening   Listening to evaluate or analyze.

criticism   The act of passing judgment on someone or something.

criticism (in Gottman's model)   Complaints about another person or the person's behaviors.

cultivation theory   The theory that television encourages or cultivates a distorted view of the world among heavy viewers.

culture   The totality of learned, shared symbols, language, values, and norms that distinguish one group of people from another.

cyberbullying   Using the Internet to inflict emotional or psychological harm.

D

database   An electronic storehouse of specific information that people can search.

deception   The act of leading others to believe something the speaker knows to be untrue.

decode   To interpret or give meaning to a message.

deductive reasoning   A form of reasoning in which one starts with a general conclusion and then uses it to explain specific individual cases.

defamation   Language that harms a person's reputation or image.

defensiveness   Seeing oneself as a victim and denying responsibility for one's behaviors.

defused power structure   Occurs when the ability to make decisions is spread more evenly among the organization's members, with no one member or group holding excessive power.

defining   Providing the meaning of a word or concept.

democratic style   A leadership style in which every member of a group has the right to participate in decision making.

demonstrating   Showing how to do something by doing it as it is explained.

denotative meaning   The literal meaning of a word.

depth   The degree of intimacy of our self-disclosures.

describing   Using words to depict or portray a person, a place, an object, or an experience.

desensitization   The process of confronting frightening situations directly, to reduce the stress they cause.

desensitization theory   The theory that people's acceptance of real-life violence grows as they see more violence reflected in the media.

diagnosis   A determination of the medical problems a person has.

dialectical tensions   Conflicts between two important but opposing relational needs or desires.

differentiating stage   The stage of relationship dissolution at which partners begin to view their differences as undesirable or annoying.

disconfirming messages   Behaviors that imply a lack of respect or value for others.

divorce   The legal discontinuation of a marriage.

doctor-patient privilege   The assurance that health professionals will keep patient information confidential.

downward communication   Messages we send to people at lower levels of the organizational hierarchy, such as subordinates, interns, and staff members who report to us.

E

either/or fallacy   A statement that identifies two alternatives and falsely suggests that if one is rejected, the other must be accepted.

e-mail   Electronic mail messages exchanged through a computer network—one of the earliest mass uses of the Internet.

emblems   Gestures that have a direct verbal translation.

emoticons   Textual representations of facial expressions.

empathic listening   Listening to experience what the speaker thinks or feels.

empathy   The ability to think and feel as others do.

encode   To put an idea into language or gesture.

enculturation   The process of acquiring a culture.

enthymeme   A syllogism in which one of the premises is already so widely known and accepted that it is omitted.

equal time rule   Requires stations to offer competing political parties equal access to the airwaves.

equity theory   Theory that a good relationship is one in which a person's ratio of costs and benefits is equal to his or her partner's.

e-therapy   The use of communication technology for delivering or receiving psychotherapy.

ethics   Principles that guide judgments about whether something is morally right or wrong.

ethnicity   People's perceptions of ancestry or heritage.

ethnocentrism   The tendency to judge other cultures' practices as inferior to one's own.

ethos   A speaker's respectability, trustworthiness, and moral character.

etymology The origin or history of a word.

euphemism A vague, mild expression that symbolizes and substitutes for something blunter or harsher.

exit interview A conversation about an employee's experiences with an organization that he or she is leaving.

experimenting stage The stage of relationship development at which people converse to learn more about each other.

expert opinion Recommendations of individuals who have expertise in a particular area that are sometimes the basis of a group's decision-making process.

expert power A form of power that stems from having expertise in a particular area.

explaining Revealing why something occurred or how something works.

explicit rules Rules that have been clearly articulated.

extemporaneous speech A speech that is carefully prepared to sound as though it is being delivered spontaneously.

external communication Communication with people outside the organization.

extroversion A personality trait shared by people who are friendly, assertive, and outgoing with others.

F

face A person's desired public image.

face needs Important components of one's desired public image.

face-threatening act Any behavior that threatens one or more face needs.

facework The behaviors people use to establish and maintain their desired public image with others.

facial displays Facial expressions that are an important source of information in nonverbal communication.

fairness doctrine A law that required broadcasters to air all sides of a public issue.

false consensus An outcome where some members of a group say they support the unanimous decision even though they do not.

false-cause fallacy A statement asserting that if an event occurs before some outcome, the event therefore caused that outcome.

family of origin The family in which one grows up, usually consisting of parents and siblings.

family of procreation The family one starts as an adult, usually consisting of a spouse or romantic partner and children.

family rituals Repetitive activities that have special meaning for a family.

feedback Verbal and nonverbal responses to a message.

fellowship face The need to be liked and accepted by others.

feminine culture A culture in which people cherish traditionally feminine qualities and prefer little differentiation in the roles of women and men.

fight-or-flight response A reaction that helps prepare the body either to confront or to avoid a stressor.

fireside chats Evening radio speeches President Franklin D. Roosevelt made to the United States between 1933 and 1944.

fluency The smoothness of a speaker's delivery.

formal communication Messages that come from the organization and relate to its operations.

formal outline A structured set of all the points and subpoints in a speech.

formal roles Roles that involve functions prescribed by the organization itself.

forms of rhetorical proof Ways to support a persuasive argument, including ethos, pathos, and logos.

fundamental attribution error The tendency to attribute others' behaviors to internal rather than external causes.

G

general search engine A website on which one can search for other websites containing information on a specified topic.

George Gerbner Communication professor who was a leading researcher on media violence. He estimated that by the age of 18, the average U.S. viewer had witnessed 32,00 murders and 40,000 attempted murders on television.

Gerald Levin A young executive at *Time* magazine who developed the idea for a cable television network in the 1970s.

gesticulation The use of arm and hand movements to communicate.

glazing over Daydreaming or allowing the mind to wander while another person is speaking.

globalization The increasing interconnectedness of societies and their economies as a result of developments in transportation and communication.

gossip Informal, and frequently judgmental, talk about people who are not present.

grapevine   A metaphor used to indicate that informal messages are often conveyed in upward, downward, and lateral directions simultaneously.

graphic slide   An electronic display of information in a visually compelling format.

groupthink   A situation in which group members seek unanimous agreement despite their individual doubts.

H

halo effect   A predisposition to attribute positive qualities to physically attractive people.

haptics   The study of the sense of touch.

hasty generalization   A broad claim that is based on insufficient evidence.

hate speech   Language used to degrade, intimidate, or dehumanize specific groups of people.

Hays Code   Same as the Motion Picture Production Code, which distinguished acceptable from unacceptable content for movies in the United States.

health campaigns   Coordinated media messages that encourage the audience to take specific steps to increase or protect physical and mental health.

health care providers   Professional caregivers.

Health Insurance Portability and Accountability Act (HIPAA)   A law giving patients access to, and control over, their personal health information.

hearing   The sensory process of receiving and perceiving sounds.

hierarchy   The division of people into levels of authority.

high-context culture   A culture in which people are taught to speak in an indirect, inexplicit way.

high-power-distance culture   A culture in which certain groups, such as the royal family or the members of the ruling political party, have much greater power than the average citizen.

hostile audience   An audience in which listeners are predisposed to disagree with the speaker.

HURIER model   A model describing the stages of effective listening as hearing, understanding, remembering, interpreting, evaluating, and responding.

I

I-statement   A statement that claims ownership of the communicator's feelings or thoughts.

ideawriting   An idea-generating process in which each member adds three or four ideas to a pile and then offers comments on others' ideas. Afterward, members respond to comments made about their ideas and generate a master list of ideas worthy of consideration.

identity   The set of perceptions a person has about who he or she is; also known as *self-concept*.

illustrators   Gestures that go along with a verbal message to clarify it.

image   The way one wishes to be seen or perceived by others.

image management   The process of projecting one's desired public image.

immediacy behaviors   Nonverbal signals of affection and affiliation.

implicit rules   Rules that have not been clearly articulated but are nonetheless understood.

impromptu speech   A speech delivered with little or no preparation.

individualistic culture   A culture in which people believe that their primary responsibility is to themselves.

inductive reasoning   A form of reasoning in which one considers evidence and then draws general conclusions from it.

infidelity   Romantic or sexual interaction with someone outside one's romantic relationship.

informal communication   Communication that is not sanctioned by an organization but arises from the social interactions of its members.

informal roles   Functions that are adopted by specific people rather than dictated by the organization.

information hunger   The desire to learn.

information overload   The state of being overwhelmed by the enormous amount of information encountered each day.

information-seeking behavior   A series of action to find out more about a health issue.

information-transfer approach   Model of organizational communication in which communication is seen as a pipeline through which information flows from one source to another.

informational listening   Listening to learn.

informational power   A form of power that stems from the ability to control access to information.

informative speaking   Publicly addressing others to increase their knowledge, understanding, or skills.

in-groups   Groups of people with which a person identifies.

initiating stage   The stage of relationship development at which people meet and interact for the first time.

instant messaging   A form of text communication that occurs simultaneously between two or more connected users on a computer.

instrumental needs   Practical, everyday needs.

integrating stage   The stage of relationship development at which a deep commitment has formed, and the partners share a strong sense that the relationship has its own identity.

intensifying stage   The stage of relationship development at which people move from being acquaintances to being close friends.

interaction model   A model describing communication as a process shaped by feedback and context.

interdependence (groups)   With respect to groups, a state in which each member of a group affects, and is affected by, every other member.

interdependence   The state in which what happens to one person affects everyone else in the relationship.

internal communication   The messages people within the workplace convey to one another.

interpersonal attraction   The force that draws people together.

interpersonal communication   Communication that occurs between two people in the context of their relationship.

interpretation   The process of assigning meaning to information that has been selected for attention and organized.

interview   A structured conversation in which one person poses questions to which another person responds.

intimacy   Significant emotional closeness experienced in a relationship, whether romantic or not.

intimate distance   The zone of space willingly occupied only with intimate friends, family members, and romantic partners.

intrapersonal communication   Communication with oneself.

introversion   A personality trait shared by people who are shy, reserved, and aloof.

investment   The commitment of one's energies and resources to a relationship.

J

jargon   Technical vocabulary of a certain occupation or profession.

Johannes Gutenberg   German publisher who invented the printing press in the 1440s.

Johari window   A visual representation of components of the self that are known or unknown to the self and to others.

K

kinesics   The study of movement.

L

laissez-faire style   A leadership style in which leaders offer minimal supervision.

language   A structured system of symbols used for communicating meaning.

lateral communication   Messages we share with peers or anyone who occupies the same position in the organizational hierarchy as we do.

legitimate power   A form of power in which leaders' status or position gives them the right to make requests with which others must comply.

life story   A way of presenting oneself to others that is based on one's self-concept but is also influenced by other people.

line chart   A graphic display of numbers in the form of a line or lines that connect various data points.

listening   The active process of making meaning out of another person's spoken message.

loaded language   Words with strongly positive or negative connotations.

logical fallacy   A line of reasoning that, even if it makes sense, does not genuinely support a speaker's point.

logos   Listeners' ability to reason.

low-context culture   A culture in which people are expected to be direct and to say what they mean.

low-power-distance culture   A culture in which people believe that no one person or group should have excessive power.

M

main point   A statement expressing a specific idea or theme related to the speech topic.

mainstream media   Those media channels that reach the broadest audiences.

majority rule   A decision-making process that follows the will of the majority.

masculine culture   A culture in which people cherish traditionally masculine values and prefer sex-specific roles for women and men.

mass communication   Communication to a large audience that is transmitted by media.

media   A collection of various channels of communication.

media activism Coordinated efforts to express displeasure with media messages and to force changes in their content.

media effects The influences media have on people's everyday lives.

media literacy An assessment of your competence in evaluating media messages and their effects.

media sites Websites on which people can share audio-visual messages.

memorized speech A speech composed word for word and then delivered from memory.

message Verbal and nonverbal elements of communication to which people give meaning.

metacommunication Communication about communication.

microblogging A combination of blogging and texting supported by the website Twitter.

mindful Aware—as in being aware of how other cultures' behaviors and ways of thinking are likely to differ from one's own.

minority rule A decision-making process in which a small number of members makes a decision on behalf of the group.

mnemonics Devices that can aid short- and long-term memory.

model (in public speaking) A representation of an object.

model A formal description of a process.

monochronic culture A culture that sees time as a valuable commodity that should be used wisely and not wasted.

monogamy The state of being in only one romantic relationship at a time and avoiding romantic or sexual involvement with others outside that relationship.

Monroe's motivated sequence A way of organizing a persuasive speech consisting of appeals to attention, need, satisfaction, visualization, and then action.

Motion Picture Production Code Distinguished acceptable and unacceptable content for movies in the United States.

motion picture rating system A means of evaluating a film's suitability for various audiences.

N

narration Describing a series of events in sequence.

nationality One's status as a citizen of a particular country.

need to belong theory A psychological theory proposing a fundamental human inclination to bond with others.

neutral audience An audience lacking strong feelings for or against the topic of a speech.

noise Anything that distracts people from listening to what they wish to listen to.

nominal group technique (NGT) An idea-generating process in which group members generate their initial ideas silently and independently and then combine them and consider them as a group.

nonverbal channels The various behavioral forms that nonverbal communication takes.

nonverbal communication Behaviors and characteristics that convey meaning without the use of words.

norm of reciprocity The social expectation that favors should be reciprocated.

O

objective Based on facts rather than opinions.

oculesics The study of eye behavior.

olfactics The study of the sense of smell.

open systems Organizations that communicate and share information with other people or groups, including government offices, media outlets, advertisers, and benefactors.

opinion Evaluation about what is good and bad.

organization The process of categorizing information that has been selected for attention.

organizational communication The interactions within structural groups of people that help them to accomplish their goals.

organizational culture The values, customs, and communication behaviors that organization members share and that reflect the organization's distinct identity.

organizational rites Ceremonial acts and practices that convey characteristics of an organization's culture.

organizational rituals Repeated behaviors that provide a familiar routine to an organization's experiences.

out-groups Groups of people with which a person does not identify.

over-benefited A state in which one's relational benefits outweigh one's costs.

P

paralanguage Vocalic behaviors that communicate meaning along with verbal behavior.

pathos Listeners' emotions.

peer A person similar to us in status or power.

perception The process of making meaning from environmental experiences.

perceptual schema   A mental framework for organizing information.

perceptual set   A person's predisposition to perceive only what he or she wants or expects to perceive.

personal distance   The zone of space occupied with close friends and relatives.

persuasion   An attempt to motivate others, through communication, to adopt or to maintain a specific manner of thinking or doing.

persuasion   The process of convincing people to think or act in a certain way.

persuasive interview   A conversation intended to affect beliefs, opinions, or behaviors.

persuasive speaking   Public speech that aims to influence listeners' beliefs, attitudes, and actions.

physical attraction   Attraction to someone's appearance.

physical traits   The body's physical attributes.

physician-centered communication   A model in which medical professionals dictate the duration and scope of communication with patients.

pie chart   A graphic display of numbers in the form of a circle that is divided into segments, each of which represents a percentage of the whole.

pilot test   A small-scale version of a health campaign meant to spot problems and generate feedback.

plagiarism   Knowingly using information from another source without giving proper credit to that source.

political advertising   Media messages designed to influence people's political decisions.

polychronic culture   A culture that views time as holistic, fluid, and infinite.

polygamy   The state of having two or more spouses at once.

power   The ability to influence or control people or events.

presentation aids   Anything used in conjunction with a speech or presentation to stimulate listeners' senses.

preview   A statement alerting listeners that a speaker is about to shift to a new topic.

primacy effect   The tendency to emphasize the first impression over later impressions when forming a perception.

problem-solution pattern   A pattern of organizing the main points of a speech so that they describe a problem and then offer solutions for it.

problem-solving pattern   A way of organizing a pervasive speech in which the speaker establishes the existence of a problem and then proposes a solution to it.

problem-solving interview   A discussion conducted to identify solutions to a problem or conflict.

product placement   An advertising strategy involving featuring particular brands in the storyline of a movie, television show, book, or even comic strip.

profanity   Language considered to be vulgar, rude, or obscene.

prognosis   A prediction of the course of a medical condition and the chance of recovery.

proportionality   The relative sizes of facial or body features.

proposition   That which a persuasive speech attempts to convince an audience to accept.

proposition of fact   A claim that a particular argument is supported by the best available evidence and should therefore be taken as factual.

proposition of policy   A claim about what should be done.

proposition of value   A claim that evaluates the worth of a person, an object, or an idea.

proxemics   The study of the use of space.

proximity   Closeness, as in how closely together people live or work.

pseudolistening   Pretending to listen.

psychosocial traits   Characteristics of one's personality and ways of relating to others.

public communication   Communication directed at an audience that is larger than a small group.

public distance   The zone of space maintained during a public presentation.

public speaking anxiety (stage fright)   Nervousness or fear brought on by performing in front of an audience.

purpose statement   A declaration of the specific goal for a speech.

Q

questionnaire   A written instrument containing questions for people to answer.

R

real time   When participants in a videoconference can see and hear one another as they are communicating.

reason   To make judgments about the world based on evidence rather than emotion or intuition.

rebuttal tendency   The propensity to debate a speaker's point and formulate a reply while that person is still speaking.

receiver   The party who interprets a message.

recency effect   The tendency to emphasize the most recent impression over earlier impressions when forming a perception.

receptive audience   An audience composed of people who already accept and agree with all or most of what a speaker plans to say.

red herring fallacy   A statement that responds to an argument by introducing an irrelevant detail to divert attention from the point of the argument.

referent power   A form of power that derives from attraction to the leader.

refutational approach   A way of organizing a persuasive speech in which the speaker begins by presenting the main arguments against his or her position and then immediately refutes those arguments.

regulators   Gestures that control the flow of conversation.

relational dimension   Signals about the relationship in which a message is being communicated.

relational maintenance behaviors theory   Theory specifying the primary behaviors people use to maintain their relationships.

relational needs   The essential elements people seek in their relationships with others.

representation   Describing something in terms of its physical or psychological attributes.

research search engine   A website on which one can search for research published in books, academic journals, and other periodicals.

resources   Assets that enable a group to be productive.

résumé   A short document listing a person's employment qualifications.

reward power   A form of power based on the leader's ability to reward another for doing what the leader says.

rites   Ceremonial acts and practices that convey one or more characteristics of a workplace's culture.

rituals   Repeated behaviors that provide a familiar routine to a workplace's experiences.

role   A pattern of behavior that defines a person's function within a group, such as a family.

rule of division   A rule of speech organization specifying that if a point is divided into subpoints, it must have at least two subpoints.

rule of parallel wording   A rule of speech organization specifying that all points and subpoints in an outline should have the same grammatical structure.

rule of subordination   A rule of speech organization specifying that some concepts in the speech are more important than others.

S

Sapir-Whorf hypothesis   A theory that language shapes a person's views of reality.

scripted speech   A speech composed word for word on a manuscript and then read aloud exactly as it is written.

selection   The process of paying attention to a certain stimulus.

selection interview   A conversation intended to help the interviewer choose the most appropriate person for a position, an assignment, a promotion, or an award.

selective attention   Listening only to what one wants to hear and ignoring the rest.

selective exposure   A process by which we seek media messages that match our values rather than those that do not.

self-concept   The set of perceptions a person has about who he or she is; also known as *identity*.

self-disclosure   Act of intentionally giving others information about oneself that one believes is true but thinks others don't already have.

self-efficacy   A belief that one can perform a desired action.

self-esteem   One's subjective evaluation of one's value and worth as a person.

self-fulfilling prophecy   An expectation that gives rise to behaviors that cause the expectation to come true.

self-monitoring   Awareness of one's behavior and how it affects others.

self-serving bias   The tendency to attribute one's successes to stable internal causes and one's failures to unstable external causes.

service-oriented interview   A conversation oriented toward helping people with a product or service they have purchased.

sexual harassment   Unsolicited, unwelcomed behavior of a sexual nature in the workplace.

signposts   Single words and phrases that distinguish one point in a presentation from another and help listeners follow the speaker's path.

skepticism   An attitude that involves raising questions or having doubts.

slang   Informal and unconventional words often understood only within a particular group.

slippery slope fallacy   A statement that attacks an argument by taking it to such an extreme that it appears ludicrous.

small group A collection of people working interdependently to accomplish a task; small groups typically include 3 to 20 members.

small group communication Communication occurring within small groups of three or more people.

social attraction Attraction to someone's personality.

social distance The zone of space occupied with casual acquaintances.

social exchange theory Theory suggesting that people seek to maintain relationships in which their benefits outweigh their costs.

social loafing The tendency of some members of a group to contribute less to the group than the average member does, particularly as the group grows in size.

social media User-generated websites offering content that individual users construct for delivery to mass audiences, allowing people to build and maintain social connections.

social network sites Websites (such as Facebook) that allow users to meet, communicate, and share information online.

social penetration theory Theory suggesting that the depth and breadth of self-disclosure help us learn about a person we're getting to know.

social support The verbal and nonverbal behaviors people enact when they are trying to be helpful to others.

social validation principle The idea that people will comply with requests if they believe that others are also complying.

societies Groups of people who share common symbols, language, values, and norms.

source The originator of a thought or an idea.

space pattern A pattern of organizing the main points of a speech according to areas.

spam E-mail messages sent indiscriminately to thousands of recipients at once, often to advertise a product or service.

speaking notes An abbreviated version of a formal speech outline.

stage fright Anxiety or fear brought on by performing in front of an audience.

stagnating stage The stage of relationship dissolution at which the relationship stops growing and the partners feel as if they are just "going through the motions."

stalemate An outcome where members' opinions are so sharply divided that consensus is impossible to achieve.

stereotype A generalization about a group or category of people that is applied to individual members of that group.

stonewalling Withdrawing from a conversation.

strategic ambiguity Leaving parts of a message open to different interpretations intentionally, to accomplish a specific goal.

strategic control approach Model of organizational communication that recognizes that people in an organization can use communication to control their environments.

straw man fallacy A statement that refutes a claim that was never made.

stress The body's reaction to any type of perceived threat.

stressor Any event that causes a perceived threat to well-being.

stuttering A speech disorder that disrupts the flow of words with repeated or prolonged sounds and involuntary pauses.

subjective Biased toward a specific conclusion.

summary A statement that briefly reminds listeners of points a speaker has already made.

survey A method of collecting data by asking people directly about their experiences.

survey interview An interaction aimed at gathering information.

syllogism A three-line argument consisting of a major premise, a minor premise, and a conclusion.

symbol A representation of an idea.

symmetry The similarity between the left and right sides of a face or body.

symptom A sign of a potential health problem.

synergy A collaboration that produces more than the sum of its parts.

synonyms Words that have the same meaning.

T

table The display of words or numbers in a format of columns and rows.

task attraction Attraction to someone's abilities or dependability.

Telecommunications Act of 1996 A federal law requiring (among othe things) that all television sets 13 inches or larger manufactured after January 1, 2000, include a V-chip.

telemedicine The use of communication technology for health consultation.

terminating stage The stage of relationship dissolution at which the relationship is officially deemed to be over.

text slide An electronic display of text used to accompany a speech.

texting Instant messaging with a cell phone.

theory of structuration Anthony Giddens's theory that all human behavior, including communication behavior, is influenced by an ever-present tension between creativity (or *agency*) and constraint (*structure*).

thesis statement   A one-sentence version of the message in a speech.

Thomas Edison   U.S. inventor who greatly influenced the lives of people worldwide in the 1800s with his inventions of the incandescent light bulb, the phonograph, and a motion picture camera, among many other patents that he held.

threat   A declaration of the intention to harm someone.

time pattern   A pattern of organizing the main points of a speech in chronological order.

topic pattern   A pattern of organizing the main points of a speech to represent different categories.

traits   Defining characteristics of a person that are often relatively enduring and not easily changeable.

transaction model   A model describing communication as a process in which everyone is simultaneously a sender and a receiver.

transactional approach   A model of organizational communication which makes no distinctions between senders and receivers of messages. According to this approach, everyone in an interaction is simultaneously encoding and decoding.

transition   A statement that connects one point in a speech to the next.

treatment plan   A course of action to remedy or manage a medical condition.

TV parental guidelines   A system for rating the content of television shows.

U

unanimous consensus   Uncontested support for a decision—sometimes the only option in a group's decision-making process.

uncertainty avoidance   The extent to which people try to avoid situations that are unstructured, unclear, or unpredictable.

uncertainty reduction theory   Theory suggesting that people find uncertainty to be unpleasant, so they are motivated to reduce their uncertainty by getting to know others.

under-benefited   A state in which one's relational costs outweigh one's benefits.

upward communication   Messages we send to people at higher levels of the organizational hierarchy than we occupy.

uses and gratification   A theory that leads researchers to explore needs other than validation that media messages fulfill for people.

V

V-chip   A device allowing television owners to block access to certain types of programs, such as those featuring excessive violence or adult themes.

verbal footnote   A statement giving credit for quoted words in a speech to their original source.

vested interest   An inherent motivation to pay attention.

visualization   Developing a mental image, such as an image of oneself giving a successful performance.

vividness effect   The tendency of dramatic, shocking events to distort one's perceptions of reality.

vocalics   Characteristics of the voice that communicate meaning.

W

work/life conflict   The pressure of balancing the demands of work with those of nonwork life.

workplace communication   The interactions people have as part of their employment.

workplace culture   The values, customs, and communication behaviors that workplace members share and that reflect their organization's distinct identity.

Y

you-statement   A statement that shifts responsibility for the communicator's feelings or thoughts to the other party in the communication.

Chapter 1

1. http://bits.blogs.nytimes.com/2011/10/12/ anonymous-messaging-app-vibe-gets-boost-from-occupy-wall-street/

2. See Rubin, B. D. (2005). Linking communication scholarship and professional practice in colleges and universities. *Journal of Applied Communication Research, 33,* 294–304.

3. DeWall, C. N., & Bushman, B. J. (2011). Social acceptance and rejection: The sweet and the bitter. *Current Directions in Psychological Science, 20,* 256–260.

4. Kross, E., Berman, M. G., Mischel, W., Smith, E. E., & Wager, T. D. (2011). Social rejection shares somatosensory representations with physical pain. *Proceedings of the National Academy of Sciences, 108,* 6270–6275.

5. Perry, B. D. (2002). Childhood experience and the expression of genetic potential: What childhood neglect tells us about nature and nurture. *Brain and Mind, 3,* 79–100.

6. Ardiel, E. L., & Rankin, C. H. (2010). The importance of touch in development. *Paediatrics & Child Health, 15,* 153–156.

7. Hawkley, L. C., & Cacioppo, J. T. (2010). Loneliness matters: A theoretical and empirical review of consequences and mechanisms. *Annals of Behavioral Medicine, 40,* 218–27; Iecovich, E., Jacobs, J. M., & Stessman, J. (2011). Loneliness, social networks, and mortality: 18 years of follow-up. *The International Journal of Aging and Human Development, 72,* 243–263.

8. Kiecolt-Glaser, J. K., Loving, T. J., Stowell, J. R., Malarkey, W. B., Lemeshow, S., Dickinson, S. L., & Glaser, R. (2005). Hostile marital interactions, proinflammatory cytokine production, & wound healing. *Archives of General Psychiatry, 62,* 1377–1384; Cohen, S., Doyle, W. J., Skoner, D. P., Rabin, B. S., & Gwaltney, J. M. (1997). Social ties and susceptibility to the common cold. *Journal of the American Medical Association, 277,* 1940–1944.

9. Rubin, R. B., Perse, E. M., & Barbato, C. A. (1988). Conceptualization and measurement of interpersonal communication motives. *Human Communication Research, 14,* 602–628.

10. Knapp, M. L., & Daly, J. A. (Eds.). (2011). *The handbook of interpersonal communication* (4th ed.). Thousand Oaks, CA: Sage.

11. Wang, H., & Wellman, B. (2010). Social connectivity in America: Changes in adult friendship network size from 2002 to 2007. *American Behavioral Scientist, 53,* 1148–1169.

12. See, e.g., Usita, P. M., & Blieszner, R. (2002). Immigrant family strengths: Meeting communication challenges. *Journal of Family Issues, 23,* 266–286.

13. Barnes, C. D., Carvallo, M., Brown, R. P., & Osterman, L. (2010). Forgiveness and the need to belong. *Personality and Social Psychology Bulletin, 36,* 1148–1160; Baumeister, R. F., & Leary, M. R. (1995). The need to belong: Desire for interpersonal attachments as a fundamental human motivation. *Psychological Bulletin, 117,* 497–529.

14. Kringelbach, M. L., & Berridge, K. C. (2010). The neuroscience of happiness and pleasure. *Social Research: An International Quarterly, 77,* 659–678.

15. Popenoe, D. (2007). *The state of our unions: The social health of marriage in America.* Piscataway, NJ: The National Marriage Project.

16. Whisman, M. A., & Schonbrun, Y. C. (2010). Marital distress and relapse prevention for depression. In C. S. Richards & M. G. Perri (Eds.), *Relapse prevention for depression* (pp. 251–269). Washington, D.C.: American Psychological Association.

17. Yeung, K.-T., & Martin, J. L. (2003). The looking glass self: An empirical test and elaboration. *Social Forces, 81,* 843–879.

18. Astin, A. W., Astin, H. S., & Lindholm, J. A. (2010). *Cultivating the spirit: How college can enhance students' inner lives.* San Francisco: Jossey-Bass.

19. Kenrick, D. T., Griskevicius, V., Neuberg, S. L., & Schaller, M. (2010). Renovating the pyramid of needs: Contemporary extensions built upon ancient foundations. *Perspectives on Psychological Science, 5,* 292–314; Maslow, A. H. (1970). *Motivation and personality* (2nd ed.). New York: Harper & Row.

20. Shannon, C. E., & Weaver, W. (1949). *The mathematical theory of communication.* Urbana: University of Illinois Press.

21. Laswell, H. (1948). The structure and function of communication in society. In L. Bryson (Ed.), *The communication of ideas.* New York: Harper.

22. See, e.g., Schramm, W. (1954). How communication works. In W. Schramm (Ed.), *The process and effects of mass communication.* Urbana: University of Illinois Press.

23. Barnlund, D. C. (1970). A transactional model of communication. In K. K. Sereno & C. D. Mortensen (Eds.), *Foundations of communication theory* (pp. 83–102). New York: Harper & Row.

24. Sun, S., Hullman, G., & Wang, Y. (2010). Communicating in the multichannel age: Interpersonal communication motivation, interaction involvement and channel affinity. *Journal of Media and Communication Studies, 3,* 7–15.

25. Watzlawick, T., Beavin, J., & Jackson, D. (1967). *The pragmatics of human communication.* New York: Norton.

26. Motley, M. T. (1990). On whether one can(not) communicate: An examination via traditional communication postulates. *Western Journal of Speech Communication, 54,* 1–20.

27. This position is usually attributed to Watzlawick, Beavin, & Jackson, 1967.

28. Shimanoff, S. B. (1980). *Communication rules: Theory and research.* Beverly Hills, CA: Sage.

29. Floyd, K. (2012). *Interpersonal communication* (2nd ed.). New York: McGraw-Hill.

30. National Communication Association. (1999). *How Americans communicate* [online]. Retrieved April 16, 2006, from www.natcom.org/research/ Roper/how_americans_communicate.htm.

31. Gottman, J. M., & Silver, N. (1999). *The seven principles for making marriage work.* New York: Crown.

32. For a classic text, see Katriel, T., & Philipsen, G. (1981). "What we need is communication": "Communication" as a cultural category in some American speech. *Communication Monographs, 48,* 300–317.

33. McDaniel, S. H., Beckman, H. B., Morse, D. S., Silberman, J., Seaburn, D. B., & Epstein, R. M. (2007). Physician self-disclosure in primary care visits: Enough about you, what about me? *Archives of Internal Medicine, 167,* 1321-1326.

34. Chesley, N. (2005). Blurring boundaries? Linking technology use, spillover, individual distress, and family satisfaction. *Journal of Marriage and the Family, 67,* 1237–1248.

35. National Association of Colleges and Employers. (2009). *Job outlook 2009: Spring update.* Bethlehem, PA: Author.

36. Graduates are not prepared to work in business. (1997, June). *Association Trends,* 4; Windsor, J. L., Curtis, D. B., & Stephens, R. D. (1997). National preferences in business and communication education: A survey update. *Journal of the Association for Communication Administration, 3,* 170–179; Work Week. (1998, December 29). *Wall Street Journal,* A1.

37. Beatty, M. J., Marshall, L. A., & Rudd, J. E. (2001). A twins study of communicative adaptability: Heritability of individual differences. *Quarterly Journal of Speech, 87,* 366–377; Beatty, M. J., McCroskey, J. C., & Heisel, A. D. (1998). Communication apprehension as temperamental expression: A communibiological paradigm. *Communication Monographs, 65,* 197–219.

38. Spitzberg, B. H. (2000). What is good communication? *Journal of the Association for Communication Administration, 29,* 103–119.

39. Spitzberg, B. H., & Cupach, W. (1989). *Handbook of interpersonal competence research.* New York: Springer-Verlag.

40. Chen, G. M., & Starosta, W. J. (1996). Intercultural communication competence: A synthesis. In B. R. Burleson & A. W. Kunkel (Eds.), *Communication yearbook 19* (pp. 353–383). Thousand Oaks, CA: Sage.

41. Schraw, G. (1998). Promoting general metacognitive awareness. *Instructional Science, 26,* 113–125; Sypher, B. D., & Sypher, H. E. (1983). Perceptions of communication ability: Self-monitoring in an organizational setting. *Personality and Social Psychology Bulletin, 9,* 297–304.

42. Suler, J. R. (2004). The online disinhibition effect. *CyberPsychology and Behavior, 7,* 321–326.

43. Goleman, D. (2006). *Social intelligence: The new science of human relationships.* New York: Bantam; Goleman, D. (1996). *Emotional intelligence: Why it can matter more than IQ.* New York: Bantam.

44. Stamp, G. H. (1999). A qualitatively constructed interpersonal communication model: A grounded theory analysis. *Human Communication Research, 25,* 531–547.

45. Ifert, D. E., & Roloff, M. E. (1997). Overcoming expressed obstacles to compliance: The role of sensitivity to the expressions of others and ability to modify self-presentation. *Communication Quarterly, 45,* 55–67.

46. Burleson, B. R., & Caplan, S. E. (1998). Cognitive complexity. In J. C. McCroskey, J. A. Daly, M. M. Martin, & M. J. Beatty (Eds.), *Communication and personality: Trait perspectives* (pp. 233–286). Cresskill, NJ: Hampton.

Chapter 2

1. Meeus, J., Duriez, B., Vanbeselaere, N., & Boen, F. (2010). The role of national identity representation in the relation between in-group identification and out-group derogation: Ethnic versus civic representation. *British Journal of Social Psychology, 49,* 305–320.

2. Levitt, M. J., Lane, J. D., & Leavitt, J. (2005). Immigration stress, social support, and adjustment in the first postmigration year: An inter-generational analysis. *Research in Human Development, 2,* 159–177.

3. Öhman, L., Bergdahl, J., Nyberg, L., & Nilsson, L.-G. (2007). Longitudinal analysis of the relation between moderate long-term stress and health. *Stress and Health, 23,* 131–138.

4. Rushton, J. P. (2005). Ethnic nationalism, evolutionary psychology and Genetic Similarity Theory. *Nations and Nationalism, 11,* 489–507.

5. McConnell, A. R., & Leibold, J. M. (2001). Relations among the Implicit Association Test, discriminatory behavior, and explicit measures of racial attitudes. *Journal of Experimental Social Psychology, 37,* 435–442.

6. Suransky-Polakov, S. (2002). Denmark: Rebuffing immigrants. Retrieved July 27, 2007, from www.worldpress.org/Europe/642.cfm.

7. Padden, C., & Humphries, T. (1988). *Deaf in America: Voices from a culture.* Cambridge, MA: Harvard University Press.

8. Hamill, A. C., & Stein, C. H. (2011). Culture and empowerment in the Deaf community: An analysis of internet weblogs. *Journal of Community & Applied Social Psychology, 21,* 388–406.

9. Nomeland, M. M., & Nomeland, R. E. (2012). *The deaf community in America: History in the making.* Jefferson, NC: McFarland & Company, Inc.

10. groups.google.com/group/sightseernewsletter/about

11. Gordon, R. G. (Ed.). (2005). *Ethnologue: Languages of the world* (15th ed.). Dallas: SIL International.

12. Office of the New York State Comptroller: www.osc.state.ny.us/.

13. Foundation for Endangered Languages: www.ogmios.org/home.htm.

14. See Cohen, A. B. (2009). Many forms of culture. *American Psychologist, 64,* 194–204.

15. Yin, L. (2009). Cultural difference of politeness in English and Chinese. *Asian Social Science, 5*(6), retrieved February 5, 2010, from www.ccsenet. org/journal/index.php/ass/article/view/2492/2338.

16. Yoon, K.–I. (2010). The cultural effects of individualism and collectivism on social capital. *International Area Studies Review, 13,* 187–212; see also Triandis, H. C. (1990). Cross-cultural studies of individualism and collectivism. In J. Berman (Ed.), *Nebraska symposium on motivation* (pp. 41–133). Lincoln: University of Nebraska Press.

17. Hofstede, G. (2003). *Culture's consequences: Comparing values, behaviors, institutions, and organizations across nations* (2nd ed.). Thousand Oaks, CA: Sage.

18. Piot, C. (1999). *Remotely global: Village modernity in West Africa.* Chicago: University of Chicago Press.

19. Hofstede, 2003.

20. Cai, D. A., & Fink, E. L. (2002). Conflict style differences between individualists and collectivists. *Communication Monographs, 69,* 67–87.

21. Burgoon, J. K., Guerrero, L. K., & Floyd, K. (2010). *Nonverbal communication.* Boston: Allyn & Bacon.

22. Kittler, M. G., Rygl, D., & Mackinnon, A. (2011). Beyond culture or beyond control? Reviewing the use of Hall's high-low-context concept. *International Journal of Cross Cultural Management, 11,* 63–82.

23. Ambady, N., Koo, J., Lee, F., & Rosenthal, R. (1996). More than words: Linguistic and nonlinguistic politeness in two cultures. *Journal of Personality and Social Psychology, 70,* 996–1011.

24. Hofstede, 2003.

25. Hofstede, D., & Hofstede, G. J. (2001). *Cultures and organizations: Software of the mind* (2nd ed.). Boston: McGraw-Hill.

26. Matsumoto, D., & Juang, L. (2013). *Culture & psychology* (5th ed.). Belmont, CA: Wadsworth, Cengage Learning.

27. Yook, E. L., & Albert, R. D. (1998). Perceptions of the appropriateness of negotiation in educational settings: A cross-cultural comparison among Koreans and Americans. *Communication Education, 47,* 18–29.

28. Hofstede & Hofstede, 2004.

29. Hofstede & Hofstede, 2004.

30. Hall, E. T., & Hall, M. R. (1990). *Understanding cultural differences: Germans, French, and Americans.* Boston: Intercultural.

31. Hall, E. T. (1990). *The silent language.* New York: Anchor.

32. Heereman, J., & Walla, P. (2011). Stress, uncertainty and decision confidence. *Applied Psychophysiology and Biofeedback, 36,* 273–279.

33. Hofstede, G. (1986). Cultural differences in teaching and learning. *International Journal of Intercultural Relations, 10,* 301–320.

34. Lee, W. S. (1994). On not missing the boat: A processual method for intercultural understanding of idioms and lifeworld. *Journal of Applied Communication Research, 22,* 141–161.

35. Pease, A., & Pease, B. (2004). *The definitive book of body language: The secret meaning behind people's gestures.* London: Orion.

36. Berger, C. R. (1988). Uncertainty and information exchange in developing relationships. In S. Duck & D. F. Hay (Eds.), *Handbook of personal relationships: Theory, research and intervention* (pp. 239–255). New York: Wiley.

37. Rainie, L., Madden, M., Boyce, A., Lenhart, A., Horrigan, J., Allen, K., & O'Grady, E. (2003, April 16). *The ever-shifting Internet population: A new look at Internet access and the digital divide.* Pew Internet & American Life Project. Retrieved February 17, 2010, from www.pewinternet.org/Reports/2003/The-EverShifting-Internet-Population-A-new-look-at-Internet-access-and-the-digital-divide.aspx.

38. See Gallois, C., Ogay, T., & Giles, H. (2005). Communication accommodation theory: A look back and a look ahead. In W. Gudykunst (Ed.), *Theorizing about intercultural communication* (pp. 121–148). Thousand Oaks, CA: Sage.

39. Natalie, M. (1975). Convergence of mean vocal intensity in dyadic communication as a function of social desirability. *Journal of Personality and Social Psychology, 32,* 790–804.

Chapter 3

1. Ambady, N., Bernieri, F. J., & Richeson, J. A. (2000). Toward a histology of social behavior: Judgmental accuracy from thin slices of the behavioral stream. *Advances in Experimental Social Psychology, 32,* 201–271; Borkenau, P., Mauer, N., Riemann, R., Spinath, F. M., & Angleitner, A. (2004). Thin slices of behavior as cues of personality and intelligence. *Journal of Personality and Social Psychology, 86,* 599–614.

2. Kenny, D. A. (1994). *Interpersonal perception: A social relations analysis.* New York: Guilford.

3. Schermerhorn, J. R., Hunt, J. H., & Osborn, R. N. (2003). *Organizational behavior* (8th ed.). New York: Wiley.

4. Goldstein, E. B. (2007). *Sensation and perception* (7th ed.). Pacific Grove, CA: Wadsworth.

5. Floyd, K., Ramirez, A., & Burgoon, J. K. (2008). Expectancy violations theory. In L. K. Guerrero, J. A. DeVito, & M. L. Hecht (Eds.), *The nonverbal communication reader: Classic and contemporary readings* (3rd ed., pp. 503–510). Prospect Heights, IL: Waveland.

6. Zajonc, R. B. (2001). Mere exposure: A gateway to the subliminal. *Current Directions in Psychological Science, 10,* 224–228.

7. Goldstein, 2007.

8. Floyd, K., Mikkelson, A. C., & Hesse, C. (2007). *The biology of human communication* (2nd ed.). Florence, KY: Thomson/Cengage.

9. Andersen, P. A. (1998). *Nonverbal communication: Forms and functions.* New York: McGraw-Hill.

10. Sowa, J. F. (2000). *Knowledge representation: Logical, philosophical, and computational foundations.* Pacific Grove, CA: Brooks/Cole.

11. Funder, D. C. (1999). *Personality judgment: A realistic approach to person perception.* San Diego: Academic.

12. Kelley, H. H. (1967). Attribution theory in social psychology. In D. Levine (Ed.), *Nebraska symposium on motivation* (vol. 15, pp. 192–238). Lincoln: University of Nebraska Press.

13. Jones, E. E., & Davis, K. E. (1965). From acts to dispositions: The attribution process in person perception. In L. Berkowitz (Ed.), *Advances in experimental social psychology* (vol. 2, pp. 219–266). New York: Academic.

14. See, e.g., Manusov, V. (1993). It depends on your perspective: Effects of stance and beliefs about intent on person perception. *Western Journal of Communication, 57,* 27–41.

15. Andersen, 1998.

16. Ji, L. K., Peng, K., & Nisbett, R. E. (2000). Culture, control, and perception of relationships in the environment. *Journal of Personality and Social Psychology, 78,* 943–955; Knowles, E. D., Morris, M. W., Chiu, C.-Y., & Hong, Y.-Y. (2001). Culture and the process of person perception: Evidence for automaticity among East Asians in correcting for situational influences on behavior. *Personality and Social Psychology Bulletin, 27,* 1344–1356.

17. Luszcz, M. A., & Fitzgerald, K. M. (1986). Understanding cohort differences in cross-generational, self, and peer perceptions. *Journal of Gerontology, 41,* 234–240.

18. Farwell, L., & Weiner, B. (2000). Bleeding hearts and the heartless: Popular perceptions of liberal and conservative ideologies. *Personality and Social Psychology Bulletin, 26,* 845–852.

19. Lepore, L., & Brown, R. (1997). Category and stereotype activation: Is prejudice inevitable? *Journal of Personality and Social Psychology, 72,* 275–287.

20. Buttney, R. (1997). Reported speech in talking race on campus. *Human Communication Research, 23,* 477–506; Nelson, T. D. (2005). Ageism: Prejudice against our featured future self. *Journal of Social Issues, 61,* 207–221.

21. See, e.g., Hendrix, K. G. (2002). "Did being Black introduce bias into your study?" Attempting to mute the race-related research of black scholars. *Howard Journal of Communication, 13,* 153–171; Hughes, P. C., & Baldwin, J. R. (2002). Communication and stereotypical impressions. *Howard Journal of Communication, 13,* 113–128.

22. Aronson, J., Lustina, M. J., Good, C., & Keough, K. (1999). When white men can't do math: Necessary and sufficient factors in stereotype threat. *Journal of Experimental Social Psychology, 35,* 29–46.

23. Snyder, M., & Uranowitz, S. (1978). Reconstructing the past: Some cognitive consequences of person perception. *Journal of Personality and Social Psychology, 36,* 941–950.

24. Allen, M. (1998). Methodological considerations when examining a gendered world. In D. J. Canary & K. Dindia (Eds.), *Handbook of sex differences and similarities in communication* (pp. 427–444). Mahwah, NJ: Lawrence Erlbaum Associates.

25. Lee, Y. -T., Jussim, L. J., & McCauley, C. R. (1996). *Stereotype accuracy: Toward appreciating group differences.* Washington, D.C.: American Psychological Association.

26. Tetlock, P. E. (1983). Accountability and the perseverance of first impressions. *Social Psychology Quarterly, 46,* 285–292.

27. Asch, S. (1946). Forming impressions of personality. *Journal of Abnormal and Social Psychology, 41,* 258–290.

28. Parsons, C. K., Liden, R. C., & Bauer, T. N. (2001). Personal perception in employment interviews. In M. London (Ed.), *How people evaluate others in organizations* (pp. 67–90). Mahwah, NJ: Lawrence Erlbaum Associates.

29. Luchins, A. (1957). Primacy-recency in impression formation. In C. Hovland (Ed.), *The order of presentation in persuasion.* New Haven, CT: Yale University Press.

30. Baddeley, A. D., & Hitch, G. (1993). The recency effect: Implicit learning with explicit retrieval? *Memory and Cognition, 21,* 146–155.

31. McCann, C. D., Higgins, E. T., & Fondacaro, R. A. (1991). Primacy and recency in communication and self-persuasion: How successive audiences and multiple encodings influence subsequent evaluative judgments. *Social Cognition, 9,* 47–66.

32. Schyns, P. G., & Oliva, A. (1999). Dr. Angry and Mr. Smile: When categorization flexibly modifies the perception of faces in rapid visual presentations. *Cognition, 69,* 243–265.

33. Stern, M., & Karraker, K. H. (1989). Sex stereotyping of infants: A review of gender labeling studies. *Sex Roles, 20,* 501–522.

34. King, D. E., & Bushwick, B. (1994). Beliefs and attitudes of hospital inpatients about faith healing and prayer. *Journal of Family Practice, 39,* 349–352.

35. Floyd, K. (2000). Affectionate same-sex touch: Understanding the influence of homophobia on observers' perceptions. *Journal of Social Psychology, 140,* 774–788.

36. Floyd, K., & Yoshimura, C. G. (2002). The extended self-serving bias in attribution making about communication behavior. In A. V. Stavros (Ed.), *Advances in communications and media research* (vol. 1, pp. 129–138). Hauppauge, NY: Nova Science.

37. Manusov, V., & Harvey, H. J. (Eds.). (2001). *Attribution, communication behavior, and close relationships.* Cambridge, England: Cambridge University Press.

38. Weiner, B. (2000). Intrapersonal and interpersonal theories of motivation from the attributional perspective. *Educational Psychology Review, 12,* 1–14.

39. Pascarella, E. T., Edison, M., Hagedorn, L. S., Nora, A., & Terenzini, P. T. (1996). Influences on students' internal locus of attribution for academic success in the first year of college. *Research in Higher Education, 37,* 731–756.

40. Weiner, B. (1985). An attributional theory of achievement motivation and emotion. *Psychological Review, 92,* 548–573.

41. Hooley, J. M., & Campbell, C. (2002). Control and controllability: Beliefs and behaviour in high and low expressed emotion relatives. *Psychological Medicine, 32,* 1091–1099.

42. Block, J., & Funder, D. C. (1986). Social roles and social perception: Individual differences in attribution and error. *Journal of Personality and Social Psychology, 51,* 1200–1207.

43. Sedikides, C., Campbell, W. K., Reeder, G. D., & Elliott, A. J. (1998). The self-serving bias in relational context. *Journal of Personality and Social Psychology, 74,* 378–386.

44. Sillars, A., Roberts, L. J., Dun, T., & Leonard, K. (2001). Stepping into the stream of thought: Cognition during marital conflict. In V. Manusov & J. H. Harvey (Eds.), *Attribution, communication behavior, and close relationships* (pp. 193-201). Cambridge, England: Cambridge University Press.

45. Ross, L. (1977). The intuitive psychologist and his shortcomings: Distortions in the attribution process. In L. Berkowitz (Ed.), *Advances in experimental social psychology* (vol. 10, pp. 173–220). New York: Academic; Tetlock, P. E. (1985). Accountability: A social check on the fundamental attribution error. *Social Psychology Quarterly, 48,* 227–236.

46. Luft, J., & Ingham, H. (1955). The Johari window: A graphic model of interpersonal awareness. *Proceedings of the Western Training Laboratory in Group Development.* Los Angeles: UCLA.

47. Reported in Myers, D. G. (1980). *The inflated self.* New York: Seabury.

48. Brown, J. D., & Mankowski, T. A. (1993). Self-esteem, mood, and self-evaluation: Changes in mood and the way you see you. *Journal of Personality and Social Psychology, 64,* 421–430; Campbell, J. D. (1990). Self-esteem and clarity of the self-concept. *Journal of Personality and Social Psychology, 59,* 538–549.

49. Tarlow, E. M., & Haaga, D. A. F. (1996). Negative self-concept: Specificity to depressive symptoms and relation to positive and negative affectivity. *Journal of Research in Personality, 30,* 120–127.

50. Kolligan, J. (1990). Perceived fraudulence as a dimension of perceived incompetence. In R. J. Sternberg & J. Kolligan (Eds.), *Competence considered* (pp. 261–285). New Haven, CT: Yale University Press; Downey, G., & Feldman, S. I. (1996). Implications of rejection sensitivity for intimate relationships. *Journal of Personality and Social Psychology, 70,* 1327–1343.

51. Campbell, J. D., & Lavallee, L. F. (1993). Who am I? The role of self-concept confusion in understanding the behavior of people with low self-esteem. In R. F. Baumeister (Ed.), *Self-esteem: The puzzle of low self-regard* (pp. 3–20). New York: Plenum.

52. Buhrmester, D., Furman, W., Wittenberg, M. T., & Reis, H. T. (1988). Five domains of interpersonal competence in peer relations. *Journal of Personality and Social Psychology, 55,* 991–1008; Murray, S. L., Rose, P., Bellavia, G., Holmes, J. G., & Kusche, A. (2002). When rejection stings: How self-esteem constrains relationship-enhancement processes. *Journal of Personality and Social Psychology, 83,* 556–573.

53. Baumeister, R. F. (2001). Violent pride: Do people turn violent because of self-hate, or self-love? *Scientific American, 284*(4), 96–101; Olweus, D. (1994). *Bullying at school: What we know and what we can do.* Malden, MA: Blackwell.

54. Baumeister, R. F., Campbell, J. D., Krueger, J. I., & Vohs, K. D. (2003). Does high self-esteem cause better performance, interpersonal success, happiness, or healthier lifestyles? *Psychological Science in the Public Interest, 4,* 1–44.

55. Bishop, J., & Inderbitzen-Nolan, H. M. (1995). Peer acceptance and friendship: An investigation of their relation to self-esteem. *Journal of Early Adolescence, 15,* 476–489; Rusbult, C. E., Morrow, G. D., & Johnson, D. J. (1987). Self-esteem and problem solving behavior in close relationships. *British Journal of Social Psychology, 26,* 293–303.

56. McAdams, D. P. (1996). Personality, modernity, and the storied self: A contemporary framework for studying persons. *Psychological Inquiry, 7,* 295–321.

57. Donath, J. S. (1999). Identity and deception in the virtual community. In P. Kollock & A. S. Smith (Eds.), *Communities in Cyberspace* (pp. 29–59). London: Routledge.

58. Kendall, L. (1998). Meaning and identity in "Cyberspace": The performance of gender, class, and race online. *Symbolic Interaction, 21,* 129–153.

59. Herring, S. C., Scheidt, L. A., Bonus, S., & Wright, E. (2004). Bridging the gap: A genre analysis of weblogs. *Proceedings of the 37th Hawaii International Conference on System Sciences (HICSS-37).* Los Alamitos, CA: IEEE. Retrieved October 15, 2009, from http://csdl.computer.org/comp/proceedings/hicss/2004/2056/04/205640101b.pdf.

60. Huffaker, D. A., & Calvert, S. L. (2005). Gender, identity, and language use in teenage blogs. *Journal of Computer-Mediated Communication, 10*(2), article 1. http://jcmc.indiana.edu/vol10/issue2/huffaker.html.

61. Goldschmidt, M. M. (2004). Good person stories: The favor narrative as a self-presentation strategy. *Qualitative Research Reports in Communication, 5,* 28–33.

62. See Ting-Toomey, S., Oetzel, J. G., & Yee-Jung, K. (2001). Self-construal types and conflict management styles. *Communication Reports, 14,* 87–104; Ting-Toomey, S., & Oetzel, J. G. (2001). *Managing intercultural conflict effectively.* Thousand Oaks, CA: Sage.

63. Goffman, E. (1959). *The presentation of the self in everyday life.* New York: Doubleday; see also Brown, P., & Levinson, S. C. (1987). *Politeness: Some universals in language usage.* Cambridge, England: Cambridge University Press.

64. Lim, T. S., & Bowers, J. W. (1991). Facework: Solidarity, approbation, and tact. *Human Communication Research, 17,* 415–449.

65. Cupach, W. R., & Metts, S. (1994). *Facework.* Thousand Oaks, CA: Sage.

66. Brocklehurst, J., & Dickinson, E. (1996). Autonomy for elderly people in long-term care. *Age and Aging, 25,* 329–332.

67. See, e.g., Takahashi, L. M. (1998). *Homelessness, AIDS, and stigmatization: The NIMBY syndrome in the United States at the end of the twentieth century.* New York: Oxford University Press.

Chapter 4

1. Baker, M. C. (2002). *The atoms of language: The mind's hidden rules of grammar.* New York: Basic.

2. Pinker, S. (2007). *The stuff of thought: Language as a window into human nature.* New York: Viking.

3. Ogden, C. K., & Richards, I. A. (1927). *The meaning of meaning: A study of the influence of language upon thought and of the science of symbolism* (2nd ed.). Orlando: Harcourt Brace.

4. British Council. (2004). Mum's the word: British Council announces results of 70 most beautiful words survey. Retrieved online September 23, 2006, from: http://www.britishcouncil.de/e/about/70words.htm

5. Bryson, B. (1990). *The mother tongue: English and how it got that way.* New York: William Morrow.

6. Hayakawa, S. I., & Hayakawa, A. R. (1991). *Language in thought and action.* San Diego: Harcourt.

7. Gudykunst, W., & Lee, C. (2002). Cross-cultural communication theories. In W. Gudykunst & B. Mody (Eds.), *The handbook of international and intercultural communication* (2nd ed., pp. 25–50). Thou- sand Oaks, CA: Sage.

8. Schultz, E. A. (1990). *Dialogue at the margins: Whorf, Bakhtin, and linguistic relativity.* Madison: University of Wisconsin Press.

9. Gumperz, J. J., & Levinson, S. C. (Eds.). (1996). *Rethinking linguistic relativity.* New York: Cambridge University Press.

10. For more detail on the Sapir-Whorf hypothesis, see Pütz, M., & Verspoor, M. (Eds.). (2000). *Explorations in linguistic relativity.* Amsterdam: John Benjamins Publishing Company.

11. Marcus, M. G. (1976, October). The power of a name. *Psychology Today, 9,* 75–77, 106.

12. Steele, K. M., & Smithwick, L. E. (1989). First names and first impressions: A fragile relationship. *Sex Roles, 21,* 517–523.

13. See Bertrand, M., & Mullainathan, S. (2004). Are Emily and Greg more employable than Lakisha and Jamal? A field experiment on labor market discrimination. *American Economic Review, 94,* 991–1013; but see Fryer, R. G., & Levitt, S. D. (2004). The causes and consequences of distinctively black names. *Quarterly Journal of Economics, 119,* 767–805.

14. Giles, H., & Wiemann, J. M. (1987). Language, social comparison and power. In C. R. Berger & S. H. Chaffee (Eds.), *The handbook of communication science* (pp. 350–384). Newbury Park, CA: Sage.

15. Bavelas, J. B., Black, A., Bryson, L., & Mullett, J. (1988). Political equivocation: A situational explanation: *Journal of Language and Social Psychology, 7*, 137–145; Bavelas, J. B., Black, A., Chovil, N., & Mullett, J. (1990). *Equivocal communication.* Newbury Park, CA: Sage.

16. Hamilton, M. A., & Mineo, P. J. (1998). A framework for understanding equivocation. *Journal of Language and Social Psychology, 17*, 3–35.

17. Daly, J. A., Diesel, C. A., & Weber, D. (1994). Conversational dilemmas. In W. R. Cupach & B. H. Spitzberg (Eds.), *The dark side of interpersonal communication* (pp. 127–156). Mahwah, NJ: Lawrence Erlbaum Associates.

18. Huston, T. L., Caughlin, J. P., Houts, R. M., Smith, S. E., & George, L. J. (2001). The connubial crucible: Newlywed years as predictors of marital delight, distress, and divorce. *Journal of Personality and Social Psychology, 80*, 237–252.

19. Floyd, K., & Riforgiate, S. (2008). Affectionate communication received from spouses predicts stress hormone levels in healthy adults. *Communication Monographs, 75*, 351–368.

20. Floyd, K., Mikkelson, A. C., Tafoya, M. A., Farinelli, L., La Valley, A. G., Judd, J., Davis, K. L., Haynes, M. T., & Wilson, J. (2007). Human affection exchange: XIV. Relational affection predicts resting heart rate and free cortisol secretion during acute stress. *Behavioral Medicine, 32*, 151–156.

21. Floyd, K., Boren, J. P., Hannawa, A. F., Hesse, C., McEwan, B., & Veksler, A. E. (2009). Kissing in marital and cohabiting relationships: Effects on blood lipids, stress, and relationship satisfaction. *Western Journal of Communication, 73*, 113–133; Floyd, K., Mikkelson, A. C., Hesse, C., & Pauley, P. M. (2007). Affectionate writing reduces total cholesterol: Two randomized, controlled trials. *Human Communication Research, 33*, 119–142.

22. Floyd, K., Mikkelson, A. C., Tafoya, M. A., Farinelli, L., La Valley, A. G., Judd, J., Haynes, M. T., Davis, K. L., & Wilson, J. (2007). Human affection exchange: XIII. Affectionate communication accelerates neuroendocrine stress recovery. *Health Communication, 22*, 123–132.

23. Floyd, K., Hesse, C., & Haynes, M. T. (2007). Human affection exchange: XV. Metabolic and cardiovascular correlates of trait expressed affection. *Communication Quarterly, 55*, 79–94.

24. Floyd, K. (2002). Human affection exchange: V. Attributes of the highly affectionate. *Communication Quarterly, 50*, 135–154; Floyd, K., Hess, J. A., Miczo, L. A., Halone, K. K., Mikkelson, A. C., & Tusing, K. J. (2005). Human affection exchange: VIII. Further evidence of the benefits of expressed affection. *Communication Quarterly, 53*, 285–303; Hesse, C., & Floyd, K. (2008). Affectionate experience partially mediates the effects of alexithymia on mental health and interpersonal relationships. *Journal of Social and Personal Relationships, 25*, 793–810.

25. Jorm, A. F., Dear, K. B. G., Rodgers, B., & Christensen, H. (2003). Interaction between mother's and father's affection as a risk factor for anxiety and depression symptoms. *Social Psychiatry and Psychiatric Epidemiology, 38*, 173–179; Schwartz, G. E., & Russek, L. G. (1998). Family love and lifelong health? A challenge for clinical psychology. In D. K. Routh & R. J. DeRubeis (Eds.), *The science of clinical psychology: Accomplishments and future directions* (pp. 121–146). Washington, DC: American Psychological Association.

26. ASD/AMD Merchandise Group. (2006). Greeting card marketers and retailers struggle. Retrieved September 18, 2006, from: http://www.merchandisegroup.com/merchandise/newsletter/newsletter_display.jsp?vnu_content_id=1001306530

27. www.bluemountain.com

28. Dunbar, R. (1996). *Grooming, gossip, and the evolution of language.* Cambridge, MA: Harvard University Press.

29. McAndrew, F. T., Bell, E. K., & Garcia. C. M. (2007). Who do we tell and whom do we tell on? Gossip as a strategy for status enhancement. *Journal of Applied Social Psychology, 37*, 1562–1577.

30. See De Backer, C. J. S., Nelissen, M., Vyncke, P., Braeckman, J., & McAndrew, F. T. (2007). Celebrities: From teachers to friends. A test of two hypotheses on the adaptiveness of celebrity gossip. *Human Nature, 18*, 334–354.

31. Feinberg, M., Willer, R., Steller, J., & Keltner, D. (in press 2012). The virtues of gossip: Reputational information sharing as prosocial behavior. *Journal of Personality and Social Psychology*; see also McAndrew, F. T., & Milenkovic, M. A. (2002). Of tabloids and family secrets: The evolutionary psychology of gossip. *Journal of Applied Social Psychology, 32*, 1064–1082.

32. Figure is current as of December 2011 according to "Yahoo! Advertising Solutions," available online at: http://advertising.yahoo.com/article/omg.html

33. Martin, P. S. (2004). Inside the black box of negative campaign effects: Three reasons why negative campaigns mobilize. *Political Psychology, 25*, 545–562.

34. Freedman, P., & Goldstein, K. (1999). Measuring media exposure and the effects of negative campaign ads. *American Journal of Political Science, 43*, 1189–1208.

35. Burger, J. M. (1986). Increasing compliance by improving the deal: The that's-not-all technique. *Journal of Personality and Social Psychology, 31*, 277–283.

36. Gouldner, A. W. (1960). The norm of reciprocity: A preliminary statement. *American Sociological Review, 25*, 161–178.

37. Cialdini, R. B. (1994). Interpersonal influence. In S. Shavitt & T. C. Brock (Eds.), *Persuasion: Psychological insights and perspectives* (pp. 195–218). Boston: Allyn & Bacon.

38. Cody, M. J., Seiter, J., & Montagne-Miller, Y. (1995). Women and men in the marketplace. In P. Kalbfleisch & M. J. Cody (Eds.), *Gender, power, and communication in human relationships* (pp. 305–328). Hillsdale, NJ: Lawrence Erlbaum Associates.

39. Wiseman, R. (2002). *Laughlab: The scientific search for the world's funniest joke.* London: Random House.

40. Goel, V., & Dola, R. J. (2001). The functional anatomy of humor: Segregating cognitive and affective components. *Nature Neuroscience, 4*, 237–238.

41. Mobbs, D., Greicius, M. D., Abdel-Azim, E., Menon, V., & Reiss, A. L. (2003). Humor modulates the mesolimbic reward centers. *Neuron, 40*, 1041–1048.

42. Norrick, N. R. (1993). *Conversational joking: Humor in everyday talk.* Indianapolis: Indiana University Press.

43. Keller, K. (1984). *Humor as therapy.* Wauwatosa, WI: Med-Psych.

44. eingold, A. (1992). Gender differences in mate selection preferences: A test of the parental investment model. *Psychological Bulletin, 112*, 125–139.

45. Alberts, J. K. (1992). Teasing and sexual harassment: Double bind communication in the workplace. In L. A. Perry, H. Sterk, & L. Turner (Eds.), *Constructing and reconstructing gender* (pp. 150–120). Albany: SUNY Press.

46. Makin, V. S. (2004). Face management and the role of interpersonal politeness variables in euphemism production and comprehension. *Dissertation Abstracts International, 64*, 4077; McGlone, M. S., & Batchelor, J. A. (2003). Looking out for number one: Euphemism and face. *Journal of Communication, 53*, 251–264.

47. Butler, J. (1997). *Excitable speech: A politics of the performative.* New York: Routledge.

48. Waltman, M. S., & Haas, J. W. (2007). Advertising hate on the Internet. In D. W. Schumann & E. Thorson (Eds.), *Internet advertising: Theory and practice* (pp. 397–426). Mahwah, NJ: Lawrence Erlbaum Associates.

49. Bryant, S. (2006). Feds retrieve Google records after Gmail used for hate speech. Retrieved September 6, 2006, from: http://googlewatch.eweek.com/blogs/google_watch/archive/2006/07/27/11852.aspx

Chapter 5

1. Nierenberg, G. (1990). *How to read a person like a book.* New York: Pocket; Calero, H. H. (2005). *The power of non-verbal communication: What you do is more important than what you say.* Lansdowne, PA: Silver Lake.

2. Mehrabian, A. (1968). Communication without words. *Psychology Today, 2*, 51–52.

3. Burgoon, J. K., & Hoobler, G. (2002). Nonverbal signals. In M. L. Knapp & J. A. Daly (Eds.), *Handbook of interpersonal communication* (3rd ed., pp. 240–299). Thousand Oaks, CA: Sage.

4. Burgoon, J. K. (1985). Nonverbal signals. In M. L. Knapp & G. R. Miller (Eds.), *Handbook of interpersonal communication* (pp. 344–390). Beverly Hills, CA: Sage.

5. See Hall, J. A. (2006). How big are nonverbal sex differences? The case of smiling and nonverbal sensitivity. In K. Dindia & D. J. Canary (Eds.), *Sex differences and similarities in communication* (2nd ed., pp. 59–81). Mahwah, NJ: Lawrence Erlbaum Associates.

6. Ekman, P., & Friesen, W. V. (1975). *Unmasking the face: A field guide to recognizing emotions from facial clues.* Englewood Cliffs, NJ: Prentice Hall.

7. Ekman, P. (1972). Universals and cultural differences in facial expressions of emotion. In J. Cole (Ed.), *Nebraska symposium on motivation, 1971* (vol. 19, pp. 207–282). Lincoln: University of Nebraska Press.

8. Boucher, J. D., & Carlson, G. E. (1980). Recognition of facial expression in three cultures. *Journal of Cross-Cultural Psychology, 11*, 263–280; Cüceloglu, D. M. (1970). Perception of facial expressions in three cultures. *Ergonomics, 13*, 93–100; Ekman, P., Friesen, W. V., O'Sullivan, M., Chan, A., Diacoyanni-Tarlatzis, I., Heider, K., Krause, R., LeCompte, W. A., Pitcairn, T., Ricci-Bitti, P. E., Scherer, K., Tomita, M., & Tzavaras, A. (1987). Universals and cultural differences in the judgments of facial expressions of emotion. *Journal of Personality and Social Psychology, 53*, 712–717; Izard, C. E. (1971). *The face of emotion.* New York: Appleton-Century-Crofts; McAndrew, F. T. (1986). A cross-cultural study of recognition thresholds for facial expression of emotion. *Journal of Cross-Cultural Psychology, 17*, 211–224; Niit, T., & Valsiner, J. (1977). Recognition of facial expressions: An experimental investigation of Ekman's model. *Acta et Commentationes Universitatis Tarvensis, 429*, 85–107.

9. Elfenbein, H. A., & Ambady, N. (2002). On the universality and cultural specificity of emotion recognition: A meta-analysis. *Psychological Bulletin, 128*, 203–235.

10. Kappas, A., Hess, U., & Scherer, K. R. (1991). Voice and emotion. In R. S. Feldman & B. Rimé (Eds.), *Fundamentals of nonverbal communication* (pp. 200–237). Cambridge, England: Cambridge University Press.

11. Bavelas, J. B., Coates, L., & Johnson, T. (2002). Listener responses as a collaborative process: The role of gaze. *Journal of Communication, 52,* 566–580.

12. Guerrero, L. K., & Floyd, K. (2006). *Nonverbal communication in close relationships.* Mahwah, NJ: Lawrence Erlbaum Associates.

13. See, e.g., Carroll, L., & Gilroy, P. J. (2002). Role of appearance and nonverbal behavior in the perception of sexual orientation among lesbians and gay men. *Psychological Reports, 91,* 155–122; Douglas Creed, W. E., Scully, M. A., & Austin, J. R. (2002). Clothes make the person? The tailoring of legitimating accounts and the social construction of identity. *Organization Science, 13,* 475–496; Schötz, S. (2003). Towards synthesis of speaker age: A perceptual study with natural, synthesized, and resynthesized stimuli. *PHONUM, 9,* I–X.

14. Cha, A., Hecht, B. R., Nelson, K., & Hopkins, M. P. (2004). Resident physician attire: Does it make a difference to our patients? *American Journal of Obstetrics and Gynecology, 190,* 1484–1488.

15. See Morry, M. M. (2007). The attraction-similarity hypothesis among cross-sex friends: Relationship satisfaction, perceived similarities, and self-serving perceptions. *Journal of Social and Personal Relationships, 24,* 117–138; Watkins, L. M., & Johnston, L. (2000). Screening job applicants: The impact of physical attractiveness and application quality. *International Journal of Selection and Assessment, 8,* 76–84.

16. Ekman, P., Friesen, W. V., & Scherer, K. R. (1976). Body movement and voice pitch in deceptive interaction. *Semiotica, 16,* 23–27.

17. Ekman, P., Friesen, W. V., & O'Sullivan, M. (1997). Smiles when lying. In P. Ekman & E. L. Rosenberg (Eds.), *What the face reveals: Basic and applied studies of spontaneous expression using the facial affect coding system (FACS)* (pp. 201–214). New York: Oxford University Press.

18. Vrij, A., Semin, G. R., & Bull, R. (1996). Insight into behavior displayed during deception. *Human Communication Research, 22,* 544–562.

19. Knapp, M. L. (1978). *Nonverbal communication in human interaction* (2nd ed.). New York: Holt.

20. Ellis, H. D., & Young, A. W. (1989). Are faces special? In A. W. Young & H. D. Ellis (Eds.), *Handbook of research on face processing* (pp. 1–26). Amsterdam: North-Holland.

21. Smith, C., Lentz, E. M., & Mikos, K. (1988). *Signing naturally.* San Diego: DawnSign.

22. Iverson, J. M., Tencer, H. L., Lany, J., & Goldin-Meadow, S. (2000). The relation between gesture and speech in congenitally blind and sighted language-learners. *Journal of Nonverbal Behavior, 24,* 105–130.

23. Floyd, K. (2006). *Communicating affection: Interpersonal behavior and social context.* Cambridge, England: Cambridge University Press.

24. Field, T. M. (Ed.). (1995). *Touch in early development.* Mahwah, NJ: Lawrence Erlbaum Associates.

25. Zuckerman, M., & Miyake, K. (1993). The attractive voice: What makes it so? *Journal of Nonverbal Behavior, 17,* 119–135.

26. Wolvin, A., & Coakley, C. (1996). *Listening.* Dubuque, IA: Brown & Benchmark.

27. Burgoon, J. K., Guerrero, L. K., & Floyd, K. (2010). *Nonverbal communication.* Boston: Allyn & Bacon.

28. Hall, E. T. (1959). *The silent language.* Garden City, NY: Doubleday; Hall, E. T. (1963). System for the notation of proxemic behavior. *American Anthropologist, 65,* 1003–1026.

29. Dion, K. K., Berscheid, E., & Walster, E. (1972). What is beautiful is good. *Journal of Personality and Social Psychology, 24,* 285–290; Eagley, A. E., Ashmore, R. D., Makhijani, M. G., & Longo, L. C. (1991). What is beautiful is good, but . . . : A meta-analytic review of research on the physical attractiveness stereotype. *Psychological Bulletin, 110,* 109–139; Kuhlenschmidt, S., & Conger, J. C. (1988). Behavioral components of social competence in females. *Sex Roles, 18,* 107–112.

30. O'Grady, K. E. (1989). Physical attractiveness, need for approval, social self-esteem, and maladjustment. *Journal of Social and Clinical Psychology, 8,* 62–69; Curran, J. P., & Lippold, S. (1975). The effects of physical attraction and attitude similarity on attraction in dating dyads. *Journal of Personality, 43,* 528–539.

31. Efran, M. G. (1974). The effect of physical appearance on the judgment of guilt, interpersonal attraction, and severity of recommended punishment in a simulated jury task. *Journal of Experimental Research in Personality, 8,* 45–54; Efran, M. G., & Patterson, E. (1974). Voters vote beautiful: The effect of physical appearance on a national debate. *Canadian Journal of Behavioral Science, 6,* 352–356; West, S. G., & Brown, T. J. (1975). Physical attractiveness, the severity of the emergency and helping: A field experiment and interpersonal simulation. *Journal of Experimental Social Psychology, 11,* 531–538.

32. Nowak, K. L., & Rauh, C. (2006). The influence of the avatar on online perceptions of anthropomorphism, androgyny, credibility, homophily, and attraction. *Journal of Computer-Mediated Communication, 11,* 153–178.

33. Jandt, F. E. (1995). *Intercultural communication: An introduction.* Thousand Oaks, CA: Sage.

34. Burgoon et al., 2010.

35. Feghali, E. K. (1997). Arab cultural communication patterns. *International Journal of Intercultural Relations, 21,* 345–378.

36. Watson, O. M. (1970). *Proxemic behavior: A cross-cultural study.* The Hague: Mouton.

37. Iizuka, Y. (1994). Gaze during speaking as related to shyness. *Perceptual and Motor Skills, 78,* 1259–1264; Larsen, R. J., & Shackelford, T. K. (1996). Gaze avoidance: Personality and social judgments of people who avoid direct face-to-face contact. *Personality and Individual Differences, 21,* 907–917.

38. Matsumoto, D. (2006). Culture and nonverbal behavior. In V. Manusov & M. L. Patterson (Eds.), *The Sage handbook of nonverbal communication* (pp. 219–236). Thousand Oaks, CA: Sage.

39. Ekman, P. (1993). Facial expression and emotion. *American Psychologist, 48,* 384–392; Ekman, P., & Friesen, W. V. (1986). A new pan-cultural facial expression of emotion. *Motivation and Emotion, 10,* 159–168; Scherer, K. R., & Wallbott, H. G. (1994). Evidence for universality and cultural variation of differential emotion response patterning. *Journal of Personality and Social Psychology, 66,* 310–328.

40. Matsumoto, D. (1991). Cultural influences on facial expressions of emotion. *Southern Communication Journal, 56,* 128–137; Matsumoto, 2006.

41. Burgoon et al., 2010.

42. Hall, E. T., & Hall, M. R. (1990). *Understanding cultural differences: Germans, French, and Americans.* Yarmouth, ME: Intercultural.

43. Levine, R., & Wolff, E. (1985, March). Social time: The heartbeat of culture. *Psychology Today,* 28–35.

44. McDaniel, E. R., & Andersen, P. A. (1998). Intercultural variations in tactile communication: A field study. *Journal of Nonverbal Behavior, 22,* 59–75; see also Field, T. (1999). American adolescents touch each other less and are more aggressive toward their peers as compared with French adolescents. *Adolescence, 34,* 753–758.

45. Andersen, P. A. (2008). *Nonverbal communication: Forms and functions* (2nd ed.). Long Grove, IL: Waveland; Andersen, P. A., & Wang, H. (2006). Unraveling cultural cues: Dimensions of non-verbal communication across cultures. In L. A. Samovar, R. E. Porter, & E. R. McDaniel (Eds.), *Intercultural communication: A reader* (pp. 250–266). Belmont, CA: Wadsworth.

46. Kramsch, C. (1998). *Language and culture.* New York: Oxford University Press.

47. Fridlund, A. J. (1994). *Human facial expression: An evolutionary view.* San Diego: Academic.

48. Grieser, D. L., & Kuhl, P. K. (1988). Maternal speech to infants in a tonal language: Support for universal prosodic features in motherese. *Developmental Psychology, 24,* 14–20.

49. Wood, J. T. (2009). *Gendered lives: Communication, culture, and gender* (8th ed.). Belmont, CA: Cengage/Wadsworth.

50. Floyd, K., Mikkelson, A. C., & Hesse, C. (2007). *The biology of human communication* (2nd ed.). Florence, KY: Thomson.

51. Burgoon, J. K., & Bacue, A. (2003). Nonverbal communication skills. In B. R. Burleson & J. O. Greene (Eds.), *Handbook of communication and social interaction skills* (pp. 179–219). Mahwah, NJ: Lawrence Erlbaum Associates.

52. Floyd, 2006. (See note 24.)

53. Blier, M. J., & Blier-Wilson, L. A. (1989). Gender differences in sex-rated emotional expressiveness. *Sex Roles, 21,* 287–295.

54. Nolen-Hoeksema, S. (1987). Sex differences in unipolar depression: Evidence and theory. *Psychological Bulletin, 101,* 259–282.

55. Coats, E. J., & Feldman, R. S. (1996). Gender differences in nonverbal correlates of social status. *Personality and Social Psychology Bulletin, 22,* 1014–1022.

56. Burrowes, B. D., & Halberstadt, A. G. (1987). Self- and family-expressiveness styles in the experience and expression of anger. *Journal of Nonverbal Behavior, 11,* 254–268.

57. Mulac, A., Studley, L. B., Wiemann, J. W., & Bradac, J. J. (1987). Male/female gaze in same-sex and mixed-sex dyads: Gender-linked differences and mutual influence. *Human Communication Research, 13,* 323–344.

58. Wada, M. (1990). The effects of interpersonal distance change on nonverbal behaviors: Mediating effects of sex and intimacy levels in a dyad. *Japanese Psychological Research, 32,* 86–96.

59. Exline, R. V. (1963). Explorations in the process of person perception: Visual interaction in relation to competition, sex, and the need for affiliation. *Journal of Personality, 31,* 1–20.

60. Mulac et al., 1987.

61. Patterson, M. L., & Schaeffer, R. E. (1977). Effects of size and sex composition on interaction distance, participation, and satisfaction in small groups. *Small Group Behavior, 8,* 433–442.

62. Shaffer, D. R., & Sadowski, C. (1975). This table is mine: Respect for marked barroom tables as a function of gender of spatial marker and desirability of locale. *Sociometry, 38,* 408–419.

63. Marieb, E. N. (2003). *Essentials of human anatomy and physiology* (7th ed.). San Francisco: Benjamin Cummings.

64. Fitzpatrick, M. A., Mulac, A., & Dindia, K. (1994, July). *Convergence and reciprocity in male and female communication patterns in spouse and stranger interaction.* Paper presented at the Fifth International Conference on Language and Social Psychology, Brisbane, Australia.

65. Major, B., Schmidlin, A. M., & Williams, L. (1990). Gender patterns in social touch: The impact of setting and age. *Journal of Personality and Social Psychology, 58,* 634–643.

66. Major et al., 1990.

67. See Dortch, S. (1997). Women at the cosmetics counter. *American Demographics, 19,* 4.

68. Gray, J. (1992). *Men are from Mars, women are from Venus: A practical guide to improving communication and getting what you want in your relationships.* New York: HarperCollins.

69. Dindia, K. (2006). Men are from North Dakota, women are from South Dakota. In K. Dindia & D. J. Canary (Eds.), *Sex differences and similarities in communication* (2nd ed., pp. 3–20). Mahwah, NJ: Lawrence Erlbaum Associates.

70. See, e. g., Hall, J. A. (2006). How big are nonverbal sex differences? The case of smiling and nonverbal sensitivity. In K. Dindia & D. J. Canary (Eds.), *Sex differences and similarities in communication* (2nd ed., pp. 59–81). Mahwah, NJ: Lawrence Erlbaum Associates.

71. Ekman, P., & Friesen, W. V. (1982). Felt, false, and miserable smiles. *Journal of Nonverbal Behavior, 6,* 238–252.

72. Riggio, R. E. (2005). The Social Skills Inventory (SSI): Measuring nonverbal and social skills. In V. Manusov (Ed.), *The sourcebook of nonverbal measures: Going beyond words* (pp. 25–34). Mahwah, NJ: Lawrence Erlbaum Associates.

73. Riggio, R. E. (2006). Nonverbal skills and abilities. In V. Manusov & M. L. Patterson (Eds.), *The Sage handbook of nonverbal communication* (pp. 79–96). Thousand Oaks, CA: Sage.

74. Riggio, R. E. (1986). Assessment of basic social skills. *Journal of Personality and Social Psychology, 51,* 649–660.

75. See Friedman, H. S., & Riggio, R. E. (1981). Effects of individual differences in nonverbal expressiveness on transmission of emotion. *Journal of Nonverbal Behavior, 6,* 96–102.

76. Friedman, H. S., Prince, L. M., Riggio, R. E., & DiMatteo, M. R. (1980). Understanding and assessing nonverbal expressiveness: The Affective Communication Test. *Journal of Personality and Social Psychology, 39,* 333–351.

Chapter 6

1. See Ames, D., Maissen, L. B., & Brockner, J. (2012). The role of listening in interpersonal influence. *Journal of Research in Personality, 46,* 345-349.

2. Emmert, P. (1996). President's perspective. *ILA Listening Post, 56,* 2–3.

3. Dindia, K., & Kennedy, B. L. (2004, November). *Communication in everyday life: A descriptive study using mobile electronic data collection.* Paper presented at the annual conference of the National Communication Association, Chicago, IL.

4. Barker, L., Edwards, R., Gaines, C., Gladney, K., & Holley, F. (1980). An investigation of proportional time spent in various communicating activities by college students. *Journal of Applied Communication Research, 8,* 101–109; Hargie, O., Saunders, C., & Dickson, D. (1994). *Social skills in interpersonal communication* (3rd ed.). New York: Routledge.

5. Windsor, J. L., Curtis, D. B., & Stephens, R. D. (1997). National preferences in business and communication education: An update. *Journal of the Association for Communication Administration, 3,* 170–179.

6. See Vangelisti, A. L. (Ed.). (2012). *Handbook of family communication* (2nd ed.). New York: Taylor & Francis.

7. Miller, R., Perlman, D., & Brehn, S. (2006). *Intimate relationships.* New York: McGraw-Hill.

8. Brownell, J. (1990). Perceptions of effective listeners: A management study. *Journal of Business Communication, 27,* 401–415.

9. Carrell, L. J., & Willmington, S. C. (1996). A comparison of self-report and performance data in assessing speaking and listening competence. *Communication Reports, 9,* 185–191.

10. See Lane, K., Balleweg, B. J., Suler, J. R., Fernald, P. S., & Goldstein, G. S. (2000). Acquiring skills—Undergraduate students. In M. E. Ware & D. E. Johnson (Eds.), *Handbook of demonstrations and activities in the teaching of psychology: Vol. 3. Personality, abnormal, clinical-counseling, and social* (2nd ed., pp. 109–124). Mahwah, NJ: Lawrence Erlbaum Associates.

11. Brownell, J. (2010). The skills of listening-centered communication. In A. D. Wolvin (Ed.), *Listening and human communication in the 21st Century* (pp. 141–157). Oxford, England: Wiley-Blackwell.

12. Wolvin, A. D. (1987, June). *Culture as a listening variable.* Paper presented at the summer conference of the International Listening Association, Toronto, Ontario, Canada.

13. Chen, G.-M., & Chung, J. (1997). The "Five Asian Dragons": Management behaviors and organization communication. In L. A. Samovar &

R. E. Porter (Eds.), *Intercultural communication: A reader* (pp. 317–328). Belmont, CA: Wadsworth.

14. Egan, G. (1998). *The skilled helper* (6th ed.). Pacific Grove, CA: Brooks/Cole.

15. Brownell, J. (2002). *Listening attitudes, principles, and skills* (2nd ed.). Boston: Allyn & Bacon.

16. Mar, R. A. (2011). The neural bases of social cognition and story comprehension. *Annual Review of Psychology, 62,* 103–134.

17. Thomas, L. T., & Levine, T. R. (1994). Disentangling listening and verbal recall: Separate but related constructs? *Human Communication Research, 21,* 103–127.

18. Benoit, S. S., & Lee, J. W. (1986). Listening: It can be taught. *Journal of Education for Business, 63,* 229–232.

19. Gross, A. L., Parisi, J. M., Spira, A. P., Kuelder, A. M., Ko, J. Y., Sacynski, J. S., et al. (2012). Memory training interventions for older adults: A meta-analysis. *Aging & Mental Health 16,* 722–734.

20. Tice, M., & Henetz, T. (2011). Reading between the turns: Social perceptions of turn-taking cues in conversation. *Journal of the Acoustical Society of America, 130,* 2443.

21. Kuhn, J. L. (2001). Toward an ecological humanistic psychology. *Journal of Humanistic Psychology, 41,* 9–24.

22. Bernhardt, B. C., & Singer, T. (2012). The neural basis of empathy. *Annual Review of Neuroscience, 35,* 1–23.

23. Woltin, K.–A., Corneille, O., Yzerbyt, V. Y., & Förster, J. (2011). Narrowing down to open up for other people's concerns: Empathic concern can be enhanced by inducing detailed processing. *Journal of Experimental Social Psychology, 47,* 418–424.

24. Sarampalis, A., Kalluri, S., Edwards, B., & Hafter, E. (2009). Objective measures of listening effort: Effects of background noise and noise reduction. *Journal of Speech, Language, and Hearing Research, 52,* 1230–1240.

25. Kekäläinen, P., Niemelä, R., Tuomainen, M., Kemppilä, S., Palonen, J, Riuttala, H., et al. (2010). Effect of reduced summer indoor temperature on symptoms, perceived work environment and productivity in office work: An intervention study. *Intelligent Buildings International, 2,* 251–266.

26. Ball, S. A., & Zuckerman, M. (1992). Sensation seeking and selective attention: Focused and divided attention on a dichotic listening task. *Journal of Personality and Social Psychology, 63,* 825–831.

27. Toffler, A. (1970). *Future shock.* New York: Random House.

28. American Academy of Pediatrics. (2006). Children, adolescents, and advertising. *Pediatrics, 118,* 2563–2569.

29. Bhasin, K. (2012). This is how information overload destroys your productivity. Retrieved online May 29, 2012, from www.businessinsider.com/infographic-how-information-overload-affects-you-in-the-workplace-2012-2.

30. American Psychiatric Association. *Diagnostic and statistical manual of mental disorders* (4th ed.). Washington, D.C.: Author.

31. Attention-deficit hyperactivity disorder: ADHD in adults. Retrieved online March 8, 2008, from www.webmd.com/add-adhd/guide/adhd-adults.

32. Versfeld, N. J., & Dreschler, W. A. (2002). The relationship between the intelligibility of time-compressed speech and speech-in-noise in young and elderly listeners. *Journal of the Acoustical Society of America, 111,* 401–408; Wolvin, A., & Coakley, C. (1996). *Listening.* Dubuque, IA: Brown & Benchmark.

33. Golen, S. (1990). A factor analysis of barriers to effective listening. *Journal of Business Communication, 27,* 25–36.

34. Golen, 1990.

35. Watson, K. W., & Smeltzer, L. R. (1984). Barriers to listening: Comparisons between students and practitioners. *Communication Research Reports, 1,* 82–87.

36. Golen, 1990.

37. Nelson, A., & Brown, C. D. (2012). *The gender communication handbook: Conquering conversational collisions between men and women.* San Francisco: Wiley.

38. Redeker, G., & Maes, A. (1996). Gender differences in interruptions. In D. Slobin, J. Gerhardt, A. Kyratzis, & J. Guo (Eds.), *Social interaction, social context, and language* (pp. 579–612). Mahwah, NJ: Lawrence Erlbaum Associates.

39. Gilovich, T. (1997, March/April). Some systematic biases of everyday judgment. *Skeptical Inquirer,* 31–35.

40. Guadagno, R., E., Rhoads, K. V. L., & Sagarin, B. J. (2011). Figural vividness and persuasion: Capturing the "elusive" vividness effect. *Social Psychology Bulletin, 37,* 626–638.

42. Glassman, J. K. (1998, May 29). Put shootings in proper perspective. *San Jose Mercury News,* B7.

43. Ruggeiro, V. (1988). *Teaching thinking across the curriculum.* New York: Harper & Row.

44. Tannen, D. (1990). *You just don't understand: Women and men in conversation.* New York: Ballantine.

45. Pollak, K. I., Arnold, R. M., Jeffreys, A. S., Alexander, S. C., Olsen, M. K., Abernethy, A. P., Skinner, C. S., Rodriguez, L. K., & Tulsky, J. A. (2007).

Oncologist communication about emotion during visits with patients with advanced cancer. *Journal of Clinical Oncology, 25,* 5748–5752.

46. Floyd, K. (2006). *Communicating affection: Interpersonal behavior and social context.* Cambridge, England: Cambridge University Press.

Chapter 7

1. Parks, M. R. (2007). *Personal relationships and personal networks.* Mahwah, NJ: Lawrence Erlbaum Associates; quote is from page 1.
2. See Fiske, A. P. (1992). The four elementary forms of sociality: Framework for a unified theory of social relations. *Psychological Review, 99,* 689–723.
3. Baumeister, R. F. (2012). Need-to-belong theory. In P. Van Lange, A. Kruglanski, & E. T. Higgins (Eds.), *Handbook of social psychological theories* (Vol. 2, pp. 121–140). London: Sage.
4. See Metzner, J. L., & Fellner, J. (2010). Solitary confinement and mental illness in U.S. prisons: A challenge for medical ethics. *Journal of the American Academy of Psychiatry and the Law, 38,* 104–108.
5. Schumm, W. R., Bell, D. B., Knott, B., & Rice, R. E. (1996). The perceived effect of stressors on marital satisfaction among civilian wives of enlisted soldiers deployed to Somalia for Operation Restore Hope. *Military Medicine, 161,* 601–606.
6. Dykstra, P. A., van Tilburg, T. G., & De Jong-Gierveld, J. (2005). Changes in older adult loneliness: Results from a seven-year longitudinal study. *Research on Aging, 27,* 725–747; Sorkin, D., Rook, K. S., & Lu, J. L. (2002). Loneliness, lack of emotional support, lack of companionship, and the likelihood of having a heart condition in an elderly sample. *Annals of Behavioral Medicine, 24,* 290–298; Tijhuis, M. A., De Jong-Gierveld, J., Feskins, E. J., & Kromhout, D. (1999). Changes in and factors related to loneliness in older men: The Zutphen Elderly Study. *Age and Ageing, 28,* 491–495.
7. Parks, M. R., & Floyd, K. (1996). Making friends in cyberspace. *Journal of Communication, 46,* 80–97.
8. Davis, K. (2012). Friendship 2.0: Adolescents' experience of belonging and self-disclosure online. *Journal of Adolescence, 35,* 1527–1536.
9. Whitty, M. (2001). Age/sex/location: Uncovering the social cues in the development of online relationships. *CyberPsychology & Behavior, 4,* 623–630.
10. Schiffrin, H., Edelman, A., Falkenstern, M., & Stewart, C. (2010). The associations among computer-mediated communication, relationships, and well-being. *Cyberpsychology, Behavior, and Social Networking, 13,* 299–306.
11. Chan, D. K.-S., & Cheng, G. H.-L. (2004). A comparisons of offline and online friendship qualities at different stages of relationship development. *Journal of Social and Personal Relationships, 21,* 305–320.
12. Mesch, G. S., & Talmuc, I. (2006). Online friendship formation, communication channels, and social closeness. *International Journal of Internet Science, 1,* 29–44.
13. See, e.g., Halsen, M., Wollebergh, W., & Meeus, W. (2000). Social support from parents and friends and emotional problems in adolescence. *Journal of Youth and Adolescence, 29,* 319–335.
14. Rawlins, W. K. (1992). *Friendship matters: Communication, dialectics, and the life course.* New York: Aldine de Gruyter.
15. Cohen, S., Doyle, W. J., Turner, R., Alper, C. M., & Skoner, D. P. (2003). Sociability and susceptibility to the common cold. *Psychological Science, 14,* 389–395.
16. Ruberman, W., Weinblatt, E., Goldberg, J. D., & Chaudhary, B. S. (1984). Psychosocial influences on mortality after myocardial infarction. *New England Journal of Medicine, 311,* 552–559.
17. House, J. S., Landis, K. R., & Umberson, D. (1988). Social relationships and health. *Science, 241,* 540–545.
18. See, e.g., Schnurr, P. P., & Green, B. L. (Eds.). (2004). *Trauma and health: Physical health consequences of exposure to extreme stress.* Washington, D.C.: American Psychological Association.
19. Gallant, M. P. (2003). The influence of social support on chronic illness self-management: A review and directions for research. *Health Education & Behavior, 30,* 170–195.
20. Duck, S. W. (2012). Interpersonal attraction and personal relationships. In V. S. Ramachandran (Ed.), *Encyclopedia of human behavior* (2nd ed.). New York: Academic Press.
21. Adams, G. R., & Roopnarine, J. L. (1994). Physical attractiveness, social skills, and same-sex peer popularity. *Journal of Group Psychotherapy, Psychodrama and Sociometry, 47,* 15–35; Speed, A., & Gangestad, S. W. (1997). Romantic popularity and mate preferences: A peer-nomination study. *Personality and Social Psychology Bulletin, 23,* 928–936.
22. Mehrabian, A., & Blum, J. S. (2003). Physical appearance, attractiveness, and the mediating role of emotions. In N. J. Pallone (Ed.), *Love, romance, sexual interaction: Research perspectives from current psychology* (pp. 1–29). New Brunswick, NJ: Transaction.

23. Hume, D. K., & Montgomerie, R. (2001). Facial attractiveness signals different aspects of "quality" in women and men. *Evolution and Human Behavior, 22,* 93–112.
24. Festinger, L., Schachter, S., & Back, K. W. (1963). *Social pressures in informal groups: A study of human factors in housing.* Stanford, CA: Stanford University Press.
25. Selfhout, M., Burk, W., Branje, S., Denissen, J. Van Aken, M., & Meeus, W. (2010). Emerging late adolescent friendship networks and Big Five personality traits: A social network approach. *Journal of Personality, 78,* 509–538.
26. See Byrne, D. (1997). An overview (and underview) of research and theory within the attraction paradigm. *Journal of Social and Personal Relationships, 14,* 417–431.
27. For an extended discussion, see Guerrero, L. K., & Floyd, K. (2006). *Nonverbal communication in close relationships.* Mahwah, NJ: Lawrence Erlbaum Associates.
28. Dutilleux, J. P. (1994). *L'indien blanc: Vingt ans de sortilege amazonien* [The white Indian: Twenty years of the Amazonian curse]. Paris: R. Laffont.
29. Thesander, M. (1997). *The feminine ideal.* London: Reaktion.
30. Singh, D., Dixson, B. J., Jessop, T. S., Morgan, B., & Dixson, A. F. (2010). Cross-cultural consensus for waist-hip ratio and women's attractiveness. *Evolution and Human Behavior, 31,* 176–181.
31. Singh, D. (1995). Female judgment of male attractiveness and desirability for relationships: Role of waist-to-hip ratio and financial status. *Journal of Personality and Social Psychology, 69,* 1089–1101.
32. Workman, L., & Reader, W. (2004). *Evolutionary psychology: An introduction.* Cambridge, England: Cambridge University Press.
33. Berger, C. R., & Calabrese, R. J. (1975). Some explorations in initial interaction and beyond: Toward a developmental theory of interpersonal communication. *Human Communication Research, 1,* 99–112.
34. Brashers, D. E. (2007). A theory of communication and uncertainty management. In B. Whaley & W. Samter (Eds.), *Explaining communication theory* (pp. 201–218). Mahwah, NJ: Lawrence Erlbaum Associates.
35. Sunnafrank, M. (1986). Predicted outcome values: Just now and then? *Human Communication Research, 13,* 39–40.
36. Sunnafrank, M. (1990). Predicted outcome value and uncertainty reduction theories: A test of competing perspectives. *Human Communication Research, 17,* 76–103.
37. See Keaten, J. A., Kelly, L., Pribyl, C. B., & Sakamoto, M. (2009). Fear and competence in Japan and the U.S.: Fear of negative evaluation, affect for communication channels, channel competence and use of computer mediated communication. *Journal of Intercultural Communication Research, 38,* 23–39.
38. Derlega, V. J., Winstead, B. A., & Greene, K. (2008). Self-disclosure and starting a close relationship. In S. Sprecher, A. Wenzel, & J. Harvey (Eds.), *Handbook of relationship initiation* (pp. 153–174). New York: Psychology Press.
39. Gergen, K. J., Greenbert, M. S., & Willis, R. H. (1980). *Social exchange: Advances in theory and research.* New York: Plenum; Thibaut, J. W., & Kelley, H. H. (1959). *The social psychology of groups.* New York: Wiley.
40. See, e.g., Lloyd, S. A., Cate, R. M., & Henton, J. M. (1984). Predicting premarital relationship stability: A methodological refinement. *Journal of Marriage and the Family, 46,* 71–76.
41. Messick, R. M., & Cook, K. S. (Eds.). (1983). *Equity theory: Psychological and sociological perspectives.* New York: Praeger.
42. Stafford, L. (2011). Measuring relationship maintenance behaviors: Critique and development of the revised relationship maintenance behavior scale. *Journal of Social and Personal Relationships, 28,* 287–303.
43. Ledbetter, A. M. (2009). Family communication patterns and relational maintenance behavior: Direct and mediated associations with friendship closeness. *Human Communication Research, 35,* 130–147.
44. See Hecht, M. L., Shepard, T., & Hall, T. J. (1979). Multivariate indices of the effects of self-disclosure. *Western Journal of Speech Communication, 43,* 235–245.
45. Argyle, M., & Henderson, M. (1984). The rules of friendship. *Journal of Social and Personal Relationships, 1,* 211–237.
46. Milardo, R. M. (1986). Personal choice and social constraint in close relationships: Application of network analysis. In V. J. Derlega & B. A. Winstead (Eds.), *Friendship and social interaction* (pp. 145–166). New York: Springer-Verlag.
47. Coltrane, S. (1996). *Family man.* New York: Oxford University Press.
48. Floyd, K., & Morman, M. T. (1997). Affectionate communication in nonromantic relationships: Influences of communicator, relational, and contextual factors. *Western Journal of Communication, 61,* 279–298.
49. Altman, I., & Taylor, D. (1973). *Social penetration: The development of interpersonal relationships.* New York: Holt.
50. Gouldner, A. W. (1960). The norm of reciprocity: A preliminary statement. *American Sociological Review, 25,* 161–178.
51. Miller, L. C., & Kenny, D. A. (1986). Reciprocity of self-disclosure at the individual and dyadic levels: A social relations analysis. *Journal of Personality and Social Psychology, 50,* 713–719.

52. Derlega, V. J., Metts, S., Petronio, S., & Margulis, S. T. (1993). *Self-disclosure*. Newbury Park, CA: Sage.

53. See Wood, J. T. (2007). *Gendered lives: Communication, gender, and culture* (7th ed.). Belmont, CA: Wadsworth.

54. Dindia, K., & Allen, M. (1992). Sex differences in self-disclosure: A meta-analysis. *Psychological Bulletin, 112*, 106–124.

55. See, e.g., Triandis, H. C. (1989). The self and social behavior in differing cultural contexts. *Psychological Review, 96*, 506–520.

56. Dindia, K. (2000). Sex differences in self-disclosure, reciprocity of self-disclosure, and self-disclosure and liking: Three meta-analyses reviewed. In S. Petronio (Ed.), *Balancing the secrets of private disclosures* (pp. 21–35). Mahwah, NJ: Lawrence Erlbaum Associates.

57. Lippert, T., & Prager, K. J. (2001). Daily experiences of intimacy: A study of couples. *Personal Relationships, 8*, 283–298.

58. Dindia, K. (2002). Self-disclosure research: Knowledge through meta-analysis. In M. Allen & R. W. Preiss (Eds.), *Interpersonal communication research: Advances through meta-analysis* (pp. 169–185). Mahwah, NJ: Lawrence Erlbaum Associates.

59. Kelly, A. E., Klusas, J. A., von-Weiss, R. T., & Kenny, C. (2001). What is it about revealing secrets that is beneficial? *Personality and Social Psychology Bulletin, 27*, 651–665.

60. See Kacewicz, E., Slatcher, R. B., & Pennebaker, J. W. (2007). Expressive writing: An alternative to traditional methods. In L. L' Abate (Ed.), *Low-cost approaches to promote physical and mental health: Theory, research, and practice* (pp. 271–284). New York: Springer.

61. Helgeson, V. S., & Gottlieb, B. H. (2000). Support groups. In S. Cohen, L. G. Underwood, & B. H. Gottlieb (Eds.), *Social support measurement and intervention* (pp. 221–245). New York: Oxford University Press.

62. Wright, P. H. (1984). Self-referent motivation and the intrinsic quality of friendship. *Journal of Social and Personal Relationships, 1*, 115–130.

63. See Shimanoff, S. B. (1980). *Communication rules: Theory and research.* Beverly Hills, CA: Sage.

64. Argyle, M., & Henderson, M. (1984). The rules of friendship. *Journal of Social and Personal Relationships, 1*, 211–237.

65. Parks, M. R., & Floyd, K. (1996). Meanings for closeness and intimacy in friendship. *Journal of Social and Personal Relationships, 15*, 517–537.

66. Wood, J. T., & Inman, C. C. (1993). In a different mode: Masculine styles of communicating closeness. *Journal of Applied Communication Research, 21*, 279–295.

67. Floyd, K. (1995). Gender and closeness among friends and siblings. *Journal of Psychology, 129*, 193–202; see also Morman, M. T., & Floyd, K. (1998). "I love you, man": Overt expressions of affection in male-male interaction. *Sex Roles, 38*, 871–881.

68. Galupo, M. P. (2009). Cross-category friendship patterns: Comparison of heterosexual and sexual minority adults. *Journal of Social and Personal Relationships, 26*, 811–831.

69. Tillmann-Healy, L. M. (2001). *Between gay and straight: Understanding friendship across sexual orientation.* Walnut Creek, CA: AltaMira Press.

70. Price, J. (1999). *Navigating differences: Friendships between gay and straight men.* New York: Harrington Press.

71. O'Boyle, C. G., & Thomas, M. D. (1996). Friendships between lesbian and heterosexual women. In J. S. Weinstock & E. D. Rothblum (Eds.), *Lesbian friendships* (pp. 240–248). New York: New York University Press.

72. See, e.g., Galupo, M. P., & St. John, S. (2001). Benefits of cross-sexual orientation friendships among adolescent females. *Journal of Adolescence, 24*, 83–93.

73. Sapadin, L. A. (1988). Friendship and gender: Perspectives of professional men and women. *Journal of Social and Personal Relationships, 5*, 387–403.

74. Rawlins, W. K. (1992). *Friendship matters: Communication, dialectics, and the life course.* New York: Aldine de Gruyter.

75. Kaplan, D. L., & Keys, C. B. (1997). Sex and relationship variables as predictors of sexual attraction in cross-sex platonic friendships between young heterosexual adults. *Journal of Social and Personal Relationships, 14*, 191–206; Sapadin, 1988.

76. Egland, K. I., Spitzberg, B. G., & Zormeier, M. M. (1996). Flirtation and conversational competence in cross-sex platonic and romantic relationships. *Communication Reports, 9*, 105–118.

77. Fuiman, M., Yarab, P., & Sensibaugh, C. (1997, July). *Just friends? An examination of the sexual, physical, and romantic aspects of cross-gender friendships.* Paper presented at the biennial meeting of the International Network on Personal Relationships, Oxford, OH.

78. Afifi, W. A., & Faulkner, S. L. (2000). On being "just friends": The frequency and impact of sexual activity in cross-sex friendships. *Journal of Social and Personal Relationships, 17*, 205–222.

79. Werking, K. J. (1997). *We're just good friends: Women and men in nonromantic relationships.* New York: Guilford.

80. Hughes, M., Morrison, K., & Asada, K. J. K. (2005). What's love got to do with it? Exploring the impact of maintenance rules, love attitudes, and network support on friends with benefits relationships. *Western Journal of Communication, 69*, 49–66.

81. Messman, S. J., Canary, D. J., & Hause, K. S. (2000). Motives to remain platonic, equity, and the use of maintenance strategies in opposite-sex friendships. *Journal of Social and Personal Relationships, 17*, 67–94.

82. Rumens, N. (2008). The complexities of friendship: Exploring how gay men make sense of their workplace friendships with straight women. *Culture and Organization, 14*, 79–95.

83. Moon, D. (1995). Insult and inclusion: The term *fag hag* and gay male "community." *Social Forces, 74*, 487–510.

84. Rose, S. M. (1985). Same- and cross-sex friendships and the psychology of homosociality. *Sex Roles, 12*, 63–74.

85. Sias, P. M., Krone, K. J., & Jablin, F. M. (2002). An ecological systems perspective on workplace relationships. In M. L. Knapp & J. A. Daly (Eds.), *Handbook of interpersonal communication* (3rd ed., pp. 615–642). Thousand Oaks, CA: Sage.

86. Sias, P. M., & Cahill, D. J. (1998). From co-workers to friends: The development of peer friendships in the workplace. *Western Journal of Communication, 62*, 273–300.

87. Marks, S. R. (1994). Intimacy in the public realm: The case of co-workers. *Social Forces, 72*, 843–858.

88. Winstead, B. A., Derlega, V. J., Montgomery, M. J., & Pilkington, C. (1995). The quality of friendships at work and job satisfaction. *Journal of Social and Personal Relationships, 12*, 199–215.

89. Zorn, T. E. (1995). Bosses and buddies: Constructing and performing simultaneously hierarchical and close friendship relationships. In J. T. Wood & S. Duck (Eds.), *Under-studied relationships: Off the beaten track* (pp. 122–147). Thousand Oaks, CA: Sage.

90. Largent, R. N. (1987). *The relationship of friendship with a supervisor to job satisfaction and satisfaction with the supervisor.* Unpublished master's thesis, University of North Dakota, Grand Forks, ND.

91. See Fiedler, F. E. (1957). A note on leadership theory: The effect of social barriers between leaders and followers. *Sociometry, 20*, 87–94.

92. Zorn, 1995.

93. Adelman, M. B., Ahuvia, A., & Goodwin, C. (1994). Beyond smiling. In R. T. Rust & R. L. Oliver (Eds.), *Service quality: New directions in theory and practice* (pp. 139–171). Thousand Oaks, CA: Sage; Locke, K. (1996). A funny thing happened! The management of consumer emotions in service encounters. *Organizational Science, 7*, 40–59.

94. Gwinner, K. P., Gremler, D. D., & Bitner, M. J. (1998). Relational benefits in service industries: The customer's perspective. *Journal of the Academy of Marketing Science, 26*, 101–114.

95. American College of Physicians. *Ethics manual.* Retrieved February 9, 2008, from www.acponline.org/running_practice/ethics/.

Chapter 8

1. Guerrero, L. K., La Valley, A. G., & Farinelli, L. (2008). The experience and expression of anger, guilt, and sadness in marriage: An equity theory explanation. *Journal of Social and Personal Relationships, 25*, 699–724.

2. Baxter, L. A., & Braithwaite, D. O. (2009). Relational dialectics theory, applied. In S. W. Smith & S. R. Wilson (Eds.), *New directions in interpersonal communication research* (pp. 48–68). Thousand Oaks, CA: Sage.

3. Peterson, G. W., & Bush, K. R. (1999). Predicting adolescent autonomy from parents: Relationship connectedness and restrictiveness. *Sociological Inquiry, 69*, 431–457.

4. U.S. Census Bureau. (2012). Marriage and divorce. Downloaded May 29, 2012, from www.census.gov/hhes/socdemo/marriage/

5. Kaplan, R. M., & Kronick, R. G. (2006). Marital status and longevity in the United States population. *Journal of Epidemiology and Community Health, 60*, 760–765; Manzoli, M., Villarti, P., Pirone, G. M., & Boccia, A. (2007). Marital status and mortality in the elderly: A systematic review and meta-analysis. *Social Science & Medicine, 64*, 77–94.

6. Macintyre, S. (1992). The effects of family position and status on health. *Social Science & Medicine, 35*, 453–464.

7. Duncan, G., Wilkerson, B., & England, P. (2006). Cleaning up their act: The effects of marriage and cohabitation in licit and illicit drug use. *Demography, 43*, 691–710.

8. Bachman, J. G., Wadsworth, K. N., O'Malley, P. M., Johnston, L. D., & Schulenberg, J. E. (1997). *Smoking, drinking, and drug use in young adulthood: The impacts of new freedoms and new responsibilities.* Mahwah, NJ: Lawrence Erlbaum Associates.

9. Kim, H. K., & McKenry, P. (2002). The relationship between marriage and psychological well-being. *Journal of Family Issues, 23*, 885–911; Lamb, K. A., Lee, G. R., & DeMaris, A. (2003). Union formation and depression: Selection and relationship effects. *Journal of Marriage and Family, 65*, 953–962.

10. See Umberson, D., Crosnoe, R., & Reczek, C. (2010). Social relationships and health behavior across life course. *Annual Review of Sociology, 36*, 139–157.

11. Waldron, I., Hughes, M. E., & Brooks, T. L. (1996). Marriage protection and marriage selection—Prospective evidence for reciprocal effects of marital status and health. *Social Science & Medicine, 43*, 113–123.

12. Fierman, D. M., & Poulsen, S. S. (2011). Open relationships: A culturally and clinically sensitive approach. In J. Malpas & A. I. Lev (Eds.), *At the edge: Exploring gender and sexuality in couples and families* (pp. 16–24). Washington, D.C.: American Family Therapy Academy.

13. Anapol, D. (2010). *Polyamory in the 21st century: Love and intimacy with multiple partners.* Lanham, MD: Rowman & Littlefield.

14. Rust, P. C. (2003). Monogamy and polyamory: Relationship issues for bisexuals. In L. Garnets & D. Kimmel (Eds.), *Psychological perspectives on lesbian, gay, and bisexual experiences* (pp. 475–495). New York: Columbia University Press.

15. Bettinger, M. (2004). Polyamory and gay men: A family systems approach. *Journal of GLBT Family Studies, 1,* 97–116; Blasband, D., & Peplau, L. A. (1985). Sexual exclusivity versus openness in gay male couples. *Archives of Sexual Behavior, 14,* 395–412.

16. Munson, M., & Stelbourn, J. P. (Eds.). (1999). *The lesbian polyamory reader: Open relationships, non-monogamy, and casual sex.* Binghamton, NY: Haworth.

17. eBizMBA. (2012). Top 15 most popular dating websites, May 2012. Accessed May 29, 2012, from www.ebizmba.com/articles/dating-websites.

18. See Uebelacker, L. A., Courtnage, E. S., & Whisman, M. A. (2003). Correlates of depression and marital dissatisfaction: Perceptions of marital communication style. *Journal of Social and Personal Relationships, 20,* 757–769.

19. Previti, D., & Amato, P. R. (2003). Why stay married? Rewards, barriers, and marital stability. *Journal of Marriage and Family 65,* 561–573.

20. Dion, K. K., & Dion, K. L. (1996). Cultural perspectives on romantic love. *Personal Relationships, 3,* 5–17.

21. Amato, P. R., & Previti, D. (2003). People's reasons for divorcing. *Journal of Family Issues 24,* 602–626.

22. Smock, P. J., Manning, W. D., & Porter, M. (2005). "Everything's there except money": How money shapes decisions to marry among cohabitors. *Journal of Marriage and Family, 67,* 680–696.

23. Compton, J., & Pollak, R. A. (2007). Why are power couples increasingly concentrated in large metropolitan areas? *Journal of Labor Economics, 25,* 475–512.

24. Kurdek, L. A. (2004). Are gay and lesbian cohabiting couples *really* different from heterosexual married couples? *Journal of Marriage and Family, 66,* 880–900.

25. Kurdek, L. A. (1998). Relationship outcomes and their predictors: Longitudinal evidence from heterosexual married, gay cohabiting, and lesbian cohabiting couples. *Journal of Marriage and the Family, 60,* 553–568.

26. Kurdek, L. A. (1994). Conflict resolution styles in gay, lesbian, heterosexual nonparent, and heterosexual parent couples. *Journal of Marriage and the Family, 56,* 705–722.

27. Kurdek, L. A. (1994). Areas of conflict for gay, lesbian, and heterosexual couples: What couples argue about influences relationship satisfaction. *Journal of Marriage and the Family, 56,* 923–934.

28. Kurdek, L. A., & Schmitt, J. P. (1987). Perceived emotional support from family and friends in members of homosexual, married, and heterosexual cohabiting couples. *Journal of Homosexuality, 14,* 57–68.

29. Kurdek, L. A. (1993). The allocation of household labor in gay, lesbian, and heterosexual married couples. *Journal of Social Issues, 49,* 127–139.

30. Balsam, K. F., Beauchaine, T. P., Rothblum, E. D., & Solomon, S. E. (2008). Three-year follow-up of same-sex couples who had civil unions in Vermont, same-sex couples not in civil unions, and heterosexual married couples. *Developmental Psychology, 44,* 102–116; Roisman, G. I., Clausell, E., Holland, A., Fortuna, K., & Elieff, C. (2008). Adult romantic relationships as contexts of human development: A multi-method comparison of same-sex couples with opposite-sex dating, engaged, and married dyads. *Developmental Psychology, 44,* 91–101.

31. Fierman, D. M., & Poulsen, S. S. (2011). Open relationships: A culturally and clinically sensitive approach. In J. Malpas & A. I. Lev (Eds.), *At the edge: Exploring gender and sexuality in couples and families* (pp. 16–24). Washington, D.C.: American Family Therapy Academy.

32. Levine, R. B. (1993). Is love a luxury? *American Demographics, 15,* 27–28.

33. Hsu, F. L. K. (1981). The self in cross-cultural perspective. In A. J. Marsella, B. De Vos, & F. L. K. Hsu (Eds.), *Culture and self* (pp. 24–55). London: Tavistock; quote is from p. 50.

34. Knapp, M. L. (1978). *Social intercourse: From greeting to goodbye.* Boston: Allyn & Bacon; see also Knapp, M. L., & Vangelisti, A. L. (2000). *Interpersonal communication and human relationships* (4th ed.). Boston: Allyn & Bacon.

35. Peplau, L. A. (2003). Lesbian and gay relationships. In L. Garnets & D. Kimmel (Eds.), *Psychological perspectives on lesbian, gay, and bisexual experiences* (pp. 395–419). New York: Columbia University Press.

35. Sautter, J. M., Tippett, R. M., & Morgan, S. P. (2010). The social demography of Internet dating in the United States. *Social Science Quarterly, 91,* 554–575.

36. See, e.g., Donn, J. A., & Sherman, R. C. (2002). Attitudes and practices regarding the formation of romantic relationships on the Internet. *Cyber-Psychology & Behavior, 5,* 107–123; Parks, M. R., & Roberts, L. D. (1988).

"Making MOOsic": The development of personal relationships online and a comparison to their off-line counterparts. *Journal of Social and Personal Relationships, 15,* 517–537.

38. Sanders, J. V. (2012, March 13). The participation divide: Separate and unequal in digital media? *The Pew Internet & American Life Project.* Downloaded April 17, 2012, from http://pewinternet.org/Media-Mentions/2012/The-Participation-Divide.aspx.

39. Zickuhr, K., & Smith, A. (2012, April 13). Digital differences. *The Pew Internet & American Life Project.* Downloaded April 17, 2012, from http://pewinternet.org/Reports/2012/Digital-differences/Overview.aspx.

40. James, J. (2012). Which developing countries have done the most to close the digital divide? *Telematics and Informatics, 29,* 2–10.

41. Gibbs, J. L., Ellison, N. B., & Heino, R. D. (2006). Self-presentation in online personals: The role of anticipated future interaction, self-disclosure, and perceived success in Internet dating. *Communication Research, 33,* 1–26.

42. Toma, C., Hancock, J. T., & Ellison, N. (2008). Separating fact from fiction: An examination of deceptive self-presentation in online dating profiles. *Personality and Social Psychology Bulletin, 34,* 1023–1036.

43. Hancock, J. T., & Toma, C. L. (2009). Putting your best face forward: The accuracy of online dating photography. *Journal of Communication, 59,* 367–386.

44. Sautter et al., 2010.

45. Subscription Site Insider. (2011). *Dating and matchmaking site benchmark report.* Newport, RI: Anne Holland Ventures.

46. See Walther, J. B. (2010). Computer-mediated communication. In C. R. Berger, M. E. Roloff, & D. R. Roskos-Ewoldsen (Eds.), *Handbook of communication science* (2nd ed., pp. 489–505). Los Angeles: Sage.

47. Wilmot, W. W., & Hocker, J. L. (2001). *Interpersonal conflict.* New York: McGraw-Hill.

48. Gottman, J. M., & Levenson, R. W. (1992). Marital processes predictive of later dissolution: Behavior, physiology, and health. *Journal of Personality and Social Psychology, 63,* 221–233.

49. Gottman, J. M. (1994). *What predicts divorce?* Hillsdale, NJ: Lawrence Erlbaum Associates.

50. Holman, T. B., & Jarvis, M. O. (2003). Hostile, volatile, avoiding, and validating couple-conflict types: An investigation of Gottman's couple-conflict types. *Personal Relationships, 10,* 267–282.

51. Petronio, S. (2002). *Boundaries of privacy.* Albany: SUNY Press.

52. Derlega, V. J., Winstead, B. A., & Greene, K. (2008). Self-disclosure and starting a close relationship. In S. Sprecher, A. Wenzel, & J. Harvey (Eds.), *Handbook of relationship initiation* (pp. 153–174). New York: Psychology Press.

53. Cordova, J. V., Gee, C. B., & Warren, L. Z. (2005). Emotional skillfulness in marriage: Intimacy as a mediator of the relationship between emotional skillfulness and marital satisfaction. *Journal of Social and Clinical Psychology, 24,* 218–235.

54. Mirgain, S. A., & Cordova, J. V. (2007). Emotion skills and marital health: The association between observed and self-reported emotion skills, intimacy, and marital satisfaction. *Journal of Social and Clinical Psychology, 26,* 983–1009.

55. Gottman, J. M., & Levenson, R. W. (1986). Assessing the role of emotion in marriage. *Behavioral Assessment, 8,* 31–48.

56. Carstensen, L. L., Gottman, J. M., & Levenson, R. W. (1995). Emotional behavior in long-term marriage. *Psychology and Aging, 10,* 140–149.

57. Gottman, J. M. (1994). *What predicts divorce?* Hillsdale, NJ: Lawrence Erlbaum Associates.

58. Gottman & Levenson, 1986; Gottman, 1994.

59. See Alberts, J. K., Tracy, S. J., & Trethewey, A. (2011). An integrative theory of the division of domestic labor: Threshold level, social organizing and sensemaking. *Journal of Family Communication, 11,* 21–38.

60. Alberts, J. K., Yoshimura, C. G., Rabby, M., & Loschiavo, R. (2005). Mapping the topography of couples' daily conversation. *Journal of Social and Personal Relationships, 22,* 299–322.

61. Kluwer, E. S., Heesink, J. A. M., & Van de Vliert, E. (1996). Marital conflict about the division of household labor and paid work. *Journal of Marriage and the Family, 58,* 958–969.

62. Coltrane, S. (2000). Research on household labor: Modeling and measuring the social embeddedness of routine family work. *Journal of Marriage and the Family, 62,* 1208–1233; Coltrane, S., & Adams, M. (2001). Men's family work: Child-centered fathering and the sharing of domestic labor. In R. Hertz & N. L. Marshall (Eds.), *Working families: The transformation of the American home* (pp. 72–99). Berkeley and Los Angeles: University of California Press.

63. Minnotte, K. L., Minnotte, M. C., Pedersen, D. E., Mannon, S. E., & Kiger, G. (2010). His and her perspectives: Gender ideology, work-to-family conflict, and marital satisfaction. *Sex Roles, 63,* 425–438.

64. Minnotte et al., 2010.

65. Mannino, C. A., & Deutch, F. M. (2007). Changing the division of household labor: A negotiated process between partners. *Sex Roles, 56,* 309–324.

66. Johnson, E. M., & Huston, T. L. (1998). The perils of love, or why wives adapt to husbands during the transition to parenthood. *Journal of Marriage and the Family, 60,* 195–204; Kluwer, E. S., Heesink, J. A. M., & Van de Vliert, E. (2000). The division of labor in close relationships: An asymmetrical conflict issue. *Personal Relationships, 7,* 263–282.

67. Kluwer, E. S. (1998). Responses to gender inequality in the division of family work: The status quo effect. *Social Justice Research, 11,* 337–357.

68. Boren, J. P. (2007, November). *Negotiating the division of household labor in same-sex romantic partnerships.* Paper presented at the annual meeting of the National Communication Association, Chicago.

69. Knapp, M. L., & Vangelisti, A. L. (2008). *Interpersonal communication and human relationships* (6th ed.). Boston: Allyn & Bacon.

70. Duck, S. (1987). How to lose friends without influencing people. In M. E. Roloff & G. R. Miller (Eds.), *Interpersonal processes: New directions in communication research* (pp. 278–298). Beverly Hills, CA: Sage.

71. Kellerman, K., Reynolds, R., & Chen, J. B. (1991). Strategies of conversational retreat: When parting is not sweet sorrow. *Communication Monographs, 58,* 362–383.

72. Kreider, R. M., & Ellis, R. (2011). *Number, timing, and duration of marriages and divorces, 2009.* Washington, D.C.: U.S. Census Bureau.

73. Amato, P. R. (2000). The consequences of divorce for adults and children. *Journal of Marriage and the Family, 62,* 1269–1287.

74. Hetherington, E. M., & Stanley-Hagen, M. (1999). The adjustment of children with divorced parents: A risk and resiliency perspective. *Journal of Child Psychology and Psychiatry, 40,* 129–140.

75. Gross, D. (2010, November 4). Facebook knows when you'll break up. Retrieved February 29, 2012, from www.cnn.com/2010/TECH/social.media/11/02/facebook.breakups/index.html.

76. American Bar Association. (1996). *Guide to family law.* New York: Times Books.

77. General Accounting Office. (1997). Memo B-275860, from www.gao.gov/archiva/1997/og97016.pdf.

78. Satir, V. (1972). *Peoplemaking.* Palo Alto, CA: Science and Behavior Books.

79. Kreider, R. M., & Ellis, R. (2011). *Living arrangements of children: 2009.* Washington, D.C.: U.S. Census Bureau.

80. Satir, 1972.

81. Braithwaite, D. O., Baxter, L. A., & Harper, A. M. (1998). The role of rituals in the management of dialectical tensions of "old" and "new" in blended families. *Communication Studies, 49,* 105–120.

82. Braithwaite et al., 1998; quote is from page 113.

83. Stone, E. (1989). *Black sheep and kissing cousins: How our family stories shape us.* New York: Penguin.

84. Vangelisti, A. L., & Caughlin, J. P. (1997). Revealing family secrets: The influence of topic, function, and relationships. *Journal of Social and Personal Relationships, 14,* 679–705.

85. Aron, A., Norman, C. C., Aron, E. N., McKenna, C., & Heyman, R. E. (2000). Couples' shared participation in novel and arousing activities and experienced relationship quality. *Journal of Personality and Social Psychology, 78,* 273–284.

86. Ellis, K. (2002). Perceived parental confirmation: Development and validation of an instrument. *Southern Communication Journal, 67,* 319–334.

87. Gibb, J. R. (1961). Defensive communications. *Journal of Communication, 3,* 141–148.

88. Gottman, J. (2003). Why marriages fail. In K. M. Galvin & P. J. Cooper (Eds.), *Making connections: Readings in relational communication* (pp. 258–266). Los Angeles: Roxbury.

89. Gottman, J. M. (1994). *What predicts divorce?* Hillsdale, NJ: Lawrence Erlbaum Associates.

90. Gottman, 1994.

91. Kiecolt-Glaser, J. K., Glaser, R., Cacioppo, J. T., & Malarkey, W. B. (1998). Marital stress: Immunologic, neuroendocrine, and autonomic correlates. *Annals of the New York Academy of Sciences, 840,* 656–663.

92. Kiecolt-Glaser, J. K., Loving, T. J., Stowell, J. R., Malarkey, W. B., Lemeshow, S., Dickinson, S., & Glaser, R. (2005). Hostile marital interactions, proinflammatory cytokine production, and wound healing. *Archives of General Psychiatry, 62,* 1377–1384; Kiecolt-Glaser, J. K., Newton, T., Cacioppo, J. T., MacCallum, R. C., Glaser, R., & Malarkey, W. B. (1996). Marital conflict and endocrine function: Are men really more physiologically affected than women? *Journal of Consulting and Clinical Psychology, 64,* 324–332.

93. Baxter, L. A., & Braithwaite, D. O. (2009). Relational dialectics theory, applied. In S. W. Smith & S. R. Wilson (Eds.), *New directions in interpersonal communication research* (pp. 48–68). Thousand Oaks, CA: Sage.

Chapter 9

1. Relethford, J. (2003). *Reflections of our past: How human history is revealed in our genes.* New York: Basic.

2. www.habitat.org

3. Myers, S. A., & Anderson, C. M. (2008). *The fundamentals of small group communication.* Thousand Oaks, CA: Sage.

4. Beebe, S. A., & Masterson, J. T. (2009). *Communication in small groups: Principles and practices* (9th ed.). Boston: Allyn & Bacon.

5. Harris, T. E., & Sherblom, J. C. (2010). *Small group and team communication* (5th ed.). Boston: Allyn & Bacon.

6. Rothwell, J. D. (2009). *In mixed company: Small group communication* (7th ed.). Belmont, CA: Wadsworth.

7. Henman, L. D. (2003). Groups as systems. In R. Y. Hirokawa, R. S. Cathcart, L. A. Samovar, & L. D. Henman (Eds.), *Small group communication theory & practice: An anthology* (8th ed., pp. 3–7). Los Angeles: Roxbury.

8. Carron, A. V., & Brawley, L. R. (2000). Cohesion: Conceptual and measurement issues. *Small Group Research, 31,* 89–106.

9. See Rovio, E., Esokla, J., Kozub, S. A., Duda, J. L., & Lintunen, T. (2009). Can high group cohesion be harmful? A case study of a junior ice-hockey team. *Small Group Research, 40,* 421–435.

10. Kjormo, O., & Halvari, H. (2002). Two ways related to performance in elite sport: The path of self-confidence and competitive anxiety and the path of group cohesion and group goal-clarity. *Perceptual and Motor Skills, 94,* 950–966.

11. Craig, T. Y., & Kelly, J. R. (1999). Group cohesiveness and creative performance. *Group Dynamics: Theory, Research, and Practice, 3,* 243–256.

12. Fujishin, R. (2007). *Creating effective groups: The art of small group communication* (2nd ed.). Lanham, MD: Rowman & Littlefield.

13. Riddle, B. L., Anderson, C. M., & Martin, M. M. (2000). Small group socialization scale: Development and validity. *Small Group Research, 31,* 554–572.

14. Wittenbaum, G. M., Hollingshead, A. B., Paulus, P. B., Hirokawa, R. Y., Ancona, D. G., Peterson, R. S., Jehn, K. A., & Yoon, K. (2004). The functional perspective as a lens for understanding groups. *Small Group Research, 35,* 17–43.

15. Mayer, M. E. (1998). Behaviors leading to more effective decisions in small groups embedded in organizations. *Communication Reports, 11,* 123–132.

16. Southwell, D., & Twist, S. (2007). *Secret societies.* New York: Rosen; see also Bond, M. (2007). The dining Freemasons: Security protocols for secret societies. *Lecture Notes in Computer Science, 4631,* 266–275.

17. See, e.g., Newer, H. (1999). *From wrongs of passage: Fraternities, sororities, hazing, and binge drinking.* Bloomington: Indiana University Press.

18. Decker, S. H., & Van Winkle, B. (1996). *Life in the gang: Family, friends, and violence.* Cambridge, England: Cambridge University Press.

19. www.redhatsociety.com

20. Frey, L. R., & Sunwolf. (2005). The communication perspective on group life. In S. A. Whelan (Ed.), *The handbook of group research and practice* (pp. 158–186). Thousand Oaks, CA: Sage.

21. Harris, T. E., & Sherblom, J. C. (2010). *Small group and team communication* (5th ed.). Boston: Allyn & Bacon.

22. Staples, D. S., & Webster, J. (2007). Exploring traditional and virtual team members' "best practices." *Small Group Research, 38,* 60–97.

23. Schiller, S. Z., & Mandviwalla, M. (2007). Virtual team research: An analysis of theory use and a framework for theory appropriation. *Small Group Research, 38,* 12–59.

24. Johnson, S. K., Bettenhausen, K., & Gibbons, E. (2009). Realities of working in virtual teams: Affective and attitudinal outcomes of using computer-mediated communication. *Small Group Research, 40,* 623–649.

25. Hardin, A. M., Fuller, M. A., & Davison, R. M. (2007). I know I can, but can we? Culture and efficiency beliefs in global virtual teams. *Small Group Research, 38,* 130–155.

26. Majchrzak, A., Malhotra, A., Stamps, J., & Lipnack, J. (2004). Can absence make a team grow stronger? *Harvard Business Review,* May 2004, 1–8.

27. http://www.9-11commission.gov/

28. National Commission on Terrorist Attacks Upon the United States. (2004). *The 9/11 Commission report: Final report of the National Commission on Terrorist Attacks Upon the United States.* New York: Norton.

29. Grossman, M. (2000). *Encyclopedia of the United States cabinet.* Santa Barbara, CA: ABC-Clio.

30. Langford, J., & McDonagh, D. (Eds.). (2002). *Focus groups: Supporting effective product development.* London: Taylor & Francis.

31. www.riaa.com/goldandplatinumdata.php?resultpage=1&table=tblTopArt&action=

32. www.kiwanis.org

33. www.lionsclubs.org

34. Davison, K. P., Pennebaker, J. W., & Dickerson, S. S. (2000). Who talks? The social psychology of illness support groups. *American Psychologist, 55,* 205–217.

35. Goodwin, P. J., Leszcz, M., Ennis, M., Koopmans, J., Vincent, L., Guther, H., Drysdale, E., Hundleby, M., Chochinov, J. M., Navarro, M., Speca, M., Masterson, J., Dohan, L., Sela, R., Warren, B., Patterson, A., Pritchard, K. I., Arnold, A., Doll, R., O'Reilley, S. E., Quirt, G., Hood, N., & Hunter, J. (2001). The effect of group psychosocial support on survival in metastatic breast cancer. *New England Journal of Medicine, 345,* 1719–1726; see also Gilden, J. C., Hendryx, M. S., Clar, S., & Singh, S.

P. (1992). Diabetes support groups improve health care of older diabetic patients. *Journal of the American Geriatrics Society, 40,* 147–150.

36. Wright, K. B., & Bell, S. B. (2003). Health-related support groups on the Internet: Linking empirical findings to social support and computer-mediated communication theory. *Journal of Health Psychology, 8,* 39–54.

37. Based on the number of hits from a Google search conducted in May 2012 using the phrase "online support group."

38. McPherson, M., Smith-Lovin, L., & Cook, J. M. (2001). Birds of a feather: Homophily in social networks. *Annual Review of Sociology, 27,* 415–444.

39. Peris, R., Gimeno, M. A., Pinazo, D., Ortet, G., Carrero, V., Sanchiz, M., & Ibáñez, I. (2002). Online chat rooms: Virtual spaces of interaction for socially oriented people. *CyberPsychology & Behavior, 5,* 43–51.

40. For discussion, see Ellison, N. B., Steinfield, C., & Lampe, C. (2007). The benefits of Facebook "friends": Social capital and college students' use of online social network sites. *Journal of Computer-Mediated Communication, 12,* 1143–1168.

41. www.collegequizbowl.org

42. Gokhale, A. A. (1995). Collaborative learning enhances critical thinking. *Journal of Technology Education, 7,* 22–30.

43. See Young, C. B., & Henquinet, J. A. (2000). A conceptual framework for designing group projects. *Journal of Education for Business, 76,* 56–60.

44. Keyton, J., Harmon, N., & Frey, L. R. (1996, November). *Grouphate: Implications for teaching small group communication.* Paper presented at the annual meeting of the Speech Communication Association, San Diego.

45. Louis, M. R. (1980). Surprise and sense making: What newcomers experience in entering unfamiliar organizational settings. *Administrative Science Quarterly, 25,* 226–251.

46. Moreland, R. L. (1985). Social categorization and the assimilation of "new" group members. *Journal of Personality and Social Psychology, 48,* 1173–1190.

47. Sinclair-James, L., & Stohl, C. (1997). Group endings and new beginnings. In L. R. Frey & J. K. Barge (Eds.), *Managing group life: Communicating in decision-making groups* (pp. 308–334). Boston: Houghton Mifflin.

48. Keyton, J. (1993). Group termination: Completing the study of group development. *Small Group Research, 24,* 84–100.

49. Baker, D. F., & Campbell, C. M. (2004). When is there strength in numbers? A study of undergraduate task groups. *College Teaching, 53,* 14–18.

50. Sunwolf. (2002). Getting to "groupaha!": Provoking creating processes in task groups. In L. R. Frey (Ed.), *New directions in group communication* (pp. 203–217). Thousand Oaks, CA: Sage.

51. Williams, K., Harkins, S., & Latané, B. (1981). Identifiability as a deterrent to social loafing: Two cheering experiments. *Journal of Personality and Social Psychology, 40,* 303–311.

52. Hung, T.-K., Chi, N.-W., & Lu, W.-L. (2009). Exploring the relationships between perceived coworker loafing and counterproductive work behaviors: The mediating role of a revenge motive. *Journal of Business and Psychology, 24,* 257–270.

53. Høigaard, R., Säfvenbom, R., & Tønnessen, F. E. (2006). The relationship between group cohesion, group norms, and perceived social loafing in soccer teams. *Small Group Research, 37,* 217–232.

54. Wheelan, S. A., & McKeage, R. L. (1993). Developmental patterns in small and large groups. *Small Group Research, 24,* 60–83.

55. Engleberg, I. N., & Wynn, D. R. (2009). *Working in groups* (5th ed.). Boston: Allyn & Bacon.

56. Myers, S. A., & Anderson, C. M. (2008). *The fundamentals of small group communication.* Thousand Oaks, CA: Sage.

57. Hess, J. A. (1993). Assimilating newcomers into an organization: A cultural perspective. *Journal of Applied Communication Research, 21,* 189–210.

58. See Moreland, R. L., & Levine, J. M. (2002). Socialization and trust in work groups. *Group Processes & Intergroup Relations, 5,* 185–201.

59. Keyton, J. (2000). Introduction: The relational side of groups. *Small Group Research, 31,* 387–396.

60. Mullen, B., & Cooper, C. (1994). The relation between group cohesiveness and performance: An integration. *Psychological Bulletin, 115,* 210–227; Welch, B. A., Mossholder, K. W., Stell, R. P., & Bennett, N. (1998). Does work group cohesiveness affect individuals' performance and organizational commitment? *Small Group Research, 29,* 472–494.

Chapter 10

1. Fok, S. (2009, February 17). Group of downtown retailers brainstorm ideas to battle recession. *Hanford Sentinel.* Available online: http://www.hanfordsentinel.com/articles/2009/02/17/news/doc499b090a5e4eb299711745.prt.

2. Litchfield, R. C. (2008). Brainstorming reconsidered: A goal-based view. *The Academy of Management Review, 33,* 649–668.

3. Kohn, N. W., & Smith, S. M. (2011). Collaborative fixation: Effects of others' ideas on brainstorming. *Applied Cognitive Psychology, 25,* 359–371.

4. Putman, V. L., & Paulus, P. B. (2009). Brainstorming, brainstorming rules and decision making. *The Journal of Creative Behavior, 43,* 29–40.

5. Gautschi, T. F. (1990). How to improve group decisions. *Design News, 47*(17), 188.

6. MacPhail, A. (2001). Nominal group technique: A useful method for working with young people. *British Educational Research Journal, 27,* 161–170.

7. Peña, A., Estrada, C. A., Soniat, D., Taylor, B., & Burton, M. (2012). Nominal group technique: A brainstorming tool for identifying areas to improve pain management in hospitalized patients. *Journal of Hospital Medicine, 7,* 416–420.

8. Jefferson, W. K., Zunker, C., Feucht, J. C., Fitzpatrick, S. L., Greene, L. F., Shewchuk, R. M., et al. (2010). Use of the Nominal Group Technique (NGT) to understand the perceptions of the healthiness of foods associated with African Americans. *Evaluation and Program Planning, 33,* 343–348.

9. Watkins, P. J. (2005). Idea writing: Generating solutions for effective change. *Planning and Changing, 36,* 40–46.

10. Moore, C. M. (1987). *Group techniques for idea building.* Newbury Park, CA: Sage.

11. See Adler, R. B., & Elmhorst, J. M. (2008). *Communicating at work: Principles and practices for business and the professions* (9th ed.). New York: McGraw-Hill.

12. Eagly, A. H., & Karau, S. J. (2002). Role congruity theory of prejudice toward female leaders. *Psychological Review, 109,* 573–598.

13. Koch, S. C. (2005). Evaluative affect display toward male and female leaders of task-oriented groups. *Small Group Research, 36,* 678–703.

14. Eagly, A. H., Makhijani, M. G., & Klonsky, B. G. (1992). Gender and the evaluation of leaders: A meta-analysis. *Psychological Bulletin, 111,* 3–22.

15. Koch, S. C. (2005). Evaluative affect display toward male and female leaders II: Transmission among group members and leader reactions. *Journal of Articles in Support of the Null Hypothesis, 3,* 51–72.

16. Koch, 2005.

17. Cohen, A. (2009). *The tall book.* New York: Bloomsbury.

18. See Burgoon, J. K., & Dunbar, N. E. (2006). Nonverbal expressions of dominance and power in human relationships. In V. L. Manusov & M. L. Patterson (Eds.), *The Sage handbook of nonverbal communication* (pp. 279–297). Thousand Oaks, CA: Sage; see also Frieze, I. H., Olson, J. E., & Good, D. C. (1990). Perceived and actual discrimination in the salaries of male and female managers. *Journal of Applied Social Psychology, 20,* 46–67; Montepare, J. M. (1995). The impact of variations in height on young children's impressions of men and women. *Journal of Nonverbal Behavior, 19,* 31–47.

19. Judge, T. A., & Cable, D. M. (2004). The effect of physical height on workplace success and income: Preliminary test of a theoretical model. *Journal of Applied Psychology, 89,* 428–441.

20. See Kane, J. N., Anzovin, S., & Podell, J. (2001). *Facts about the presidents: A compilation of biographical and historical information.* Bronx, NY: Wilson.

21. Judge & Cable, 2004.

22. Sczesny, S., Spreeman, S., & Stahlberg, D. (2006). Masculine = competent? Physical appearance and sex as sources of gender-stereotypic attributions. *Swiss Journal of Psychology, 65,* 15–23.

23. Sczesny, S., & Kühnen, U. (2004). Meta-cognition about biological sex and gender stereotypic physical appearance: Consequences for the assessment of leadership competence. *Personality and Social Psychology Bulletin, 30,* 13–21.

24. Cherulnik, P. D., Turns, L. C., & Wilderman, S. K. (2006). Physical appearance and leadership: Exploring the role of appearance-based attribution in leader emergence. *Journal of Applied Social Psychology, 20,* 1530–1539.

25. Paglis, L. L., & Green, S. G. (2002). Leadership self-efficacy and managers' motivation for leading change. *Journal of Organizational Behavior, 23,* 215–235; see also House, R. J., & Aditya, R. N. (1997). The social scientific study of leadership: Quo vadis? *Journal of Management, 23,* 409–473.

26. Chemers, M. M., Watson, C. B., & May, S. T. (2000). Dispositional affect and leadership effectiveness: A comparison of self-esteem, optimism, and efficacy. *Personality and Social Psychology Bulletin, 26,* 267–277.

27. Özalp Türetgen, I., Unsal, P., & Erdem, I. (2008). The effects of sex, gender role, and personality traits on leader emergence: Does culture make a difference? *Small Group Research, 39,* 588–615; see also Ellis, R. J., Adamson, R. S., Deszca, G., & Cawsey, T. F. (1988). Self-monitoring and leadership emergence. *Small Group Research, 19,* 312–324; Miller, J. S., & Cardy, R. L. (2000). Self-monitoring and performance appraisal: Rating outcomes in project teams. *Journal of Organizational Behavior, 21,* 609–626.

28. Ellis, R. J. (1988). Self-monitoring and leadership emergence in groups. *Personality and Social Psychology Bulletin, 14,* 681–693.

29. Judge, T. A., Bono, J. E., Ilies, R., & Gerhardt, M. W. (2002). Personality and leadership: A qualitative and quantitative review. *Journal of Applied Psychology, 87,* 765–780.

30. Hawkins, K., & Stewart, R. A. (1991). Effects of communication apprehension on perceptions of leadership and intragroup attraction in small task-oriented groups. *Southern Communication Journal, 57*, 1–10.

31. O'Hair, D., & Wiemann, M. O. (2004). *The essential guide to group communication.* Boston: Bedford/St. Martin's.

32. Van Vugt, M., Jepson, S. F., Hart, C. M., & De Cremer, D. (2004). Autocratic leadership in social dilemmas: A threat to group stability. *Journal of Experimental Social Psychology, 40*, 1–13.

33. Hackman, M. Z., & Johnson, C. E. (2004). *Leadership: A communication perspective* (4th ed.). Long Grove, IL: Waveland.

34. Foels, R., Driskell, J. E., Mullen, B., & Salas, E. (2000). The effects of democratic leadership on group member satisfaction: An integration. *Small Group Research, 31*, 676–701.

35. Huffaker, D. (2010). Dimensions of leadership and social influence in online communities. *Human Communication Research, 36*, 593–617.

36. Dunbar, N. E., & Burgoon, J. K. (2005). Perceptions of power and interactional dominance in interpersonal relationships. *Journal of Social and Personal Relationships, 22*, 207–233.

37. French, J. P. R., & Raven, B. H. (1959). The bases of social power. In D. Cartwright & A. Zander (Eds.), *Group dynamics* (pp. 607–623). New York: Harper & Row; Raven, B. H. (1965). Social influences and power. In I. D. Steiner & M. Fishbein (Eds.), *Current studies in social psychology* (pp. 371–381). New York: Holt, Rinehart & Winston.

38. Alonzo, M. (2012). Paul Babeu's Mexican exlover says sheriff's attorney threatened him with deportation. *Phoenix New Times News*, Retrieved June 2, 2012, from www.phoenixnewtimes.com/2012-02-16/news/paul-babeu-s-mexican-ex-lover-says-sheriff-s-attorney-threatened-him-with-deportation/.

39. Baron, J. N., & Pfeffer, J. (1994). The social psychology of organizations and inequality. *Social Psychology Quarterly, 57*, 190–209.

40. Gaski, J. F. (1986). Intercorrelations among a channel entity's power sources: Impact of the exercise of reward and coercion on expert, referent, and legitimate power sources. *Journal of Marketing Research, 23*, 62–77.

41. Till, B. D., & Busler, M. (2000). The match-up hypothesis: Physical attractiveness, expertise, and the role of fit on brand attitude, purchase intent and brand beliefs. *Journal of Advertising, 29*, 1–13.

42. Andreoni, J., & Petrie, R. (2008). Beauty, gender and stereotypes: Evidence from laboratory experiments. *Journal of Economic Psychology, 29*, 73–93.

43. See Clegg, S. R. (1989). Radical revisions: Power, discipline, and organizations. *Organization Studies, 10*, 97–115.

44. Blake, R. R., & Mouton, J. S. (1984). *The managerial grid III* (3rd ed.). Houston: Gulf.

45. Messman, S. J., & Mikesell, R. L. (2000). Competition and interpersonal conflict in dating relationships. *Communication Reports, 13*, 21–34.

46. Olson, L. N., & Braithwaite, D. O. (2004). "If you hit me again, I'll hit you back": Conflict management strategies of individuals experiencing aggression during conflicts. *Communication Studies, 55*, 271–285.

47. Cahn, D. D. (1992). *Conflict in intimate relationships.* New York: Guilford.

48. Wilmot, W. W., & Hocker, J. L. (2007). *Interpersonal conflict* (7th ed.). New York: McGraw-Hill.

49. Oetzel, J. G., & Ting-Toomey, S. (2003). Face concerns in interpersonal conflict: A cross-cultural empirical test of the face negotiation theory. *Communication Research, 30*, 599–625.

50. Solomin, M. (2006). Groupthink versus The Wisdom of Crowds: The social epistemology of deliberation and dissent. *Southern Journal of Philosophy, 44*, 28–42.

51. Janis, I. L. (1972). *Victims of groupthink.* Boston: Houghton Mifflin.

52. See McCauley, C. (1998). Group dynamics in Janis's theory of groupthink: Backward and forward. *Organizational Behavior and Human Decision Processes, 73*, 142–162.

53. Schafer, M., & Crichlow, S. (1996). Antecedents of groupthink: A quantitative study. *Journal of Conflict Resolution, 40*, 415–435; Vaughan, D. (1996). *The Challenger launch decision: Risky technology, culture, and deviance at NASA.* Chicago: University of Chicago Press.

54. Courtright, J. A. (1978). A laboratory investigation of groupthink. *Communication Monographs, 45*, 229–246.

55. Ginnett, R. (2005, May/June). What can leaders do to avoid groupthink? *Leadership in Action, 25*(2), 14.

Chapter 11

1. www.politicususa.com/jon-stewart-fox-ratings/

2. www.marketingcharts.com/television/academy-awards-fewest-viewers-in-39-years-3612/

3. factfinder.census.gov

4. DeNavas-Walt, C., Proctor, B. D., & Smith, J. C. (2008). *U.S. Census Bureau current population reports, P60–235: Income, poverty, and health insurance coverage in the United States: 2007.* Washington, D.C.: U.S. Government Printing Office.

5. Lupia, A. (2002). Who can persuade whom? Implications from the nexus of psychology and rational choice theory. In J. H. Kuklinski (Ed.), *Thinking about political psychology* (pp. 51–88). New York: Cambridge University Press.

Chapter 12

1. www.sportsbusinessjournal.com/index.cfm?fuseaction=article.preview&articleid=61260

2. Comadena, M. E., Hunt, S. K., & Simonds, C. J. (2007). The effects of teacher clarity, nonverbal immediacy, and caring on student motivation, affective, and cognitive learning. *Communication Research Reports, 24*, 241–248.

3. Titsworth, B. S. (2004). Students' notetaking: The effects of teacher immediacy and clarity. *Communication Education, 53*, 305–320.

4. Houser, M. L. (2006). Expectancy violations of instructor communication as predictors of motivation and learning: A comparison of traditional and nontraditional students. *Communication Quarterly, 54*, 331–349; see also Chesebro, J. L. (2003). Effects of teacher clarity and nonverbal immediacy on student learning, receiver apprehension, and affect. *Communication Education, 52*, 135–147.

Chapter 13

1. Wolvin, A. D. (2010). Listening engagement: Intersecting theoretical perspectives. In A. D. Wolvin (Ed.), *Listening and human communication in the 21st Century* (pp. 7–30). Chichester, England: John Wiley & Sons.

2. See Hayes, D. P. (1988). Speaking and writing: Distinct patterns of word choice. *Journal of Memory and Language, 27*, 572–585.

3. Gallup, G. (Ed.). (2001). *The 2001 Gallup poll: Public opinion.* Lanham, MD: Rowman & Littlefield.

4. Blöte, A. W., Kint, M. J. W., Miers, A. C., & Westernberg, P. M. (2009). The relationship between public speaking anxiety and social anxiety: A review. *Journal of Anxiety Disorders, 23*, 305–313.

5. Payne, C. (2011, September 6). Adele talks stage fright. Retrieved April 23, 2012, from www.billboard.com/news/adele-talks-stage-fright-i-puke-quite-a-1005339512.story#/news/adele-talks-stage-fright-i-puke-quite-a-1005339512.story.

6. McCroskey, J. C. (2006). Oral communication apprehension: A summary of recent theory and research. *Human Communication Research, 1*, 70–96.

7. Ogden, J. S. (2010). *Public speaking anxiety, test anxiety, and academic achievement in undergraduate students.* Unpublished master's thesis, College of Education, Bucknell University. Retrievable from: http://digitalcommons.bucknell.edu/masters_theses/51.

8. Heimberg, R. G., Stein, M. B., Hiripi, E., & Kessler, R. C. (2000). Trends in the prevalence of social phobia in the United States: A synthetic cohort analysis of changes over four decades. *European Psychiatry, 15*, 29–37.

9. von Dawans, B., Fischbacher, U., Kirschbaum, C., Fehr, E., & Heinrichs, M. (2012). The social dimension of stress reactivity: Acute stress increases prosocial behavior in humans. *Psychological Science, 23*, 651–660.

10. Behnke, R. R., & Sawyer, C. R. (1998). Conceptualizing speech anxiety as a dynamic trait. *Southern Communication Journal, 63*, 160–168.

11. Behnke, R. R., & Sawyer, C. R. (1999). Milestones of anticipatory public speaking anxiety. *Communication Education, 48*, 165–172.

12. Witt, P. L., & Behnke, R. R. (2006). Anticipatory speech anxiety as a function of public speaking assignment type. *Communication Education, 55*, 167–177.

13. MacIntyre, P. D., & Thivierge, K. A. (1995). The effects of speaker personality on anticipated reactions to public speaking. *Communication Research Reports, 12*, 125–133.

14. Freeman, T., Sawyer, C. R., & Behnke, R. R. (1997). Behavioral inhibition and the attribution of public speaking state anxiety. *Communication Education, 46*, 175–187.

15. MacIntyre & Thivierge, 1995.

16. Mladenka, J. D., Sawyer, C. R., & Behnke, R. R. (1998). Anxiety sensitivity and speech trait anxiety as predictors of state anxiety during public speaking. *Communication Quarterly, 46*, 417–429.

17. Behnke, R. R., & Sawyer, C. R. (2000). Anticipatory anxiety patterns for male and female public speakers. *Communication Education, 49*, 187–195.

18. Hollander, E., Liebowitz, M. R., Cohen, B., & Gorman, J. M. (1989). Prolactin and sodium lactate-induced panic. *Psychiatry Research, 28*, 181–191.

19. Kunimatsu, M. M., & Marsee, M. A. (2012). Examining the presence of anxiety in aggressive individuals: The illuminating role of fight-or-flight mechanisms. *Child and Youth Care Forum, 41*, 247–258.

20. Floyd, K., Mikkelson, A. C., & Hesse, C. (2007). *The biology of human communication* (2nd ed.). Florence, KY: Thomson.

21. Roberts, J. B., Sawyer, C. R., & Behnke, R. R. (2004). A neurological representation of speech state anxiety: Mapping salivary cortisol levels of public speakers. *Western Journal of Communication, 68*, 219–231.

22. Arch, J. J., & Craske, M. G. (2006). Mechanisms of mindfulness: Emotion regulation following a focused breathing induction. *Behaviour Research and Therapy, 44*, 1849–1858.

23. Fredrikson, M., & Gunnarsson, R. (1992). Psychobiology of stage fright: The effect of public performance on neuroendocrine, cardiovascular, and subjective reactions. *Biological Psychology, 33*, 51–61.

24. Scott, S. (2007). College hats or lecture trousers? Stage fright and performance anxiety in university teachers. *Ethnography and Education, 2*, 191–207.

25. Witt, P. L., Brown, K. C., Roberts, J. B., Weisel, J., Sawyer, C. R., & Behnke, R. R. (2006). Somatic anxiety patterns before, during, and after giving a public speech. *Southern Communication Journal, 71*, 87–100; see also Roberts, Sawyer, & Behnke, 2004.

26. Finn, A. N., Sawyer, C. R., & Behnke, R. R. (2009). A model of anxious arousal for public speaking. *Communication Education, 58*, 417–432.

27. Bouma, E. M. C., Riese, H., Ormel, J., Verhulst, F. C., & Oldehinkel, A. J. (2009). Adolescents' cortisol responses to awakening and social stress: Effects of gender, menstrual phase and oral contraceptives. The TRIALS study. *Psychoneuroendocrinology, 34*, 884–893.

28. Traustadóttir, T., Bosch, P. R., & Matt, K. S. (2003). Gender differences in cardiovascular and hypothalamic-pituitary-adrenal axis responses to psychological stress in healthy older adult men and women. *Stress, 6*, 133–140.

29. Heponiemi, T., Keltikangas-Järvinen, K., Kettunen, J., Puttonen, S., & Ravaja, N. (2004). BIS-BAS sensitivity and cardiac autonomic stress profiles. *Psychophysiology, 41*, 37–45.

30. See Russell, J. J., Moskowitz, D. S., Zuroff, D. C., Bleau, P., Pinard, G., & Young, S. N. (2011). Anxiety, emotional security and the interpersonal behavior of individuals with social anxiety disorder. *Psychological Medicine, 41*, 545–554.

31. Clevinger, T., & King, T. R. (1961). A factor analysis of the visible symptoms of stage fright. *Speech Monographs, 28*, 296–298.

32. Bulleted list was adapted from Table 1 of Mulac, A., & Sherman, A. R. (1974). Behavioral assessment of speech anxiety. *Quarterly Journal of Speech, 60*, 134–143.

33. See Beatty, M. J., Heisel, A. D., Lewis, R. J., Pence, M. E., Reinhart, A., & Tian Y. (2011). Communication apprehension and resting alpha range asymmetry in the anterior cortex. *Communication Education, 60*, 441–460.

34. Moons, W. G., Eisenberger, N. I., & Taylor, S. E. (2010). Anger and fear responses to stress have different biological profiles. *Brain, Behavior, and Immunity, 24*, 215–219.

35. Porges, S. W. (2009). The polyvagal theory: New insights into adaptive reactions of the autonomic nervous system. *Cleveland Clinic Journal of Medicine, 76* Suppl 2, S86–S90.

36. Ayres, J., & Hopf, T. (1992). Visualization: Reducing speech anxiety and enhancing performance. *Communication Reports, 5*, 1–10.

37. Ayres, J., Hopf, T., & Ayres, D. M. (1994). An examination of whether imaging ability enhances the effectiveness of an intervention designed to reduce speech anxiety. *Communication Education, 43*, 252–258.

38. Hopf, T., & Ayres, J. (1992). Coping with public speaking anxiety: An examination of various combinations of systematic desensitization, skills training, and visualization. *Journal of Applied Communication Research, 20*, 183–198.

39. Jönsson, P., Wallergård, Österberg, K., Hansen, Å. M., Johansson, G., & Karlson, B. (2010). Cardiovascular and cortisol reactivity and habituation to a virtual reality version of the Trier Social Stress Test: A pilot study. *Psychoneuroendocrinology, 35*, 1397–1403.

40. Garland, E. L., Fredrickson, B., Kring, A. M., Johnson, D. P., Meyer, P. S., & Penn, D. L. (2010). Upward spirals of positive emotions counter downward spirals of negativity: Insights from the broaden-and-build theory and affective neuroscience on the treatment of emotion dysfunctions and deficits in psychopathology. *Clinical Psychology Review, 30*, 849–864.

41. Knapp, M. L. (2009). *Lying and deception in human interaction.* Boston: Pearson.

42. Mehu, M., Mortillaro, M., Bänziger, T., & Scherer, K. R. (2012). Reliable facial muscle activation enhances recognizability and credibility of emotional expression. *Emotion, 12*, 701–715.

43. Yokoyama, H., & Daibo, I. (2012). Effects of gaze and speech rate on receivers' evaluations of persuasive speech. *Psychological Reports, 110*, 663–676.

44. van Straaten, I., Holland, R. W., Finkenauer, C., Hollenstein, T., & Engels, R. C. M. E. (2010). Gazing behavior during mixed-sex interactions: Sex and attractiveness effects. *Archives of Sexual Behavior, 39*, 1055–1062.

45. Vincze, L. (2009). Gesture and gaze in persuasive political discourse. *Multimodal Signals: Cognitive and Algorithmic Issues, 5398*, 187–196.

46. Burgoon, J. K. (1991). Relational message interpretations of touch, conversational distance, and posture. *Journal of Nonverbal Behavior, 15*, 233–259.

47. Munhall, K. G., Jones, J. A., Callan, D. E., Kuratate, T., & Vatikiotis-Bateson, E. (2004). Visual prosody and speech intelligibility: Head movement improves auditory speech perception. *Psychological Science, 15*, 133–137

48. Pelachaud, C. (2009). Studies on gesture expressivity for a virtual agent. *Speech Communication, 51*, 630–639.

49. Elsbach, K. D. (2004). Managing images of trustworthiness in organizations. In K. M. Roderick & K. S. Cook (Eds.), *Trust and distrust in organizations* (pp. 275–292). New York: Russell Sage Foundation.

50. Wolvin, A. D. (Ed.). (2010). *Listening and human communication in the 21st Century.* Chichester, England: John Wiley & Sons.

51. See Jones, C., Berry, L., & Stevens, C. (2007). Synthesized speech intelligibility and persuasion: Speech rate and non-native listeners. *Computer Speech & Language, 21*, 641–651.

52. Simonds, B. K., Meyer, K. R., Quinlan, M. M., & Hunt, S. K. (2006). Effects of instructor speech rate on student affective learning, recall, and perceptions of nonverbal immediacy, credibility, and clarity. *Communication Research Reports, 23*, 187–197.

53. Rockwell, P., & Hubbard, A. E. (1999). The effect of attorneys' nonverbal communication on perceived credibility. *Journal of Credibility Assessment and Witness Psychology, 2*, 1–13.

54. Ray, G. B. (1986). Vocally cued personality prototypes: An implicit personality theory approach. *Communication Monographs, 53*, 266–276.

55. Miley, W. M., & Gonsalves, S. (2003). What you don't know can hurt you: Students' perceptions of professors' annoying teaching habits. *College Student Journal, 37*, 447–455.

56. Miller, G. R., & Hewgill, M. A. (1964). The effect of variations in nonfluency on audience ratings of source credibility. *Quarterly Journal of Speech, 50*, 36–44.

57. Kalinowski, J. S., & Saltuklaroglu, T. (2006). *Stuttering.* San Diego: Plural.

58. Reilly, S., Onslow, M., Packman, A., Wake, M., Bavin, E. L., Prior, M., et al. (2009). Predicting stuttering onset by the age of 3 years: A prospective, community cohort study. *Pediatrics, 123*, 270–277.

59. Guitar, B. (2005). *Stuttering: An integrated approach to its nature and treatment.* San Diego: Lippincott, Williams & Wilkins.

60. Kragh, S. U., & Bislev, S. (2005). Universities and student values across nations. *Journal of Intercultural Communication, 9.* Retrieved June 6, 2012, from www.immi.se/intercultural/nr9/kragh.htm.

61. Stewart, E. C., & Bennett, M. J. (1991). *American cultural patterns: A cross-cultural perspective.* Yarmouth, ME: Intercultural Press. Quote is from p. 155.

62. Alley, M. (2003). *The craft of scientific presentations: Critical steps to succeed and critical errors to avoid.* New York: Springer.

63. Kim, D., & Gilman, D. A. (2008). Effects of text, audio, and graphic aids in multimedia instruction for vocabulary learning. *Educational Technology & Society, 11*, 114–126.

64. Zayas-Baya, E. P. (1997). Instructional media in the total language picture. *International Journal of Instructional Media, 5*, 145–150.

Chapter 14

1. Tolani, A. T., & Yen, S. (2009, March). *Many websites fail to dispel myths about IUDs, emergency contraception, birth control, and proper timing of pap smears.* Paper presented at the annual meeting of the Society for Adolescent Medicine, Los Angeles.

2. www.teachforamerica.org

3. Allen, R. R., & McKerrow, R. E. (1985). *The pragmatics of public communication* (3rd ed.). Dubuque, IA: Kendall/Hunt.

4. Garner, R. (1992). Learning from school texts. *Educational Psychologist, 27*, 53–63; see also Miller, R. B., & McCown, R. R. (1986). Effects of text coherence and elaboration on recall of sentences within paragraphs. *Contemporary Educational Psychology, 11*, 127–138.

5. Fransden, K. D., & Clement, D. A. (1984). The functions of human communication in informing: Communicating and processing information. In C. C. Arnold & J. W. Bowers (Eds.), *Handbook of rhetorical and communication theory* (pp. 338–399). Boston: Allyn & Bacon.

6. Pascarella, E., Edison, M., Nora, A., Hagedorn, L. S., & Braxton, J. (1996). Effects of teacher organization/preparation and teacher skill/clarity on general cognitive skills in college. *Journal of College Student Development, 37*, 7–19.

7. Thompson, F., & Grundgenett, D. (1999). Helping disadvantaged learners build effective learning skills. *Education, 120*, 130–135.

8. See Cacioppo, J. T., & Petty, R. E. (1979). Effects of message repetition and position on cognitive response, recall, and persuasion. *Journal of Personality and Social Psychology, 37*, 97–109.

9. Garner, R. L. (2006). Humor in pedagogy: How ha-ha can lead to aha! *College Teaching, 54*, 177–180.

Chapter 15

1. Perloff, R. M. (2010). *The dynamics of persuasion: Communication and attitudes in the 21st Century* (4th ed.). New York: Taylor & Francis.

2. Homer, P. M. (2006). Relationships among ad-induced affect, beliefs, and attitudes: Another look. *Journal of Advertising, 35*, 35–51.

3. Priester, J. R., & Petty, R. E. (1995). Source attributions and persuasion: Perceived honesty as a determinant of message scrutiny. *Personality and Social Psychology Bulletin, 21*, 637–654.

4. Hannah, S. T., & Avolio, B. J. (2011). Leader character, ethos, and virtue: Individual and collective considerations. *The Leadership Quarterly, 22,* 989–994.

5. Stewart, R. A. (1994). Perceptions of a speaker's initial credibility as a function of religious involvement and religious disclosiveness. *Communication Research Reports, 11,* 169–176.

6. See Koob, G. F., & Volkow, N. D. (2010). Neurocircuitry of addiction. *Neuropsychopharmacology, 35,* 217–238.

7. See, e.g., Rothman, A. J., Salovey, P., Turvey, C., & Fishkin, S. A. (1993). Attributions of responsibility and persuasion: Increasing mammography utilization among women over 40 with an internally oriented message. *Health Psychology, 12,* 39–47.

8. Crick, N. (2004). Conquering our imagination: Thought experiments and enthymemes in scientific argument. *Philosophy and Rhetoric, 37,* 21–41.

9. Rydell, R. J., Sherman, S. J., Boucher, K. L., & Macy, J. T. (2012). The role of motivational and persuasive message factors in changing implicit attitudes toward smoking. *Basic and Applied Social Psychology, 34,* 1–7.

10. Prestwich, A., Perugini, M., & Hurling, R. (2010). Can implementation intentions and text messages promote brisk walking? A randomized trial. *Health Psychology, 29,* 40–49.

11. DiSanza, J. R., & Legge, N. J. (2002). *Business and professional communication: Plans, processes, and problems* (2nd ed.). Boston: Allyn & Bacon.

12. Lau, R. L., Sigelman, L., Heldman, C., & Babbit, P. (1999). The effects of negative political advertisements: A meta-analytic assessment. *American Political Science Review, 93,* 851–875.

13. Burgoon, J. K., Guerrero, L. K., & Floyd, K. (2010). *Nonverbal communication.* Boston: Allyn & Bacon.

14. Kouzes, J. M., & Pozner, B. Z. (2011). *Credibility: How leaders gain and lose it, why people demand it.* New York: John Wiley & Sons.

15. Burgoon, J. K., & Hale, J. L. (1988). Nonverbal expectancy violations: Model elaboration and application to immediacy behaviors. *Communication Monographs, 55,* 58–79.

16. http://pressroom.toyota.com/pr/tms/default.aspx

Chapter 16

1. Conrad, C., & Poole, M. (2004). *Strategic organizational communication: Into the twenty-first century* (7th ed.). Fort Worth, TX: Harcourt Brace.

2. Trice, H., & Beyer, J. (1984). Studying organizational cultures through rites and ceremonials. *Academy of Management Review, 9,* 653–669.

3. Mokros, H. (2006). Composing relationships at work. In J. T. Wood & S. W. Duck (Eds.), *Composing relationships: Communication in everyday life* (pp. 175–185). Belmont, CA: Thomson Wadsworth.

4. Islam, G., & Zyphur, M. J. (2009). Rituals in organizations: A review and expansion of current theory. *Group & Organization Management, 34,* 114–139.

5. Mumby, D. K. (2006). Constructing working-class masculinity in the workplace. In J. T. Wood & S. W. Duck (Eds.), *Composing relationships: Communication in everyday life* (pp. 89–95). Belmont, CA: Thomson Wadsworth.

6. www.hhs.gov/ocr/privacy/

7. www.ed.gov/policy/gen/guid/fpco/ferpa/index.html

8. Montana, J. C. (2004). E-mail, voice mail, and instant messaging: A legal perspective. *Information Management Journal, 38,* 37–41.

9. Snyder, J. L., & Cornetto, K. M. (2009). Employee perceptions of e-mail monitoring from a boundary management perspective. *Communication Studies, 60,* 476–492.

10. Holmes, J., & Marra, M. (2002). Having a laugh at work: How humour contributes to workplace culture. *Journal of Pragmatics, 34,* 1683–1710.

11. Morreall, J. (2008). Applications of humor: Health, the workplace, and education. In V. Raskin (Ed.), *The primer of humor research* (pp. 449–478). New York: Mouton de Gruyter.

12. Lang, J. C., & Lee, C. H. (2010). Workplace humor and organizational creativity. *The International Journal of Human Resource Management, 21,* 46–60.

13. Mesmer-Magnus, J., Glew, D. J., & Viswesvaran, C. (2012). A meta-analysis of positive humor in the workplace. *Journal of Managerial Psychology, 27,* 155–190.

14. Fisher, W. R. (1984). Narration as human communication paradigm: The case of public moral argument. *Communication Monographs, 51,* 1–22.

15. Pacanowsky, M., & O'Donnell-Trujillo, N. (1983). Organizational communication as cultural performance. *Communication Monographs, 30,* 126–147.

16. Conrad, C., & Poole, M. (2004). *Strategic organizational communication: Into the twenty-first century* (7th ed.). Fort Worth, TX: Harcourt Brace.

17. Schultz, H. (1997). *Pour your heart into it: How Starbucks built a company one cup at a time.* New York: Hyperion.

18. Cockburn-Wootten, C., & Zorn, T. (2006). Cabbages and headache cures: Work stories within the family. In J. T. Wood & S. W. Duck (Eds.), *Composing relationships: Communication in everyday life* (pp. 137–145). Belmont, CA: Thomson Wadsworth.

19. See Axley, S. (1984). Managerial and organizational communication in terms of the conduit metaphor. *Academy of Management Review, 9,* 428–437.

20. Eisenberg, E. M., Goodall, H. L., & Trethewey, A. (2009). *Organizational communication: Balancing creativity and constraint* (6th ed.). Boston: Bedford/St. Martin's. Quote is from page 29.

21. Wenberg, J., & Wilmot, W. (1973). *The personal communication process.* New York: John Wiley & Sons.

22. Axley, 1984.

23. Tracy, K., & Eisenberg, E. (1991). Giving criticism: A multiple goals case study. *Research on Language and Social Interaction, 24,* 37–70.

24. Donnellon, A., Gray, B., & Bougon, M. (1986). Communication, meaning, and organized action. *Administrative Science Quarterly, 31,* 43–55.

25. Weick, K. (1995). *Sensemaking in organizations.* Newbury Park, CA: Sage.

26. Eisenberg, E. (1986). Ambiguity as strategy in organizational communication. *Communication Monographs, 51,* 227–242.

27. Giddens, A. (1984). *The constitution of society: Outline of the theory of structuration.* Berkeley and Los Angeles: University of California Press.

28. Eisenberg, Goodall, & Trethewey, 2009.

29. Gould, E. W. (2009). "I heard it on the grapevine"—Blogging, Facebook, YouTube, and student self-organization during a faculty strike. *Lecture Notes in Computer Science, 5621,* 336–345.

30. Smith, B. (1996). Care and feeding of the office grapevine. *Management Review, 85,* 6.

31. Michaelson, G., Iterson, A. V., & Waddington, K. (2010). Gossip in organizations: Contexts, consequences, and controversies. *Group & Organization Management, 35,* 371–390; Hellweg, S. A. (1992). Organizational grapevines. In K. L. Hutchinson (Ed.), *Readings in organizational communication* (pp. 159–172). Dubuque, IA: William C. Brown.

32. Pew Internet & American Life Project. (2009). *Networked workers.* Retrieved December 24, 2009, from www.pewinternet.org/. Reports/2008/Networked-Workers.aspx?r=1.

33. Radicati, S. (2011). *Email statistics report, 2011–2015.* Palo Alto, CA: The Radicati Group.

34. Harford, T. (2007, February 3). If telecommuting is so easy, why do we travel for work more than ever? *Slate.* Retrieved December 24, 2009, from www.slate.com/id/2158571; see also Holland, K. (2006, December 3). Under new management: When work time isn't face time. *The New York Times.* Retrieved December 24, 2009, from www.nytimes.com/2006/12/03/business/yourmoney/03mgmt.html?ex=1322802000&en=84c055647a8e11f9&ei=5088&partner=rssnyt&emc=rss&pagewanted=print.

35. Forrester Research, Inc. (2012). U.S. online retail forecast, 2011 to 2016. Retrieved June 4, 2012, from www.forrester.com/US+Online+Retail+Forecast+2011+To+2016/fulltext/-/E-RES60672?docid=60672/.

36. Belanger, F., Hiller, J. S., & Smith, W. J. (2002). Trustworthiness in electronic commerce: The role of privacy, security, and site attributes. *The Journal of Strategic Information Systems, 11,* 245–270.

37. Ferguson, A. J. (2005). Fostering e-mail security awareness: The West Point Carronade. *Educause Quarterly, 28,* 54–57.

38. See Orrange, R. (2002). Aspiring law and business professionals' orientations to work and family life. *Journal of Family Issues, 23,* 287–317.

39. Voydanoff, P. (1988). Work role characteristics, family structure demands and work/family conflict. *Journal of Marriage and the Family, 50,* 749–761.

40. See Tracy, S. J. (2005). Locking up emotion: Moving beyond dissonance for understanding emotion labor discomfort. *Communication Monographs, 72,* 261–283.

41. Höge, T. (2009). When work strain transcends psychological boundaries: An inquiry into the relationship between time pressure, irritation, work-family conflict and psychosomatic complaints. *Stress & Health, 25,* 41–51.

42. Geiger-Brown, J., Trinkoff, A., & Rogers, V. E. (2011). The impact of work schedules, home, and work demands on self-reported sleep in registered nurses. *Journal of Occupational & Environmental Medicine, 53,* 303–307.

43. Rantanen, M., Mauno, S., Kinnunen, U., & Rantanen, J. (2011). Do individual coping strategies help or harm in the work-family conflict situation? Examining coping as a moderator between work-family conflict and well-being. *International Journal of Stress Management, 18,* 24–48.

44. Hostetler, A. J., Desrochers, S., Kopko, K., & Moen, P. (2012). Marital and family satisfaction as a function of work-family demands and community resources: Individual- and couple-level analyses. *Journal of Family Issues, 33,* 316–340.

45. Michel, J. S., Mitchelson, J. K., Pichler, S., & Cullen, K. L. (2010). Clarifying relationships among work and family social support, stressors, and work-family conflict. *Journal of Vocational Behavior, 76,* 91–104.

46. Eby, L. T., Maher, C. P., & Butts, M. M. (2010). The intersection of work and family life: The role of affect. *Annual Review of Psychology, 61,* 599–622.

47. Petitta, L., & Vecchione, M. (2011). Job burnout, absenteeism, and extra role behaviors. *Journal of Workplace Behavioral Health, 26,* 97–121.

48. Neuman, J. H. (2004). Injustice, stress, and aggression in organizations. In R. W. Griffin & A. M. O'Leary-Kelly (Eds.), *The dark side of organizational behavior* (pp. 62–102). San Francisco: Jossey-Bass.

49. Dessy, E. (2009). Effective communication in difficult situations: Preventing stress and burnout in the NICU. *Early Human Development, 85,* S39–S41.

50. Schweitzer, T. (2007). Seven out of 10 employees admit to abusing office computers, phones. *Inc.* Retrieved December 24, 2009, from www.inc.com/news/articles/200701/workers.html.

51. Earley, P., & Gibson, C. (2002). *Multinational work teams.* Mahwah, NJ: Lawrence Erlbaum Associates; Padavic, I., & Reskin, B. (2002). *Women and men at work.* Thousand Oaks, CA: Sage.

52. Farr, J. (Ed.). (2003). Stereotype threat effects in employment settings. [Special issue.] *Human Performance, 16.*

53. Friedman, D. E., & Greenhaus, J. H. (2000). *Work and family—Allies or enemies? What happens when business professionals confront life choices?* New York: Oxford University Press.

54. Friedman, S., & Lobel, S. (2003). The happy workaholic: A role model for employees. *Academy of Management Executive, 17,* 87–98.

55. Friedman & Greenhaus, 2000.

56. Rotondo, D. M., Carlson, D. S., & Kincaid, J. F. (2003). Coping with multiple dimensions of work-family conflict. *Personnel Review, 32,* 275–296.

57. Kirby, E. L., & Krone, K. J. (2003). For the community. Suggestions for practitioners based on E. L. Kirby & K. J. Krone (2002) approved by the National Communication Association Legislative Council to pilot an online journal.

58. Albrecht, T. L., Irey, K. V., & Mundy, A. K. (1982). Integration in a communication network as a mediator of stress. *Social Work, 27,* 229–234.

59. Ray, E. B., & Miller, K. I. (1991). The influence of communication structure and social support on job stress and burnout. *Management Communication Quarterly, 4,* 506–527.

60. Barsade, S. G. (2002). The ripple effect: Emotional contagion and its influence on group behavior. *Administrative Science Quarterly, 47,* 644–65.

61. Frost, P. J. (2004). Handling toxic emotions: New challenges for leaders and their organizations. *Organizational Dynamics, 33,* 111–127.

Chapter 17

1. Vivian, J. (2011). *The media of mass communication* (10th ed.). Boston: Allyn & Bacon.

2. Whitfield, R., Farrer, A., Vainker, S. J., & Rawson, J. (1990). *The caves of the thousand Buddhas: Chinese art from the silk route.* New York: George Braziller.

3. Eisenstein, E. L. (2005). *The printing revolution in early modern Europe* (2nd rev. ed.). Cambridge: Cambridge University Press.

4. American Society of Magazine Editors. (2012). Number of magazines by category 1999-now. Retrieved June 12, 2012, from www.magazine.org/ASME/EDITORIAL_TRENDS/1145.aspx.

5. Engadget.com. (2011, October 4). Apple: 16 billion iTunes songs downloaded, 300 million iPods sold. Retrieved June 4, 2012, from www.engadget.com/2011/10/04/apple-16-billion-itunes-songs-downloaded-300-million-ipods-sol/.

6. SiriusXM. Corporate overview. Retrieved February 28, 2011, from www.siriusxm.com/corporate.

7. Federal Communications Commission. FCC V-chip fact sheet. Retrieved February 28, 2011, from www.fcc.gov/Bureaus/Mass_Media/Factsheets/factvchip.html.

8. Vivian, 2011.

9. National Cable and Telecommunications Association. (2010). NCTA industry data. Retrieved February 28, 2011, from www.ncta.com/Statistics.aspx.

10. de Moraes, L. (2012, February 6). Super Bowl XLVI: Biggest TV audience ever. *The Washington Post.* Retrieved June 4, 2012, from www.washingtonpost.com/blogs/tv-column/post/super-bowl-xlvi-no-tv-ratings-record/2012/02/06/gIQAVAD6tQ_blog.html.

11. Kerr, D. (2012, March 19). Teens prefer texting over phone calls, e-mail. Retrieved June 4, 2012, from http://news.cnet.com/8301-1023_3-57400439-93/teens-prefer-texting-over-phone-calls-e-mail/.

12. The Nation. (2012, April 25). Hits 900m users, values $77b. Retrieved June 4, 2012, from www.nation.com.pk/pakistan-news-newspaper-daily-english-online/entertainment/25-Apr-2012/hits-900m-users-values-77b.

13. Billboard Magazine. (2011, February 24). Eminem overtakes Lady Gaga as most 'liked' living artist on Facebook. Source: www.billboard.biz/bbbiz/industry/digital-and-mobile/eminem-overtakeslady-gaga-as-most-liked-1005047232.story.

14. Weber, H. (2012, March 21). With 140 million active users & 340 million tweets per day, Twitter is officially mainstream. Retrieved June 4, 2012, from http://thenextweb.com/socialmedia/2012/03/21/twitter-has-over-140-million-active-users-sending-over-340-million-tweets-a-day/.

15. Nielsen Company. (2009). Television audience 2009.Retrieved June 12, 2012, from http://blog.nielsen.com/nielsenwire/media_entertainment/more-than-half-the-homes-in-us-have-three-or-more-tvs/.

16. Nielsen Company. (2008). Average U.S. home now receives a record 118.6 TV channels. Retrieved June 12, 2012, from www.nielsen.com/us/en/insights/press-room/2008/average_u_s__home.html.

17. Nielsen Company. (2011). Who watches what (and how much)? U.S. TV trends by ethnicity. Retrieved June 12, 2012, from http://blog.nielsen.com/nielsenwire/consumer/who-watches-what-and-how-much-u-s-tv-trends-by-ethnicity/.

18. Anderson, J. (2010). *Understanding the changing needs of the U.S. online consumer, 2010.* Cambridge, MA: Forrester Research.

19. RadioInsights. (2010, April 7). How much do people listen? Really? Retrieved June 12, 2012, from www.radioinsights.com/2010/04/how-much-do-people-listen.html.

20. Bureau of Labor Statistics. (2011, June 22). American Time Use Survey. Retrieved June 12, 2012, from www.bls.gov/news.release/atus.nr0.htm.

21. Cooper, J. (2007). *Cognitive dissonance: 50 years of a classic theory.* London: Sage.

22. For an excellent review, see Stroud, N. J. (2011). *Niche news: The politics of news choice.* New York: Oxford University Press.

23. Knobloch-Westerwick, S., & Meng, J. (2009). Selective exposure to attitude-consistent and counterattitudinal political information. *Communication Research, 36,* 426–448.

24. McQuail, D. (2010). *McQuail's mass communication theory* (6th ed.). London: Sage.

25. According to the Pew Research Center, stories about the economy accounted for 14 percent of all news stories in 2010, more than any other topic.

26. Several public opinion polls showed the economy to be the top issue for voters in the 2010 midterm elections, including the Gallup Poll described here: www.gallup.com/poll/127247/voters-rate-economytop-issue-2010.aspx.

27. McCombs, M. (2005). The agenda-setting function of the press. In G. Overholser & K. H. Jamieson (Eds.), *The press* (pp. 156–168). Oxford: Oxford University Press.

28. Lowry, D. T., Nio, T. C. J., & Leitner, D. W. (2003). Setting the public fear agenda: A longitudinal analysis of network TV crime reporting, public perceptions of crime and FBI crime statistics. *Journal of Communication, 53,* 61–73.

29. Spillius, A. (2010, June 7). BP oil spill: Mississippi governor says press coverage is more damaging than slick. *The Telegraph,* retrieved March 5, 2011, from www.telegraph.co.uk/finance/newsbysector/energy/oiland-gas/7807579/BP-oil-spill-Mississippi-governor-sayspress-coverage-is-more-damaging-than-slick.html.

30. Gerbner, G., Gross, L., Morgan, M., Signorielli, N., & Shanahan, J. (2002). Growing up with television: Cultivationprocesses. In J. Bryant & D. Zillman (Eds.), *Media effects: Advances in theory and research* (2nd ed., pp. 43–68). Mahwah, NJ: Lawrence Erlbaum Associates.

31. See Bryant, J., & Zillman, D. (Eds.). (2008). *Media effects: Advances in theory and research* (3rd ed.). New York: Taylor & Francis.

32. Ellis, B. (2012, January 12). Class of 2011 scores higher-paying jobs. *CNN Money.* Retrieved June 4, 2012, from http://money.cnn.com/2012/01/12/pf/college/salaries/index.htm.

33. Romer, D., Jamieson, K. H., & Aday, S. (2003). Television news and the cultivation of fear of crime. *Journal of Communication, 53,* 88–104.

34. Center for Communication and Social Policy, University of California, Santa Barbara. (1998). *National Television Violence Study Executive Summary, Vol. 3.* Santa Barbara: Author.

35. Federal Bureau of Investigation. (2010). *Preliminary semiannual uniform crime report, January–June, 2010.* Washington, D.C.: Author.

36. Evans, D. S. (2008). The economics of the online advertising industry. *Review of Network Economics, 7,* 359–391.

37. Kantar Media. (2010, September 13). Kantar Media reports U.S. advertising expenditures increased 5.7% in the first half of 2010. Retrieved March 7, 2011, from http://kantarmediana.com/intelligence/press/kantar-media-reports-us-advertising-expenditures-increased-57-firsthalf-2010.

38. Baumer, K. (2011, March 2). The asking price for Super Bowl XLVI ads is $3.5 million. *Business Insider.* Retrieved March 7, 2011, from www.businessinsider.com/ad-price-super-bowl-xlvi-2011-3#ixzz1FUYVMyk1. 1967 figure is adjusted for inflation; figure is $40,000 in 1967 dollars.

39. Google Annual Report, 2010. Retrieved June 4, 2012, from investor.google.com/pdf/2010_google_annual_report.pdf.

40. Saladino, M. P. (2008). The proliferation of product placement as a means of advertising communication. *Journal of International Business Ethics, 1,* 100–106.

41. Serjeant, J. (2011, February 22). Apple deemed top of movie product placement charts. Los Angeles: Reuters. Retrieved March 11, 2011, from www.reuters.com/article/2011/02/22/us-productplacement-idUSTRE71L69920110222.

42. See Nord, D. P. (2006). *Communities of journalism: A history of American newspapers and their readers*. Champaign: University of Illinois Press.

43. Ryfe, D. M. (1999). Franklin Roosevelt and the fireside chats. *Journal of Communication, 49*, 80–103.

44. Fettman, E., & Lomazow, S. (2010). *FDR's deadly secret*. New York: PublicAffairs.

45. See Rorabaugh, W. J. (2009). *The real making of the president: Kennedy, Nixon, and the 1960 election*. Lawrence: University Press of Kansas; Donaldson, G. A. (2007). *The first modern campaign: Kennedy, Nixon, and the election of 1960*. Lanham, MD: Rowman & Littlefield.

46. Grossman, M., Lipsitz, K., Sides, J., & Trost, C. (2005). What voters want from political campaign communication. *Political Communication, 22*, 337–354.

47. Lau, R. R., & Rovner, I. B. (2009). Negative campaigning. *Annual Journal of Political Science, 42*, 573–595.

48. Bipartisan Campaign Reform Act of 2002, 2 U.S.C. § 441b

49. *Citizens United v. Federal Election Commission*, 130 S. Ct. 876 (2010).

50. Gerbner, G., & Signorielli, N. (1990). *Violence profile, 1967 through 1988–1989: Enduring patterns*. Manuscript, University of Pennsylvania, Annenberg School of Communication.

51. Haugen, D. M., & Musser, S. (Eds.). (2008). *Media violence (opposing viewpoints)*. Farmington Hills, MI: Greenhaven Press.

52. See Tilley, D. S., & Brackely, M. (2005). Men who batter intimate partners: A grounded theory study of the development of male violence in intimate partner relationships. *Issues in Mental Health Nursing, 26*, 281–297.

53. Bartholow, B. D., Bushman, B. J., & Sestir, M. A. (2006). Chronic violent video game exposure and desensitization to violence: Behavioral and event-related brain potential data. *Journal of Experimental Social Psychology, 42*, 532–539.

54. Carnagey, N. L., Anderson, C. A., & Bushman, B. J. (2007). The effect of video game violence on physiological desensitization to real life violence. *Journal of Experimental Social Psychology, 43*, 489–496.

55. Funk, J. B., Baldacci, H. B., Pasold, T., & Baumgardner, J. (2004). Violence exposure in real-life, video games, television, movies, and the Internet: Is there desensitization? *Journal of Adolescence, 27*, 23–39.

56. Anderson, C. A., & Bushman, B. J. (2001). Effects of violent video games on aggressive behavior, aggressive cognition, aggressive affect, physiological arousal, and prosocial behavior: A meta-analytic review of the scientific literature. *Psychological Science, 12*, 353–359; Paik, H., & Comstock, G. (1994). The effects of television violence on antisocial behavior: A meta-analysis. *Communication Research, 21*, 516–546.

57. Cooper, C. A. (2007). *Violence in the media and its influence on criminal defense*. Jefferson, NC: McFarland & Company.

58. Starcevic, V., & Porter, G. (2010). Virtual violence: The games people play. In E. Aboujaoude & L. M. Koran (Eds.), *Impulse control disorders* (pp. 182–188). Cambridge: Cambridge University Press.

59. See, e.g., Huesmann, L. R., & Taylor, L. D. (2006). The role of media violence in violent behavior. *Annual Review of Public Health, 27*, 393–415; Phillips, D. P., & Hensley, J. E. (1984). When violence is rewarded or punished: The impact of mass media stories on homicide. *Journal of Communication, 34*, 101–116; Eron, L. D., Huesmann, L. R., Lefkowitz, M. M., & Walder, L. O. (1972). Does television violence cause aggression? *American Psychologist, 27*, 253–263.

60. Nathanson, A. (2004). Factual and evaluative approaches to modifying children's responses to violent television. *Journal of Communication, 54*, 321–336.

61. www.fcc.gov

62. 47 U.S.C. § 315(a).

63. Telecommunications Act of 1996, Pub. LA. No. 104–104, 110 Stat. 56 (1996).

64. 47 U.S.C. § 315 (1970); 47 C.F.R. § 76.209(d) (1975).

65. Carroll, W. K., & Hackett, R. A. (2006). Democratic media activism through the lens of social movement theory. *Media, Culture & Society, 28*, 83–104.

66. Dixon, T. L., & Linz, D. (2000). Overrepresentation and underrepresentation of African Americans and Latinos as lawbreakers on television news. *Journal of Communication, 50*, 131–154.

67. Tuchman, G. (2000). The symbolic annihilation of women by the mass media. In L. Crothers & C. Lockhart (Eds.), *Culture and politics: A reader* (pp. 150–174). New York: St. Martin's Press.

68. Gross, L. (2001). Out of the mainstream: Sexual minorities and the mass media. In M. G. Durham & D. M. Kellner (Eds.), *Media and cultural studies: Key works* (pp. 405–423). Malden, MA: Blackwell Publishers.

69. The Motion Picture Production Code of 1930 (Hays Code). Retrieved March 17, 2011, from www.artsreformation.com/a001/hays-code.html.

Chapter 18

1. Hollon, M. F. (2005). Direct-to-consumer advertising: A haphazard approach to health promotion. *Journal of the American Medical Association, 293*, 2030–2033.

2. Berger, C. R., & Calabrese, R. J. (1975). Some explorations in initial interaction and beyond: Toward a developmental theory of interpersonal communication. *Human Communication Research, 1*, 99–112.

3. Mengel, M. B., Holleman, W. L., & Fields, S. A. (Eds.). (2002). *Fundamentals of clinical practice* (2nd ed.). New York: Plenum.

4. See Glas, A. S., Lijmer, J. G., Prins, M. H., Bonsel, G. J., & Bossuyt, P. M. M. (2003). The diagnostic odds ratio: A single indicator of test performance. *Journal of Clinical Epidemiology, 56*, 1129–1135.

5. Babrow, A. S. (2001). Uncertainty, value, communication, and problematic integration. *Journal of Communication, 51*, 553–573.

6. Rahman, A., & Isenberg, D. A. (2008). Systemic lupus erythematosus. *New England Journal of Medicine, 358*, 929–939.

7. *Upjohn Co. v. United States*, 449 U.S. 383, 389 (1981).

8. Federally Authorized Tax Practitioner Privilege of 1998 (P.L. 105–206).

9. *Wolfe v. United States*, 291 U.S. 7 (1934).

10. *People v. Phillips* (1 Southwest L. J., 90 [1813]).

11. Health Insurance Portability and Accountability Act (HIPAA) of 1996 (P.L. 104–191).

12. Smith, M. B., Christensen, N., Strohecker, J., Anderson, J. L., Horne, B. D., Day, J. D., Weiss, J. P., Crandall, B. G., Osborn, J. S., Muhlstein, J. B., Lappe, D. L., Moss, H., Oliver, J., Viau, K., & Bunch, T. J. (2010). Poor understanding and compliance among AF patients on warfarin who use herbal and dietary supplements. *Circulation, 111*, A16326.

13. Jung, B., & Reidenberg, M. M. (2007). Physicians being deceived. *Pain Medication, 8*, 433–437.

14. McDermott, B., & Feldman, M. (2007). Malingering in the medical setting. *Psychiatric Clinics of North America 30*, 645–662.

15. Rudolph, J. (2008, March 7). Bonding with patients when time is scarce: Even the busiest physician can find time to convey caring and concern. *Medical Economics, 85*(5), 50–51.

16. Probst, J. C., Greenhouse, D. L., & Selassie, A. W. (1997). Patient and physician satisfaction with an outpatient care visit. *Journal of Family Practice, 45*, 418–426.

17. See Wiedenmayer, K., Summers, R. S., Mackle, C. A., Gous, A. G. S., Everard, M., & Tromp, D. (2006). *Developing pharmacy practice: A focus on patient care*. Geneva: World Health Organization and International Pharmaceutical Federation.

18. Mangione, S., Kane, G. C., Caruso, J. W., Gonnella, J. S., Nasca, T. J., & Hojat, M. (2002). Assessment of empathy in different years of internal medicine training. *Medical Teacher, 24*, 370–373.

19. Hojat, M., Mangione, S., Nasca, T. J., Rattner, S., Erdmann, J. B., Gonnella, J. S., & Magee, M. (2004). An empirical study of decline in empathy in medical school. *Medical Education, 38*, 934–941.

20. Bonvicini, K. A., Perlin, M. J., Bylund, C. L., Carroll, G., Rouse, R. A., & Goldstein, M. G. (2009). Impact of communication training on physician expression of empathy in patient encounters. *Patient Education and Counseling, 75*, 3–10.

21. Silvester, J., Patterson, F., Koczwara, A., & Ferguson, E. (2007). "Trust me . . .": Psychological and behavioral predictors of perceived physician empathy. *Journal of Applied Psychology, 92*, 519–527.

22. Bylund, C. L., & Makoul, G. (2002). Empathic communication and gender in the physician–patient encounter. *Patient Education and Counseling, 48*, 207–216.

23. Exposure to stress: Occupational hazards in hospitals. (2008, July). Atlanta: Centers for Disease Control and Prevention (CDC). Retrieved April 29, 2011, from www.cdc.gov/niosh/docs/2008-136/default.html.

24. Ornish, D., Scherwitz, L. W., Billings, J. H., Gould, K. L., Merritt, T. A., Sparler, S., Armstrong, W. T., Ports, T. A., Kirkeeide, R. L., Hogeboom, C., & Brand, R. J. (1998). Intensive lifestyle changes for reversal of coronary heart disease. *Journal of the American Medical Association, 280*, 2001.

25. Halbesleben, J. R., & Rathert, C. (2008). Linking physician burnout and patient outcomes: Exploring the dyadic relationship between physicians and patients. *Health Care Management Review, 33*, 29–39.

26. Bullman, W. (1996). The National Council on Patient Information and Education: Focusing on communication, compliance, FDA Medguide proposal in 1996. *Formulary, 31*, 389–396.

27. See, e.g., Wright, K. B., Sparks, L., & O'Hair, H. D. (2008). *Health communication in the 21st century*. Malden, MA: Blackwell Publishing.

28. Wanzer, M. B., Booth-Butterfield, M., & Gruber, K. (2004). Perceptions of health care providers' communication: Relationships between patient-centered communication and satisfaction. *Health Communication, 16*, 363–384.

29. Larsen, K. M., & Smith, K. C. (1981). Assessment of nonverbal communication in the patient–physician interview. *Journal of Family Practice, 12*, 481–488.

30. Burgoon, J. K., Pfau, M., Parrott, R., Birk, T., Coker, R., & Burgoon, M. (1987). Relational communication, satisfaction, compliance–gaining strategies, and compliance in communication between physicians and patients. *Communication Monographs, 54*, 307–324.

31. Klingle, R. S. (1993). Bringing time into physician compliance gaining research: Toward a reinforcement expectancy theory of strategy effectiveness. *Health Communication, 5*, 283–308.

32. Klingle, R. S. (1996). Physician communication as a motivational tool for long-term patient compliance: Reinforcement expectancy theory. *Communication Studies, 47*, 206–217.

33. Klingle, R. S., & Burgoon, M. (1995). Patient compliance and satisfaction with physician influence attempts: A reinforcement expectancy approach to compliance-gaining over time. *Communication Research, 22*, 148–187.

34. Liaison Committee on Medical Education. (1998). *Functions and structure of a medical school.* Washington, D.C.: Author; Batalden, P., Leach, D., Swing, S., Dreyfus, H., & Dreyfus, S. (2002). General competencies and accreditation in graduate medical education. *Health Affairs, 21*, 103–111.

35. Makoul, G., & Curry, R. H. (2007). The value of assessing and addressing communication skills. *Journal of the American Medical Association, 298*, 1057–1059.

36. Street, R. L., & Millay, B. (2001). Analyzing patient participation in medical encounters. *Health Communication, 13*, 61–73.

37. Pahal, J. S. (2006). The dynamics of resident–patient communication: Data from Canada. *Communication & Medicine, 3*, 161–170.

38. Dyche, L., & Swiderski, D. (2005). The effect of physician solicitation approaches on ability to identify patient concerns. *Journal of General Internal Medicine, 20*, 267–270.

39. Walker, K. L., Arnold, C. L., Miller-Day, M., & Webb, L. M. (2002). Investigating the physician–patient relationship: Examining emerging themes. *Health Communication, 14*, 45–68.

40. See Smith, R. C., & Hoppe, R. B. (1991). The patient's story: Integrating the patient- and physician-centered approaches to interviewing. *Annals of Internal Medicine, 115*, 470–477.

41. Geller, G., Bernhardt, B. A., Carrese, J., Rushton, C. H., & Kolodner, K. (2008). What do clinicians derive from partnering with their patients? Reliable and valid measure of "personal meaning in patient care." *Patient Education and Counseling, 72*, 293–300.

42. Schmid Mast, M., Hall, J. A., & Roter, D. (2008). Caring and dominance affect participants' perceptions and behaviors during a virtual medical visit. *Journal of General Internal Medicine, 23*, 523–527.

43. Balint, J., & Shelton, W. (1996). Regaining the initiative: Forging a new model of the patient–physician relationship. *Journal of the American Medical Association, 275*, 887–892.

44. Laine, C., & Davidoff, F. (1996). Patient-centered medicine: A professional evolution. *Journal of the American Medical Association, 275*, 152–155.

45. Rimal, R. N., Ratzan, S. C., Arnston, P., & Freimuth, V. S. (1997). Reconceptualizing the "patient": Health care promotion as increasing citizens' decision-making competencies. *Health Communication, 9*, 61–74.

46. Poirier, M. A., Clark, M. M., Cerhan, J. H., Pruthi, S., Geda, Y. E., & Dale, L. C. (2004). Teaching motivational interviewing to first-year medical students to improve counseling skills in health behavior change. *Mayo Clinic Proceedings, 79*, 327–331.

47. van Zanten, M., Boulet, J. R., & McKinley, D. (2007). Using standardized patients to assess the interpersonal skills of physicians: Six years' experience with a high-stakes certification examination. *Health Communication, 22*, 195–205.

48. Stewart, M., Brown, J. B., Donner, A., McWhinney, I. R., Oates, J., Weston, W. W., & Jordan, J. (2000). The impact of patient-centered care on outcomes. *The Journal of Family Practice, 49*, 796–804.

49. Mallinger, J. B., Griggs, J. J., & Shields, C. G. (2005). Patient centered care and breast cancer survivors' satisfaction with information. *Patient Education and Counseling, 57*, 342–349.

50. Zandbelt, L., Smets, E. M. A., Oort, F. J., Godfried, M. H., & de Haes, H. C. J. M. (2007). Medical specialists' patient-centered communication and patient-reported outcomes. *Medical Care, 45*, 330–339.

51. Kulich, K. R., Berggren, U., & Hallberg, L. R. M. (2003). A qualitative analysis of patient-centered dentistry in consultations with dental phobic patients. *Journal of Health Communication, 8*, 171–187.

52. Roter, D. L., Stewart, M., Putnam, S. M., Lipkin, M., Stiles, W., & Inui, T. S. (1997). Communication patterns of primary care physicians. *Journal of the American Medical Association, 277*, 350–356.

53. Levinson, W., Roter, D. B., Mullooly, J. B., Dull, V. T., & Frankel, R. M. (1997). The relationship with malpractice claims among primary care physicians and surgeons. *Journal of the American Medical Association, 277*, 553–559.

54. Linzer, M., Konrad, T. R., Douglas, J., McMurray, J. E., Pathman, D. E., Williams, E. S., Schwartz, M. D., Gerrity, M., Scheckler, W., Bigby, J. A., & Rhodes, E. (2000). Managed care, time pressure, and physician job satisfaction: Results from the Physician Worklife Study. *Journal of General Internal Medicine, 15*, 441–450.

55. American Telemedicine Association: www.americantelemed.org.

56. Reece, S. (2008, April 18). Pick up the mouse, put down the phone: Trading e-mails with patients is easier than playing phone tag, and you may even get paid for it. *Medical Economics, 85*, 24–28.

57. Wright, K. B. (2008). New technologies and health communication. In K. B. Wright & S. D. Moore (Eds.), *Applied health communication* (pp. 63–84). Cresskill, NJ: Hampton Press.

58. Whitten, P., Sypher, B. D., & Patterson, J. D. (2000). Transcending the technology of telemedicine: An analysis of telemedicine in North Carolina. *Health Communication, 12*, 109–135.

59. Roter, D. L., Larson, S., Sands, D. Z., Ford, D. E., & Houston, T. (2008). Can e-mail messages between patients and physicians be patient-centered? *Health Communication, 23*, 80–86.

60. Baur, C. (2000). Limiting factors in the transformative powers of e-mail in patient-physician relationships: A critical analysis. *Health Communication, 12*, 239–259.

61. D'Arcy, J., Reynolds, J. R., Stiles, W. B., & Grohol, J. M. (2006). An investigation of session impact and alliance in Internet-based psychotherapy: Preliminary results. *Counselling & Psychotherapy Research, 6*, 164–168.

62. www.onlinetherapyinstitute.com

63. Andersson, G., Strömgren, T., Ström, L., & Lyttkens, L. (2002). Randomized controlled trial of Internet-based cognitive behavior therapy for distress associated with tinnitus. *Psychosomatic Medicine, 64*, 810–816.

64. www.ismho.org

65. First FW Red Cross volunteer leaves to help tornado victims. (2011, April 28). Retrieved May 2, 2011, from www.indianasnewscenter.com/news/local/First-FW-Red-Cross-Volunteer-Leaves-To-Help-Tornado-Victims-120896989.html.

66. Volunteers pour into South after tornadoes. (2011, April 30). Retrieved April 30, 2011, from www.reuters.com/article/2011/04/30/us-usa-weather-volunteers-idUSTRE73T1ZR20110430.

67. Jones, N. (2010). Stressors of school: Take time to relax. *The Voice.* Retrieved April 29, 2011, from www.buvoice.com/stressors-ofschool-1.1675102.

68. Pryor, J. H., Hurtado, S., DeAngelo, L., Palucki Blake, L., & Tran, S. (2011). *The American freshman: National norms for fall 2010.* Los Angeles: Higher Education Research Institute, University of California, Los Angeles.

69. Cohen, S., Janicki-Deverts, D., & Miller, G. E. (2007). Psychological stress and disease. *Journal of the American Medical Association, 298*, 1685–1687.

70. Jansen, A. S., Nguyen, A. V., Karpitsky, V., Mettenleiter, T. C., & Loewy, A. D. (1995). Central command neurons of the sympathetic nervous system: Basis of the fight-or-flight response. *Science, 270*, 644–646.

71. Floyd, K., Mikkelson, A. C., & Hesse, C. (2007). *The biology of human communication* (2nd ed.). Florence, KY: Thomson Learning.

72. Lovallo, W. R. (2004). *Stress & health: Biological and psychological interactions* (2nd ed.). Thousand Oaks, CA: Sage.

73. Contrada, R. J., & Baum, A. (Eds.). (2010). *The handbook of stress science: Biology, psychology, and health.* New York: Springer.

74. Potempa, K. (1984). An overview of the role of cardiovascular reactivity to stressful challenges in the etiology of hypertension. *Journal of Cardiovascular Nursing, 8*, 27–38.

75. Hotz, S. B. (1995). Stress and cardiovascular disease risk behaviors: Implications for health behavioral change. *Canadian Journal of Cardiology, 11*, 8A–11A.

76. Roy, M. P., Kirschbaum, C., & Steptoe, A. (2001). Psychological, cardiovascular, and metabolic correlates of individual differences in cortisol stress recovery in young men. *Psychoneuroendocrinology, 26*, 375–391.

77. Maes, M., Bosmans, E., Suy, E., Minner, B., & Raus, J. (1991). A further exploration of the relationships between immune parameters and the HPA axis activity in depressed inpatients. *Psychological Medicine, 21*, 313–320.

78. Yehuda, R., Boisoneau, D., Mason, J. W., & Giller, E. L. (1993). Glucocorticoid receptor number and cortisol excretion in mood, anxiety, and psychotic disorders. *Biological Psychiatry, 34*, 18–25.

79. Kiecolt-Glaser, J. K., Glaser, R., Shuttleworth, E. C., Dyer, C. S., Ogrocki, P., & Speicher, C. E. (1987). Chronic stress and immunity in family caregivers of Alzheimer's disease victims. *Psychosomatic Medicine, 49*, 523–535.

80. Torres, S. J., & Nowson, C. A. (2007). Relationship between stress, eating behavior, and obesity. *Nutrition, 23*, 887–894.

81. Hall, M., Thayer, J. F., Germain, A., Moul, D., Vasko, R., Puhl, M., Miewald, J., & Buysse, D. J. (2007). Psychological sleep is associated with heightened physiological arousal during NREM sleep in primary insomnia. *Behavioral Sleep Medicine, 5*(3), 178–193.

82. Cohen, S., Tyrell, D. A., & Smith, A. P. (1993). Negative life events, perceived stress, negative affect, and susceptibility to the common cold. *Journal of Personality and Social Psychology, 64*, 131–140.

83. Clover, R. D., Abell, T., Becker, L. A., Crawford, S., & Ramsey, C. N. (1989). Family functioning and stress as predictors of influenza B infection. *Journal of Family Practice, 28,* 535–539.

84. Folkman, S. (Ed.). (2010). *The Oxford handbook of stress, health, and coping.* New York: Oxford University Press.

85. Burleson, B. R., & MacGeorge, E. L. (2002). Supportive communication. In M. L. Knapp & J. A. Daly (Eds.), *Handbook of interpersonal communication* (3rd ed., pp. 374–422). Thousand Oaks, CA: Sage.

86. Goldsmith, D. J. (2004). *Communicating social support.* Cambridge: Cambridge University Press.

87. Barrera, M. (2000). Social support research in community psychology. In J. Rappaport & E. Seidman (Eds.), *Handbook of community psychology* (pp. 215–245). New York: Kluwer Academic/Plenum Publishers.

88. Windle, M. (1992). A longitudinal study of stress buffering for adolescent problem behaviors. *Developmental Psychology, 28,* 522–530.

89. Cohen, S., Sherrod, D. R., & Clark, M. S. (1986). Social skills and the stress-protective role of social support. *Journal of Personality and Social Psychology, 50,* 963–973.

90. Thorsteinsson, E. B., & James, J. E. (1999). A meta-analysis of the effects of experimental manipulations of social support during laboratory stress. *Psychology and Health, 14,* 869–886.

91. Floyd, K., Mikkelson, A. C., Tafoya, M. A., Farinelli, L., La Valley, A. G., Judd, J., Davis, K. L., Haynes, M. T., & Wilson, J. (2007). Human affection exchange: XIV. Relational affection predicts resting heart rate and free cortisol secretion during acute stress. *Behavioral Medicine, 32,* 151–156.

92. Floyd, K., Pauley, P. M., & Hesse, C. (2010). State and trait affectionate communication buffer adults' stress reactions. *Communication Monographs, 77,* 618–636.

93. Cohen, S., Doyle, W. J., Turner, R., Alper, C. M., & Skoner, D. P. (2003). Sociability and susceptibility to the common cold. *Psychological Science, 14,* 389–395.

94. Carver, C. S. (2011). Coping. In R. J. Contrada & A. Baum (Eds.), *The handbook of stress science: Biology, psychology, and health* (pp. 221–230). New York: Springer.

95. Kohn, P. M. (1996). On coping adaptively with daily hassles. In M. Zeidner & N. S. Endler (Eds.), *Handbook of coping* (pp. 181–201). New York: John Wiley & Sons.

96. O'Donnell, K., Badrick, E., Kumari, M., & Steptoe, A. (2008). Psychological coping styles and cortisol over the day in healthy older adults. *Psychoneuroendocrinology, 33,* 601–611; See also Mikolajczak, M., Roy, E., Luminet, O., Fillée, C., & de Timary, P. (2007). The moderating impact of emotional intelligence on free cortisol responses to stress. *Psychoneuroendocrinology, 32,* 1000–1012.

97. Lehman, D. R., Ellard, J. H., & Wortman, C. B. (1986). Social support for the bereaved: Recipients and providers' perspectives on what is helpful. *Journal of Counseling and Clinical Psychology, 54,* 438–446.

98. www.dailymail.co.uk/news/article-1199447/Two-year-oldgirl-saves-mothers-life–seeing-999-episode-Tweenies.html

99. Brodie, M., Hamel, E., C., Altman, D., Blendon, R., & Benson, J. M. (2003). Health news and the American public, 1996–2002. *Journal of Health Politics, Policy and Law, 28,* 927–950.

100. Cram, P., Fendrick, A. M., Inadomi, J., Cowen, M. E., Carpenter, D., & Vijan, S. (2003). The impact of a celebrity promotional campaign on the use of colon cancer screening: The Katie Couric effect. *Archives of Internal Medicine, 163,* 1601–1605.

101. Cooper, C. P., & Roter, D. L. (2000) "If it bleeds it leads"? Attributes of TV health news stories that drive viewer attention. *Public Health Reports, 115,* 331–338.

102. http://healthnewsreview.org/review.html?review_id=2089

103. Berry, T. R., Wharf-Higgins, J., & Naylor, P. J. (2007). SARS wars: An examination of the quantity and construction of health information in the news media. *Health Communication, 21,* 35–44.

104. Miniño, A. M., Heron, M. P., Murphy, S. L., & Kochanek, K. D. (2007). *Deaths: Final data for 2004.* Atlanta: Centers for Disease Control and Prevention, Division of Vital Statistics.

105. Slater, M. D., Long, M., Bettinghaus, E. P., & Reineke, J. B. (2008). News coverage of cancer in the U.S.: A national sample of newspapers, television, and magazines. *Journal of Health Communication, 13,* 523–537.

106. Frost, K., Frank, E., & Maibach, E. (1997). Relative risk in the news media: A quantification of misrepresentation. *American Journal of Public Health, 87,* 842–845.

107. Gagnon, M.-A., & Lexchin, J. (2008). The cost of pushing pills: A new estimate of pharmaceutical promotion expenditures in the United States. *PLoS Medicine, 5*(1): e1. doi:10/1371/journal/pmed.0050001.

108. Calfee, J. E. (2002). Direct-to-consumer advertising of prescription drugs: Evaluating regulatory policy in the United States and New Zealand. *Journal of Public Policy & Marketing, 21*(2), 174.

109. Cline, R. J. W., & Young, H. N. (2004). Marketing drugs, marketing health care relationships: A content analysis of visual cues in direct-to-consumer prescription drug advertising. *Health Communication, 16,* 131–157.

110. Ibid, p. 151.

111. Public Health Cigarette Smoking Act of 1969 (P.L. 91-289).

112. Family Smoking Prevention and Tobacco Control Act of 2009 (P.L. 111-1256).

113. See Nelson, J. P. (2006, July). Alcohol advertising in magazines: Do beer, wine, and spirits ads target youth? *Contemporary Economic Policy,* 357–369.

114. Hether, H. J., Huang, G. C., Beck, V., Murphy, S. T., & Valente, T. W. (2008). Entertainment-education in a media-saturated environment: Examining the impact of single and multiple exposures to breast cancer storylines on two popular medical dramas. *Journal of Health Communication: International Perspectives, 13,* 808–823.

115. O'Connor, S., Deeks, J. J., Hawton, K., Simkin, S., Keen, A., Altman, D. G., Philo, G., & Bulstrode, C. (1999). Effects of a drug overdose in a television drama on knowledge of specific dangers of self-poisoning: Population based surveys. *British Medical Journal, 318,* 978–979.

116. McNeilly, D. P., & Wengel, S. P. (2001). The "ER" seminar: Teaching psychotherapeutic techniques to medical students. *Academic Psychiatry, 25,* 193–200.

117. Goodman, K. (2007, March). Imagining doctors: Medical students and the TV medical drama. *Virtual Mentor: American Medical Association Journal of Ethics, 9*(3), 182–187.

118. Harris, D., & Willoughby, H. (2009). Resuscitation on television: Realistic or ridiculous? A quantitative observational analysis of the portrayal of cardiopulmonary resuscitation in television medical drama. *Resuscitation, 80,* 1275–1279.

119. Diem, S. J., Lantos, J. D., & Tulsky, J. A. (1996). Cardiopulmonary resuscitation on television: Miracles and misinformation. *New England Journal of Medicine, 334,* 1578–1582.

120. Van den Bulck, J. J. M. (2002). The impact of television fiction on public expectations of survival following in hospital cardiopulmonary resuscitation by medical professionals. *European Journal of Emergency Medicine, 9,* 325–329.

121. Sandroni, C., Nolan, J., Cavallaro, F., & Antonelli, M. (2007). In hospital cardiac arrest: Incidence, prognosis, and possible measures to improve survival. *Intensive Care Medicine, 33,* 237–245.

122. Morgan, S. E., Harrison, T. R., Chewning, L., Davis, L., & DiCorcia, M. (2007). Entertainment (mis)education: The framing of organ donation in entertainment television. *Health Communication, 22,* 143–151.

123. Aldea, A., López, B., Moreno, A., Riaño, D., & Valls, A. (2001). A multiagent system for organ transplant co-ordination. *Artificial Intelligence in Medicine, 2101,* 413–416.

124. www.foxnews.com/health/2011/05/06/having-sex-blowingnose-cause-brain-bleed/

125. http://thechart.blogs.cnn.com/2011/02/20/yes-oral-sex-is-sex-andit-can-boost-cancer-risk/

126. www.msnbc.msn.com/id/39265727/ns/health-food_safety/

127. Barnes, M., Penrod, C., Neiger, B., Merrill, R., Eggett, D., & Thomas, E. (2003). Measuring the relevance of evaluation criteria among health information seekers on the Internet. *Journal of Health Psychology, 8,* 71–82.

128. Wright, K. B., Sparks, L., & O'Hair, H. D. (2008). *Health communication in the 21st century.* Malden, MA: Blackwell Publishing.

129. McMullan, M. (2006). Patients using the Internet to obtain health information: How this affects the patient-health professional relationships. *Patient Education and Counseling, 63,* 24–28.

130. www.docshop.com/2009/01/20/height-and-weight-ofamericas-top-female-celebrities-how-do-you-compare-to-your-favoritehollywood-starlets

131. Odgen, C. L., Fryar, C. D., Carroll, M. D., & Flegal, K. M. (2004, October 27). *Mean body weight, height, and body mass index, United States 1960–2002.* Atlanta: Centers for Disease Control and Prevention.

132. Neighbors, L. A., & Sobol, J. (2007). Prevalence and magnitude of body weight and shape dissatisfaction among university students. *Eating Disorders, 8,* 429–439.

133. Brown, J. D., & Walsh-Childers, K. (2002). Effects of media on personal and public health. In J. Bryant & D. Zillman (Eds.), *Media effects: Advances in theory and research* (pp. 453–488). Mahwah, NJ: Lawrence Erlbaum Associates; Harrison, K. (2000). The body electric: Thin-ideal media and eating disorders in adolescents. *Journal of Communication, 50,* 119–143.

134. Neighbors & Sobol, 2007.

135. Hudson, J. I., Hiripi, E., Pope, H. G., & Kessler, R. C. (2007). The prevalence and correlates of eating disorders in the National Comorbidity Survey Replication. *Biological Psychiatry, 61,* 348–358.

136. National Institute on Drug Abuse. (2007, December). *InfoFacts: High school and youth trends.* Bethesda, MD: Author.

137. Cohen, J., Collins, R., Darkes, J., & Gwartney, D. (2007). A league of their own: Demographics, motivations and patterns of use of 1,955 male adult non-medical anabolic steroid users in the United States. *Journal of the International Society of Sports Nutrition, 4,* 1–14.

138. Ibid; Råstam, M. (1992). Anorexia nervosa in 51 Swedish adolescents: Premorbid problems and comorbidity. *Journal of the American Academy of Child & Adolescent Psychiatry, 31,* 819–829.

139. Nestle, M. (1997, March–April). Alcohol guidelines for chronic disease prevention: From prohibition to moderation. *Nutrition Today, 32,* 86–92.

140. U.S. Department of Health and Human Services, Office of the Surgeon General. (2007). *The Surgeon General's call to action to prevent and reduce underage drinking*. Washington, D.C.: Author.

141. Alcohol Concern. (2007, July). *Not in front of the children—Child protection and advertising*. London: Author.

142. Ibid.

143. Stacy, A. W., Zogg, J. B., Unger, J. B., & Dent, C. W. (2004). Exposure to televised alcohol ads and subsequent alcohol use. *American Journal of Health Behavior, 28*, 498–509.

144. Hetsroni, A. (2007). Four decades of violent content on prime-time network programming: A longitudinal meta-analytic review. *Journal of Communication, 57*, 759–784.

145. Smith, S. L., Nathanson, A. I., & Wilson, B. J. (2002). Prime-time television: Assessing violence during the most popular viewing hours. *Journal of Communication, 52*, 84–111.

146. Oliver, M. B., & Kalyanaraman, S. (2002). Appropriate for all viewing audiences? An examination of violent and sexual portrayals in movie previews featured on video rentals. *Journal of Broadcasting & Electronic Media, 46*, 283–299.

147. Pesky, S., & Blascovich, J. (2007). Immersive virtual environments versus traditional platforms: Effects of violent and nonviolent video game play. *Media Psychology, 10*, 135–156.

148. Gerbner, G., & Signorielli, N. (1990). *Violence profile, 1967 through 1988–1989: Enduring patterns*. Manuscript, University of Pennsylvania, Annenberg School of Communication.

149. Anderson, C. A., & Bushman, B. J. (2001). Effects of violent video games on aggressive behavior, aggressive cognition, aggressive affect, physiological arousal, and prosocial behavior: A meta-analytic review of the scientific literature. *Psychological Science, 12*, 353–359; Paik, H., & Comstock, G. (1994). The effects of television violence on antisocial behavior: A meta-analysis. *Communication Research, 21*, 516–546.

150. Huesmann, L. R., Moise-Titus, J., Podolski, C., & Eron, L. D.(2003). Longitudinal relations between children's exposure to TV violence and their aggressive and violent behavior in young adulthood: 1977–1992. *Developmental Psychology, 39*, 201–221.

151. Farrar, K. M., Krcmar, M., & Nowak, K. L. (2006). Contextual features of violent video games, mental models, and aggression. *Journal of Communication, 56*, 387–405.

152. Haridakis, P. M. (2006). Men, women, and televised violence: Predicting viewer aggression in male and female television viewers. *Communication Quarterly, 54*, 227–255.

153. Kunkel, D., Eyal, K., Donnerstein, E., Farrar, K. M., Biely, E., & Rideout, V. (2007). Sexual socialization messages on entertainment television: Comparing content trends 1997–2002. *Media Psychology, 9*, 595–622.

154. Kunkel, D., Eyal, K., Finnerty, K., Biely, E., & Donnerstein, E. (2005). *Sex on TV4*. Menlo Park, CA: Henry J. Kaiser Family Foundation.

155. Olson, B. (1994). Sex and the soaps: A comparative content analysis of health issues. *Journalism Quarterly, 71*, 840–850.

156. Collins, R. L., Elliott, M. N., Berry, S. H., Kamouse, D. E., Kunkel, D., Hunter, D. B., & Miu, A. (2004). Watching sex on television predicts adolescent initiation of sexual behavior. *Pediatrics, 114*, e280–e289.

157. Sexual health of adolescents and young adults in the United States. (2008, September). Menlo Park, CA: Henry J. Kaiser Family Foundation. Retrieved May 9, 2011, from www.kff.org/womenshealth/upload/3040_04.pdf.

158. Ibid.

159. Stretcher, V. J., & Rosenstock, I. M. (1997). The health belief model. In K. Glanz, F. M. Lewis, & B. K. Rimer (Eds.), *Health behavior and health education* (pp. 41–59). San Francisco: Jossey-Bass.

160. Bandura, A. (1994). Social cognitive theory of mass communication. In J. Bryant & D. Zillman (Eds.), *Media effects: Advances in theory and research* (pp. 61–90). Hillsdale, NJ: Lawrence Erlbaum Associates.

161. Ajzen, I., & Fishbein, M. (1980). *Understanding attitudes and predicting behavior*. Englewood Cliffs, NJ: Prentice-Hall.

162. Ajzen, I. (1991). The theory of planned behavior. *Organizational Behavior and Human Decision Processes, 50*, 179–211.

163. Prochaska, J. O., & DiClemente, C. C. (1983). Stages and processes of self-change of smoking: Toward an integrative model of change. *Journal of Consulting and Clinical Psychology, 51*, 390–395.

Appendix

1. Fortado, B. (2011). A field exploration of informal workplace communication. *Sociology Mind, 1*, 212-220.

2. Gould, E. W. (2009). "I heard it on the grapevine"—Blogging, Facebook, YouTube, and student self-organization during a faculty strike. *Lecture Notes in Computer Science, 5621*, 336–345; Smith, B. (1996). Care and feeding of the office grapevine. *Management Review, 85*, 6.

3. Michaelson, G., Iterson, A. V., & Waddington, K. (2010). Gossip in organizations: Contexts, consequences, and controversies. *Group & Organization Management, 35*, 371–390; Hellweg, S. A. (1992). Organizational grapevines. In K. L. Hutchinson (Ed.), *Readings in organizational communication* (pp. 159–172). Dubuque, IA: Brown.

4. Trice, H., & Beyer, J. (1984). Studying organizational cultures through rites and ceremonials. *Academy of Management Review, 9*, 653–669.

5. Mokros, H. (2006). Composing relationships at work. In J. T. Wood & S. W. Duck (Eds.), *Composing relationships: Communication in everyday life* (pp. 175–185). Belmont, CA: Thomson Wadsworth.

6. Islam, G., & Zyphur, M. J. (2009). Rituals in organizations: A review and expansion of current theory. *Group & Organization Management, 34*, 114–139.

7. Mumby, D. K. (2006). Constructing working-class masculinity in the workplace. In J. T. Wood & S. W. Duck (Eds.), *Composing relationships: Communication in everyday life* (pp. 89–95). Belmont, CA: Thomson Wadsworth.

8. Holmes, J., & Marra, M. (2002). Having a laugh at work: How humour contributes to workplace culture. *Journal of Pragmatics, 34*, 1683–1710.

9. Morreall, J. (2008). Applications of humor: Health, the workplace, and education. In V. Raskin (Ed.), *The primer of humor research* (pp. 449–478). New York: Mouton de Gruyter.

10. Lang, J. C., & Lee, C. H. (2010). Workplace humor and organizational creativity. *The International Journal of Human Resource Management, 21*, 46–60.

11. Mesmer-Magnus, J., Glew, D. J., & Viswesvaran, C. (2012). A meta-analysis of positive humor in the workplace. *Journal of Managerial Psychology, 27*, 155–190.

12. Pew Internet & American Life Project. (2009). *Networked workers*. Retrieved December 24, 2009, from www.pewinternet.org/Reports/2008/Networked-Workers.aspx?r=1.

13. Radicati, S. (2011). *Email statistics report, 2011–2015*. Palo Alto, CA: The Radicati Group.

14. Rubin, L. (2011, November 28). Employees cyber shopping—The boss could be watching. American News Report, retrieved June 17, 2012, from http://americannewsreport.com/employees-cyber-shopping-the-boss-could-be-watching-8812240.html.

15. Ibid

16. See Orrange, R. (2002). Aspiring law and business professionals' orientations to work and family life. *Journal of Family Issues, 23*, 287–317.

17. Höge, T. (2009). When work strain transcends psychological boundaries: An inquiry into the relationship between time pressure, irritation, work-family conflict and psychosomatic complaints. *Stress & Health, 25*, 41–51.

18. Geiger-Brown, J., Trinkoff, A., & Rogers, V. E. (2011). The impact of work schedules, home, and work demands on self-reported sleep in registered nurses. *Journal of Occupational & Environmental Medicine, 53*, 303–307.

19. Rantanen, M., Mauno, S., Kinnunen, U., & Rantanen, J. (2011). Do individual coping strategies help or harm in the work-family conflict situation? Examining coping as a moderator between work-family conflict and well-being. *International Journal of Stress Management, 18*, 24–48.

20. Hostetler, A. J., Desrochers, S., Kopko, K., & Moen, P. (2012). Marital and family satisfaction as a function of work-family demands and community resources: Individual- and couple-level analyses. *Journal of Family Issues, 33*, 316–340.

21. Michel, J. S., Mitchelson, J. K., Pichler, S., & Cullen, K. L. (2010). Clarifying relationships among work and family social support, stressors, and work-family conflict. *Journal of Vocational Behavior, 76*, 91–104.

22. Eby, L. T., Maher, C. P., & Butts, M. M. (2010). The intersection of work and family life: The role of affect. *Annual Review of Psychology, 61*, 599–622.

23. Petitta, L., & Vecchione, M. (2011). Job burnout, absenteeism, and extra role behaviors. *Journal of Workplace Behavioral Health, 26*, 97–121.

24. Neuman, J. H. (2004). Injustice, stress, and aggression in organizations. In R. W. Griffin & A. M. O'Leary-Kelly (Eds.), *The dark side of organizational behavior* (pp. 62–102). San Francisco: Jossey-Bass.

25. Dessy, E. (2009). Effective communication in difficult situations: Preventing stress and burnout in the NICU. *Early Human Development, 85*, S39–S41.

26. Earley, P., & Gibson, C. (2002). *Multinational work teams*. Mahwah, NJ: Lawrence Erlbaum Associates; Padavic, I., & Reskin, B. (2002). *Women and men at work*. Thousand Oaks, CA: Sage.

27. Farr, J. (Ed.). (2003). Stereotype threat effects in employment settings. [Special issue.] *Human Performance, 16*.

28. www.eeoc.gov/types/sexual_harassment.cfm

29. Lumsden, G., & Lumsden, D. (2004). *Communicating in groups and teams* (4th ed.). Belmont, CA: Wadsworth.

30. Rockoff, J. E., Staiger, D. O., Kane, T. J., & Taylor, E. S. (2010, July). Information and employee evaluation: Evidence from a randomized intervention in public schools. National Bureau of Economic Research working paper no. 16240. Retrieved May 8, 2012 from www.nber.org/papers/w16240.

31. Coulehan, J. L., & Block, M. L. (2006). *The medical interview: Mastering skills for clinical practice*. Philadelphia: Davis.

32. Stewart, C. J., & Cash, W. B. (2007). *Interviewing: Principles and practices* (12th ed.). New York: McGraw-Hill.

Photos

Front Matter

p. iv: Kory Floyd; p. v: © Ryan McVay/Getty Images RF; p. vi-xi: iStockphoto; p. xii: iStockphoto; p. xiii-xv: iStockphoto; p. xvii. © Photodisc/Getty Images RF; p. xix: iStockphoto; xxvi: iStockphoto.

Chapter 1

Opener: © Associated Press/AP Wide World; p. 5 (top): © The McGraw-Hill Companies; (bottom): © Fancy Photography/Veer RF; p. 6: © Purestock/Alamy RF; p. 7: © Melba Photo Agency/Alamy RF; p. 9: © Pixtal/AGE Fotostock RF; p. 10: © Ingram Publishing RF; p. 11: © Thinkstock/Getty Images RF; p. 13: © AFP/Getty Images; p. 14: © George Doyle/Getty Images RF; p. 16: © Thinkstock RF; p. 18: © Courtesy Everett Collection; p. 19 (top): © altrendo images/Stockbyte/Getty Images RF; (bottom): © istockphoto; p. 22: © Abel Mitja Varela/The Agency Collection/Getty Images RF; p. 23: © Ghislain and Marie David de Lossy/Cultura/Getty Images RF; p. 24 (competent communicator): © Design Pics/Don Hammond RF; p. 25: © Ozier Muhammad/The New York Times/Redux; p. 26: © Hybrid Images/Cultura/Getty Images RF.

Chapter 2

Opener: © Getty Images; p. 30: © AP Photo/Lynne Sladky; p. 31: © NASA/NOAA/SPL/Getty Images RF; p. 32: © Dimitri Vervitsiotis/Getty Images RF; p. 33: David McNew/Getty Images; p. 34 (top): © Brand X Pictures/PunchStock RF; (bottom): © James Woodson/Getty Images RF; p. 35: © Michael Newman/PhotoEdit; p. 36 (top, left): © Comstock/Getty Images RF; (top, right): © AP Photo/Brainerd Dispatch, Steve Kohls; (bottom): © Eyewire (Photodisc)/PunchStock RF; p. 37 (top): © MEHDI FEDOUACH/Getty Images; (bottom): © Image Source/Getty Images RF; p. 40: © Getty Images; p. 42: © Tim Graham/Getty Images; p. 43: © Hugh Sitton/Getty Images; (bottom): © Design Pics/Don Hammond RF; p. 45: © AP Photo/CP, Winnipeg Free Press-Ken Gigliotti; p. 46: © Marku Kirchgessner/laif/Redux; p. 47 (Competent Communicator): © Design Pics/Don Hammond RF; p. 48: © Image Source/Getty Images RF.

Chapter 3

Opener: © WireImage/Getty Images; p. 56: © AP Photo/Chris Gardner; p. 58: © Comstock Images/Punchstock RF; p. 59 (top): © Photomondo /Getty Images RF; (bottom): © Glow Images/Alamy RF; p. 60: © Joe Raedle/Getty Images; p. 61 (top): © Brand X Pictures/Punchstock RF; (bottom, left): © Ethan Miller/Getty Images; (bottom, middle): © Ingram Publishing RF; (bottom, right): © Ron Chapple/Taxi/Getty Images; p. 62: © Lions Gate/courtesy Everett Collection; p. 63 (top): © Ingram Publishing RF; (bottom): © FilmMagic/Getty Images; p. 64: © Jeff Kravitz/FilmMagic/Getty Images; p. 65: © Stockbyte/Getty Images RF; p. 66: Tetra Images/Getty Images RF; p. 68 & 69: © Image Source/Getty Images RF; p. 70: © Design Pics/Don Hammond RF; p. 71: © Walt Disney Studios Motion Pictures/Courtesy Everett Collection; p. 73 (top): Design Pics/Don Hammond RF; (bottom): © John Lund/Marc Romanelli/Blend Images LLC RF; p. 74: © Larry Hirshowitz/Corbis.

Chapter 4

Opener: Josh Anderson/The New York Times/Redux; p. 81 (top): © ABC via Getty Images; (bottom): © Tim O'Hara/Corbis RF; p. 82: © Blend Images/Getty Images RF; p. 83 top: © Ryan McVay/Getty Images RF p.83 bottom:© BananaStock/ PunchStock RF; p. 86: © Flying Colours/Iconica/Getty Images; p. 87: © Brand X/Getty Images RF; p. 88: Soft drink map designed by Matthew Campbell under the direction of Dr. Gregory Plumb, Department of Cartography & Geography, East Central University; p. 89: Luedke and Sparrow/Digital Vision/Getty Images RF; p. 90 (top): © AP Photo/Lawrence Jackson; (bottom): © Dave and Les Jacobs/Blend Images LLC RF; p. 91: © Ingram Publishing RF; p. 93 (top): © Felipe Trueba/epa/Corbis; (bottom): © Glow Images RF; p. 94: © Lifesize/Getty Images RF; p. 95: © FilmMagic/Getty Images; p. 97: © Jim West/The Image Works; p. 99: © Design Pics/Don Hammond RF; p. 100: © Purestock/SuperStock RF.

Chapter 5

Opener: © Getty Images; p. 104: © Photofest; p. 105: © Stephen Mullon/The Image Bank/Getty Images; p. 107 (top): © Martial Colomb/Getty Images RF; (bottom): © CBS via Getty Images; p. 108: © Creatas Images/Jupiter Images RF; 5.2: Courtesy Martin Gruendl; 5.3: © Kory Floyd; p. 112 (left): © Erik Isakson/Blend Images/Getty Images RF; (right): © Bob Thomas/Photodisc/Getty Images RF; p. 113 (top): © Dougal Waters/Getty Images RF; (bottom): © Getty Images; p. 115 (top): © Dougal Waters/Getty Images RF; (bottom): © Keith Brofsky/Getty Images RF; p. 116: © Siri Stafford/Getty Images RF; p. 117: © BBS United/Photodisc/Getty Images RF; p. 118: © Martin Hunter/Stringer/Getty Images; p. 119 (top): © Getty Images; (bottom): © Jon Feingersch/The Image Bank/Getty Images; p. 122 (top): © CBS via Getty Images; (bottom): U.S. Air Force photo by Staff Sgt. Marcus McDonald; p. 124: © Design Pics/Don Hammond RF.

Chapter 6

Opener: Campaign for the Fair Sentencing of Youth; 6.1: Design Pics/Kristy-Anne Glubish RF; p. 129: © Brand X Pictures/PunchStock RF; p. 130: © Royalty-Free/Corbis; p. 134: © Eric Audras/Getty Images RF; p. 135 (top): © Digital Vision/Getty Images RF; (bottom): © Universal/courtesy Everett Collection; p. 136: Design Pics/Don Hammond RF; p. 138 (top): © Katrina Wittkamp/Getty Images RF; (bottom): © C Squared Studios/Getty Images RF; p. 140 (top): © INSADCO Photography/Alamy RF; (bottom): © Photodisc Collection/Getty Images RF; p. 142: © Lifesize/Getty Images RF; p. 145: © Derek Berwin/The Image Bank/Getty Images; p. 148: © Design Pics/Don Hammond RF.

Chapter 7

Opener: © Grant Halverson/Associated Press; p. 152: © Glow Images RF; p. 153: © Getty Images/Image Source RF; p. 155 (top): © The Bakersfield Californian/ZUMA; (bottom): © Alexander Walter/Getty Images RF; p. 156: © Masterfile; p. 158: © Design Pics/Don Hammond RF; p. 160: © The McGraw-Hill Companies, Inc./Barry Barker, photographer; p. 162: © Paul Burns/Corbis RF; p. 163: © Image Source/Getty Images RF; p. 164: © Rubberball/Getty Images RF; p. 167: © Author's Image/PunchStock RF; p. 168: © Juli Balla/Stockbyte/Getty Images; p. 169: © Brand X Pictures/PunchStock RF; p. 170: © Yellow Dog Productions/The Image Bank/Getty Images RF; p. 171: © BananaStock Ltd. RF; p. 172: © AP Photo/M. Spencer Green; p. 173: © Ingram Publishing/Super-Stock RF; p. 175: © Dynamic Graphics Group/PunchStock RF.

Chapter 8

Opener: © Martha Manning; p. 180: © Paul Barton/Corbis; p. 181 (top): © Image Source/Getty Images RF; (bottom): © Klaus Tiedge/Corbis RF; p. 182 (top): © Ryan McVay/Getty Images RF; (bottom): © Image Sources/Getty Images RF; p. 183 (top): © Chris Noble/

Stone/Getty Images; (bottom): © Stockdisc/PunchStock RF; p. 184: © Photo Japan/Alamy; p. 185 (left): © Jim Wilson/The New York Times/Redux; (right): AFP/Getty Images; p. 186: © Jack Hollingsworth/Photodisc/Getty Images RF; p. 187: © Design Pics/Don Hammond RF; p. 189: © Stock4B-RF/Getty Images RF; p. 190: © Tom Stewart/Corbis; p. 191 (top): © SW Productions/Brand X Pictures/Getty Images RF; (bottom): © Brandon Harman/Taxi/Getty Images; p. 192 (top): © Buena Vista Images/Stockbyte/Getty Images RF; (bottom): © Ryan McVay/Getty Images RF; p. 193 (top): © WireImage/Getty Images; (bottom): © Blend Images/Alamy RF; p. 194: © Sean Justice/Corbis RF; p. 195: © ABC via Getty Images; p. 196: © 2009 Jupiterimages Corporation RF; p. 197 (top): © Getty Images/Foodcollection RF; (bottom): © Lars A. Niki RF; p. 199: © Digital Vision RF; p. 200: © Exactostock/SuperStock RF.

Chapter 9

Opener: © ABC via Getty Images; p. 208: © Mark Wilson/Getty Images; p. 209: Purestock/SuperStock RF; p. 210: © Image100/Photolibrary RF; p. 211 (top): © Don Smith/Getty Images; (bottom): © Paramount/Courtesy Everett Collection; p. 212: © John G. Mabanglo/AFP/Getty Images; p. 213: © AP Photo/Sentinel-Tribute, Michael Lehmkuhle; p. 215 (top): Ross Anania/Photographer's Choice/Getty Images; (bottom): © Samuel Zuder/laif/Redux; Fig 9.1 (compete): © Design Pics/Don Hammond RF; (Focus on discrete tasks): © Tim Pannell/ Corbis RF; (Evaluate and advise): © Getty Images; (Provide service and support): © AP Photo/The Ames Tribune, Jon Britton; (Help us learn): © Alberto Pomares/Getty Images RF; (create art and ideas): © Redferns via Getty Images; (promote social networking): © Blend Images/PunchStock; p. 218: © Comstock/JupiterImages RF; p. 220 (top): © S. Meltzer/PhotoLink/Getty Images RF; (bottom): © Stockdisc/PunchStock RF; p. 222: © Getty Images/Blend Images RF; p. 223: © CBS via Getty Images; p. 225: © Blend Images/SuperStock RF; p. 227 (competent communicator): © Design Pics/Don Hammond RF; p. 229: © FogStock/Alamy RF.

Chapter 10

Opener: © AFP/Getty Images; p. 234: © Author's Image/PunchStock RF; p. 235: Photodisc/PunchStock RF; p. 236: © Ryan Mcay/Getty Images RF; p. 239: © AP Photo/Karim Kadim; p. 240: © Jackson Vereen/Cole Group/Getty Images RF; p. 242 (competent communicator): © Design Pics/Don Hammond RF; p. 243: © Thony Belizaire/AFP/Getty Images; p. 245: © E. Audras/PhotoAlto RF; p. 246: © Associated Press; p. 247 (top): © Scott Olson/Getty Images; (bottom): © Jose Luis Pelaez Inc/Blend Images LLC RF; p. 248: © Royalty-Free/Corbis; p. 249: © Adrian Weinbrecht/Stone/Getty Images; p. 250: © Rim Light/PhotoLink/Getty Images RF; p. 251 (top): Ko Sasaki/The New York Times/Redux; (bottom): © Ingram Publishing RF; p. 253 (top): © The McGraw-Hill Companies Inc./Ken Cavanagh Photographer; (bottom): NASA Headquarters - Greatest Images of NASA (NASA-HQ-GRIN); p. 255: © Royalty-Free/Corbis.

Chapter 11

Opener: © AFP/Getty Images; p. 260: © Kevin Winter/Getty Images; p. 261 (top): © Mike Cardew/MCT/Landov; (bottom): © WireImage Getty Images; p. 262: © Maria Teijeiro/Getty Images RF; p. 263: © Dimitri Vervitsiotis/Digital Vision/Getty Images RF; p. 264: © Uppercut RF/Getty Images RF; p. 266: © Design Pics/Don Hammond RF; p. 267: © Hill Street Studios/Blend Images/Getty Images; p. 269: © Ethan Miller/Getty Images; p. 270: © AP Photo/Darryl Bush; p. 271 (top): © Win McNamee/Getty Images; (bottom): © Photodisc Collection/Getty Images RF; p. 272 (top): © JupiterImages/Comstock Images/Alamy RF; (bottom): © SW Productions/Photodisc/PunchStock RF; p. 274: © moodboard/Corbis RF; p. 276: © W. Wayne Lockwood, M.D./Corbis; p. 278: © The McGraw-Hill Companies, Inc./Jill Braaten, photographer; p. 279: © Hill Street Studios/Getty Images RF; p. 280: © Burke/Triolo Productions/Brand X/Corbis RF.

Chapter 12

Opener: © Pete Souza/White House/Handout/Corbis; p. 284: Spike Mafford/Getty Images RF; p. 286: © AP Photo/Paul Spinelli; p. 287: © moodboard/Corbis RF; p. 288: Big Cheese Photo/ Jupiter Images RF; p. 289: © David Muir/Photo Disc/Getty Images RF; p. 290: Copyright © Foodcollection RF; p. 291: © Ryan McVay/Getty Images RF; p. 292: © Hulton Archives/Getty Images; p. 294: © Flip Schulke/Corbis; p. 296 (top): © PictureNet/Corbis; (bottom): © Image Source/SuperStock RF; p. 301: © Design Pics/Don Hammond RF; p. 302: © Goodshoot/PunchStock RF; p. 303: © Nicole Hill/Rubberball/Corbis RF; p. 304: © Lawrence Bender Prods./The Kobal Collection/Art Resource; p. 306: © Corbis RF.

Chapter 13

Opener: © Everett Collection, Inc; p. 312: Digital Vision Ltd./SuperStock RF; p. 314 (top): © McGraw-Hill Companies, Inc./Jill Braaten, photographer RF; (bottom): © Bloomberg via Getty Images; p. 315: © WireImage Getty Images; p. 317: © Colin Anderson/Getty Images RF; p. 319 (left): © Erin Patrice O'Brien/Digital Vision/Getty Images RF; (right): © Bryan Allen/Corbis; p. 320 (top): © Comstock Images/JupiterImages RF; (bottom): © Shelb Ross/Riser/Getty Images; p. 321: © Tina Stallard/Getty Images; p. 322: © Pixtal/AGE Fotostock RF; p. 323 (top): © Photodisc Collection/Getty Images RF; (bottom): © Royalty-Free/Corbis; p. 324: © Design Pics /Don Hammond RF; p. 325: © Ingram Publishing RF; p. 328: © Royalty-Free/Corbis; p. 330: © Brand X Pictures/Punchstock; p. 331: © Glow Images RF; p. 332: © Tom Kola/Stock Image/Getty Images; p. 333: © Jeff Jacobson.

Chapter 14

Opener: Courtesy of Lucile Packard Children's Hospital; p. 338: © Thomas Barwick/Getty Images RF; p. 340 (top): © John Wang/Getty Images; (bottom): © Rex Features via AP Images; p. 341: Copyright © FoodCollection RF; p. 342: © Pixtal/AGE Fotostock RF; p. 343 (top): © Associated Press; (bottom): © Royalty Free/Corbis; p. 345: Huntstock/Getty Images RF; p. 346: © Design Pics/Don Hammond RF; p. 347: © Ryan McVay/Getty Images RF; p. 349: © wonderlandstock/Alamy RF; p. 350 (top): © Ingram Publishing RF; (bottom): © Design Pics/Don Hammond RF; p. 351: © AP Photo/Eric Risberg.

Chapter 15

Opener: © AP Photo/Bebeto Matthews; p. 358: © Gabriel Bouys/AFP/Getty Images; p. 359: © Alex Wong/Getty Images; p. 360: Library of Congress, Prints & Photographs Division, photograph by Carol M. Highsmith [reproduction number, LC-HS503- 2800]; p. 361: © Image Source/Getty Images RF; p. 362: Jose Luis Pelaez Inc/Blend Images LLC RF; p. 363: © The McGraw-Hill Companies; p. 366: © Jon Feingersh /Blend Images/Corbis RF; p. 368: © Keith Brofsky/Getty Images RF; p. 369: © Stockbyte/Getty Images RF; p. 370: Kevin Winter/Getty Images; p. 371: © Design Pics/Don Hammond RF; p. 373: © AP Photo/Gerald Herbert; p. 374: Radius Images/Getty Images RF; p. 376: (top) © Martin Shields/Science Source/Photo Researchers, Inc.; (bottom): © Susan See Photography RF.

Chapman, Chris, 179–180
character, 375–376
charisma, 376
chart, 328
chat rooms, 218
Cheesecake Factory, 378
chemotherapy, 448
children of deaf adults
    (CODAs), 344
China, 131, 343
chronemics, 116
*The Chronicles of Narnia: The Voyage
    of the Dawn Treader* (film), 419
Cingular, 130
circumscribing stage, 192
clarity, 84
Clark, Dick, 329
class
    dialect and, 87
    power distance and, 42
classroom response system, 349
clichés, 87
clicker technology, 349
clients, relationships with, 175
Cline, Rebecca, 449
Clinical Skills Assessment, 442
Clinton, Bill, *243*
Clinton, Hillary, 419
closed systems, 385
closed-mindedness, 140, 143*t*
closedness, 183
Cobain, Kurt, 95
Cobern, Kristi, 332
co-cultures
    bases of, 34–35
    components of, 36–39
    deaf, 34–35
    definition of, 34
    distinctive features of, 39
    identification with multiple,
        35–36
    jargon, 39
    online, 35, 39
    perception and, 60–61
    slang, 94–95
    uncertainty avoidance, 44
CODAs. *See* children of deaf adults
Code of Medical Ethics (AMA), 438
code-switching, 48
coercive power, 246, 247
cognitive complexity, 24–25
Cohen, Sheldon, 155
cohesion, 210, 228–230
Colbert, Stephen, *81*, 419
Coldplay, 217
Coleridge, Samuel Taylor, 175
collaborating style, of conflict,
    251–252

collaborative communication, 442
collectivistic cultures, 40
    decision making in, 239
College Board, 68
collegial stories, 390
Collins, Suzanne, 413
Colmes, Alan, 413
The Color Purple (film), 411
comedians, 3–4
Comindex, 279
commitment, 180–181
communication. *See also
    specific types*
    action model of, 8–9
    behaviors as, 15
    break down, 18
    characteristics of, 12–13
    consciousness-raising,
        213–214
    CPM theory, 190
    cultural awareness, 44–51
    culture affecting, 39–44
    in cyberspace, 5
    definition of, 4
    image management and,
        71–74
    interaction model of, 10–11
    myths of, 17–20
    nature/types of, 8–17
    reasons for, 4–7
    transaction model of, 10–11
    types of, 16–17
communication accommodation
    theory, 87
communication apprehension, 243
communication codes
    gestures, 48–49
    idioms, 48
    jargon, 48
communication competence,
    20–26
communication privacy manage-
    ment (CPM) theory, 190
communication technology,
    5, 50, A–8
    effective use of, 404
    health and, 442–444
    organizational communica-
        tion challenges, 399–402
comparative advantage
    method, 367
compare-and-contrast
    definitions, 339
comparison level, 161, 162*f*
comparison level for alternatives,
    161, 162*f*
competence, 20–26, 375
competence face, 75

competing style, of conflict, 250
competition, small group, 218
competitive interrupting,
    140–141, 143*t*
complementarity, attraction to, 157
compromising style, of
    conflict, 251
conclusion, of speech, 293–294
conditional information, 437
confidentiality, 438–439
confirmation bias, 143
confirming messages, 199, 199*t*
conflict
    accommodating, 250–521
    avoiding, 250
    collaborating, 251–252
    competing, 250
    compromising, 251
    constructive handling of,
        199–201, 250–252
    GLBT styles of, 190
    in intimate relationships,
        189–190
    management in groups,
        250–252
    in romantic relationships,
        189–190
    within small groups, 224–225
    work/life, A–9
conflict-avoiding couples, 189
connection
    autonomy *vs.*, 182–183
    language and, 89–90
connotative meaning, 82, 339
Conrad, Charles, 384
consciousness-raising
    communication, 213–214
consensus, 237
constraint, 392–393
constructive criticism, 91
constructs, 58
consumers, 396, A–3
contempt, 200
content dimension, 13
context, 9–10
    adapting to, 11–12
    appropriateness and, 21–22
    channel-lean, 12
    channel-rich, 12
    culture, low *vs.* high, 41
    decision making and,
        239–240
    language and, 84–85
    nonverbal communication,
        105
    physical, 10
    presentation aids, 331–332
    psychological, 10

small groups and, 214, 223–224
workplace, A–9–A–11
divorce, 193
Dixon, Travis, 427
doctor-patient privilege, 438
documentaries, 414
Dole, Elizabeth, 249
Doodle.com, 226
downward communication, 394–395, A–2
Dr. Phil (television show), 20
Dreamgirls (film), 340
DreamWorks, 414
Drudge Report (website), 427
dual-career families, A–9
dysfunctional groups, 211

E

eating disorders, 117, 451–452
e-commerce, 401
ECPA. *See* Electronic Communications Privacy Act
Edison, Thomas, 413
EEOC. *See* Equal Employment Opportunity Commission
effectiveness, 20–21, 220
listening stages, 131–134
efficiency, 440
Egypt, 417
either/or fallacy, 369
Ekman, Paul, 107
Electronic Communications Privacy Act (ECPA), 400, A–8
electronic media, 415–417
electronic presentation aids, 328–329
electronic print materials, 278
electronic spying, 418
Ellis, C. P., 151–152
Ellison, Keith, 343
Elway, John, 261–262
e-mail, 81, 416
distractions and, A–8
emoticons, 105f
message privacy addendum, 400f, A–8, A–9f
security risks, 401–402
emblems, 112, 118
Eminem, 417
emoticons, 105f
emotions
facial displays and, 109
nonverbal communication and, 107–108
persuasion and, 361
social relationships and, 154–155

emotional abuse, 247
emotional appeals, 360–362, 362f
emotional commitment, 180
emotional communication, 190–191
emotional expressiveness, 120
emotional support, 445
emotion-focused coping, 446
empathic concern, 135
empathic listening, 134–135, 146–147, 148
empathizing, 133
empathy, 23, 24, 440
employers, researching potential, A–15
employment law, A–18–A–20
encounter communication, 213–214
encounter phase, 222
enculturation, 33
entertainment
health messages in, 450
speaking and, 261
entertainment needs, 420
enthymeme, 363
Entourage (television series), 415
Equal Employment Opportunity Commission (EEOC), 401, A–10
equal time rule, 426
equity theory, 160, 162–163
equivocation, 87–88
ER (television series), 450
ERIC, 279
esteem support, 445
ET (film), 414
e-therapy, 443–444
ethics, 25–26
in informative speaking, 349–350
of presentation aids, 332–333
ethnicity, 32
ethnocentrism, 46–47
ethos, 360
E*TRADE, 422
etymology, 339
euphemisms, 94
evaluating, 133
examples, in speech, 302
defining by, 339
exit interview, A–11
exit phase, 222
expectations
humor and, 93
listening and, 131
in relationships, 201
experience, 17
experimenting stage, 186

expert opinion, 238
expert power, 247
expertise, 17
explaining, 340–341
explicit rules, 14, 387–388
extemporaneous speech, 312–313
external communication, 396–397, A–3–A–4
extroversion, 243
eye behaviors, 111–112
eye contact, 8, 119, 120, 322

F

face. *See also* image
autonomy, 75
competence, 75
defining, 74
facework, 74
fellowship, 75
needs, 74–75
threats, 75
Facebook, 4, 9, 193, 218, 393, 412, 416–418, 422
as channel-lean context, 400
culture, 32t
in-groups and out-groups, 31
face-threatening act, 75
facework, 74
facial displays, 109, 110f, 119
emoticons, 105f
facial primacy principle, 109
facts, opinions *vs.*, 97–98
FAIR. *See* Fairness & Accuracy in Reporting
Fair Isaac Corporation, 338
Fairness & Accuracy in Reporting (FAIR), 427
fairness doctrine, 427
false authority, 370
false consensus, 237
false dichotomy, 351
false-cause fallacy, 369
families
blended, 195
communicating in, 193–198
definition of, 193–195
genes, 194
identical twins, *194*
legal obligations, 194
nuclear, 195, 196
rituals, 197
roles in, 194–195, 196–197
secrets, 198
single-parent, 195
stories, 197–198
types of, 195–196

speech of recognition, 263
speed dating, 56
Spencer, Octavia, 71
spiritual needs, 7, 346
Spitzberg, William, 20, 181
stability, 65
Stafford, Laura, 163
stage fright, 315
stagnating stage, 192
stalemate, 237
Stamps, Jeffrey, 214
Star Wars (film), 414
Starbucks, 389
State of the Union address, 283
statistics, in speech, 302
STDs. *See* sexually transmitted
    diseases
Steamboat Willie (film), 414
stereotypes, 61–62, 427
steroid abuse, 451–452
Stewart, Charles, A–19–A–20
Stewart, Jon, 260
stigma, 73, 75
Stone, Elizabeth, 198
stonewalling, 133, 201
stories
    collegial, 390
    corporate, 389–390
    family, 197–198
    organizational, 389–390
    personal, 390
Stossel, John, 325
strain-based stress, 402
strategic ambiguity, 392
strategic control approach, 392
straw man fallacy, 370
streaming media, 414
stress, 315–318, 402, 444–445
    process, 444–445
    social support and, 446, 447
stress buffering effect, 446
stress hormones, 316, 317
stressor, 445
study groups, 218
stuttering, 326
subjectivity, 341
Sullivan, Anthony, 261
summary, of speech, 293–294
summary transition, 295
The Sun (newspaper), 412
Sunnafrank, Michael, 160
Super Bowl, 286
support groups, 217–218
supporting, 133
    nonverbal, 147
supporting materials. *See* speaking/
    speech, supporting materials for
Surgeon General, U.S., 303

survey interview, A–12
surveys, 279–280
swear words. *See* profanity
Sweden, 32
Swift, Taylor, 64
Swivel Sweeper, 261
syllogisms, 363
symbols, 13
    cultural, 36
    language and, 80–81
symmetry, 109, 110*f*, 159
sympathetic listening, 135
symptoms, 436
synergy, 223
synonyms, 339
syntactic rules, 82
systems theory, 209

T

table (presentation aid), 328
taboo topics, 344
talk radio, 413
talking. *See also* speaking/speech
    tone of voice, 9, 12, 41, 132
talking down, 98, 274
task cohesion, 210
tasks
    sharing, 163
    small groups, 210
tasks attraction, 156
Tate, Lionel, 425
Taylor, Dalmas, 164
Teach for America, 338
TeacherJobs.com, A–12
Tebow, Tim, 103
Telecommunications Act of
    1996, 426
telemedicine, 443–444
television, 415
    advertising on, 422
    health messages, 450
    ratings, 427–428, 428*f*
    reality, 107
terminating stage, 192–193
terminator statements, 147
text messages, 89*t*
    emoticons, 105*f*
    e-therapy via, 443–444
text slide, 328
textbooks, 413
texting, 416
thank you notes, A–17–A–18
theory of planned behavior, 454
theory of reasoned action, 454
theory of structuration, 392
thesis statement, 286, 287*t*
thought, language and, 86

threats, 91
    face, 75
Tillmann-Healy, Lisa, 170
time
    audience availability, 273–274
    culture and, 119
    pattern, 292
    use of, 116–117
Time (magazine), 413
time management, 43
time orientation, 240
time-based stress, 402
Titanic (film), 414
toasting, 262. *See also* speaking/
    speech
tobacco, 450
Toffler, Alvin, 138
tone of voice, 9, 12, 41, 132
topic pattern, 292
topics. *See* speaking/speech, topics
touch, 4, 120
touch behaviors, 113–114
Toy Story (film), 414
Toyota, 376–377
tracking software, 418
trade books, 413
traits, 240–243
transaction model, 10–11
transactional approach, 391–392
transitions in speech, 294–296
Transportation Security
    Administration, U.S., 387
transtheoretical model, 454
Travel Channel, 343
Treatise on Rhetoric (Aristotle), 360
treatment plan, 437
Trice, Harrison, 386, A–5
Trojan horse, 401
trust, self-disclosure and, 165–168
trust markers, 401
truth, 349
truthiness, *81*
Turnitin, 306
TV parental guidelines, 427
Twitter, 4, 72, 89*t*, 95, 412, 417
    as channel-lean context,
        12–13

U

unanimous consensus, 237
uncertainty avoidance, 43–44
uncertainty reduction theory, 160
uncontrollable attribution, 65
under-benefited, 162
understanding
    culture and language, 131
    in listening, 132